XI'AN

西安 统计年鉴

STATISTICAL YEARBOOK

2020

中英文对照 Chinese/English

中国统计出版社
China Statistics Press

西安市统计局
XI'AN MUNICIPAL BUREAU OF STATISTICS
国家统计局西安调查队
NBS SURVEY OFFICE IN XI'AN

图书在版编目（CIP）数据

西安统计年鉴. 2020 = Xi'an Statistical Yearbook 2020 : 汉英对照 / 西安市统计局, 国家统计局西安调查队编. -- 北京 : 中国统计出版社, 2020.9
ISBN 978-7-5037-9235-9

Ⅰ. ①西… Ⅱ. ①西… ②国… Ⅲ. ①统计资料一西安一2020一年鉴一汉、英 Ⅳ. ①C832.411-54

中国版本图书馆CIP数据核字(2020)第151979号

西安统计年鉴—2020

作　　者/ 西安市统计局 国家统计局西安调查队
责任编辑/ 钟　钰
装帧设计/ 西安乐成品牌策划设计有限公司
出版发行/ 中国统计出版社有限公司
地　　址/ 北京市丰台区西三环南路甲6号
邮政编码/ 100073
电　　话/ 邮购（010）63376909 书店（010）68783171
网　　址/ http://www.zgtjcbs.com
印　　刷/ 西安第一印刷厂
经　　销/ 新华书店
开　　本/ 890mm × 1240mm 1/16
字　　数/ 1525千字
印　　张/ 43
版　　别/ 2020年9月第1版
版　　次/ 2020年9月第1次印刷
定　　价/ 260.00元 Price: 260.00yuan(RMB)

本书附同版本CD-ROM一张，光盘内容以书面文字为准。
如有印装差错，由本社发行部调换。

《西安统计年鉴—2020》编辑部

总编辑：张民伟　程海营
副总编辑：秦来生　赵群洁　李　红　陈瑾瑜　谷晓春　朱　强　陈立民
焦卫冬　董　军　张　敏
主编：赵群洁
副主编：刘　婷　李　芬
编辑：（以姓氏笔划为序）
丁抗玲　马建华　马　琰　王义龙　冯军魁　白　敏　边可为
刘栋婷　孙国伟　安海军　张　静　李　娜　李　航　连　鹏
陈　英　罗延庆　罗朝晖　赵　晖　席锋旭　栾立森　贾薪蓉
贾海宇　高　唯　高小琴　黄雪冰　曾文元　雷麦鸽　薛　丰
执行编辑：康　敏　赵　博　侯计平　孟　刚　罗　茜　张　熠
英文翻译：董　骋

XI'AN STATISTICAL YEARBOOK-2020
EDITORLAL STAFF

Editor-in-chief: Zhang Minwei　Cheng Haiying
Associate Editors-in-chief: Qin Laisheng　Zhao Qunjie　Li Hong　Chen Jinyu　Gu Xiaochun　Zhu Qiang
Chen Limin　Jiao Weidong　Dong Jun　Zhang Min
Editor-in-Chief: Zhao Qunjie
Deputy Editors-in-Chief: Liu Ting　Li Fen
Editorial Staff: Ding Kangling　Ma Jianhua　Ma Yan　Wang Yilong　Feng Junkui　Bai Min
Bian Kewei　Liu Dongting　Sun Guowei　An Haijun　Zhang Jing　Li Na　Li Hang
Lian Peng　Chen Ying　Luo Yanqing　Luo Zhaohui　Zhao Hui　Xi Fengxu　Luan Lisen
Jia Xinrong　Jia Haiyu　Gao Wei　Gao Xiaoqin　Huang Xuebing　Zeng Wenyuan
Lei Maige　Xue Feng
Executive Editor: Kang Min　Zhao Bo　Hou Jiping　Meng Gang　Luo Qian　Zhang Yi
English Translater: Dong Cheng

编者说明

一、《西安统计年鉴—2020》系统收录了全市、区县及开发区2019年经济、社会各方面统计数据，以及重要历史年份主要统计数据，是一部全面记载西安市国民经济和社会发展情况的大型连续性统计文献资料和重要工具书。

二、本年鉴正文内容分为二十二个篇章：（一）综合；（二）基本单位；（三）国民经济核算；（四）人口、从业人员与职工工资；（五）固定资产投资；（六）财政；（七）物价指数；（八）人民生活；（九）城市公用事业；（十）环境保护；（十一）农业；（十二）工业；（十三）能源；（十四）建筑业；（十五）运输、邮电和信息化；（十六）国内贸易；（十七）对外经济贸易和旅游；（十八）规模以上服务业；（十九）金融业；（二十）教育和科技；（二十一）文化、体育、卫生、社会福利和其他；（二十二）企业调查。同时，为方便读者使用，各篇章前设有简要说明和主要统计指标，对本篇章的主要内容、资料来源、以及历史变动情况予以简要概述，篇末附有《主要统计指标解释》。

三、本年鉴统计资料的统计标准，按当时国家统计制度执行，有关指标的涵义、口径、范围、计算方法等，在不同时期可能有所不同，使用时请注意。如国民经济行业分类按GB/T4754—2017标准执行。

四、为便于国内外读者查阅，本年鉴全部内容均采用中英文对照编辑。

五、本年鉴中，国民经济核算部分的2018年数据为全国第四次经济普查数据，2003-2017年数据为第四次经济普查修订数据；工业部分的2018年数据为第四次经济普查上报数据；国内贸易部分的2003—2018年为第四次经济普查修订数据；农业部分的2007-2017年农林牧渔业总产值、产量等和2013-2017年畜产品等为依据第三次农业普查调整后数据；固定资产投资数据主要为增长速度等相对指标数据；科技数据（除部门数据）为2018年数据。

六、数据口径：本年鉴中2017年起全市数据中，基本单位、国民经济核算、农业（除个别指标）、工业、建筑业、国内贸易、服务业、能源、固定资产投资、常住人口、从业人员和职工工资、信息化、企业调查、城市公用事业（除城市公共交通部分等）、财政、教育、文化、卫生、社会福利和行政区划等指标数据包含西咸新区；2018年起人民生活、利用外资等指标包含西咸新区；2019年起证券、气象等指标包含西咸新区。物价指数（除部分指标）、运输邮电、环境保护、对外贸易和旅游(除部分指标)、银行和保险、体育、户籍人口、土地面积等指标数据为西安原口径或不包含西咸新区数据，具体情况见表下附注。

七、本年鉴中的部分指标合计数或相对数由于单位取舍不同产生的计算误差均未作机械调整。

八、本年鉴所使用的计量单位均依据2019年相关统计报表制度。

九、本年鉴使用的符号说明："…"表示数据不足本表最小单位；"空白"表示该项统计指标无数据或数据不详；"#"表示其中项；"*"表示另有注解。

感谢社会各界长期以来对《西安统计年鉴》的广泛关注和大力支持。为进一步做好工作，更好地为广大读者服务，希望社会各界提出宝贵意见。

PREFACE

I. *Xi'an Statistical Yearbook 2020* is a periodical statistic yearbook which record economic and social development of Xi'an all-around in 2019 and some selected data series in historical important years. With its features of comprehensive and intensive information, this practically provides data covering the situation of social and economic developments in Xi'an.

II. The book contains twenty-two parts, 1.General Survey; 2.Basic Unit; 3.National Economic Account; 4.Population, Employment and Wages; 5.Investment in Fixed Assets; 6.Government Finance; 7.Price Indices; 8.People's Livelihood; 9.Urban Public Utilities; 10.Environmental Protection; 11.Agriculture; 12.Industry; 13.Energy; 14.Construction; 15.Transportation, Post and Informatization; 16.Domestic Trade; 17.Foreign Trade; 18. Service Industry; 19.Financial Intermediation; 20.Education, Science and Technology; 21.Culture, Sports, Public Health, Social Welfare and Other Social Activities; 22.Enterprises Investigation. Meanwhile, for the convenience of the reader, a brief explanation and major statistical indicators are provided before each chapter, the main contents, sources and historical changes of this chapter are briefly summarized. The final part is accompanied by the interpretation of major statistical indicators.

III. The data of various years in conformity to the statistical standards prescribed by national statistical system of the time. The meaning, scope and calculating method of indicators may have some difference in different periods, which readers must pay attention to. For example, national industries classification is carried out according to standard GB/T4754 -2017.

IV. For the convenience of being consulted by foreigners, the book is Chinese-English bilingual edition.

V. In this yearbook, the data of 2018 at the part of National Economic Accounting and Industry is the results of Fourth National Economic Census, the data from 2003 to 2017 at the part of National Economic Account have adjusted by Fourth National Economic Census. The data of industry in 2018 is revised for The Fourth National Economic Census; The domestic trade part of 2003-2018 is based on the adjusted data of The Fourth National Economic Census. The agricultural output, the total output value, output of agriculture, forestry, animal husbandry and fishery in 2007-2017 and the livestock products and aquatic products in 2013-2017 are based on the adjusted data of the third agricultural census. The per capita disposable income of urban residents and rural residents is revised based on the new caliber in 2018; Fixed asset investment data are mainly relative indicator data such as growth rate.

VI. Statistical scope: in this yearbook, the data from 2017 about the basic unit, the national economic accounting, agriculture, industry, construction industry, domestic trade, services, energy, investment in fixed assets, labor wages, informatization, enterprise survey, urban public utilities, finance, education, culture, health and social welfare contains Xixian New District. Since 2018, the indicators such as people's living and utilization of foreign capital include Xixian New District. Since 2019, the indicators such as securities and meteorology include Xixian New District. The price index (except for individual indicators), transportation, post and telecommunications, environmental protection, foreign trade and tourism (except for some indicators), Banking and Insurance, sports, household registration, land area and other indicators are Xi'an original caliber data or does not include Xixian New District. See the notes under the table for details.

VII. Statistical discrepancies due to rounding are not adjusted automatically in this yearbook.

VIII. Unit of measurement is used in this yearbook according to 2019 statistics system.

IX. Explanations on symbols used in this yearbook:

"..." indicates the data is less than the minimum unit in this table;

(Blank) indicates the data not available;

\# indicates the items of the total;

* indicates some other explanatory note.

Here we would like to express our sincere thanks to the people for their concerning and support to the Xi'an statistical yearbook. In order to do better and provide better service to readers, we hope that the whole society fields can propose constructive advices.

生产总值（亿元）

Gross Domestic Product (100 million yuan)

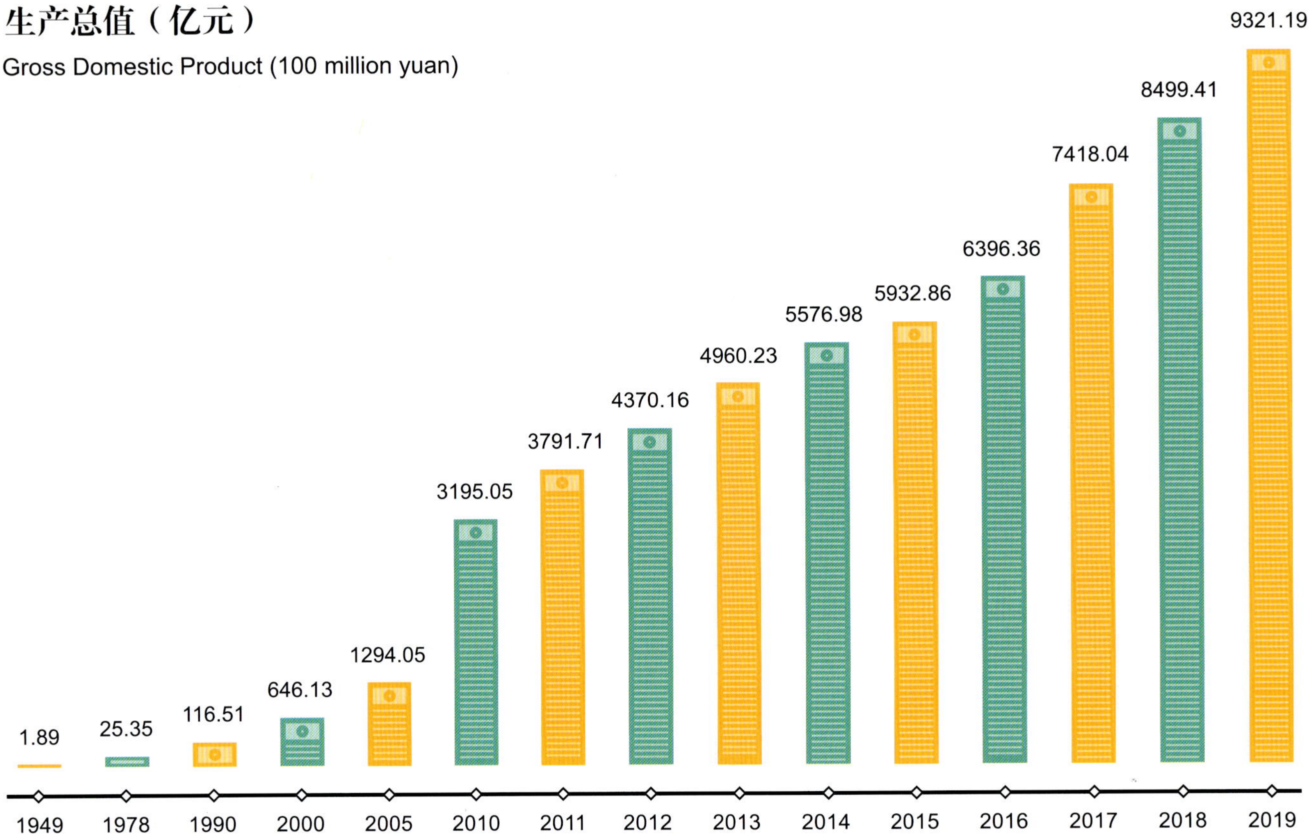

生产总值指数（以上年为100）

Indices of Gross Domestic Product (preceding year = 100)

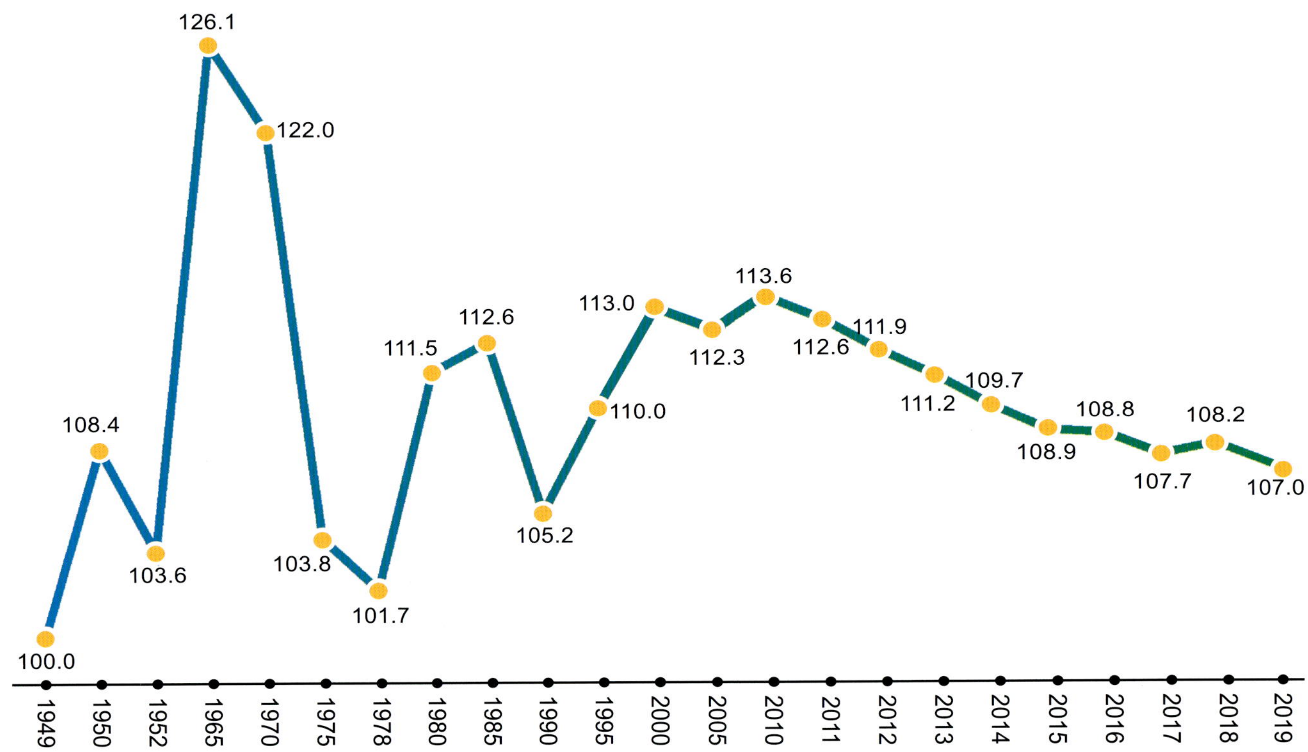

生产总值构成(%)
Composition of Gross Domestic Product (%)

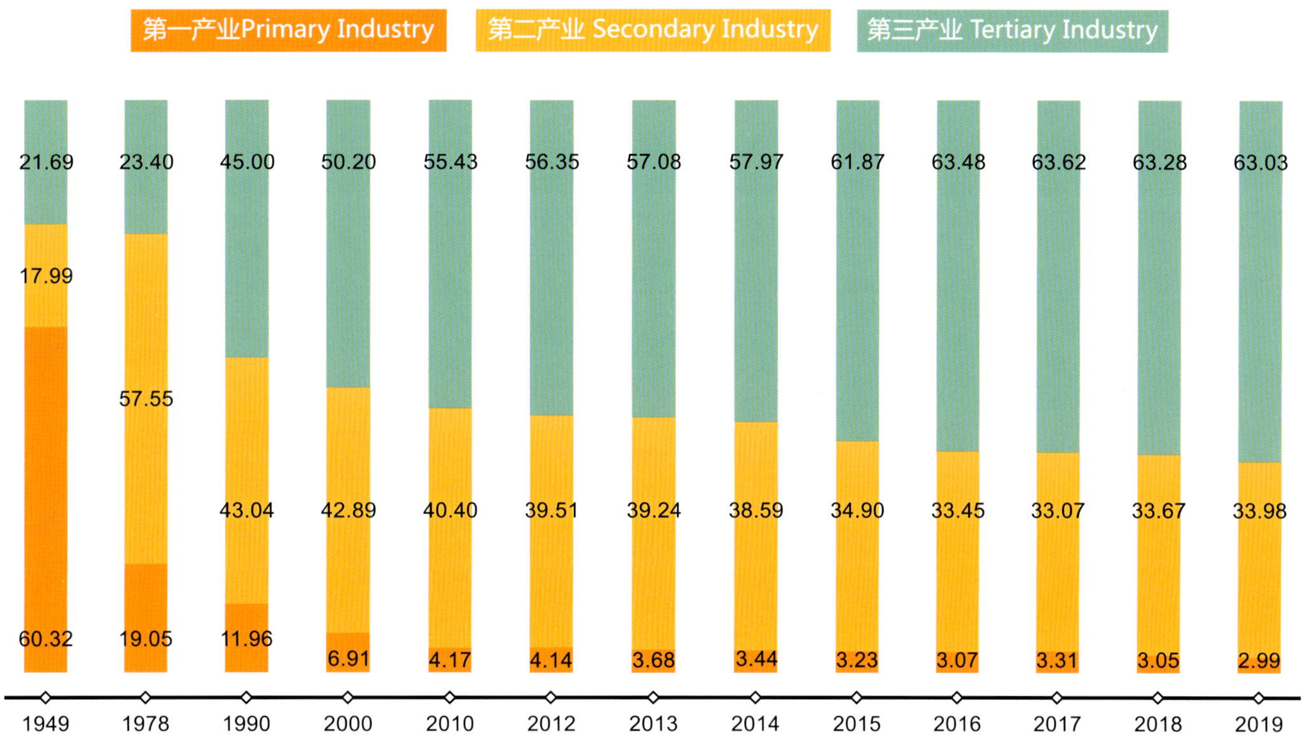

人均GDP（元/人）
Per Capita GDP(yuan/person)

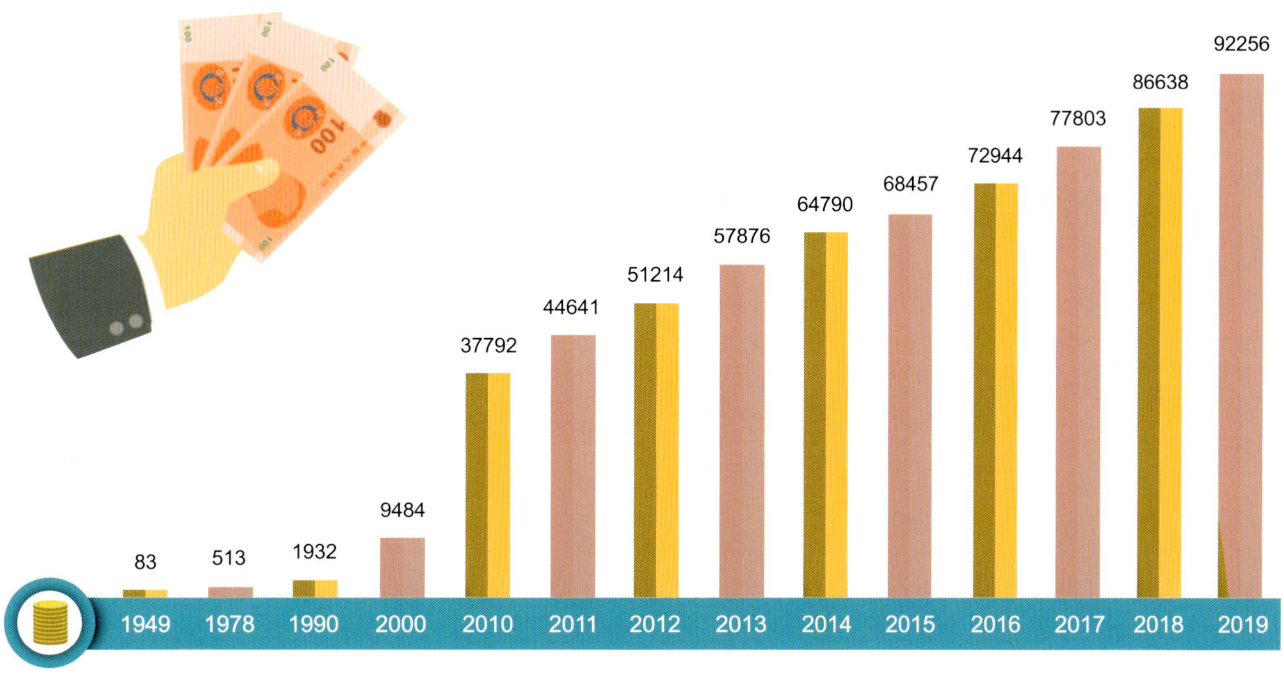

年末常住人口（万人）

Year-end Permanent Population(10000 persons)

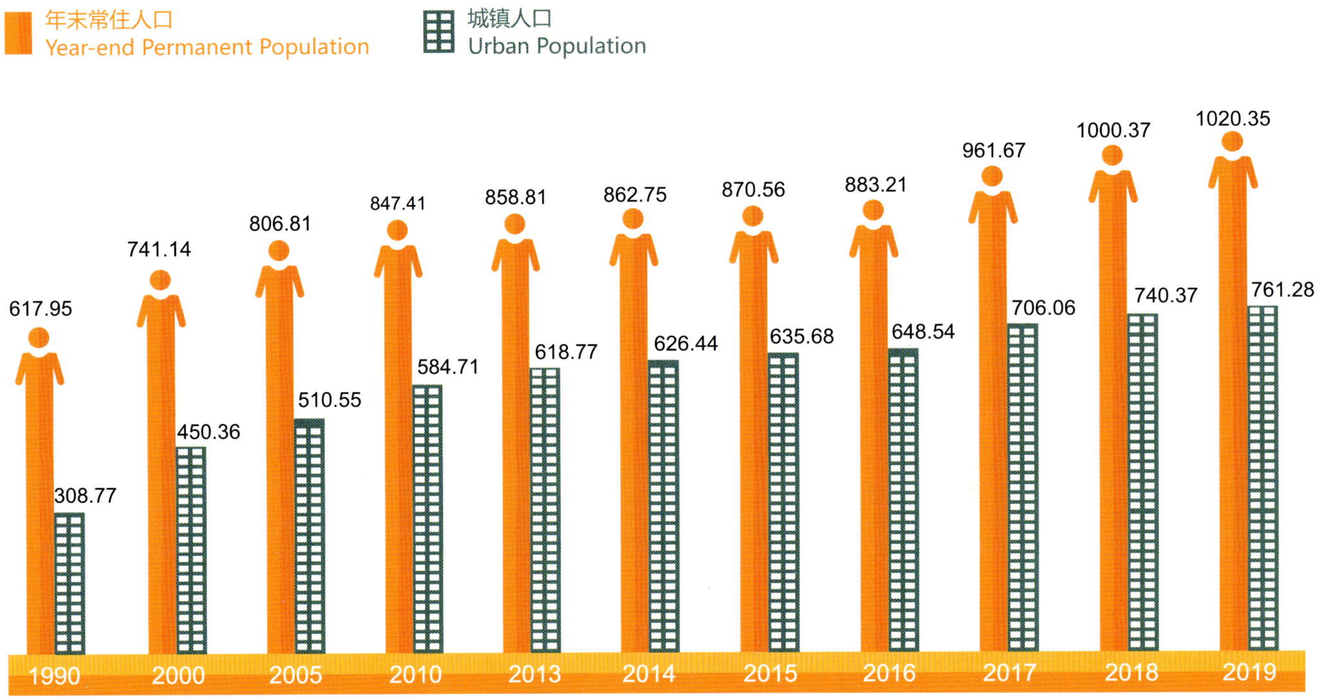

社会从业人数（万人）

Social Workers(10000 persons)

固定资产投资增长速度（%）

Growth Rates of Investment in Fixed Assets (%)

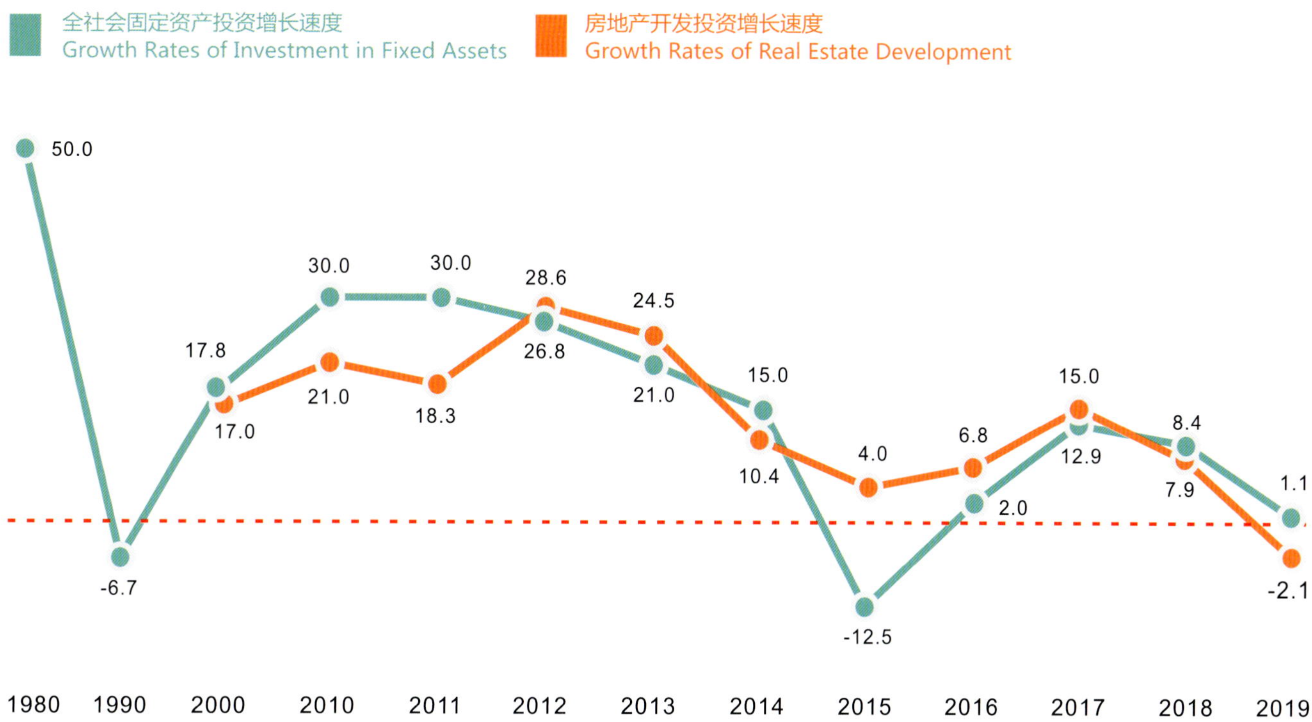

商品房销售面积（万平方米）

Floor Space of Commercialized Buildings Sold(10 000sq.m)

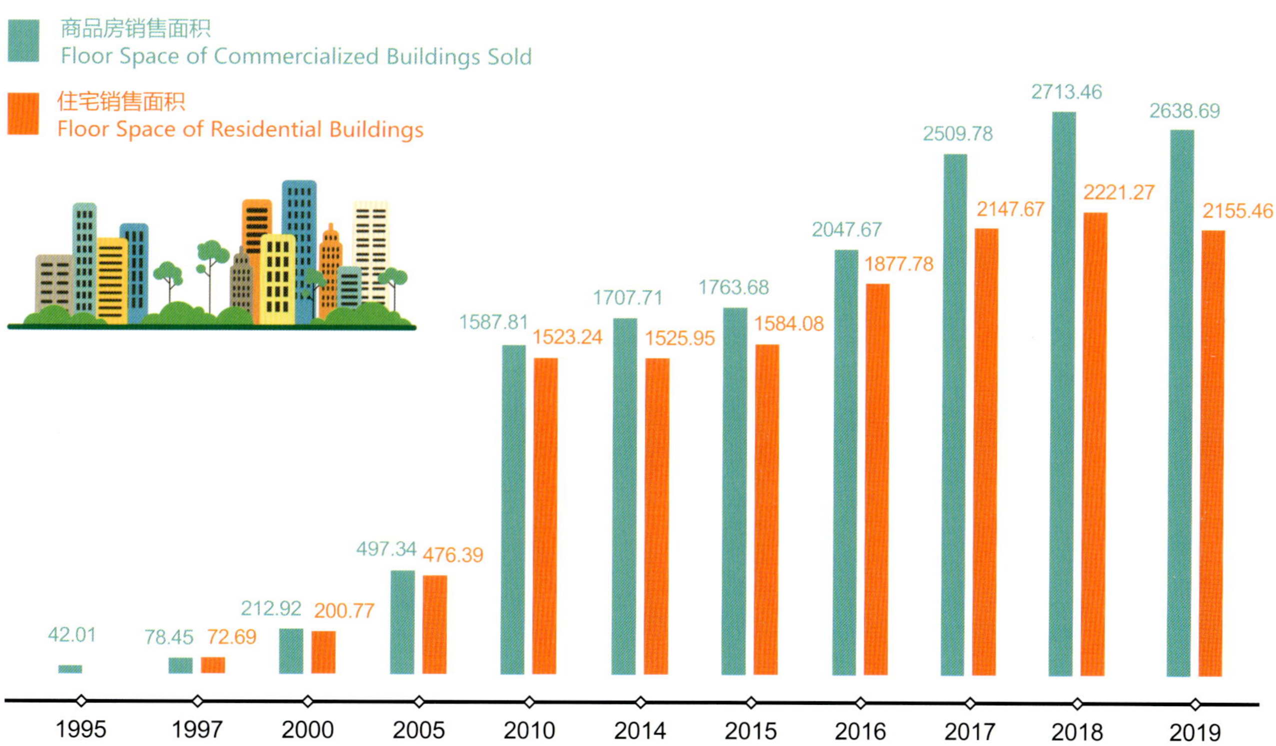

农林牧渔业总产值（亿元）

Gross Output Value of Farming,Forestry,
Animal Husbandry and Fishery (100 million yuan)

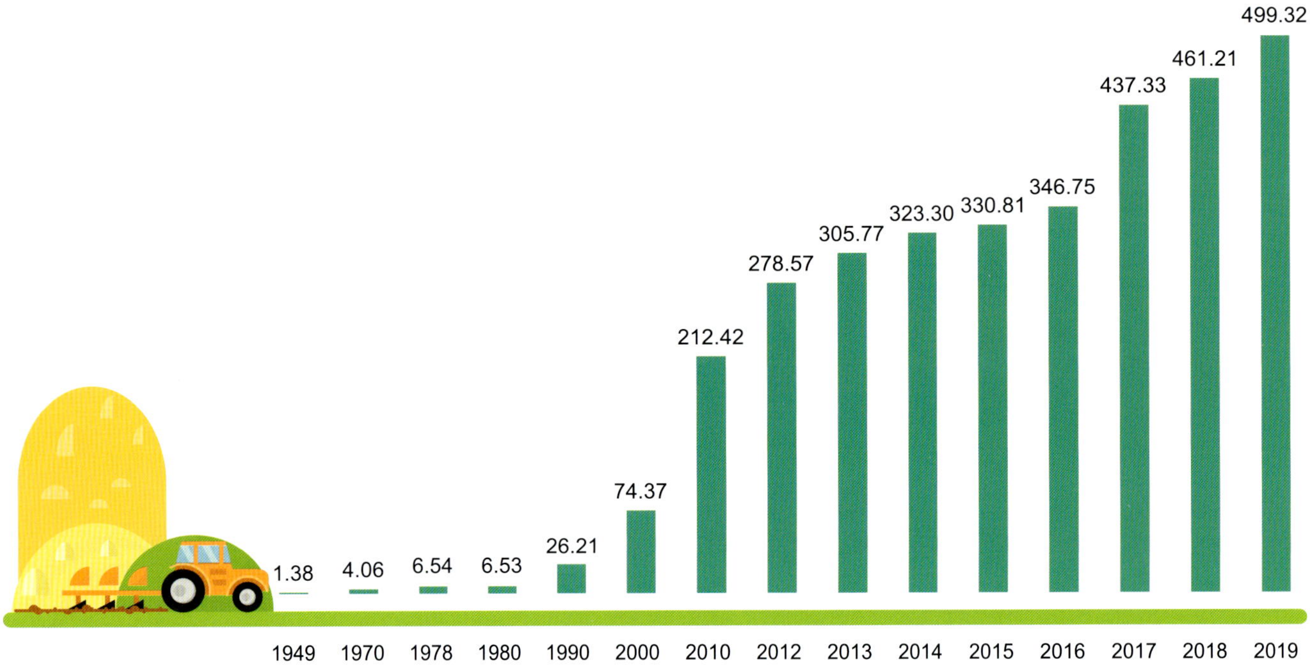

粮食产量（万吨）

Grain Product(10000 tons)

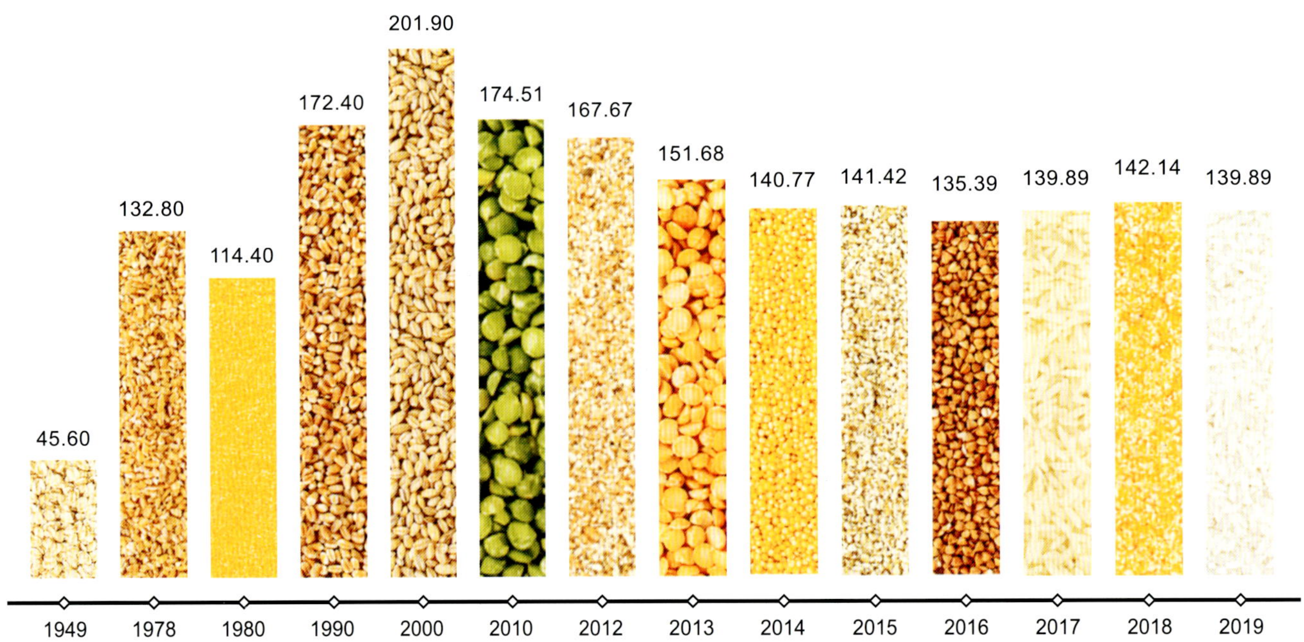

蔬菜产量（万吨）

Vegetables Product(10000 tons)

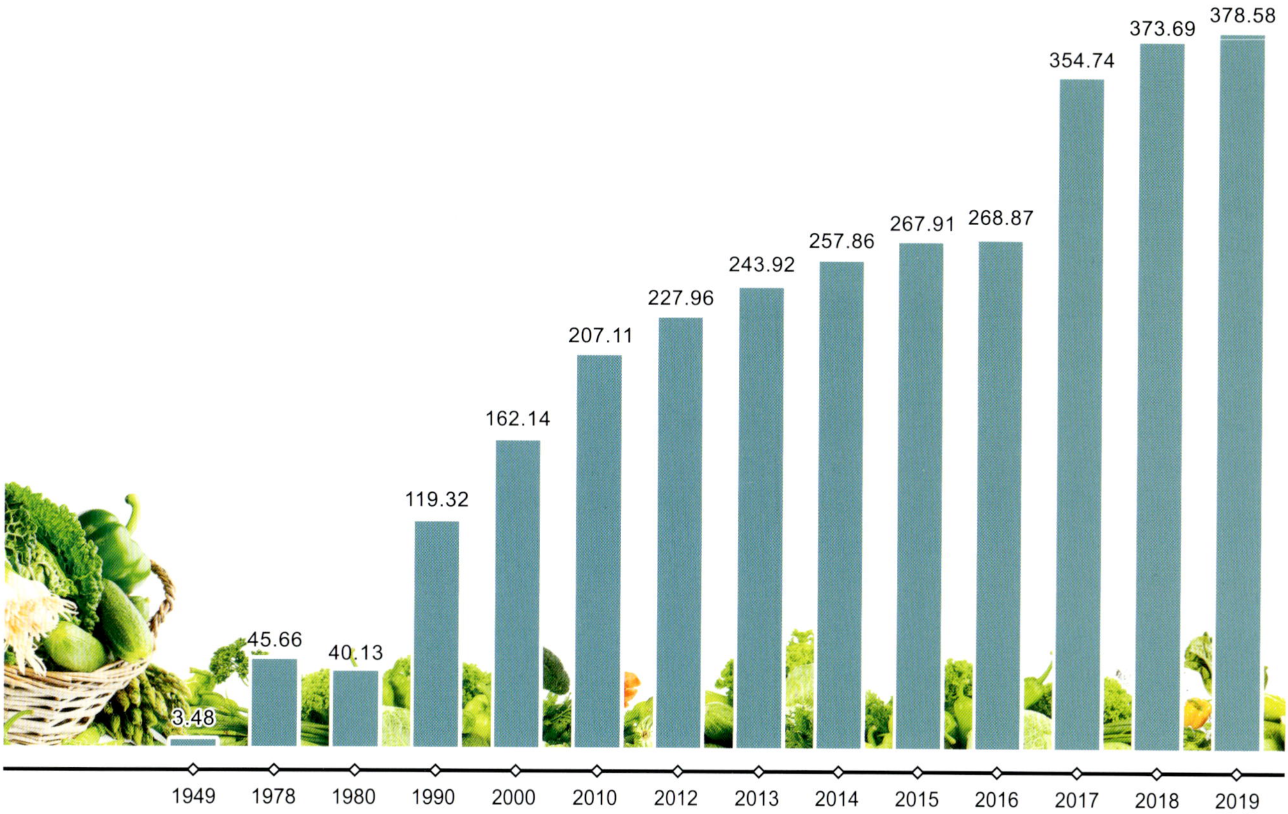

规模以上工业企业主要产品产量

Output of Major Industrial Products Of Enterprises Above Designated Size

汽车（万辆）
Motor Vehicle(10000units)

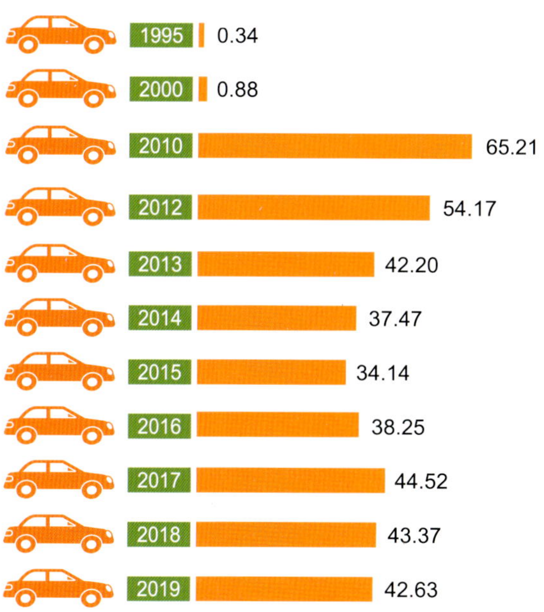

变压器（万千伏安）
Transformer (10000kwa)

交通
Traffic

等级公路（公里）
Expressways and Clas I to IV Highways(KM)

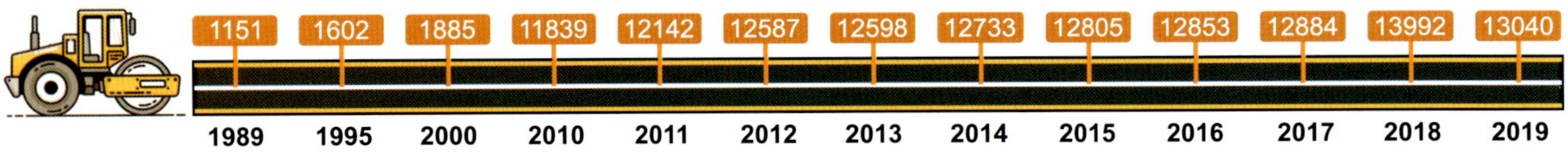

高速公路（公里）
Expressway(KM)

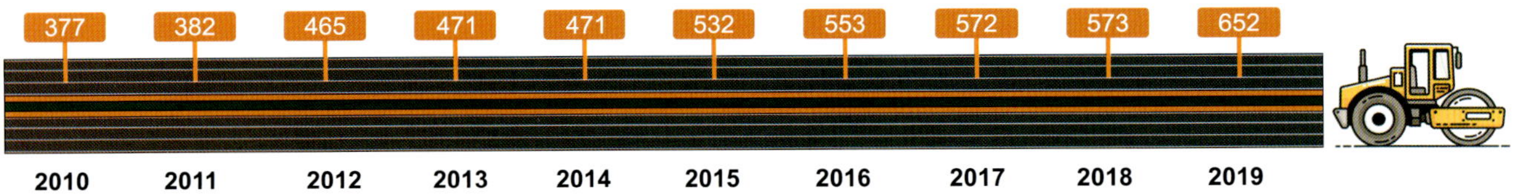

全社会车辆数（万辆）
Possession of Civil Vehicles(10000 units)

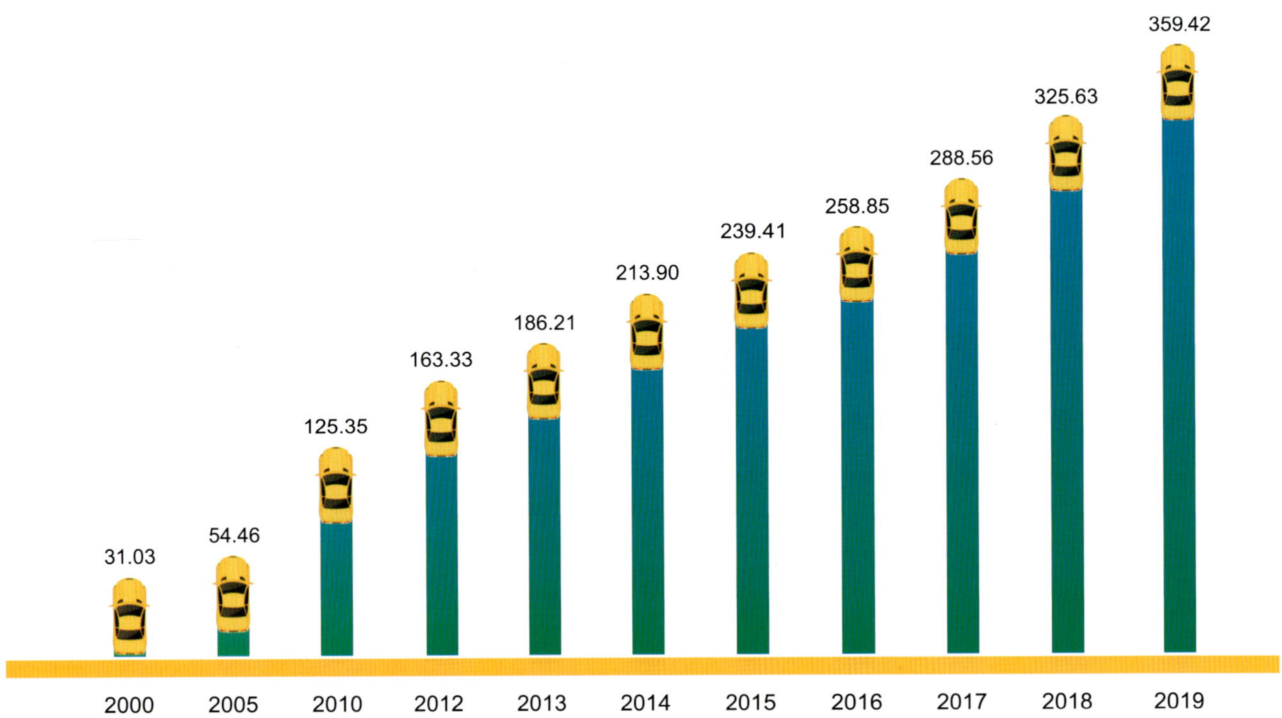

社会消费品零售总额（亿元）
Total Retail Sales of Consumer Goods(100 million yuan)

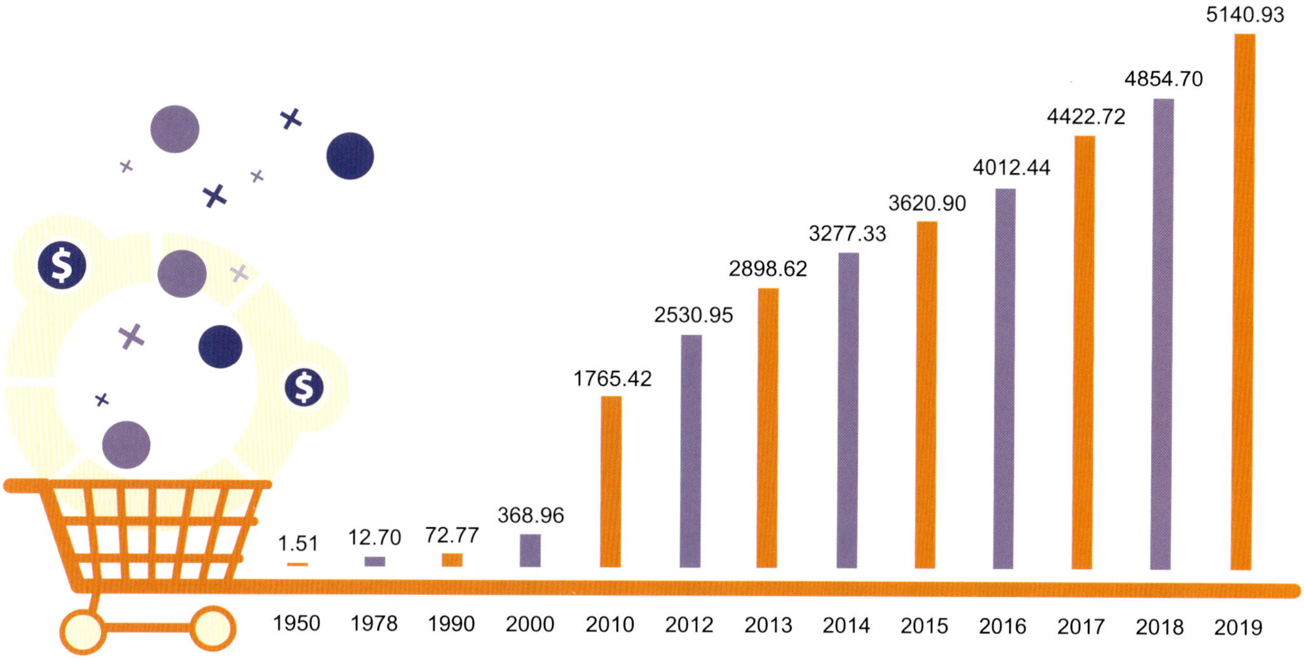

实际利用外商直接投资额（亿美元）
Foreign Direct Investment(USD 100 million)

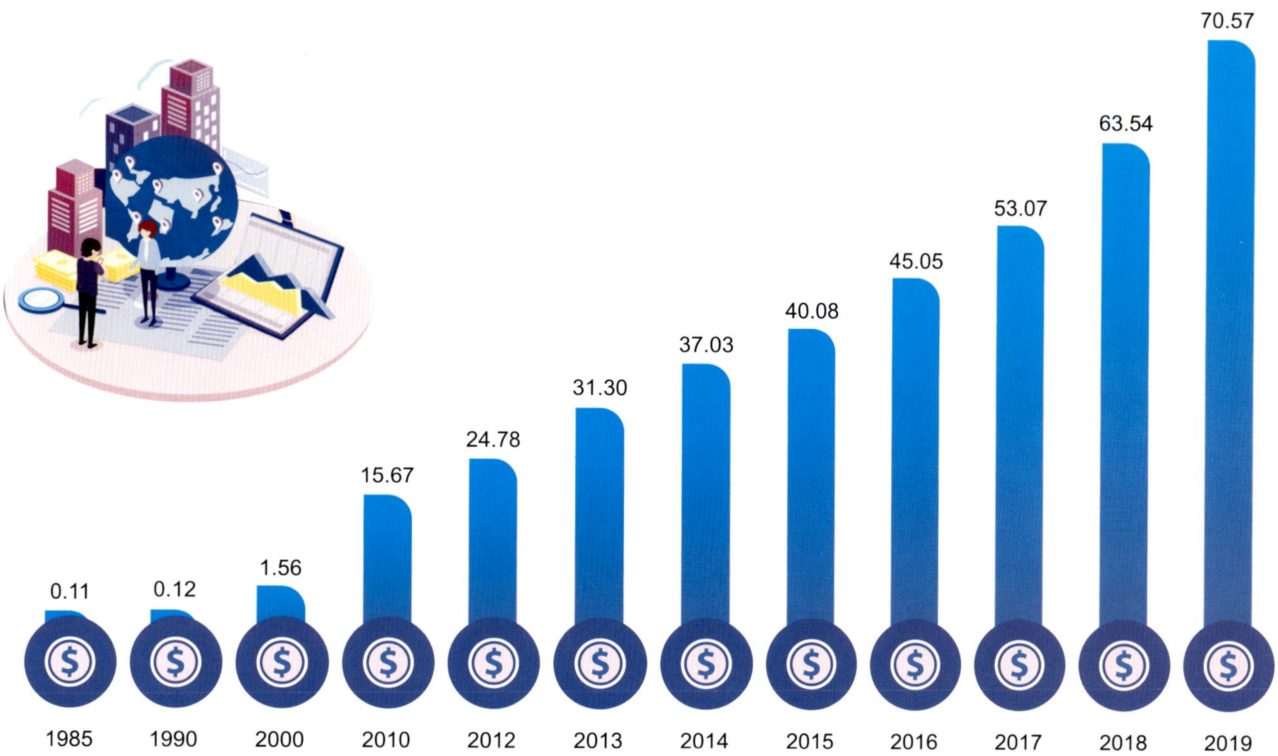

进出口总值（亿美元）

Total Value of Imports and Exports(USD 100 million)

	1987	1990	2000	2010	2012	2013
进出口总值	1.36	3.82	17.37	103.92	130.14	179.85
出口总值	0.75	2.83	10.61	53.17	72.99	84.78
进口总值	0.61	0.99	6.76	50.75	57.15	95.07

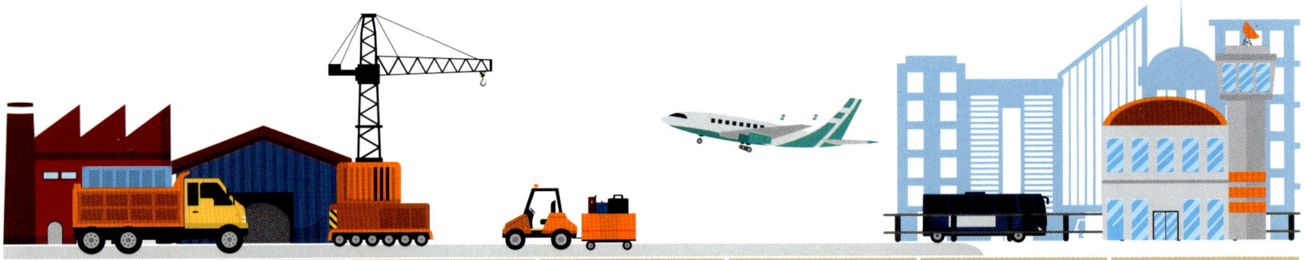

	2014	2015	2016	2017	2018	2019
进出口总值	1532.15	1761.69	1829.95	2545.08	3303.24	3242.51
出口总值	734.68	819.88	947.31	1552.22	1957.17	1730.28
进口总值	797.47	941.81	882.64	992.86	1346.07	1512.23

注：2014年起单位为人民币亿元

旅游人数及收入

Number of Tourists and Tourism Income

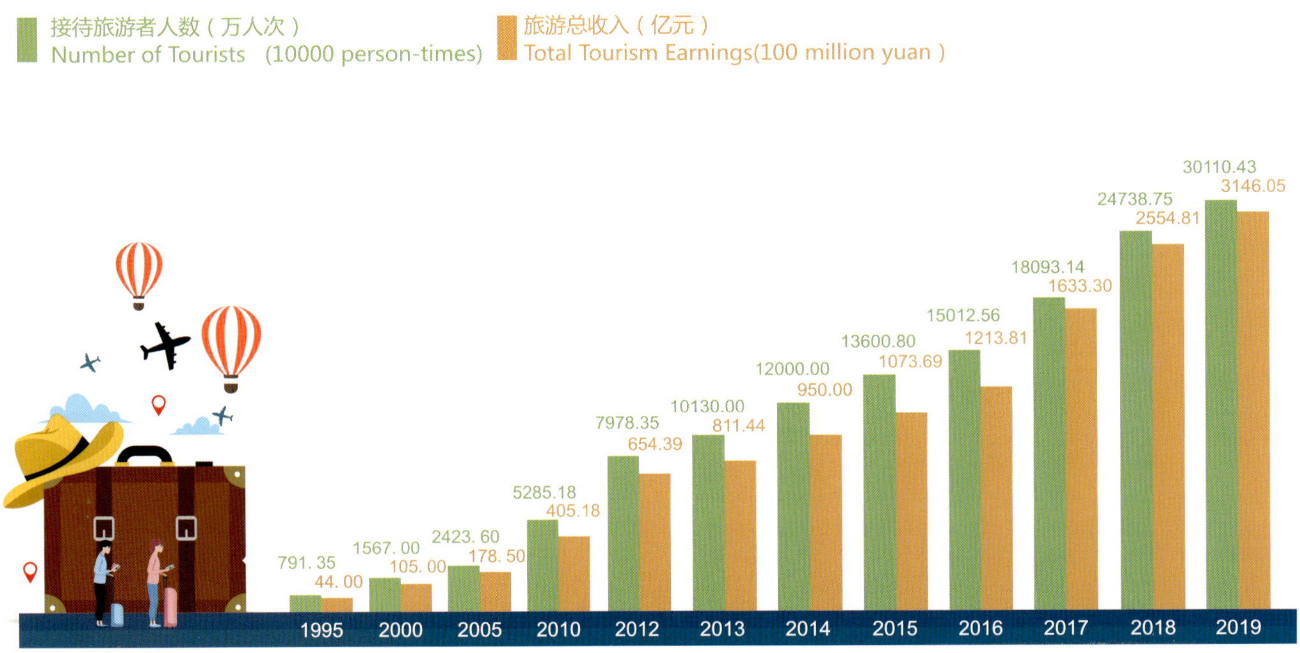

财政收支（亿元）

Govement Revenue and Expenditure(100 million yuan)

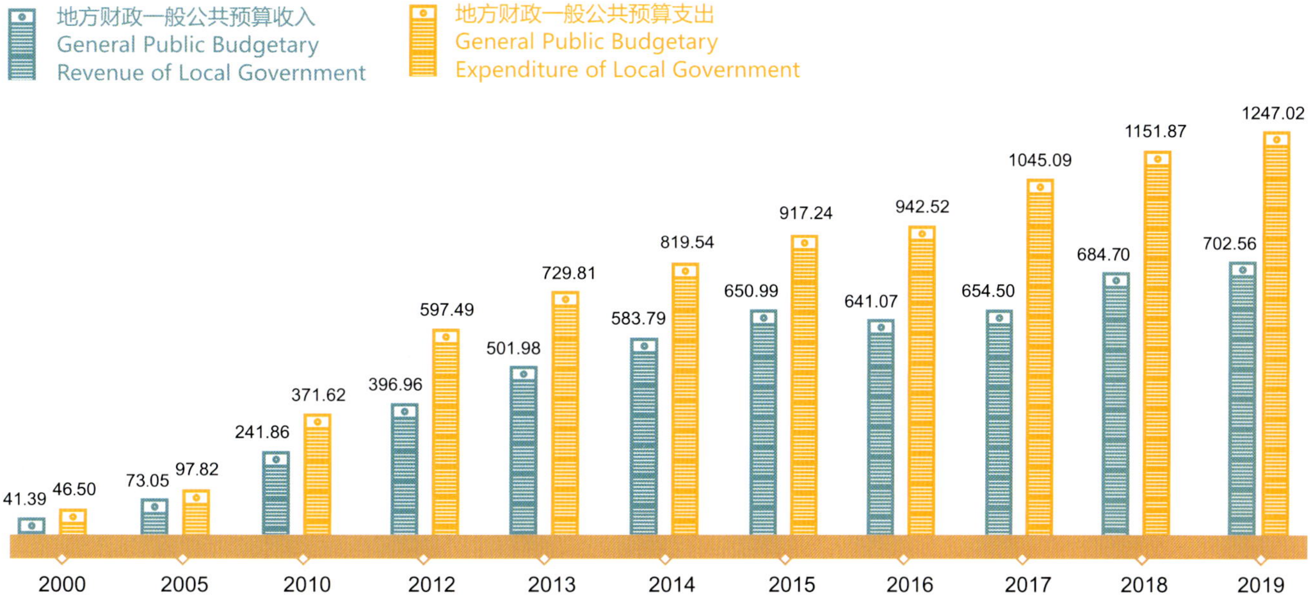

金融机构人民币存贷款年末余额（亿元）

Year-end Deposit and Loans in Financial Institutions (100 million yuan)

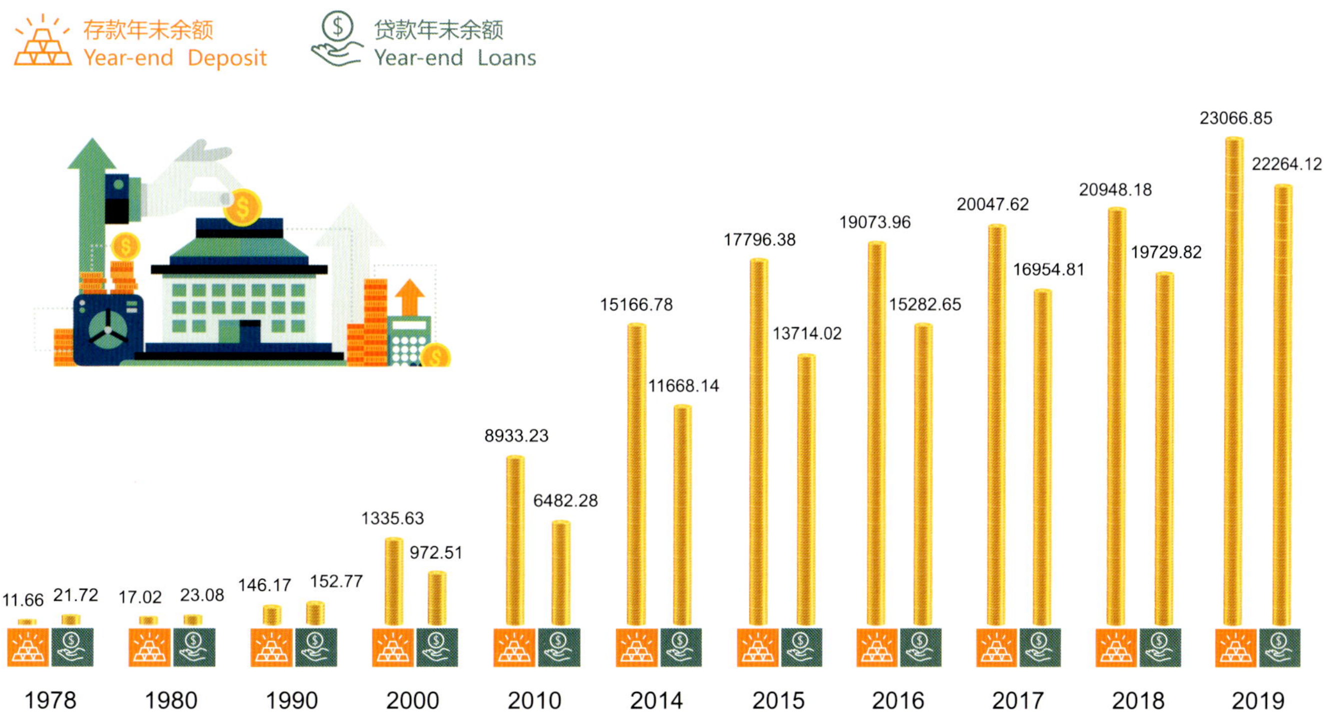

城市公共运营车辆（辆）

City Operating Vehicles(unit)

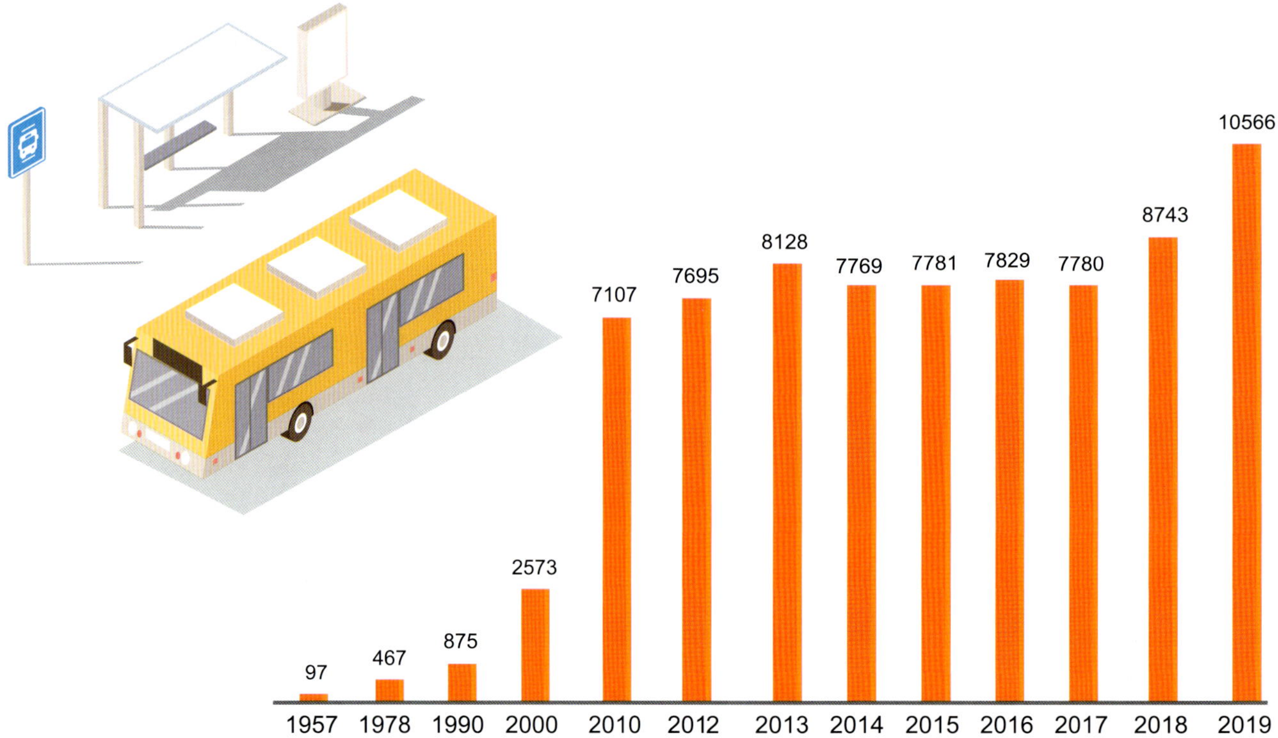

天然气供气总量（万立方米）

Total Natural Gas Supply(10000 cu.m)

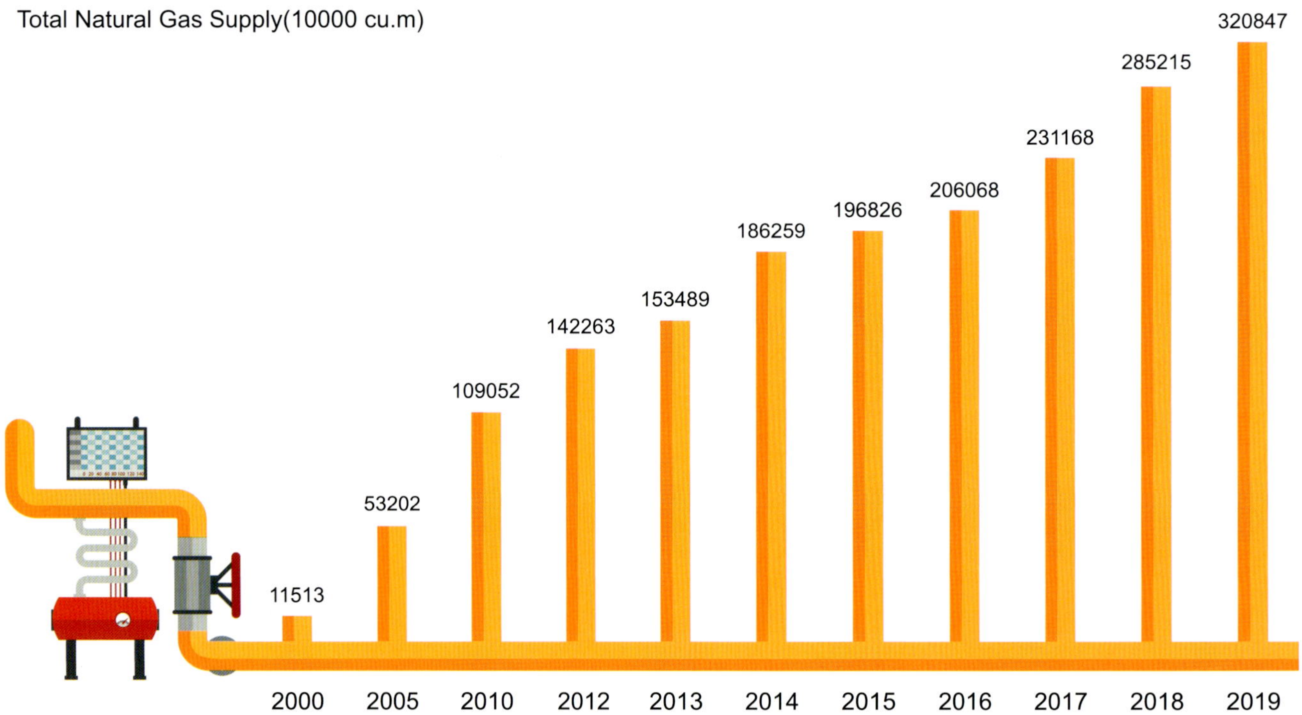

园林绿地面积（公顷）

Total Area of Park，Gardens and Green Area（hectare）

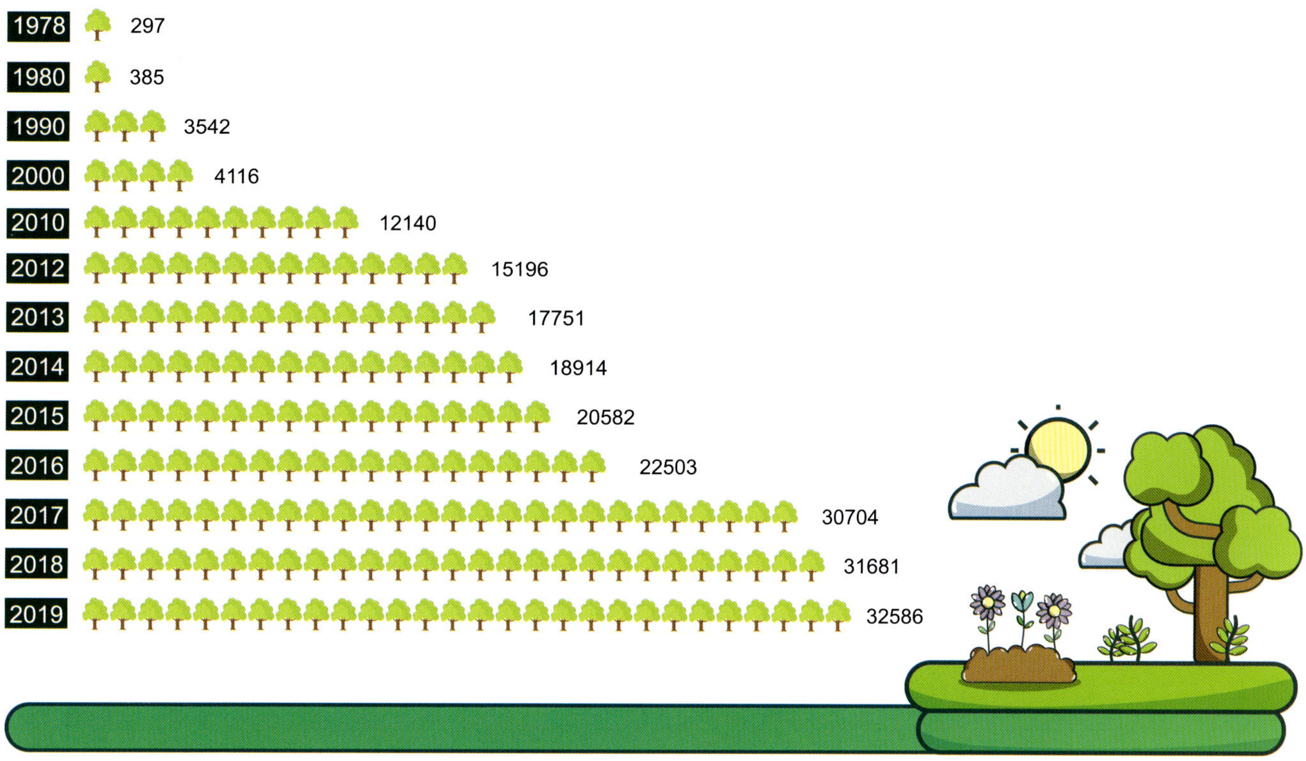

普通教育在校学生（万人）

Total Enrollment of Regular Education（10000 persons）

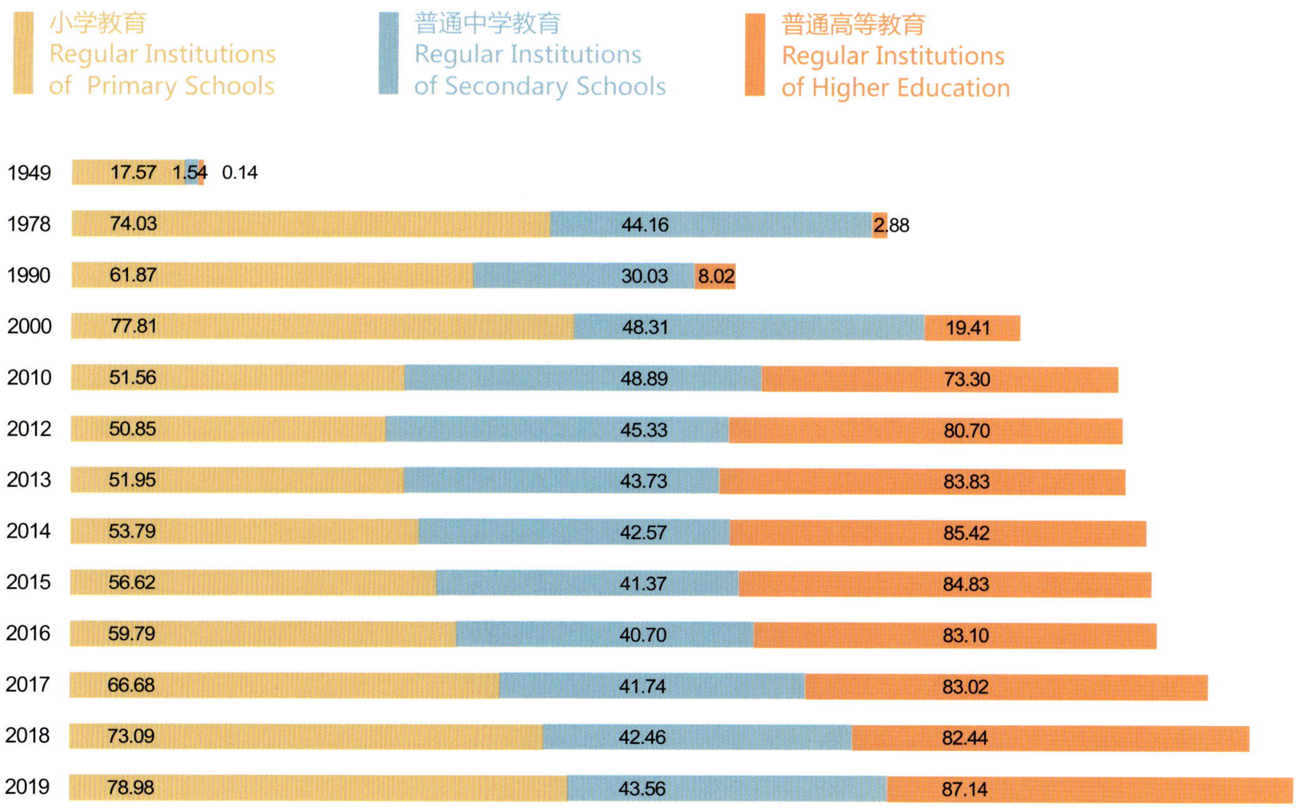

专任教师（万人）

Full-time Teachers (10000 persons)

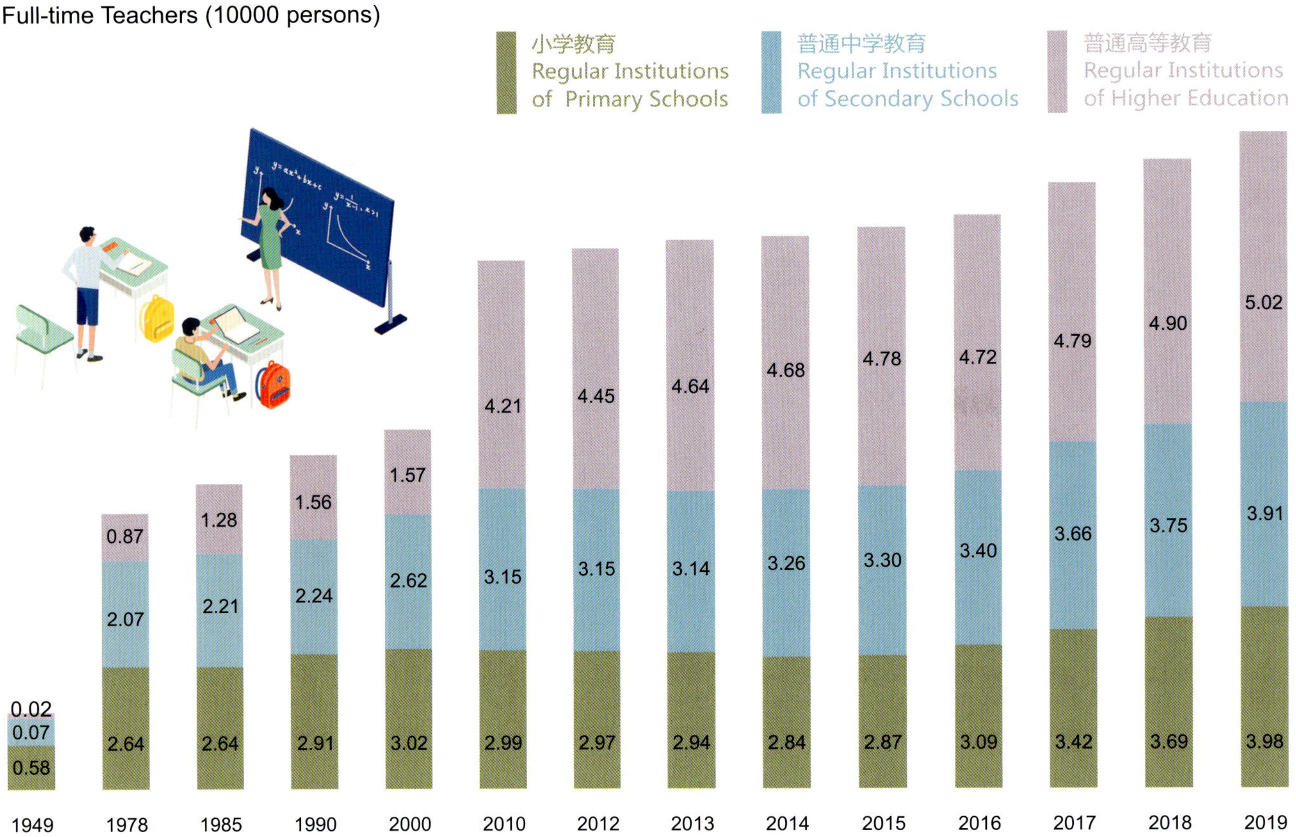

价格指数（以上年价格为100）

Price Indices(the price of preceding year=100)

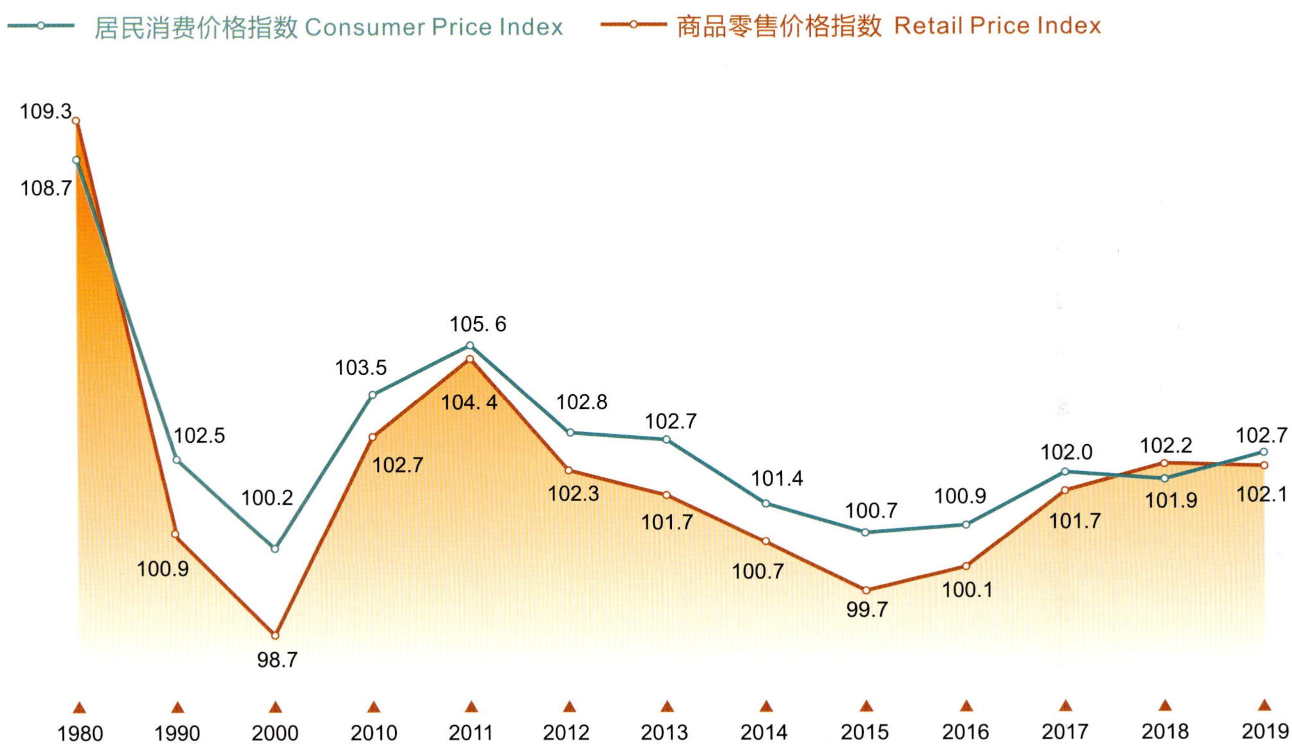

目 录

CONTENTS

一、综 合

GENERAL SURVEY

二、基本单位

BASIC UNIT

三、国民经济核算

NATIONAL ECONOMIC ACCOUNTS

四、人口、从业人员与职工工资

POPULATION，EMPLOYMENT AND WAGES

五、固定资产投资

INVESTMENT IN FIXED ASSETS

六、财　政

GOVERNMENT FINANCE

七、物价指数

PRICE INDICES

八、人民生活

PEOPLE'S LIVELIHOOD

九、城市公用事业

URBAN PUBLIC UTILITIES

十、环境保护

ENVIRONMENT PROTECTION

十一、农　　业

AGRICULTURE

十二、工　业

INDUSTRY

十三、能　源
ENERGY

十四、建筑业
CONSTRUCTION

十五、运输邮电和信息化

TRANSPORT，POSTAL TELECOMMUNICATION SERVICE AND INFORMATIZATION

十六、国内贸易

DOMESTIC TRADE

十七、对外经济贸易和旅游

FOREIGN TRADE AND ECONOMIC COOPERATION TOURISM

十八、规模以上服务业

SERVICE INDUSTRY OBOVE DESIGNATED SIZE

十九、金融业

FINANCIAL INTERMEDIATION

二十、教育和科技

EDUCATION，SCIENCE AND TECHNOLOGY

二十一、文化、体育、卫生、社会福利和其他
CULTURE, SPORTS, PUBLIC HEALTH, SOCIAL WELFARE INSTITUTIONS AND OTHER SOCIAL ACTIVITIES

二十二、企业调查

ENTERPRISES INVESTIGATION

西安市2019年国民经济和社会发展统计公报[1]

西安市统计局　国家统计局西安调查队

2020年3月23日

2019年，面对国内外风险挑战明显上升的复杂局面，全市上下以习近平新时代中国特色社会主义思想为指引，紧扣追赶超越定位和“五个扎实”要求，谋划启动“十项重点工作”，统筹做好稳增长、促改革、调结构、惠民生、防风险、保稳定各项工作，经济运行稳中有进，经济结构继续优化，发展质量稳步提升，民生福祉持续增进，社会事业繁荣发展，生态环境整体改善，实现了经济平稳健康发展与社会和谐稳定，开创建设国家中心城市新局面，建设具有历史文化特色的国际化大都市迈出新步伐。

一、综合

初步核算，全年地区生产总值[2]（GDP）9321.19亿元，比上年增长7.0%。其中，第一产业增加值279.13亿元，增长4.3%；第二产业增加值3167.44亿元，增长7.6%；第三产业增加值5874.62亿元，增长6.8%。三次产业构成为3.0:34.0:63.0。按常住人口计算，全年人均生产总值92256元，比上年增长3.9%。

全年非公有制经济增加值5066.18亿元，占生产总值的比重为54.4%，比上年提高1.0个百分点。

全年居民消费价格比上年上涨2.7%，其中，食品烟酒价格上涨4.1%。商品零售价格上涨2.1%。工业生产者出厂价格上涨1.6%，工业生产者购进价格持平。新建商品住宅销售价格上涨21.1%。

图1：2019年居民消费价格月度涨跌幅度（%）

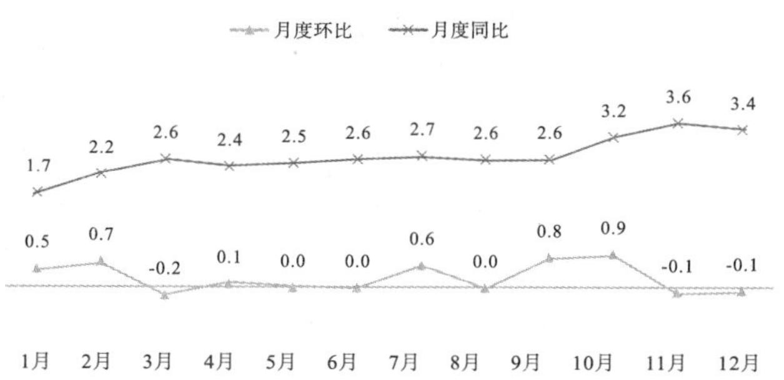

表1：2019年居民消费价格比上年涨跌幅度（%）

指　标	涨跌幅度（%）
居民消费价格	2.7
食品烟酒	4.1
衣着	3.1
居住	2.6
生活用品及服务	1.5
交通和通信	-0.7
教育文化和娱乐	4.2
医疗保健	0.9
其他用品和服务	3.9

全年新增城镇就业16.12万人，城镇失业人员再就业6.27万人。年末城镇登记失业率为3.27%。

全年新登记各类市场主体88.31万户，比上年增长62.6%。其中，新登记企业13.06万户，增长3.2%；新登记个体工商户75.17万户，增长81.0%。

全年地方财政一般公共预算收入702.56亿元，比上年增长2.6%，其中，税收收入580.75亿元，增长4.3%。全年地方财政一般公共预算支出1247.99亿元，比上年增长8.3%。

二、农业

全年粮食种植面积409.71万亩，比上年下降2.3%；蔬菜种植面积107.72万亩，与上年持平；瓜果种植面积14.73万亩，下降1.3%；油料种植面积4.66万亩，增长1.1%；棉花种植面积0.12万亩，增长31.1%。

全年粮食产量139.90万吨，比上年下降1.6%，其中，夏粮70.63万吨，秋粮69.27万吨。蔬菜产量378.58万吨，增长1.3%；水果产量97.18万吨，增长9.0%。

表2：2019年主要农产品产量及其增长速度

产品名称	单位	产量	比上年增长（%）
粮食	万吨	139.90	-1.6
蔬菜	万吨	378.58	1.3
水果	万吨	97.18	9.0
肉类	万吨	5.14	-5.6
#猪肉	万吨	3.35	-6.7
奶类	万吨	12.37	7.4
禽蛋	万吨	5.39	2.4
猪年末存栏数	万头	29.66	-5.2
牛年末存栏数	万头	5.16	2.0
羊年末存栏数	万只	7.19	-3.1
家禽年末存栏数	万只	643.67	2.9

三、工业、建筑业和能耗

全年全部工业增加值1868.86亿元，比上年增长6.6%。规模以上工业[3]增加值增长6.9%。在规模以上工业中，轻工业增加值下降3.8%，重工业增加值增长9.1%。

图2：2018–2019年规模以上工业增加值增长速度（%）

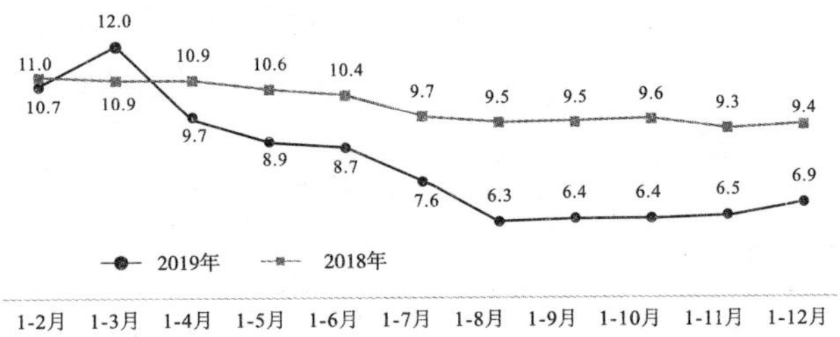

全年规模以上工业中，装备制造业[4]增加值增长9.3%，占规模以上工业增加值的比重为65.7%。其中，铁路、船舶、航空航天和其他运输设备制造业增长9.2%，计算机、通信和其他电子设备制造业增长15.9%，电气机械和器材制造业增长6.7%，汽车制造业下降1.0%，仪器仪表制造业增长19.7%，通用设备制造业增长9.9%，专用设备制造业增长11.3%，金属制品、机械和设备修理业增长13.0%。六大高耗能行业[5]增加值增长4.3%，其中，非金属矿物制品业增长4.9%，有色金属冶炼和压延加工业增长3.5%，黑色金属冶炼和压延加工业下降2.5%，石油加工、炼焦和核燃料加工业下降12.0%，化学原料和化学制品制造业增长8.9%，电力、热力生产和供应业增长1.6%。

表3：2019年10大行业增加值增长速度

行业名称	比上年增长（%）
规模以上工业增加值	6.9
10个行业合计	7.6
通用设备制造业	9.9
专用设备制造业	11.3
汽车制造业	-1.0
铁路、船舶、航空航天和其他运输设备制造业	9.2
电气机械和器材制造业	6.7
计算机、通信和其他电子设备制造业	15.9
仪器仪表制造和金属制品业	7.0
食品制造业	6.2
医药制造业	-5.8
电力、热力生产和供应业	1.6

全年规模以上工业中，战略性新兴产业[6]总产值比上年增长9.6%，占规模以上工业比重为42.5%；高技术制造业[7]总产值增长14.9%，占规模以上工业比重为26.3%，其中，电子及通信设备制造业总产值增长22.7%，占高技术制造业的比重为70.3%，信息化学品制造业下降74.2%，航空、航天器及设备制造业增长4.3%，计算机及办公设备制造业下降4.3%。

工业新产品产量快速增长。单晶硅176.36万千克，比上年增长2.3倍；多晶硅1030.20万千克，增长2.0倍；锂离子电池1761.04万只，增长17.1%；光电子器件427.20万只，增长22.8%。

表4：2019年主要工业产品产量及其增长速度

产品名称	单位	产量	比上年增长（%）
发电量	亿千瓦小时	155.00	-10.5
饮料	万吨	207.59	22.7
小麦粉	万吨	44.01	-20.8
饲料	万吨	74.28	-7.2
乳制品	万吨	72.64	-3.0
中成药	万吨	1.25	16.7
交流电动机	万千瓦	261.32	0.5
变压器	万千伏安	17365.29	31.2
汽车	万辆	42.63	-1.7
其中：载货汽车	万辆	19.23	5.0
轿车	万辆	14.14	-21.8
运动型多用途乘用车(SUV)	万辆	9.26	33.5
新能源汽车	万辆	9.35	-32.5
单晶硅	万千克	176.36	225.3
电力电缆	万千米	14.09	-39.6
光纤	万千米	564.61	-29.6
光缆	万芯千米	676.75	-22.5
锂离子电池	万只	1761.04	17.1
智能手机	万台	1141.21	-31.1
光电子器件	万只	427.20	22.8
电子元件	亿只	45.84	-10.4
集成电路圆片	万片	143.30	-4.5

规模以上工业企业主营业务收入5740.80亿元，比上年增长7.7%。实现利润总额298.70亿元，下降16.7%。

全年全社会建筑业增加值1358.48亿元，比上年增长9.1%。全市具有资质等级的总承包和专业承包建筑业企业实现建筑业总产值4514.38亿元，增长15.8%，其中，国有及国有控股企业产值3467.90亿元，增长14.6%。所有资质等级企业签订合同额12669.45亿元，增长25.2%。

全年规模以上工业综合能源消费量634.77万吨标准煤，比上年下降8.4%。其中，高耗能行业综合能源消费量485.64万吨标准煤，比上年下降10.8%。非高耗能行业综合能源消费量149.13万吨标准煤，增长0.4%。规模以上工业煤炭消费1068.14万吨，比上年减少130.98万吨。其中，非电力企业煤炭消费305.39万吨，比上年减少50.14万吨。

四、服务业

全年批发和零售业增加值777.86亿元，比上年增长8.5%；交通运输、仓储和邮政业增加值330.54亿元，增长6.7%；住宿和餐饮业增加值178.49亿元，增长5.2%；金融业增加值998.94亿元，增长7.9%；房地产业增加值729.52亿元，增长0.8%；其他服务业增加值2768.82亿元，增长7.5%。全年规模以上服务业[8]企业营业收入2454.36亿元，比上年增长11.4%。

全年货物运输总量2.74亿吨，比上年增长3.8%；货物运输周转量519.01亿吨公里，与上年持平。旅客运输总量2.63亿人次，增长1.0%；旅客运输周转量387.51亿人公里，增长6.9%。国际（地区）航线88条，境外航班通航架次23991架。年末全市机动车保有量359.42万辆，比上年末增长12.3%。其中，私人汽车保有量308.26万辆，增长10.3%。

全年邮政业务总收入79.44亿元,比上年增长28.8%。电信业务总收入146.53亿元，下降2.5%。年末全市固定电话用户250.08万户，移动电话用户1711.37万户，固定互联网宽带接入用户[9]438.65万户。

五、固定资产投资

全年全社会固定资产投资比上年增长1.1%。其中，固定资产投资（不含农户）增长1.1%。

图3：2019年固定资产投资（不含农户）增长速度（%）

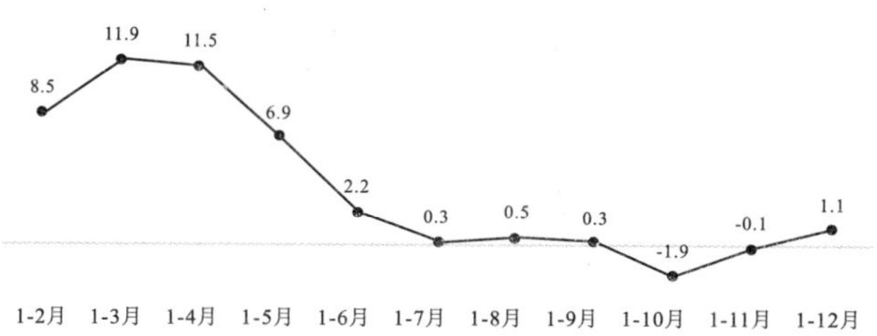

在固定资产投资（不含农户）中，第一产业投资比上年下降21.0%；第二产业投资增长1.5%，其中，工业投资增长2.0%；第三产业投资增长1.3%。民间固定资产投资[10]比上年下降3.5%，占固定资产投资（不含农户）的比重为43.7%。

表5：2019年分行业固定资产投资（不含农户）增长速度（%）

行业	比上年增长	行业	比上年增长（%）
固定资产投资（不含农户）	1.1	金融业	-82.2
#农、林、牧、渔业	-21.6	房地产业[11]	-4.7
采矿业	156.8	租赁和商务服务业	38.8
制造业	4.2	科学研究和技术服务业	-29.0
电力、热力、燃气及水的生产和供应业	-14.1	水利、环境和公共设施管理业	12.0
建筑业	-70.2	居民服务和其他服务业	24.9
批发和零售业	-31.2	教育	27.0
交通运输、仓储和邮政业	1.6	卫生和社会工作	0.9
住宿和餐饮业	0.8	文化、体育和娱乐业	16.7
信息传输、软件和信息技术服务业	-30.1	公共管理和社会组织	-15.7

全年房地产开发投资比上年下降2.1%。其中，住宅投资增长9.0%，办公楼投资下降9.0%，商业营业用房投资下降39.4%。房屋施工面积17475.02万平方米，增长8.9%；房屋竣工面积1057.69万平方米，增长8.2%。

表6：2019年房地产开发和销售主要指标及其增长速度

指标	绝对数（万平方米）	比上年增长（%）
房屋施工面积	17475.02	8.9
其中：住宅	12450.59	11.1
房屋竣工面积	1057.69	8.2
其中：住宅	761.59	22.2
商品房销售面积	2638.69	-2.8
其中：住宅	2155.46	-3.0
商品房待售面积	202.71	-15.6
其中：住宅	55.57	-7.4

六、国内贸易

全年社会消费品零售总额比上年增长6.0%。其中，限额以上企业（单位）消费品零售额[12]增长0.2%。按经营地统计，城镇消费品零售额增长5.9%；乡村消费品零售额增长7.4%。按消费形态统计，商品零售额增长5.8%；餐饮收入增长7.7%。

限额以上企业（单位）消费品零售额中，网上商品零售额[13]421.50亿元，占限额以上消费品零售额的

16.9%，比上年提高5.4个百分点；比上年增长21.7%，增速高于限额以上消费品零售额21.5个百分点。

在限额以上企业（单位）商品零售额中，粮油、食品类零售额比上年增长13.8%，服装、鞋帽、针、纺织品类下降1.8%，化妆品类增长16.0%，金银珠宝类增长25.3%，日用品类增长3.0%，体育、娱乐用品类增长2.0%，电子出版物及音像制品类持平，家用电器和音像器材类下降2.3%，通讯器材类增长2.3%，家具类增长22.1%，石油及制品类增长1.8%，建筑及装潢材料类增长5.6%，汽车类下降5.5%。

七、对外经济

全年进出口总值3243.06亿元，比上年下降1.8%。其中，出口1730.21亿元，下降11.6%；进口1512.85亿元，增长12.4%。

图4：2015-2019年进出口总值及其增长速度

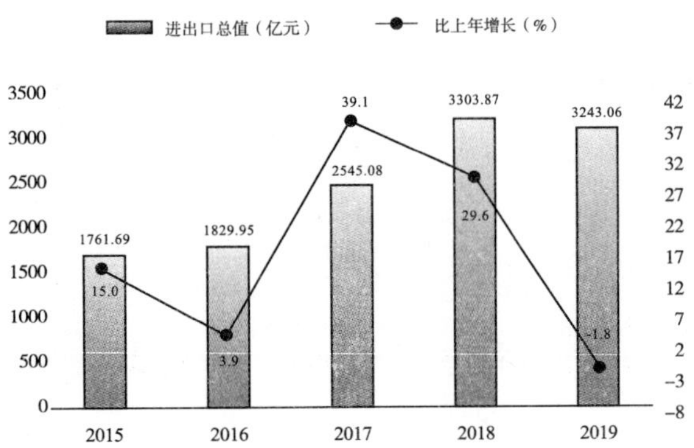

在进出口总值中，加工贸易进出口2030.88亿元，下降7.7%，占进出口总值的62.6%；一般贸易进出口657.65亿元，增长9.1%，占进出口总值的20.3%。

主要进口商品有，机电产品进口1222.39亿元，增长11.3%；精炼铜进口61.75亿元，增长14.9%；矿砂进口32.45亿元，下降25.8%；医药品进口30.29亿元，增长17.9%。主要出口商品有，机电产品出口1592.83亿元，下降11.8%；单晶硅片出口25.74亿元，增长6.5%；农产品出口18.68亿元，下降24.1%；有机化学品出口18.58亿元，增长6.1%。

全年实际使用外资70.57亿美元，比上年增长11.1%。

八、金融

年末全市金融机构本外币存款余额23340.84亿元，比上年末增长9.8%。人民币存款余额23066.85亿元，增长10.1%，其中，住户存款余额9653.29亿元，增长14.0%。金融机构本外币贷款余额22436.65亿元，增长12.8%。人民币贷款余额22264.12亿元，增长12.8%。

表7：2019年末金融机构本外币存贷款余额及其增长速度

指标	年末数（亿元）	比上年增长（%）
期末金融机构存款余额	23340.84	9.8
#住户存款	9653.29	14.0
非金融企业存款	8912.70	7.0
机关团体存款	3636.41	1.7
财政性存款	195.89	29.6
非银行业金融机构存款	914.66	24.8
期末金融机构贷款余额	22436.65	12.8
#住户贷款	6313.55	21.2
非金融企业及机关团体贷款	16103.90	9.8
非银行业金融机构贷款	0.19	0.0

全年证券市场各类证券交易总额45228.64亿元，比上年增长37.5%。年末全市拥有境内上市公司37家，比上年新增5家，其中，科创板首批上市公司2家。新三板挂牌企业125家，比上年新增6家。上市总股本615.18亿股，总市值5667.12亿元。

年末全市共有保险机构67家。全年保费收入523.13亿元，比上年增长9.3%。全年支付各类赔款给付142.37亿元，比上年增长8.8%。

九、教育、科技、文化旅游和体育

全市高等教育学校[14]75所，其中，普通高等学校63所，成人高等学校12所。各类高等教育在校学生137.36万人，毕业生39.68万人。其中，普通高等学校（本专科）在校学生73.86万人，毕业生19.18万人。另有研究生培养机构43所，在校学生13.20万人，毕业生2.86万人。

国家级高新技术企业数3673家，比上年增加1053家。全年技术市场合同交易额1364亿元。全年专利申请量72377件，其中，发明专利申请量29297件。

全市博物馆（不含民营）128座，各级别文物保护单位428处。公共图书馆14个，市级群众艺术馆1个，文化馆14个，文化站185个。地市广播电视台2座，县级广播电视台8座。电视及广播人口覆盖率均达到100%。全年举办各类会展活动283个，其中，举办国际性会展活动68个；全年参展参会人数278万人次。

全年接待国内外游客30110.43万人次，比上年增长21.7%；旅游业总收入3146.05亿元，增长23.1%。

全年举办各类群众体育展示表演和竞赛活动共计300项次，体育社团举办和承办体育赛事300项次，其中，国际性和全国性赛事28项次。更新社区全民健身路径72个。全市新增社会体育指导员1958名。我市培养输送运动员参加国际、国内各项比赛获得金牌72枚、银牌63枚、铜牌60枚。

十、卫生健康和社会服务

年末全市共有各类卫生机构7011个，其中，医院359个，社区卫生服务中心（站）244个，卫生院118个。各类卫生技术人员11.22万人，其中，执业（含助理）医师3.85万人。各类卫生机构床位7.25万张。

全市提供住宿的法定社会服务机构156个，床位2.64万张，年末收养人数12961人。年末城市低保对象1.50万户、2.24万人，发放低保金2.09亿元；农村低保对象2.49万户、6.86万人，发放低保金4.24亿元。6639人享受农村特困人员救助供养，发放供养金7364万元。

十一、人口、人民生活和社会保障

年末全市常住人口1020.35万人，比上年末净增加19.98万人，其中，男性人口521.46万人，占51.1%；女性人口498.89万人，占48.9%，性别比为104.5（以女性为100，男性对女性的比例）。全年出生人口12.45万人，出生率为12.32‰；死亡人口5.59万人，死亡率为5.53‰；自然增长率为6.79‰。城镇人口761.28万人，占常住人口比重（常住人口城镇化率）74.61%；农村人口259.07万人，占25.39%。

图5：2016-2019年常住人口城镇化率（%）

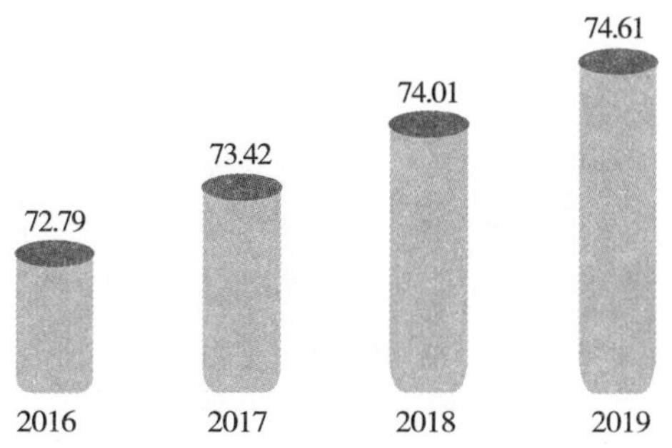

全年全市居民人均可支配收入34064元，比上年增长8.5%，其中，城镇常住居民人均可支配收入41850元，增长8.1%，农村常住居民人均可支配收入14588元，增长9.8%。

年末全市城镇基本医疗保险参保人数598.30万人；基本养老保险参保人数719.04万人，其中，城镇企业职工养老保险参保人数442.69万人；失业保险参保人数219.99万人，工伤保险参保人数266.89万人，职工生育保险参保人数252.68万人。年末农村新型合作医疗参保人数435.31万人。

十二、城市建设、环境和应急管理

全年完成城市建设维护投资826亿元。年末建成区面积729.14平方公里。年末污水日处理能力328.10万吨，比上年末提高5.8%。

全年空气质量优良天数225天。二氧化硫年平均浓度为9微克/标立方米，二氧化氮年平均浓度为48微克/标立方米。颗粒物（PM10）年平均浓度为96微克/标立方米，颗粒物（PM2.5）年平均浓度为57微克/标立方米。全市集中式饮用水源地的水质达标率为100%。区域环境噪声等效声级均值为55.8分贝，道路交通噪声等效声级均值为70.5分贝。

全年发生各类生产安全事故319起，死亡190人。其中，交通运输和仓储业事故290起，死亡158人；工矿商贸事故28起，死亡31人；农林牧渔业事故1起，死亡1人。

注释：

[1]本公报中2019年数据为初步统计数，生产总值、规模以上工业增加值、建筑业增加值及其分类项目等按照2018年第四次全国经济普查新基数测算。部分数据因四舍五入的原因，存在着分项与合计不等的情况。

[2]生产总值、各行业增加值和人均生产总值绝对数按现价计算，增长速度按可比价格计算。

[3]规模以上工业统计标准为年主营业务收入2000万元及以上的工业法人单位。

[4]装备制造业包括金属制品业，通用设备制造业，专用设备制造业，汽车制造业，铁路、船舶、航空航天和其他运输设备制造业，电气机械和器材制造业，计算机、通信和其他电子设备制造业，仪器仪表制造业。

[5]六大高耗能行业包括石油加工、炼焦和核燃料加工业，化学原料和化学制品制造业，非金属矿物制品业，黑色金属冶炼和压延加工业，有色金属冶炼和压延加工业，电力、热力生产和供应业。

[6]工业战略性新兴产业包括新一代信息技术产业，高端装备制造产业，新材料产业，生物产业，新能源汽车产业，新能源产业，节能环保产业七大产业中的工业相关行业。

[7]高技术制造业包括医药制造业，航空、航天器及设备制造业，电子及通信设备制造业，计算机及办公设备制造业，医疗仪器设备及仪器仪表制造业，信息化学品制造业。

[8]规模以上服务业统计范围包括年营业收入1000万元及以上，或年末从业人员50人及以上的交通

运输、仓储和邮政业，信息传输、软件和信息技术服务业，房地产业（不含房地产开发经营），租赁和商务服务业，科学研究和技术服务业，水利、环境和公共设施管理业，教育，卫生和社会工作；年营业收入500万元及以上，或年末从业人员50人及以上的居民服务、修理和其他服务业，文化、体育和娱乐业法人单位。

[9]固定互联网宽带接入用户是指报告期末在电信企业登记注册，通过xDSL、FTTx+LAN、FTTH/0以及其他宽带接入方式和普通专线接入公众互联网的用户。

[10]民间固定资产投资是指具有集体、私营、个人性质的内资企事业单位以及由其控股（包括绝对控股和相对控股）的调查单位建造或购置固定资产的投资。

[11]房地产业投资除房地产开发投资外，还包括物业管理、中介服务、租赁经营和其他房地产业。

[12]限额以上企业（单位）消费品零售额的统计标准为年主营业务收入2000万元及以上的批发业企业（单位）、500万元及以上的零售额业企业（单位）、200万元及以上的住宿和餐饮业企业（单位）。

[13]网上商品零售额是指企业（单位）通过公共网络交易平台（包括自建网站和第三方平台）取得订单，售给个人、社会集团非生产、非经营用的实物商品金额（含增值税），付款可以在网上进行，也可以在网下进行。公共网络包括计算机互联网、移动互联网等。

[14]高等教育学校包含普通高等学校和成人高等学校。各类高等教育在校学生和毕业生包括研究生、普通高等教育本专科学生、成人高等教育学生和网络本专科学生。

数据口径：本公报中2019年进出口、交通运输、电信、环境监测等指标数据为西安原口径数据，未包含西咸的咸阳片区；居民人均可支配收入、就业、市场主体、财政、利用外资、邮政、证券、会展、旅游、教育、体育、博物馆、文化、卫生、社会服务、低保、农村特困人员救助供养、人口、城市建设、安全生产、生产总值、农业、工业、建筑业、固定资产投资、国内贸易等指标数据为包含西咸新区数据。物价数据中，2019年居民消费价格、商品零售价格、新建商品住宅销售价格为西安原口径数据，工业生产者出厂价格、工业生产者购进价格为包含西咸新区数据。金融数据中，保险保费、金融机构数为西安原口径数据，未包含西咸的咸阳片区；上市挂牌企业数、证券数据为包含西咸新区数据。科技数据中，技术市场合同交易额和专利数据为西安原口径数据，高新技术企业为包含西咸新区数据。社会保障数据中，城镇企业职工养老保险参保人数为西安原口径数据，城镇基本医疗保险、失业保险、工伤保险和职工生育保险参保人数、农村新型合作医疗参保人数为包含西咸新区数据。

资料来源：本公报中物价、居民人均可支配收入数据来自国家统计局西安调查队；城镇新增就业、登记失业率、社会保障数据来自西安市人力资源和社会保障局；市场主体、专利数据来自市市场监管局；财政数据来自市财政局；进出口数据来自西安海关；利用外资数据来自市投资合作局；旅游、博物馆、公共图书馆、群众艺术馆、文化馆、广播、电视数据来自市文化旅游局；铁路运输数据来自西安铁路局；公路运输数据来自市交通局；民航运输数据来自西安咸阳国际机场；机动车数据来自市车管所；邮政业务数据来自市邮政管理局；电信业务数据来自中国移动西安分公司、中国电信西安分公司、中国联通西安分公司；货币金融数据来自中国人民银行西安分行营业管理部；证券、保险数据来自市金融工作局；教育数据来自市教育局；科技数据来自市科技局；会展数据来自市商务局；体育数据来自市体育局；医疗保险、新农合数据来自市医疗保障局；卫生数据来自市卫生和健康委员会；社会服务、低保、农村特困人员救助供养数据来自市民政局；城市建设数据来自市住房和城乡建设局；环境监测数据来自市生态环境局；安全生产数据来自市应急管理局；其他数据均来自市统计局。

Statistical Communique of Xi'an City On 2019 National Economic and Social Development[1]

Xi'an Municipal Bureau of Statistics and NBS Survey Office in Xi'an

Mar.22th，2020

In 2019, in the face of increased risk challenge of complicated situation at home and abroad, the whole city to Xi Jinping, the new times the thought of socialism with Chinese characteristics as guidance, closely pursued beyond orientation and "five solid" requirement, planning to start the "10 major key work", make overall steady growth, promoting the reform, restructuring, livelihood, prevent risks, maintaining stability, all work in the stability of economic operation, continue to optimize the economic structure, development quality steadily improve, continue to improve, people's livelihood welfare social undertakings prosperity development, overall improve ecological environment, realize the health steady economic development and social harmony and stability, create a new situation that the construction of national center city,New steps have been taken to build an international metropolis with historical and cultural characteristics.

I. General Outlook

Preliminary accounting, annual gross domestic product[2]GDP reached 932.119 billion yuan, an increase of 7.0% over the previous year.Of this, the added value of the primary industry reached 27.913 billion yuan, up 4.3%;The added value of the secondary industry was 316.744 billion yuan, up 7.6%;The added value of the tertiary industry reached 587.462 billion yuan, up 6.8%.The three industries constitute 3.0:34.0:63.0.Based on the resident population, the annual per capita GDP was 92,256 yuan, an increase of 3.9% over the previous year.

The added value of the non-public sector was 506.618 billion yuan, accounting for 54.4% of GDP, an increase of 1.0 percentage points over the previous year.

The consumer price index rose by 2.7%, of which the prices of food, tobacco and alcohol rose by 4.1%. Retail prices rose 2.1%. Producer prices rose by 1.6% and producer prices were flat. New residential sales prices rose 21.1%.

Table 1 The Rate of Increase and Decrease of CPI in 2019(%)

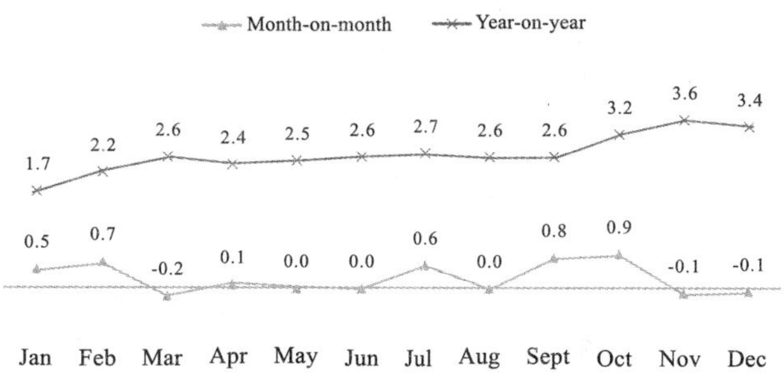

Sheet 1 Increase and decrease rate of consumer price ratio in 2019 (%)

Item	Rise or fall（%）
Consumer price Index	2.7
Food alcohol and tobacco	4.1
dress	3.1
live	2.6
Articles and services for daily use	1.5
Transportation and Communications	-0.7
Education, culture and entertainment	4.2
Health care	0.9
Other supplies and services	3.9

A total of 161,200 urban jobs were created, and 62,700 unemployed urban workers were re-employed. The registered urban unemployment rate was 3.27% at the end of the year.

Last year, 883,100 new market entities of various types were registered, an increase of 62.6% over the previous year. Among them, 130,600 were newly registered enterprises, up 3.2%. The number of newly registered individual businesses reached 751,700, an increase of 81.0%.

Revenue in the general public budgets of local governments totaled 70.256 billion yuan, an increase of 2.6% over the previous year, including 58.075 billion yuan in tax revenue, an increase of 4.3%. Local governments spent 124.799 billion yuan in general public budgets last year, an increase of 8.3% over the previous year.

II. Agriculture

The total area planted with grain was 4,097,100 mu, down 2.3% from the previous year.The vegetable planting area was 1.0772 million mu, the same as last year.Melon and fruit planting area 147,300 mu, down 1.3%;Oil planting area of 46,600 mu, up 1.1%;Cotton planting area of 1,200 mu, an increase of 31.1%.

Grain output for the whole year was 1.3990 million tons, down 1.6% from the previous year, including 706,300 tons for summer grain and 692,700 tons for autumn grain. Vegetable output reached 3,785,800 tons, up 1.3%; The output of fruit was 971,800 tons, up 9.0%.

Sheet 2 The main Product of Agriculture Production in 2019

Name of Product	Units	Output	Increase over the last year (%)
Grain	10,000 tons	139.90	-1.6
Vegetable	10,000 tons	378.58	1.3
Fruit	10,000 tons	97.18	9.0
Meat	10,000 tons	5.14	-5.6
# Pork	10,000 tons	3.35	-6.7
Milk	10,000 tons	12.37	7.4
Poultry egg	10,000 tons	5.39	2.4
Year-end Pig on hand	10,000 head	29.66	-5.2
Year-end Ox on hand	10,000 head	5.16	2.0
Year-end Sheep on hand	10,000 head	7.19	-3.1
Year-end Fowl on hand	10,000 head	643.67	2.9

III.Industry and Construction

The total added value of industry reached 186.886 billion yuan, an increase of 6.6% over the previous year.Above scale industry[3]Added value increased by 6.9% .Among industries above designated size, the added value of light industry fell by 3.8% , while that of heavy industry rose by 9.1% .

Table 2 The Growth of Above–Scale Industrial added Value 2018–2019 (%)

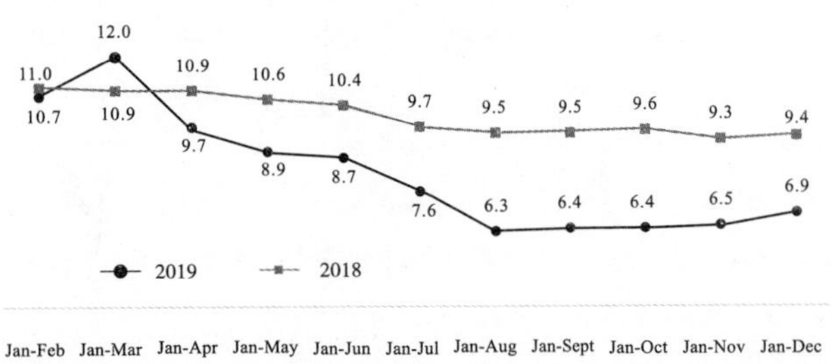

Annual scale above the industry, equipment manufacturing industry[4]The value added increased by 9.3%, accounting for 65.7% of the value added of industries above designated size.Among them, railway, shipbuilding, aerospace and other transportation equipment manufacturing industry grows 9.2%, computers, communications and other electronic equipment manufacturing growth 15.9%, electrical machinery and equipment manufacturing industry to grow 6.7%, a 1.0% drop in auto manufacturing, instrument manufacturing growth 19.7%, general equipment manufacturing growth 9.9%, special equipment manufacturing growth 11.3%, metal products, machinery and equipment repair industry increased by 13.0%.Six energy-intensive industries[5]Added value growth of 4.3%, among them, non-metallic mineral products increased by 4.9%, non-ferrous metal smelting and rolling processing industry to grow 3.5%, a 2.5% drop in black metal smelting and rolling processing industry, oil processing and coking and nuclear fuel processing industry fell by 12.0%, chemical raw materials and chemical products manufacturing growth 8.9%, electricity, heat production and supply industry growth rate of 1.6%.

Sheet 3 The Growth of 10 Major Industrial added Value and Their Proportion to Industrial Enterprises above Designated Size in 2019

Item	Increase over the last year (%)
Growth of Industrial added Value above Designated Size	6.9
Total：10 Major Industrial Enterprises	7.6
Manufacture of General Purpose Machinery	9.9
Manufacture of Special Purpose Machinery	11.3
Manufacture of Automobiles	-1.0
Manufacture of Railway, Ship, Aerospace and Other Transportation Equipments	9.2
Manufacture of Electrical Machinery and Apparatus	6.7
Manufacture of Computers, Communication and Other Electronic Equipment	15.9
Manufacture of Mental Products,Measuring Instruments and Machinery	7.0
Manufacture of Food	6.2
Manufacture of Medicines	-5.8
Production and Supply of Electric Power and Heat Power	1.6

Above the annual scale of the industry, strategic emerging industries [6] The total output value increased by 9.6% over the previous year, accounting for 42.5% of the total industrial output value. High-tech manufacturing industry [7] Total output value increased by 14.9%, accounting for 26.3% of industries above the industrial scale. Among them, the total output value of electronic and communication equipment manufacturing increased by 22.7%, accounting for 70.3% of high-tech manufacturing, information chemicals manufacturing decreased by 74.2%, aviation, spacecraft and equipment manufacturing increased by 4.3%, and computer and office equipment manufacturing decreased by 4.3%.

The output of new industrial products grew rapidly. Monocrystalline silicon 1,763,600 kg, an increase of 2.3 times over the previous year; Polysilicon 10,302,000 kg, an increase of 2.0 times;17,610,400 lithium ion batteries, up 17.1%; There were 4.272 million optoelectronic devices, an increase of 22.8%.

Sheet 4 Output of Major Industrial Products above Designated Size in Xi'an(2019)

Name of Product	Units	Output	Increase over the last year(%)
Electricity	100 million kilo watt-hour	155.00	-10.5
Soft Drink	10,000 tons	207.59	22.7
Wheat Meal	10,000 tons	44.01	-20.8
Feed	10,000 tons	74.28	-7.2
Dairy	10,000 tons	72.64	-3.0
Chinese Patent Medicine	10,000 tons	1.25	16.7
AC Motors	10,000Kilowatt	261.32	0.5
Transformer	10,000 kilovolt amperes	17365.29	31.2
Motor Vehicle	10,000 units	42.63	-1.7
Truck	10,000 units	19.23	5.0
Car	10,000 units	14.14	-21.8
Sports Utility Vehicle	10,000 units	9.26	33.5
New Energy Vehicle	10,000 units	9.35	-32.5
Monocrystalline Silicon	10,000kg	176.36	225.3
Electric Cable	10,000km	14.09	-39.6
Optical Fiber	10,000km	564.61	-29.6
Optical Cable	10,000 core kilometers	676.75	-22.5
Lithium Ion Battery	10,000 units	1761.04	17.1
Smart Phone	10,000 units	1141.21	-31.1
Optoelectronic Devices	10,000 units	427.20	22.8
Electronic Component	10,000 units	45.84	-10.4
Integrated Circuit Chip	10,000 chips	143.30	-4.5

The main business income of industrial enterprises above designated size reached 574.080 billion yuan, up 7.7% over the previous year. The total profit reached 29.87 billion yuan, down 16.7%.

The added value of the construction industry reached 135.848 billion yuan, an increase of 9.1% over the previous year.The total output value of general contracting and specialized contracting construction enterprises with qualification grades reached 451.438 billion yuan, up 15.8%, among which the output value of state-owned and state-holding enterprises was 346.790 billion yuan, up 14.6%.The value of contracts signed by enterprises of all levels of qualification reached 1,266.945 billion yuan, up 25.2%.

The overall energy consumption of industries above designated size was 6,347,700 tons of standard coal, 8.4% lower than that of the previous year.Among them, the comprehensive energy consumption of the energy-intensive industries was 4.8564 million tons of standard coal, down 10.8% from the previous year.The comprehensive energy consumption of non-energy-intensive industries was 1,491,300 tons of standard coal, up 0.4%. Industrial coal consumption above designated size was 10,681,400 tons, a decrease of 1,309,800 tons over the previous year. Among them, the coal consumption of non-power enterprises was 3.0539 million tons, 501,400 tons less than that of the previous year.

IV. Service Industry

The added value of wholesale and retail businesses amounted to 77.786 billion yuan, an increase of 8.5% over the previous year.Transportation, warehousing and postal services added 33.054 billion yuan, up 6.7%;The added value of the accommodation and catering industry reached 17.849 billion yuan, up 5.2%;The added value of the financial sector reached 99.894 billion yuan, up 7.9%;The added value of the real estate industry reached 72.952 billion yuan, up 0.8%;The added value of other services is 276.882 billion yuan, up 7.5%.Annual scale above the service sector[8]The operating revenue of enterprises reached 245.436 billion yuan, up 11.4% over the previous year.

Cargo transport totaled 274 million tons last year, an increase of 3.8% over the previous year.Cargo transport turnover reached 51.901 billion ton-km, the same as the previous year.The total number of passenger trips reached 263 million, up 1.0%;Passenger traffic amounted to 38.751 billion passenger-km, up by 6.9%.There were 88 international (regional) routes and 23,991 overseas flights.At the end of the year, the number of motor vehicles in the city was 3,594,200, an increase of 12.3%

over that at the end of the previous year.Among them, the number of private car PARC reached 3,082,600, up 10.3%.

The total revenue of postal services reached 7.944 billion yuan, up 28.8% over the previous year.The total revenue of telecom business reached 14.653 billion yuan, down 2.5%.By the end of the year, there were 2,500,800 fixed telephone users and 17.1137 million mobile phone users, as well as fixed Internet broadband access users[9]4.3865 million households.

V. Investment in Fixed Assets

Investment in fixed assets rose by 1.1% over the previous year.Of this, fixed asset investment (excluding rural households) rose by 1.1%.

Table 3 Investment in Fixed Assets(excluding by rural households)Growth Rate in 2019 (%)

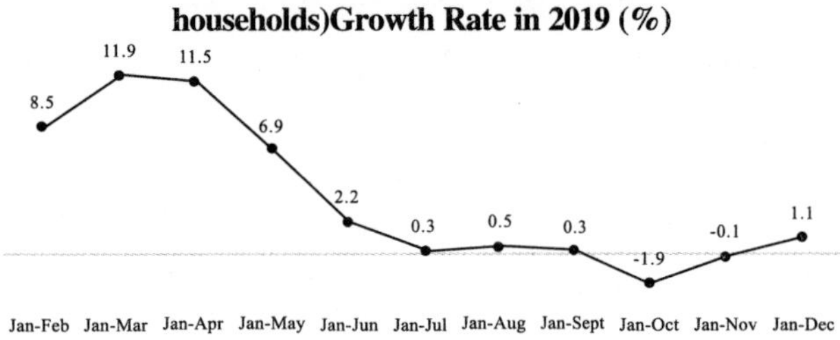

In fixed asset investment (excluding rural households), investment in the primary industry decreased by 21.0% compared with the previous year.Investment in the secondary industry increased by 1.5%, of which industrial investment increased by 2.0%.Investment in the tertiary industry increased by 1.3%.Private investment in fixed assets[10]This was 3.5% lower than the previous year, and accounted for 43.7% of fixed asset investment (excluding rural households).

Sheet 5 The Investment in Fixed Assets and Growth Rate in Main Industries in 2019

Industries	Growth rate(%)	Industries	Growth rate(%)
Investment Fixed Assets (excluding farmers)	1.1	TheFinancialSector	-82.2
Agriculture, Forestry, Animal husbandry and Fishery	-21.6	The Real Estate Industry[11]	-4.7
The MiningIndustry	156.8	Leasing and Business Services	38.8
Manufacturing	4.2	Scientific Research and Technical Services	-29.0
Production and Supply of Electricity, Heat, Gas and Water	-14.1	Water, Environmental and Public utility Management Industries	12.0
The Construction Industry	-70.2	Residential Services and Other Services	24.9
Wholesale and Retail	-31.2	Education	27.0
Transportation, Warehousing and Postal Services	1.6	Health and Social Work	0.9
Accommodation and Catering	0.8	Culture, Sports and Entertainment	16.7
Information Transmission, Software and Information Technology Services	-30.1	Public Administration and Social Organization	-15.7

Investment in real estate development decreased by 2.1% over the previous year.Investment in residential buildings increased by 9.0%, investment in office buildings fell by 9.0%, and investment in commercial buildings fell by 39.4%.The area under construction was 174,750,200 square meters, an increase of 8.9%;The completed housing area was 10,576,900 square meters, up 8.2%.

Sheet 6 The Main Indicators of Real Estate Development and Sales in 2019

Item	Absolute logarithm (10,000 square meters)	Increase over the last year (%)
Construction area	17475.02	8.9
Among them: Residence	12450.59	11.1
Floor area completed	1057.69	8.2
Among them: Residence	761.59	22.2
Commercial housing sales area	2638.69	-2.8
Among them: Residence	2155.46	-3.0
Commercial housing area for sale	202.71	-15.6
Among them: Residence	55.57	-7.4

VI. Domestic trade

The total retail sales of consumer goods increased by 6.0% over the previous year.Among them, the quota above enterprises (units) retail sales of consumer goods[12]Growth of 0.2%.According to local statistics, the retail sales of consumer goods in urban areas increased by 5.9%.Rural retail sales of consumer goods grew by 7.4%.According to consumption patterns, retail sales of goods increased by 5.8%;Food and beverage revenue rose 7.7%.

Above the quota of enterprises (units) retail sales of consumer goods, online retail sales of goods[13]42.15 billion yuan, accounting for 16.9% of the retail sales of consumer goods above designated quotas and 5.4 percentage points higher than that of the previous year.The growth rate was 21.7% over the previous year, 21.5 percentage points higher than the retail sales of consumer goods above the quota.

In the above designated enterprises (units) the retail sales of goods, grain and oil, food, retail sales growth of 13.8% over the previous year, a 1.8% drop in clothing, shoes and hats, the needle, textiles, cosmetics class increases by 16.0%, 25.3% gold and silver jewelry, daily necessities grew 3.0% in the class, sports and entertainment products rose 2.0%, electronic publications and audio-visual products, household appliances and audio-visual equipment fell by 2.3%, 2.3% growth communications equipment class, class furniture rose 22.1%, oil and products rose 1.8%, building and decoration materials increased by 5.6%, a 5.5% drop in motor vehicles.

VII. *Foreign Economic Relation*

Imports and exports totaled 324.306 billion yuan, down 1.8% from the previous year. Among them, exports reached 173.021 billion yuan, down 11.6%; Imports reached 151.285 billion yuan, up 12.4%.

Table 4 Total Value of Import and Export of Goods and the Growth Rates 2015–2019

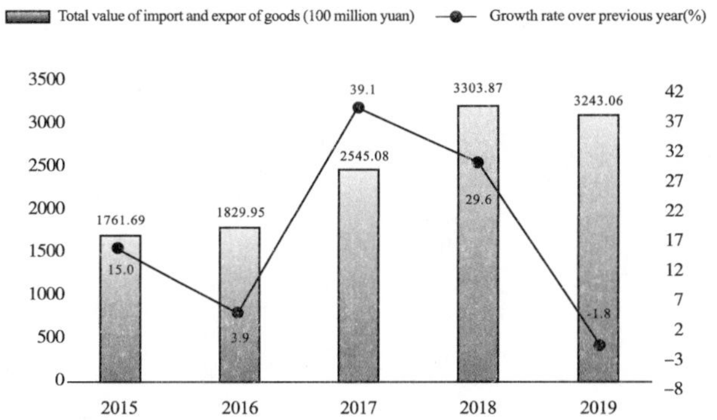

Of the total value of imports and exports, processing trade totaled 203.088 billion yuan, down 7.7% and accounting for 62.6% of the total value. Imports and exports in general trade totaled 65.765 billion yuan, up 9.1% and accounting for 20.3% of the total value of imports and exports.

The main imports included mechanical and electrical products, which reached 122.239 billion yuan, up 11.3%;Imports of refined copper reached 6.175 billion yuan, up 14.9%;Ore imports reached 3.245 billion yuan, down 25.8%;The import of pharmaceuticals and pharmaceuticals reached 3.029 billion yuan, up 17.9%.The main exports were mechanical and electrical products, which totaled 159.283 billion yuan, down 11.8%;Exports of monocrystallone silicon wafers reached 2.574 billion yuan, up 6.5%;The export of agricultural products reached 1.868 billion yuan, down 24.1%;The export of organic chemicals came to 1.858 billion yuan, up 6.1%.

The actual use of foreign capital reached 7.057 billion US dollars, an increase of 11.1% over the previous year.

VIII. *Financial*

At the end of the year, the balance of local and foreign currency deposits of financial institutions in Tianjin was 3334.084 billion yuan, an increase of 9.8% over that at the end of the previous year.The deposit balance of RMB was 2,306.685 billion yuan, up by 10.1%, among which, the household deposit balance was 965.329 billion yuan, up by 14.0%.The balance of domestic and foreign currency loans of financial institutions was 2,243.665 billion yuan, up 12.8%.The balance of RMB loans is 2,226.412 billion yuan, up 12.8%.

Sheet 7 Savings Deposit and Loans in RMB and Foreign Currencies in All Financial Institutions and the Growth Rates at the End of 2019

Item	Year–end–figure (100 million yuan)	Increase over the last year(%)
Total Deposits	23340.84	9.8
# Household Deposit	9653.29	14.0
Non-Financial Enterprise Deposits	8912.70	7.0
Corporate deposit	3636.41	1.7
Fiscal deposits	195.89	29.6
Deposits in non-banking financial institutions	914.66	24.8
The balance of loans to financial institutions at the end of the period	22436.65	12.8
# Household Loans	6313.55	21.2
Group loans to non-financial enterprises and government agencies	16103.90	9.8
Non-bank Financial Institution Loans	0.19	

All kinds of securities traded on the stock market totaled 4522.864 billion yuan last year, an increase of 37.5% over the previous year.At the end of the year, the city had 37 domestic listed companies, 5 more than the previous year, among which 2 were the first batch of listed companies on the Science and Innovation Board.There were 125 listed companies on the New Third Board, six more than the previous year.The total listed capital is 61.518 billion shares and the total market value is 566.712 billion yuan.

At the end of the year, there were 67 insurance institutions in the city. The annual premium income was 52.313 billion yuan, an increase of 9.3% over the previous year. The government paid 14.237 billion yuan in reparations, an increase of 8.8% over the previous year.

IX. Education, Science and Technology, Cultural Tourism and Sports

The city's higher education schools[14]are 75. Among them, there are 63 ordinary institutions of higher learning and 12 adult institutions of higher learning.There were 1,373,600 students in all types of higher education, and 396,800 graduates.Of these, 738,600 were enrolled in regular institutions of higher learning and 191,800 were graduates.In addition, there are 43 post-graduate training institutions with 132,000 students and 28,600 graduates.

There were 3,673 state-level high-tech enterprises, an increase of 1,053 over the previous year. The total contract value of the technology market was 136.4 billion yuan. The number of patent applications was 72,377, including 29,297 for invention.

The city has 128 museums (excluding private ones) and 428 cultural relic protection units at all levels.There are 14 public libraries, 1 municipal mass art gallery, 14 cultural centers and 185 cultural stations.Prefectural city radio and television station 2, county level radio and television station 8.Both television and radio coverage reached 100%.283 exhibition events were held throughout the year, 68 of which were international events.The annual number of participants reached 2.78 million.

China received 301,104,300 domestic and foreign tourists, an increase of 21.7% over the previous year. The total revenue of tourism reached 314.605 billion yuan, up 23.1%.

A total of 300 mass sports exhibitions and competitions were held throughout the year, and 300 sports events were held or organized by sports associations, among which 28 were international and national events.72 community fitness paths have been updated.The city's new social sports instructors 1958.Our city trains and trains athletes to participate in international and domestic competitions and win 72 Gold medals, 63 Silver medals and 60 Bronze medals.

X. Health and Social Services

By the end of the year, there were 7,011 health institutions of all kinds in the city, among which 359 were hospitals, 244 were community health service centers (stations) and 118 were health centers.There were 112,200 health technicians of all kinds, including 38,500 practicing doctors (including assistant doctors).There are 72,500 beds in various health institutions.

The city has 156 legal social service institutions providing accommodation, with 26,400 beds, and 12,961 adoptions at the end of the year.At the end of the year, 209 million yuan of subsistence allowances were paid to 15,000 urban households and 22,400 people.A total of 424 million yuan was paid to 24,900 rural households and 68,600 people receiving subsistence allowances.A total of 6,639 people were provided with assistance to people living in extreme poverty in rural areas, and a grant of 73.64 million yuan was granted.

XI. Population, Living Conditions and Social Security

At the end of the year, the city's permanent resident population was 10.2035 million, a net increase of 199,800 over that at the end of the previous year, among which the male population was 5,214,600, accounting for 51.1%.The female population was 4,988,900, accounting for 48.9%, with a sex ratio of 104.5 (female was 100, male to female ratio).There were 124,500 births last year, with a birth rate of 12.32 per thousand.55,900 people died, with a mortality rate of 5.53 per thousand;The natural growth rate was 6.79 per thousand.The urban population was 7.6128 million, accounting for 74.61% of the permanent population (the urbanization rate of permanent population).The rural population was 2.5907 million, accounting for 25.39%.

Table 5 Urbanization Rate of Permanent Residents 2016–2019 (%)

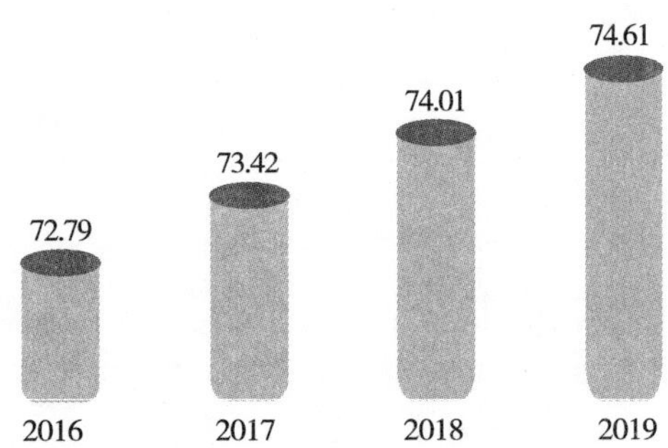

The per capita disposable income of urban residents was 34,064 yuan, an increase of 8.5% over the previous year, of which the per capita disposable income of urban residents was 41,850 yuan, an increase of 8.1%, and the per capita disposable income of rural residents was 14,588 yuan, an increase of 9.8%.

At the end of the year, 5.983 million people participated in urban basic medical insurance.A total of 7.1904 million people participated in basic old-age insurance, including 4,426,900 urban enterprise employees.2.1999 million people were covered by unemployment insurance, 2.6689 million were covered by work-related injury insurance, and 2,526,800 were covered by maternity insurance.By the end of the year, 4.3531 million rural residents were covered by the new cooperative medical care system.

XII. *Urban Construction, Environment and Work Safety*

The total investment in urban construction and maintenance reached 82.6 billion yuan. The end of the built-up area of 729.14 square kilometers. At the end of the year, the daily sewage treatment capacity was 3.281 million tons, an increase of 5.8% over that at the end of the previous year.

There are 225 days with good air quality throughout the year.The average annual concentration of SO_2 was 9 MCG/M3 and that of nitrogen dioxide was 48 MCG/m3.The average annual concentration of particulate matter (PM10) was 96 MCG/M3 and that of particulate matter (PM2.5) was 57 MCG/m3.The water quality of centralized drinking water source in the whole city reaches the standard rate of 100%.The average equivalent sound level of regional environmental noise is 55.8 dB, and the average equivalent sound level of road traffic noise is 70.5 dB.

There were 319 production safety accidents and 190 deaths. Among them, there were 290 traffic and storage accidents, with 158 deaths;28 industrial, mining and trade accidents, 31 deaths;1 farming, forestry, animal husbandry and fishery accident, 1 death.

Note:

[1] The 2019 data in this communique are preliminary statistics. Gross domestic product (GDP), added value of industries above designated size, added value of construction industry and their classified items are calculated based on the new base of the fourth national Economic census in 2018.Some of the data is rounded, there is a breakdown and total unequal.

[2] Gross domestic product, added value of industries and per capita GDP are calculated in absolute terms at current prices, and growth rates are calculated at comparable prices.

[3] The statistical standards for industries above the scale are industrial legal entities with annual main business income of 20 million yuan or more.

[4] Equipment manufacturing industry includes metal products industry, general equipment manufacturing industry, special equipment manufacturing industry, automobile manufacturing industry, railway, ship, aerospace and other transportation equipment manufacturing industry, electrical machinery and equipment manufacturing industry, computer, communication and other electronic equipment manufacturing industry, instrument and meter manufacturing industry.

[5] The six energy-intensive industries include petroleum processing, coking and nuclear fuel processing, chemical raw material and chemical products manufacturing, non-metallic mineral products, ferrous metal smelting and rolling processing, non-ferrous metal smelting and rolling processing, electric power and thermal production and supply.

[6] Industrial strategic emerging industries include new generation information technology industry, high-end equipment manufacturing industry, new materials industry, biological industry, new energy automobile industry, new energy industry, energy conservation and environmental protection industry.

[7] High-tech manufacturing includes pharmaceutical manufacturing, aviation, spacecraft and equipment manufacturing, electronic and communication equipment manufacturing, computer and office equipment manufacturing, medical instrument equipment and instrumentation manufacturing, and information chemicals manufacturing.

[8] scale above services statistics scope including the annual business income is 10 million yuan and above, or at the end of the staff more than 50 people and transportation, warehousing and postal service, information transmission, software and information technology services, real estate (including real estate development business), leasing and business services, scientific research and technical services, water conservancy, environment and public facilities management, education, health and social work;A legal entity of resident service, repair and other service industry, culture, sports and entertainment industry with an annual operating income of 5 million yuan or above or with 50 or more employees at the end of the year.

[9] Fixed Internet broadband access users refer to those who are registered with telecommunications enterprises at the end of the reporting period and access the public Internet through xDSL, FTTx+LAN, FTTH/0 and other broadband access methods and ordinary dedicated lines.

[10] Private fixed assets investment refers to the investment in the construction or purchase of fixed assets by domestic funded enterprises and institutions with the nature of collective, private and individual, and the survey units that are controlled by them (including absolute holding and relative holding).

[11] In addition to real estate development investment, real estate investment also includes property management, intermediary services, leasing operations and other real estate industries.

[12] The statistical standards of retail sales of consumer goods for enterprises above designated size are wholesale enterprises (units) with annual main business income of 20 million yuan or above, retail sales enterprises (units) with annual retail sales of 5 million yuan or above, and accommodation and catering enterprises (units) with annual sales of 2 million yuan or above.

[13] Retail sales of online goods refer to the amount of

physical goods (including VALUE-ADDED tax) sold to individuals and social groups for non-production and non-business use through public online trading platforms (including self-built websites and third-party platforms) that enterprises (units) obtain orders from. Payment can be made online or offline.Public network includes computer Internet, mobile Internet and so on.

[14] Higher education schools include ordinary institutions of higher learning and adult institutions of higher learning.All kinds of higher education students and graduates include graduate students, general higher education undergraduate students, adult higher education students and network undergraduate students.

Data calibres: The 2019 import and export, transportation, telecommunications, environmental monitoring and other index data in this communique are the original calibres of Xi 'an, excluding Xianyang district of Xi Xian;Per capita disposable income, employment and market main body, finance, foreign capital utilization, postal and securities, exhibition, tourism, education, sports, museums, culture, health, social services, low income, rural strands personnel assistance support, population, urban construction, safety production, GDP, agriculture, industry, construction industry, investment in fixed assets, such as domestic trade index data to include west salty new district.Among the price data, consumer price, retail price and sales price of new commercial housing in 2019 are the original data of Xi 'an, while producer price and industrial producer purchase price include the data of Xi Xian New Area.Among the financial data, the insurance premium and financial institutions are the original data of Xi 'an, excluding Xianyang district of Xi Xian.The number of listed enterprises and securities data include the data of Xi Xian New Area.Among the scientific and technological data, the contract turnover and patent data of the technology market are the original caliber data of Xi 'an, while the high-tech enterprises include the data of Xi Xian New Area.Among the social security data, the number of employees participating in the old-age insurance of urban enterprises is the original standard data of Xi 'an, the number of urban basic medical insurance, unemployment insurance, work-related injury insurance and maternity insurance of employees, and the number of rural new cooperative medical insurance are the data of Xi Xian New Area.

Source: Price and per capita disposable income data in this communique are from the Xi 'an Survey Team of the National Bureau of Statistics.New urban employment, registered unemployment rate and social security data are from Xi 'an Human Resources and Social Security Bureau.Market entities and patent data are from mBAS;The financial data are from the municipal Finance Bureau; Import and export data from Xi 'an Customs; Data on utilization of foreign capital came from municipal Investment cooperation Bureau; Tourism, museums, public libraries, mass art galleries, cultural centers, radio and TELEVISION data from the Municipal Cultural Tourism Bureau;Railway transport data from Xi 'an Railway Bureau; Road transport data from the Municipal Transportation Bureau; Civil aviation traffic data from Xi 'an Xianyang International Airport; Motor vehicle data from the municipal Vehicle administration; The postal service data are from the municipal Postal administration ; The telecom business data came from Xi 'an Branch of China Mobile, Xi 'an Branch of China Telecom and Xi 'an Branch of China Unicom. The monetary and financial data are from the Operation Management Department of Xi 'an Branch of the People's Bank of China. The data of securities and insurance are from the Municipal Finance Work Bureau;The education data came from the municipal Education Bureau; The science and technology data are from the municipal Science and Technology Bureau; Exhibition data from municipal Bureau of Commerce;The sports data are from the municipal Sports Bureau;Data of medical insurance and new rural cooperative medical care came from municipal Medical Security Bureau.Health data from the municipal Health and Health Commission;Data on social services, subsistence allowances and assistance and support for people in extreme poverty in rural areas are from the Civil Affairs Bureau.Urban construction data from the Municipal Bureau of Housing and Urban-Rural Development;Environmental monitoring data from municipal Bureau of Ecology and Environment; The safety production data comes from the municipal Emergency management Bureau; Other data are from the municipal Bureau of Statistics.

1 综 合

GENERAL SURVEY

资料整理：李　芬
Data management：Li Fen
数据审核：刘　婷
Data audit：Liu Ting

第一部分　综合

一、简要说明

本章资料主要包括西安市行政区划、自然地理、自然资源、气象、国民经济和社会发展等综合资料，由西安市统计局综合处根据局内各专业处及有关部门统计资料进行整理和编辑。

二、主要指标

生产总值（亿元）	9321.19	比上年增长	7.0%
农林牧渔业总产值（亿元）	499.32	比上年增长	4.3%
全社会固定资产投资额（亿元）	–	比上年增长	1.1%
社会消费品零售总额（亿元）	5140.93	比上年增长	6.0%
财政一般公共预算收入（亿元）	702.56	比上年增长	2.6%
财政一般公共预算支出（亿元）	1247.02	比上年增长	8.3%
进出口总值（亿元）	3242.52	比上年下降	1.8%
城镇常住居民人均可支配收入（元）	41850	比上年增长	8.1%
农村常住居民人均可支配收入（元）	14588	比上年增长	9.8%

1　GENERAL SURVEY

Ⅰ.Brief Introduction

This chapter consists of mainly unified data of administrative divisions, natural geography, natural resources, meteorology, national economy and social development of Xi'an city. It is compiled by Integration Division according to the reported data from other divisions of the Xi'an Bureau of Statistics and other departments of the municipal government.

Ⅱ. Major Indicators

		Increase over Preceding Year
Gross Domestic Product (100 mil. Yuan)	9321.19	7.0%
Gross Output Value of Farming, Forestry, Animal, Husbandry and Fishery (100 mil. Yuan)	499.32	4.3%
Total Investment In Fixed Assets (100 mil. Yuan)	–	1.1%
Total Retail Sales of Consumer Goods (100 mil. Yuan)	5140.93	6.0%
Government General Public Budgetary Revenue (100 mil. Yuan)	702.56	2.6%
Government General Public Budgetary Expenditures (100 mil. Yuan)	1247.02	8.3%
Total Value of Imports and Exports (RMB 100 mil.Yuan)	3242.52	-1.8%
Per Capita Annual Disposable Income of Urban Households (Yuan)	41850	8.1%
Per Capita Annual Disposable Income of Rural Households (Yuan)	14588	9.8%

1-1 行政区划（2019年）

Administrative Division (2019)

单位：个 (unit)

地　区	Region	乡镇及街道办 Township and Urban Subdistrict Office	镇数 Town	街道办事处 Urban Subdistrict Office	村民委员会 Villagers' Committee	社区居委会 Neighbourhood Committee
西安市	**Xi'an**	**187**	**48**	**139**	**2064**	**1106**
新城区	Xincheng	9		9		101
碑林区	Beilin	8		8		98
莲湖区	Lianhu	9		9		131
灞桥区	Baqiao	9		9	113	76
未央区	Weiyang	10		10	52	153
雁塔区	Yanta	10		10	61	193
阎良区	Yanliang	7		7	73	27
临潼区	Lintong	23		23	226	43
长安区	Chang'an	21		21	294	118
高陵区	Gaoling	7		7	86	17
鄠邑区	Huyi	13	6	7	245	20
蓝田县	Lantian	19	18	1	337	10
周至县	Zhouzhi	20	19	1	264	17
西咸新区	Xixian	22	5	17	313	102

注：本表数据来源市民政局。

1-2 土地面积和常住人口密度（2019年）

Statistics on Land Area and Density of Permanent Population（2019）

地 区	Region	土地面积 Area 绝对数（平方公里） Absolute Value (sq.km)	比重（%） Proportion （%）	常住人口（万人） Total of Permanent Population (10 000 persons)	常住人口密度（人/平方公里） Density of Permanent Population (person/sq.km)
西安市	**Xi 'an**	**10096.81**	**100.0**	**1020.35**	
市区	**Urban**	**5145.66**	**51.0**	**803.55**	
新城区	Xincheng	30.13	0.3	64.72	21482
碑林区	Beilin	23.37	0.2	68.77	29421
莲湖区	Lianhu	38.32	0.4	78.33	20439
灞桥区	Baqiao	324.50	3.2	70.39	2169
未央区	Weiyang	264.41	2.6	82.73	
雁塔区	Yanta	151.44	1.5	138.53	9148
阎良区	Yanliang	244.55	2.4	30.45	1245
临潼区	Lintong	915.97	9.1	70.04	765
长安区	Chang'an	1588.53	15.7	106.42	
高陵区	Gaoling	285.03	2.8	36.71	1288
鄠邑区	Huyi	1279.42	12.7	56.46	
二县	**Two Counties**	**4951.15**	**49.0**	**112.90**	**228**
蓝田县	Lantian	2005.95	19.9	53.61	267
周至县	Zhouzhi	2945.20	29.2	59.29	201
西咸新区	**Xixian**			**103.90**	

注：1.本表土地面积数据来源市自然资源和规划局，为西安原口径数据。表中土地面积数据为2018年数据。
2.全市常住人口数据包含西咸新区。
3.由于全市、市区及相关区县常住人口包含西咸新区，土地面积为原口径，暂不计算人口密度。

1-3 自然状况和资源（2019年）

Nature Conditions and Resources（2019）

指　标	Item	2019
一、自然状况	**Nature Conditions**	
土地总面积（平方公里）	Total Land Area (sq.km)	10096.81
#市区面积	Urban Area	5145.66
气候（市区）	Climate (Urban)	
年平均气温（℃）	Average Annual Temperature (℃)	15.3
年降水量（毫米）	Total Annual Precipitation (mm)	593.0
日照总时数（小时）	Total Sunshine Time (hour)	1751.8
平均风速（米/秒）	Average Wind-speed (m/sec.)	2.2
二、自然资源	**Natural Resources**	
年末常用耕地面积（千公顷）	Cultivated Area Year-end （1 000 hectare)	240.89
林业用地面积（千公顷）	Area of Forestry (1 000 hectare)	480.49
全市水面面积（千公顷）	Whole Water Area (1 000 hectare)	3.97
水资源总量（亿立方米）	Total Water Resource (0.1 billion cu.m)	24.45
#天然地表水资源总量	Total Savageness Surface Water Resource	20.31
地下水资源总量（亿立方米）	Total Underground Water Resource (0.1 billion cu.m)	9.27

注：1.全市水面面积包括湖泊、水库、鱼塘、城市段河流面积等。
2.本表数据来源市气象局、自然资源和规划局、水务局等。
3.本表年末常用耕地面积含西咸新区，其他指标数据均为西安原口径数据。
4.本表林业用地面积数据为2018年调整数据。土地面积为2018年数据。

1-4 气象情况（2019年）

Climate Condition（2019）

地　区	Region	平均气温（℃）Average Temperature（℃）	日照时数（小时）Sunshine Time (hour)	降水天数（天）Raining days (day)	年降水量（毫米）Total Annual Precipitation (mm)	平均风速（米/秒）Average Wind-speed (m/second)
市　区	Urban	15.3	1751.8	83	593.0	2.2
灞桥区	Baqiao	13.5		97	758.0	1.5
阎良区	Yanliang	15.5	1830.5	87	545.8	1.2
临潼区	Lintong	15.0	1848.7	82	666.4	1.7
长安区	Chang'an	13.7	1795.4	102	800.9	1.3
高陵区	Gaoling	14.6	1833.4	101	501.7	1.9
鄠邑区	Huyi	14.3	1671.4	120	742.5	1.6
蓝田县	Lantian	13.7	1740.4	105	808.4	1.5
周至县	Zhouzhi	13.9	1655.1	99	798.1	1.4
西咸新区	Xixian	14.2	1935.7	90	608.3	1.9

注：本表数据来源市气象局，灞桥区未开展日照观测。

1-5 市区及远郊区县各月平均气温（2019年）

Average Temperature of Xi'an and the Districts and Outer Suburban of Each Month（2019）

单位：℃　　　　(℃)

月　份	Month	市区 Urban	灞桥区 Baqiao	阎良区 Yanliang	临潼区 Lintong	长安区 Chang'an	高陵区 Gaoling	鄠邑区 Huyi	蓝田县 Lantian	周至县 Zhouzhi	西咸新区 Xixian
一月	January	1.0	-0.3	-0.9	0.7	-0.4	-0.2	0.3	-1.1	0.0	-0.5
二月	February	3.5	1.3	2.1	2.9	2.4	2.8	2.8	1.9	2.5	2.5
三月	March	12.5	10.8	10.8	12.1	10.3	11.2	11.2	10.0	10.9	11.1
四月	April	17.5	15.9	16.5	17.2	15.9	16.7	16.6	16.6	16.6	16.8
五月	May	21.0	18.5	20.3	20.9	19.1	20.4	19.9	19.7	19.3	19.9
六月	June	25.5	23.0	25.4	25.6	23.7	25.4	24.2	24.3	23.6	24.4
七月	July	27.5	25.2	27.2	27.2	25.7	27.4	26.4	26.4	25.6	26.7
八月	August	26.7	24.2	26.0	26.1	25.1	26.3	25.7	24.9	24.9	26.1
九月	September	20.9	19.0	20.3	20.4	19.4	20.5	20.0	19.7	19.4	20.2
十月	October	14.5	12.7	14.0	14.2	13.3	14.0	14.0	13.4	13.5	13.6
十一月	November	8.8	8.8	7.7	8.6	7.9	7.9	8.1	7.4	7.7	7.5
十二月	December	3.9	3.0	1.7	3.6	2.0	2.4	2.7	1.6	2.4	2.0

注：本表数据来源于市气象局。

1-6 市区及远郊区县各月日照时数（2019年）

Sunshine Duration of Xi'an and the Districts and Outer Suburban of Each Month (2019)

单位：小时 (hour)

月 份	Month	市区 Urban	灞桥区 Baqiao	阎良区 Yanliang	临潼区 Lintong	长安区 Chang'an	高陵区 Gaoling	鄠邑区 Huyi	蓝田县 Lantian	周至县 Zhouzhi	西咸新区 Xixian
一月	January	80.5		96.3	96.1	57.7	96.6	81.6	57.7	76.9	67.9
二月	February	92.0		86.0	82.8	40.7	95.2	76.8	59.9	61.9	65.0
三月	March	226.1		225.3	243.4	193.7	210.6	204.3	171.1	180.4	205.4
四月	April	174.2		209.0	220.9	148.5	197.1	178.4	161.9	180.6	183.2
五月	May	161.3		172.5	170.9	146.8	174.2	154.6	164.5	166.3	173.1
六月	June	130.8		139.7	139.2	130.7	140.3	132.4	138.7	135.3	141.2
七月	July	204.6		209.2	207.9	205.7	213.7	203.4	195.3	204.5	216.1
八月	August	176.1		181.1	179.4	162.3	183.0	167.4	200.6	172.4	180.0
九月	September	163.3		170.7	170.9	154.8	170.5	143.2	173.1	139.7	158.9
十月	October	85.3		85.6	86.0	171.5	92.4	77.1	82.0	77.0	168.0
十一月	November	102.2		99.6	100.2	158.9	99.0	97.7	132.5	97.6	161.9
十二月	December	155.4		155.3	151.0	224.1	160.8	154.5	203.1	162.5	215.0

注：本表数据来源市气象局。灞桥区未开展日照观测。

1-7 市区及远郊区县各月降水天数（2019年）

Precipitation Days of Xi'an and the Districts and Outer Suburan of Each Month (2019)

单位：天 (day)

月 份	Month	市区 Urban	灞桥区 Baqiao	阎良区 Yanliang	临潼区 Lintong	长安区 Chang'an	高陵区 Gaoling	鄠邑区 Huyi	蓝田县 Lantian	周至县 Zhouzhi	西咸新区 Xixian
一月	January	3	3	5	2	3	4	3	3	3	3
二月	February	3	7	4	5	9	7	7	4	8	5
三月	March	2	3	3	2	3	2	4	3	3	2
四月	April	8	9	12	7	11	9	10	10	10	9
五月	May	11	10	15	10	10	13	14	12	8	10
六月	June	8	9	10	8	9	11	13	10	9	9
七月	July	7	9	11	7	12	13	12	9	11	8
八月	August	7	12	10	8	9	9	10	10	8	8
九月	September	12	13	17	13	14	13	15	14	13	12
十月	October	15	16	15	14	15	16	17	17	14	16
十一月	November	6	5	6	5	5	9	12	9	10	6
十二月	December	1	1	1	1	2	2	3	4	2	2

注：本表数据来源市气象局。

1-8 市区及远郊区县各月降水量（2019年）

Amount of Precipitation of Xi'an and the Districts and Outer Suburan of Each Month (2019)

单位：毫米 (mm)

月 份	Month	市区 Urban	灞桥区 Baqiao	阎良区 Yanliang	临潼区 Lintong	长安区 Chang'an	高陵区 Gaoling	鄠邑区 Huyi	蓝田县 Lantian	周至县 Zhouzhi	西咸新区 Xixian
一月	January	6.6	17.2	6.3	13.0	8.1	6.8	6.1	13.8	8.4	6.4
二月	February	9.1	11.6	9.5	8.2	13.3	7.9	17.6	8.8	17.6	11.9
三月	March	1.3	3.9	2.1	3.5	3.4	1.3	5.3	4.7	9.7	2.6
四月	April	56.7	72.6	43.2	54.1	72.0	49.1	82.2	66.7	86.1	56.8
五月	May	21.2	59.1	57.7	29.3	37.9	19.8	44.0	33.4	58.5	27.4
六月	June	112.6	114.4	130.9	97.5	118.8	85.7	122.4	124.6	111.3	102.0
七月	July	55.6	46.5	50.7	63.5	102.3	42.0	59.9	46.5	127.2	48.7
八月	August	80.8	155.2	85.5	123.8	154.0	65.6	99.5	185.4	107.1	89.2
九月	September	163.7	190.8	157.2	180.7	207.5	148.9	219.0	232.6	215.9	173.5
十月	October	75.3	82.7	101.0	83.6	55.6	66.5	54.1	73.9	39.4	75.4
十一月	November	9.7	3.3	7.6	8.6	22.2	8.0	30.0	15.6	13.9	13.0
十二月	December	0.4	0.7	0.1	0.6	5.8	0.1	2.4	2.4	2.9	1.4

注：本表数据来源市气象局。

1-9 市区及远郊区县各月平均风速（2019年）

Average Wind Velocity of Xi'an and the Districts and Outer Suburban Districts (2019)

单位：米/秒 (m/s)

月 份	Month	市区 Urban	灞桥区 Baqiao	阎良区 Yanliang	临潼区 Lintong	长安区 Chang'an	高陵区 Gaoling	鄠邑区 Huyi	蓝田县 Lantian	周至县 Zhouzhi	西咸新区 Xixian
一月	January	2.0	1.5	1.7	1.6	1.4	1.6	1.5	1.3	1.3	1.6
二月	February	2.2	1.5	2.1	1.6	1.4	1.9	1.3	1.4	1.3	1.8
三月	March	2.2	1.8	2.1	1.9	1.5	2.0	1.8	1.7	1.8	2.0
四月	April	2.8	1.7	2.7	2.0	1.2	2.6	1.8	1.7	2.0	2.3
五月	May	2.2	1.8	2.3	1.8	1.4	1.9	1.9	1.7	1.8	2.1
六月	June	2.2	1.6	2.3	1.9	1.2	2.1	1.8	1.6	1.7	2.0
七月	July	2.2	1.4	2.2	1.9	1.1	1.9	1.7	1.6	1.5	2.0
八月	August	2.3	1.4	2.0	1.8	1.2	2.0	1.7	1.4	1.6	2.2
九月	September	2.2	1.3	2.0	1.7	1.0	1.8	1.6	1.4	1.3	1.9
十月	October	1.8	1.5	1.8	1.6	1.0	1.7	1.5	1.3	1.3	1.7
十一月	November	1.9	1.4	1.9	1.6	1.3	1.7	1.4	1.3	1.3	1.7
十二月	December	2.0	1.4	2.0	1.7	1.3	1.7	1.5	1.4	1.4	1.9

注：本表数据来源市气象局。

1-10 主要年份国有土地使用权出让、划拨情况

The Transfer and Allocation of State-Owned Land Use Right in Representative Years

项　目	Item	2010	2012	2013	2014	2015	2016	2017	2018	2019
国有土地使用权出让	**Lease of the Use Right of State-owned Land**									
出让地块(宗)	Land leased (item)	386	581	550	506	416	457	397	387	540
协议	Agreement	173	80	90	109	72	82	69	79	116
招标	Invitation for Bid	3								
拍卖	Auction	11						25	203	171
挂牌交易	Listed Transaction	199	500	460	397	344	375	303	105	253
出让面积（公顷）	Area of Totally Leased Land (hectare)	1364	1853	2195	1789	1294	1599	1736	1623	2157
土地使用权出让总收入（万元）	**Total Revenue from Leasing of the Use Right(10 000 yuan)**	**358098**	**218817**	**292945**	**183901**	**109116**	**2832632**	**3988818**	**5738433**	**8221571**
国有土地使用权划拨	**Administrative Allocation of the Use Right of State-owned Land**									
划拨地块（宗）	Land Allocated (item)	108	154	234	152	141	132	130	116	205
划拨面积（公顷）	Area of Land Allocated(hectare)	1027	1617	1986	1739	1209	1135	1411	3099	4605

注：1.本表数据来自市自然资源和规划局。
2.2016年起土地使用权出让总收入，包括协议出让和招拍挂出让收入。
3.2019年起包含西咸新区。

1-11 主要年份国民经济和社会发展总量与速度指标

指　标	Item	总量指标 Total quantity index 1995	2000	2005	2010
人口与就业	**Population and Employment**				
人口	**Population**				
年底户籍总人口（万人）	Population at the Year-end （10 000 persons）	648.21	688.01	741.73	782.73
城镇人口	Urban Population	255.71	285.79	333.14	374.64
乡村人口	Rural Population	392.50	402.22	408.59	408.09
男性人口	Male Population	334.75	355.18	382.02	398.80
女性人口	Female Population	313.46	332.83	359.71	383.93
就业	**Employment**				
全社会从业人员数（万人）	Employment（10 000 persons）	372.60	389.10	415.83	477.58
#全部单位在岗职工人数	Number of Employed Staff and Workers	141.17	109.62	119.73	130.70
城镇登记失业人数（万人）	Registered Unemployed in Urban Areas（10 000 persons）	5.92	3.85	8.45	10.46
宏观经济	**Macroeconomic Indicator**				
国民经济核算（亿元）	**National Accounts（100 mil. yuan）**				
生产总值（亿元）	Gross Domestic Product（100 mil. yuan）	330.35	646.13	1294.05	3195.05
第一产业	Primary Industry	41.40	44.65	66.01	133.22
第二产业	Secondary Industry	135.33	277.13	511.19	1290.93
第三产业	Tertiary Industry	153.62	324.35	716.86	1770.89
工业	Industry	112.50	218.44	393.51	875.97
建筑业	Construction	22.83	58.69	117.68	414.96
固定资产投资	**Investment in Fixed Assets**				
全社会固定资产投资总额（亿元）	Total Investment in Fixed Assets（100 mil. yuan）	103.42	232.37	835.10	3250.56
按类别分：	By classification:				
固定资产投资（不含农户）	Investment in Fixed Assets （excluding farmers）	88.50	203.01	776.33	3104.92
#房地产开发投资	Real Estate Investment	21.65	51.85	225.23	842.34
农户投资	Farmer Investment	14.92	29.36	58.77	145.64
按经济成分划分:	By Economic Component				
国有单位	State-owned	69.08	159.60	373.70	1348.76
集体单位	Collective-Owned	9.78	14.65	59.23	326.44
个体经济	Self-employed Individual	11.13	24.40	79.04	54.73
其他经济	Other	13.43	33.72	323.13	1520.63
财政	**Public Finance**				
地方财政一般公共预算收入（亿元）	General Public Budgetary Revenue of Local Government （100 mil. yuan）	18.21	41.39	73.05	241.86
地方财政一般公共预算支出（亿元）	General Public Budgetary Expenditure of Local Government （100 mil. yuan）	18.42	46.50	97.82	371.62
物价指数（上年=100）	**Price Indices（preceding year=100）**				
商品零售价格指数	Retail Price Index	114.6	98.7	99.7	102.7
居民消费价格指数	Consumer Price Index	117.0	100.2	100.3	103.5
工业生产者出厂价格指数	Producer Price Indices （PPI） for Manufactured Goods	110.8	99.4	103.9	102.3
利用外资	**Utilization of Foreign Capital**				
利用外资签定协议额（万美元）	Amount of Foreign Capital for Utilization Through Signed Contracts or Agreements（USD 10 000）	28956	54123	121499	119689
外商实际直接投资额（万美元）	Amount of Foreign Capital Actually Utilized （USD 10 000）	18653	15633	57113	156653

注：1.国民经济核算2003—2017年为全国第四次经济普查修订数据，2018年为全国第四次经济普查数据，2019年为初步核算数。本部分其他相关数据也进行了相应调整。
2.2009年及以前年份财政收支为一般预算收支与基金预算收支之和。部分历史年份数据有所修订。
3.由于2010年固定资产投资起报点的变化，指数和平均增长速度为可比口径计算。
4.2015年，市公安局提供户籍人口分类为“城镇人口”和“乡村人口”，2015年之前，分类为“非农业人口”和“农业人口”。
5.2015年，国家取消了城乡投资分组，“农户投资”2014年之前为原来的“农村投资”。
6.由于2017年部分指标包含有西咸新区数据，速度指标为同口径计算数据。
7.本表数据2019年数据口径情况详见总说明和相关章节表下注释。
8.农业部分数据依据三农普数据对2007-2017进行了修订。畜牧业数据2013-2017年为三农普修订数据。下同。
9.投资有关数据2018年起为相对数据，与投资总量相关的指标，暂不计算。下同。
10.全部单位在岗职工人数统计范围为城镇非私营单位。

Total and Speed Index of National Economy and Social Development in Representative Years

				速度指标（%）				Indices and Growth Rates（%）		
				指数（2019比以下各年）（2019 as percentage of the following years）				平均增长速度 Average Annual Growth Rate		
2015	2017	2018	2019	2005	2010	2015	2018	2006-2010	2011-2015	2016-2019
815.66	845.09	922.82	956.74	129.0	122.1	117.2	103.7	1.1	0.8	4.0
545.95	567.26	639.62	668.57	200.6	178.4	122.4	104.5	2.4	7.8	5.2
269.71	277.83	283.20	288.17	70.5	70.6	106.9	101.8	…	-7.9	1.7
412.23	424.98	461.51	477.13	124.9	119.6	115.7	103.4	0.9	0.7	3.7
403.43	420.11	461.31	479.61	133.3	125.0	118.9	104.0	1.3	1.0	4.4
528.06	596.21	621.22	645.86	143.9	125.3	113.4	104.0	2.8	2.0	3.2
181.86	188.42	181.76	192.14	158.2	144.9	104.1	105.7	1.8	6.8	1.0
10.74	11.51	12.48	12.52	147.9	119.6	116.4	100.3	4.4	0.5	3.9
5932.86	7418.04	8499.41	9321.19	434.8	227.1	135.7	107.0	13.9	10.9	7.9
191.91	245.26	258.98	279.13	199.0	149.5	116.8	104.3	5.9	5.0	4.0
2070.47	2452.92	2861.86	3167.44	371.2	206.3	129.9	107.6	12.5	9.7	6.8
3670.48	4719.86	5378.56	5874.62	508.0	247.7	140.2	106.8	15.5	12.1	8.8
1242.18	1436.72	1707.90	1868.86	338.3	205.3	131.1	106.6	10.5	11.2	7.0
857.40	1047.34	1210.79	1358.48	502.0	217.3	130.2	109.1	18.2	17.0	6.8
5165.98	7556.47			985.8	253.3	126.3	101.1	31.2	14.9	6.0
5086.93	7463.31			1074.0	268.5	128.1	101.1	31.9	15.9	6.4
1831.67	2333.34			1055.2	282.1	129.7	97.9	30.2	16.8	6.7
79.05	93.16			141.4	57.0	105.1	98.0	19.9	-11.5	1.3
1826.62	4127.66			871.4	241.5	141.3	105.1	29.3	11.3	9.0
158.14	153.36			164.4	29.8	48.7	144.2	40.7	-9.4	-16.5
80.47	93.94							-7.1	13.2	
3100.75	3181.51			1265.9	269.0	104.8	96.7	36.6	20.7	1.2
650.99	654.50	684.70	702.56	1300.0	389.4	138.7	102.6	27.3	22.9	8.5
917.24	1045.09	1151.87	1247.02	1243.5	327.0	131.4	108.3	30.6	20.0	7.1
99.7	101.7	102.2	102.1					2.5	1.7	1.5
100.7	102.0	101.9	102.7					3.1	2.6	1.9
98.5	100.3	101.1	101.6					2.2	0.1	0.2
193684	464954	475508	196410	80.6	81.8	50.6	41.3	-0.3	10.1	-15.7
400833	530680	635370	705738	1186.2	432.5	169.0	111.1	22.4	20.7	14.0

1-11 续表1

指 标	Item	总量指标 Total quantity index			
		1995	2000	2005	2010
产 业	**Industry**				
农业	**Agriculture**				
耕地面积（万亩）	Cultivated Areas（10 000 hectares）	463.97	443.37	400.17	383.32
农林牧渔业总产值 （亿元）	Gross Output Value of Farming，Forestry, Animal Husbandry and Fishery（100 mil yuan）	75.46	74.37	106.54	212.42
主要农产品产量（万吨）	Output of Major Farm Products（10 000 tons）				
粮 食	Grain	175.30	201.90	205.50	174.51
奶 类	Milk				
蔬 菜	Vegetables	133.60	162.14	195.70	207.11
水 果	Fruits	24.10	34.36	51.29	66.11
肉 类	Meat				
水产品	Aquatic Products	0.85	1.14	0.94	1.19
工业	**Industry**				
规模以上工业企业主要经济指标（亿元）	Main Economic Indicators of Industrial Enterprises above Designated Size（100 mil. yuan）				
资产总计	Total Assets		958.05	1503.85	3592.13
主营业务收入	Revenue from Principal Business		420.42	980.97	3011.19
利润总额	Profits		16.11	28.72	245.37
从业人员年平均人数 （万人）	Annual Average Employees（10 000 persons）		43.25	37.92	47.11
主要工业产品产量	Output of Major Industrial Products				
布（亿米）	Cloth（100 mil.m）	3.03	2.48	2.70	2.38
机制纸及纸板（万吨）	Machine-Made Paper（10 000ton）	36.44	5.47	22.19	49.60
发电量（亿千瓦时）	Electricity（100 million kwh）	22.00	19.00	48.00	96.94
钢材（万吨）	Steel Products（10 000ton）	31.44	10.00	24.02	110.77
汽车（万辆）	Motor Vehicle （10 000 units）	0.30	0.90	4.10	65.21
建筑业	**Construction**				
建筑业企业从业人数（人）	Number of Employed Persons（person）		136718	158311	539000
建筑业总产值（亿元）	Gross Output Value（100 mil. yuan）	42.55	105.93	326.65	1334.00
房屋建筑施工面积 （万平方米）	Floor Space of Buildings under Construction （10 000 sq.m）	601.70	793.30	1801.20	4592.57
房屋建筑竣工面积 （万平方米）	Floor Space of Buildings Completed （10 000 sq.m）	177.15	336.80	569.01	1391.91

注：1.规模以上工业2018年为全国第四次经济普查上报数据。
2.由于2010年规模以上工业起报点的变化，指数和平均增长速度为可比口径计算。

continued 1

2015	2017	2018	2019	速度指标（%） 指数（2019比以下各年）（2019 as percentage of the following years） 2005	2010	2015	2018	Indices and Growth Rates（%） 平均增长速度 Average Annual Growth Rate 2006-2010	2011-2015	2016-2019
356.89	374.45	367.61	361.33	81.9	85.4	91.8	98.3	-9.0	-1.4	-2.1
330.81	437.33	461.21	499.32	215.5	154.3	117.9	104.3	6.8	5.5	4.2
141.42	139.89	142.14	139.89	81.6	75.7	92.7	98.4	1.5	-4.0	-1.9
7.68	11.65	11.52	12.37	125.4	83.6	83.0	107.4	8.5	0.1	-4.6
267.91	354.74	373.69	378.58	192.8	149.1	113.4	101.3	5.3	5.6	3.2
73.33	89.80	89.15	97.18	236.2	143.0	115.2	109.0	10.6	4.4	3.6
7.21	5.87	5.45	5.14	78.0	103.9	88.1	94.3	-5.6	3.4	-3.1
1.42	1.38	1.35	1.36	144.6	114.2	95.8	100.7	5.7	3.6	-1.1
6740.26	7862.59	8294.07	9449.95	640.9	268.2	142.9	113.9	19.0	13.4	9.3
4374.11	5710.70	6021.12	6483.80	624.6	203.6	140.1	107.7	25.1	7.8	8.8
206.88	367.77	402.44	325.60	977.9	114.5	135.8	80.9	53.6	-3.4	8.0
50.59	51.11	51.40	49.75	120.5	97.0	90.4	96.8	4.4	1.4	-2.5
1.04	1.27	1.28	1.21	44.8	50.9	116.5	95.3	-2.5	-15.3	3.9
12.22	18.62	15.39	11.38	34.9	15.6	63.3	74.0	17.5	-24.4	-10.8
158.68	176.74	172.76	155.00	276.8	137.1	83.7	89.5	15.1	10.4	-4.4
37.03	54.91	33.40	31.47	235.6	51.1	152.9	117.5	35.8	-19.7	11.2
34.14	44.52	43.37	42.63	1039.3	65.4	124.8	98.3	73.9	-12.1	5.7
596245	703169	740351	835995	521.4	153.2	138.5	112.9	27.8	2.0	8.5
2650.41	3304.54	3925.72	4514.38	1377.7	337.4	169.9	115.0	41.0	14.7	14.2
11979.16	13491.49	15855.39	17174.05	936.6	367.2	140.9	108.3	20.6	21.1	9.0
2712.01	2553.10	2755.17	2726.28	449.5	183.7	94.3	99.0	19.6	14.3	-1.5

1-11 续表2

指 标	Item	总量指标 Total quantity index			
		1995	2000	2005	2010
交通运输	**Transportation**				
货运量（万吨）	Freight Traffic（10 000 tons）	9590	6999	12051	34323
铁 路	Railways	3317	3101	540	706
公 路	Highways	6268	3890	11505	33610
民用航空	Civil Aviation	5	8	6	7
客运量（万人次）	Passenger Traffic（10 000 persons-times）	9069	8068	10479	30294
铁 路	Railways	2678	2130	1796	2781
公 路	Highways	6128	5578	8294	26536
民用航空	Civil Aviation	263	360	389	977
邮电通信业	**Post and Telecommunication Services**				
邮电业务总量（亿元）	Total Business Revenue（100 mil. yuan）	7.65	46.16	132.04	323.11
函 件（万件）	Number of Letters Delivered（10 000 pieces）	14647	8230	9526	8176
本地电话局用交换机容量（万门）	Capacity of Local Office Telephone Exchanges（10 000 line）	58.30	204.80	457.30	449.00
本地电话年末用户（万户）	Local fixed telephone end users （million）	29.95	124.26	321.48	261.77
城市电话用户	Urban Telephone Subscribers	29.11	107.24	271.40	228.26
乡村电话用户	Rural Telephone Subscribers	0.84	17.02	50.08	33.50
移动电话用户（万户）	Number of Mobile Telephone Subscribers（10 000 subscribers）		73.10	419.96	1423.08
互联网年末宽带用户（万户）	Number of Subscribers of Intemet Services（10 000 subscribers）			33.93	146.18
国内贸易	**Domestic Trade**				
社会消费品零售总额（亿元）	Total Retail Sales of Consumer Goods（100 mil. yuan）	188.35	368.96	698.37	1765.42
对外经济贸易	**Foreign Trade**				
进出口总值（万美元）	Total Value of Exports and Imports（USD 10 000）	137510	173696	390146	1039273
出口总值	Exports	110163	106062	263441	531729
进口总值	Imports	27347	67634	126705	507544
旅游	**Tourism**				
旅游者人数（万人次）	Number of Tourists（10 000 persons）	791.35	1567.00	2423.60	5285.18
旅游总收入（亿元）	Earnings from Tourism （10 000yuan）	44.00	105.00	178.50	405.18
金融业	**Financial Intermediation**				
金融机构（不含外资）人民币存款余额（亿元）	Balance of Deposits in Domestic Funded Financial Institutions （100 mil. yuan）	359.51	1335.63	3599.70	8863.36
金融机构（不含外资）人民币贷款余额（亿元）	Balance of Loans in Domestic Funded Financial Institutions （100 mil. yuan）	334.50	972.52	2158.10	6420.72
保险公司保费收入（亿元）	Insurance premium income （100 million Yuan）	4.70	13.58	44.94	129.38
保险公司赔款及付给金额（亿元）	Indemnity Insurance and Amount Paid（100 million yuan）	1.70	1.39	9.50	26.39

注：1.2006年铁路数据按新口径统计；2018年起铁路数据为西铁局西安口径数据。
2.2006年国际互联网络用户改为互联网宽带用户。
3.1993—2018年社会消费品零售总额为全国第四次经济普查修订数据。本部分其他相关数据也进行了相应调整。
4.2014年起，海关不发布进出口美元口径数据，为了数据可持续性，使用年均汇率折算为美元口径。

continued 2

				速度指标（%）				Indices and Growth Rates（%）		
2015	2017	2018	2019	指数（2019比以下各年）（2019 as percentage of the following years）				平均增长速度 Average Annual Growth Rate		
				2005	2010	2015	2018	2006-2010	2011-2015	2016-2019
46270	25497	26219	27426				104.6	23.3		
848	994	497	487				98.0	5.5		
45401	24477	25691	26901				104.7	23.9		
21	26	31	38				122.6	3.1		
26904	24287	26057	26315				101.0	23.7		
3982	4500	6037	6332				104.9	9.1		
19625	15601	15555	15261				98.1	26.2		
3297	4186	4465	4722				105.8	20.2		
331.53	439.85	739.53	1421.70	1076.9	440.1	428.8	192.2	19.6	0.5	43.9
1707	1360	1081	1028	10.7	12.6	60.3	95.1	-3.0	-26.9	-11.9
145.10								-0.4	-20.2	
292.08	273.22	262.28	250.08	77.8	95.5	85.6	95.3	-4.0	2.2	-3.8
261.44	243.81	237.78	229.46	84.4	100.4	87.7	96.5	-3.4	2.8	-3.2
30.63	29.41	24.50	20.62	41.3	61.6	67.4	84.2	-7.7	-1.8	-9.4
1767.00	1854.21	1858.09	1711.36	407.4	120.3	96.8	92.1	27.6	4.4	-0.8
289.97	346.79	392.48	438.65	1293.7	300.3	151.4	111.8	33.9	14.7	10.9
3620.90	4422.72	4854.70	5140.93	767.4	306.7	151.1	106.0	20.1	15.2	10.9
2828479	3769490	4991748	4700323	1204.9	452.3	166.2	94.2	21.6	39.6	13.5
1316350	2298972	2957605	2508203	951.4	471.4	190.4	84.8	15.1	35.3	17.5
1512129	1470518	2034142	2192120	1731.2	432.2	145.1	107.8	32.0	43.9	9.8
13600.80	18093.14	24738.75	30110.43	1242.1	569.4	221.3	121.7	21.6	37.0	22.0
1073.69	1633.30	2554.81	3146.05	1763.0	776.6	293.0	123.1	15.1	38.4	30.8
17682.94	19943.41	20811.95	22891.88	636.2	258.4	129.6	110.0	19.7	14.8	6.7
13604.89	16831.48	19610.88	22135.23	1025.4	344.7	162.7	112.9	24.4	16.2	12.9
263.02	421.10	478.56	522.85	1164.0	404.3	198.9	109.3	23.6	15.2	18.8
87.62	118.71	130.82	141.42	1488.4	535.7	161.4	108.1	24.8	27.1	12.7

1-11 续表3

指 标	Item	总量指标 Total quantity index 1995	2000	2005	2010
教育、科技、文化	**Education, Science and Technology and Culture**				
教育	**Education**				
专任教师数（人）	Full-time Teachers（person）				
#普通高等学校	Institutions of Higher Education	15914	15679	29498	42098
普通中等专业学校	Regular Specialized Secondary Schools	2533	3172	2130	1845
普通中学	Regular Middle Schools	21984	26230	31094	31506
小 学	Primary Schools	30270	30215	29647	29944
在校学生数（万人）	Students Enrollment（10 000 person）				
#普通高等学校	Institutions of Higher Education	11.67	19.41	53.06	73.30
普通中等专业学校	Regular Specialized Secondary Schools	3.74	6.02	6.16	6.75
普通中学	Regular Schools	32.32	48.31	55.74	48.89
小 学	Primary Schools	79.36	77.81	60.47	51.56
科技	**Science and Technology**				
国家级高新技术企业数（个）	Hi-tech Enterprises （unit）				827
企事业单位累计授权专利数（件）	Accumulated patents awarded（unit）	3164	6139	11670	31999
文化	**Cultural**				
图书馆总藏量（千册件）	Total Collections in Library （1000 Volume-time）	2830	3214	3671	4465
文化馆、站（个）	Cultural Centers or Stations （unit）	201	251	192	197
电视节目制作时间（小时）	Time for TV Programs Production（hour）	5738	11871	27377	29626
家庭、生活、环境	**Family, People's Livelihood and Environment**				
家庭	**Family**				
家庭总户数（户籍人口）（万户）	Total Number of Households（10 000 household）	171.25	187.08	203.04	226.71
城镇常住居民平均每户家庭人口（人）	Average Household Size in Urban Areas（person）	3.88	2.99	2.93	2.81
农村常住居民平均每户家庭人口（人）	Average Household Size in Rural Areas（person）	4.60	4.30	4.22	3.94
婚姻	**Marriages and Divorces**				
结婚（对）	Number of Marriages（couple）	47236	46415	49962	83645
离婚（对）	Number of Divorces（couple）	4296	5161	12747	19060
居住	**Housing**				
城镇居民人均现住房建筑面积（平方米）	Per Capita Building Area of Urban Residents （sq.m）	13.05	14.82	16.38	28.70
农村居民人均现住房建筑面积（平方米）	Per Capita Building Area of Rural Residents（sq.m）	21.77	28.31	36.73	66.73

注：1.2008年及以前图书馆总藏量为图书馆藏书量。
2.2005年以前城镇居民人均现住房总建筑面积为城镇人均住房使用面积。
3.2014年城乡居民人均住房面积为城乡住户调查一体化改革后新口径数据，与往年不可比。
4.结婚和离婚对数2018年数据含西咸新区与往年不可比，增速暂不计算。

continued 3

2015	2017	2018	2019	速度指标（%） Indices and Growth Rates（%） 指数（2019比以下各年）(2019 as percentage of the following years) 2005	2010	2015	2018	平均增长速度 Average Annual Growth Rate 2006-2010	2011-2015	2016-2019
47768	47917	49018	50236	170.3	119.3	105.2	102.5	7.4	2.6	1.3
1228	998	958	918	43.1	49.7	74.7	95.8	-2.8	-7.8	-7.0
33014	36565	37539	39143	118.5	116.8	111.5	104.3	0.3	0.9	2.8
28748	34163	36878	39836	123.9	122.6	129.3	108.0	0.2	-1.1	6.6
84.83	83.02	82.44	87.14	164.3	118.9	102.7	105.7	6.7	3.0	0.7
3.47	2.74	2.48	2.79	45.2	41.3	80.3	112.5	1.9	-12.5	-5.3
41.37	41.74	42.46	43.56	75.2	85.8	101.5	102.6	-2.6	-3.3	0.4
56.62	66.68	73.09	78.98	123.6	145.1	132.1	108.1	-3.1	1.9	7.2
1316	1839	2620	3673		443.9	279.1	140.2		9.7	29.3
103910	175063	206703	240826	2064.4	752.8	231.8	116.5	22.4	26.6	23.4
6522	7340	7711	8012	218.4	179.6	122.9	103.9	4.0	7.9	5.3
199	202	202	202	94.7	92.4	91.5	100.0	0.6	0.2	-2.2
43563	49001	45731	58427	213.3	197.1	134.2	127.8	1.6	8.0	7.6
253.13	267.68	290.41	300.95	148.1	132.8	118.9	103.6	2.2	2.2	4.4
2.80	2.80	2.80	2.80	95.6	99.6	100.0	100.0	-0.8	-0.1	
3.60	3.60	3.70	3.70	87.7	94.0	102.8	100.0	-1.6	-1.8	0.7
80790	70954	93007	87315				93.9	10.9	-0.7	
22748	28811	42034	45329				107.8	8.4	3.6	
32.10	33.70	34.40	34.80			108.5	101.2	11.9		2.1
50.70	52.40	51.40	49.10			96.8	95.5	12.7		-0.8

1-11 续表4

指　标	Item	总量指标 Total quantity index 1995	2000	2005	2010
生活	**People's Livelihood**				
城镇居民人均可支配收入（元）	Per Capita Annual Disposable Income of Urban Households（yuan）	4153	6364	9628	22244
农村居民人均可支配收入（元）	Per Capita Annual Disposable Income of Rural Residents（yuan）	1353	2344	3460	7750
住户存款（亿元）	Household deposits（100 mil. yuan）	291.46	675.83	1716.76	3641.09
工资	**Wages**				
在岗职工工资总额（亿元）	The Gross Salary of Workers （100 mil. yuan）	67.23	101.68	211.14	501.76
城镇非私营单位从业人员年平均工资（元）	Aunual Average Wage of Stuff and Workers in Urban Non-privite Enterprises（yuan）	4763	9179	17728	37870
卫生	**Health Care**				
医院、卫生院（个）	Number of Hospitals（unit）	368	426	479	412
执业（助理）医师（人）	Licensed （Assistant） Doctors （person）	18846	18750	17730	18763
医院、卫生院床位数（张）	Number of Hospital Beds（unit）	28265	28697	30087	36796
市政建设	**City Construction**				
自来水供应量（万立方米）	Volume of Tap Water Supply（10 000 cu.m）	35885	30273	35776	41089
自来水供水管道长度（公里）	Length of Water Supply Pipelines（km）	1066	2237	2315	2416
城市天然气供气总量 （万立方米）	Volume of Natural Gas Supply in Urban Areas（10 000 cu.m）	8419	11513	53202	109052
城市公共运营车辆（辆）	Total Number of Public Buses and Trolley Buses（unit）	977	2573	4762	7107
道路长度（公里）	Length of Paved Roads（km）	835	975	1382	2662
绿地面积（公顷）	Areas of Green Land（hectare）	5603	4116	4867	12140
环境、灾害	**Environment and Disaster**				
工业废水排放量（万吨）	Volume of Waste Water up to the Standard for Discharge（10 000 tons）	12479	9145	16969	13840
火灾发生数（起）	Number of Fire Disasters（case）	426	1040	2664	1825
火灾事故损失额（万元）	Fire Loss（10 000 yuan）	742	472	1566	2224
交通事故发生数（起）	Number of Traffic Accidents（case）	3065	4099	4903	2323
交通事故损失额（万元）	Loss of Traffic Accidents（10 000 yuan）	1103	1116	2024	737

注：1.城镇非私营单位从业人员年平均工资2012年前为城镇非私营单位在岗职工年平均工资。
2.2014年及以后城乡居民人均收入为新口径数据。2013年及以前“农村居民人均可支配收入”为“农村居民人均纯收入”。依据2018年新口径对2017年城乡居民收入进行了衔接，其他年份不可比。
3.部门对住户存款部分历史年代数据进行了修订。2015年之前住户存款为储蓄存款。
4.市政建设大部分指标2017年起包含西咸新区，与以前年份不可比，故不计算相关增速指标。

continued 4

2015	2017	2018	2019	速度指标（%） Indices and Growth Rates（%） 指数（2019比以下各年）（2019 as percentage of the following years） 2005	2010	2015	2018	平均增长速度 Average Annual Growth Rate 2006-2010	2011-2015	2016-2019
33188	35837	38729	41850	550.1	238.1	135.8	108.1	18.2	15.1	8.0
14072	12190	13286	14588	641.2	286.4	140.7	109.8	17.5	15.3	8.9
6571.18	7497.30	8360.33	9553.29	557.1	262.7	145.5	114.3	13.3	12.5	9.8
1202.01	1488.71	1622.72	1903.84	871.1	366.7	153.1	117.3	18.9	19.1	11.2
60557	75262	83821	92359	523.7	245.2	153.3	110.2	16.4	9.8	11.3
395	448	462	477	89.3	103.8	108.4	103.2	-3.0	-0.8	2.0
26626	30820	33776	38469	209.5	197.8	139.4	113.9	1.1	7.3	8.7
51345	60513	65552	69107	219.4	179.3	128.5	105.4	4.1	6.9	6.5
56055	89216	90394	75392				83.4	2.8	6.4	
4371	4900	4960	4977				100.3	0.9	12.6	
196826	231168	285215	320847				112.5	15.4	12.5	
7781	7780	8743	10566	222.1	148.8	135.9	120.9	8.3	1.8	8.0
3571	4399	4712	5142				109.1	14.0	6.1	
20582	30704	31681	32586				102.9	20.1	11.1	
5204	4248	4163	3914	24.3	29.6	78.7	94.0	-4.0	-17.8	-5.8
2590	2353	2066	1871	70.2	102.6	72.2	90.6	-7.3	7.3	-7.8
2402	1659	1783	1887	120.7	84.9	78.6	105.8	7.3	1.5	-5.8
2392	2858	3153	2973	60.6	128.0	124.2	94.3	-13.9	0.6	5.6
1470	1777	2191	1809	89.3	245.5	123.0	82.5	-18.3	14.8	5.3

1-12 主要年份国民经济和社会发展结构指标

单位：%

指　　标	Item	1995	2000	2005
人口与就业	**Population and Employment**			
人 口	**Population**			
城乡结构	Structure			
城镇人口	Urban Population	39.45	41.54	44.91
乡村人口	Rural Population	60.55	58.46	55.09
性别结构	Sexual Structure			
男	Male	51.64	51.62	51.50
女	Female	48.36	48.38	48.50
就 业	**Employment**			
全社会从业人员产业结构	Industrial Structure of the Whole Society			
第一产业	Primary Industry	41.17	37.78	32.78
第二产业	Secondary Industry	29.43	27.57	27.46
第三产业	Tertiary Industry	29.40	34.65	39.76
宏观经济	**Macro Economy**			
国民经济核算	**National Accounting**			
生产总值产业结构	Industrial Structure			
第一产业	Primary Industry	12.53	6.91	5.10
第二产业	Secondary Industry	40.97	42.89	39.50
第三产业	Tertiary Industry	46.50	50.20	55.40
投 资	**Investment**			
全社会固定资产投资结构	Structure of Total Investment in Fixed Assets			
报表种类结构	By classification			
固定资产投资（不含农户）	Investment in Fixed Assets (excluding farmers)	85.57	87.36	92.96
#房地产开发投资	Real Estate Investment	20.93	22.31	27.00
农户投资	Farmer Investment	14.43	12.64	7.04
经济成分结构	Registion Status Composition			
国有经济	State-owned Enterprises Investment	66.79	68.68	44.75
集体经济	Collective-owned Enterprises Investment	9.46	6.30	7.09
个体经济	Self-employed Individual	10.76	10.50	9.46
其他经济	Other	12.99	14.51	38.69
财 政	**Government Finance**			
财政收入结构	Structure of Government Revenue			
中　央	Central Government		31.94	58.30
地　方	Local Governments		68.06	41.70

注：1.2015年，市公安局提供户籍人口分类为“城镇人口”和“乡村人口”，2015年之前，分类为“非农业人口”和“农业人口”。
2.本表2008年以后财政收入结构中地方指地方财政一般公共预算收入。

Structural Indicators of National Economic and Social Development in Representative Years

(%)

2010	2012	2013	2014	2015	2016	2017	2018	2019
47.86	50.05	50.79	51.29	66.93	66.94	67.12	69.31	69.88
52.14	49.95	49.21	48.71	33.07	33.06	32.88	30.69	30.12
50.95	50.75	50.66	50.59	50.54	50.49	50.29	50.01	49.87
49.05	49.25	49.34	49.41	49.46	49.51	49.71	49.99	50.13
25.65	22.33	20.81	19.71	20.39	19.50	18.98	16.30	15.70
29.65	31.55	28.55	28.49	24.53	23.72	22.73	24.79	25.48
44.70	46.12	50.64	51.80	55.08	56.78	58.29	58.91	58.83
4.17	4.14	3.68	3.44	3.23	3.07	3.31	3.05	2.99
40.40	39.51	39.24	38.59	34.90	33.45	33.07	33.67	33.98
55.43	56.35	57.08	57.97	61.87	63.48	63.62	63.28	63.03
95.52	96.80	97.03	96.25	98.47	98.18	98.77		
25.91	30.21	31.08	29.84	35.46	37.67	30.88		
4.48	3.20	2.97	3.75	1.53	1.52	1.23		
41.49	39.15	34.49	32.46	35.36	44.92	54.62		
10.04	4.59	4.28	3.44	3.06	2.93	2.03		
1.68	1.95	1.64	1.41	1.56	1.57	1.24		
46.78	54.31	59.58	62.69	60.02	50.58	42.10		
37.28	32.37	30.80	29.61	28.94	31.68	35.63	39.86	40.83
47.36	52.71	55.60	57.25	58.39	56.45	47.96	46.88	45.80

1-12 续表1

单位：%

指　　标	Item	1995	2000	2005
产　业	**Industry**			
农　业	**Agriculture**			
农林牧渔业	Structure of Gross Output Value of Farming,			
总产值结构	Forestry,Animal Husbandry and Fishery			
农　业	Farming	68.03	69.23	61.69
林　业	Forestry	0.96	1.14	1.23
牧　业	Animal Husbandry	30.29	28.58	30.96
渔　业	Fishery	0.72	1.05	0.69
农林牧渔专业及辅助性活动	Farming,Forestry,Animal Husbandry and Fishery			5.43
建筑业	**Construction**			
建筑业总产值结构	Structure of Gross Output Value of Construction Industry			
房屋建筑业	Building Construction	12.84	9.28	34.05
土木工程建筑业	Civil Engineering Construction	86.27	88.50	56.59
建筑安装业	Installation of Construction			
建筑装饰和其他建筑业	Decoration and others	0.89	2.22	9.36
交通运输业	**Transportation**			
客运量结构	Structure of Passenger Traffic			
铁　路	Railways	29.53	26.40	17.14
公　路	Highways	67.57	69.14	79.15
民　航	Civil Aviation	2.90	4.46	3.71
货运量结构	Structure of Freight Traffic			
铁　路	Railways	34.59	44.30	26.92
公　路	Highways	65.36	55.58	73.04
民　航	Civil Aviation	0.05	0.12	0.04
国内贸易	**Domestic Trade**			
社会消费品零售总额结构	Composition of Retail Sales of Consumer Goods			
城　镇	Urban Area	88.95	87.99	90.17
农　村	Rural Area	11.05	12.01	9.83
教育文化、卫生、人民生活	**Education and Culture，Health Care，People's Livelihood**			
教　育	**Education**			
在校学生结构	Structure of Student Enrollment			
#普通高等学校	Institutions of Higher Education	8.81	12.44	28.48
普通中等专业学校	Regular Specialized Secondary Schools	2.84	3.84	3.33
普通中学	Regular Schools	24.55	30.93	29.89
小 学	Primary Schools	59.91	49.89	32.45

continued 1

(%)

2010	2012	2013	2014	2015	2016	2017	2018	2019
65.40	65.61	66.66	67.95	68.06	68.00	68.81	70.04	69.97
1.26	2.24	2.62	2.69	2.96	2.95	3.10	3.67	3.70
25.35	23.09	21.22	19.60	18.54	17.93	16.67	14.74	14.56
0.60	0.71	0.74	0.74	0.59	0.57	0.52	0.57	0.44
7.39	8.34	8.75	9.02	9.85	10.56	10.90	10.98	11.33
24.63	43.03	43.03	41.58	38.41	36.69	36.64	37.73	39.84
68.61	47.57	47.86	49.43	51.84	53.63	54.13	54.84	52.80
4.39	6.49	5.86	5.32	5.91	6.61	6.30	4.88	4.79
2.37	2.91	3.25	3.67	3.84	3.07	2.93	2.55	2.56
9.18	8.07	8.02	13.65	14.80	17.74	18.53	23.17	24.06
87.59	85.45	85.18	74.97	72.95	66.63	64.24	59.70	57.99
3.23	6.48	6.80	11.38	12.25	15.63	17.24	17.14	17.94
2.06	1.84	1.71	2.14	1.83	3.58	3.90	1.90	1.78
97.92	98.13	98.25	97.81	98.12	96.32	96.00	97.99	98.09
0.02	0.04	0.04	0.05	0.05	0.10	0.10	0.12	0.14
96.00	96.92	96.89	96.85	96.70	96.61	96.43	98.05	98.02
4.00	3.08	3.11	3.15	3.30	3.39	3.57	1.95	1.98
32.60	31.00	33.09	33.16	32.78	31.38	29.13	27.52	27.44
3.02	2.08	1.84	1.58	1.34	1.17	0.96	0.83	0.88
21.74	17.40	17.26	16.53	16.00	15.37	14.65	14.18	13.72
22.95	19.52	20.51	20.88	21.88	22.58	23.40	24.40	24.87

1–12 续表2

单位：%

指　标	Item	1995	2000	2005
专任教师结构	Structure of Full-time Teachers			
#普通高等学校	Institutions of Higher Education	21.25	19.89	29.93
普通中等专业学校	Regular Specialized Secondary Schools	3.38	4.02	2.16
普通中学	Regular Middle Schools	29.37	33.21	31.55
小 学	Primary Schools	40.41	38.34	30.08
人民生活	**People's Livelihood**			
城镇居民消费结构	Consumption Structure of Urban Residents			
食品烟酒	Food,Tobacco and Alcohol	44.68	36.46	37.04
衣 着	Clothing	12.67	8.13	9.03
居 住	Residence	6.49	11.23	9.10
生活用品及服务	Living Articles and Services	13.75	11.33	4.73
交通和通信	Transport and Communication Services	5.58	6.93	9.67
教育文化娱乐	Recreation, Education and Culture Services	9.05	13.74	17.18
医疗保健	Medical and Health Care Services	3.27	7.23	9.45
其他用品和服务	Other Commodities and Services	4.51	4.95	3.80
农村居民消费结构	Consumption Structure of Rural Residents			
食品烟酒	Food,Tobacco and Alcohol	50.31	36.63	36.34
衣 着	Clothing	8.39	6.65	6.11
居 住	Residence	5.92	21.41	17.76
生活用品及服务	Living Articles and Services	5.17	5.47	5.11
交通和通信	Transport and Communication Services	8.09	4.21	8.19
教育文化娱乐	Recreation, Education and Culture Services	18.53	14.49	16.15
医疗保健	Medical and Health Care Services	1.78	6.93	8.19
其他用品和服务	Other Commodities and Services	1.81	4.21	2.15
卫 生	**Health Care**			
卫生技术人员结构	Medical Technical Personnel by Types			
执业（助理）医师	Licensed（Assistant） Doctors	45.42	44.82	41.96
注册护士	Registered Nurses	32.68	34.29	33.14
药 师	Junior Paramedics	8.78	8.31	7.30
技 师	Technicians	5.21	5.21	5.33
其 他	Others	7.91	7.37	12.27

注：2014年及以后为城乡住户调查一体化改革后数据，居民消费结构与2014年之前不可比。

continued 2

(%)

2010	2012	2013	2014	2015	2016	2017	2018	2019
32.47	32.96	33.91	33.87	34.52	32.63	30.90	30.74	29.97
1.42	1.18	1.08	0.97	0.89	0.84	0.64	0.60	0.55
24.30	23.36	22.95	23.62	23.86	23.50	23.58	23.54	23.35
23.10	21.97	21.49	20.57	20.52	21.41	22.03	23.13	23.76
31.29	32.48	32.44	29.21	29.59	29.26	29.44	27.08	26.80
11.11	12.17	12.02	9.09	8.78	8.22	8.12	7.91	7.65
9.33	8.47	7.82	17.89	17.78	17.87	17.84	20.01	21.00
7.56	7.87	7.80	7.21	7.42	7.59	7.57	7.86	7.26
12.06	14.26	14.01	14.16	13.31	13.67	13.00	11.74	11.85
14.66	14.33	14.17	12.60	12.48	12.29	12.61	13.93	13.69
9.50	8.52	7.99	7.32	7.92	8.14	8.28	8.97	8.95
4.49	1.91	3.76	2.53	2.72	2.96	3.15	2.50	2.79
32.54	33.83	32.96	29.93	28.18	26.86	27.27	24.43	25.45
6.55	7.42	7.87	7.44	7.12	6.65	6.50	5.94	6.25
24.41	21.91	19.82	21.99	23.28	23.38	23.54	23.60	23.10
6.53	7.46	7.76	6.97	6.60	7.59	7.85	7.67	7.22
8.45	10.19	9.86	10.66	10.70	10.76	10.69	11.71	11.85
11.20	10.20	10.56	10.26	11.68	11.86	11.90	13.26	13.15
8.54	8.85	8.41	11.07	10.68	11.17	10.47	12.05	11.46
1.78	0.14	2.77	1.68	1.76	1.73	1.79	1.34	1.51
33.16	34.46	33.58	32.66	32.69	32.30	32.71	33.28	34.27
40.01	41.61	42.13	42.28	42.74	43.50	44.15	45.77	46.22
5.36	5.05	4.99	4.88	4.86	4.72	4.54	4.36	4.20
8.11	5.91	5.75	5.63	5.76	5.86	5.94	5.95	5.91
13.36	12.97	13.55	14.56	13.97	13.62	12.66	10.64	9.40

1-13 主要年份国民经济和社会发展比例和效益指标

指　　标	Item	1995
人口与就业	**Population and Employment**	
人口	**Population**	
出生率（‰）	Birth Rate（‰）	11.95
死亡率（‰）	Death Rate（‰）	4.98
自然增长率（‰）	Natural Growth Rate（‰）	6.79
就业	**Employment**	
就业者负担人口	Dependency Ratio	1.7
三次产业就业者比例	Employment Ratio by Type of Industry	
（以第一产业为100）	（Employment in primary industry=100）	
第一产业	Primary Industry	100
第二产业	Secondary Industry	71.5
第三产业	Tertiary Industry	71.4
城镇登记失业率(%)	Unemployment Rate in Urban Areas(%)	3.1
宏观经济	**Macro Economy**	
国民经济核算	**National Accounting**	
三次产业增加值比例	Ratio of Value-added by Type of Industry	
（以第一产业为100）	（Employment in primary industry=100）	
第一产业	Primary Industry	100
第二产业	Secondary Industry	326.9
第三产业	Tertiary Industry	371.1
全社会劳动生产率(元／人)	Overall Labor Productivity（yuan/person）	8963
第一产业	Primary Industry	2698
第二产业	Secondary Industry	12404
第三产业	Tertiary Industry	14488
人均生产总值(元)	Per Capita GDP（yuan）	5131
固定资产投资	**Investment in Fixed Assets**	
全社会固定资产投资相当于生产总值比例(%)	Proportion of Investment in fixed Assets to GDP(%)	31.3
房屋建筑面积竣工率(%)	Rate of Floor Space of Buildings Completed in Construction(%)	33.4
固定资产交付使用率(%)	Rate of Fixed Assets Completed in Capital Construction and Put into Use(%)	70.7
建设项目建成投产率(%)	Rate of Projects Completed in Capital Construction and Put into Use(%)	43.7
财政	**Finance**	
财政总收入相当于生产总值比例(%)	Proportion of Government Revenue to GDP(%)	5.5
一般公共预算支出相当于生产总值比例(%)	Proportion of Government General Public Budgeary Expenditures to GDP(%)	5.6
利用外资	**Utilization of Foreign Capital**	
外商实际直接投资额相当于利用外资协议金额比例(%)	Proportion of Foreign Capital Actually Used to Total Amount of Foreign Capital for Utilization by Signed Contracts or Agreements(%)	64.4

注：本表财政收入数据2009年及以前为一般预算财政收入和基金收入之和。依据部门历史年份修订结果对财政相关数据进行了重新计算。

Proportions of National Economic and Social Development and Benefit Index in Representative Years

	2000	2005	2010	2012	2013	2014	2015	2016	2017	2018	2019
	13.07	9.58	9.73	10.13	9.57	10.11	10.15	11.54	12.62	12.47	12.32
	5.96	5.16	5.34	5.57	5.37	5.47	5.51	5.40	5.42	5.48	5.53
	7.11	4.42	4.39	4.56	4.20	4.64	4.64	6.14	7.20	6.99	6.79
	1.8	1.8	1.8	1.7	1.6	1.6	1.6	1.6	1.6	1.6	1.6
	100	100	100	100	100	100	100	100	100	100	100
	73.0	83.8	124.0	141.3	137.2	144.6	120.3	121.7	119.7	152.1	162.3
	91.7	121.3	183.3	206.5	243.3	262.9	270.1	291.3	307.1	361.4	374.8
	3.4	4.3	4.2	3.5	3.4	3.4	3.4	3.3	3.3	3.3	3.3
	100	100	100	100	100	100	100	100	100	100	100
	620.7	774.4	969.0	953.3	1066.0	1123.5	1078.9	1087.9	1000.1	1105.1	1134.8
	726.4	1086.0	1329.3	1359.5	1550.4	1687.5	1912.6	2064.6	1924.4	2076.8	2104.6
	16367	31356	67973	86490	94907	104867	111837	119867	130668	139628	147129
	2960	4747	11129	15351	16204	17783	18045	18483	22470	24156	27552
	25443	45258	93218	110093	124045	141911	147176	166245	186251	197683	198860
	24024	44611	83586	106847	111886	118682	129488	136009	144404	150770	157518
	9484	16158	37792	51214	57876	64790	68457	72944	77803	86638	92256
	36.0	64.5	101.7	97.1	103.5	105.9	87.1	81.2	101.9		
	42.0	28.1	6.9	8.7	13.2	11.4	6.8	9.9	11.2	6.4	6.3
	74.0	52.8	38.4	42.4	37.1	42.5	40.3	38.3	43.4	26.9	33.6
	44.2	54.2	53.9	56.1	56.1	62.5	61.0	64.6	62.4	36.3	55.3
	9.5	12.7	16.0	17.2	18.2	18.3	18.8	17.8	18.4	17.2	16.5
	7.2	7.6	11.6	13.7	14.7	14.7	15.5	14.7	14.1	13.6	13.4
	28.9	47.0	130.9	68.8	124.3	145.0	207.0	441.2	114.1	133.6	359.3

1-13 续表1

指　　标	Item	1995
能　　源	**Energy**	
单位生产总值能耗降低率（%）	Decreasing Rate of Energy Consumption per Unit GDP（%）	
产　　业	**Industries**	
农业	**Agriculture**	
农业从业者人均耕地面积（公顷）	Cultivated Land per Agricultural Laborer（hectare）	0.20
每公顷耕地农业机械总动力（千瓦）	Total Power of Agricultural Machinery per Hectare of Cultivated Land（kw）	5.23
每公顷耕地化肥施用量（公斤）	Chemical Fertilizer Consumption per Hectare of Cultivated Land（kg）	536
每公顷耕地生产的农业总产值（元）	Agricultural Output Value per Hectare of Cultivated Land（yuan）	24396
每个农林牧渔业劳动力农产品生产量（公斤）	Output of Farm Products per Farming,Forestry,Animal Husbandry and Fishery Husbandry and Fishery Laborer （kg）	
粮食	Grain	1150
蔬菜	Vegetables	877
禽蛋	Poultry Eggs	
肉类	Meat	
水产品	Aquatic Products	6
每公顷播种面积农产品产量（公斤）	Output of Farm Crops per Hectare of Sown Area（kg）	
粮食	Grain	3806
油料	Oil-bearing Crops	1753
蔬菜	Vegetables	34800
工业	**Industrial**	
规模以上工业企业经济效益	**Economic Benefit of Industrial Enterprises above Designated Size**	
总资产贡献率（%）	Ratio of Total Assets to Industrial Output Value （%）	
资产负债率（%）	Assets-Liability Ratio （%）	
流动资产周转次数（次 /年）	Rate of Annual Turnover Working Capitals（times/year）	
成本费用利润率（%）	Ratio of Profits to Cost （%）	
产品销售率（%）	Proportion of Industrial Products Sold（%）	
全员劳动生产率（元/人）	Overall Labor Productivity （yuan/person）	
建筑业	**Construction**	
机械装备率（元 / 人）	Value of Machinery per Laborer（yuan/person）	5990
产值利润率（%）	Ratio of Per-tax Profits to Gross Output Value（%）	3.5
全员劳动生产率（元 / 人）（按总产值计算）	Overall Labor Productivity（yuan/person）（in terms of gross output value per employee）	37689
邮电通信业	**Post and Communication Services**	
电话普及率（含移动电话） （部/百人）	Access to Telephones, National（include mobilphone）（set/100 persons）	7.9
移动电话普及率（部/百人）	Access to Mobilphones （set/100 persons）	0.48

continued 1

2000	2005	2010	2012	2013	2014	2015	2016	2017	2018	2019
		2.06	3.51	3.57	5.89	3.20	3.83	4.61	5.99	4.78
0.20	0.22	0.22	0.22	0.23	0.22	0.23	0.22	0.22	0.25	0.25
6.78	8.39	10.48	12.1	12.73	13.32	13.68	11.31	10.19	9.91	10.2
664	794	922	987	982	1045	1035	1050	1023	1031	1013
25161	39937	83123	112961	125238	134435	139040	149979	175189	188192	207284
1382	1493	1497	1480	1398	1276	1346	1323	1267	1456	1430
1110	1421	1777	2012	2249	2338	2549	2628	3214	3827	3870
				45	43	49	61	48	54	55
				61	64	69	67	53	56	53
8	7	10	12	13	13	14	13	13	14	14
4342	4796	4682	4949	4886	4831	5132	5052	4947	5082	5122
1526	1821	1950	1992	1948	1519	2099	1408	2173	2180	2157
37797	35231	39798	42990	45271	38085	48711	39152	50851	52027	52717
	8.4	12.2	7.7	8.5	7.4	5.7	6.4	7.2	7.3	5.4
65.0	65.0	57.6	59.4	59.5	59.7	57.3	55.7	53.0	54.5	53.9
1.0	1.3	1.7	1.5	1.5	1.4	1.3	1.3	1.4	1.3	1.2
4.2	3.1	8.8	4.5	5.2	5.2	4.8	6.0	6.6	6.8	5.1
97.1	97.5	97.1	96.7	95.7	94.9	94.5	96.0	97.3	96.2	94.0
29496	82815	188483	230032	264324	275288	268182	277240	294393		
6805	13332	9461	12216	10339		12712	14193	10051	10005	7964
3.4	4.8	4.4	2.8	2.6	2.3	2.3	3.1	2.8	3.0	2.5
74347	206337	321340	479232	354419	347000	406962	422421	411690	457700	467200
31.2	100.0	199.0	247.2	288.7	270.3	236.5	229.1	221.2	212.0	192.2
10.62	56.62	168.00	210.87	251.59	234.75	203.00	197.00	192.80	185.74	167.70

1-13 续表2

指　　标	Item	1995
国内贸易	**Domestic Trade**	
人均批发零售和住宿餐饮业消费品零售额（元）	Per Capita Retail Sales of Wholesale,Retail Trade and Accommodation Catering Trade(yuan)	1997
对外经济贸易	**Foreign Trade**	
进出口总值相当于地区生产总值比例（%）	Proportion of Total Imports & Exports to GDP（%）	34.76
国际旅游	**International Tourism**	
每一来华游客花费（元）	Expenditure per International Tourist in China(yuan)	556
金融业	**Finance and Insurance**	
金融机构存款相当于生产总值比例（%）	Bank Deposits as Percentage of GDP（%）	108.83
金融机构贷款相当于生产总值比例（%）	Bank Loans as Percentage of GDP（%）	101.26
教育、科技、文化	**Education, Science and Technology and Culture**	
教育	**Education**	
毕业率（%）	Graduation Rate（%）	
小学	Primary Schools	
初中	Junior Schools	
学校教师负担系数	Student-teacher Ratio	
高等学校	Colleges and Universities	6.83
中等学校	Secondary Schools	14.42
小学	Primary Schools	26.22
文化	**Culture**	
每百万人有艺术表演团体（个）	Number of Troupes per Million Persons（unit）	3.39
每百万人有公共图书馆（个）	Number of Public Libraries per Million Persons（unit）	2.31
家庭、生活、环境	**Family, People's Livelihood and Environment**	
家庭	**Family**	
城市居民家庭	Urban Households	
平均每一劳动力负担人口（人）	Persons supported by Each Laborer（person）	1.8
农村居民家庭	Rural Households	
平均每一劳动力负担人口（人）	Persons supported by Each Laborer（person）	1.6
卫生	**Health Care**	
每万人医院数（个）	Number of Hospitals per 10 000 Persons(unit)	0.60
每万人医生数（人）	Number of Doctors per 10 000 Persons（person）	29.10
每万人医院床位数（张）	Number of Hospital Beds per 10 000 Persons（unit）	43.60
市政建设	**City Construction**	
城市自来水普及率（%）	Percentage of Households with Access to Tap Water（%）	
城市用气普及率（%）	Percentage of Households with Access to Tap Gas（%）	
人均公园绿地面积（平方米）	Per Capita Public Green Areas (sq.m)	3.80

continued 2

2000	2005	2010	2012	2013	2014	2015	2016	2017	2018	2019
4122	9160	20882	29659	33821	38074	41780	45758	47946	49486	50882
22.25	24.79	21.54	18.72	22.11	27.47	29.69	28.61	34.31	38.86	34.79
645	737	767	820	801	792	789	809	903	1033	1045
206.71	278.17	277.41	275.61	275.51	270.11	298.05	296.38	268.85	244.86	245.59
150.51	166.77	200.96	195.86	200.19	207.57	229.31	237.00	226.90	230.73	237.47
		100.4	100.2	99.8	99.6	99.6	99.8	99.8	100.0	99.8
		99.7	98.7	99.3	99.9	98.3	98.7	98.3	100.0	99.0
12.38	17.99	17.41	18.15	18.05	18.27	17.76	17.62	17.33	16.82	17.35
17.84	18.47	17.78	16.43	15.07	14.01	13.88	13.05	12.78	13.10	13.06
25.75	20.38	17.22	17.15	17.66	18.94	19.94	11.98	11.42	11.31	11.13
3.20	2.56	1.53	2.22	2.10	2.09	2.07	2.04	1.87	1.80	1.76
2.18	2.02	1.77	1.75	1.75	1.74	1.49	1.47	1.35	1.30	1.27
2.2	2.1	1.9	1.9	1.8	1.3	1.3	1.3	1.3	1.3	1.3
1.6	1.6	1.5	1.5	1.5	1.4	1.4	1.4	1.4	1.5	1.6
0.57	0.59	0.49	0.44	0.44	0.44	0.45	0.44	0.47	0.46	0.47
25.30	21.98	22.14	26.95	27.81	28.77	30.58	31.55	32.05	33.76	37.70
38.72	37.29	43.42	47.45	51.45	54.56	58.98	60.02	62.92	65.53	67.73
98.95	99.00	98.77	100	100	100	100	100	99.25	97.85	98.27
81.51	91.30	97.02	98.19	98.68	98.71	98.79	98.89	96.07	99.90	99.96
5.12	5.63	9.11	10.22	10.70	11.22	11.47	11.61	12.04	9.97	9.97

1-14 主要年份平均每天主要社会经济活动

指　　标	Item	1995	2000
一、每天创造的财富	**Daily Production**		
生产总值（万元）	Gross Domestic Product（10 000 yuan）	9050.7	17702.2
第一产业	Primary Industry	1134.3	1223.3
第二产业	Secondary Industry	3707.7	7592.6
第三产业	Tertiary Industry	4208.8	8886.3
工业	Industry	3082.2	5984.7
建筑业	Construction	625.5	1608.0
批发和零售业	Wholesale and Retail Trade	909.6	1804.7
交通运输、仓储和邮政业	Transport, Storage, Post & Telecommunication Services	674.0	1178.4
住宿和餐饮业	Hotels and Catering Services		505.8
财政总收入（万元）	Total Government Revenue（10 000 yuan）	498.8	1686.8
财政一般公共预算支出（万元）	Government General Public Budgetary Expenditures（10 000 yuan）	504.7	1274.0
粮食（吨）	Grain（ton）	4801	5532
奶类（吨）	Milk（ton）		
蔬菜（吨）	Vegetables（ton）	3660	4442
肉类（吨）	Meat（ton）		
水产品（吨）	Aquatic Products（ton）	23	31
布（万米）	Cloth（10 000 m）	83	77
发电量（万千瓦小时）	Electricity（10 000 kwh）	610	534
钢材（吨）	Steel（ton）	861	274
汽车（辆）	Motor Vehicle（unit）	8	25
二、每天消费量	**Daily National Consumption**		
社会消费品零售总额（万元）	Total Retail Sales of Consumer Goods （10 000 yuan）	5160	10108
三、每天其他经济活动	**Other Daily Economic Activities**		
竣工住宅面积（平方米）	Floor Space of Buildings Completed （sq.m）	6927	14930
货运量（万吨）	Freight Traffic（10 000 tons）	26.3	19.2
客运量（万人次）	Passenger Traffic（10 000 person-times）	24.8	22.1
邮电业务总量（万元）	Business Volume of Postal and Telecommunications Services（10 000 yuan）	209.6	1264.7
进出口总值（万美元）	Total Value of Imports and Exports （USD 10 000）	110.2	475.9
出口值	Exports	82.5	290.6
进口值	Imports	27.7	185.3
外商实际直接投资额（万美元）	Foreign Capital Actually Used（USD 10 000）	51.1	42.8
旅游者人数（人次）	Number of Tourists （person-time）	21681	42932
四、每天人口变动和婚姻	**Daily Population Changes and Marriages**		
出 生（人）	Births（person）	211	247
死 亡（人）	Deaths（person）	88	113
结 婚（对）	Marriages（couple）	129	129
离 婚（对）	Divorces（couple）	12	14

注：本表财政收入数据2009年及以前为一般预算财政收入和基金收入之和。依据部门历史年份修订结果对财政相关数据进行了重新计算。

Major Social and Economic Activities Per Day in Representative Years

2005	2010	2012	2013	2014	2015	2016	2017	2018	2019
35453.4	87535.6	119730.4	135896.7	152794.0	162544.1	175242.7	203234.0	232860.5	255375.1
1808.5	3649.9	4962.2	5002.7	5248.8	5257.8	5387.9	6719.5	7095.3	7647.4
14005.2	35367.9	47306.8	53331.0	58970.7	56725.2	58616.2	67203.3	78407.1	86779.2
19640.0	48517.5	67461.6	77563.0	88574.5	100561.1	111238.6	129311.2	147357.8	160948.5
10781.1	23999.2	31255.6	34745.8	38000.8	34032.3	34326.3	39362.2	46791.8	51201.6
3224.1	11368.8	16051.2	19138.1	21688.8	23490.4	25206.8	28694.2	33172.3	37218.6
3823.8	9026.8	12604.1	14034.5	15131.8	16146.0	16413.2	17903.8	19429.0	21311.2
1619.7	3679.2	5046.3	5335.1	5803.6	6565.2	7366.8	8151.8	8674.8	9055.9
1303.8	2628.2	3407.9	3315.1	3448.2	3887.1	3927.1	4204.1	4498.4	4890.1
4489.6	13991.5	20632.1	24733.3	27936.7	30547.4	31114.5	37389.3	40010.7	42024.4
2680.0	10181.4	16369.6	19994.8	22453.2	25129.9	25822.5	28632.6	31558.1	34164.9
5631	4781	4594	4156	3857	3875	3709	3833	3894	3833
			202	222	210	217	319	316	339
5362	5674	6245	6683	7065	7340	7366	9719	10238	10372
			181	194	198	188	161	149	141
26	33	38	39	39	39	37	38	37	37
74	65	39	38	33	29	33	35	35	33
1316	2656	2726	5055	4920	4347	4411	4842	4733	4247
658	3035	857	1488	1175	1015	1203	1504	915	862
112	1787	1484	1156	1027	935	1048	1220	1188	1168
19133	48368	69341	79414	89790	99203	109930	121170	133005	140847
16400	12287	24762	23014	40078	22632	36472	36683		
33.0	94.0	123.1	137.3	115.2	126.8	65.4	69.9	71.8	75.1
28.7	83.0	99.1	104.9	70.5	73.7	64.9	66.5	71.4	72.1
3617.7	8852.3	5923.6	6793.0	8016.4	9083.1	10496.2	12050.7	20261.1	38950.7
1068.9	2847.3	3565.6	4927.5	6833.5	7749.3	7547.9	10327.4	13676.0	12877.6
721.8	1456.8	1999.7	2322.8	3276.7	3606.4	3907.3	6298.6	8103.0	6871.8
347.1	1390.5	1565.9	2604.7	3556.8	4142.8	3640.6	4028.8	5573.0	6005.8
156.5	429.2	678.9	857.5	1014.5	1098.2	1234.2	1453.9	1740.7	1933.5
66400	144799	218585	277534	328767	372625	411303	495702	677774	824943
210	225	237	225	238	241	277	330	335	341
63	124	130	126	129	131	130	142	147	153
137	229	246	244	250	221	212	194	255	239
35	52	51	56	60	62	70	79	115	124

1-15 各区县国民经济和社会发展主要指标（2019年）

指 标	Item	新城区 Xincheng	碑林区 Beilin	莲湖区 Lianhu
一、年底总人口（常住人口）（万人）	Population at the Year-end Permanent population(10 000 persons)	64.72	68.77	78.33
二、生产总值（亿元）	Gross Domestic Product(100 mil. yuan)	605.93	1013.97	789.05
第一产业	Primary Industry			
第二产业	Secondary Industry	212.93	232.79	257.36
第三产业	Tertiary Industry	393.00	781.18	531.69
三、全社会固定资产投资增长速度（%）	The growth rate of Total Investment in Fixed Assets（%）	16.3	-19.5	-29.4
固定资产投资（不含农户）增长速度	The growth rate of Investment in Fixed Assets (excluding farmers)	16.3	-19.5	-29.4
#房地产开发投资增长速度	The growth rate of Real Estate	32.8	-26.7	-43.3
四、财政一般公共预算收入（万元）	General Public Budgetary Revenue(10 000 yuan)	227250	367845	389740
财政一般公共预算支出（万元）	General Public Budgetary Expenditure(10 000 yuan)	229618	290175	358792
五、农林牧渔业总产值（万元）	Gross Output Value of Farming，Forestry Animal Husbandry and Fishery(10 000 yuan)			
主要农产品产量（万吨）	Output of Major Farm Products(10 000 tons)			
粮食	Grain			
蔬菜	Vegetables			
瓜果	Melon and Fruit			
肉类(吨)	Meat (Ton)			
奶类(吨)	Milk (Ton)			
六、规模以上工业总产值（亿元）	Gross industrial Output Value(100 mil. yuan)	320.28	16.70	429.36
七、建筑业	Construction			
房屋建筑施工面积（万平方米）	Floor Space of Buildings under Construction (10 000 sq.m)	337.14	5082.11	2460.93
房屋建筑竣工面积（万平方米）	Floor Space of Buildings Completed(100 mil. yuan)	69.54	825.27	318.36
八、社会消费品零售总额（亿元）	Total Retail Sales of Consumer Goods (100 mil. yuan)	293.11	622.29	553.76
九、城镇居民人均可支配收入（元）	Per Capita Annual Disposable Income of Urban Households (yuan)	48208	47977	47995
农村居民人均可支配收入（元）	Per Capita Disposable Income of Rural Households (yuan)			
十、医疗机构数（个）	Number of Health Care Institutions(unit)			
卫生技术人员（人）	Number of Medical Technical Personnel (person)	12913	14785	13244
床位数（张）	Number of Beds(unit)	7976	9326	8788

Major Indicators of National Economy and Social Development by Region（2019）

灞桥区 Baqiao	未央区 Weiyang	雁塔区 Yanta	阎良区 Yanliang	临潼区 Lintong	长安区 Chang'an	高陵区 Gaoling	鄠邑区 Huyi	蓝田县 Lantian	周至县 Zhouzhi	西咸新区 Xixian
70.39	82.73	138.53	30.45	70.04	106.42	36.71	56.46	53.61	59.29	103.9
489.19	1255.07	2271.01	255.06	242.69	1001.21	374.44	180.23	149.23	137.15	520.72
19.23	0.28		28.86	36.20	28.73	27.19	27.71	28.35	35.88	46.72
137.73	562.46	522.76	106.37	70.97	547.03	210.41	51.68	35.43	16.12	185.21
332.23	692.33	1748.25	119.83	135.52	425.45	136.84	100.84	85.45	85.15	288.79
-0.3	-12.0	4.5	-7.9	-12.5	32.9	-27.3	-33.7	-6.0	-35.2	10.1
-0.3	-12.0	4.5	-8.0	-13.3	33.4	-27.6	-35.8	-6.2	-42.3	10.3
-12.4	-30.1	-20.8	-2.1	13.7	24.7	-0.7	-5.7	20.5	66.1	47.7
182840	311884	459339	70143	131584	208071	120553	74905	27218	25099	718509
355428	335458	353002	224871	458230	504679	355325	338450	427514	424000	1260679
332266	6419		489024	666124	492276	528830	483560	519089	643428	832203
2.47			11.50	33.26	15.75	12.29	19.59	17.10	12.02	15.91
12.28	0.07		74.07	53.13	20.58	62.33	28.65	10.94	22.88	93.65
0.19	0.01		27.13	9.56	3.72	1.09	4.88	2.72	0.27	2.87
1788			2297	15932	4832	3676	5830	8488	6759	1835
3449	41		20771	51948	6244	12605	7287	14317	3349	3700
151.91	1101.03	733.17	366.14	242.48	1554.18	1075.02	376.83	64.32	38.68	376.06
399.96	4057.41	3058.76	43.49	71.46	202.14	111.60	63.47	102.24	21.86	1161.47
3.70	590.01	437.24	17.92	14.72	35.19	67.98	32.63	82.78	7.75	223.22
448.66	904.20	1162.36	38.33	64.77	251.33	142.11	46.78	47.63	40.85	524.74
40328	44628	48685	40631	30810	42051	38794	24788	23893	22407	25270
17969			15808	14659	15928	16370	13632	14731	13137	14027
4760	11566	16928	2588	3564	8364	3188	4264	2584	2890	3869
3184	6977	8951	1890	2934	6821	2361	3209	1869	2052	2656

主要统计指标解释

行政区划 指国家对行政区域的划分。根据有关法规规定，我国的行政区域划分如下：（1）全国分为省、自治区、直辖市；（2）省、自治区分为自治州、县、自治县、市；（3）自治州分为县、自治县、市；（4）县、自治县分为乡、民族乡、镇；（5）直辖市和较大的市分为区、县；（6）国家在必要时设立的特别行政区。

气候 指地球与大气之间长期能量交换与质量交换所形成的一种自然环境状态，它是多种因素综合作用的结果。气候既是人类生活和生产的环境要素之一，又是供给人类生活和生产的重要资源。气温、降水、湿度等气象要素的多年平均值是用来描述一个地区气候状况的主要参数，而各种气象要素某年、某月的平均值（或总量）则可以反映出该时期天气气候状况的重要特征。

自然资源 指人类可以直接从自然界获得，并用于生产和生活的物质资源。自然资源一般可以分成可再生资源和非再生资源两大类。可再生资源指在较短时间内可以再生、可以循环利用的资源，包括土地资源、水资源、气候资源、生物资源和海洋资源等。非再生资源指在使用后不能再生的资源，包括矿产资源和地热能源。

土地资源 土地指陆地的表层部分，它主要由岩石、岩石的风化物和土壤构成。土地资源按利用类型可以分为农用地、建筑用地和未利用地。农用地包括耕地、园地、林地、牧草地和水面。建筑用地包括居民点及工矿用地、交通用地和水利设施用地。未利用地指农用地和建筑用地以外的土地，包括滩涂、荒漠、戈壁、冰川和石山等。

耕地面积 指经过开垦用以种植农作物并经常进行耕耘的土地面积。包括种有作物的土地面积、休闲地、新开荒地和抛荒未满三年的土地面积。

森林面积 指由乔木树种构成，郁闭度0.2以上（含0.2）的林地或冠幅宽度10米以上的林带的面积，即有林地面积。森林面积包括天然起源和人工起源的针叶林面积、阔叶林面积、针阔混交林面积和竹林面积，不包括灌木林地面积和疏林地面积。

林业用地面积 指生长乔木、竹类、灌木、沿海红树林等林木的土地面积，包括有林地、灌木林、疏林地、未成林造林地、迹地、苗圃等。

水资源总量 指评价区内降水形成的地表和地下产水总量，即地表产流量与降水入渗补给地下水量之和，不包括过境水量。

地表水资源量 指评价区内河流、湖泊、冰川等地表水体中可以逐年更新的动态水量，即当地天然河川径流量。

地下水资源量 指评价区内降水和地表水对饱水岩土层的补给量，包括降水入渗补给量和河道、湖库、渠系、渠灌田间等地表水体的入渗补给量。

气温 指空气的温度，我国一般以摄氏度（℃）为单位表示。气象观测的温度表是放在离地面约1.5米处通风良好的百叶箱里测量的，因此，通常说的气温指的是离地面1.5米处百叶箱中的温度。其统计计算方法为：

月平均气温是将全月各日的平均气温相加，除以该月的天数而得。

年平均气温是将12个月的月平均气温累加后除以12而得。

降水量 指从天空降落到地面的液态或固态（经融化后）水，未经蒸发、渗透、流失而在地面上积聚的深度。其统计计算方法为：

月降水量是将全月各日的降水量累加而得。

年降水量是将12个月的月降水量累加而得。

日照时数 指太阳实际照射地面的时间。其统计方法与降水量相同。

平均增长速度 平均增长速度表明社会经济现象在一个较长的时期内逐期平均增长变化的程度，它不能根据各个环比增长速度直接求得，但与平均发展速度之间存在着一定的数量关系：平均增长速度 = 平均发展速度 - 1。

平均发展速度 是一种根据环比发展速度计算的序时平均数,由于各时期对比的基础不同，所以计算平均发展速度不能采用一般的序时平均数的计算方法，计算方法分为水平法和累计法。水平法，又称几何平均法，即将环比发展速度按连乘法用几何平均数公式计算。累计法，也称方程法，根据一段时期内各年发展水平总和与基期水平的关系，列出方程式计算平均发展速度。水平法着重考虑最后一年所达到的发展水平；累计法着重考虑整个时期累计发展水平的总量。

本《年鉴》内所列的平均增长速度，均用“水平法”计算。从某年到某年平均增长速度的年份，均不包括基期年在内。如建国六十年以来的平均增长速度是以1949年为基期计算的，则写为1950–2009年平均增长速度，其余类推。

Explanatory Notes on Main Statistical Indicators

Divisions of Administrative Areas refers to the division of administrative areas by the State. The relative laws stipulate that (1)the whole country is divided into provinces, autonomous regions and municipalities directly under the Central Government;(2)provinces and autonomous regions are further divided into autonomous prefectures, counties, autonomous counties and cities; (3)autonomous prefectures are further divided into counties, autonomous counties and cities; (4)counties and autonomous counties are further divided into townships, ethnic townships and towns; (5)municipalities directly under the Central Government and large cities are divided into districts and counties, (6)the State shall, when necessary, establish special administrative regions.

Climate refers to the natural environmental status formed by the long-term exchange of energy and mass between the earth and the atmosphere, and is the result of interaction of many factors. Climate is both one of the environment factors and also the important resources for living and production activities of the human being. The average values across several years of meteorological factors such as temperature, rainfall and humidity are used as important parameters to describe the climate of a region, while the average values (or total values)of a given year or month of meteorological factors reflect the key characteristics of climate for that period of time.

Natural Resources refer to material resources that could be obtained from the nature by human being and used for production and living. Natural resources in general can be classified as renewable resources and non-renewable resources. Renewable resources refer to resources that could be renewed and recycled during a relatively short period of time, including land resource, water resource, climate resource, biology resource and marine resource. Non-renewable resources include resources that could not be renewed, such as minerals and geothermal resource.

Land Resource Land refers to the surface of the earth, consisting of mainly rocks and its whethering and earth. Land resource can be classified, by its utilization, as land for agriculture, land for construction and unused land. Land for agriculture includes cultivated land, plantation land, forestland, grassland and waters. Land for construction includes land for residential purpose, for manufacturing and mining, for transportation and for water-conservancy projects. Unused land refers to land other than land for agriculture and.construction, including beaches, deserts, Gobi, glaciers and rock mountains.

Area of Cultivated Land refers to area of land reclaimed for the regular cultivation of various farm crops, including crop-cover land, fallow, newly reclaimed land and land laid idle for less than 3 years.

Forest Area refers to the area of trees and bamboo grow with canopy density above 0.2, the area of shrubby tree according to regulations of the government, the area of forest land inside farm land and the area of trees planted by the side of villages, farm houses and along roads and rivers.

Area of Afforested Land refers to area for land for trees bamboo, bushes and mangrove, including forest-covered land, bush-covered land, sparse forest land, land planned for afforestation and nurseries of young trees.

Total Water Resources refers to total volume of water resources measured as run-off for surface water from rainfall and recharge for groundwater in a given area, excluding transit water.

Surface Water Resources refers to total renewable resources which exist in rivers, lakes, glaciers and other collectors from rainfall and are measured as run-off of rivers.

Groundwater Resources refers to replenishment of aquifers with rainfall and surface water.

Temperature refers to the air temperature. China uses centigrade as the unit. The thermometry used for weather observation is put in a breezy shutter, which is 1.5 meters high from the ground. Therefore, the commonly used temperature refers to the temperature in the breezy shutter 1.5 meters away from the ground. The calculation method is as follows:

Monthly average temperature is the summation of average daily temperature of one month divided by the actual days of that particular month.

Annual average temperature is the summation of monthly average of a year divided by 12 months.

Volume of Precipitation refers to the deepness of liquid state or solid state (thawed)water falling from the sky to the ground that has not been evaporated, infiltrated or run off. The calculation method is as follows:

Monthly precipitation is the summation of daily precipitation of a month.

Annual precipitation is the summation of 12 months precipitation of a year.

Sunshine Hours refer to the actual hours of sun irradiating the earth. The calculation method is the same as that of the precipitation.

Average Annual Growth Rate shows the average growth rate of social and economic development during a longer period. It can not be directly calculated by chain based growth rate. The relation is:

Average Annual Growth Rate=Average Speed of Development - 1

Average speed of development is the time series average of speed which calculated by chain based.Because the reference bases during the different periods are not same, average speed of development can not be calculated by the general method. Level approach and accumulative approach for calculating average speed of development rate are applied. The "level approach" , or the method of calculating the geometric average, is derived by the formula of geometric average of the chain-based speeds of development, or comparing the level of the last year of the interval with that of the beginning year; the other is called the "accumulative approach" or the "algebraic average" , "equation" method, which is derived by the summation of the actual figure of each year in the interval divided by the figure in the base year. The level approach focuses on the level of the last year, while the accumulative approach emphasizes the aggregate development in the duration.

The average annual growth rates listed in the Yearbook are calculated by the level approach except for the growth rate of investment in fixed assets. The base year is not listed in the duration for which average annual growth rates are computed. For instance, the average annual growth rate of the 60 years since 1949 is shown as the average annual growth rate of 1950-2009 without showing the base year 1949.

2 基本单位

BASIC UNIT

资料整理：张　奇　张　斌
Data management：Zhang Qi　Zhang Bin
数据审核：曾文元
Data audit：Zeng Wenyuan

第二部分　基本单位

一、简要说明

本章资料主要包括法人单位、产业活动单位和企业一套表调查单位数等资料，由西安市统计局普查中心提供。本年统计年鉴一套表单位数为年报数，使用时请注意。

二、主要指标

法人单位数（个）	254898	比上年增长	51.0%
产业活动单位数（个）	275797	比上年增长	51.2%
规模以上工业企业数（个）	1598	比上年增长	10.9%
限额以上批发零售住宿餐饮业企业数（个）	2662	比上年增长	27.7%
资质内建筑业企业数（个）	1288	比上年增长	6.5%
房地产开发经营企业数（个）	1115	比上年增长	-1.2%
规模以上服务业企业数（个）	2075	比上年增长	24.3%

2　BASIC UNIT

Ⅰ.Brief Introduction

This chapter consists of unified data of enterprises and industrial active unites and investigation unit in "Enterprises Data in One sheet", provided by census center of Xi'an Municipal Bureau of statistics . Data of "Enterprises Data in One Sheet" in this Yearbook is the number of annual reports, please note that when used.

Ⅱ.Major Indicators

		Increase over Preceding Year
Number of Enterprises (unit)	254898	51.0%
Number of Industrial Active Units (unit)	275797	51.2%
Number of Industrial Enterprises above Designed Size (unit)	1598	10.9%
Number of Enterprises about Wholesale、Retail、Accommodation and Catering above Designed Size (unit)	2662	27.7%
Number of Qualified Construction Enterprises (unit)	1288	6.5%
Number of Real Estate Development Enterprises (unit)	1115	-1.2%
Number of service Enterprises above Designed Size (unit)	2075	24.3%

2-1 按登记注册类型分法人单位数（2019年）

Impersonal Entities by Status of Registion（2019）

单位：个 (unit)

分 组	Classify	法人单位数 Number of Enterprises	企业 Enterprises
总 计	**Total**	**254898**	**234189**
#非公有制企业法人	Non-public corporate	229499	229499
按登记注册类型分	**Grouped by Status of Registion**		
（一）内资	Domestic Funded Enterprises	253868	233159
国有	State-owned Enterprises	6085	930
集体	Collective-owned Enterprises	1619	928
股份合作	Cooperative Enterprises	138	114
联营	Joint Ownership Enterprises	80	47
国有联营	State Joint Ownership Enterprises	9	6
集体联营	Collective Joint Ownership Enterprises	43	28
国有与集体联营	Joint State-collective Ownership Enterprises	6	5
其他联营	Other Joint Ownership Enterprises	22	8
有限责任公司	Limited Liability Corporations	13099	13023
国有独资公司	State Sole Funded Corporations	577	577
其他有限责任公司	Other Limited Liability Corporations	12522	12446
股份有限公司	Share-holding Corporations Limited	698	695
私营	Private Enterprises	218452	217367
私营独资企业	Private-funded Enterprises	4355	3773
私营合伙	Private Partnership Enterprises	1222	1015
私营有限责任公司	Private Limited Liability Corporations	211414	211122
私营股份有限公司	Private Share-holding Corporations Ltd.	1461	1457
其他	Other Domestic Funded Enterprises	13697	55
（二）港、澳、台商投资企业	Enterprises with Funds from Hong Kong, Macau and Taiwan	394	394
与港、澳、台商合资经营	Joint-venture with Funds from Hong Kong,Macau and Taiwan	118	118
与港、澳、台商合作经营	Cooperative Enterprises with Funds from Hong Kong Macau and Taiwan	8	8
港澳台商独资经营	Enterprises with Sole Investment from Hong Kong Macau and Taiwan	205	205
港澳台商投资股份有限公司	Share-holding Corporations Ltd. with funds from Hong Kong, Macau & Taiwan	9	9
其他港澳台商投资	Other Enterprises with Funds from Hong Kong, Macau and Taiwan	54	54
（三）外商投资	Foreign Funded Enterprises	636	636
中外合资经营	Sino-foreign Joint Ventures	197	197
中外合作经营	Sino-Foreign Cooperation Enterprises	5	5
外资企业	Foreign Owned Enterprises	366	366
外商投资股份有限公司	Limited Company Funded by Foreign Investment	28	28
其他外商投资	Other Foreign Funded Enterprises	40	40

2-2 按国民经济行业分法人单位数（2019年）

Impersonal Entities by Industry of the National Economy（2019）

单位：个 (unit)

分 组	Classify	法人单位数 Number of Enterprises	企业 Enterprises
总 计	**Total**	**254898**	**234189**
（一）农、林、牧、渔业	Agriculture,Forestry,Animal Husbandry and Fishery	5149	1772
农业	Farming	2166	635
林业	Forestry	639	231
畜牧业	Animal Husbandry	1187	480
渔业	Fishery	38	18
农、林、牧、渔专业及辅助性活动	Agriculture, Forestry, Animal husbandry, Fishery and Auxiliary Activities	1119	408
（二）采矿业	Mining	136	136
煤炭开采和洗选业	Mining and Washing of Coal	6	6
石油和天然气开采业	Extraction of Petroleum and Natural Gas	10	10
黑色金属矿采选业	Mining of Ferrous Metal Ores	6	6
有色金属矿采选业	Mining of Non-ferrous Metal Ores	6	6
非金属矿采选业	Mining and Processing of Nonmetal Ores	25	25
开采专业及辅助性活动	Mining Professional and Auxiliary Activities	74	74
其他采矿业	Mining of Other Ores	9	9
（三）制造业	Manufacturing	17612	17578
农副食品加工业	Processing of Food from Agricultural Products	540	520
食品制造业	Manufacture of Foods	509	507
酒、饮料和精制茶制造业	Manufacture of Beverages	263	262
烟草制品业	Manufacture of Tobacco	5	5
纺织业	Manufacture of Textile	141	139
纺织服装、服饰业	Manufacture of Textile Wearing Apparel	185	182
皮革、毛皮、羽毛及其制品和制鞋业	Manufacture of Leather, Fur, Feather and Related Products and Footware	18	17
木材加工和木、竹、藤、棕、草制品业	Timber Processing,Bamboo,Cane, Palm Fiber and Straw Products	270	270
家具制造业	Manufacture of Furniture	516	516
造纸及纸制品业	Manufacture of Paper and Paper Products	370	370
印刷和记录媒介复制业	Printing,Reproduction of Recording Media	559	559
文教、工美、体育和娱乐用品制造业	Manufacture of Articles For Culture, Education and Sport Activities	302	301

2-2 续表1 continued 1

单位：个 (unit)

分 组	Classify	法人单位数 Number of Enterprises	企业 Enterprises
石油、煤炭及其他燃料加工业	Processing of Petroleum, Coking, Processing of Nuclear Fuel	66	66
化学原料和化学制品制造业	Manufacture of Raw Chemical Materials and Chemical Products	787	787
医药制造业	Manufacture of Medicines	306	306
化学纤维制造业	Manufacture of Chemical Fibers	15	15
橡胶和塑料制品业	Manufacture of Rubber and Manufacture of Plastics	545	544
非金属矿物制品业	Manufacture of Non-metallic Mineral Products	1534	1533
黑色金属冶炼和压延加工业	Smelting and Pressing of Ferrous Metals	154	154
有色金属冶炼和压延加工业	Smelting and Pressing of Non-ferrous Metals	181	181
金属制品业	Manufacture of Metal Products	1443	1443
通用设备制造业	Manufacture of General Purpose Machinery	2584	2584
专用设备制造业	Manufacture of Special Equipment	1597	1597
汽车制造业	Manufacture of Motor Vehicle	299	299
铁路、船舶、航空航天和其他运输设备制造业	Railways,Shipbuilding,Aerospace and Other Transportation Equipment Manufacturing Industry	394	394
电气机械和器材制造业	Manufacture of Electric Equipment and Machinery	1386	1386
计算机、通信和其他电子设备制造业	Manufacture of Communication Equipment, Computers and other Electronic Equipment	1051	1051
仪器仪表制造业	Manufacture of Measuring Instruments and Machinery	712	712
其他制造业	Other Manufacturing	119	119
废弃资源综合利用	Recycling and Disposal of Waste	93	93
金属制品、机械和设备修理业	Metal Products,Machinery and Equipment Repair Industry	668	666
（四）电力、热力、燃气及水的生产供应业	Production and Distribution of Electricity,Heat ,Gas and Water	575	569
电力、热力生产和供应业	Production and Supply of Electric Power and Heat Power	342	339
燃气生产和供应业	Gas mining and supplying industry	66	65
水的生产和供应业	Production and Supply of Water	167	165
（五）建筑业	Construction	34155	34154
房屋建筑业	Construction of Building	8517	8517
土木工程建筑业	Civil Engineering	8442	8442
建筑安装业	Architectural Installation	5105	5105
建筑装饰、装修和其他建筑业	Architectural Decoration and Other Construction	12091	12090
（六）批发和零售业	Wholesale and Retail Trades	77617	75288

2-2 续表2 continued 2

单位：个 (unit)

分组	Classify	法人单位数 Number of Enterprises	企业 Enterprises
批发业	Wholesale Trade	41239	39310
零售业	Retail Trade	36378	35978
（七）交通运输、仓储和邮政业	Traffic, Transport, Storage and Post	5006	4712
铁路运输业	Transport Via Railway	10	10
道路运输业	Transport Via Road	3394	3369
水上运输业	Water Transport	2	2
航空运输业	Air Transport	76	75
管道运输业	Transport Via Pipeline	3	3
多式联运和运输代理业	Multimodal Transport and Transportation Agency	538	537
装卸搬运和仓储业	Loading,Unloading,portage,storge and management of Land industry	842	576
邮政业	Post	141	140
（八）住宿和餐饮业	Hotels and Catering Services	5072	5070
住宿业	Hotels	1906	1904
餐饮业	Catering Services	3166	3166
（九）信息传输、软件和信息技术服务业	Information Transmission, Computer Services and Software	15860	15824
电信、广播电视和卫星传输服务	Telecom & Other Information Transmission Services	690	689
互联网和相关服务	Internet and Relevant Services	2397	2389
软件和信息技术服务	Software Industry	12773	12746
（十）金融业	Financial Intermediation	1332	1328
货币金融服务	Monetary and Financial Services	455	453
资本市场服务	Capital Market Services	409	408
保险业	Insurance	181	181
其他金融业	Other Financial Intermediation	287	286
（十一）房地产业	Real Estate	12290	12278
房地产业	Real Estate	12290	12278
（十二） 租赁和商务服务业	Leasing and Business Services	32779	31882
租赁业	Leasing	3126	3121
商务服务业	Business Services	29653	28761
（十三）科学研究和技术服务业	Scientific Research, Technical Sevice	17253	16606
研究与试验发展	Research and Experimental Development	2360	2273
专业技术服务业	Professional Technical Services	10148	9921

2-2 续表3 continued 3

单位：个 (unit)

分　组	Classify	法人单位数 Number of Enterprises	企业 Enterprises
科技推广和应用服务业	Services of Science and Technology Exchanges and Promotion	4745	4412
（十四）水利、环境和公共设施管理业	Management of Water Conservancy, Environment and Public Facilities	1581	1396
水利管理业	Management of Water Conservancy	132	57
生态保护和环境治理业	Environmental Management	250	223
公共设施管理业	Management of Public Facilities	1114	1040
土地管理业	Lang management	85	76
（十五）居民服务、修理和其他服务业	Services to Households and Other Services	6460	6397
居民服务业	Services to Households	2522	2470
机动车、电子产品和日用产品修理业	The Repair Service Industry for Motor Vehicle、Electronic	2960	2958
其他服务业	Other Services	978	969
（十六）教育	Education	5666	1761
教育	Education	5666	1761
（十七）卫生和社会工作	Health, Social Security	2677	1007
卫生	Health	2221	921
社会工作	Social	456	86
（十八）文化、体育和娱乐业	Culture, Sports and Entertainment	6825	6431
新闻和出版业	Journalism and Publishing Activities	170	145
广播、电视、电影和录音制作业	Broadcasting,Movies,Television and Audiovisual Activities	1307	1292
文化艺术业	Cultural and Art Activities	1525	1253
体育	Sports Activities	689	643
娱乐业	Entertainment	3134	3098
（十九）公共管理、社会保障和社会组织	Public Management and Social Organizaion	6853	
中国共产党机关	Organs of Communist Party of China	178	
国家机构	Government Agencies	1782	
人民政协、民主党派	People's Political Consultative Conference and Democratic Parties	21	
社会保障	Social Security	56	
群众团体、社会团体和其他成员组织	Mass organizations、Social Groups and other members of the organization	1738	
基层群众自治组织	Grass-roots Mass Self-Government Organizations	3078	
（二十）国际组织	International Organizations		
国际组织	International Organizations		

2-3 各区县法人单位数（2019年）

Impersonal Entities by Region and Development Zone (2019)

单位：个 (unit)

区 县	Region	法人单位数 Number of Enterprises	企业 Enterprises
总 计	**Total**	**254898**	**234189**
新城区	Xincheng	10799	10078
碑林区	Beilin	23725	22761
莲湖区	Lianhu	19222	18247
灞桥区	Baqiao	14677	13756
未央区	Weiyang	54770	53750
雁塔区	Yanta	65004	63559
阎良区	Yanliang	3634	2926
临潼区	Lintong	5684	3943
长安区	Chang'an	12853	10998
高陵区	Gaoling	5721	4731
鄠邑区	Huyi	7220	4712
蓝田县	Lantian	4117	2372
周至县	Zhouzhi	6379	2906
西咸新区	Xixian	21093	19450

注：西安市行政区不包含西咸新区单位数，西咸新区单位数按统计局代码汇总。

2-4 按登记注册类型分产业活动单位数（2019年）

Industrial Active Units by Status of Registion（2019）

单位：个 (unit)

分 组	Classify	产业活动单位数 Number of Industrial Active Units	企业 Enterprises
总计	**Total**	**275797**	**253142**
按登记注册类型分	Grouped by Status of Registion		
（一）内资	Domestic Funded Enterprises	273284	250629
国有	State-owned Enterprises	8523	1691
集体	Collective-owned Enterprises	1929	1113
股份合作	Cooperative Enterprises	152	128
联营	Joint Ownership Enterprises	92	59
国有联营	State Joint Ownership Enterprises	14	11
集体联营	Collective Joint Ownership Enterprises	45	30
国有与集体联营	Joint State-collective Ownership Enterprises	8	7
其他联营	Other Joint Ownership Enterprises	25	11
有限责任公司	Limited Liability Corporations	16397	16321
国有独资公司	State Sole Funded Corporations	713	713
其他有限责任公司	Other Limited Liability Corporations	15684	15608
股份有限公司	Share-holding Corporations Limited	2855	2852
私营	Private Enterprises	229482	228392
私营独资企业	Private-funded Enterprises	4455	3870
私营合伙	Private Partnership Enterprises	1256	1048
私营有限责任公司	Private Limited Liability Corporations	222065	221772
私营股份有限公司	Private Share-holding Corporations Ltd.	1706	1702
其他	Other Enterprises	13854	73

2-4 续表 continued

单位：个 (unit)

分 组	Classify	产业活动单位数 Number of Industrial Active Units	企业 Enterprises
（二）港、澳、台商投资企业	Enterprises with Funds from Hong Kong,Macau and Taiwan	754	754
与港、澳、台商合资经营	Joint-venture with Funds from Hong Kong,Macau and Taiwan	153	153
与港、澳、台商合作经营	Cooperative Enterprises with Funds from Hong Kong Macau and Taiwan	14	14
港澳台商独资经营	Enterprises with Sole Investment from Hong Kong Macau and Taiwan	413	413
港澳台商投资股份有限公司	Share-holding Corporations Ltd. with funds from Hong Kong, Macau & Taiwan	61	61
其他港澳台商投资	Other Enterprises with Funds from Hong Kong,Macau and Taiwan	113	113
（三）外商投资	Foreign Funded Enterprises	1759	1759
中外合资经营	Sino-foreign Joint Ventures	305	305
中外合作经营	Sino-Foreign Cooperation Enterprises	8	8
外资企业	Foreign Owned Enterprises	1105	1105
外商投资股份有限公司	Limited Company Funded by Foreign Investment	187	187
其他外商投资	Other Foreign Funded Enterprises	154	154

2-5 按国民经济行业分产业活动单位数（2019年）

Industrial Active Units by Industry of the National Economy（2019）

单位：个 (unit)

分 组	Classify	产业活动单位数 Number of Industrial Active Units	企业 Enterprises
总 计	**Total**	**275797**	**253142**
（一）农、林、牧、渔业	Agriculture,Forestry,Animal Husbandry and Fishery	5209	1788
农业	Farming	2175	644
林业	Forestry	640	231
畜牧业	Animal Husbandry	1189	481
渔业	Fishery	39	19
农、林、牧、渔专业及辅助性活动	Agriculture, Forestry, Animal husbandry, Fishery and Auxiliary Activities	1166	413
（二）采矿业	Mining	146	146
煤炭开采和洗选业	Mining and Washing of Coal	6	6
石油和天然气开采业	Extraction of Petroleum and Natural Gas	12	12
黑色金属矿采选业	Mining of Ferrous Metal Ores	6	6
有色金属矿采选业	Mining of Non-ferrous Metal Ores	6	6
非金属矿采选业	Mining and Processing of Nonmetal Ores	25	25
开采专业及辅助性活动	Mining Professional and Auxiliary Activities	82	82
其他采矿业	Mining of Other Ores	9	9
（三）制造业	Manufacturing	18157	18122
农副食品加工业	Processing of Food from Agricultural Products	560	539
食品制造业	Manufacture of Foods	538	536
酒、饮料和精制茶制造业	Manufacture of Beverages	269	268
烟草制品业	Manufacture of Tobacco	5	5
纺织业	Manufacture of Textile	146	144
纺织服装、服饰业	Manufacture of Textile Wearing Apparel	197	194
皮革、毛皮、羽毛及其制品和制鞋业	Manufacture of Leather, Fur, Feather and Related Products and Footware	20	19
木材加工和木、竹、藤、棕、草制品业	Timber Processing,Bamboo,Cane, Palm Fiber and Straw Products	275	275
家具制造业	Manufacture of Furniture	529	529
造纸及纸制品业	Manufacture of Paper and Paper Products	379	379
印刷和记录媒介复制业	Printing,Reproduction of Recording Media	575	575
文教、工美、体育和娱乐用品制造业	Manufacture of Articles For Culture, Education and Sport Activities	308	307

2-5 续表1 continued 1

单位：个 (unit)

分组	Classify	产业活动单位数 Number of Industrial Active Units	企业 Enterprises
石油、煤炭及其他燃料加工业	Processing of Petroleum, Coking, Processing of Nuclear Fuel	68	68
化学原料和化学制品制造业	Manufacture of Raw Chemical Materials and Chemical Products	813	813
医药制造业	Manufacture of Medicines	322	322
化学纤维制造业	Manufacture of Chemical Fibers	15	15
橡胶和塑料制品业	Manufacture of Rubber and Manufacture of Plastics	563	562
非金属矿物制品业	Manufacture of Non-metallic Mineral Products	1594	1593
黑色金属冶炼和压延加工业	Smelting and Pressing of Ferrous Metals	157	157
有色金属冶炼和压延加工业	Smelting and Pressing of Non-ferrous Metals	185	185
金属制品业	Manufacture of Metal Products	1487	1487
通用设备制造业	Manufacture of General Purpose Machinery	2637	2637
专用设备制造业	Manufacture of Special Equipment	1641	1641
汽车制造业	Manufacture of Motor Vehicle	312	312
铁路、船舶、航空航天和其他运输设备制造业	Railways,Shipbuilding,Aerospace and Other Transportation Equipment Manufacturing Industry	402	402
电气机械和器材制造业	Manufacture of Electric Equipment and Machinery	1445	1445
计算机、通信和其他电子设备制造业	Manufacture of Communication Equipment, Computers and other Electronic Equipment	1072	1072
仪器仪表制造业	Manufacture of Measuring Instruments and Machinery	730	730
其他制造业	Other Manufacturing	126	126
废弃资源综合利用	Recycling and Disposal of Waste	93	93
金属制品、机械和设备修理业	Metal Products,Machinery and Equipment Repair Industry	694	692
（四）电力、热力、燃气及水的生产供应业	Production and Distribution of Electricity,Heat ,Gas and Water	658	649
电力、热力生产和供应业	Production and Supply of Electric Power and Heat Power	396	390
燃气生产和供应业	Gas mining and supplying industry	82	81
水的生产和供应业	Production and Supply of Water	180	178
（五）建筑业	Construction	35186	35185
房屋建筑业	Construction of Building	8857	8857
土木工程建筑业	Civil Engineering	8682	8682
建筑安装业	Architectural Installation	5294	5294
建筑装饰、装修和其他建筑业	Architectural Decoration and Other Construction	12353	12352
（六）批发和零售业	Wholesale and Retail Trades	84636	82302

2-5 续表2 continued 2

单位：个 (unit)

分组	Classify	产业活动单位数 Number of Industrial Active Units	企业 Enterprises
批发业	Wholesale Trade	42250	40318
零售业	Retail Trade	42386	41984
（七）交通运输、仓储和邮政业	Traffic, Transport, Storage and Post	5800	5495
铁路运输业	Transport Via Railway	33	33
道路运输业	Transport Via Road	3722	3686
水上运输业	Water Transport	3	3
航空运输业	Air Transport	95	94
管道运输业	Transport Via Pipeline	5	5
多式联运和运输代理业	Multimodal Transport and Transportation Agency	668	667
装卸搬运和仓储业	Loading,Unloading,portage,storge and management of Land industry	877	611
邮政业	Post	397	396
（八）住宿和餐饮业	Hotels and Catering Services	6156	6153
住宿业	Hotels	2110	2108
餐饮业	Catering Services	4046	4045
（九）信息传输、软件和信息技术服务业	Information Transmission, Computer Services and Software	16660	16622
电信、广播电视和卫星传输服务	Telecom & Other Information Transmission Services	956	954
互联网和相关服务	Internet and Relevant Services	2474	2465
软件和信息技术服务	Software Industry	13230	13203
（十）金融业	Financial Intermediation	3915	3905
货币金融服务	Monetary and Financial Services	2087	2079
资本市场服务	Capital Market Services	633	632
保险业	Insurance	855	855
其他金融业	Other Financial Intermediation	340	339
（十一）房地产业	Real Estate	13495	13483
房地产业	Real Estate	13495	13483
（十二）租赁和商务服务业	Leasing and Business Services	34760	33819
租赁业	Leasing	3292	3287
商务服务业	Business Services	31468	30532
（十三）科学研究和技术服务业	Scientific Research, Technical Sevice	18172	17472
研究与试验发展	Research and Experimental Development	2418	2330
专业技术服务业	Professional Technical Services	10824	10558

2-5 续表3 continued 3

单位：个 (unit)

分 组	Classify	产业活动单位数 Number of Industrial Active Units	企业 Enterprises
科技推广和应用服务业	Services of Science and Technology Exchanges and Promotion	4930	4584
（十四）水利、环境和公共设施管理业	Management of Water Conservancy, Environment and Public Facilities	1689	1459
水利管理业	Management of Water Conservancy	159	64
生态保护和环境治理业	Environmental Management	263	230
公共设施管理业	Management of Public Facilities	1173	1084
土地管理业	Lang management	94	81
（十五）居民服务、修理和其他服务业	Services to Households and Other Services	6832	6763
居民服务业	Services to Households	2684	2629
机动车、电子产品和日用产品修理业	The Repair Service Industry for Motor Vehicle、Electronic	3142	3140
其他服务业	Other Services	1006	994
（十六）教育	Education	6378	1978
教育	Education	6378	1978
（十七）卫生和社会工作	Health, Social Security	2869	1121
卫生	Health	2405	1032
社会工作	Social	464	89
（十八）文化、体育和娱乐业	Culture, Sports and Entertainment	7107	6680
新闻和出版业	Journalism and Publishing Activities	179	152
广播、电视、电影和录音制作业	Broadcasting,Movies,Television and Audiovisual Activities	1362	1346
文化艺术业	Cultural and Art Activities	1578	1278
体育	Sports Activities	766	720
娱乐业	Entertainment	3222	3184
（十九）公共管理、社会保障和社会组织	Public Management and Social Organizaion	7972	
中国共产党机关	Organs of Communist Party of China	182	
国家机构	Government Agencies	2833	
人民政协、民主党派	People's Political Consultative Conference and Democratic Parties	21	
社会保障	Social Security	68	
群众团体、社会团体和其他成员组织	Mass organizations、Social Groups and other members of the organization	1759	
基层群众自治组织	Grass-roots Mass Self-Government Organizations	3109	
（二十）国际组织	International Organizations		
国际组织	International Organizations		

2-6 各区县产业活动单位数（2019年）

Industrial Active Units by Region and Development Zone (2019)

单位：个 (unit)

区 县	Region	产业活动单位数 Number of Industrial Active Units	企业 Enterprises
总 计	**Total**	**275797**	**253142**
新城区	Xincheng	11868	11144
碑林区	Beilin	26015	25031
莲湖区	Lianhu	20912	19917
灞桥区	Baqiao	15826	14794
未央区	Weiyang	58147	57060
雁塔区	Yanta	69826	68300
阎良区	Yanliang	4213	3356
临潼区	Lintong	6688	4569
长安区	Chang'an	13818	11876
高陵区	Gaoling	6544	5298
鄠邑区	Huyi	7875	5204
蓝田县	Lantian	4810	2671
周至县	Zhouzhi	6887	3285
西咸新区	Xixian	22368	20637

注:西安市行政区不含西咸新区单位，西咸新区单位按统计局代码汇总。

2-7　各区县、开发区企业一套表调查单位数（2019年）

Number of Survey Units of “One Sheet”by Region and Development Zone（2019）

单位：个　　　　　　　　　　　　　　　　　　　　　　　　　　　　(unit)

区县、开发区	Region	合计 Total	规模以上工业 Industrial Enterprises above Designed Size	限额以上批发零售住宿餐饮业 Above wholesale and Retail Accommodation and Catering Industry	资质内建筑业 Qualified Construction Enterprises	房地产开发经营企业 Real Estate Development Enterprises	规模以上服务业 Service Enterprises above Designed Size
全　市	**Total**	**8738**	**1598**	**2662**	**1288**	**1115**	**2075**
新城区	Xincheng	438	10	209	67	34	118
碑林区	Beilin	733	7	322	151	47	206
莲湖区	Lianhu	535	23	188	94	74	156
灞桥区	Baqiao	205	61	38	34	41	31
未央区	Weiyang	384	29	135	86	59	75
雁塔区	Yanta	580	39	178	146	65	152
阎良区	Yanliang	200	71	51	26	29	23
临潼区	Lintong	207	85	43	36	17	26
长安区	Chang'an	229	27	89	31	46	36
高陵区	Gaoling	240	102	58	19	33	28
鄠邑区	Huyi	223	95	65	12	34	17
蓝田县	Lantian	134	56	30	13	16	19
周至县	Zhouzhi	128	29	50	12	23	14
西咸新区	Xixian	804	209	260	68	162	105
高新区	GaoXin	1347	378	258	235	94	382
经开区	JingKai	1216	249	402	162	86	317
曲江新区	Qujiang	386		64	48	85	189
航空基地	Aviation Industry Base	89	48	12	5	13	11
航天基地	Aerospace Base	221	56	53	16	52	44
浐灞生态区	Chanba Eco-District	258	4	82	21	88	63
国际港务区	International Trade &Logistic Park	181	20	75	6	17	63

注：由于统计口径不同，一套表调查单位数与各专业有差异。

2-8 各区县企业一套表调查单位数（2019年）

Number of Survey Units of "One Sheet" by Region and Development Zone (2019)

单位：个 (unit)

区 县	Region	合计 Total	规模以上工业 Industrial Enterprises above Designed Size	限额以上批发零售住宿餐饮业 Above wholesale and Retail Accommodation and Catering Industry	资质内建筑业 Qualified Construction Enterprises	房地产开发经营企业 Real Estate Development Enterprises	规模以上服务业 Service Enterprises above Designed Size
全 市	**Total**	**8738**	**1598**	**2662**	**1288**	**1115**	**2075**
新城区	Xincheng	436	8	210	65	36	117
碑林区	Beilin	731	6	324	147	47	207
莲湖区	Lianhu	542	24	190	95	75	158
灞桥区	Baqiao	542	86	165	55	104	132
未央区	Weiyang	1601	197	550	257	186	411
雁塔区	Yanta	2057	257	475	410	222	693
阎良区	Yanliang	289	118	63	31	42	35
临潼区	Lintong	224	85	45	36	28	30
长安区	Chang'an	611	188	162	62	101	98
高陵区	Gaoling	347	186	67	20	37	37
鄠邑区	Huyi	270	132	69	16	36	17
蓝田县	Lantian	134	56	30	13	16	19
周至县	Zhouzhi	150	46	52	13	23	16
西咸新区	Xixian	804	209	260	68	162	105

2-9 按区县和国民经济行业分法人单位数（2019年）

单位：个

区 县	Region	合计 Total	农、林、牧、渔业 Agriculture Forestry Animal Husbandry and Fishery	采矿业 Mining	制造业 Manufacturing	电力、燃气及水的生产和供应业 Production and Distribution of Electricity Gas and Water
全　市	**Total**	254898	5149	136	17612	575
新城区	Xincheng	10799		2	284	5
碑林区	Beilin	23725		4	205	10
莲湖区	Lianhu	19222			284	3
灞桥区	Baqiao	14677	301	3	1323	39
未央区	Weiyang	54770	88	42	2424	90
雁塔区	Yanta	65004	129	32	3520	95
阎良区	Yanliang	3634	125		696	21
临潼区	Lintong	5684	721		726	22
长安区	Chang'an	12853	585	5	1394	39
高陵区	Gaoling	5721	578	12	979	22
鄠邑区	Huyi	7220	970	8	1607	35
蓝田县	Lantian	4117	489	4	450	74
周至县	Zhouzhi	6379	802	9	317	33
西咸新区	Xixian	21093	361	15	3403	87

注：1.西安市行政区不包含西咸新区单位数，西咸新区单位数按统计局代码汇总；
　　2.建筑业房地产专业按照注册地区划汇总。

Impersonal Entities by Region and Development Zone and Industry of the National Economy (2019)

(unit)

建筑业 Construction	批发和零售业 Wholesale and Retail Trades	交通运输、仓储和邮政业 Traffic Transport Storage and Post	住宿和餐饮业 Hotels and Catering Services	信息传输、软件和信息技术服务业 Information Transmission Software and Information Technology Services	金融业 Financial Intermediation
34155	77617	5006	5072	15860	1332
1025	4692	244	374	361	58
2883	8800	194	649	1308	99
1842	7526	374	535	1004	72
2190	4906	541	206	551	192
8802	22606	1062	821	2375	229
8883	14851	571	1352	7980	508
415	731	161	73	89	19
810	913	116	107	118	14
2042	2166	205	305	847	54
732	1215	215	94	145	6
671	884	127	80	123	23
395	1034	47	68	28	5
431	2243	366	85	65	8
3034	5050	783	323	866	45

2-9 续表

单位：个

区 县	Region	房地产业 Real Estate	租赁和商务服务业 Leasing and Business Services	科学研究和技术服务业 Scientific Research Technical Services	水利、环境和公共设施管理业 Management of Water Conservancy, Environment and Public Facilities
全 市	**Total**	12290	32779	17253	1581
新城区	Xincheng	582	1226	519	58
碑林区	Beilin	1336	4020	1614	67
莲湖区	Lianhu	1052	2820	1624	88
灞桥区	Baqiao	623	1559	677	93
未央区	Weiyang	2683	6555	3206	279
雁塔区	Yanta	3530	10691	6437	298
阎良区	Yanliang	185	304	130	44
临潼区	Lintong	160	480	171	57
长安区	Chang'an	565	1440	959	124
高陵区	Gaoling	308	435	188	56
鄠邑区	Huyi	209	454	389	77
蓝田县	Lantian	81	245	86	70
周至县	Zhouzhi	111	245	98	101
西咸新区	Xixian	865	2305	1155	169

continude

(unit)

居民服务、修理和其他服务业 Services to Households Repairs and Other Services	教育 Education	卫生和社会工作 Health and Social Work	文化、体育和娱乐业 Culture Sports and Entertainment	公共管理、社会保障和社会组织 Public Administration Social Security and Social Organizations	国际组织 International Orgnizations
6460	5666	2677	6825	6853	
319	298	149	246	357	
674	507	216	723	416	
544	427	183	433	411	
378	290	104	354	347	
1246	577	233	908	544	
1625	967	368	2674	493	
88	120	102	64	267	
133	285	225	149	477	
341	490	177	421	694	
161	174	46	102	253	
94	315	468	117	569	
42	235	66	72	626	
58	427	174	114	692	
757	554	166	448	707	

2-10 按区县和机构类型分法人单位数（2019年）

Impersonal Entities by Agencies Types of Legal Entities Corporate Units and Region and Development Zone (2019)

单位：个 (unit)

区 县	Region	法人单位数 Number of Enterprises	企业法人 Business Entity	事业法人 Institution Entity	机关法人 Government Entity	社会团体 Social Organization	其他 Other
全 市	**Total**	**254898**	**234189**	**4171**	**1083**	**1354**	**14101**
新城区	Xincheng	10799	10078	237	89	110	285
碑林区	Beilin	23725	22761	287	70	175	432
莲湖区	Lianhu	19222	18247	285	74	130	486
灞桥区	Baqiao	14677	13756	176	62	35	648
未央区	Weiyang	54770	53750	329	124	91	476
雁塔区	Yanta	65004	63559	335	99	140	871
阎良区	Yanliang	3634	2926	139	50	66	453
临潼区	Lintong	5684	3943	304	71	42	1324
长安区	Chang'an	12853	10998	521	90	51	1193
高陵区	Gaoling	5721	4731	139	51	36	764
鄠邑区	Huyi	7220	4712	339	64	104	2001
蓝田县	Lantian	4117	2372	262	87	96	1300
周至县	Zhouzhi	6379	2906	416	66	203	2788
西咸新区	Xixian	21093	19450	402	86	75	1080

注：西安市行政区不包含西咸新区单位数，西咸新区单位数按统计局代码汇总。

2-11 按区县和登记注册类型分企业法人单位数（2019年）

The Corporate Units by Types of Corporate Registration and Region and Development Zone (2019)

单位：个 (unit)

区 县	Region	企业单位数 Number of Enterprises	内资企业 Domestic Investment Enterprises	国有企业 State-owned Enterprises	集体企业 Collective-owned Enterprises	股份合作企业 Share-holding Corperative Enterprises	联营企业 Joint Ownership Enterprises
全 市	**Total**	**234189**	**233159**	**930**	**928**	**114**	**47**
新城区	Xincheng	10078	10060	108	126	7	6
碑林区	Beilin	22761	22697	136	108	12	4
莲湖区	Lianhu	18247	18214	144	119	7	8
灞桥区	Baqiao	13756	13687	45	62	9	2
未央区	Weiyang	53750	53590	62	57	10	1
雁塔区	Yanta	63559	63136	167	86	37	4
阎良区	Yanliang	2926	2907	26	38	7	1
临潼区	Lintong	3943	3928	41	62	4	3
长安区	Chang'an	10998	10907	51	68	2	2
高陵区	Gaoling	4731	4709	33	22	2	3
鄠邑区	Huyi	4712	4696	28	52	5	2
蓝田县	Lantian	2372	2366	23	27	3	4
周至县	Zhouzhi	2906	2900	35	33	1	2
西咸新区	Xixian	19450	19362	31	68	8	5

2-11 续表 continued

区 县	Region	有限责任公司 Limited Liability Corporations	股份有限公司 Share-holding Corperation Ltd.	私营企业 Private Enterprises	港、澳、台商投资企业 Enterprises with Funds from Hong Kong, Macao and Taiwan	外商投资企业 Enterprises with Foreign Investment
全 市	**Total**	**13023**	**695**	**217367**	**394**	**636**
新城区	Xincheng	857	45	8911	10	8
碑林区	Beilin	622	51	21762	32	32
莲湖区	Lianhu	879	54	17002	14	19
灞桥区	Baqiao	1501	40	12027	42	27
未央区	Weiyang	1989	81	51383	71	89
雁塔区	Yanta	3810	220	58808	129	294
阎良区	Yanliang	168	15	2651	6	13
临潼区	Lintong	137	6	3675	8	7
长安区	Chang'an	1091	51	9639	25	66
高陵区	Gaoling	324	22	4303	7	15
鄠邑区	Huyi	196	14	4399	7	9
蓝田县	Lantian	193	30	2086	2	4
周至县	Zhouzhi	98	15	2706	6	
西咸新区	Xixian	1158	51	18015	35	53

注：西安市行政区不包含西咸新区单位数，西咸新区单位数按统计局代码汇总。

主要统计指标解释

企业（单位）登记注册类型 企业或企业产业活动单位的登记注册类型，依据在市场监管部门登记注册的类型划分。机关、事业单位和社会团体及其他组织的登记注册类型，依据主要经费来源和管理方式，根据实际情况进行划分。

国有企业 指企业全部资产归国家所有，并按《中华人民共和国企业法人登记管理条例》规定登记注册的非公司制的经济组织。不包括有限责任公司中的国有独资公司。

集体企业 指企业资产归集体所有，并按《中华人民共和国企业法人登记管理条例》规定登记注册的经济组织。

股份合作企业 指以合作制为基础，由企业职工共同出资入股，吸收一定比例的社会资产投资组建，实行自主经营，自负盈亏，共同劳动，民主管理，按劳分配与按股分红相结合的一种集体经济组织。

联营企业 指两个及两个以上相同或不同所有制性质的企业法人或事业单位法人，按自愿、平等、互利的原则，共同投资组成的经济组织。联营企业包括国有联营企业、集体联营企业、国有与集体联营企业和其他联营企业。

有限责任公司 指根据《中华人民共和国公司登记管理条例》规定登记注册，由两个以上、五十个以下的股东共同出资，每个股东以其所认缴的出资额对公司承担有限责任，公司以其全部资产对其债务承担责任的经济组织。有限责任公司包括国有独资公司以及其他有限责任公司。

股份有限公司 指根据《中华人民共和国公司登记管理条例》规定登记注册，其全部注册资本由等额股份构成并通过发行股票筹集资本，股东以其认购的股份对公司承担有限责任，公司以其全部资产对其债务承担责任的经济组织。

私营企业 指由自然人投资设立或由自然人控股，以雇佣劳动为基础的营利性经济组织。包括按照《公司法》、《合伙企业法》、《私营企业暂行条例》规定登记注册的私营有限责任公司、私营股份有限公司、私营合伙企业和私营独资企业。

其他企业 指上述企业之外的其他内资经济组织。

与港澳台商合资经营企业 指港澳台地区投资者与内地企业依照《中华人民共和国中外合资经营企业法》及有关法律的规定，按合同规定的比例投资设立、分享利润和分担风险的企业。

与港澳台商合作经营企业 指港澳台地区投资者与内地企业依照《中华人民共和国中外合作经营企业法》及有关法律的规定，依照合作合同的约定进行投资或提供条件设立、分配利润和分担风险的企业。

港澳台商独资经营企业 指依照《中华人民共和国外资企业法》及有关法律的规定，在内地由港澳台地区投资者全额投资设立的企业。

港澳台商投资股份有限公司 指根据国家有关规定，经原外经贸部依法批准设立，其中港、澳、台商的股本占公司注册资本的比例达25%以上的股份有限公司。凡其中港、澳、台商的股本占公司注册资本的比例小于25%的，属于内资企业中的股份有限公司。

中外合资经营企业 指外国企业或外国人与中国内地企业依照《中华人民共和国中外合资经营企业法》及有关法律的规定，按合同规定的比例投资设立、分享利润和分担风险的企业。

中外合作经营企业 指外国企业或外国人与中国内地企业依照《中华人民共和国中外合作经营企业法》及有关法律的规定，依照合作合同的约定进行投资或提供条件设立、分配利润、分担风险和亏损的企业。

外资企业 指依照《中华人民共和国外资企业法》及有关法律的规定，在中国内地由外国投资者全额投资设立的企业。

外商投资股份有限公司 指根据国家有关规定，经原外经贸部依法批准设立，其中外资的股本占公司注册资本的比例达25%以上的股份有限公司。凡其中外资股本占公司注册资本的比例小于25%的，属于内资企业中的股份有限公司。

行政机关、事业单位和社会团体

行政机关：包括国家权力机关、国家行政机关、国家监察机关、司法机关、政党机关、政协组织和其他机关法人；机关法人单位的本部，以及国家权力机关分支机构、国家行政机关分支或派出机构、监察机关分支机构、人民法院分支机构、人民检察院分支机构等。

①国家权力机关：指全国人民代表大会及其常务委员会、地方各级人民代表大会及其常务委员会和办事机构。

②国家行政机关：指国务院和地方各级人民政府及其工作部门，以及地区行政行署。

③国家监察机关：指行使监察职能的机关。

④国家司法机关：指国家审判机关和检察机关。

⑤政党机关：指中国共产党各级机关和所属办事机

构、各民主党派各级机关和办事机构。

⑥政协组织：指中国人民政治协商会议全国委员会和地方各级委员会及其办事机构。

事业单位 包括①经机构编制部门批准成立和登记或备案，领取《事业单位法人证书》，取得法人资格的单位；②事业法人单位的本部及分支机构或派出机构。

社会团体 指中国公民自愿组成，为实现会员共同意愿，按照其章程开展活动的非营利性社会组织。包括①经各级民政部门核准登记，领取《社会团体法人登记证书》的各类社会团体；②由各级机构编制管理部门直接管理其机构编制的群众团体；③经国务院批准可以免于登记的社会团体。

Explanatory Notes on Main Statistical Indicators

The types of registration of enterprises (units) The types of registration of enterprises or industrial activity units of enterprises shall be divided into the types of registration of government organs, public institutions, social organizations and other organizations according to the types of registration registered in the market supervision departments, and shall be divided according to the main sources of funds and ways of management according to the actual situation.

State-owned Enterprises refer to non-corporation economic units where the entire assets are owned by the State and which have been registered in accordance with the Regulation of the People's Republic of China on the Management of Registration of Corporate Enterprises. Not included from this category are solely State-funded corporations in the limited liability corporations.

Collective-owned Enterprises refer to economic units where the assets are owned collectively and which have been registered in accordance with the Regulation of the People's Republic of China on the Management of Registration of Corporate Enterprises.

Cooperative Enterprises refer to a form of collective economic units (enterprises)where capitals come mainly from employees as their shares, with certain proportion of capital from the outside, where production is organized on the basis of independent operation, independent accounting for profits and losses, joint work, democratic management, and a distribution system that integrates remuneration according to work with dividend according to capital share.

Joint Ownership Enterprises refer to economic units established by two or more corporate enterprises or corporate institutions of the same or different ownership, through joint investment on the basis of voluntary participation, equality, and mutual benefits. They include State joint ownership enterprises; collective joint ownership enterprises; joint State-collective enterprises; and other joint ownership enterprises.

Limited Liability Corporations refer to economic units established with investment from 2-50 investors and registered in accordance with the Regulation of the People's Republic of China on the Management of Registration of Corporations, each investor bearing limited liability to the corporation depending on its share of investment, and the corporation bearing liability to its debt to the maximum of its total assets. Limited liability corporations include solely State-funded limited liability corporations and other limited liability corporations.

Share-holding Corporations Ltd. refer to economic units registered in accordance with the Regulation of the People's Republic of China on the Management of Registration of Corporations, with total registered capital divided into equal shares and raised through issuing stocks. Each investor bears limited liability to the corporation depending on the holding of shares, and the corporation bears liability to its debt to the maximum of its total assets.

Private Enterprises refer to profit-making economic units invested and established by natural persons, or controlled by natural persons using employed labour~ Included in this category are private limited liability corporations, private share-holding corporations Ltd., private partnership enterprises and private-funded enterprises registered in accordance with the Company Law, the Law on Partnership Business and Interim Regulations on Private Enterprises.

Other Domestic-funded Enterprises refer to domestic-funded economic units other than those mentioned above.

Joint Venture Enterprises with Funds from Hong Kong, Macau and Taiwan are enterprises established by investors from Hong Kong, Macau and Taiwan with enterprises in the mainland of China in accordance with the Law of the People's Republic of China on Sino-foreign Equity Joint Ventures and other relevant laws, where the establishment of the investment and the sharing of profits and risks are stipulated under joint venture contracts.

Cooperative Enterprises with Funds from Hong Kong, Macan and Taiwan established by investors from Hong Kong, Macau and Taiwan with enterprises in the mainland of China in accordance with the Law of the People's Republic of China on Sino-foreign Contractual Joint Venture and other relevant laws, where the investment or provision of facilities and the sharing of profits and risks are stipulated under cooperative contracts.

Enterprises with Sole (exclusive)Investment from Hong Kong, Macau and Taiwan refer to enterprises established in the mainland of China with exclusive investment from investors from Hong Kong, Macau and Taiwan in accordance with the Law of the People's Republic of China on Wholly Foreign-owned Enterprises and other relevant laws.

Share-holding Corporations Ltd. with Investment from Hong Kong, Macau and Taiwan refer to share- holding corporations Ltd. established with the approval from the former Ministry of Foreign Trade and Economic Relations in line with relevant State regulations, where the share of investment from Hong Kong, Macau or Taiwan businessmen exceeds 25% of the total registered capital of the corporation. In case the share of investmentfrom Hong Kong, Macau or Taiwan is less than 25% of thetotal registered capital, the enterprise is to be classified as domestic-funded share-holding corporation Ltd.

Joint Venture Enterprises with Foreign Investment refer to enterprises jointly established byforeign enterprises or foreigners with enterprises in themainland of China in accordance with the Law of thePeople's Republic of China on Sino-foreign Equity JointVentures and other relevant laws, where the sharing ofinvestment, profits and risks is stipulated under contract.

Cooperative Enterprises with Foreign Investment refer to enterprises jointly established by foreign enterprises or foreigners with enterprises in the mainland of China in accordance with the Law of the People's Republic of China on Sino-foreign Contractual Joint Venture and other relevant laws, According to the enterprise that invests or provides conditions for establishment in accordance with the terms of the cooperation contract, distributes profits and shares risks and losses.

Enterprises with Sole (exclusive)Foreign Investment refer to enterprises established in the mainland of China with exclusive investment from foreign investors in accordance with the Law of the People's Republic of China on Wholly Foreign-owned Enterprises and other relevant laws.

Share-holding Corporations Ltd. with Foreign Investment refer to share-holding corporations Ltd. established with the approval from the former Ministry of Foreign Trade and Economic Relations in line with relevant State regulations, where the share of investment from foreign investors exceeds 25% of the total registered capital of the corporation. In case the share of foreign investment is less than 25% ofthe total registered capital, the enterprise is to be classified as domestic-funded share-holding corporation Ltd.

Administrative Organization, Institutions and Social organizations

Administrative organization including organs of state power, organs of state administration, organs of state supervision, judicial organs, organs of political parties, organizations of the CPPCC and other organs as legal persons; The headquarters of a legal entity of a state organ, a branch of a state organ of power, a branch of a state administrative organ or its dispatched organ, a branch of a supervisory organ, a branch of a people's court, a branch of a people's procuratorate, etc.

(1)The organs of state power: The National People's Congress and its Standing Committee, the local people's congresses at various levels and their standing committees and administrative bodies.

(2)State administrative organs: refer to the State Council and local people's governments at various levels and their working departments, as well as regional administrative agencies.

(3)State supervisory organs refer to organs that exercise supervisory functions.

(4) National judicial organs: refers to the national judicial organs and procurator organs.

Political party organs: refer to the organs and subordinate offices of the Communist Party of China at all levels, and the organs and offices of the democratic parties at all levels.

The CPPCC refers to the National Committee of the Chinese People's Political Consultative Conference (CPPCC) and local committees at all levels and their administrative bodies.

Public institutions include approved by the establishment of institutions and registration or record, get the "institution legal person certificate", obtain the legal person status of the unit; (2) The headquarters and branches or dispatched offices of the institution as legal person.

Social organizations refer to non-profit social organizations formed by Chinese citizens voluntarily to carry out activities in accordance with their articles of association in order to realize the common wishes of members. Including (1) approved by the civil affairs departments at all levels to register, get the "social organization legal person registration certificate" of all kinds of social organizations; (2) The establishment management departments at all levels shall directly manage the mass organizations with their establishment; Social organizations which may be exempted from registration with the approval of the State Council.

3 国民经济核算

NATIONAL ECONOMIC ACCOUNTS

资料整理：张　洁　段　斐　刘晓敏
Data management：Zhang Jie Duan Fei Liu Xiaomin
数据审核：连　鹏
Data audit：Lian Peng

第三部分　国民经济核算

一、简要说明

1.本章资料反映西安市国民经济核算情况。

2.本章资料包括西安市生产总值、构成和指数，非公有制经济增加值及占比等。生产总值是根据不同产业部门、不同行业的特点和资料来源情况而采用不同方法计算的。非公有制经济增加值测算执行的是《陕西省统计局关于非公有制经济增加值测算的暂行办法（修订版）》。

3.本年鉴公布的国内生产总值以及与之有关的指标数据，如果遇到普查或者重大核算方法改革，在能够获得更详细的基础资料的情况下，国内生产总值的历史数据还会发生变动。

2016年，国家统计局改革研发支出的核算方法，将能够为所有者带来经济利益的研发支出不再作为中间消耗，而是作为固定资本形成处理。根据新的核算方法，在四经普修订时对以前年份进行了调整性修订。

2019年数据为初步核算数，2003年–2018年为第四次经济普查修订数据。

4.2012年，根据国家质检总局和国家标准委颁布的《国民经济行业分类》（GB／T 4754—2011），国家统计局对《三次产业划分规定》进行了修订，将“农、林、牧、渔业”中的“农、林、牧、渔服务业”，“采矿业”中的“开采辅助活动”，“制造业”中的“金属制品、机械和设备修理业”等三个大类一并调入第三产业。2013年（含）之后三次产业分类执行国家统计局2012年制定的新《三次产业划分规定》。

5.2004年（含）之前人均GDP按户籍人口计算，2005年（含）之后按常住人口计算。

6.国民经济核算数据绝对数按当年价格计算，指数按可比价格计算。

二、主要指标

生产总值（亿元）	9321.19	比上年增长	7.0%
第一产业	279.13	比上年增长	4.3%
第二产业	3167.44	比上年增长	7.6%
第三产业	5874.62	比上年增长	6.8%
人均生产总值（元/人）	92256	比上年增长	3.9%

3 NATIONAL ECONOMIC ACCOUNTS

I.Brief introduction

1.Data in this chapter reflects the National Economic accounting situation of Xi'an.

2.Data in this chapter includes Xi'an GDP, composition, index, the added value and the proportion of the non-public sectors of the economy, etc.Data of GDP are based on different approaches in accordance with different features of various sectors, industry and data sources. The estimation of the non-public sectors of the economy is based on Interim Measures of Shaanxi Provincial Bureau on the Estimation of Value Added of the Non-Public Sectors of the Economy (Revised Edition).

3.For data of GDP and related indicators published in the Yearbook, if there are census or reformation of significant accounting method, historical data of GDP may also undergo change under the circumstance that more specific data can be obtained.

In 2016, National Bureau of Statistics reforms the Methodology of Research and Development Expenditure. It regulates that R&D expenditure which will bring economic benefit for the owners should be treated as Fixed Assets instead of Intermediate Consumption. According to new accounting method,the previous years were revised in the fourth national economic census.

Data of 2019 is preliminary accounting data, the fourth economic census was revised from 2013 to 2018.

4.Classification Rules of Three Strata of Industry was adjusted by National Bureau of Statistics of China in accordance with Industrial Classification for National Economic Activities (GB/T 4754-2011) in 2012, which was promulgated by AQSIQ and SAC. Services in support of agriculture, forestry, animal husbandry and fishery, support activities for mining, repair service of metal products, machinery and equipment are categorized into the Tertiary Industry. Industrial classification is based on adjusted Classification Rules of Three Strata of Industry (2012) since 2013.

5.Per capita GDP was calculated by register population before 2005, but since 2005 it is based on permanent resident population.

6.Data on national accounts are calculated at current prices, and the indices are calculated at constant prices.

Ⅱ.Major Indicators

		Increase over Preceding Year
Gross Domestic Product(100 mil. yuan)	9321.19	7.0%
Primary Industry	279.13	4.3%
Secondary Industry	3167.44	7.6%
Tertiary Industry	5874.62	6.8%
Per Capita Gross Domestic Product (yuan/person)	92256	3.9%

3-1 主要年份生产总值

Gross Domestic Product in Representative Years

(本表按当年价格计算)　　　　(Data in the table are calculated at current prices)
单位：亿元　　　　(100 million yuan)

年份 Year	生产总值 Gross Domestic Product	第一产业 Primary Industry	第二产业 Secondary Industry	第三产业 Tertiary Industry	人均国内生产总值 (元/人) Per Capita GDP (yuan/person)
1952	3.37	1.59	0.88	0.90	135
1965	12.76	2.62	7.22	2.92	323
1970	17.76	3.13	10.96	3.67	412
1975	21.33	4.14	12.63	4.56	448
1978	25.35	4.83	14.59	5.93	513
1980	31.66	4.73	18.69	8.24	623
1983	35.89	5.22	20.14	10.53	674
1984	44.14	7.45	24.17	12.52	817
1985	57.58	8.76	30.83	17.99	1049
1986	65.78	9.59	33.86	22.33	1178
1987	80.16	10.73	37.69	31.74	1409
1988	99.22	11.47	46.58	41.17	1711
1989	109.38	12.78	48.91	47.69	1861
1990	116.51	13.94	50.15	52.42	1932
1991	136.14	17.17	57.06	61.91	2224
1992	164.85	18.78	69.22	76.85	2662
1993	229.56	22.58	110.88	96.10	3661
1994	289.82	31.68	128.27	129.87	4563
1995	330.35	41.40	135.33	153.62	5131
1996	406.95	46.94	161.63	198.38	6246
1997	488.82	51.33	197.97	239.52	7424
1998	525.85	51.91	216.32	257.62	7906
1999	577.29	45.53	243.35	288.41	8599
2000	646.13	44.65	277.13	324.35	9484
2001	734.86	45.87	312.90	376.09	10628
2002	826.68	47.77	353.58	425.33	11831
2003	926.12	50.72	402.22	473.18	13052
2004	1092.35	60.21	464.95	567.19	15155
2005	1294.05	66.01	511.19	716.86	16158
2006	1512.56	70.44	612.69	829.42	18567
2007	1857.75	82.42	763.07	1012.26	22476
2008	2313.26	102.46	940.42	1270.38	27736
2009	2689.06	106.09	1105.01	1477.96	31994
2010	3195.05	133.22	1290.93	1770.89	37792
2011	3791.71	165.43	1516.30	2109.98	44641
2012	4370.16	181.12	1726.70	2462.35	51214
2013	4960.23	182.60	1946.58	2831.05	57876
2014	5576.98	191.58	2152.43	3232.97	64790
2015	5932.86	191.91	2070.47	3670.48	68457
2016	6396.36	196.66	2139.49	4060.21	72944
2017	7418.04	245.26	2452.92	4719.86	77803
2018	8499.41	258.98	2861.86	5378.56	86638
2019	9321.19	279.13	3167.44	5874.62	92256

注：1.2004年（含）之前人均GDP按户籍人口计算，2005年（含）之后按常住人口计算。
2.2013年（含）之后三次产业分类依据国家统计局2012年制定的新《三次产业划分规定》。
3.2017年开始西咸新区由西安代管，统计范围发生变化，之前年份则不含（下同）。
4.2003年−2017年数据为第四次经济普查修订结果（下同）。2018年数据为第四次经济普查数据。
5.2019年数据为初步核算数（下同）。

3-2 主要年份生产总值指数（上年＝100）

Indices of Gross Domestic Product in Representative Years(preceding year = 100)

(本表按可比价格计算) (Data in the table are calculated at constant prices)

年 份	Year	生产总值 Gross Domestic Product	第一产业 Primary Industry	第二产业 Secondary Industry	第三产业 Tertiary Industry	人均生产总值 Per Capita GDP
1952		103.6	92.2	137.5	123.7	
1965		126.1	134.1	133.0	106.7	
1970		122.0	109.4	140.0	100.1	
1975		103.8	92.6	107.1	107.5	
1978		101.7	101.6	99.4	108.2	
1980		111.5	83.3	119.7	116.5	
1985		112.6	107.5	111.8	116.9	
1986		111.4	107.7	108.4	118.8	
1987		113.6	100.8	109.1	126.6	
1988		111.4	81.2	115.5	114.7	
1989		106.7	103.0	104.5	110.8	
1990		105.2	103.0	102.5	109.6	
1991		109.8	118.6	108.6	108.6	108.2
1992		115.6	109.4	118.1	115.0	114.3
1993		123.9	112.5	142.7	108.4	122.3
1994		110.3	98.4	110.6	113.2	108.8
1995		110.0	104.5	112.1	108.6	108.5
1996		114.9	106.8	118.8	111.7	113.5
1997		114.4	109.1	116.7	112.4	113.2
1998		113.3	106.5	117.5	108.8	112.1
1999		112.2	97.4	115.7	110.1	111.2
2000		113.0	103.5	115.1	111.5	111.4
2001		113.1	102.5	115.3	112.6	111.4
2002		113.3	103.1	115.0	113.0	112.1
2003		113.1	101.8	117.5	110.5	111.4
2004		113.1	106.2	115.5	111.7	111.4
2005		112.3	107.5	109.8	115.1	110.5
2006		112.9	106.8	110.5	115.2	111.0
2007		115.1	104.5	113.0	117.4	113.4
2008		114.8	107.6	113.2	116.4	113.8
2009		113.0	104.9	110.7	115.1	112.2
2010		113.6	105.7	115.0	113.2	112.9
2011		112.6	105.4	111.7	113.9	112.1
2012		111.9	106.0	110.4	113.4	111.4
2013		111.2	104.4	112.6	110.7	110.7
2014		109.7	105.0	109.4	110.2	109.2
2015		108.9	104.4	104.6	112.1	108.1
2016		108.8	103.3	107.2	110.0	107.6
2017		107.7	105.0	105.1	109.4	106.0
2018		108.2	103.3	107.1	109.1	105.1
2019		107.0	104.3	107.6	106.8	103.9
平均每年增长	**Yearly Average Growth Rates**					
“一五”时期	**The First Five-Year Plan Period**	**15.8**	**5.9**	**37.7**	**16.9**	
“二五”时期	**The Second Five-Year Plan Period**	**2.0**	**-3.7**	**2.5**	**8.4**	
1963-1965年	**Readjust Period**	**14.2**	**16.1**	**23.4**	**0.3**	
“三五”时期	**The Third Five-Year Plan Period**	**7.1**	**0.1**	**11.7**	**5.4**	
“四五”时期	**The Fourth Five-Year Plan Period**	**5.0**	**4.0**	**5.3**	**5.0**	
“五五”时期	**The Fifth Five-Year Plan Period**	**6.0**	**-0.7**	**6.5**	**10.1**	
“六五”时期	**The Sixth Five-Year Plan Period**	**10.7**	**7.9**	**10.4**	**12.9**	
“七五”时期	**The Seventh Five-Year Plan Period**	**9.6**	**-1.3**	**7.9**	**15.9**	
“八五”时期	**The Eighth Five-Year Plan Period**	**13.8**	**8.5**	**17.8**	**10.7**	**12.3**
“九五”时期	**The Ninth Five-Year Plan Period**	**13.6**	**4.6**	**16.8**	**10.9**	**12.3**
“十五”时期	**The Tenth Five-Year Plan Period**	**13.0**	**4.2**	**14.6**	**12.6**	**11.4**
“十一五”时期	**The Eleventh Five-Year Plan Period**	**13.9**	**5.9**	**12.5**	**15.5**	**12.7**
“十二五”时期	**The Twelve Five-Year Plan Period**	**10.9**	**5.0**	**9.7**	**12.1**	**10.3**

3-3 主要年份生产总值指数（1952年=100）

Indices of Gross Domestic Product in Representative Years(1952= 100)

(本表按可比价格计算) (Data in the table are calculated at constant prices)

年　份 Year	生产总值 Gross Domestic Product	第一产业 Primary Industry	第二产业 Secondary Industry	第三产业 Tertiary Industry
1952	100.0	100.0	100.0	100.0
1965	341.6	173.3	1048.3	329.2
1970	481.6	174.3	1821.0	428.6
1975	614.2	211.9	2362.5	547.9
1978	678.7	231.3	2560.8	643.8
1980	821.4	204.2	3237.2	885.2
1983	988.4	222.5	3846.2	1154.4
1984	1213.6	278.2	4748.8	1388.7
1985	1366.8	299.1	5310.6	1632.4
1986	1523.1	322.3	5756.7	1928.9
1987	1730.0	324.9	6280.6	2441.6
1988	1926.3	263.7	7256.6	2801.2
1989	2054.8	271.6	7583.1	3104.6
1990	2162.5	279.7	7772.7	3403.6
1991	2374.4	331.7	8441.2	3696.3
1992	2744.8	362.9	9969.1	4250.7
1993	3400.8	408.2	14225.9	4607.8
1994	3751.1	401.8	15733.8	5216.0
1995	4126.2	419.9	17637.6	5664.6
1996	4741.0	448.5	20953.5	6327.4
1997	5423.7	489.3	24452.7	7112.0
1998	6145.1	521.1	28731.9	7737.9
1999	6894.8	507.6	33242.8	8519.4
2000	7791.1	525.4	38262.5	9499.1
2001	8811.7	538.5	44116.7	10696.0
2002	9983.7	555.2	50734.2	12086.5
2003	11294.6	565.2	59612.7	13355.6
2004	12778.7	600.2	68852.7	14918.2
2005	14345.3	645.3	75600.2	17170.8
2006	16198.7	689.1	83538.2	19780.8
2007	18644.8	720.1	94398.2	23222.7
2008	21407.9	774.9	106858.8	27031.2
2009	24195.2	812.8	118292.7	31112.9
2010	27478.5	859.2	136036.6	35219.8
2011	30951.8	905.6	151952.8	40115.3
2012	34625.8	959.9	167755.9	45490.8
2013	38514.2	1002.1	188893.2	50358.3
2014	42250.1	1052.2	206649.1	55494.8
2015	46001.9	1098.5	216155.0	62209.7
2016	50063.9	1134.8	231718.1	68430.7
2017	53913.8	1191.8	243508.6	74863.2
2018	58318.6	1231.1	260797.7	81675.8
2019	62400.9	1284.0	280618.3	87229.8

3-4 主要年份生产总值构成

Composition of Gross Domestic Product in Representative Years

(本表按当年价格计算) (Data in the table are calculated at current prices)

单位：% (%)

年 份	Year	生产总值 Gross Domestic Product	第一产业 Primary Industry	第二产业 Secondary Industry	第三产业 Tertiary Industry
1952		100	47.18	26.11	26.71
1965		100	20.53	56.58	22.89
1970		100	17.62	61.71	20.67
1975		100	19.41	59.21	21.38
1978		100	19.05	57.55	23.40
1980		100	14.94	59.03	26.03
1985		100	15.21	53.54	31.25
1986		100	14.58	51.47	33.95
1987		100	13.39	47.02	39.59
1988		100	11.56	46.95	41.49
1989		100	11.68	44.72	43.60
1990		100	11.96	43.04	45.00
1991		100	12.61	41.91	45.48
1992		100	11.39	41.99	46.62
1993		100	9.84	48.30	41.86
1994		100	10.93	44.26	44.81
1995		100	12.53	40.97	46.50
1996		100	11.53	39.72	48.75
1997		100	10.50	40.50	49.00
1998		100	9.87	41.14	48.99
1999		100	7.89	42.15	49.96
2000		100	6.91	42.89	50.20
2001		100	6.24	42.58	51.18
2002		100	5.78	42.77	51.45
2003		100	5.48	43.43	51.09
2004		100	5.51	42.56	51.93
2005		100	5.10	39.50	55.40
2006		100	4.66	40.51	54.83
2007		100	4.44	41.07	54.49
2008		100	4.43	40.65	54.92
2009		100	3.95	41.09	54.96
2010		100	4.17	40.40	55.43
2011		100	4.36	39.99	55.65
2012		100	4.14	39.51	56.35
2013		100	3.68	39.24	57.08
2014		100	3.44	38.59	57.97
2015		100	3.23	34.90	61.87
2016		100	3.07	33.45	63.48
2017		100	3.31	33.07	63.62
2018		100	3.05	33.67	63.28
2019		100	2.99	33.98	63.03
"一五"时期	**The First Five-Year Plan Period**	**100**	**32.88**	**43.92**	**23.20**
"二五"时期	**The Second Five-Year Plan Period**	**100**	**18.08**	**58.63**	**23.29**
1963-1965年	**Readjust Period**	**100**	**19.36**	**55.38**	**25.26**
"三五"时期	**The Third Five-Year Plan Period**	**100**	**18.60**	**57.33**	**24.07**
"四五"时期	**The Fourth Five-Year Plan Period**	**100**	**20.46**	**59.59**	**19.95**
"五五"时期	**The Fiifth Five-Year Plan Period**	**100**	**18.41**	**57.69**	**23.90**
"六五"时期	**The Sixth Five-Year Plan Period**	**100**	**16.03**	**55.01**	**28.96**
"七五"时期	**The Seventh Five-Year Plan Period**	**100**	**12.42**	**46.11**	**41.47**
"八五"时期	**The Eighth Five-Year Plan Period**	**100**	**11.44**	**43.52**	**45.04**
"九五"时期	**The Ninth Five-Year Plan Period**	**100**	**9.09**	**41.45**	**49.46**
"十五"时期	**The Tenth Five-Year Plan Period**	**100**	**5.55**	**41.95**	**52.50**
"十一五"时期	**The Eleventh Five-Year Plan Period**	**100**	**4.28**	**40.74**	**54.98**
"十二五"时期	**The Twelve Five-Year Plan Period**	**100**	**3.71**	**38.21**	**58.08**

3-5 主要年份分行业增加值

The Value added by Industry in Representative Years

单位：亿元 （100 million yuan）

年 份 Year	地区生产总值 Gross Domestic Product Domestic Product	农、林、牧、渔业 Farming Forestry Animal Husbandry Fishery	工业 Industry	建筑业 Construction	批发和零售业 Wholesale and Retail Trades
1992	164.85	18.78	61.33	7.89	18.16
1993	229.56	22.58	98.88	12.00	22.63
1994	289.82	31.68	110.52	17.75	27.83
1995	330.35	41.40	112.50	22.83	33.20
1996	406.95	46.94	132.52	29.11	44.51
1997	488.82	51.33	161.97	36.00	59.31
1998	525.85	51.91	175.00	41.32	64.93
1999	577.29	45.53	194.00	49.35	70.27
2000	646.13	44.65	218.44	58.69	65.87
2001	734.86	45.87	246.90	66.00	78.38
2002	826.68	47.77	280.20	73.38	91.57
2003	926.12	50.72	319.26	82.96	94.95
2004	1092.35	60.21	372.18	92.77	123.27
2005	1294.05	66.01	393.51	117.68	139.57
2006	1512.56	70.44	465.70	146.99	164.33
2007	1857.75	82.42	569.08	193.99	184.91
2008	2313.26	102.46	672.60	267.82	225.20
2009	2689.06	106.09	763.81	341.20	278.87
2010	3195.05	133.22	875.97	414.96	329.48
2011	3791.71	165.43	1009.29	507.01	406.26
2012	4370.16	181.12	1140.83	585.87	460.05
2013	4960.23	197.76	1268.22	698.54	512.26
2014	5576.98	207.89	1387.03	791.64	552.31
2015	5932.86	209.58	1242.18	857.40	589.33
2016	6396.36	216.34	1252.91	920.05	599.08
2017	7418.04	270.83	1436.72	1047.34	653.49
2018	8499.41	286.33	1707.90	1210.79	709.16
2019	9321.19	309.68	1868.86	1358.48	777.86

注：1999年（含）之前，批发和零售业与住宿和餐饮业无法分类，故1999年（含）之前批发和零售业数据为批发和零售业与住宿和餐饮业合计数。

3-5 续表 continued

单位：亿元 （100 million yuan）

年 份 Year	交通运输、仓储和邮政业 Transport，Storage and Post	住宿和餐饮业 Accommodation and Catering Trade	金融业 Financial Intermediation	房地产业 Real Estate	其他服务业 Others Services
1992	15.21		16.28	1.58	25.62
1993	18.01		20.59	1.97	32.90
1994	22.02		31.19	3.76	45.07
1995	24.60		35.20	4.90	55.72
1996	32.73		40.15	7.42	73.57
1997	43.02		37.50	8.74	90.95
1998	48.64		32.95	11.95	99.15
1999	55.35		30.37	14.42	118.00
2000	43.01	18.46	33.00	16.96	147.05
2001	45.50	21.97	36.21	21.38	172.65
2002	48.25	25.27	43.48	26.90	189.86
2003	46.99	25.34	47.96	32.39	225.55
2004	49.06	35.03	58.05	37.68	264.11
2005	59.12	47.59	79.33	45.90	345.36
2006	69.07	53.60	95.95	55.31	391.17
2007	78.02	67.89	141.69	70.93	468.83
2008	98.93	81.61	170.78	92.18	601.69
2009	110.55	79.27	198.58	124.92	685.79
2010	134.29	95.93	237.40	188.10	785.70
2011	160.29	114.66	278.09	245.14	905.54
2012	184.19	124.39	350.92	280.17	1062.63
2013	194.73	121.00	446.54	303.30	1217.89
2014	211.83	125.86	597.14	343.69	1359.59
2015	239.63	141.88	683.26	427.42	1542.19
2016	268.89	143.34	743.09	474.39	1778.27
2017	297.54	153.45	834.19	562.78	2161.71
2018	316.63	164.19	916.94	658.64	2528.84
2019	330.54	178.49	998.94	729.52	2768.82

3-6 主要年份分行业增加值指数（上年＝100）

Indices of the Value added by Industry in Representative Years（preceding year = 100）

(本表按可比价格计算) (Data in the table are calculated at constant prices)

年 份 Year	地区生产总值 Gross Domestic Product Domestic Product	农、林、牧、渔业 Farming Forestry Animal Husbandry Fishery	工业 Industry	建筑业 Construction	批发和零售业 Wholesale and Retail Trades
1992	115.6	109.4	118.1	118.2	130.7
1993	123.9	112.5	143.7	135.6	108.0
1994	110.3	98.4	106.8	141.3	103.1
1995	110.0	104.5	108.1	136.6	109.6
1996	114.9	106.8	117.1	126.8	116.0
1997	114.4	109.1	116.4	117.8	124.0
1998	113.3	106.5	116.1	123.4	110.7
1999	112.2	97.4	114.0	122.8	106.4
2000	113.0	103.5	113.8	120.1	111.4
2001	113.1	102.5	116.3	111.8	110.5
2002	113.3	103.1	116.4	109.3	115.3
2003	113.1	101.8	115.7	124.9	112.0
2004	113.1	106.2	114.5	119.3	109.0
2005	112.3	107.5	106.7	121.1	110.5
2006	112.9	106.8	108.5	117.2	112.9
2007	115.1	104.5	111.7	117.3	113.3
2008	114.8	107.6	111.8	117.5	114.0
2009	113.0	104.9	106.7	121.9	121.7
2010	113.6	105.7	114.0	117.3	110.9
2011	112.6	105.4	111.9	111.2	117.7
2012	111.9	106.0	110.8	109.4	111.2
2013	111.2	104.8	112.4	113.9	108.4
2014	109.7	105.2	108.3	112.3	107.6
2015	108.9	105.1	103.7	107.3	105.0
2016	108.8	104.1	108.2	106.3	103.9
2017	107.7	104.8	105.0	104.8	104.6
2018	108.2	103.5	108.3	107.1	106.1
2019	107.0	104.4	106.6	109.1	108.5

注：1999年（含）之前，批发和零售业与住宿和餐饮业无法分类，故1999年（含）之前批发和零售业数据为批发和零售业与住宿和餐饮业合计数。

3-6 续表 continued

(本表按可比价格计算)　　(Data in the table are calculated at constant prices)

年 份 Year	交通运输、仓储和邮政业 Transport，Storage and Post	住宿和餐饮业 Accommodation and Catering Trade	金融业 Financial Intermediation	房地产业 Real Estate	其他服务业 Others Services
1992	111.3		107.6	119.5	112.2
1993	102.7		109.7	107.4	111.4
1994	102.5		126.9	160.7	114.8
1995	102.6		103.7	119.7	113.6
1996	115.1		98.7	130.8	114.2
1997	122.4		87.0	109.6	115.1
1998	114.4		88.8	138.3	110.3
1999	111.9		90.6	118.6	117.0
2000	111.7	111.7	107.7	116.6	111.7
2001	111.6	114.2	103.6	123.5	114.2
2002	106.1	116.5	104.6	106.0	116.5
2003	110.5	112.3	111.1	105.7	110.2
2004	112.3	116.9	108.4	107.7	112.5
2005	112.4	123.4	110.7	108.8	117.8
2006	112.6	116.5	109.5	118.7	117.3
2007	110.9	116.1	123.2	123.1	118.3
2008	109.2	107.5	112.3	108.7	121.6
2009	110.6	103.2	121.2	130.8	111.5
2010	116.3	112.0	114.3	133.4	110.6
2011	112.7	109.4	114.7	117.9	111.8
2012	110.4	105.4	125.4	110.8	112.7
2013	104.6	100.3	124.0	113.2	108.2
2014	105.8	100.2	120.4	107.0	109.5
2015	109.3	110.5	116.4	113.5	113.1
2016	109.0	101.2	111.9	110.9	111.9
2017	106.8	103.9	106.5	109.1	113.6
2018	106.1	104.7	105.3	105.8	112.3
2019	106.7	105.2	107.9	100.8	107.5

3-7 主要年份三次产业贡献率

Three Industries Contribution Rate in Representative Years

(本表按可比价格计算)　　　　(Data in the table are calculated at constant prices)

单位：%　　　　(%)

年 份 Year	生产总值 Gross Domestic Product	第一产业 Primary Industry	第二产业 Secondary Industry	第三产业 Tertiary Industry
2000	100	1.8	66.9	31.3
2001	100	1.3	50.4	48.3
2002	100	1.5	49.4	49.1
2003	100	0.8	59.2	40.0
2004	100	2.4	54.3	43.3
2005	100	2.9	37.6	59.5
2006	100	2.7	32.2	65.1
2007	100	1.4	33.3	65.3
2008	100	2.2	33.9	63.9
2009	100	1.6	30.8	67.6
2010	100	1.6	40.4	58.0
2011	100	1.8	37.4	60.8
2012	100	2.0	35.0	63.0
2013	100	1.3	43.9	54.8
2014	100	1.7	38.4	59.9
2015	100	1.5	20.6	77.9
2016	100	1.2	28.6	70.2
2017	100	2.2	23.4	74.4
2018	100	1.4	29.8	68.8
2019	100	2.1	38.5	59.4

3-8 主要年份三次产业对生产总值增长的拉动

Contribution of the Three Strata of Industry to GDP Growth in Representative Years

(本表按可比价格计算)　　(Data in the table are calculated at constant prices)
单位：百分点　　(percentage points)

年份 Year	生产总值 Gross Domestic Product	第一产业 Primary Industry	第二产业 Secondary Industry	第三产业 Tertiary Industry
2000	13.0	0.2	8.7	4.1
2001	13.1	0.2	6.6	6.3
2002	13.3	0.2	6.6	6.5
2003	13.1	0.1	7.8	5.2
2004	13.1	0.3	7.1	5.7
2005	12.3	0.4	4.6	7.3
2006	12.9	0.3	4.2	8.4
2007	15.1	0.2	5.0	9.9
2008	14.8	0.3	5.0	9.5
2009	13.0	0.2	4.0	8.8
2010	13.6	0.2	5.5	7.9
2011	12.6	0.2	4.7	7.7
2012	11.9	0.2	4.2	7.5
2013	11.2	0.1	4.9	6.2
2014	9.7	0.2	3.7	5.8
2015	8.9	0.1	1.8	7.0
2016	8.8	0.1	2.5	6.2
2017	7.7	0.2	1.8	5.7
2018	8.2	0.1	2.4	5.7
2019	7.0	0.1	2.7	4.2

3-9 分行业增加值

Value added by Industry

单位：亿元 (100 million yuan)

指 标	Item	增加值 Value Added		指数（上年=100） Index	
		2018	2019	2018	2019
地区生产总值	**Gross Domestic Product**	**8499.41**	**9321.19**	**108.2**	**107.0**
农、林、牧、渔业	Farming Forestry Animal Husbandry Fishery	286.33	309.68	103.5	104.4
工业	Industry	1707.90	1868.86	108.3	106.6
建筑业	Construction	1210.79	1358.48	107.1	109.1
批发和零售业	Wholesale and Retail Trades	709.16	777.86	106.1	108.5
交通运输、仓储及邮政业	Transport,Storage and Post	316.63	330.54	106.1	106.7
住宿和餐饮业	Accommodation and Catering Trade	164.19	178.49	104.7	105.2
金融业	Financial Intermediation	916.94	998.94	105.3	107.9
房地产业	Real Estate	658.64	729.52	105.8	100.8
其他服务业	Others Services	2528.84	2768.82	112.3	107.5
第一产业	Primary Industry	258.98	279.13	103.3	104.3
第二产业	Secondary Industry	2861.86	3167.44	107.1	107.6
第三产业	Tertiary Industry	5378.56	5874.62	109.1	106.8

3-10 各区县生产总值（2019年）

Gross Domestic Product by Region（2019）

单位：亿元 （100 million yuan）

区 县	Region	生产总值 Gross Domestic Product	第一产业 Primary Industry	第二产业 Secondary Industry	第三产业 Tertiary Industry	人均生产总值（元） Per Capita GDP （yuan）
全 市	**Total**	**9321.19**	**279.13**	**3167.44**	**5874.62**	**92256**
新城区	Xincheng	605.93		212.93	393.00	94052
碑林区	Beilin	1013.97		232.79	781.18	148306
莲湖区	Lianhu	789.05		257.36	531.69	101688
灞桥区	Baqiao	489.19	19.23	137.73	332.23	70836
未央区	Weiyang	1255.07	0.28	562.46	692.33	156424
雁塔区	Yanta	2271.01		522.76	1748.25	166466
阎良区	Yanliang	255.06	28.86	106.37	119.83	84220
临潼区	Lintong	242.69	36.20	70.97	135.52	34737
长安区	Chang'an	1001.21	28.73	547.03	425.45	95037
高陵区	Gaoling	374.44	27.19	210.41	136.84	102628
鄠邑区	Huyi	180.23	27.71	51.68	100.84	32092
蓝田县	Lantian	149.23	28.35	35.43	85.45	27818
周至县	Zhouzhi	137.15	35.88	16.12	85.15	23109
西咸新区	Xixian	520.72	46.72	185.21	288.79	50501

注：本表数据为初步核算数。

3-11 各区县生产总值指数（2019年）（上年=100）

Indices of Gross Domestic Product by Region (2019) (preceding year = 100)

(本表按可比价格计算) (Data in the table are calculated at constant prices)

区 县	Region	生产总值 Gross Domestic Product	第一产业 Primary Industry	第二产业 Secondary Industry	第三产业 Tertiary Industry	人均生产总值 Per Capita GDP
全 市	**Total**	**107.0**	**104.3**	**107.6**	**106.8**	**103.9**
新城区	Xincheng	106.5		107.6	105.8	104.3
碑林区	Beilin	106.3		112.7	104.7	103.5
莲湖区	Lianhu	105.1		104.4	105.4	101.9
灞桥区	Baqiao	108.3	101.3	110.2	107.8	103.3
未央区	Weiyang	107.2	70.5	106.7	107.7	98.8
雁塔区	Yanta	108.0		109.7	107.4	102.8
阎良区	Yanliang	105.9	105.0	106.5	105.6	104.2
临潼区	Lintong	107.5	105.7	111.8	105.6	106.7
长安区	Chang'an	108.2	103.7	113.1	103.1	105.4
高陵区	Gaoling	104.2	104.7	101.5	109.3	102.8
鄠邑区	Huyi	102.0	104.9	90.3	107.6	100.6
蓝田县	Lantian	103.6	103.0	95.3	108.3	103.3
周至县	Zhouzhi	100.2	106.8	68.2	106.5	99.9
西咸新区	Xixian	110.6	102.9	109.1	113.3	107.9

注：本表数据为初步核算数。

3-12 主要年份非公有制经济增加值

The Added Value of Non-public-owned Economic in Representative Years

年 份 Year	非公有制经济增加值 （亿元） the Added Value of Non-public-owned Economic (100 million yuan)	非公有制经济增加值 占GDP比重（%） the Added Value of Non-public-owned Economic Percentage to GDP(%)
2005	560.32	43.3
2006	673.09	44.5
2007	854.57	46.0
2008	1101.11	47.6
2009	1309.57	48.7
2010	1587.94	49.7
2011	1916.95	50.6
2012	2246.26	51.4
2013	2589.24	52.2
2014	2939.07	52.7
2015	3132.55	52.8
2016	3377.28	52.8
2017	3931.72	53.0
2018	4539.52	53.4
2019	5066.18	54.4

注：1.2005-2018年数据根据第四次经济普查GDP修订结果相应进行了调整。
2.2019年数据为初步核算数。

主要统计指标解释

生产总值（GDP） 是按市场价格计算的一个地区（或国家）所有常住单位在一定时期内生产活动的最终成果。生产总值有三种表现形态，即价值形态、收入形态和产品形态。从价值形态看，它是所有常住单位在一定时期内生产的全部货物和服务价值超过同期中间投入的全部非固定资产货物和服务价值的差额，即所有常住单位的增加值之和；从收入形态看，它是所有常住单位在一定时期内创造并分配给常住单位和非常住单位的初次收入分配之和；从产品形态看，它是所有常住单位在一定时期内最终使用的货物和服务价值与货物和服务净出口价值之和。在实际核算中，生产总值有三种计算方法，即生产法、收入法和支出法。三种方法分别从不同的方面反映生产总值及其构成。

人均生产总值 即"人均GDP"，常作为发展经济学中衡量经济发展状况的指标，是最重要的宏观经济指标之一，它是人们了解和把握一个国家或地区的宏观经济运行状况的有效工具。将一个国家核算期内（通常是一年）实现的国内生产总值与这个国家的常住人口（或户籍人口）相比进行计算，得到人均生产总值。

三次产业 指根据社会生产活动历史发展的顺序对产业结构的划分。目前我国的三次产业划分是：

第一产业是指农、林、牧、渔业（不含农、林、牧、渔服务业）。

第二产业是指采矿业（不含开采辅助活动），制造业（不含金属制品、机械和设备修理业），电力、热力、燃气及水生产和供应业，建筑业。

第三产业即服务业，是指除第一产业、第二产业以外的其他行业。

劳动者报酬 指劳动者因从事生产活动所获得的全部报酬。包括劳动者获得的各种形式的工资、奖金和津贴，既包括货币形式的，也包括实物形式的，还包括劳动者所享受的公费医疗和医药卫生费、上下班交通补贴、单位支付的社会保险费、住房公积金等。

生产税净额 指生产税减生产补贴后的余额。生产税指政府对生产单位从事生产、销售和经营活动以及因从事生产活动使用某些生产要素（如固定资产、土地、劳动力）所征收的各种税、附加费和规费。生产补贴与生产税相反，指政府对生产单位的单方面转移支出，因此视为负生产税，包括政策亏损补贴、价格补贴等。

固定资产折旧 指一定时期内为弥补固定资产损耗按照规定的固定资产折旧率提取的固定资产折旧，或按国民经济核算统一规定的折旧率虚拟计算的固定资产折旧。它反映了固定资产年当期生产中的转移价值。各类企业和企业化管理的事业单位的固定资产折旧是指实际计提的折旧费；不计提折旧的政府机关、非企业化管理的事业单位和居民住房的固定资产折旧是按照统一规定的折旧率和固定资产原值计算的虚拟折旧。原则上，固定资产折旧应按固定资产当期的重置价值计算，但是目前我国尚不具备对全社会固定资产进行重估价的基础，所以暂时只能采用上述办法。

营业盈余 指常住单位创造的增加值扣除劳动者报酬、生产税净额和固定资产折旧后的余额。它相当于企业的营业利润加上生产补贴，但要扣除从利润中开支的工资和福利等。

三次产业贡献率 各产业不变价增加值增量与不变价GDP增量之比。

三次产业拉动率 GDP增长速度与各产业贡献率之乘积。

非公有制经济 非公有制经济是指国民经济中除国有经济和集体经济以外的部分，对其中的混合制经济要依据实收资本之间的比例，按经济成分对各主要经济总量进行划分。

Explanatory Notes on Main Statistical Indicators

Gross Domestic Product (GDP) refers to the final products at market prices produced by all resident units in a country (or a region) during a certain period of time. Gross domestic product is expressed in three different perspectives, namely value, income, and products respectively. GDP in its value perspective refers to the total value of all goods and services produced by all resident units during a certain period of time, minus the total value of input of goods and services of the nature of non-fixed assets; in other words, it is the sum of the value-added of all resident units. GDP from the perspective of income includes the primary income created by all resident units and distributed to resident and non-resident units. GDP from the perspective of products refers to the value of all goods and services for final demand by all resident units plus the net exports of goods and services during a given period of time. In the practice of national accounting, gross domestic product is calculated from three approaches, namely production approach, income approach and expenditure approach, which reflect gross domestic product and its composition from different angles.For a region, it is called as Gross Regional Product (GRP) or regional GDP.

Per capita gross domestic product: "per capita GDP", often used as a measure of economic development in development economics, it is one of the most important macroeconomic indicators, and people's understanding and grasp of a country or a region effective tool of macroeconomic performance. The gross domestic product (GDP) of a country's accounting period (usually one year) is divided by the country's resident population (or household population), resulting in per capita GDP.

Three Strata of Industry Classification of economic activities into three strata of industry is a common practice in the world, although the grouping varies to some extent from country to country. In China economic activities are categorized into the following three strata of industry:

Primary industry refers to agriculture, forestry, animal husbandry and fishery and services in support of these industries.

Secondary industry refers to mining and quarrying, manufacturing, production and supply of electricity, water and gas, and construction.

Tertiary industry refers to all other economic activities not included in the primary or secondary industries.

Compensation of Employees refers to the total payment of various forms to employees for the productive activities they are engaged in. It includes wages, bonuses and allowances, which the employees earn in cash or in kind. It also includes the free medical services provided to the employees and the medicine expenses, transport subsidies and social insurance, and housing fund paid by the employers.

Net Taxes on Production refers to taxes on production less subsidies on production. The taxes on production refers to the various taxes, extra charges and fees levied on the production units on their production, sale and business activities as well as on the use of some factors of production, such as fixed assets, land and labour in the production activities they are engaged in. In contrast to taxes on production, subsidies on production refer to the unilateral government transfer to the production units and are therefore regarded as negative taxes on production. They include subsidies on the loss due to implementation of government policies, price subsidies, etc.

Depreciation of Fixed Assets refers to the depreciation of fixed assets in a given period, drawn in accordance with the stipulated depreciation rate for the purpose of compensating the wear-and-tear loss of the fixed assets or the depreciation of fixed assets imputed in accordance with the stipulated unified depreciation rate in the national economic accounting system. It reflects the value of transfer of the fixed assets in the production of the current period. The depreciation of fixed assets in various enterprises and institutions managed as enterprises refers to the depreciation expenses actually drawn. In government agencies and institutions not managed as enterprises which do not draw the depreciation expenses, as well as for the houses of residents, the depreciation of fixed assets is the imputed depreciation, which is calculated in accordance with the stipulated unified depreciation rate. In principle, the depreciation of fixed assets should be calculated on the basis of the re-purchased value of the fixed assets. However, currently the conditions in China do not facilitate the revaluation of all the fixed assets. Therefore, only the above-mentioned methods can be adopted at present.

Operating Surplus refers to the balance of the value added created by the resident units after deducting the labourers remuneration, net taxes on production and the depreciation of fixed assets. It is equivalent to the business profit of the enterprises plus subsidies to production, but the wages and welfare expenses paid from the profits should be deducted.

Three Industry Contribution Rate The ratio of all industries incremental value added to GDP increment at constant prices.

Three Industries Pulling Rate The product of GDP growth rate and the contribution rate of each industry.

Non–public Economy It refers to the part of in addition to state-owned economy and collective economy in the national economy,On which the mixed-economy should be divided according to the major economic components of total economic output based on the proportion in paid-in capital.

4 人口、从业人员与职工工资

POPULATION,EMPLOYMENT AND WAGES

资料整理：张　叶　张　磊
Data management：Zhang Ye Zhang Lei
数据审核：冯军魁
Data audit：Feng Junkui

第四部分　人口、从业人员与职工工资

一、简要说明

（一）人口部分反映西安市人口发展变化基本情况。

1.年末常住人口、性别比例、年龄比例、城镇人口比例以及人口出生率、人口死亡率和人口自然增长率等数据，根据人口普查、1%人口抽样调查或年度人口变动情况抽样调查推算所得，2006–2009年年末常住人口根据2010年第六次全国人口普查数据进行了调整。

2. 户籍人口资料数据来源于西安市公安局人口统计年报，为西安原口径数据。

3.人口统计调查方法。目前人口统计调查有：在逢“0”的年份进行全国人口普查；在逢“5”的年份进行全国1%人口抽样调查；其余年份进行人口变动情况抽样调查。

（二）就业部分

1.反映西安市劳动就业与工资的基本情况。主要内容包括全社会从业人员数、城镇非私营单位从业人员数、城镇非私营单位从业人员工资、城镇登记失业率等。（城镇登记失业人数及失业率资料由市人力资源局提供并整理）

2.统计范围和调查方法

（1）城镇非私营单位是指城镇地区全部非私营法人单位，具体包括国有单位、集体单位、联营经济、股份制经济、外商投资经济、港澳台投资经济等单位。工资统计是统计单位的从业人员，而个体从业人员、自由职业者等非单位从业人员不在工资统计范围内。

根据国家统计局制定的《企业一套表统计调查制度》和《劳动工资统计调查制度》，对城镇非私营法人单位采用全面调查的方法。

（2）城镇私营单位主要是指在内资法人单位中由自然人投资设立或由自然人控股，以雇佣劳动为基础的营利性经济组织，包括按照《公司法》《合伙企业法》《私营企业暂行条例》规定登记注册的私营有限责任公司、私营股份有限公司、私营合伙企业和私营独资企业。

根据国家统计局制定的《企业一套表统计调查制度》和《劳动工资统计调查制度》，对私营单位工资统计采用全面调查和抽样调查相结合的方法。

二、主要指标

年末户籍人口（万人）	956.74	比上年增长	3.7%
人口自然增长率（‰）	6.79	比上年下降	0.2个千分点
常住人口（万人）	1020.35	比上年增长	2.0%
男女性别比（以女性为100）	104.52	比上年下降	0.23个百分点
户籍人口密度（人／平方公里）	948	比上年增加	34人/平方公里
城镇非私营单位在岗职工年平均工资（元）	96867	比上年增长	11.2%

4 POPULATION,EMPLOYMENT AND WAGES

Ⅰ.Brief Introduction

I. Population part reflects the basic conditions of development and changes of population in Xi'an.

1. Permanent population at the year–end, proportion of population by sex, proportion of population by age, proportion of urban population, birth rate, death rate and natural growth rate of population. The data are estimated by Xi'an Bureau of Statistics on the basis of population censuses, the one percent sample survey on population, or annual sample surveys on population changes. Permanent Population at the Year–end from 2006 to 2009 have been adjusted in accordance with the flash sums of the 6th National Population Census in 2010.

2. The total population with residence registration are obtained from the annual reports of population of Xi'an Public Security Bureau. It is the original caliber data of Xi'an.

3. Investigation methods. The statistical surveys on population are as follows:

The national populationcensus is conducted in the year ending with 0; the national 1 percent population sample survey is conducted in the year ending with 5; sample survey on population changes are conducted in the rest of the years.

II. Employment part

1. This part reflects the basic conditions of labour employment and wages of Xi'an, mainly including the number of all employed persons, number of urban non–private units, wages of urban non–private units employed persons, registered urban unemployment rate and etc. (the number of registered urban unemployment and registered urban unemployment rate are obtained from the Xi'an municipal human resources bureau).

2. The statistical coverage and investigation methods.

a) The urban non–private units: are non–private legal units in urban area, including state–owned units, urban collective–owned units, joint ownership units, cooperative units, foreign funded units and units with funds from Hong Kong, Macao & Taiwan etc. Wage of employed persons in urban non–private units are the persons employed in those units, except self–employed and freelancers.

In accordance withA Set of Statistical Survey System for Enterprises and The Survey System on Labour Wageby National Bureau of Statistics of China, the investigation method of non–private legal units in urban area is comprehensive survey.

b) The urban private units: are established by natural person or controlled by natural person in legal units invested by domestic, are for–profit units based on wage–labor, including private limited liability corporations, private share holding corporations Ltd., partnership corporations and private sole proprietorship corporations registered in accordance with the Company Law,Partnership Enterprise Law and Provisional Regulations.

In accordance with A Set of Statistical Survey System for Enterprises and The Survey System on Labour Wageby National Bureau of Statistics of China, the investigation method of wage of employed persons in private legal units is combined with comprehensive survey and sampling survey.

Ⅱ.Major Indicators

		Increase over Preceding Year
Total registered Population of Year–end(10 000 persons)	956.74	3.7%
Natural Growth Rate(‰)	6.79	–0.2 per thousand
Permanent Population(10 000 persons)	1020.35	2.0%
Sex Ratio (Female=100)	104.52	–0.23 percentage points
Density of Population (person/sq.km)	948	34 person/sq.km
Annual Average Wage of Staff and Workers in Urban Non–privite Enterprises(yuan)	96867	11.2%

4-1 主要年份人口数、人口密度和人口发展情况

Population, Population Density and Population Development in Representative Years

单位：万人 (10 000 persons)

年份 Year	总人口 Total Population	市区 Urban Area	女性人口 Number of Female	城镇人口 Urban Population	人口密度（人/平方公里） Density of Population (person/sq.km)	总人口指数（上年为100）Total Population Index (100 for preceding year) 全市 Whole City	市区 Urban Area
1952	252.92	92.42	118.81	57.61	254	102.6	103.1
1965	400.05	179.88	190.72	136.39	401	102.5	103.4
1970	435.12	188.12	210.47	139.12	436	101.9	101.4
1978	498.10	210.15	241.82	159.98	499	101.7	102.7
1980	511.91	221.19	249.26	172.85	513	101.4	102.6
1985	553.11	245.76	268.40	201.90	554	101.6	102.2
1986	563.97	251.80	273.30	205.92	565	102.0	102.5
1987	574.46	257.69	278.12	210.25	575	101.9	102.3
1988	585.85	264.94	283.68	216.99	587	102.0	102.8
1989	597.36	270.80	289.44	222.54	598	102.0	102.2
1990	608.89	275.69	295.29	226.98	610	101.9	101.8
1991	615.48	419.29	298.13	230.85	617	101.1	152.1
1992	623.20	429.54	301.92	236.45	624	101.3	102.4
1993	630.91	435.41	305.30	240.85	632	101.2	101.4
1994	639.45	442.30	309.17	248.35	641	101.4	101.6
1995	648.21	448.65	313.46	255.71	645	101.4	101.4
1996	654.87	454.68	316.60	261.28	653	101.0	101.3
1997	662.06	461.17	320.18	267.52	663	101.1	101.4
1998	668.22	466.31	323.20	271.75	669	100.9	101.1
1999	674.50	463.56	326.12	276.14	676	100.9	99.4
2000	688.01	483.10	332.83	285.79	689	102.0	104.2
2001	694.84	489.88	336.04	292.62	696	101.0	101.4
2002	702.59	497.38	339.51	300.05	704	101.1	101.5
2003	716.58	510.26	346.26	312.88	718	102.0	102.6
2004	725.01	516.30	350.85	318.50	717	101.2	101.2
2005	741.73	533.21	359.71	333.14	734	102.3	103.3
2006	753.11	540.97	365.74	343.78	745	101.5	101.5
2007	764.25	549.19	371.84	353.85	756	101.5	101.5
2008	772.30	554.73	376.76	363.87	764	101.1	101.0
2009	781.67	561.58	382.39	370.66	773	101.2	101.2
2010	782.73	562.65	383.93	374.64	774	100.1	100.2
2011	791.83	568.77	389.31	391.31	783	101.2	101.1
2012	795.98	572.76	392.04	398.40	788	100.5	100.7
2013	806.93	580.60	398.15	409.82	799	101.4	101.4
2014	815.29	587.16	402.83	418.16	807	101.0	101.1
2015	815.66	588.43	403.43	545.95	808	100.0	100.2
2016	824.93	629.24	408.39	552.21	817	101.1	106.9
2017	845.09	649.08	420.11	567.26	837	102.4	103.2
2018	922.82	725.58	461.31	639.62	914	109.2	111.8
2019	956.74	821.31	479.61	668.57	948	103.7	113.2

注：本表为公安年报数据，系户籍人口。2016年起公安年报调整至11月30日，市区数1991年增加临潼、长安，2016年增加高陵，行政区划面积自2012年发生变更，调整了2012年和2013年户籍人口密度。2015年公安局户籍改革，按统计上城乡划分标准统计城镇与乡村人口。户籍人口为西安原口径数据。2019年计算的人口密度所使用的土地面积为2018年数据。

4-2 主要年份人口自然变动情况

Natural Population Movements in Representative Years

单位：万人 (10 000 persons)

年份 Year	出生 Birth 人数 Population	出生率（‰）Birth Rate（‰）	死亡 Death 人数 Population	死亡率（‰）Death Rate（‰）	自然增长率（‰）Natural Growth Rate（‰）	迁入人口 Immigrant Population	迁出人口 Emigrant Population
1985	8.95	16.30	3.01	5.48	10.82	11.60	8.74
1986	10.14	18.15	2.78	4.97	13.18	11.79	8.39
1987	9.76	17.14	2.83	4.97	12.17	12.58	9.26
1988	9.42	16.24	2.89	4.98	11.26	13.54	8.97
1989	11.78	19.92	3.04	5.13	14.79	12.73	10.15
1990	12.40	20.55	3.45	5.72	14.83	11.82	9.86
1991	8.73	14.25	3.26	5.33	8.92	8.98	6.09
1992	8.98	14.49	3.39	5.48	9.01	13.94	9.54
1993	9.25	14.75	3.37	5.38	9.37	11.50	8.33
1994	8.08	12.71	3.16	4.97	7.74	13.40	8.59
1995	7.69	11.95	3.21	4.98	6.97	14.41	8.85
1996	7.26	11.15	3.41	5.24	5.91	11.94	8.88
1997	6.84	10.38	3.12	4.75	5.63	12.58	8.62
1998	6.40	9.62	3.10	4.66	4.96	10.89	8.36
1999	6.19	9.22	3.88	5.78	3.44	12.58	9.23
2000	8.90	13.07	4.06	5.96	7.11	17.12	9.23
2001	5.11	7.39	2.89	4.19	3.20	15.16	10.83
2002	5.34	7.64	3.08	4.41	3.23	13.90	9.41
2003	6.02	8.48	3.32	4.68	3.80	20.60	9.15
2004	6.63	9.19	4.23	5.87	3.32	15.56	10.19
2005	7.67	9.58	4.13	5.16	4.42	22.61	9.46
2006	8.13	9.98	4.45	5.46	4.52	17.23	11.75
2007	8.27	10.00	4.53	5.48	4.52	19.90	14.01
2008	8.47	10.15	4.65	5.57	4.58	18.49	15.04
2009	8.47	10.08	4.73	5.63	4.45	16.84	13.14
2010	8.23	9.73	4.51	5.34	4.39	14.09	13.50
2011	8.25	9.71	4.57	5.38	4.33	14.21	11.74
2012	8.64	10.13	4.75	5.57	4.56	12.55	13.10
2013	8.20	9.57	4.60	5.37	4.20	10.83	8.60
2014	8.70	10.11	4.71	5.47	4.64	9.10	7.61
2015	8.80	10.15	4.78	5.51	4.64	8.08	11.61
2016	10.12	11.54	4.74	5.40	6.14	6.21	4.68
2017	12.03	12.62	5.17	5.42	7.20	25.22	4.94
2018	12.23	12.47	5.38	5.48	6.99	76.53	8.02
2019	12.45	12.32	5.59	5.53	6.79	30.81	6.21

注：2004年以前为公安年报数据。迁入人口和迁出人口为公安年报数据。公安数据为西安原口径数据。2010年出生、死亡、自然增长率根据第六次人口普查数据推算得出。2005-2009、2011-2019年出生、死亡、自然增长率为人口变动抽样调查推算数据。

4-3 人口年龄构成和抚养比

Population Age Composition and Dependency Ratio

单位：% (%)

年 份 Year	各年龄段人口比重 Proportion of Population of All Ages 0-14岁 0-14 year old	15-64岁 15-64 year old	65岁及以上 65 year old and above	总抚养比 Total Dependency Ratio	少年儿童 Children	老年人口 Elderly Population
1990	25.71	69.08	5.21	44.76	37.21	7.55
2000	22.27	71.26	6.47	40.33	31.25	9.08
2010	12.89	78.65	8.46	27.15	16.39	10.76
2011	12.57	78.33	9.10	27.66	16.04	11.62
2012	12.54	78.02	9.44	28.17	16.07	12.10
2013	12.46	77.88	9.66	28.40	16.00	12.40
2014	12.52	77.46	10.02	29.10	16.16	12.94
2015	12.56	76.94	10.50	29.98	16.33	13.65
2016	12.76	76.35	10.89	30.97	16.71	14.26
2017	13.63	75.20	11.17	32.97	18.12	14.85
2018	13.75	74.96	11.29	33.40	18.34	15.06
2019	13.90	74.41	11.69	34.39	18.68	15.71

注：1990、2000、2010年数据根据人口普查数据加工整理，2011-2019年数据根据人口变动抽样调查数据推算，自2017年起为纳入西咸新区咸阳片区后的结构。抚养比指0-14岁、65岁及以上人口占15-64岁人口的比重。

4-4 全市及各区县人口数和户数（2019年）

Population and Households by Region（2019）

单位：万人 (10 000 persons)

区 县	Region	总户数（万户） Number of Households (10 000 households)	总人口 Total Population	城填人口 Urban Population	按性别划分Grouped by Sex 男 Male	女 Female	迁入人口(人) Immigrant Population (person)	迁出人口(人) Emigrant Population (person)
全 市	**Total**	**300.95**	**956.74**	**668.57**	**477.13**	**479.61**	**308124**	**62102**
新城区	Xincheng	18.33	53.73	53.73	26.61	27.12	17287	3518
碑林区	Beilin	23.11	73.40	73.40	36.35	37.05	30589	8302
莲湖区	Lianhu	26.83	76.13	76.13	37.34	38.79	33341	5151
灞桥区	Baqiao	21.42	65.51	65.23	31.93	33.58	22485	2734
未央区	Weiyang	31.56	97.80	97.80	47.48	50.32	67606	9129
雁塔区	Yanta	40.12	127.75	127.75	62.53	65.22	75693	12885
阎良区	Yanliang	8.64	27.39	12.63	13.71	13.68	3550	1635
临潼区	Lintong	22.95	73.00	23.94	36.91	36.09	4433	1791
长安区	Chang'an	39.31	126.18	59.06	62.66	63.52	28633	5662
高陵区	Gaoling	11.49	36.60	24.20	18.10	18.50	6252	1016
鄠邑区	Huyi	19.07	63.83	20.32	32.68	31.15	8252	2066
蓝田县	Lantian	19.52	65.61	18.16	34.07	31.54	3194	4308
周至县	Zhouzhi	18.61	69.81	16.22	36.76	33.05	6809	3905

注：本表均为公安年报数据，为西安原口径数据。总户数未机械配平。

4-5 全市及各区县常住人口数和人口变动情况（2019年）

Permanent Population and Population Changes by Region（2019）

区 县	Region	常住人口（万人） Permanent Population (10 000 persons)	城镇 Urban	出生率（‰） Birth Rate（‰）	死亡率（‰） Death Rate（‰）	自然增长率（‰） Natural Growth Rate（‰）
全 市	**Total**	**1020.35**	**761.28**	**12.32**	**5.53**	**6.79**
新城区	Xincheng	64.72	64.72	9.21	3.72	5.49
碑林区	Beilin	68.77	68.77	11.17	4.21	6.96
莲湖区	Lianhu	78.33	78.33	10.96	3.97	6.99
灞桥区	Baqiao	70.39	67.03	12.88	5.64	7.24
未央区	Weiyang	82.73	80.60	12.97	5.51	7.46
雁塔区	Yanta	138.53	138.53	12.19	4.61	7.58
阎良区	Yanliang	30.45	17.63	11.25	5.65	5.60
临潼区	Lintong	70.04	24.79	11.96	5.78	6.18
长安区	Chang'an	106.42	65.41	13.56	7.05	6.51
高陵区	Gaoling	36.71	23.89	13.15	5.98	7.17
鄠邑区	Huyi	56.46	24.21	13.12	6.31	6.81
蓝田县	Lantian	53.61	18.24	13.75	7.22	6.53
周至县	Zhouzhi	59.29	20.46	13.45	7.33	6.12
西咸新区	Xixian	103.90	68.67	12.45	5.58	6.87

注：本表数据均为人口变动抽样调查推算数据。自2017年起常住口径数据含西咸新区。

4-6 主要年份常住人口数

Permanent Population in Representative Years

单位：万人 (10 000 persons)

年 份 Year	年末常住人口 Permanent Population（year-end）	城镇 Urban	乡村 Rural
2000	741.14	450.36	290.78
2005	806.81	510.55	296.26
2006	822.52	530.94	291.58
2007	830.54	548.99	281.55
2008	837.52	565.16	272.36
2009	843.46	581.40	262.06
2010	847.41	584.71	262.70
2011	851.34	596.79	254.55
2012	855.29	611.62	243.67
2013	858.81	618.77	240.04
2014	862.75	626.44	236.31
2015	870.56	635.68	234.88
2016	883.21	648.54	234.67
2017	961.67	706.06	255.61
2018	1000.37	740.37	260.00
2019	1020.35	761.28	259.07

注：2000年常住人口为普查数据。2010年常住人口为年末常住人口数，根据第六次人口普查数据推算得出。2005-2009、2011-2019年常住人口为人口变动抽样调查推算数据。自2017年起常住口径数据为大西安范围，含西咸新区。

4–7 主要年份社会从业人数

Number of Social Laborers in Representative Years

单位：万人　　　　　　　　　　　　　　　　　　　　　　　　　　　　(10 000 persons)

年　份 Year	合计 Total	一、按城乡分 Grouped by Urban Area and Rural Area					二、按三次产业分 Grouped by Industry		
		1.城镇 Urban	国有经济 State-owned Enterprises	集体经济 Collective Enterprises	其他经济 Others	2.乡村 Village	第一产业 Primary Industry	第二产业 Secondary Industry	第三产业 Tertiary Industry
1985	**296.80**	129.07	96.80	29.07	3.20	167.73	135.89	98.61	62.30
1986	**299.45**	132.82	101.28	28.43	3.11	166.63	127.46	100.61	71.38
1987	**312.16**	138.56	104.58	30.72	3.26	173.60	130.36	107.75	74.05
1988	**327.76**	142.24	106.46	30.73	5.05	185.52	138.87	108.12	80.77
1989	**332.65**	145.65	108.80	30.44	6.41	187.00	142.21	106.40	84.04
1990	**343.06**	147.93	110.95	29.78	7.20	195.13	149.64	106.74	86.68
1991	**347.65**	149.48	111.87	29.80	7.81	198.17	152.24	108.19	87.22
1992	**357.51**	151.67	113.19	29.97	8.51	205.84	154.75	110.22	92.54
1993	**363.70**	155.72	112.98	29.77	12.97	207.98	154.02	114.02	95.66
1994	**364.56**	154.88	113.39	27.97	13.52	209.68	153.51	108.53	102.52
1995	**372.60**	158.80	113.79	25.58	19.43	213.80	153.39	109.67	109.54
1996	**379.29**	164.54	113.29	24.82	26.43	214.75	153.43	109.17	116.69
1997	**385.14**	169.52	112.44	23.52	33.56	215.62	153.23	109.46	122.45
1998	**393.95**	177.20	106.06	21.50	49.64	216.75	153.00	110.45	130.50
1999	**400.43**	180.27	105.08	20.50	54.69	220.16	154.64	110.58	135.21
2000	**389.10**	176.45	103.46	18.40	54.59	212.65	147.03	107.26	134.81
2001	**389.30**	177.94	100.47	17.10	60.37	211.36	145.09	108.96	135.25
2002	**397.16**	181.85	100.54	16.90	64.41	215.31	143.04	111.62	142.50
2003	**404.92**	183.23	94.51	16.78	71.94	221.69	146.67	109.09	149.16
2004	**409.57**	187.53	93.43	15.41	78.69	222.04	141.81	111.70	156.06
2005	**415.83**	192.53	93.27	14.47	84.79	223.30	136.31	114.20	165.32
2006	**422.15**	196.16	84.46	14.41	97.29	225.99	135.10	116.09	170.96
2007	**436.36**	214.27	90.58	11.88	111.81	222.09	133.33	125.06	177.97
2008	**448.05**	224.20	90.17	10.60	123.43	223.85	127.87	130.23	189.95
2009	**462.52**	239.39	90.83	7.63	140.93	223.13	122.13	131.57	208.82
2010	**477.58**	252.54	94.01	5.48	153.05	225.04	117.27	145.40	214.91
2011	**495.99**	265.43	91.62	5.33	168.48	230.56	121.05	151.33	223.61
2012	**514.57**	287.65	95.33	5.10	187.22	226.92	114.92	162.35	237.30
2013	**530.71**	308.04	86.06	7.29	214.69	222.67	110.45	151.50	268.76
2014	**532.92**	316.59	84.83	6.67	225.09	216.33	105.02	151.85	276.05
2015	**528.06**	327.68	84.52	5.29	237.87	200.38	107.68	129.51	290.87
2016	**539.18**	335.07	87.15	4.85	243.07	204.11	105.12	127.88	306.18
2017	**596.21**	370.33	86.06	4.46	279.81	225.88	113.17	135.52	347.52
2018	**621.22**	398.23	80.83	3.53	313.87	222.99	101.25	154.02	365.95
2019	**645.86**	421.75	75.84	3.28	342.63	224.11	101.37	164.54	379.95

注：第一产业从业人员中包括城镇农林牧渔及服务业企业人员。

4-8 按国民经济行业分从业人数（2019年）

单位：万人

行　业	Sector	合计 Total
总计	**Total**	**645.86**
（一）农、林、牧、渔业	Agriculture ,Forestry,Animal Husbandry and Fishery	101.37
（二）采矿业	Mining	2.13
（三）制造业	Manufacturing	86.47
（四）电力、热力、燃气及水生产和供应业	Production and Supply of Electricity,Gas,Heat and Water	6.80
（五）建筑业	Construction	69.13
（六）批发和零售业	Wholesale and Retail Trades	96.19
（七）交通运输、仓储和邮政业	Traffic,Transport,Storage and Post	38.02
（八）住宿和餐饮业	Hotels and Catering Services	51.14
（九）信息传输、软件和信息技术服务业	Information Transmission,Software and Information Technology Services	15.10
（十）金融业	Financial Intermediation	17.00
（十一）房地产业	Real Estate	17.49
（十二）租赁和商务服务业	Leasing and Business Services	24.67
（十三）科学研究和技术服务业	Scientific Research and Technical Services	16.23
（十四）水利、环境和公共设施管理业	Management of Water Conservancy, Environment and Public Facilities	3.83
（十五）居民服务、修理和其他服务业	Services to Households, Repairs and Other Services	26.19
（十六）教育	Education	32.49
（十七）卫生和社会工作	Health and Social Work	21.86
（十八）文化、体育和娱乐业	Culture, Sports and Entertainment	5.14
（十九）公共管理、社会保障和社会组织	Public Administration, Social Security and Social Organizations	14.61
（二十）国际组织	International Organizations	

Number of Employed Persons Grouped by Industry of the National Economy (2019)

(10 000 persons)

国有经济 State-owned Enterprises	集体经济 Collective Enterprises	城镇其他经济 Urban Other Enterprises	城镇私营经济及个体劳动者 Urban Private Enterprises and Individual Labors	乡村从业人员 Rural Employed Persons
75.84	**3.28**	**132.20**	**210.43**	**224.11**
0.28		0.04	3.22	97.83
		1.27	0.87	
12.04	0.22	30.47	27.47	16.26
2.99		2.85	0.96	
1.27	1.60	20.63	27.54	18.08
0.73	0.13	10.14	63.18	22.01
11.21	0.12	5.45	9.16	12.08
0.22	0.02	4.88	33.17	12.85
0.09		10.64	3.38	0.99
1.96	0.03	13.44	0.74	0.83
0.48	0.10	8.57	8.35	
0.95	0.56	5.09	8.32	9.75
5.87	0.08	6.14	3.36	0.79
1.22		1.70	0.91	
0.33	0.10	0.42	11.65	13.69
14.55	0.18	6.62	3.40	7.74
7.64	0.12	2.40	1.95	9.75
1.08	0.01	1.34	2.71	
12.93	0.01	0.11	0.09	1.46

4-9 城镇非私营单位从业人员情况（2019年）

单位：人

分　组	Classify	单位从业人员 Employed Persons	女性 Female
总计	**Total**	**2113143**	**839720**
一、按机构类型分组	**Grouped by Organization Type**		
#企业	Enterprises	1653422	593126
事业	Public Institutions	290193	167706
机关	Government Units	112874	37398
二、按国民经济行业分组	**Grouped by Economic Sector**		
（一）农、林、牧、渔业	Agriculture ,Forestry,Animal Husbandry and Fishery	3144	938
（二）采矿业	Mining	12650	2993
（三）制造业	Manufacturing	427337	132698
（四）电力、热力、燃气及水生产和供应业	Production and Supply of Electricity,Gas,Heat and Water	58426	17800
（五）建筑业	Construction	235075	35852
（六）批发和零售业	Wholesale and Retail Trades	109979	57177
（七）交通运输、仓储和邮政业	Traffic,Transport,Storage and Post	167794	44508
（八）住宿和餐饮业	Hotels and Catering Services	51194	30254
（九）信息传输、软件和信息技术服务业	Information Transmission,Software and Information Technology Services	107344	39808
（十）金融业	Financial Intermediation	154288	97671
（十一）房地产业	Real Estate	91454	37596
（十二）租赁和商务服务业	Leasing and Business Services	66020	26986
（十三）科学研究和技术服务业	Scientific Research and Technical Services	120877	36002
（十四）水利、环境和公共设施管理业	Management of Water Conservancy, Environment and Public Facilities	29182	11813
（十五）居民服务、修理和其他服务业	Services to Households, Repairs and Other Services	8501	4228
（十六）教育	Education	213432	135115
（十七）卫生和社会工作	Health and Social Work	101653	73221
（十八）文化、体育和娱乐业	Culture, Sports and Entertainment	24291	11460
（十九）公共管理、社会保障和社会组织	Public Administration, Social Security and Social Organizations	130502	43600
（二十）国际组织	International Organizations		

注：自2018年开始，表名中“全部单位”改为“城镇非私营单位”。下同。

Basic Facts on Employees in Urban Non-Private Units（2019）

(person)

在岗职工合计 Total Fully Employed Staff and Workers	其他从业人员 Other Employed Persons	单位从业人员平均人数 Average Employment	在岗职工合计 Staff and Workers	其他从业人员 Other Employed Persons
1921379	**191764**	**2157393**	**1965404**	**191989**
1485730	167692	1704229	1536055	168174
277682	12511	286155	273555	12600
103996	8878	111488	102743	8745
3075	69	3157	3088	69
11922	728	16096	15326	770
417765	9572	474028	465058	8970
57202	1224	67521	66216	1305
206279	28796	231055	200230	30825
105516	4463	110260	105381	4879
163834	3960	166832	162366	4466
46195	4999	51005	45351	5654
106288	1056	108505	107770	735
66553	87735	148254	63962	84292
88533	2921	91968	88712	3256
49927	16093	68255	51277	16978
117383	3494	119576	116021	3555
27271	1911	30673	28749	1924
8357	144	9055	8908	147
204397	9035	208163	199509	8654
97584	4069	98785	94744	4041
22814	1477	25092	23549	1543
120484	10018	129113	119187	9926

4-10 城镇国有单位从业人员情况（2019年）

单位：人

分　组	Classify	单位从业人员 Employed Persons	女性 Female
总计	**Total**	**758381**	**312903**
一、按机构类型分组	**Grouped by Organization Type**		
#企业	Enterprises	368175	115609
事业	Public Institutions	275456	158762
机关	Government Units	112137	37049
二、按国民经济行业分组	**Grouped by Economic Sector**		
（一）农、林、牧、渔业	Agriculture ,Forestry,Animal Husbandry and Fishery	2764	796
（二）采矿业	Mining		
（三）制造业	Manufacturing	120445	37750
（四）电力、热力、燃气及水生产和供应业	Production and Distribution of Electricity,Gas and Water	29903	8885
（五）建筑业	Construction	12670	2204
（六）批发和零售业	Wholesale and Retail Trades	7340	4186
（七）交通运输、仓储和邮政业	Traffic,Transport,Storage and Post	112115	27247
（八）住宿和餐饮业	Hotels and Catering Services	2160	1307
（九）信息传输、软件和信息技术服务业	Information Transmission,Software and Information Technology Services	892	320
（十）金融业	Financial Intermediation	19589	10707
（十一）房地产业	Real Estate	4773	1646
（十二）租赁和商务服务业	Leasing and Business Services	9532	4032
（十三）科学研究和技术服务业	Scientific Research and Technical Services	58712	18184
（十四）水利、环境和公共设施管理业	Management of Water Conservancy, Environment and Public Facilities	12187	5021
（十五）居民服务、修理和其他服务业	Services to Households, Repairs and Other Services	3336	1518
（十六）教育	Education	145452	85926
（十七）卫生和社会工作	Health and Social Work	76424	54994
（十八）文化、体育和娱乐业	Culture, Sports and Entertainment	10806	5004
（十九）公共管理、社会保障和社会组织	Public Administration, Social Security and Social Organizations	129281	43176
（二十）国际组织	International Organizations		

Basic Facts on Employees in State-owned Units（2019）

(person)

在岗职工合计 Total Fully Employed Staff and Workers	其他从业人员 Other Employed Persons	单位从业人员平均人数 Average Employment	在岗职工合计 Staff and Workers	其他从业人员 Other Employed Persons
730613	**27768**	**791935**	**764378**	**27557**
360825	7350	406982	399787	7195
263991	11465	271585	260042	11543
103259	8878	110772	102027	8745
2696	68	2779	2711	68
119380	1065	145749	144878	871
29896	7	39057	39050	7
12325	345	12403	12038	365
7123	217	7460	7244	216
110403	1712	111417	109294	2123
2003	157	2205	2029	176
889	3	936	933	3
17596	1993	21132	19606	1526
4452	321	5159	4763	396
8750	782	10989	10207	782
57720	992	58313	57338	975
10545	1642	13363	11729	1634
3277	59	3938	3879	59
140104	5348	143008	137660	5348
73967	2457	75328	72853	2475
10183	623	10798	10150	648
119304	9977	127901	118016	9885

4-11 城镇集体单位从业人员情况（2019年）

单位：人

分　组	Classify	单位从业人员 Employed Persons	女性 Female
总计	**Total**	**32792**	**8140**
一、按机构类型分组	**Grouped by Organization Type**		
#企业	Enterprises	29551	5987
事业	Public Institutions	2707	1751
机关	Government Units	3	1
二、按国民经济行业分组	**Grouped by Economic Sector**		
（一）农、林、牧、渔业	Agriculture ,Forestry,Animal Husbandry and Fishery	7	4
（二）采矿业	Mining		
（三）制造业	Manufacturing	2234	761
（四）电力、热力、燃气及水生产和供应业	Production and Distribution of Electricity,Gas and Water	31	10
（五）建筑业	Construction	16021	1899
（六）批发和零售业	Wholesale and Retail Trades	1283	496
（七）交通运输、仓储和邮政业	Traffic,Transport,Storage and Post	1183	303
（八）住宿和餐饮业	Hotels and Catering Services	198	129
（九）信息传输、软件和信息技术服务业	Information Transmission,Software and Information Technology Services	16	4
（十）金融业	Financial Intermediation	298	72
（十一）房地产业	Real Estate	963	323
（十二）租赁和商务服务业	Leasing and Business Services	5570	1261
（十三）科学研究和技术服务业	Scientific Research and Technical Services	725	310
（十四）水利、环境和公共设施管理业	Management of Water Conservancy, Environment and Public Facilities	4	1
（十五）居民服务、修理和其他服务业	Services to Households, Repairs and Other Services	993	323
（十六）教育	Education	1829	1305
（十七）卫生和社会工作	Health and Social Work	1231	870
（十八）文化、体育和娱乐业	Culture, Sports and Entertainment	94	42
（十九）公共管理、社会保障和社会组织	Public Administration, Social Security and Social Organizations	112	27
（二十）国际组织	International Organizations		

Basic Facts on Employees in Urban Collective-owned Units（2019）

(person)

在岗职工合计 Total Fully Employed Staff and Workers	其他从业人员 Other Employed Persons	单位从业人员 平均人数 Average Employment	在岗职工合计 Staff and Workers	其他从业人员 Other Employed Persons
31378	**1414**	**32340**	**30955**	**1385**
28313	1238	29101	27892	1209
2539	168	2706	2538	168
3		3	3	
7		7	7	
2034	200	2253	2058	195
31		31	31	
15432	589	15417	14849	568
1112	171	1289	1118	171
1141	42	1175	1134	41
163	35	198	164	34
16		12	12	
298		290	290	
830	133	961	829	132
5544	26	5706	5680	26
677	48	735	687	48
4		4	4	
993		998	998	
1740	89	1823	1734	89
1158	73	1235	1162	73
91	3	94	91	3
107	5	112	107	5

4-12 城镇非私营其他经济类型单位从业人员情况（2019年）

单位：人

分 组	Classify	单位从业人员 Employed Persons	女性 Female
总计	**Total**	**1321970**	**518677**
一、按机构类型分组	**Grouped by Organization Type**		
#企业	Enterprises	1255696	471530
事业	Public Institutions	12030	7193
机关	Government Units	734	348
二、按国民经济行业分组	**Grouped by Economic Sector**		
（一）农、林、牧、渔业	Agriculture ,Forestry,Animal Husbandry and Fishery	373	138
（二）采矿业	Mining	12650	2993
（三）制造业	Manufacturing	304658	94187
（四）电力、热力、燃气及水生产和供应业	Production and Supply of Electricity,Gas,Heat and Water	28492	8905
（五）建筑业	Construction	206384	31749
（六）批发和零售业	Wholesale and Retail Trades	101356	52495
（七）交通运输、仓储和邮政业	Traffic,Transport,Storage and Post	54496	16958
（八）住宿和餐饮业	Hotels and Catering Services	48836	28818
（九）信息传输、软件和信息技术服务业	Information Transmission,Software and Information Technology Services	106436	39484
（十）金融业	Financial Intermediation	134401	86892
（十一）房地产业	Real Estate	85718	35627
（十二）租赁和商务服务业	Leasing and Business Services	50918	21693
（十三）科学研究和技术服务业	Scientific Research and Technical Services	61440	17508
（十四）水利、环境和公共设施管理业	Management of Water Conservancy, Environment and Public Facilities	16991	6791
（十五）居民服务、修理和其他服务业	Services to Households, Repairs and Other Services	4172	2387
（十六）教育	Education	66151	47884
（十七）卫生和社会工作	Health and Social Work	23998	17357
（十八）文化、体育和娱乐业	Culture, Sports and Entertainment	13391	6414
（十九）公共管理、社会保障和社会组织	Public Administration, Social Security and Social Organizations	1109	397
（二十）国际组织	International Organizations		

Basic Facts on Employees in Urban Non-Private Other Units (2019)

(person)

在岗职工合计 Total Fully Employed Staff and Workers	其他从业人员 Other Employed Persons	单位从业人员 平均人数 Average Employment	在岗职工合计 Staff and Workers	其他从业人员 Other Employed Persons
1159388	**162582**	**1333118**	**1170071**	**163047**
1096592	159104	1268146	1108375	159771
11152	878	11864	10975	889
734		713	713	
372	1	371	370	1
11922	728	16096	15326	770
296351	8307	326026	318122	7904
27275	1217	28433	27135	1298
178522	27862	203235	173343	29892
97281	4075	101511	97019	4492
52290	2206	54240	51938	2302
44029	4807	48602	43158	5444
105383	1053	107557	106825	732
48659	85742	126832	44066	82766
83251	2467	85848	83120	2728
35633	15285	51560	35390	16170
58986	2454	60528	57996	2532
16722	269	17306	17016	290
4087	85	4119	4031	88
62553	3598	63332	60115	3217
22459	1539	22222	20729	1493
12540	851	14200	13308	892
1073	36	1100	1064	36

4-13 主要年份城镇非私营单位分行业从业人员年平均工资

单位：元

分　组	Classify	2010	2011
总计	**Grouped by Economic Sector**	**37870**	**41679**
（一）农、林、牧、渔业	Agriculture ,Forestry,Animal Husbandry and Fishery	21436	23567
（二）采矿业	Mining	32154	38551
（三）制造业	Manufacturing	26663	34698
（四）电力、热力、燃气及水生产和供应业	Production and Distribution of Electricity,Gas and Water	39508	47705
（五）建筑业	Construction	26875	29773
（六）批发和零售业	Wholesale and Retail Trades	25103	27996
（七）交通运输、仓储和邮政业	Traffic,Transport,Storage and Post	41737	48231
（八）住宿和餐饮业	Hotels and Catering Services	19647	22925
（九）信息传输、软件和信息技术服务业	Information Transmission,Software and Information Technology Services	45904	51135
（十）金融业	Financial Intermediation	63952	72195
（十一）房地产业	Real Estate	45273	34626
（十二）租赁和商务服务业	Leasing and Business Services	30267	31549
（十三）科学研究和技术服务业	Scientific Research and Technical Services	55456	64448
（十四）水利、环境和公共设施管理业	Management of Water Conservancy, Environment and Public Facilities	25322	26009
（十五）居民服务、修理和其他服务业	Services to Households, Repairs and Other Services	26443	23993
（十六）教育	Education	53084	54442
（十七）卫生和社会工作	Health and Social Work	44035	48836
（十八）文化、体育和娱乐业	Culture, Sports and Entertainment	31925	34717
（十九）公共管理、社会保障和社会组织	Public Administration, Social Security and Social Organizations	39964	42163
（二十）国际组织	International Organizations		

Average Wages of Urban Non-private Employees by Industry in Representative Years

(yuan)

2012	2013	2014	2015	2016	2017	2018	2019
44533	**49350**	**54573**	**60557**	**67205**	**75262**	**83821**	**92359**
31846	36658	42881	43426	48626	52020	72890	81373
33489	40605	42116	46645	108827	118026	99400	106393
38957	44321	49482	56686	61434	66067	73733	80703
55409	59955	61252	65887	69092	77674	70021	75545
35828	39507	48275	52783	60475	68025	73963	81621
34382	37362	40915	46203	48210	55793	62362	68787
48760	54147	59189	62816	63583	69469	88547	97746
26637	29497	30914	33746	37507	41147	42970	46523
63328	67495	100550	109448	137210	142407	150081	167240
75652	97140	104433	106807	108569	114884	108643	114753
37567	44832	48120	52423	56979	57970	65726	72780
34291	42109	46828	52637	54395	53474	54940	62628
68274	69951	69958	72731	79539	86199	103604	118277
29938	38429	43033	45356	44062	48277	54127	59967
25103	32066	32478	37019	35721	35979	56707	62097
54581	59143	58451	63761	71635	86672	98158	103991
56764	61602	59892	61623	74797	86521	99523	108493
40833	50201	57239	61561	65974	70202	74588	81117
47691	49893	47000	51681	59437	77660	84567	90877

4-14 主要年份城镇非私营单位从业人数及工资总额

Number of Urban Non-Private Employees and Remuneration in Representative Years

年 份 year	单位从业人员（万人） Number of Employed Persons (10 000 persons)	从业人员工资总额（亿元） Remuneration of Employed Persons (100mil. yuan)	城镇非私营单位从业人员年平均工资（元） Annual Average Wage of Employees in Urban Non-private Units(yuan)	城镇国有单位从业人员年平均工资（元） Annual Average Wage of Employees in State-owned Units(yuan)	城镇集体单位从业人员年平均工资（元） Annual Average Wage of Employees in Urban Collective Units(yuan)	城镇非私营其它经济类型单位从业人员年平均工资（元） Average Wages of Urban Non-private Basic Facts on Employees in other Units(yuan)
1978	93.56	6.28	688	705	609	
1980	103.09	8.17	818	849	699	
1985	127.04	14.17	1148	1215	923	1409
1986	132.78	16.87	1311	1388	1048	1659
1987	135.48	19.13	1446	1544	1107	1583
1988	137.56	22.81	1702	1842	1216	2065
1989	139.86	25.64	1873	2010	1385	2188
1990	141.55	29.48	2133	2290	1545	2044
1991	142.86	26.88	2276	2435	1657	2966
1992	144.51	30.80	2545	2758	1709	3504
1993	146.03	43.25	2999	3274	1910	3551
1994	142.37	58.87	4172	4588	2337	5243
1995	141.17	67.23	4763	5168	2837	5863
1996	140.60	75.64	5407	5858	3216	6225
1997	138.89	80.83	5785	6204	3437	7487
1998	138.78	82.85	6900	7445	3964	6942
1999	115.88	90.13	7764	8238	4374	8217
2000	112.45	103.80	9179	9742	5178	9451
2001	113.93	123.12	10786	11570	5431	10781
2002	115.77	138.88	12138	12877	6230	12543
2003	116.68	155.95	13504	14217	6892	14215
2004	118.15	184.63	15473	15994	7428	17030
2005	123.66	215.67	17728	18420	7612	19066
2006	125.10	250.87	20475	21392	8494	21859
2007	129.40	319.23	25012	25696	9768	27400
2008	130.85	379.29	29749	30246	10834	33344
2009	135.64	450.48	34032	34611	11940	37307
2010	140.38	520.88	37870	38122	12505	40721
2011	154.33	658.73	41679	45217	23241	37643
2012	165.59	770.86	44533	47493	29988	41218
2013	198.42	1031.46	49350	52782	34591	47462
2014	199.41	1151.53	54573	54138	41006	55766
2015	198.46	1255.75	60557	60301	43291	61590
2016	199.19	1358.95	67205	66295	48098	68847
2017	202.29	1542.35	75262	76682	54755	74999
2018	196.23	1677.57	83821	87096	53048	82239
2019	211.31	1992.54	92359	101187	49998	88142

注：因1989年以前，西安市行政区划有几次调整，本表按1989年西安行政区划对1989年前的历史数据进行了调整。

4-15 城镇非私营单位从业人员工资总额（2019年）

Total Wages of Urban Non-Private Units Employees（2019）

单位：万元 （10 000yuan）

分 组	Classify	单 位 从业人员 工资总额 Total Wages of Employment	在岗职工 工资总额 Total Wages of Employed Staff and Workers
总计	**Total**	**19925425**	**19038357**
一、按机构类型分组	**Grouped by Organization Type**		
#企业	Enterprises	15432814	14641052
事业	Public Institutions	3158462	3104252
机关	Government Units	1030430	1002517
二、按国民经济行业分组	**Grouped by Economic Sector**		
（一）农、林、牧、渔业	Agriculture ,Forestry,Animal Husbandry and Fishery	25689	25524
（二）采矿业	Mining	171250	165216
（三）制造业	Manufacturing	3825539	3776581
（四）电力、热力、燃气及水生产和供应业	Production and Supply of Electricity, Gas,Heat and Water	510090	506201
（五）建筑业	Construction	1885894	1688059
（六）批发和零售业	Wholesale and Retail Trades	758442	731777
（七）交通运输、仓储和邮政业	Traffic,Transport,Storage and Post	1630720	1599083
（八）住宿和餐饮业	Hotels and Catering Services	237289	224146
（九）信息传输、软件和信息技术服务业	Information Transmission,Software and Information Technology Services	1814639	1809979
（十）金融业	Financial Intermediation	1701260	1362075
（十一）房地产业	Real Estate	669343	654855
（十二）租赁和商务服务业	Leasing and Business Services	427469	362729
（十三）科学研究和技术服务业	Scientific Research and Technical Services	1414312	1392923
（十四）水利、环境和公共设施管理业	Management of Water Conservancy, Environment and Public Facilities	183936	177815
（十五）居民服务、修理和其他服务业	Services to Households, Repairs and Other Services	56229	55889
（十六）教育	Education	2164698	2118169
（十七）卫生和社会工作	Health and Social Work	1071747	1053165
（十八）文化、体育和娱乐业	Culture, Sports and Entertainment	203540	193487
（十九）公共管理、社会保障和社会组织	Public Administration, Social Security and Social Organizations	1173342	1140684
（二十）国际组织	International Organizations		

4-15 续表 continued

单位：万元 (10 000 yuan)

分 组	Classify	其他从业人员工资总额 Remuneration of Other Employed Persons	从业人员年平均工资（元） Average Wages of Employees (yuan)
总计	**Total**	**887068**	**92359**
一、按机构类型分组	**Grouped by Organization Type**		
#企业	Enterprises	791762	90556
事业	Public Institutions	54210	110376
机关	Government Units	27913	92425
二、按国民经济行业分组	**Grouped by Economic Sector**		
（一）农、林、牧、渔业	Agriculture ,Forestry,Animal Husbandry and Fishery	165	81373
（二）采矿业	Mining	6034	106393
（三）制造业	Manufacturing	48958	80703
（四）电力、热力、燃气及水生产和供应业	Production and Supply of Electricity, Gas,Heat and Water	3889	75545
（五）建筑业	Construction	197835	81621
（六）批发和零售业	Wholesale and Retail Trades	26665	68787
（七）交通运输、仓储和邮政业	Traffic,Transport,Storage and Post	31637	97746
（八）住宿和餐饮业	Hotels and Catering Services	13143	46523
（九）信息传输、软件和信息技术服务业	Information Transmission,Software and Information Technology Services	4660	167240
（十）金融业	Financial Intermediation	339185	114753
（十一）房地产业	Real Estate	14488	72780
（十二）租赁和商务服务业	Leasing and Business Services	64740	62628
（十三）科学研究和技术服务业	Scientific Research and Technical Services	21389	118277
（十四）水利、环境和公共设施管理业	Management of Water Conservancy, Environment and Public Facilities	6121	59967
（十五）居民服务、修理和其他服务业	Services to Households, Repairs and Other Services	340	62097
（十六）教育	Education	46529	103991
（十七）卫生和社会工作	Health and Social Work	18582	108493
（十八）文化、体育和娱乐业	Culture, Sports and Entertainment	10053	81117
（十九）公共管理、社会保障和社会组织	Public Administration, Social Security and Social Organizations	32658	90877
（二十）国际组织	International Organizations		

4-16 城镇国有单位从业人员工资总额（2019年）

Total Average of Urban State-owned Units Employees（2019）

单位：万元 （10 000yuan）

分组	Classify	单位从业人员工资总额 Total Wages of Employment	在岗职工工资总额 Total Wages of Employed Staff and Workers
总计	**Total**	**8013371**	**7894969**
一、按机构类型分组	**Grouped by Organization Type**		
#企业	Enterprises	3940533	3898447
事业	Public Institutions	3022419	2974444
机关	Government Units	1024839	996926
二、按国民经济行业分组	**Grouped by Economic Sector**		
（一）农、林、牧、渔业	Agriculture ,Forestry,Animal Husbandry and Fishery	23097	22934
（二）采矿业	Mining		
（三）制造业	Manufacturing	1235548	1231246
（四）电力、热力、燃气及水生产和供应业	Production and Distribution of Electricity, Gas and Water	250000	249979
（五）建筑业	Construction	85802	83372
（六）批发和零售业	Wholesale and Retail Trades	55052	54166
（七）交通运输、仓储和邮政业	Traffic,Transport,Storage and Post	1162201	1142210
（八）住宿和餐饮业	Hotels and Catering Services	10474	9639
（九）信息传输、软件和信息技术服务业	Information Transmission,Software and Information Technology Services	10553	10533
（十）金融业	Financial Intermediation	391296	388597
（十一）房地产业	Real Estate	33525	32420
（十二）租赁和商务服务业	Leasing and Business Services	79199	75969
（十三）科学研究和技术服务业	Scientific Research and Technical Services	660527	654490
（十四）水利、环境和公共设施管理业	Management of Water Conservancy, Environment and Public Facilities	78817	74063
（十五）居民服务、修理和其他服务业	Services to Households, Repairs and Other Services	33191	33129
（十六）教育	Education	1750219	1726130
（十七）卫生和社会工作	Health and Social Work	893235	882186
（十八）文化、体育和娱乐业	Culture, Sports and Entertainment	96906	92683
（十九）公共管理、社会保障和社会组织	Public Administration, Social Security and Social Organizations	1163730	1131222
（二十）国际组织	International Organizations		

4-16 续表 continued

单位：万元 (10 000yuan)

分 组	Classify	其他从业人员工资总额 Remuneration of Other Employed Persons	从业人员年平均工资（元） Average Wages of Employees (yuan)
总计	**Total**	**118402**	**101187**
一、按机构类型分组	**Grouped by Organization Type**		
#企业	Enterprises	42086	96823
事业	Public Institutions	47975	111288
机关	Government Units	27913	92518
二、按国民经济行业分组	**Grouped by Economic Sector**		
（一）农、林、牧、渔业	Agriculture ,Forestry,Animal Husbandry and Fishery	163	83111
（二）采矿业	Mining		
（三）制造业	Manufacturing	4302	84772
（四）电力、热力、燃气及水生产和供应业	Production and Distribution of Electricity, Gas and Water	21	64009
（五）建筑业	Construction	2430	69179
（六）批发和零售业	Wholesale and Retail Trades	886	73797
（七）交通运输、仓储和邮政业	Traffic,Transport,Storage and Post	19991	104311
（八）住宿和餐饮业	Hotels and Catering Services	835	47502
（九）信息传输、软件和信息技术服务业	Information Transmission,Software and Information Technology Services	20	112741
（十）金融业	Financial Intermediation	2699	185168
（十一）房地产业	Real Estate	1105	64983
（十二）租赁和商务服务业	Leasing and Business Services	3230	72071
（十三）科学研究和技术服务业	Scientific Research and Technical Services	6037	113273
（十四）水利、环境和公共设施管理业	Management of Water Conservancy, Environment and Public Facilities	4754	58982
（十五）居民服务、修理和其他服务业	Services to Households, Repairs and Other Services	62	84285
（十六）教育	Education	24089	122386
（十七）卫生和社会工作	Health and Social Work	11049	118579
（十八）文化、体育和娱乐业	Culture, Sports and Entertainment	4223	89744
（十九）公共管理、社会保障和社会组织	Public Administration, Social Security and Social Organizations	32508	90987
（二十）国际组织	International Organizations		

4-17 城镇集体单位从业人员工资总额（2019年）

Total Average of Basic Facts on Employees in Urban Collective-owned Units（2019）

单位：万元 （10 000yuan）

分 组	Classify	单 位 从业人员 工资总额 Total Wages of Employment	在岗职工 工资总额 Total Wages of Employed Staff and Workers
总计	**Total**	**161695**	**156760**
一、按机构类型分组	**Grouped by Organization Type**		
#企业	Enterprises	139391	135053
事业	Public Institutions	20673	20098
机关	Government Units	21	21
二、按国民经济行业分组	**Grouped by Economic Sector**		
（一）农、林、牧、渔业	Agriculture ,Forestry,Animal Husbandry and Fishery	47	47
（二）采矿业	Mining		
（三）制造业	Manufacturing	9005	8352
（四）电力、热力、燃气及水生产和供应业	Production and Distribution of Electricity, Gas and Water	137	137
（五）建筑业	Construction	72638	70299
（六）批发和零售业	Wholesale and Retail Trades	5075	4533
（七）交通运输、仓储和邮政业	Traffic,Transport,Storage and Post	6555	6530
（八）住宿和餐饮业	Hotels and Catering Services	784	655
（九）信息传输、软件和信息技术服务业	Information Transmission,Software and Information Technology Services	56	56
（十）金融业	Financial Intermediation	6019	6019
（十一）房地产业	Real Estate	4366	3976
（十二）租赁和商务服务业	Leasing and Business Services	24519	24451
（十三）科学研究和技术服务业	Scientific Research and Technical Services	6200	5973
（十四）水利、环境和公共设施管理业	Management of Water Conservancy, Environment and Public Facilities	21	21
（十五）居民服务、修理和其他服务业	Services to Households, Repairs and Other Services	4226	4226
（十六）教育	Education	13077	12730
（十七）卫生和社会工作	Health and Social Work	7803	7600
（十八）文化、体育和娱乐业	Culture, Sports and Entertainment	515	508
（十九）公共管理、社会保障和社会组织	Public Administration, Social Security and Social Organizations	654	648
（二十）国际组织	International Organizations		

4-17 续表 continued

单位：万元 (10 000 yuan)

分组	Classify	其他从业人员工资总额 Remuneration of Other Employed Persons	从业人员年平均工资（元） Average Wages of Employees (yuan)
总计	**Total**	**4935**	**49998**
一、按机构类型分组	**Grouped by Organization Type**		
#企业	Enterprises	4338	47899
事业	Public Institutions	575	76397
机关	Government Units		68333
二、按国民经济行业分组	**Grouped by Economic Sector**		
（一）农、林、牧、渔业	Agriculture ,Forestry,Animal Husbandry and Fishery		66857
（二）采矿业	Mining		
（三）制造业	Manufacturing	653	39969
（四）电力、热力、燃气及水生产和供应业	Production and Distribution of Electricity, Gas and Water		44097
（五）建筑业	Construction	2339	47115
（六）批发和零售业	Wholesale and Retail Trades	542	39371
（七）交通运输、仓储和邮政业	Traffic,Transport,Storage and Post	25	55791
（八）住宿和餐饮业	Hotels and Catering Services	129	39606
（九）信息传输、软件和信息技术服务业	Information Transmission,Software and Information Technology Services		46750
（十）金融业	Financial Intermediation		207548
（十一）房地产业	Real Estate	390	45431
（十二）租赁和商务服务业	Leasing and Business Services	68	42971
（十三）科学研究和技术服务业	Scientific Research and Technical Services	227	84348
（十四）水利、环境和公共设施管理业	Management of Water Conservancy, Environment and Public Facilities		52000
（十五）居民服务、修理和其他服务业	Services to Households, Repairs and Other Services		42340
（十六）教育	Education	347	71731
（十七）卫生和社会工作	Health and Social Work	203	63181
（十八）文化、体育和娱乐业	Culture, Sports and Entertainment	7	54819
（十九）公共管理、社会保障和社会组织	Public Administration, Social Security and Social Organizations	6	58384
（二十）国际组织	International Organizations		

4-18 城镇非私营其他经济类型单位从业人员工资总额（2019年）

Average Wages of Urban Non-private Basic Facts on Employees in other Units (2019)

单位：万元 (10 000yuan)

分组	Classify	单位从业人员工资总额 Total Wages of Employment	在岗职工工资总额 Total Wages of Employed Staff and Workers
总计	**Total**	**11750360**	**10986628**
一、按机构类型分组	**Grouped by Organization Type**		
#企业	Enterprises	11352890	10607552
事业	Public Institutions	115370	109710
机关	Government Units	5570	5570
二、按国民经济行业分组	**Grouped by Economic Sector**		
（一）农、林、牧、渔业	Agriculture ,Forestry,Animal Husbandry and Fishery	2546	2543
（二）采矿业	Mining	171250	165216
（三）制造业	Manufacturing	2580986	2536983
（四）电力、热力、燃气及水生产和供应业	Production and Distribution of Electricity, Gas and Water	259953	256085
（五）建筑业	Construction	1727455	1534389
（六）批发和零售业	Wholesale and Retail Trades	698314	673078
（七）交通运输、仓储和邮政业	Traffic,Transport,Storage and Post	461964	450343
（八）住宿和餐饮业	Hotels and Catering Services	226031	213851
（九）信息传输、软件和信息技术服务业	Information Transmission,Software and Information Technology Services	1804030	1799389
（十）金融业	Financial Intermediation	1303945	967459
（十一）房地产业	Real Estate	631452	618459
（十二）租赁和商务服务业	Leasing and Business Services	323751	262309
（十三）科学研究和技术服务业	Scientific Research and Technical Services	747585	732461
（十四）水利、环境和公共设施管理业	Management of Water Conservancy, Environment and Public Facilities	105098	103732
（十五）居民服务、修理和其他服务业	Services to Households, Repairs and Other Services	18812	18535
（十六）教育	Education	401403	379309
（十七）卫生和社会工作	Health and Social Work	170710	163379
（十八）文化、体育和娱乐业	Culture, Sports and Entertainment	106119	100296
（十九）公共管理、社会保障和社会组织	Public Administration, Social Security and Social Organizations	8958	8814
（二十）国际组织	International Organizations		

4-18 续表 continued

单位：万元 (10 000 yuan)

分 组	Classify	其他从业人员工资总额 Remuneration of Other Employed Persons	从业人员年平均工资（元） Average Wages of Employees (yuan)
总计	**Total**	**763732**	**88142**
一、按机构类型分组	**Grouped by Organization Type**		
#企业	Enterprises	745338	89524
事业	Public Institutions	5660	97244
机关	Government Units		78121
二、按国民经济行业分组	**Grouped by Economic Sector**		
（一）农、林、牧、渔业	Agriculture ,Forestry,Animal Husbandry and Fishery	3	68623
（二）采矿业	Mining	6034	106393
（三）制造业	Manufacturing	44003	79165
（四）电力、热力、燃气及水生产和供应业	Production and Distribution of Electricity, Gas and Water	3868	91426
（五）建筑业	Construction	193066	84998
（六）批发和零售业	Wholesale and Retail Trades	25236	68792
（七）交通运输、仓储和邮政业	Traffic,Transport,Storage and Post	11621	85170
（八）住宿和餐饮业	Hotels and Catering Services	12180	46506
（九）信息传输、软件和信息技术服务业	Information Transmission,Software and Information Technology Services	4641	167728
（十）金融业	Financial Intermediation	336486	102809
（十一）房地产业	Real Estate	12993	73555
（十二）租赁和商务服务业	Leasing and Business Services	61442	62791
（十三）科学研究和技术服务业	Scientific Research and Technical Services	15124	123511
（十四）水利、环境和公共设施管理业	Management of Water Conservancy, Environment and Public Facilities	1366	60729
（十五）居民服务、修理和其他服务业	Services to Households, Repairs and Other Services	277	45670
（十六）教育	Education	22094	63381
（十七）卫生和社会工作	Health and Social Work	7331	76820
（十八）文化、体育和娱乐业	Culture, Sports and Entertainment	5823	74731
（十九）公共管理、社会保障和社会组织	Public Administration, Social Security and Social Organizations	144	81440
（二十）国际组织	International Organizations		

4-19 主要年份城镇登记失业人数及失业率

Registered Unemployed Persons and Unemployment Rate in Urban Area in Representative Years

年 份 year	城镇登记失业人员数（万人） Real Number of Registered Unemployed Persons (10 000 persons)	城镇登记失业率（%） Registered Unemployment in Urban Area (%)
2002		3.7
2003		4.5
2004	8.29	4.3
2005	8.45	4.3
2006	8.74	4.3
2007	8.77	4.3
2008	9.40	4.2
2009	10.02	4.3
2010	10.46	4.2
2011	10.37	3.9
2012	9.60	3.5
2013	10.13	3.4
2014	10.84	3.4
2015	10.74	3.4
2016	11.29	3.3
2017	11.51	3.3
2018	12.48	3.3
2019	12.52	3.3

注：本表数据由西安市人力资源与社会保障局提供。

主要统计指标解释

人口数 指一定时点、一定地区范围内的有生命的个人的总和。年度统计的年末人口数，指每年12月31日24时的人口数。

常住人口 指实际经常居住在某地区一定时间（半年以上，含半年）的人口。常住人口包括户口在本辖区人也在本辖区居住的人，户口在本辖区之外但在户口登记地半年以上的人，户口待定（无户口和口袋户口）的人，户口在本辖区但离开本辖区半年以下的人。

城镇人口和乡村人口 城镇人口是指居住在城镇范围内的全部常住人口；乡村人口是除上述人口以外的全部人口。

出生率（又称粗出生率） 指在一定时期内（通常为一年）平均每千人所出生的人数的比率，一般用千分率表示。其计算公式为：

出生率＝年出生人数／年平均人数×1000‰

式中：出生人数指活产婴儿，即胎儿脱离母体时（不管怀孕月数），有过呼吸或其他生命现象。年平均人数指年初、年底人口数的平均数，也可用年中人口数代替。

死亡率（又称粗死亡率） 指在一定时期内（通常为一年）一定地区的死亡人数与同期内平均人数（或期中人数）之比，一般用千分率表示。本资料中的死亡率指年死亡率，其计算公式为：

死亡率＝年死亡人数／年平均人数×1000‰

人口自然增长率 指在一定时期内（通常为一年）人口自然增加数（出生人数减死亡人数）与该时期内平均人数（或期中人数）之比，一般用千分率表示。计算公式为：

人口自然增长率＝（本年出生人数—本年死亡人数）／年平均人数×1000‰。

从业人员 指在16周岁及以上，从事一定社会劳动并取得劳动报酬或经营收入的人员。这一指标反映了一定时期内全部劳动力资源的实际利用情况，是研究我国基本国情国力的重要指标。

单位从业人员 指在各级国家机关、政党机关、社会团体及企业、事业单位中工作，取得工资或其他形式的劳动报酬的全部人员。包括在岗职工、再就业的离退休人员、民办教师以及在各单位中工作的外方人员和港澳台方人员、兼职人员、借用的外单位人员和第二职业者。不包括离开本单位仍保留劳动关系的职工。各单位的就业人员反映了各单位实际参加生产或工作的全部劳动力。

城镇私营和个体就业人员 城镇私营就业人员指在工商管理部门注册登记，其经营地址设在县城关镇（含城关镇）以上的私营企业就业人员；包括私营企业投资者和雇工。城镇个体就业人员指在工商管理部门注册登记，并持有城镇户口或在城镇长期居住，经批准从事个体工商经营的就业人员；包括个体经营者和在个体工商户劳动的家庭帮工和雇工。

国有单位 指资产归国家所有的经济组织。包括按《中华人民共和国企业法人登记管理条例》规定登记注册的非公司制的经济组织，以及中央、地方各级国家机关、事业单位和社会团体。

集体单位 指生产资料归集体所有，并按《中华人民共和国企业法人登记管理条例》规定登记注册的经济组织。

其他单位 包括股份合作单位、联营单位、有限责任公司、股份有限公司、港澳台商投资单位以及外商投资单位等其他登记注册类型单位。

在岗职工 指在本单位工作并由单位支付工资的人员，以及有工作岗位，但由于学习、病伤产假等原因暂未工作，仍由单位支付工资的人员。

职工工资总额 指各单位在一定时期内直接支付给本单位全部职工的劳动报酬总额。工资总额的计算原则应以直接支付给职工的全部劳动报酬为根据。各单位支付给职工的劳动报酬以及其他根据有关规定支付的工资，不论是计入成本的还是不计入成本的，不论是按国家规定列入计征奖金税项目的，还是未列入计征奖金税项目的，不论是以货币形式支付的还是以实物形式支付的，均包括在工资总额内。

职工平均工资 指企业、事业、机关单位的职工在一定时期内平均每人所得的货币工资额。它表明一定时期职工工资收入的高低程度，是反映职工工资水平的主要指标。计算公式为：

职工平均工资＝报告期实际支付的全部职工工资总额/报告期全部职工平均人数

城镇登记失业人员 指有非农业户口，在一定的劳动年龄内，有劳动能力，无业而要求就业，并在当地就业服务机构进行求职登记的人员。

城镇登记失业率 指城镇登记失业人数同城镇从业人数与城镇从业人数与城镇登记失业人数之和的比。计算公式为：

$$\text{城镇登记失业率}=\frac{\text{城镇登记失业人数}}{\text{（城镇单位就业人员-使用的农村劳动力-聘用的离退休人员-聘用的港澳台及外方人员）+不在岗职工+城镇私营业主+城镇个体户主+城镇私营企业及个体就业人员+城镇登记失业人数}}\times 100\%$$

Explanatory Notes on Main Statistical Indicators

The annual statistics on total population is taken at midnight, the 31st of December, not including residents in Taiwan province, Hong Kong SAR and Macao SAR and Chinese national residing abroad.

Permanent population refers to the population of actual habitual residence in a certain area six months or over six months. Permanent popul ation include the accounts in this area which are also living in this area, accounts outside this area but with more than half a year of household registration, accounts to be determined including people without accounts or pockets of accounts, and accounts in the area but leaving this area less than six months.

Urban Population and Rural Population Urban population refers to all people residing in cities and towns, while rural population refers to population other than urban population.

Birth Rate (or Crude Birth Rate) refers to the ratio of the number of births to the average population (or mid-period population) during a certain period of time (usually one year), expressed in ‰. Birth rate in the chapter refers to annual birth rate. The following formula is used:

$$\text{Birth Rate}=\frac{\text{Number of Births}}{\text{Annual Average Population}}\times 1000‰$$

Number of births in the formula refers to live births, i.e. when a baby has breathed or showed any vital phenomena regardless of the length of pregnancy.

Annual average population is the average of the number of population at the beginning of the year and that at the end of the year. Sometimes it is substituted by the mid-year population.

Death Rate (or Crude Death Rate) refers to the ratio of the number of deaths to the average population (or mid-period population) during a certain period of time (usually one year), expressed in ‰. Death rate in the chapter refers to annual death rate. The following formula is used:

$$\text{DeathRate}=\frac{\text{Number of Deaths}}{\text{Annual Average Population}}\times 1000‰$$

Natural Growth Rate of Population refers to the ratio of natural increase in population (number of births minus number of deaths) in a certain period of time (usually one year) to the average population (or mid-period population) of the same period, expressed in ‰. The following formula is applied:

Natural Growth Rate of Population =(Number of Births-Number of Deaths)/Annual Average Population× 1000‰

Employed Persons refer to the ones aged 16 and over who are engaged in gainful employment and thus receive remuneration payment or earn business income. This indicator reflects the actual utilization of total labour force during a certain period of time and is often used for the research on China's economic situation and national power.

Persons Employed in Various Units refer to all the persons working in government agencies of various levels, political and party organizations, social organizations, enterprises and institutions, and receiving wages or other forms of payment. They include fully-employed staff and workers, re-employed retirees, teachers in the schools run by the local people, foreigners and Chinese compatriots from Hong Kong, Macao, and Taiwan working in various units, part-time employees, employees of other units working temporarily at current posts, and employees holding the second job, but do not include persons who have left their working units while keeping their labour contract (employment relation) unchanged. This indicator reflects the total number of laborers actually engaged in production or other operations in various units.

Persons Employed in Private Enterprises and Self- Employed Individuals in Urban Areas Persons employed in private enterprises refer to the persons employed in the private enterprises which have been registered at the departments of industrial and commercial administration for which the business operation are situated at a county town (i.e. a town where the county government is located), or at urban areas with administrative hierarchy higher than a county town. The self-employed individuals in urban areas refer to persons who hold the certificates of residence in urban areas or have resided in the urban areas for a long time and have been registered at the departments of industrial and commercial administration and approved to be engaged in individual industrial or commercial business, including self-employed persons as well as helpers and hired labourers who work in individual households.

State–owned Units refer to economic units whose assets are owned by the state, including non-corporation units registered according to Regulation of the People's Republic of China on the Registration of Enterprises and

Corporations, state organs, institutions and social organizations at the central-level and local levels.

Collective-owned Units refer to economic units registered according to Regulation of the People's Republic of China on the Registration of Enterprises and Corporations where the means of production are collectively owned.

Units of Other Types of Ownership refer to units registered with other types of ownership, including cooperative units, joint ownership units, limited liability corporations, share holding corporations, units funded by entrepreneurs from Hong Kong, Macao, and Taiwan, and foreign- funded units.

Employed Staff and Workers refer to persons who work in, and receive wages from their working units, including persons who have their work posts but are temporarily absent from work for reasons of study or on sick, injury or maternal leave and still receive wages from their working units.

Total Wage Bill refers to the total remuneration payment to employed persons in various units during a certain period of time. The calculation of total wage bill is based on the total remuneration payment to employed persons . Therefore, all the wages and salaries and other payments to employed persons are included in the total wage bill regardless of sources, reckoning the cost of production or not, category, listing as items of premium taxation or not, and forms, paying in cash or in kind.

Average Wage refers to the average wage in money terms per person during a certain period of time for employed persons in enterprises, institutions, and government agencies, which reflects the general level of wage income during a certain period of time and is calculated as follows:

$$\text{AverageWage}=\frac{\text{TotalWage Billof Employed Personsat Reference Time}}{\text{Average Number of Persons Employedat Reference Time}}$$

Registered Unemployed Persons in Urban Areas refer to the persons with non-agricultural household registration at certain working ages (16 years old to retirement age), who are capable of working, unemployed and willing to work, and have been registered at the local employment service agencies to apply for a job.

Registered Unemployment Rate in Urban Areas refers to the ratio of the number of the registered unemployed persons to the sum of the number of persons employed in various units (minus the employed rural labour force, re-employed retirees, and Hong Kong, Macao, Taiwan or foreign employees), laid-off staff and workers in urban units, owners of private enterprises in urban areas, owners of self-employed individuals in urban areas, employees of private enterprises in urban areas, employee of self-employed individuals in urban areas, and the registered unemployed persons in urban areas. The formula is as follows:

$$\text{Registered Unemployment rate in urban areas}=\frac{\text{numberof registered urban unemployed persons}}{\begin{array}{c}\text{number of persons employed in urbanunits-employed rurallabour force}\\ \text{re-employed retirees - HongKong, Macao,Taiwan or foreign employees}\\ \text{+ laid-off staff and workers+owners of urban private Enterprises+ owners of}\\ \text{urbanself-employed Individuals + employees ofurbanprivate Enterprises+employees of}\\ \text{urbanself- employed Individuals+ registered unemployed persons in urbanareas}\end{array}}\times 100\%$$

5 固定资产投资

INVESTMENT IN FIXED ASSETS

资料整理：席锋旭 王 峰 张 驰
Data management：Xi Fengxu Wang Feng Zhang Chi
数据审核：陈 英
Data audit：Chen Ying

第五部分　固定资产投资

一、简要说明

1.本章资料反映西安固定资产投资的基本情况、固定资产投资的结构和比例关系、固定资产投资的资金来源及固定资产投资的效果等。主要包括全社会固定资产投资、项目投资、房地产开发投资和农户投资以及分区县、开发区投资情况等。

2.固定资产投资统计的范围包括：城乡建设项目投资、房地产开发投资及农户投资。

3.固定资产投资统计的资料来源主要为国家统计局的全面统计报表。除农户固定资产投资统计采用抽样调查方法外，其他均为全面统计报表。

4.统计口径的变化。

自1997年起，除房地产开发投资、非农户投资、农户投资及城镇和工矿区私人建房投资外，固定资产投资的统计起点由5万元提高到50万元。

自2006年起，非农户固定资产投资统计改为按项目统计，调查方法由抽样调查改为全面统计报表，起点提高到50万元。城镇和工矿区私人建房投资改为按项目统计，起点为50万元。

自2011年起，除房地产开发投资、农户投资外，固定资产投资项目统计起点，由计划总投资50万元提高到500万元；统计范围从城镇扩大到农村企事业组织，并将这一统计范围定义为“固定资产投资（不含农户）”。

二、主要指标

指标		
全社会固定资产投资	比上年增长	1.1%
#国有经济单位	比上年增长	5.1%
集体经济单位	比上年增长	44.2%
#固定资产投资	比上年增长	1.1%
#房地产开发投资	比上年增长	–2.1%
商品房销售面积	比上年增长	–2.8%
全市新增固定资产	比上年增长	26.2%
全市竣工住宅面积	比上年增长	22.4%

5 INVESTMENT IN FIXED ASSETS

Ⅰ.Brief Introduction

1.This chapter reflects the scale and speed of investment in fixed assets in Xi'an, the structure and proportional relationship of investment in fixed assets, the source of funds for investment in fixed assets and the effects of them during a certain period of time by describing the quantity of fixed asset activities built and purchased in the whole society during a certain period of time, mainly including total investment in fixed assets in the whole province, project investment, real estate development, farmer investment by Region and Development Zone.

2.Statistics on the investment in fixed assets cover investments in capital construction projects in urban and rural areas, investments in real estate development and rural household investment.

3.The data sources for the statistics of investment in fixed assets mainly come from complete statistical report forms, Investment in fixed assets by farm households are calculated with sample survey, and the others come from complete statistical report forms.

4.Changes in Statistical Scope

Since 1997, the cut-off point of projects covered by statistics of investment in fixed assets are raised from an investment of 50,000 yuan to 500,000 yuan, except investment in real estate development, non-farm household investment, farm household investment and private investment in housing construction in urban areas and industrial and mining areas.

Since 2006, statistics on investments in fixed assets of rural non-farm households are changed to project-based. Survey method is changed from sample survey to the system of reporting form with complete enumeration. The cut-off point has been raised to 500,00 yuan. Statistics on private investment in housing construction in urban areas and industrial and mining areas have become project-based. The cut-off point has been raised to 500,000 yuan.

Since 2011, except investment in real estate development and rural household investment , the cut-off point of statistics on investments in fixed assets are raised, amount of intended investment are raised from 500,000 yuan to 5000,000. The scope of investment statistics expends from urban to rural enterprises, and this scope of statistics is defined "investments in fixed assets(non-farm)" .

Ⅱ.Major Indicators

	Increase over Preceding Year
Total Investment In Fixed Assets	1.1%
State-owned Enterprises	5.1%
Collective-owned Enterprises	44.2%
Project Investment	1.1%
Real Estate Development	-2.1%
Floor Space of Commercialized Buildings Sold	-2.8%
Investment Newly Increased Fixed Assets	26.2%
Total Floor Space of Building Completed	22.4%

5-1 主要年份按类别分全社会固定资产投资增长速度

The Growth Rate of Total Investment in Fixed Assets in the Whole Country by Classifications in Representative Years

单位：% (%)

年 份 Year	全社会固定资产投资 Total Investment in Fixed Assets in the Whole Country	固定资产投资 Investment in Fixed Assets	房地产开发投资 Real Estate Investment	农户投资 Farmer Investment
1980	50.0	48.8		53.3
1981	-8.7	1.8		-37.2
1982	69.8	75.9		42.7
1983	10.2	14.3		-12.2
1984	23.2	16.6		70.5
1985	43.1	35.1		81.8
1986	20.1	28.4		-9.8
1987	22.1	24.9		8.0
1988	7.7	5.5		20.8
1989	-2.9	-2.4		-5.5
1990	-6.7	-3.1		-26.1
1991	16.6	10.6	120.9	58.4
1992	25.1	28.6	65.2	8.1
1993	95.1	102.9	122.6	49.4
1994	14.0	10.2	62.7	43.9
1995	20.9	20.5	80.1	23.3
1996	10.6	9.6	13.9	16.6
1997	2.2	-1.9	0.1	24.9
1998	32.4	45.7	54.8	-25.8
1999	27.5	24.5	15.9	53.0
2000	17.8	17.6	17.0	19.0
2001	23.8	26.6	30.0	4.8
2002	17.5	19.6	17.7	0.5
2003	41.4	45.1	57.3	4.7
2004	35.3	37.3	35.9	7.1
2005	29.1	26.8	32.7	69.6
2006	27.7	25.2	26.9	61.3
2007	34.6	37.9	35.5	0.0
2008	32.8	33.3	39.5	26.4
2009	31.1	32.5	28.9	10.7
2010	30.0	31.1	21.0	9.9
2011	30.0	30.0	18.3	-5.0
2012	26.8	29.9	28.6	-1.7
2013	21.0	21.3	24.5	12.1
2014	15.0	15.2	10.4	45.5
2015	-12.5	-12.7	4.0	-64.3
2016	2.0	3.4	6.8	-0.5
2017	12.9	13.0	15.0	0.0
2018	8.4	8.5	7.9	2.1
2019	1.1	1.1	-2.1	-2.0

注：2015年国家取消了城乡投资分组，表中“农户投资”2014年以前为原先的农村投资。
2016年全社会固定资产投资不含跨省项目，固定资产投资不含跨省和跨市项目。

5-2 主要年份按经济类型分全社会固定资产投资增长速度

The Growth Rate of Total Investment in Fixed Assets in the Whole Country by Economic Type in Representative Years

单位：% (%)

年　份 Year	合计 Total	国有经济 State-owned	集体经济 Collective-owned	个体经济 Self-employed Individual	其他经济 Others
1985	43.1	34.8	72.0	79.0	
1986	20.1	29.3	-28.7	0.3	
1987	22.1	22.9	54.6	7.7	
1988	7.7	6.9	24.0	5.6	
1989	-2.9	-2.1	-21.5	1.7	
1990	-6.7	-4.3	-1.4	-24.3	
1991	16.6	10.0	56.9	48.9	
1992	25.1	31.2	-35.8	22.3	
1993	95.1	86.2	109.0	31.3	
1994	14.0	8.5	36.6	54.0	13.9
1995	20.9	6.8	136.2	10.3	102.6
1996	10.6	16.8	-10.7	12.3	-7.0
1997	2.2	-4.0	17.0	20.9	13.1
1998	32.4	46.0	-22.7	-29.9	64.7
1999	27.5	20.7	72.6	53.2	33.2
2000	17.8	16.9	7.6	50.4	8.9
2001	23.8	10.0	0.1	58.1	74.7
2002	17.5	13.9	-6.6	15.8	35.3
2003	41.4	32.4	63.0	64.3	47.4
2004	35.3	24.3	79.4	-33.3	94.5
2005	29.1	13.5	47.9	61.5	41.4
2006	27.7	7.3	86.9	35.8	38.5
2007	34.6	18.9	87.1	70.6	27.0
2008	32.8	45.7	19.2	-72.5	60.8
2009	31.1	34.3	17.4	94.1	29.0
2010	30.0	44.6	12.6	-44.1	28.9
2011	30.0	24.8	10.4	36.4	18.9
2012	26.8	37.9	-24.6	10.8	27.4
2013	21.0	6.6	12.9	2.1	32.7
2014	15.0	8.2	-7.5	-1.4	21.0
2015	-12.5	-4.7	-22.2	-3.4	-16.2
2016	2.0	15.9	-17.5	1.5	-15.3
2017	12.9	19.4	-9.9	15.0	21.2
2018	8.4	-2.9	-54.5		8.6
2019	1.1	5.1	44.2		-3.3

注：集体经济：包括城镇集体和农村集体。
个体经济：包括私营个体投资及城镇工矿区私人建房和农村私人建房。
2017年后数据为含西咸数据

5-3 主要年份按产业分全市固定资产投资增长速度

The Growth Rate of Total Investment in Fixed Assets in the Whole City by Three Strata of Industry in Representative Years

单位：% (%)

年 份 Year	全市固定资产投资 Total Investment in Fixed Assets in The Whole City	第一产业 Primary Industry	第二产业 Secondary Industry	工业 Industry	第三产业 Tertisry Industry
1980	48.8	3.2	68.5	65.0	36.1
1981	1.8	83.3	0.5	-8.0	0.9
1982	75.9	-63.6	93.8	98.4	66.4
1983	14.3	175.0	22.1	21.5	4.6
1984	16.6	72.7	-8.2	-9.5	45.2
1985	35.1	-5.3	58.3	61.7	18.5
1986	28.4	-11.1	24.4	29.8	33.5
1987	24.9	18.8	31.5	34.5	18.6
1988	5.5	-21.1	1.2	-0.5	10.6
1989	-2.4	-13.3	-0.1	2.7	-4.5
1990	-3.1	92.3	-7.6	-7.9	0.3
1991	10.6	8.0	13.1	12.8	8.3
1992	28.6	-63.0	25.0	23.3	34.0
1993	102.9	-30.0	57.1	52.3	145.4
1994	10.2	-57.1	10.4	15.2	10.3
1995	20.5	366.7	6.5	7.2	28.4
1996	9.6	-7.1	-9.9	-12.5	19.0
1997	-1.9	84.6	-8.9	-10.6	0.6
1998	45.7	100.0	49.4	37.9	44.3
1999	24.5	95.8	12.9	21.9	28.1
2000	17.6	-19.1	43.5	49.4	10.0
2001	26.6	13.2	10.7	12.7	32.9
2002	19.6	398.8	17.4	11.7	18.6
2003	45.1	-22.1	12.0	14.6	57.1
2004	37.3	1.2	17.3	22.0	42.3
2005	26.8	55.6	47.7	46.8	22.7
2006	25.2	90.9	48.0	47.0	19.4
2007	37.9	1.6	39.4	38.8	38.0
2008	33.3	132.8	24.3	24.3	34.9
2009	32.5	3.0	24.0	24.3	35.3
2010	31.1	62.8	21.3	12.6	33.1
2011	30.0	22.2	21.3	18.5	31.8
2012	29.9	130.5	41.5	48.1	26.2
2013	21.3	-26.4	46.3	50.2	17.8
2014	15.2	2.7	28.3	38.8	12.2
2015	-12.7	32.8	-8.2	-5.8	-14.7
2016	3.4	-10.1	-12.3	-12.0	8.3
2017	13.0	2.3	-10.2	-10.6	18.6
2018	8.5	20.8	28.6	28.7	5.4
2019	1.1	-21.0	1.5	2.0	1.3

5-4 按资金来源及建设性质分全市固定资产投资增长速度（2019年）

The Growth Rate of Total Investment in Fixed Assets in the Whole City by Sources of Funds and Type of Construction（2019）

单位：% (%)

指 标	Item	增长速度 Growth
一. 投资总额	**Total Investment**	**1.1**
（一）按资金来源分	Grouped by Funds Source	
1. 国家预算内投资	State Budgetary Funds	-15.3
2. 国内贷款	Domestic Loans	6.3
3. 债券	Bonds	
4. 利用外资	Utilization of Foreign Funds	-54.1
5. 自筹资金	Self-raising Funds	2.0
6. 其他资金	Others	0.5
（二）按构成分	Grouped by Composition of Funds	
1. 建筑安装工程	Construction and Installation Projects	1.6
2. 设备、工器具购置	Purchasing of Equipment and Instruments	15.3
3. 其它费用	Others	-6.9
（三）按建设性质分	Grouped by Type of Construction	
#新建	New Construction	2.4
扩建	Expansion	-30.5
改建和技术改造	Reconstruction and Technical Transformation	29.6
二. 房屋施工面积	**Floor Space Under Construction**	**7.7**

5-5 主要年份全市新增固定资产投资及房屋竣工面积增长速度

The Growth Rate of Newly Added Fixed Assets and Floor Spaces Completed of Municipal Units in Representative Years

单位：% (%)

年 份 Year	新增固定资产 Newly Increased Fixed Assets	房屋竣工面积 Floor Space of Buildings Completed	住宅 Residential Buildings
1980	44.2	38.3	41.7
1985	1.1	-4.6	-5.9
1986	55.5	22.7	20.8
1987	24.8	-11.5	-23.5
1988	0.6	-12.3	-14.1
1989	-1.4	-15.8	-14.3
1990	22.4	18.7	26.5
1991	-12.0	-12.5	-13.7
1992	25.0	10.5	17.6
1993	86.7	26.0	28.6
1994	32.8	9.7	27.3
1995	13.0	26.4	37.0
1996	-4.1	-7.1	-1.3
1997	4.7	12.7	14.8
1998	27.6	2.2	-3.8
1999	48.2	77.9	99.8
2000	26.3	5.0	-1.1
2001	11.7	-3.1	-7.8
2002	18.6	11.7	-3.2
2003	40.4	18.7	18.9
2005	-6.3	-15.4	-13.8
2004	56.4	45.7	20.1
2006	10.6	6.0	-2.6
2007	47.5	39.4	59.4
2008	8.6	-33.4	-25.4
2009	39.8	37.3	18.6
2010	17.7	-49.3	-36.7
2011	86.7	58.9	65.3
2012	36.1	32.0	38.0
2013	6.2	-31.2	-29.4
2014	32.1	66.0	74.1
2015	-17.2	-40.3	-43.5
2016	-4.7	69.9	61.2
2017	24.6	5.5	0.6
2018	-12.2	-44.5	-53.0
2019	26.2	5.6	22.4

5-6 全市固定资产投资增长速度（2019年）

The Growth Rate of Total Investment in Fixed Assets in the Whole City（2019）

单位：%

指　标	Item	固定资产投资 Investment in Fixed Assets	房地产开发投资 Real Estate Investment
一、本年完成投资	**Investment Completed This Year**	**1.1**	**-2.1**
#住宅	Residential Buildings	8.5	9.0
（一）按登记注册类型分	**Grouped by Registion Status**		
内资	Domestic Funded Enterprises	0.8	0.4
国有	State-owned Enterprises	-18.5	76.5
集体	Collective-owned Enterprises	-24.9	
股份合作	Cooperative Enterprises	-88.6	
联营	Joint Ownership Enterprises		
国有联营	State Joint Ownership Enterprises		
集体联营	Collective Joint Ownership Enterprises		
国有与集体联营	Joint State-collective Ownership Enterprises		
其他联营	Other Joint Ownership Enterprises		
有限责任公司	Limited Liability Corporations	28.5	31.4
国有独资公司	State-funded Corporations	33.6	92.5
其他有限责任公司	Other Limited Liability Corporations	27.1	28.1
股份有限公司	Stock Limited Corporation	14.3	73.0
私营	Private Enterprises	-28.0	-43.7
私营独资	Private -funded Enterprises	-27.9	
私营合伙	Private Limited Liability Corporations	-65.8	
私营有限责任公司	Private Limited Liability Corporations	-27.6	-43.8
私营股份有限公司	Private Share Holding Corporations	-43.7	-48.4
其他	Others	-37.1	
港澳台商投资	Enterprises Funded by Hong Kong, Macao and Taiwan	7.4	-36.8
与港澳台合资经营	Joint-venture Enterprises	50.4	5.1
与港澳台合作经营	Cooperative Enterprises	-52.4	-52.4
港澳台独资	Wholly Funded from Hong Kong,Macao and Taiwan	-28.3	-51.4

5-6 续表 continued

(%)

指 标	Item	固定资产投资 Investment in Fixed Assets	房地产开发投资 Real Estate Investment
港澳台投资股份有限公司	Share-holding Corporations Ltd.	-9.0	-36.1
其他港澳台投资	Investment From Hongkong,Macao,Taiwan		
外商投资	Foreign Owned Enterprises	7.6	-92.5
中外合资经营	Joint-venture Enterprises	-59.7	-81.9
中外合作经营	Cooperation Enterprises		
外资企业	Foreign Funded Enterprises	31.4	-90.8
外商投资股份有限公司	Share-holding Corporations Ltd. With Foreign Funds	-96.6	-97.2
其他外商投资	Foreign Investment		
（二）按建设性质分	**Grouped by Type of Construction**		
#新建	New Construction	2.4	
扩建	Expansion	-30.5	
改建和技术改造	Reconstruction	29.6	
（三）按构成分	**Grouped by Composition**		
1. 建筑安装工程	Construction and Installment Investment	1.6	1.2
2. 设备、工器具购置	Purchasing of Equipment and Instruments	15.3	20.0
3. 其他费用	Others	-6.9	-10.5
二、本年新增固定资产	**Newly Increase in Fixed Assets This Year**	**26.2**	**21.8**
三、房屋面积	**Floor Space**		
房屋施工面积	Floor Space of Buildings Under Construction	7.7	8.9
#住宅	Residential Buildings	11.1	11.1
房屋竣工面积	Floor Space of Buildings Completed	5.6	8.2
#住宅	Residential Buildings	22.4	22.2
四、本年房屋竣工价值	**Value of the Building Completed This Year**	**12.8**	**12.6**
#住宅	Residential Buildings	12.3	10.8

5-7 按国民经济行业分全市固定资产投资增长速度（2019年）

The Growth Rate of Investment in Fixed Assets in the Whole Country by Industry（2019）

单位：%　　　　　　　　　　　　　　　　　　　　　　　　　　　　　　　　　　　　　　（%）

行业	Sector	固定资产投资 Investment in Fixed Assets	工业企业技术改造 Technological Transformation of Industrial Enterprises
本年完成固定资产投资	**Grouped by Sector**	**1.1**	**10.2**
（一）农、林、牧、渔业	Agriculture,Forestry,Animal Husbandry and Fishery	-21.6	
（二）采矿业	Mining	156.8	132.7
（三）制造业	Manufacturing	4.2	5.0
农副食品加工业	Processing of Food from Agricultural Products	-48.5	-94.0
食品制造业	Manufacture of Foods	-0.8	48.5
酒、饮料和精制茶制造业	Wine, Soft Drinks and Refined Tea Industry	86.0	-23.5
烟草制品业	Tobacco Processing		
纺织业	Textile Industry	-77.4	-85.2
纺织服装、服饰业	Textile, Apparel Industry		
皮革、毛皮、羽毛及其制品和制鞋业	Leather, Fur, Feather (eiderdown) and Their Products Industry		
木材加工和木、竹、藤、棕、草制品业	Timber Processing,Bamboo,Cane, Palm Fiber and Straw Products	0.1	
家具制造业	Furniture Manufacturing	27.4	-92.1
造纸及纸制品业	Papermaking and Paper products	-14.0	-82.0
印刷和记录媒介复制业	Printing,Record Medium Reproduction	26.7	5.3
文教、工美、体育和娱乐用品制造业	Culture, Education, Craft Art, Sports and Entertainment Goods Manufacturing Industry	92.2	
石油、煤炭及其他燃料加工业	Oil, Coal and Other Fuel Processing Industries	-5.7	
化学原料和化学制品制造业	Raw Chemical Materials and Chemical Products	-55.2	-11.6
医药制造业	Medical and Pharmaceutical Products	-59.5	-46.0
化学纤维制造业	Chemical Fiber	3969.1	
橡胶和塑料制品业	Rubber and Plastic Products Industry	706.4	65.8
非金属矿物制品业	Nonmetal Mineral Products	20.5	50.6
黑色金属冶炼和压延加工业	Smelting and Pressing of Ferrous Metals	32.3	50.3
有色金属冶炼和压延加工业	Smelting and Pressing of Nonferrou Metals	-42.0	35.2
金属制品业	Metal Products	-64.5	-63.9

5-7 续表 continued

单位：% (%)

行　业	Sector	固定资产投资 Investment in Fixed Assets	工业企业技术改造 Technological Transformation of Industrial Enterprises
通用设备制造业	General Equipment Manufacturing Industry	-41.0	69.3
专用设备制造业	Special Purpose Equipment	31.4	45.2
汽车制造业	Automotive Manufacturing	-4.9	46.0
铁路、船舶、航空航天和其他运输设备制造业	Railroad, Marine, Aerospace and other Transportation Equipment Manufacturing	10.2	13.3
电气机械和器材制造业	Electric Equipment and Machinery	-7.6	57.8
计算机、通信和其他电子设备制造业	Communication Equipment, Computer and Other Electronic Equipment Manufacturing Industry	24.6	-21.8
仪器仪表制造业	Instrument Manufacturing Industry	-36.3	116.9
其他制造业	Other Manufacturing	-41.8	
废弃资源综合利用	Comprehensive Utilization of waste Resources	240.5	189.4
金属制品、机械和设备修理业	Metal Products, Machinery and Equipment Repair Industry	1534.8	
（四）电力、热力、燃气及水生产和供应业	Production & Supply of Electricity，Heat，Gas & Water	-14.1	25.5
（五）建筑业	Construction	-70.2	
（六）批发和零售业	Wholesale and Retail Trades	-31.2	
（七）交通运输、仓储和邮政业	Transport, Storage and Post	1.6	
（八）住宿和餐饮业	Hotels and Catering Services	0.8	
（九）信息传输、软件和信息技术服务业	Information Transmission,Computer Service and Software	-30.1	
（十）金融业	Financial Intermediation	-82.2	
（十一）房地产业	Real Estate	-4.7	
（十二） 租赁和商务服务业	Leasing and Business Services	51.1	
（十三）科学研究和技术服务业	Scientific Research,Technical Service and Geologic Prospecting	-29.0	
（十四）水利、环境和公共设施管理业	Management of Water Conservancy, Environment and Public Facilities	12.0	
（十五）居民服务、修理和其他服务业	Services to Households, Repairs and Other Services	24.9	
（十六）教育	Education	27.0	
（十七）卫生和社会工作	Health and Social Work	0.9	
（十八）文化、体育和娱乐业	Culture, Sports and Entertainment	16.7	
（十九）公共管理、社会保障和社会组织	Public Administration, Social Security and Social Organizations	-15.7	
（二十）国际组织	International Organizations		

5-8 按国民经济行业分民间投资增长速度（2019年）

The Growth Rate of Private Investment of Municipal Units by Industry（2019）

单位：%　　　　　　　　　　　　　　　　　　　　　　　　　　　　　　　　　　　　　　（%）

行　业	Sector	民间投资 Private Investment	占民间投资比重 Rate
民间投资总计	**Total**	**-3.5**	**100**
（一）农、林、牧、渔业	Agriculture, Forestry, Animal Husbandry and Fishery	-8.3	1.4
（二）采矿业	Mining	-52.9	
（三）制造业	Manufacturing	-12.5	12.7
（四）电力、热力、燃气及水生产和供应业	Production & Supply of Electricity，Heat，Gas & Water	-25.7	0.9
（五）建筑业	Construction	-33.8	
（六）批发和零售业	Wholesale and Retail Trades	-16.6	1.1
（七）交通运输、仓储和邮政业	Transportation, Storage and Post	-23.1	1.8
（八）住宿和餐饮业	Hotels and Catering Services	39.1	1.4
（九）信息传输、软件和信息技术服务业	Information Transmission, Computer Service and Software	-40.1	0.6
（十）金融业	Financial Intermediation		
（十一）房地产业	Real Estate	-4.2	66.9
（十二）租赁和商务服务业	Leasing and Business Services	218.1	3.0
（十三）科学研究和技术服务业	Scientific Research and Technical Service	-16.4	0.6
（十四）水利、环境和公共设施管理业	Management of Water Conservancy, Environment and Public Facilities	11.5	4.5
（十五）居民服务、修理和其他服务业	Services to Households, Repairs and Other Services	106.4	0.3
（十六）教育	Education	12.6	1.1
（十七）卫生和社会工作	Health and Social Work	-1.8	1.7
（十八）文化、体育和娱乐业	Culture, Sports and Entertainment	-10.8	1.8
（十九）公共管理、社会保障和社会组织	Public Administration, Social Security and Social Organizations	72.2	
（二十）国际组织	International Organizations		

5-9 按国民经济行业分基础设施投资增长速度（2019年）

The Growth Rate of Investment for Basic Infrastructure of Municipal Units by Industry (2019)

单位：%　　　　(%)

指 标	Item	比去年同期增长± Increase Over the Same Period Last Year	比重 Rate
基础设施投资总计	**Total Investment of Infrastructure**	**11.4**	**100.0**
一、电力、热力、燃气及水生产和供应业	**Production and Supply of Electricity, Heat, Gas and Water**	**17.0**	**6.1**
电力、热力的生产和供应业	The Production and Supply of Electricity and Heat	15.7	2.4
燃气的生产和供应业	The Production and Supply of Gas	9.9	0.7
水的生产和供应业	The Production and Supply of Water	19.9	3.0
二、交通运输和邮政业	**Traffic, Transport and Post**	**9.5**	**17.0**
铁路运输业	Railway Transport Industry	-15.7	1.9
道路运输业	The Road Transport Industry	8.7	13.3
水上运输业	Water Transportation		
航空运输业	The Air Transport Industry	98.2	1.2
管道运输业	Pipeline Transportation	-11.2	0.1
多式联运和运输代理服务业	Multimodal Transport and Transport Agency Services	166.2	0.3
装卸搬运	Handling Service	-59.9	
邮政业	The Postal Service	-0.6	0.1
三、信息传输业	**Information Transmission**	**-3.7**	**2.5**
电信、广播电视和卫星传输服务	Telecommunications, Radio and Television and Satellite	-5.9	2.1
互联网和相关服务	Internet and Related Services	9.5	0.4
四、水利、环境和公共设施管理业	**Management of Water Conservancy, Environment and Public Facilities**	**12.0**	**73.4**
水利管理业	Water Resources Management Industry	-61.3	1.1
生态保护和环境治理业	Ecological Protection and Environmental Control Industries	-61.9	0.5
公共设施管理业	Public Facilities Management Industry	16.9	71.8

5-10 全市固定资产投资资金来源增长速度（2019年）

The Growth Rate of Source of Funds for Total Fixed Assets Investment of Whole City (2019)

单位：%　　　　(%)

指 标	Item	固定资产投资 Investment in Fixed Assets	房地产开发 Real Estate
一、本年资金来源合计	**Total of Sources of Funds This Year**	**-0.7**	**-1.0**
1. 上年末结余资金	Balance of Last Year	1.3	5.5
2. 本年实际到位资金	Fully Funded Capital this Year	-1.0	-2.8
(1) 国家预算资金	State Budgetary Funds	-17.1	
(2) 国内贷款	Domestic Loans	4.0	-0.2
(3) 债券	Bonds		
(4) 利用外资	Utilization of Foreign Funds	-55.0	
(5) 自筹资金	Self-raising Funds	-0.2	-4.2
(6) 其他资金来源	Others	-1.7	-1.9
二、各项应付款合计	**Total Sums of Money to be Paid This Year**	**1.8**	**-4.8**

5-11 全市按行业分施工项目（2019年）

Construction Project Grouped by Industry in the Whole City（2019）

行 业	Sector	本年新增固定资产增长速度（%）The Growth Rate of Newly Increased Fixed Assets This Year（%）	施工项目个数（个）Number of Constructing Projects(unit)
总计	**Total**	**26.2**	**3460**
（一）农、林、牧、渔业	Agriculture, Forestry, Animal Husbandry and Fishery	12.0	144
（二）采矿业	Mining	145.5	5
（三）制造业	Manufacturing	-2.5	798
（四）电力、热力、燃气及水生产和供应业	Production & Supply of Electricity，Heat，Gas & Water	28.0	210
（五）建筑业	Construction		1
（六）批发和零售业	Wholesale and Retail Trades	-14.5	48
（七）交通运输、仓储和邮政业	Transportation, Storage and Post	-48.1	158
（八）住宿和餐饮业	Hotels and Catering Services	64.5	61
（九）信息传输、软件和信息技术服务业	Information Transmission, Computer Service and Software	-6.6	88
（十）金融业	Financial Intermediation		2
（十一）房地产业	Real Estate	10.7	133
（十二）租赁和商务服务业	Leasing and Business Services	110.2	79
（十三）科学研究和技术服务业	Scientific Research and Technical Service	45.9	59
（十四）水利、环境和公共设施管理业	Management of Water Conservancy, Environment and Public Facilities	80.5	1249
（十五）居民服务、修理和其他服务业	Services to Households, Repairs and Other Services	1865.2	16
（十六）教育	Education	22.8	245
（十七）卫生和社会工作	Health and Social Work	-36.5	60
（十八）文化、体育和娱乐业	Culture, Sports and Entertainment	312.4	63
（十九）公共管理、社会保障和社会组织	Public Administration, Social Security and Social Organizations	206.8	41
（二十）国际组织	International Organizations		

5-11 续表 continued

行　业	Sector	本年新开工 Newly Started This Year	本年投产项目个数（个） Projects put into Use (unit)
总计	**Total**	**1633**	**1915**
（一）农、林、牧、渔业	Agriculture, Forestry, Animal Husbandry and Fishery	85	85
（二）采矿业	Mining	4	3
（三）制造业	Manufacturing	383	513
（四）电力、热力、燃气及水生产和供应业	Production & Supply of Electricity，Heat，Gas & Water	99	81
（五）建筑业	Construction	1	5
（六）批发和零售业	Wholesale and Retail Trades	21	31
（七）交通运输、仓储和邮政业	Transportation, Storage and Post	69	113
（八）住宿和餐饮业	Hotels and Catering Services	31	26
（九）信息传输、软件和信息技术服务业	Information Transmission, Computer Service and Software	47	35
（十）金融业	Financial Intermediation		
（十一）房地产业	Real Estate	40	41
（十二） 租赁和商务服务业	Leasing and Business Services	38	42
（十三）科学研究和技术服务业	Scientific Research and Technical Service	23	34
（十四）水利、环境和公共设施管理业	Management of Water Conservancy, Environment and Public Facilities	590	708
（十五）居民服务、修理和其他服务业	Services to Households, Repairs and Other Services	12	9
（十六）教育	Education	118	85
（十七）卫生和社会工作	Health and Social Work	22	56
（十八）文化、体育和娱乐业	Culture, Sports and Entertainment	27	27
（十九）公共管理、社会保障和社会组织	Public Administration, Social Security and Social Organizations	23	21
（二十）国际组织	International Organizations		

5-12 全市固定资产投资效果（2019年）

Achievements of Total Assets Investment of Whole City（2019）

指　标	Item	固定资产投资 Investment in Fixed Assets	房地产开发投资 Real Estate Investment
一、建设项目投产率（%）	**Rate of Projects Put Into Use（%）**	**55.3**	
施工项目个数（个）	Number of Constructing Projects (unit)	3460	
本年投产项目个数（个）	Number of Projects Put into Use (unit)	1915	
二、固定资产交付使用率（%）	**Rate of Fixed Assets Put into Use（%）**	**33.6**	**20.2**
本年新增固定资产增长速度（%）	The Growth Rate of Newly Increased Fixed Assets This Year（%）	26.2	21.8
本年完成投资增长速度（%）	The Growth Rate of Investment Completed This Year（%）	1.1	-2.1
三、建设周期（年）	**Construction Period (year)**	**5.3**	**7.5**
计划总投资增长速度（%）	The Growth Rate of Total Planned Investment（%）	9.1	11.3
本年完成投资额增长速度（%）	The Growth Rate of Investment Completed This Year（%）	1.1	-2.1
四、房屋建筑面积竣工率（%）	**Completion Rate of Buildings（%）**	**6.3**	**6.1**
本年房屋施工面积增长速度（%）	The Growth Rate of Floor Space of the Constructing Buildings This Year（%）	7.7	8.9
本年房屋竣工面积增长速度（%）	The Growth Rate of Floor Space of the Buildings Completed This Year（%）	5.6	8.2

5-13 固定资产投资新增生产能力或效益（2019年）

Newly Increased Production Capacity or Project Efficiency through Investment（2019）

能源名称	Name	累计新增生产能力或效益 Cumulative Newly Increased Production Capacity or Project Efficiency
石油加工：蒸馏设备能力（处理万吨/年）	Oil Processing : Distillation Equipment Capacity (10 000 tons/year)	103
石油加工：裂变设备能力（处理万吨/年）	Oil Processing : Fission Equipment Capacity (10 000 tons/year)	
太阳能发电（万千瓦）	Solar Energy (10 000 kw)	0.63
其他发电（万千瓦）	Others (10 000 kw)	
输电线路长度（11万伏及以上）（公里）	Length of Transmission Lines (above 110 000 VA) (km)	140
载货汽车制造（辆/年）	Truck Manufacturing (car/year)	
客车制造（辆/年）	Bus Manufacturing (car/year)	
轿车制造（辆/年）	Car Manufacturing (car/year)	
其他汽车制造（辆/年）	Other cars Manufacturing (car/year)	2000
啤酒（万吨/年）	Beer (10 000 tons/year)	
白酒（万吨/年）	White Spirit (10 000 tons/year)	
其他酒（万吨/年）	Other Alcohols (10 000 tons/year)	
新建公路（公里）	Newly Highways (km)	
#高速公路（公里）	Expressway (km)	
一级公路（公里）	First Class (km)	
二级公路（公里）	Second Class (km)	
改建公路（公里）	Reconstructed Highways (km)	
新（扩）建客、货运站（个）	New (expanded) Passenger and Freight Stations （unit）	
新（扩）建公路客、货运站（平方米）	New (expanded) Road Passenger and Freight Station (square meter)	
飞机购置（驾）	Airplane Purchasing (set)	
城市自来水供水能力（万吨/日）	Tap Water Supply Capacity in City(10 000 tons/day)	1.8
城市污水处理能力（万吨/日）	Waste Water Treated Capacity in City(10 000 tons/day)	6

5-14 全市按国民经济行业分房屋建筑面积增长速度（2019年）

单位：%

行 业	Sector	本年施工房屋面积 Floor Space of Buildings Under Construction This Year	住宅 Residential Residence
总 计	**Total**	**7.7**	**11.1**
（一）农、林、牧、渔业	Agriculture, Forestry, Animal Husbandry and Fishery	15.8	-11.5
（二）采矿业	Mining	-23.4	
（三）制造业	Manufacturing	-21.5	182.6
（四）电力、热力、燃气及水生产和供应业	Production & Supply of Electricity，Heat，Gas & Water	75.1	
（五）建筑业	Construction		
（六）批发和零售业	Wholesale and Retail Trades	-5.7	-78.2
（七）交通运输、仓储和邮政业	Transportation, Storage and Post	-26.2	
（八）住宿和餐饮业	Hotels and Catering Services	-74.3	
（九）信息传输、软件和信息技术服务业	Information Transmission, Computer Service and Software	66.9	
（十）金融业	Financial Intermediation		
（十一）房地产业	Real Estate	9.2	11.1
（十二）租赁和商务服务业	Leasing and Business Services	97.5	
（十三）科学研究和技术服务业	Scientific Research and Technical Service	193.2	
（十四）水利、环境和公共设施管理业	Management of Water Conservancy, Environment and Public Facilities	-38.0	
（十五）居民服务、修理和其他服务业	Services to Households, Repairs and Other Services		
（十六）教育	Education		
（十七）卫生和社会工作	Health and Social Work	-19.6	63.6
（十八）文化、体育和娱乐业	Culture, Sports and Entertainment	-82.2	
（十九）公共管理、社会保障和社会组织	Public Administration, Social Security and Social Organizations	-79.9	63.0
（二十）国际组织	International Organizations		

The Growth Rate of Floors Space of Buildings Construction of Municipal Units by Industry (2019)

(%)

本年竣工房屋面积 Floor Space of Buildings Completed This Year	住宅 Residential Residence	本年竣工房屋价值 Value of Buildings Completed this Year	住宅 Residential Residence
5.6	**22.4**	**12.6**	**10.8**
-71.1	-27.2		
-61.5	310.4		
104.4			
-12.3			
-68.5			
7.9	21.9	12.6	10.8
218.7			
-32.4			
-18.5			
-30.8			

5-15 分区县、开发区全社会固定资产投资增长速度（2019年）

The Growth Rate of Total Investment in Fixed Assets by Region and Development Zone (2019)

单位：%　　　　(%)

区县、开发区	Region	全社会固定资产投资 Fixed Assets Investment	固定资产投资 Investment in Fixed Assets	房地产开发投资 Real Estate Investment	农户投资 Farmer Investment
全市	**Total**	1.1	1.1	-2.1	-2.0
新城区	Xincheng	16.3	16.3	32.8	
碑林区	Beilin	-19.5	-19.5	-26.7	
莲湖区	Lianhu	-29.4	-29.4	-43.3	
灞桥区	Baqiao	-0.3	-0.3	-12.4	0.8
未央区	Weiyang	-12.0	-12.0	-30.1	-22.9
雁塔区	Yanta	4.5	4.5	-20.8	
阎良区	Yanliang	-7.9	-8.0	-2.1	0.0
临潼区	Lintong	-12.5	-13.3	13.7	-1.5
长安区	Chang'an	32.9	33.4	24.7	1.6
高陵区	Gaoling	-27.3	-27.6	-0.7	-0.8
鄠邑区	Huyi	-33.7	-35.8	-5.7	-0.8
蓝田县	Lantian	-6.0	-6.2	20.5	-2.4
周至县	Zhouzhi	-35.2	-42.3	66.1	-1.6
西咸新区	Xixian	10.1	10.3	47.7	-6.5
#开发区	**Development Zones**				
高新区	GaoXin	18.3	18.3	-21.6	
经开区	JingKai	-19.9	-19.9	-40.4	
曲江新区	Qujiang	-11.7	-11.7	-26.1	
浐灞生态区	Chanba Eco-District	-12.0	-12.0	-9.3	
航空基地	Aviation Industry Base	12.2	12.2	14.8	
航天基地	Aerospace Base	-11.2	-11.2	-15.1	
国际港务区	International Trade&Logistic Park	21.3	21.3	-6.2	

5-16 分区县工业投资增长速度（2019年）

The Growth Rate of Industrial Investment by Region (2019)

单位：%　　(%)

区县	Region	工业投资 Industrial Investment	工业企业技术改造 Technological Transformation of Industrial Enterprises
全　市	**Total**	**2.0**	**10.2**
新城区	Xincheng	-52.8	-24.5
碑林区	Beilin	-73.6	-88.5
莲湖区	Lianhu	-68.1	-67.3
灞桥区	Baqiao	30.5	113.6
未央区	Weiyang	-11.7	-10.4
雁塔区	Yanta	30.5	20.2
阎良区	Yanliang	-9.5	14.3
临潼区	Lintong	-22.6	-41.5
长安区	Chang'an	30.9	-0.3
高陵区	Gaoling	-44.1	63.5
鄠邑区	Huyi	-6.0	109.0
蓝田县	Lantian	0.5	-52.9
周至县	Zhouzhi	-44.7	96.6
西咸新区	Xixian	10.8	23.4

5-17 分区县、开发区新增固定资产及房屋施工、竣工面积增长速度（2019年）

单位：%

区县、开发区	Region	本年新增固定资产 Increased Fixed Assets this Year	房屋施工面积 Floor Space of Buildings Under Construction	住宅 Residential Buildings
区县	**Region**	**12.7**	**1.3**	**4.0**
新城区	Xincheng	103.6	8.5	5.1
碑林区	Beilin	197.6	-0.8	-4.8
莲湖区	Lianhu	459.9	4.0	9.2
灞桥区	Baqiao	-39.2	10.8	11.2
未央区	Weiyang	-18.1	-1.3	0.2
雁塔区	Yanta	23.9	-7.0	-2.9
阎良区	Yanliang	-20.0	25.0	33.5
临潼区	Lintong	-1.4	4.6	1.9
长安区	Chang'an	19.0	7.4	8.2
高陵区	Gaoling	-35.3	11.5	5.2
鄠邑区	Huyi	17.2	-9.3	4.4
蓝田县	Lantian	-12.6	12.8	9.9
周至县	Zhouzhi	-71.6	-23.9	72.7
西咸新区	Xixian	80.1	69.4	76.6
开发区	**Development Zones**	**30.5**	**11.6**	**16.7**
高新区	GaoXin	6.9	-12.5	-4.7
经开区	JingKai	-34.0	-6.1	-2.8
曲江新区	Qujiang	1.2	-8.8	-9.5
浐灞生态区	Chanba Eco-District	-44.0	12.4	9.0
航空基地	Aviation Industry Base	-44.4	23.8	34.9
航天基地	Aerospace Base	114.9	8.8	12.1
国际港务区	International Trade&Logistic Park	-51.5	41.2	66.3

The Growth Rate of Newly Added Fixed Assets and Floor Space of Constructing and Completed Buildings by Region and Development Zone（2019）

（%）

本年房屋竣工面积 Floor Space of Buildings this Year Completed	住宅 Residential Buildings	本年房屋竣工价值 Value of Buildings Completed this Year	住宅 Residential Buildings	本年商品房销售面积 Floor Space of Houses Sales this year	本年商品房销售额 Sales Income of Commercial Houses this year
0.7	**19.0**	**6.9**	**8.3**	**-13.2**	**-2.6**
207.9	195.5	293.3	146.5	23.5	29.4
168.2	206.3	155.8	167.8	-55.2	-43.9
3735.9	4167.9	2614.9	4106.1	-48.3	-34.0
-80.2	-88.5	-81.0	-88.8	0.8	17.6
-52.7	-47.8	-38.8	-57.8	-15.3	-6.7
-54.0	-37.4	-56.0	-47.3	-14.7	-1.7
15.8	-23.1	57.9	-28.4	-5.3	2.6
-35.5	-95.5	-7.9	-94.6	-23.1	-22.1
16.5	-45.6	66.9	-41.8	-0.7	-1.9
-79.0				-23.3	-4.7
-31.6	233.2	-13.0	253.3	-21.4	-1.6
-38.1	-61.4	1026.7	662.0	6.1	33.0
-93.2		-92.7		58.4	92.5
661.6	1952.0	415.7	860.8	106.2	128.8
-60.1	**-78.3**	**-53.5**	**-77.0**	**15.0**	**24.3**
-80.1	-86.9	-73.2	-86.5	5.2	10.8
-74.2		-51.7		-20.7	-1.4
30.2	-31.3	-8.0	-47.0	-12.1	0.6
-84.2	-96.0	-88.6	-96.9	-8.0	-0.8
346.9	365.8	1110.0	416.0	34.1	32.5
104.2	36.2	90.2	18.8	35.7	20.7
				94.0	125.8

5-18　主要年份房地产开发投资主要指标

单位：万平方米

指　标	Item	1999	2000	2001	2002	2003	2004
本年完成投资额（亿元）	Investment Completed This Year(100 million yuan)	44.30	51.85	67.42	79.37	124.82	169.67
本年房屋施工面积	Floor Space of Buildings Under Construction This Year	793.46	763.18	743.78	1172.58	1343.12	1633.68
#住宅	Residential Buildings	649.53	619.85	580.43	964.68	943.61	1204.01
本年房屋竣工面积	Floor Space of Buildings Completed This Year	377.79	321.10	316.24	329.71	339.67	380.84
#住宅	Residential Buildings	352.28	295.55	269.61	290.30	289.56	308.06
本年房屋竣工价值（亿元）	Value of Floor Space of Buildings Completed this Year(100million yuan)	38.22	26.94	37.20	36.93	54.73	73.75
#住宅	Residential Buildings	33.02	22.97	28.62	30.46	44.01	55.58
本年商品房销售面积	Floor Space of Commercialized Buildings Sold	296.97	212.92	225.35	252.90	252.74	305.47
#住宅	Residential Buildings	284.95	200.77	192.20	237.04	230.28	279.90
本年商品房销售额（亿元）	Total Sales of Commercialized Buildings(100 million yuan)	35.19	32.52	47.22	51.35	54.29	81.35
#住宅	Residential Buildings	32.35	29.46	35.53	45.46	44.25	71.27
本年批准预售面积	Approved Pre-sale Area of This Year	30.25	253.03	67.44	61.02	52.35	176.40
#住宅	Residential Buildings	27.34	253.03	65.20	55.73	49.12	159.10
待售面积	Area for Sale	62.38	36.41	50.82	57.14	63.85	108.52
#住宅	Residential Buildings	52.32	24.02	34.18	44.70	52.34	72.76
房屋出租面积	Rental Housing Area	1.88	1.17	9.19	15.75	10.56	11.18
#住宅	Residential Buildings	0.15	0.02	0.10	1.13	5.43	5.78
本年新增固定资产（亿元）	Newly Increased Fixed Assets This Year(100 million yuan)	43.10	38.38	50.77	48.43	62.13	83.36

Main Indicators of Investment in Real Estate Development in Representative Years

(10 000sq.m)

2005	2006	2007	2008	2009	2010	2011	2012	2013	2014	2015	2016	2017	2018	2019
225.23	285.76	387.33	540.26	696.34	842.34	996.81	1281.90	1595.64	1761.88	1831.67	1955.82	2333.34	2518.01	2464.78
2174.29	2383.56	2915.95	3632.87	5708.63	6697.39	8247.69	9947.89	10454.27	12422.10	13392.94	14727.10	15843.92	16044.57	17475.02
1783.36	1890.27	2376.82	3079.13	4901.59	5777.71	7108.27	8294.92	8461.71	9727.60	9777.23	10468.80	11134.28	11208.59	12450.59
361.62	399.64	483.30	443.96	542.81	463.65	631.03	1063.70	795.35	1533.70	976.64	1560.18	1634.63	977.28	1057.69
316.52	342.15	422.47	412.46	453.49	412.44	564.59	903.82	663.20	1307.64	766.58	1259.24	1281.71	623.40	761.59
80.58	82.02	101.13	106.50	168.08	145.62	213.29	310.57	279.63	442.74	301.86	456.48	571.96	330.61	372.11
68.11	65.80	77.13	96.02	137.42	128.69	185.31	260.04	222.64	368.25	236.66	351.46	448.02	208.68	231.24
497.34	621.50	833.92	760.72	1256.02	1587.81	1778.02	1538.91	1662.75	1707.71	1763.68	2047.67	2509.78	2713.46	2638.69
476.39	584.06	782.91	715.76	1202.12	1523.24	1674.85	1383.84	1522.50	1525.95	1584.08	1877.78	2147.67	2221.27	2155.46
171.29	206.15	281.79	296.44	488.55	707.00	1091.31	1017.74	1112.87	1100.71	1146.79	1347.08	2123.34	2753.13	2989.64
158.03	179.47	251.74	268.92	450.71	661.27	973.71	858.53	976.19	928.74	985.35	1194.41	1743.43	2214.18	2462.79
300.07	428.20	491.07	569.22	1125.44	1510.20	3105.76	2627.73	1787.89	842.98	751.15	717.54	634.50	1047.65	
287.13	408.11	457.54	541.20	1095.17	1452.20	2826.79	2340.69	1597.82	727.31	583.55	508.17	515.34	865.40	
123.59	112.49	45.42	55.40	40.68	34.32	59.76	102.58	74.59	187.13	296.50	378.24	379.66	240.04	202.71
99.17	85.89	38.62	35.40	28.73	26.23	45.41	83.78	61.24	143.21	185.96	215.40	176.90	59.98	55.57
17.32	8.53	10.84	34.94	38.23	28.60	8.01	15.16	15.57	7.15	19.64	48.67	57.12	51.95	26.97
4.09	3.74	5.36	4.53	6.55	0.70	3.25	4.03	0.73	0.07	1.47	1.47		2.37	
92.78	100.22	143.17	124.02	195.71	168.20	25.53	358.03	334.41	531.44	335.91	574.54	807.26	409.04	498.31

5-19　分区县、开发区房地产开发主要指标（2019年）

单位：万元

区县、开发区	Region	企业（单位）个数（个） Number of Enterprises (unit)	本年完成投资 Investment Completed This Year	本年新增固定资产 Increased Fixed Assets This Year
全　市	**Total**	**1115**	**24647783**	**4983083**
新城区	Xincheng	36	408444	506928
碑林区	Beilin	47	271324	1166545
莲湖区	Lianhu	75	913307	815186
灞桥区	Baqiao	108	2634059	118444
未央区	Weiyang	184	2802745	1038074
雁塔区	Yanta	218	5272260	761626
阎良区	Yanliang	42	367402	20211
临潼区	Lintong	28	696964	
长安区	Chang'an	103	2713644	211620
高陵区	Gaoling	36	523011	
鄠邑区	Huyi	36	171463	151454
蓝田县	Lantian	17	132766	
周至县	Zhouzhi	23	66819	
西咸新区	Xixian	162	7673575	192995
#开发区	**Development Zones**	**435**	**9688080**	**862132**
高新区	GaoXin	94	2224724	252671
经开区	JingKai	86	1028940	303425
曲江新区	Qujiang	85	2362958	31012
浐灞生态区	Chanba Eco-District	88	2025388	98019
航空基地	Aviation Industry Base	13	229476	9800
航天基地	Aerospace Base	52	1117354	167205
国际港务区	International Trade&Logistic Park	17	699240	

Main Indicators of Real Estate Development by Region and Development Zone（2019）

(10 000 yuan)

房屋施工面积（平方米）Floor Space of Buildings Under Constmction(sq.m)	住宅 Residential Buildings	本年房屋竣工面积（平方米）Floor Space of Buildings Completed this Year(sq.m)	住宅 Residential Buildings	本年房屋竣工价值 Value of Buildings Completed this Year	住宅 Residential Buildings
174750166	**124505896**	**10576865**	**7615862**	**3721075**	**2312407**
5145100	3827233	1010639	759232	355769	186608
5993238	4116596	2827621	2210016	877141	699563
14302218	11925072	2417870	1879376	797473	580488
19310112	14455320	100681	32773	42238	9893
35319812	23432300	1850016	1194027	751744	296713
34923388	21635059	1317467	983909	496613	349244
2453531	1747024	61323	32155	16092	8916
2596764	2166853				
19446012	14115693	361493	154613	141900	46299
5508487	4629962				
1942915	1386745	230569	143061	64232	40080
1220032	955189				
892671	700027				
25695886	19412823	399186	226700	177873	94603
74510221	**49290571**	**1388527**	**398833**	**674832**	**155721**
13573488	7113759	397941	166392	191440	72769
14453483	8237254	542717		303177	
13487813	9998191	57436	45628	31012	25972
19207551	14505298	74672	13200	35736	5000
964564	512393	19000	19000	5681	5681
9080303	6289941	296761	154613	107786	46299
3743019	2633735				

5-20 房地产开发投资主要指标（2019年）

Main Indicators of Investment in Real Estate Development（2019）

单位：万元 (10 000 yuan)

指标	Item	全市合计 Total	国有 State-owned	市区 Urban	市属 Municipal
一、企业（单位）个数（个）	**Number of Enterprises(unit)**	**1115**	**62**	**957**	**1076**
二、本年完成投资	**Investment Completed This Year**	**24647783**	**2159858**	**19971536**	**23500511**
按工程用途分	Grouped by Function				
住宅	Residential Buildings	18051619	1753296	14067031	17253344
#别墅、高档公寓	Villas and Top-Grade Apartments	410267	4007	324077	370811
办公楼	Office Buildings	1896095	261147	1722586	1792088
商业营业用房	Houses for Business Use	1979943	71551	1651827	1945450
其他	Others	2720126	73864	2530092	2509629
三、本年新增固定资产	**Increased Fixed Assets This Year**	**4983083**	**343415**	**4839088**	**4983083**
四、房屋施工面积（平方米）	**Floor Space of Buildings Under Construction (sq.m)**	**174750166**	**12036889**	**157563835**	**168426226**
#住宅	Residential Buildings	124505896	8729288	111484513	120076671
五、本年房屋竣工面积（平方米）	**Floor Space of Buildings this Year Completed (sq.m)**	**10576865**	**918642**	**10245507**	**10576865**
#住宅	Residential Buildings	7615862	841369	7389162	7615862
六、本年房屋竣工价值	**Value of Buildings Completed this Year**	**3721075**	**334023**	**3592202**	**3721075**
#住宅	Residential Buildings	2312407	304210	2217804	2312407
七、本年商品房屋销售面积（平方米）	**Floor Space of Commercialized Buildings Sold this Year(sq.m)**	**26386939**	**1756045**	**23526660**	**24146955**
本年商品房销售额	Sales Income of Commercialized Buildings	29896423	1552822	27139545	27053328

5-21 商品房销售情况（2019年）

Sales of Commercial Houses（2019）

指　标	Item	全市合计 Total	国有 State-owned	市区 Urban	市属 Municipal
本年商品房销售面积（平方米）	**Floor Space of Commercialized Buildings Sold(sq.m)**	**26386939**	**1756045**	**23526660**	**24146955**
现房销售面积（平方米）	**Floor Space of Completed Apartment Sales(sq.m)**	**2163788**	**198544**	**1714088**	**2117790**
期房销售面积（平方米）	**Floor Space of Forward Delivery Housing Sales(sq.m)**	**24223151**	**1557501**	**21812572**	**22029165**
住宅	Residential Buildings	21554633	1248299	18815437	20045611
#别墅、高档公寓	Villas and High-grade Apartments	238347		215666	188276
办公楼	Office Buildings	1761540	394002	1715387	1496113
商业营业用房	Houses for Business Use	1224371	53106	1161655	1110738
其他	Others	1846395	60638	1834181	1494493
本年商品房销售额（万元）	**Real estate sales this year(10 000Yuan)**	**29896423**	**1552822**	**27139545**	**27053328**
现房销售额（万元）	**Floor Space of Completed Apartment Sales**	**1989034**	**118660**	**1587017**	**1955777**
期房销售额（万元）	**Floor Space of Forward Delivery Housing Sales**	**27907389**	**1434162**	**25552528**	**25097551**
住宅	Residential Buildings	24627867	1239166	22011996	22670563
#别墅高档公寓	Villas and High-grade Apartments	407279		368592	336838
办公楼	Office Buildings	2190223	208855	2124052	1762191
商业营业用房	Houses for Business Use	1754462	70571	1684855	1568910
其他	Others	1323871	34230	1318642	1051664
待售面积（平方米）	**Area for Sale(sq.m)**	**2027093**	**324653**	**1641526**	**2002802**
#待售一年以上（一到三年）	Being Idle for One Year	267030	2956	263995	266854
待售三年以上（含三年）	Being Idle for Three Years	356914	16412	273306	356914
住宅	Residence	555691	241344	314776	547730
#别墅高档公寓	Villas and High-grade Apartments	27302		26876	27302
办公楼	Office Buildings	266732		266732	266732
商业营业用房	Houses for Business Use	766335	40923	669775	761161
其他	Others	438335	42386	390243	427179
房屋出租面积（平方米）	**Rental area(sq.m)**	**269701**		**269701**	**269701**
住宅	Residential Buildings				
办公楼	Office Buildings	29707		29707	29707
商业营业用房	Houses for Business Use	239994		239994	239994
其他	Others				

5-22 房地产开发投资资金来源（2019年）

Source of Funds for Investment in Real Estate Development（2019）

单位：万元 (10 000 yuan)

指　标	Item	全市合计 Total	国有 State-owned	市区 Urban	市属 Municipal
一、本年资金来源合计	**Total**	**43288380**	**2939109**	**38439190**	**40726251**
1. 上年末结余资金	Balance of Last Year	9985401	618881	9519811	9558092
2. 本年实际到位资金	Fully Funded Capital this Year	33302979	2320228	28919379	31168159
(1) 国内贷款	Domestic Loans	2771066	523431	2466174	2507130
#银行贷款	Bank Loan	2318132	336900	2019187	2054196
非银行金融机构贷款	Loans from financial Institutions except Bank	452934	186531	446987	452934
(2) 自筹资金	Self-raising Funds	14423735	979160	11036429	14199018
(3) 定金及预收款	Earnest Money and Advance payment	10126944	654620	9900062	8944971
(4) 个人按揭贷款	Personal Mortgage Loan	4274194	155650	4160487	4017628
(5) 其他资金	Others	1707040	7367	1356227	1499412
二、本年各项应付款合计	**Total Sums of Money to be Paid This Year**	**6685062**	**694204**	**5801854**	**6420722**
#工程款	Project Fund	3863086	353145	3496254	3739707

5-23 房地产开发经营情况（2019年）

Running of Real Estate Development（2019）

单位：万元 （10 000 yuan）

指　标	Item	全市合计 Total	国有 State-owned	市区 Urban	市属 Municipal
一、资产负债情况	**Assets and Liabilities**				
1. 资产总计	Total Assets	146358489	17344058	130909751	136439381
2. 负债合计	Total Liabilities	127878235	13632563	114598844	119175948
3. 所有者权益合计	Total Creditor's Equity	18480254	3711495	16310906	17263433
#实收资本	Held Capital	13374618	1402380	12089667	12299531
二、损益及分配情况	**Profit or Loss and the Distribution**				
1. 主营业务收入	Revenue from Principal Business	15006722	1538439	13672008	14283332
土地转让收入	Revenue of Land Transferred	6839		6826	6839
商品房屋销售收入	Revenue of Commercial Houses Sold	13918843	1059821	12856392	13210117
自持物业收入	Self-owned Property Income	160215	20010	151944	159623
房屋出租收入	Revenue of Houses Leased	113139	5800	105281	112548
其他收入	Other Revenue	920825	458608	656846	906753
2. 主营业务成本	Cost of Principal Business	11242142	1272711	10288810	10731041
3. 主营业务税金及附加	Taxes and Other Charges on Principal Business	739487	31453	700371	707085
4. 其他业务利润	Other Business Profit	56131	2551	55568	54048
5. 销售费用	Sales Expenditures	774857	33397	661371	733544
6. 管理费用	Management Cost	629230	58539	568145	605097
7. 财务费用	Fiscal Expenditure	248253	44521	234501	257408
#利息支出	Interest Exchange	231491	61143	226903	219975
8. 营业利润	Operating Profit	2215982	168887	1993684	2081107
投资收益	Investment Revenue	170641	26416	166768	170764
营业外收入	Non-business Revenue	73350	7757	64691	70800
营业外支出	Non-business Expenditures	55004	858	52681	52687
9. 利润总额	Total Profit	2211998	174426	2001521	2080651
10. 应付职工薪酬	Salary Payable	567038	70639	498648	531795
11. 应交增值税	Value-added Tax Payable	767055	29032	642275	733699
三、全部从业人员年平均人数（人）	**Average Number of Employed（Persons）**	**91968**	**5159**	**91504**	**86832**
四、本年应付工资总额	**Total Wages This Year**	**669343**	**33525**	**667126**	**623556**

主要统计指标解释

全社会固定资产投资 是以货币形式表现的在一定时期内全社会建造和购置固定资产的工作量以及与此有关的费用的总称。该指标是反映固定资产投资规模、结构和发展速度的综合性指标，又是观察工程进度和考核投资效果的重要依据。全社会固定资产投资按登记注册类型可分为国有、集体、联营、股份制、私营和个体、港澳台商、外商、其他等。

固定资产投资(不含农户) 指城镇和农村各种登记注册类型的企业、事业、行政单位及城镇个体户进行的计划总投资500万元及500万元以上的建设项目投资和房地产开发投资，包含原口径城镇固定资产投资加上农村企事业组织项目投资，该口径自2011年起开始使用。

房地产开发投资 指各种登记注册类型的房地产开发公司、商品房建设公司及其他房地产开发法人单位和附属于其他法人单位实际从事房地产开发或经营活动的单位统一开发的包括统代建、拆迁还建的住宅、厂房、仓库、饭店、宾馆、度假村、写字楼、办公楼等房屋建筑物和配套的服务设施，土地开发工程（如道路、给水、排水、供电、供热、通讯、平整场地等基础设施工程)的投资；不包括单纯的土地交易活动。

农产投资 是指以农户为单位进行的房屋建设(主要指住宅建设)投资、农村对农、林、牧、渔及服务行业进行的投资(如农户近年广泛进行的设施农业投资)、以及农户购买生产性固定资产的投资。

固定资产投资的资金来源 根据固定资产投资的资金来源不同，分为国家预算资金、国内贷款、利用外资、自筹资金和其他资金。

（1）国家预算资金：包括一般预算、政府性基金预算、国有资本经营预算和社保基金预算等资金。

（2）国内贷款：指报告期固定资产投资单位向银行及非银行金融机构借入的用于固定资产投资的各种国内借款，包括银行利用自有资金及吸收的存款发放的贷款、上级主管部门拨入的国内贷款、国家专项贷款、地方财政专项资金安排的贷款、国内储备贷款、周转贷款等。

（3）利用外资：指报告期收到的用于固定资产建造和购置的境外资金（包括设备、材料、技术在内）。包括对外借款（外国政府、国际金融组织贷款、出口信贷、外国银行商业贷款、对外发行债券和股票）、外商直接投资及外商其他投资。不包括我国自有外汇资金（国家外汇、地方外汇、留成外汇、调剂外汇和中国银行自有资金发行的外汇贷款等）。计算利用外资时，需要折算成人民币，折算中所使用的外汇汇率按现汇计算，即按使用外汇时的汇率计算。

（4）自筹资金：指固定资产投资单位报告期收到的，由各地区、各部门及企、事业单位筹集用于固定资产投资的预算外资金，包括中央各部门、各级地方和企、事业单位的自筹资金。

（5）其他资金：指在报告期收到的除以上各种资金之外其他用于固定资产投资的资金，包括企业或金融机构通过发行各种债券筹集到的资金、社会集资、个人资金、无偿捐赠的资金及其他单位拨人的资金等。

固定资产投资按国民经济行业分 根据现有企业、事业、行政单位和建设项目建成投产后的主要产品种类或主要用途及社会经济活动性质来确定国民经济行业。一般情况下，一个建设项目或一个企业、事业单位只能属于一种国民经济行业。

固定资产投资按隶属关系分 是按建设单位或企业、事业、行政单位的主管上级机关确定的。

（1）中央：是指中共中央、人大常委会和国务院各部、委、局、总公司以及直属机构直接领导的建设项目和企业、事业、行政单位。这些单位的固定资产投资计划由国务院各部门直接编制和下达，建设中所需物资、主要设备以及建设中的问题都由中央有关部门安排和解决。

（2）地方：是由省（自治区、直辖市）、地区（州、盟、省辖市）、县（旗、县级市）三级政府及业务主管部门直接领导和管理的建设项目、企业、事业、行政单位。地方项目还包括不隶属以上各级政府及主管部门的建设项目和企业、事业单位，如外商投资企业和无主管部门的企业等。

固定资产投资按建设性质分 根据整个建设项目情况来确定。建设项目的性质一般分为新建、扩建、改建和技术改造、单纯建造生活设施、迁建、恢复、单纯购置。房地产开发单位、农户投资不划分建设性质。

（1）新建：一般指从无到有开始建设的企业、事业和行政单位或建设项目。有的单位原有基础很小，经过建设后新增的固定资产价值超过该企、事业、行政单位原有固定资产价值（原值）三倍以上的也应作为新建。

（2）扩建：指在厂内或其他地点，为扩大原有产品的生产能力（或效益）或增加新的产品生产能力，而增建主要的生产车间（或主要工程）、分厂、独立的生产线。行政、事业单位在原单位增建业务用房（如学校增建教学用房、医院增建门诊部、病房等）也作为扩建。

现有企、事业单位为扩大原有主要产品生产能力或增加新的产品生产能力，增建一个或几个主要生产车间（或主要工程）、分厂，同时进行一些更新改造工程的，也应作为扩建。

（3）改建和技术改造：指现有企业、事业单位，对原有设施进行技术改造或更新（包括相应配套的辅助性生产、生活福利设施）的建设项目。现有企业、事业单位为适应市场变化的需要，而改变企业的主要产品种类（如军工企业转产民用品等）的建设项目，应作为改建。原有产品生产作业线由于各工序（车间）之间能力不平衡，为填平补齐充分发挥原有生产能力而增建不增加本企业主要产品设计能力的车间，也应作为改建。技术改造是指企业、事业单位在现有基础上，用先进的技术代替落后的技术，用先进的工艺和装备代替落后的工艺和装备，以改变企业落后的技术经济面貌，实现以内涵为主的扩大再生产，达到提高产品质量、促进产品更新换代、节约能源、降低消耗、扩大生产规模、全面提高社会经济效益的目的。技术改造具体包括以下内容：机器设备和工具的更新改造；生产工艺改革、节约能源和原材料的改造；厂房建筑和公共设施的改造；劳动条件和生产环境的改造等。

固定资产投资按构成分 固定资产投资活动按其工作内容和实现方式分为建筑安装工程，设备工具器具购置和其他费用三个部分。

（1）建筑安装工程（建筑安装工作量）：指各种房屋、建筑物的建造工程和各种设备、装置的安装工程。包括各种房屋建造工程；各种用途设备基础和各种工业窑炉的砌筑工程及金属结构工程；为施工而进行的各种准备工作和临时工程以及完工后的清理工作等；铁路、道路的铺设，矿井的开凿及石油管道的架设等；水利工程；防空地下建筑等特殊工程；列入房屋工程预算内的暖气、卫生、通风、照明、煤气等设备的价值及装设油饰工程；列入建筑工程预算内的各种管道（蒸汽、压缩空气、石油、给排水等管道）、电力、电讯电缆导线等的敷设工程；以及各种机械设备的安装下程；为测定安装工程质量，对设备进行的试运工作；房地产开发单位进行的商品房屋开发建设工程、土地开发工程。

在建筑安装工程中，不包括被安装设备本身的价值。

（2）设备工具器具购置：指建设单位或企、事业单位购置或自制的，达到固定资产标准的设备、工具、器具的价值。新建单位及扩建单位的新建车间，按照设计或计划要求购置或自制的全部设备、工具、器具，不论是否达到固定资产标准均计入“设备工具器具购置”中。

（3）其他费用：指在固定资产建造和购置过程中发生的，除上述几项内容以外的各种应分摊计入固定资产的费用。

施工项目 指报告期内所有施工的建设项目个数，包括本年新开工的项目和以前年度开工在本年继续施工的建设项目。凡是报告期内施过工的建设项目，不论施工时间长短，均作为施工项目统计。施工项目个数可以反映一定时期固定资产投资的实际规模，与同期全部建成投产项目个数相比，可以从建设速度的角度反映固定资产投资的效果。

全部建成投产项目 指报告期内按设计文件规定的全部生产能力（或效益）建成投产，经验收合格交付使用的建设项目。

新增生产能力（或工程效益） 指通过固定资产投资活动而增加的设计能力（或工程效益）。主要指标包括建设规模、本年施工规模、自开始建设累计新增生产能力（或工程效益）、本年新增生产能力（或工程效益）等。

建设规模 指建设项目或工程设计文件中规定的全部设计能力（或工程效益）。包括已经建成投产和尚未建成投产的工程的生产能力（或工程效益）。

本年施工规模 指报告期内施工的单项工程的设计能力（或工程效益），即全部建设规模中在本年正式施工的部分。

自开始建设累计新增生产能力（或工程效益） 指自开始建设至本年底止建成投产的全部单项工程累计的新增生产能力（或工程效益）。

本年新增生产能力（或工程效益） 指在本年度内按照新增生产能力（或工程效益）的计算条件和标准，实际建成投入生产或交付使用的生产能力（或工程效益）。

施工房屋面积 指报告期内施工的全部房屋（包括地下室、半地下室以及配套房屋）建筑面积。包括本期新开工的面积和上期开工跨入本期继续施工的房屋面积，以及上期已停建在本期恢复施工的房屋面积。本期竣工和本期施工后又停缓建的房屋，其建筑面积仍计入本期房屋施工面积中。

竣工房屋面积 指在报告期内房屋建筑按照设计要求已经全部完工，达到住人和使用条件，经验收鉴定合格（或达到竣工验收标准），可正式移交使用单位的各栋房屋建筑面积的总和。

新增固定资产 指报告期内交付使用的固定资产价值。包括本年内建成投入生产或交付使用的工程投资和达到固定资产标准的设备、工具、器具的投资及有关应摊入的费用。该指标是表示固定资产投资成果的价值指标，也是反映建设进度，计算固定资产投资效果的重要指标。

项目建成投产率 指一定时期内全部建成投产项目个数与同期施工项目个数的比率。该指标是从建设单位建设速度的角度反映投资效果的指标。

固定资产交付使用率 指一定时期新增固定资产与同期完成投资额的比率。该指标是反映固定资产动用速度，衡量建设过程中宏观投资效果的综合指标。由于新增固定资产是较长时期内形成的结果，而投资额则是当年完成的，因此，该指标一般适宜于反映较长时期内固定资产的动用情况。

商品房销售面积 指报告期内出售商品房屋的合同总面积（即双方签署的正式买卖合同中所确定的建筑面积）。由现房销售建筑面积和期房销售建筑面积两部分组成。

商品房销售额 指报告期内出售商品房屋的合同总价款（即双方签署的正式买卖合同中所确定的合同总价）。该指标与商品房销售面积同口径，由现房销售额和期房销售额两部分组成。

经济适用房 指根据经济适用房计划安排建设的政策性住宅。经济是指房屋建筑造价和销售价格低于一般商品住宅；适用是指适合中低收入家庭购买使用。经济适用房主要是由地方政府统一下达投资计划，房地产公司开发，对外销售；用地一般采用行政划拨或招标投标方式，免收土地出让金；对各种经批准的收费减半征收，开发利润不超过3%；销售价格实行政府指导价。该指标可以分析房地产投资结构，反映中低收入家庭商品住宅的供求平衡情况。

Explanatory Notes on Main Statistical Indicators

Total Investment in Fixed Assets in the Whole Country refers to the volume of activities in construction and purchases of fixed assets of the whole country and related fees, expressed in monetary terms during the reference period. It is a comprehensive indicator which shows the size, structure and growth of the investment in fixed assets, providing a basis for observing the progress of construction projects and evaluating results of investment. Total investment in fixed assets in the whole country includes, by type of ownership, the investment by State-owned units, collective-owned units, joint ownership units, share-holding units, private units individuals as well as investments by entrepreneurs from Hong Kong, Macao and Taiwan, foreign investors and others.

Investment in Fixed Assets (Excluding Rural Households) refers to the investment in construction projects with a total planned investment of 5 million yuan and above by enterprises of various ownerships, public institutions, administrative units and urban self-employed individuals, and the investment in real estate development in both urban and rural areas. Since 2011, it covers the urban investment in fixed assets of original statistical ranges and project investments by rural enterprises and public institutions.

Investment in Real Estate Development refers to investment by real estate development companies, commercialized buildings construction companies and other real estate development units of various types of ownership in the construction of buildings, such as residential buildings, factory buildings, warehouses, hotels, guesthouses, holiday villages, office buildings, and the complementary service facilities and land development projects, such as roads, water supply, water drainage,power supply,heating sup ply, telecommunications, land leveling and other infrastructural projects. It does not include activities in pure land transactions.

Investmentof Rural Households refers to the Housing construction investment (mainly residential construction) taken by the Rural Households as one unit, rural investment in agriculture, forestry, animal husbandry, fishery and service industries (such as the extensive facility agriculture investment of farmers in recent years) and investment in productive fixed assets purchased by farmers.

Sources of Funds for Investment in Fixed Assets are categorized as funds from the State budget, domestic loans, foreign investment, self-raised funds, and others, depending on the sources of investment.

(1) Fund from the State budget consists of budgetary appropriation and loans from the State budget. More specifically, it includes, from the budget of the central government, capital construction fund (operation fund and non-operational fund), special expenses, loans from repayment, discount fund, expenses on innovation and trial production of new products, expenses on urban construction, expenses on temporary construction from business departments, development fund for less developed areas, as well as local budgetary fund transferred from the central budget.

(2) Domestic loans refer to loans of various forms borrowed by investing units from banks and non-bank financial institutions during the reference period for the purpose of investment in fixed assets, including loans issued by banks from their self-owned funds and deposit, loans appropriated by higher authorities, special loans by government, loans arranged by local government from special funds, domestic reserve loan, and working loan.

(3) Foreign investment refers to overseas funds received during the reference period for the construction and purchase of investment in fixed assets (covering equipment, materials and technology), including foreign borrowings (loans from foreign governments and international financial institutions, export credit, commercial loans from foreign banks, issue of bonds and stocks overseas), foreign direct investment and other foreign investments. Excluded from this category is capital in foreign exchanges owned by China (foreign exchanges owned by the central and local governments, foreign exchanges retained by enterprises, foreign exchanges by enterprises through the regulating mechanism, loans in foreign exchanges issued by the Bank of China with its own fund, etc). In calculating the utilization of foreign capital, foreign currencies are converted into Chinese Renminbi applying the current exchange rate when the foreign capitals are actually used.

(4) Self-raised funds refer to extra-budgetary funds for investment in fixed assets received during the reference period by investing units from central government ministries, local governments, enterprises and institutions, including their self-raised funds.

(5) Others refer to funds for investment in fixed assets received from sources other than those listed above, including capital raised through issuing bonds by

enterprises or financial institutions, funds raised from individuals and through donations, and funds transferred from other units.

Investment in Fixed Assets by Sector The classification of construction projects by sector is determined by enterprises, institutions, administrative units and the major products or the purpose of the projects of existing enterprises, institutional and administrative units when they are put into production or use, and by the nature of their social economic activities. In general, one project or one enterprise or institution can only be classified into one sector.

Investment in Fixed Assets by Jurisdiction of Management refers to the classification of investment by the competent authorities under which investment is made by construction units, enterprises, institutions or administrative units.

(1) Central investment refers to the investment in projects or by enterprises, institutions or administrative units which are under the direct leadership and management of the State Council and of the national commissions, ministries, agencies and State-owned large corporations. Various ministries and departments of the State Council prepare and implement plans for investment in fixed assets by those departments, and arrange and ensure the supply of materials and key equipment required for the projects.

(2) Local investment refers to the investment in projects or by enterprises, institutions or administrative units which are under the direct leadership and management of departments under the provincial, prefecture and county governments. Also included are projects by foreign-invested enterprises and enterprises without competent managing authorities.

Investment in Fixed Assets by Type of Construction Construction projects in general can be classified, by the type of construction, into new construction, expansion, reconstruction and technical transformation, purely construction of living facilities, moving, restoration and purely purchasing. However, investment by type of construction is not applied to investment by real-estate development units and investment by rural households.

(1) New construction in general refers to construction projects, which start from scratch, of enterprises, institutions, administrative agencies. In case the size of the existing unit is quite small, and the value of newly added fixed assets is more than three times of the original value, the expansion will be considered as new construction.

(2) Expansion refers to construction of new major production workshop, branch factory or independent production line within a factory or in other locations, for the purpose of increasing the production capacity (or improving efficiency) or adding new production capacity. Newly constructed accommodation for the operation of institutions and administrative organizations (such as newly constructed buildings for teaching in schools, buildings for clinics or wards in hospitals, etc.) are also classified as expansion.

Also included in expansion are investments by existing enterprises or institutions in building major production line(s) or branch factory(ies) along with some work on innovation, for the purpose of expanding the production capacity of original products or producing new products.

(3) Reconstruction and technical transformation refers to construction projects by existing enterprises or institutions in innovation or technical transformation of the old facilities (including auxiliary production equipment and welfare facilities). Also considered as reconstruction is the construction of new workshops by the existing enterprises or institutions to change the variety of products to meet the market demand (such as the production of civil products by defence industries), or to bring the designed production capacity into full play through a more balanced production process on production lines. Technical transformation refers to replacement of old technology or equipment by new technology or equipment, in order to expand the reproduction through improvement of technology contents in production, to improve product quality, to promote new products to save energy,to reduce consumption, to expand the production scale and to improve overall social-economic efficiency. Contents of technical transformation include: updating of machinery, equipment and tools; reforming production process by using energy or materials saving technology; construction of factory workshops and transformation of public facilities; improvement of working conditions and environment, etc.

Investment in Fixed Assets by Structure By their

contents and the mode of implementation, investment activities are classified into 3 categories, i.e. construction and installation, purchase of equipment and instrument, and other expenses.

(1) Construction and installation (work volume of construction and installation) refers to the construction of houses and buildings and the installation of various kinds of equipment and instruments. They include construction of houses; equipment foundations, industrial kilns and stoves, and metal structure work; preparation works and temporary works for project construction, and clearing up works post project construction; pavement of railways and roads, drilling of mines and putting up of oil pipes; construction of water conservancy; construction of underground air-raid shelters and construction of other special projects; value of equipment for heating, sanitation, ventilation, lighting, gas, painting, etc. that are covered by the budget of housing projects; laying out of various pipelines (for steam, compressed air, petroleum, tap water and sewage) and wiring and cabling for electric power and for communications; installation of various machinery and equipment; testing operation for pre- testing the quality of installation projects, and land and other development work conducted by real estate developers for commercialized housing.

The value of equipment installed is itself not included in the value of construction and installation projects.

(2) Purchase of equipment and instruments refers to the total value of equipment, tools, and instruments purchased or self-produced which come up to the cut-off point for fixed assets by the construction units or investing enterprises or institutions. Equipment, tools and instruments purchased or self-produced for new workshops by newly established or expanded units are categorized as "purchase of equipment and instruments" no matter whether they come up to the cut-off point for fixed assets.

(3) Other expenses refer to expenses arising during the construction or purchase of fixed assets other than those mentioned above.

Projects under Construction refer to number of all projects with construction activities newly started in current year or left-over from the previous year in the reference period. All projects that have construction activities undertaken during the reference period are reported as projects under construction irrespective of the length of construction work. The number of projects under construction can reflect the actual size of investment in fixed assets during a given period, and when compared with the number of projects completed and put into use during the same period, it demonstrates the results of investment in fixed assets from the angle of the speed of the construction.

Projects Completed and Put into Use refer to projects have been completed in accordance with the design documents, resulting in forming production capacity (efficiency) and have been checked and accepted after relevant tests, and have been formally delivered for use.

Newly Increased Production Capacity (or Project Efficiency) refers to the increase in design capacity (or project efficiency) through investment in fixed assets. The main indicators include: construction scale, scale of projects under construction in current year, the accumulated newly increased production capacity (project efficiency) since the start of the projects and the newly increased production capacity (project efficiency) of current year.

Construction Scale refers to the total designed production capacity (project efficiency) of the construction projects in accordance with the design document, including those have been put into operation and those that have not been completed.

Scale of Projects under Construction in Current Year refers to the designed production capacity (project efficiency) of a single project under construction in the reference period, i.e. the part of the total scale of project which is officially under construction in current year.

The Accumulated Newly Increased Production Capacity (project efficiency) since the Start of the Projects refers to the accumulated newly increased production capacity of all the single projects which have been put into use from the beginning of the projects till the end of current year.

The Newly Increased Production Capacity (project efficiency) of Current Year refers to the production capacity (project efficiency) that has been completed and put into operation in current year according to the calculation conditions and standards on newly increased production capacity (project efficiency).

Floor Space of Buildings under Construction refers to the total floor space of all the buildings (including basement, semi-basement and auxiliary buildings), including the effective area and the area occupied by the structure. This indicator is one of the important indicators in physical terms to reflect the scale and accomplishment of the construction industry and also an important basis for monitoring the progress, Calculating the cost, analyzing the efficiency and studying the supply of building materials in relation to the construction projects.

Floor Space Completed refers to the floor space of all buildings completed in the reference period, which have been appraised and accepted (or come up to the designed standards) and have been transferred to owner units.

Newly Increased Fixed Assets refer to the value of fixed that has been put into use, including investment in projects that have been completed and put into operation in current year and the investment in equipment, tools and appliance that meet the standard of fixed assets and fees that should be apportioned. This is an indicator that demonstrates the results of investment in fixed assets in monetary terms, and an important indicator to reflect the speed of construction and to calculate the efficiency of investment.

Rate of Construction Projects Completed and Put into Use refers to the ratio of the number of construction projects completed and put into use in a certain period of time to the number of projects under construction in the same period. This reflects the investment efficiency from the perspective of the speed of projects construction.

Rate of Projects of Fixed Assets Completed and Put into Operation refers to the ratio of the newly increased fixed assets to the total investment made in the same period. This is a comprehensive indicator reflecting the speed of the employment of fixed assets and the investment efficiency at the macro-level. As the newly increase fixed assets is the result of a long period while the investment is completed in the current year, this indicator is expected to be used to reflect the employment of fixed assets over a long period of time.

6 财 政

GOVERNMENT FINANCE

资料整理：孟　刚
Data management: Meng Gang
数据审核：刘　婷
Data audit: Liu Ting

第六部分 财政

一、简要说明

本章资料主要包括地方财政收入、支出总额构成及分区县情况，由西安市统计局综合处根据西安市财政局提供资料整理。

二、主要指标

财政总收入（亿元）	1533.89	比上年增长	5.0%
一般公共预算收入（亿元）	702.56	比上年增长	2.6%
一般公共预算支出（亿元）	1247.02	比上年增长	8.3%

6 GOVERNMENT FINANCE

Ⅰ.Brief Introduction

This chapter consists of primarily data on regional revenue, expenditure of the municipal government, regional revenue and expenditure of the districts and the counties. The data are provided by the Xi'an Bureau of Finance and are compiled by Integration division of the Xi'an Bureau of Statistics.

Ⅱ.Major Indicators

		Increase over Preceding Year
Total Government Revenue(100 mil. yuan)	1533.89	5.0%
General Pubilc Budgetary Revenue(100 mil. yuan)	702.56	2.6%
General Pubilc Budgetary Expenditures(100 mil. yuan)	1247.02	8.3%

6-1 主要年份地方财政一般预算收入及支出

General Public Budgetary Revenue and Expenditure of Local Finance in Representative Years

单位：亿元 （100 million yuan）

年 份 Year	财政总收入 Fiscal Revenue	一般公共预算收入 General Public Budgetary Revenue	一般公共预算支出 General Public Budgetary Expenditure	收支差额 Balance of Payments	财政总收入比上年增长（%） Fiscal Revenue Increased over the Previous Year（%）	一般公共预算收入比上年增长（%） General Public Budget Revenue Growth over the Previous Year（%）	一般公共预算支出比上年增长（%） General Public Budget Expenditures Growth over the Previous Yea r（%）
2000	61.57	41.39	46.50	-5.11		14.4	
2001	75.79	51.45	54.21	-2.76	23.1	9.9	10.2
2002	99.84	54.49	63.80	-9.32	31.7	16.9	11.3
2003	120.64	64.80	72.37	-7.57	20.8	21.6	22.6
2004	133.52	75.31	84.20	-8.88	10.7	20.0	16.3
2005	163.87	73.05	97.82	-24.76	22.7	18.2	16.2
2006	195.96	85.89	119.22	-33.33	19.6	18.6	21.9
2007	260.70	112.92	161.25	-48.33	33.0	31.5	35.3
2008	324.49	145.61	226.99	-81.38	24.5	28.9	40.8
2009	399.53	181.40	276.85	-95.45	23.4	24.6	22.0
2010	510.69	241.86	371.62	-129.76	27.6	33.3	34.2
2011	649.88	318.55	494.58	-176.03	27.3	31.7	33.1
2012	753.08	396.96	597.49	-200.53	15.9	24.6	20.8
2013	902.76	501.98	729.81	-227.84	19.9	26.5	22.1
2014	1019.69	583.79	819.54	-235.75	13.0	16.3	12.3
2015	1114.98	650.99	917.24	-266.25	9.3	16.3	12.9
2016	1135.68	641.07	942.52	-301.46	8.5	11.1	2.8
2017	1364.71	654.50	1045.09	-390.59	12.6	9.8	7.1
2018	1460.39	684.70	1151.87	-467.17	13.6	10.8	10.2
2019	1533.89	702.56	1247.02	-544.46	5.0	2.6	8.3

注：本表数据来源于市财政局，对部分历史年份数据进行了修订。

6-2 财政收入（2019年）

Government Revenue（2019）

单位：万元 （10 000 yuan）

指　　标	Item	2019
财政总收入	**Total Government Revenue**	**15338894**
#一般公共预算收入	**General Public Budgetary Revenue**	**7025624**
一、税收收入	**Total Tax Revenue**	**5807466**
1. 国内增值税	Value-added Tax	817502
2. 改征增值税	Levying VAT	1555921
3. 企业所得税	Corporate Income Tax	631472
4. 个人所得税	Individual Income Tax	227945
5. 城市建设维护税	City Maintenance and Construction Tax	510006
6. 房产税	House Property Tax	275238
7. 城镇土地使用税	Urban Land Use Tax	109314
8. 印花税	Stamp Tax	165946
9. 车船税	Tax on the Use of Vehicles and Ships	126470
10. 土地增值税	Land Appreciation Tax	627882
11. 资源税	Resource Tax	21063
12. 环境保护税	Environmental Protection Tax	578
13. 耕地占用税	Farm Land Occupatian Tax	71111
14. 契税	Deed Tax	665164
15. 其他税收收入	Other Tax Revenue	1854
二、非税收入	**Total Non-tax Revenue**	**1218158**
1. 行政事业性收费收入	Charge of Adminnistrative and Institutional Units	213151
2. 罚没收入	Penalty Receipts	165780
3. 专项收入	Special Program Receipts	521199
4. 国有资本经营收入	State-owned Assets Profit	26
5. 国有资源（资产）有偿使用收入	Revenue for the Use of State-owned Assets (Resources)	222948
6. 捐赠收入	Donation Income	76
7. 政府住房基金收入	Governmental Housing Fund Income	93459
8. 其他收入	Other Revenue	1519
政府性基金预算收入	**Governmental Fund Budgetary Revenue**	**9533803**

注：本表数据来源于市财政局。

6-3 财政支出（2019年）

Government Expenditures (2019)

单位：万元 (10 000 yuan)

指 标	Item	2019
一般公共预算支出	**General Public Budgetary Expenditure**	**12470153**
1. 一般公共服务支出	Expenditure for General Public Services	1227047
2. 国防支出	Expenditure for National Defense	8592
3. 公共安全支出	Expenditure for Public Security	780571
4. 教育支出	Expenditure for Education	2018994
5. 科学技术支出	Expenditure for Science and Technology	347911
6. 文化旅游体育与传媒支出	Expenditure for Cultural, Travel,Sports and Media	210776
7. 社会保障和就业支出	Expenditure for Social Safety Net and Employment Effort	1292821
8. 卫生健康支出	Expenditure for Medical and Health Care	919875
9. 节能环保支出	Expenditure for Energy Saving	802464
10. 城乡社区支出	Expenditure for Urban and Rural Community Affairs	2455353
11. 农林水支出	Expenditure for Agriculture, Forestry and Water Conservancy	598370
12. 交通运输支出	Expenditure for Transportation	240945
13. 资源勘探信息等支出	Expenditure for Exploration of Information	203384
14. 商业服务业等支出	Expenditure for Business Services	286907
15. 金融支出	Expenditure for Finance	17092
16. 自然资源海洋气象等支出	Natural Resources and Marine Meteorology	77747
17. 住房保障支出	Expenditure for Housing Security	494067
18. 粮油物资储备支出	Expenditure for Grain and Oil Stockpiles	19886
19. 灾害防治及应急管理支出	Expenditures for Disaster Prevention and Emergency Management	55580
20. 其他支出	Other Expenditure	106856
21. 债务付息支出	Debt Service Expenditure	303505
22. 债务发行费用支出	Debt Issuance Expenditure	1410
政府性基金预算支出	**Governmental Fund Budgetary Expenditure**	**8999411**

注：本表数据来源于市财政局。

6-4 各区县、开发区财政收入（2019年）

单位：万元

区县、开发区	Region	一般公共预算收入 General Public Budgetary Revenue	税收收入 Tax Revenue	增值税 Value Added Tax	企业所得税 Corporate Income Tax
合计	**Total**	**7025624**	**5807466**	**2373423**	**631472**
市本级合计	Sum of City Level	1362967	736784	388524	58346
新城区	Xincheng	227250	208227	67267	40514
碑林区	Beilin	367845	341998	164539	55574
莲湖区	Lianhu	389740	353887	165742	33363
雁塔区	Yanta	459339	396687	178425	43595
灞桥区	Baqiao	182840	158453	57951	23199
未央区	Weiyang	311884	284558	115816	32889
阎良区	Yanliang	70143	53427	22477	4971
临潼区	Lintong	131584	81327	32524	6958
长安区	Chang'an	208071	180627	76324	21922
高陵区	Gaoling	120553	108647	50293	7193
鄠邑区	Huyi	74905	55988	31043	3433
蓝田县	Lantian	27218	19565	10027	1081
周至县	Zhouzhi	25099	19020	10911	632
西咸新区	Xixian	718509	623379	207252	48712
全市中：高新区	Total City: Gao Xin	1032374	970229	423743	130504
经开区	JingKai	410952	368165	155409	47092
曲江新区	Qujiang	440947	405892	107205	37963
浐灞生态区	Chanba Eco-District	233946	224996	36292	14397
航天基地	Aerospace Base	76112	69468	17794	7486
航空基地	Aviation Industry Base	10526	9580	2755	807
国际港务区	International Trade&Logistic Park	142820	136562	51110	10841

注：本表数据来源于市财政局。

Government Revenue by Region and Development Zone (2019)

(10 000 yuan)

一般公共预算收入 General Public Budgetary Revenue					
税收收入 Tax Revenue					
个人所得税 Individual Income Tax	资源税 Resource Tax	城市维护建设税 City Maintenance and Construction Tax	耕地占用税 Farm Land Occupation Tax	契税 Deed Tax	其他各项税收收入 Other Tax Revenue
227945	**21063**	**510006**	**71111**	**665164**	**1307282**
19272	19953	108994			141695
9259		16945		32900	41342
29001		31302		15752	45830
21101	6	31855		44395	57425
17050	7	34207	49	51347	72007
2939	3	13281	1916	21802	37362
9368	8	24853	5444	32114	64066
3126		3016	1682	5853	12302
1879	55	6716	11856	7804	13535
5988	99	14998	1895	19698	39703
2673	1	9672	5616	7524	25675
1432	39	5229	453	3840	10519
556	34	1490	804	1203	4370
847	7	1292	744	961	3626
8973	854	44031	31965	128196	153396
68931	3	81949	4657	78668	181774
11993	-2	32176		42444	79053
6424	2	22619		83751	147928
1813	-7	7915		52874	111712
2768		5430		9613	26377
481		1785		1106	2646
2071	1	10251	4030	23319	34939

6-4 续表1

单位：万元

区县、开发区	Region	一般公共预算收入 General Public Budgetary Revenue		
		非税收入 Non-tax Revenue	专项收入 Special Program Receipts	行政事业性收费收入 Charge of Adiministrative and Institutional Units
合计	**Total**	**1218158**	**521199**	**213151**
市本级合计	Sum of City Level	626183	228353	132745
新城区	Xincheng	19023	9443	3290
碑林区	Beilin	25847	17437	2110
莲湖区	Lianhu	35853	20681	4997
雁塔区	Yanta	62652	18436	19627
灞桥区	Baqiao	24387	20131	603
未央区	Weiyang	27326	13806	7232
阎良区	Yanliang	16716	5461	3786
临潼区	Lintong	50257	3745	3773
长安区	Chang'an	27444	7546	1514
高陵区	Gaoling	11906	5142	2246
鄠邑区	Huyi	18917	3303	3506
蓝田县	Lantian	7653	1774	1346
周至县	Zhouzhi	6079	987	529
西咸新区	Xixian	95130	56455	17540
全市中：高新区	Total City: Gao Xin	62145	46830	6416
经开区	JingKai	42787	19293	711
曲江新区	Qujiang	35055	24143	347
浐灞生态区	Chanba Eco-District	8950	5438	458
航天基地	Aerospace Base	6644	5961	277
航空基地	Aviation Industry Base	946	676	98
国际港务区	International Trade&Logistic Park	6258	6158	

continued 1

（10 000 yuan）

一般公共预算收入 General Public Budgetary Revenue			政府性基金预算收入 Governmental Funds Budgetary Revenue
非税收入 Non-tax Revenue			
罚没收入 Penalty Receipts	国有资源（资产）有偿使用收入 The Revenues of the Compensation for the Use of State-owned Resoures(Assants)	其他各项非税收入 Other non-tax income	
165780	**222948**	**95080**	**9533803**
92943	89072	83070	839285
3721	2569		196
1902	4398		
3215	6960		402595
2551	22033	5	
1645	1937	71	264185
2281	3890	117	21151
1941	5528		27148
5535	37132	72	101851
14537	3725	122	198918
2277	2164	77	17730
7084	3896	1128	28130
2763	1764	6	10332
3564	919	80	19334
8999	9985	2151	3428191
2450	2838	3611	1389295
4546	15494	2743	356131
1349	7440	1776	662237
2146	908		719150
293	113		237519
38	83	51	115770
	100		694655

6-5 各区县、开发区财政支出（2019年）

单位：万元

区县、开发区	Region	一般公共预算支出 General Public Budgetary Expenditures	一般公共服务支出 General Public Services Expenditure	国防支出 Expenditure for National Defense	公共安全支出 Expenditure for Public Safety
合计	**Total**	**12470153**	**1227047**	**8592**	**780571**
市本级合计	Sum of City Level	3574080	257738	4265	419502
新城区	Xincheng	229618	18576	109	22347
碑林区	Beilin	290175	30410		24970
莲湖区	Lianhu	358792	43448	292	33141
雁塔区	Yanta	353002	36354	374	37418
灞桥区	Baqiao	355428	44733	463	24733
未央区	Weiyang	335458	36210	86	25370
阎良区	Yanliang	224871	22451	39	11186
临潼区	Lintong	458230	34408	115	19470
长安区	Chang'an	504679	48910	263	22834
高陵区	Gaoling	355325	43060	280	12356
鄠邑区	Huyi	338450	29153	418	13546
蓝田县	Lantian	427514	32369	162	11851
周至县	Zhouzhi	424000	26981	86	11623
西咸新区	Xixian	1260679	223485	1610	47540
全市中：高新区	Total City: Gao Xin	1207294	95535	30	17624
经开区	JingKai	295071	46136		7698
曲江新区	Qujiang	444479	37438		1782
浐灞生态区	Chanba Eco-District	433246	50360		5531
航天基地	Aerospace Base	106358	8157		4554
航空基地	Aviation Industry Base	32061	3844		
国际港务区	International Trade&Logistic Park	461343	57291		5495

注：本表数据来源于市财政局。

Government Expenditure by Region and Development Zone （2019）

（10 000 yuan）

一般公共预算支出 General Public Budgetary Expenditures					
教育支出 Expenditure for Education	科学技术支出 Expenditure for Science and Technology	文化旅游体育与传媒支出 Expenditure for Cultural, Travel, Sports and Media	社会保障和就业支出 Expenditure for Social Safety Net and Employment Effort	卫生健康支出 Expenditure for Medical and Health Care	节能环保支出 Expenditure for Energy Saving and Environment Protection
2018994	**347911**	**210776**	**1292821**	**919875**	**802464**
162411	72314	64638	409242	289561	243917
67060	1190	788	53924	13879	1544
73538	3934	3197	70858	19532	6072
104020	2804	2702	63690	19178	6452
105047	1236	3380	47632	32330	3950
77762	1134	2612	38076	26276	11195
104346	1903	1869	29149	24474	9745
52242	246	1733	35321	24217	4953
110013	531	8126	97471	64419	17762
145162	784	8455	63435	75440	13761
78866	709	4420	39895	46155	3940
85091	908	4900	45525	42553	19297
91004	800	7366	79380	62350	15908
111671	489	5299	51488	58394	29540
229589	15960	9381	110344	79681	60910
121531	192985	15940	42812	28780	296496
54133	31800	1434	1308	28	44581
76967		57402	1	19	3213
44166	2584	846			2976
30054	13450	120	330		3481
2000	2000	20			914
92321	150	6148	12940	12609	1857

6-5 续表1

单位：万元

区县、开发区	Region	一般公共预算支出 General Public Budgetary Expenditures			
		城乡社区支出 Expenditure for Urban and Rural Community Affairs	农林水支出 Expenditure for Agriculture, Foresty and Water Conservancy	交通运输支出 Expenditure for Transportation	资源勘探信息等支出 Expenditure for Exploration of Information
合计	**Total**	**2455353**	**598370**	**240945**	**203384**
市本级合计	Sum of City Level	849243	128386	140563	49565
新城区	Xincheng	33083	1166	1371	1890
碑林区	Beilin	52555	522	363	865
莲湖区	Lianhu	52903	2056	706	1211
雁塔区	Yanta	66793	5243	1632	1495
灞桥区	Baqiao	94468	16614	3153	1039
未央区	Weiyang	77039	8834	2184	528
阎良区	Yanliang	24589	21565	3521	7980
临潼区	Lintong	14942	51152	3944	2033
长安区	Chang'an	33158	61394	8038	1253
高陵区	Gaoling	55192	21969	12604	1227
鄠邑区	Huyi	20487	48201	7901	1195
蓝田县	Lantian	37209	63186	7463	818
周至县	Zhouzhi	23558	88145	8179	503
西咸新区	Xixian	116784	43566	36956	43202
全市中：高新区	Total City: Gao Xin	211372	20279	18	50374
经开区	JingKai	69122	200	2289	28059
曲江新区	Qujiang	227042	4821		922
浐灞生态区	Chanba Eco-District	284366	1185		565
航天基地	Aerospace Base	26956			4589
航空基地	Aviation Industry Base	10458	2036		3786
国际港务区	International Trade&Logistic Park	74034	7850	60	285

continued 1

（10 000 yuan）

一般公共预算支出 General Public Budgetary Expenditures					
商业服务业等支出 Expenditure for Business Services	金融支出 Expenditure for Finance	自然资源海洋气象等支出 Natural Resources and Marine Meteorology	住房保障支出 Expenditure for Housing Support	粮油物资储备支出 Expenditure for Grain and Oil Stockpiles	灾害防治及应急管理支出 Disaster Prevention and emergency management expenditure
286907	**17092**	**77747**	**494067**	**19886**	**55580**
68816	10621	16212	179547	16657	22853
1454	787	745	7669	34	577
877		700	720		
512		1414	18551	56	571
1224	324	1996	4901		882
591		1733	210	237	1362
1179	107	2306	102	56	789
752	206	1992	7364	630	402
292	108	3135	12474	317	1399
1174	120	6569	10421	589	1120
590		4577	23098	489	2089
633	217	2851	2830	313	547
971	111	5282	4200	348	1055
652	22	1632	2129	160	1263
22828	396	22458	68547		14484
3437	2315	1825	68114		662
1404	200		2743		2775
741	1279	6	21461		1437
9234	85	1865	23477		799
220	121	149	12697		513
	73		3962		
169326		300	18850		1

6-5 续表2 continued 2

单位：万元 （10 000 yuan）

区县、开发区	Region	一般公共预算支出 General Public Budgetary Expenditures 债务付息支出 Debt Service Expenditure	债务发行费用支出 Debt Issuance Expenditure	其他支出 Other Expenditure	政府性基金预算支出 Governmental Fund Budgetary Expenditure
合计	**Total**	**303505**	**1410**	**106856**	**8999411**
市本级合计	Sum of City Level	162723	1198	4108	1142667
新城区	Xincheng	1425			113610
碑林区	Beilin	1062			12507
莲湖区	Lianhu	5025		60	250102
雁塔区	Yanta	629		162	6397
灞桥区	Baqiao	5986		3051	110689
未央区	Weiyang	9182			22124
阎良区	Yanliang	3272		210	28041
临潼区	Lintong	4239		11880	116235
长安区	Chang'an	1654		145	141321
高陵区	Gaoling	3609		200	65130
鄠邑区	Huyi	2971		8913	39269
蓝田县	Lantian	2367		3314	13203
周至县	Zhouzhi	2179		7	32062
西咸新区	Xixian	40863	212	71883	3384055
全市中：高新区	Total City: Gao Xin	37067		98	1037113
经开区	JingKai	1161			276358
曲江新区	Qujiang	9809		139	840522
浐灞生态区	Chanba Eco-District	3513		1694	525393
航天基地	Aerospace Base	907		60	181113
航空基地	Aviation Industry Base	2068		900	116564
国际港务区	International Trade&Logistic Park	1794		32	544936

主要统计指标解释

财政收入 指国家财政参与社会产品分配所取得的收入，是实现国家职能的财力保证。主要包括：

（1）税收收入：包括增值税、消费税、企业所得税、企业所得税退税、个人所得税、资源税、城市维护建设税、房产税、印花税、城镇土地使用税、土地增值税、车船税、船舶吨税、车辆购置税、关税、耕地占用税、契税、烟叶税、环境保护税和其他税收收入。

（2）非税收入：包括专项收入、行政事业性收费收入、罚没收入、国有资本经营收入、国有资源（资产）有偿使用收入、捐赠收入、政府住房基金收入和其他收入。

财政支出 指国家财政将筹集起来的资金进行分配使用，以满足经济建设和各项事业的需要。主要包括：

（1）一般公共服务支出：指政府提供基本公共管理与服务的支出，包括人大事务、政协事务、政府办公厅（室）及相关机构事务、发展与改革事务、统计信息事务、财政事务、税收事务、审计事务、海关事务、人力资源事务、纪检监察事务、商贸事务、知识产权事务、民族事务、港澳台侨事务、档案事务、民主党派及工商联事务、群众团体事务、党委办公厅（室）及相关机构事务、组织事务、宣传事务、统战事务、对外联络事务、其他共产党事务支出、网信服务、市场监督管理实务和其他一般公共服务支出。

（2）外交支出：指政府外交事务支出，包括外交管理事务、驻外机构、对外援助、国际组织、对外合作与交流、对外宣传、边界勘界联检、国际发展合作等方面的支出。

（3）国防支出：指政府用于国防方面的支出，包括用于现役部队、国防科研事业、专项工程、国防动员等方面的支出。

（4）公共安全支出：指政府维护社会公共安全方面的支出，包括武装警察部队、公安、国家安全、检察、法院、司法、监狱、强制隔离戒毒、国家保密、缉私警察、海警等。

（5）教育支出：指政府教育事务支出，包括教育管理事务、普通教育、职业教育、成人教育、广播电视教育、留学教育、特殊教育、进修及培训、教育费附加安排的支出等。

（6）科学技术支出：指用于科学技术方面的支出，包括科学技术管理事务、基础研究、应用研究、技术研究与开发、科技条件与服务、社会科学、科学技术普及、科技交流与合作、科技重大项目等。

（7）文化旅游体育与传媒支出：指政府在文化和旅游、文物、体育、新闻出版电影、广播电视等方面的支出。

（8）社会保障和就业支出：指政府在社会保障与就业方面的支出，包括人力资源和社会保障管理事务、民政管理事务、补充全国社会保障基金、行政事业单位离退休、企业改革补助、就业补助、抚恤、退役安置、社会福利、残疾人事业、红十字事业、最低生活保障、临时救助、特困人员救助供养、补充道路交通事故社会救助基金、其他生活救助、财政对基本养老保险基金的补助、财政对其他社会保险基金的补助、退役军人管理实务等。

（9）卫生健康支出：指政府卫生健康方面的支出，包括卫生健康管理事务、公立医院、基层医疗卫生机构、公共卫生、中医药、计划生育事务、行政事业单位医疗、财政对基本医疗保险基金的补助、医疗救助、优抚对象医疗、医疗保障管理事务、老龄卫生健康事务等。

（10）节能环保支出：指政府节能环保支出，包括环境保护管理事务、环境监测与监察、污染防治、自然生态保护、天然林保护、退耕还林、风沙荒漠治理、退牧还草、已垦草原退耕还草、能源节约利用、污染减排、可再生能源、循环经济、能源管理事务等支出。

（11）城乡社区支出：指政府城乡社区事务支出，包括城乡社区管理事务、城乡社区规划与管理、城乡社区公共设施、城乡社区环境卫生、建设市场管理与监督等。

（12）农林水支出：指政府用于农林水事务支出，包括农业、林业和草原、水利、南水北调、扶贫、农业综合开发、农村综合改革、普惠金融发展支出、目标价格补贴等。

（13）交通运输支出：指政府交通运输和邮政业方面的支出，包括公路水路运输、铁路运输、民用航空运输、成品油价格改革对交通运输的补贴、邮政业支出、车辆购置税支出等。

（14）资源勘探信息等支出：指政府用于资源勘探、制造业、建筑业、工业信息等方面的支出，包括资源勘探开发、制造业、建筑业、工业和信息产业监管、国有资产监管、支持中小企业发展和管理等。

（15）商业服务业支出：指政府用于商业服务业方面的支出，包括商业流通事务、涉外发展服务等。

（16）金融支出：指政府用于金融方面的支出，包括金融部门行政支出、金融部门监管支出、金融发展、金融调控等。

（17）援助其他地区支出：指用于援助方政府安排并管理的对其他地区各类援助、捐赠等资金支出。包括一般公共服务、教育、文化体育与传媒、医疗卫生、节能环保、农业、交通运输、住房保障等支出

（18）自然资源海洋气象等支出：指政府用于自然资源、海洋管理、测绘、气象等公益服务事业方面的支出。

（19）住房保障支出：指政府用于住房方面的支出，包括保障性安居工程支出、住房改革支出、城乡社区住宅等。

（20）粮油物资储备支出：指政府用于粮油物资储备方面的支出，包括粮油事务、物资事务、能源储备、粮油储备、重要商品储备等。

（21）灾害防治及应急管理支出：指政府用于灾害防治及应急管理方面的支出，包括应急管理事务、消防事务、森林消防事务、煤矿安全、地震事务、自然灾害防治、自然灾害救灾及恢复重建支出等。

（22）债务付息支出：指政府用于归还债务利息等所发生的支出。

（23）债务发行费用支出：指政府用于债务发行兑付费用的支出。

（24）其他支出：指不能划分到上述功能科目的其他政府支出。

中央财政收入和地方财政收入 指按现行分税制财政体制划分的中央本级收入和地方本级收入。属于中央财政的收入包括关税，进口货物增值税和消费税，出口货物退增值税和消费税，消费税，铁道部门、各银行总行、各保险公司总公司等集中缴纳的城市维护建设税，增值税50%部分，纳入共享范围的企业所得税60%部分，未纳入共享范围的中央企业所得税、中央企业上交的利润，个人所得税60%部分，车辆购置税，船舶吨税，证券交易印花税，海洋石油资源税，中央非税收入等。属于地方财政的收入包括地方企业上交利润，城市维护建设税（不含铁道部门、各银行总行、各保险公司总公司集中缴纳的部分），房产税，城镇土地使用税，土地增值税，车船税，耕地占用税，契税，烟叶税，印花税（不含证券交易印花税），增值税50%部分，纳入共享范围的企业所得税40%部分，个人所得税40%部分，海洋石油资源税以外的其他资源税，地方非税收入等。

中央财政支出和地方财政支出 指根据政府在经济和社会活动中的不同职责，划分中央和地方政府的责权，按照政府的责权划分确定的支出。中央财政支出包括一般公共服务，外交支出，国防支出，公共安全支出，以及中央政府调整国民经济结构、协调地区发展、实施宏观调控的支出等。地方财政支出包括一般公共服务，公共安全支出，地方统筹的各项社会事业支出等。

Explanatory Notes on Main Statistical Indicators

Government Revenue refers to income for the government finance through participating in the distribution of social products. It is the financial guarantee to ensure government functioning. The contents of government revenue include the following main items:

(1) Tax revenue, including value added tax(VAT), consumption tax, business tax, corporate income tax, corporate income tax refund ,individual income tax, resource tax, city maintenance and construct tax, house property tax, stamp tax, urban land use tax, land appreciation tax, tax on vehicles and boat operation, ship tonnage tax, vehicle purchase tax, tariffs, farm land occupation tax, deed tax, and tobacco leaf tax, etc.

(2) Non-tax revenue, including special program receipts, charge of administrative and institutional units, penalty receipts, state-owned capital operating income, state-owned resources (assets) compensation for the use of income, donation income, government housing fund income and others non-tax receipts.

Government Expenditure refers to the distribution and use of the funds which the government finance has raised, so as to meet the needs of economic construction and various causes. It includes the following main items:

(1) Expenditure for general public services: It refers to the spending on the basic public management and services which provided by governments, including the expense on affairs of People's Congress, affairs of People's Political Consultative Conference, affairs of government general office and relative institutions, affairs of development and reform, affairs of statistics, affairs of finance, affairs of taxation, affairs of audit, affairs of customs, affairs of human resources and social security, affairs of discipline inspection and supervision, affairs of population and family planning, affairs of commerce and trade, affairs of intellectual property, affairs of administration for industry and commerce, affairs of land and resources, affairs of oceanic administration, affairs of surveying and mapping, affairs of earthquake, ethnic affairs, religious affairs, affairs of Hong Kong, Macao, Taiwan, and Overseas Chinese, affairs of archives administration, affairs of democratic parties and federation of industry and commerce, affairs of mass organization, and affairs of lottery, affairs of the general office of the Party Committee and related institutions, affairs of propaganda, affairs of united front, affairs of external liaison, affairs of expenditure on other Communist Party, other affairs of Chinese Communist Party, etc.

(2) Expenditure for foreign affairs: It refers to the spending of government on foreign affairs, including the expense on administration of foreign affairs, missions overseas, external assistance, international organizations, foreign cooperation and communication, surveying and joint inspection on borderline, etc.

(3) Expenditure for national defense: It refers to the spending of government on national defense, including the expense on active force, scientific research on national defense, special projects, mobilization of national defense, etc.

(4) Expenditure for public security: It refers to the spending of government on maintaining social and public security, including the expense on armed police force, public security, state security, prosecution, courts, justice, prison, compulsory isolation and drug treatment, state secrecy, anti-smuggling police, maritime police, etc.

(5) Expenditure for education: It refers to the spending of government on education, including the expense on the administration of education, general education, regular vocational school education, adult education, radio and television education, student abroad education, special education, education and training, education surtax arrangements spending, etc.

(6) Expenditure for science and technology: It refers to the spending of government on science and technology (S&T), including the expense on the administration of S&T, basic research, applied research, research and development, conditions and services of S&T, social science, popularization of science and technology, exchanges and cooperation of S&T, major project of S&T, etc.

(7) Expenditure for culture, sport and media: It refers to the spending of government on culture, sports, radio, film, television, press and publication, etc.

(8) Expenditure for social safety net and employment effort: It refers to the spending of government on social safety net and employment, including the expense on administration of social safety net and employment, civil affairs, subsidy on National Social Security Fund, retirees of administrative units and institutions, subsidy on enterprise reform, subsidy on employment effort, pension, placement of ex-serviceman, social welfare, the handicapped undertakings, living relief of natural disasters, affairs of Red Cross Society, minimum subsistence security, temporary assistance, relief and assistance for the residents living in extreme poverty, supplementary social assistance fund for road traffic accidents, other life assistance, financial subsidy for basic old-age insurance fund, financial subsidy for other social insurance funds, etc.

(9) Expenditure for medical health care and birth control planning: It refers to government spending on health care, including health management services, public hospitals, primary health care institutions, public health, the pharmaceutical, family planning affairs, food and drug supervision and administration affairs, medical treatment of administrative institutions, financial subsidies to basic medical insurance funds, medical assistance, preferential care for the target medical treatment, etc.

(10) Expenditure for energy saving: It refers to the government energy-saving and environmental protection expenditures, including environmental management services, environmental monitoring and surveillance, pollution control, ecological protection, natural forest protection project, forest, desert sand control, pasture, grassland of cultivated farmland, energy conservation and utilization expenditure pollution reduction, renewable energy and comprehensive utilization of resources, etc.

(11) Expenditure for urban and rural community affairs: It refers to the spending of government on urban and rural community affairs, including the expense on administration of urban and rural community, planning and management of urban and rural community, public facilities of urban and rural community, housing of urban and rural community, sanitation of urban and rural community, management and supervision on the construction market, etc.

(12) Expenditure for agriculture, forestry and water conservancy: It refers to the spending of government on agriculture, forestry and water conservancy, including the expense on agriculture, forestry, water conservancy, South-to-North Water Diversion Project, poverty alleviation, agricultural comprehensive development, comprehensive agricultural reform, inclusive financial development expenditure and target price subsidies, etc.

(13) Expenditure for transportation: It refers to the spending of government on transportation and postal services, including the expense on road transport, sea transport, rail transport, civil aviation transportation, oil price reform subsidies for transportation, postal services, vehicle purchase tax, etc.

(14) Expenditure for exploration of the power of information: It refers to the spending on exploration, manufacturing, construction, industry information and other aspects of information, including resource exploration and development, manufacturing, construction, industry and information industry regulation, safety supervision, the state-owned assets supervision and support of small and medium enterprise development and management, etc.

(15) Expenditure for business services: It refers to government spending on commercial aspects of services, including commercial distribution business, tourism management and services, foreign development services, etc.

(16) Expenditure for financial: It refers to government spending on financial aspects, including administrative of financial sector, financial sector supervision, financial development, financial control, etc.

(17) Expenditure for assistance to other parts: It refers to the various types of assistance to other regions, financial donations, donors, government expenditure and management arrangements, etc.

(18) Expenditure for Land and Marine Meteorology: It refers to government spending on land resources, marine, mapping, seismic, weather and other aspects of

public service undertakings, etc.

(19) Expenditure for housing security: It refers to government spending on housing, including affordable housing projects, housing reform, urban and rural communities housing, etc.

(20) Expenditure for Grain and Oil stockpiles: It refers to government spending on supplies of grain and oil reserves, including grain and oil services, supplies services, energy reserves, grain and oil reserves, reserves of other important commodities, etc.

(21) Expenditure on disaster prevention and emergency management: refers to the government expenditure on disaster prevention and emergency management, including expenditure on emergency management, fire control, forest fire control, coal mine safety, earthquake, natural disaster prevention and control, natural disaster relief and recovery and reconstruction, etc.

(22) Expenditure for debt interest payment: It refers to the government expenditure for repayment of interest on debts, etc.

(23) Expenditure for debt issuance: It refers to the Government expenditure on debt issuance and payment fees.

(24) Other expenditure: It refers to other government spending cannot be divided into the above functions subjects.

Revenue of the Central Government and Revenue of the Local Governments refers to the revenue collected by the Central Government and that by the local governments as defined by the decentralized taxation system. In accordance with this system, the revenue of the Central Government includes tariff, VAT and consumption tax from imports, VAT and consumption tax rebate for exports, consumption tax, city maintenance and construct tax from the Ministry of Railways, head offices of banks, head offices of insurance company, which are handed over to the government in a centralized way, 50% of the value added tax, 60% the share part of the corporate income tax, unshared part of corporate income tax of the central enterprises, profit handed in by the central enterprises, 60% of individual income tax, vehicle purchase tax, ship tonnage tax, stamp tax on securities transactions, resource tax on the offshore petroleum resources, Central Government non-tax revenue, etc. The revenue of the local governments includes profit handed in by the local enterprises, city maintenance and construct tax (excluding the part of the Ministry of Railways, head offices of banks, head offices of insurance company, which are handed over to the government in a centralized way), house property tax, urban land use tax, land appreciation tax, tax on vehicles and boat operation, farm land occupation tax, deed tax, and tobacco leaf tax, stamp tax, 50% of the value added tax, 40% the share part of the corporate income tax, 40% of individual income tax, resource tax other than the tax on offshore petroleum resources, local non-tax revenue, etc.

Expenditure of the Central Government and Expenditure of the Local Governments according to the different functions of the Central Government and local governments in economic and social activities, the rights of affairs administration are demarcated between those of the Central Government and those of local governments; and the classification of the expenditure between the Central Government and local governments are made on the basis of the classification of the rights of affairs administration between them. The expenditure of the Central Government includes the expenditure for general public services, expenditure for foreign affairs, expenditure for defense, expenditure for public security, and the expenditure of the Central Government for adjusting the national economic structure; coordinating the development among different regions; and exercising macroeconomic regulation. The expenditure of the local governments includes mainly the expenditure for general public services, expenditure for public security, and expenditures for social development which are planned by local governments, etc.

7 物价指数

PRICE INDICES

资料整理：张元园　乔兴录

Data management: Zhang Yuanyuan Qiao Xinglu

数据审核：李　航　高小琴　贾海宇

Data audit: Li Hang Gao Xiaoqin Jia Haiyu

第七部分　物价指数

一、简要说明

1.本章资料主要反映生产、流通、消费、投资与房地产等环节价格变动趋势和变动幅度。主要包括居民消费价格指数、商品零售价格指数、工业生产者出厂价格指数、工业生产者购进价格指数、固定资产投资价格指数和住宅销售价格指数。

2.本章资料由国家统计局西安调查队提供。

3.居民消费价格指数、商品零售价格指数资料的获取，是通过抽样调查和重点调查相结合的方式。在西安市区域内选定经营规模大、商品种类多的大型商场、超市、农贸市场和服务网点作为调查点，选择具有代表性的商品和服务项目作为样本，对其市场价格进行定期调查，以样本推断总体。

4.工业生产者出厂价格指数、工业生产者购进价格指数、固定资产投资价格指数，采取抽样调查和重点调查的方法。工业生产者出厂、工业生产者购进价格指数通过西安工业企业网上直报获取。固定资产投资价格指数通过西安建筑安装企业季报获取。住宅销售价格指数通过西安市月度住宅销售网签数据获取。

二、主要指标

居民消费价格总指数（上年=100）	102.7	比上年上升	0.8 个百分点
商品零售价格总指数（上年=100）	102.1	比上年下降	0.1 个百分点

7 PRICE INDICES

Ⅰ.Brief Introduction

1.The data on price indices in this chapter show the changing trends and change rates in the price of production, circulation, consumption, investment and real estate, including mainly consumer price indices, retail price indices, producer price indices for industrial producers, purchasing price indices for industrial producers, price indices for investment in fixed assets, and selling price indices of residential buildings.

2.The data are provided by NBS Survey Office in Xi'an.

3.The data for the calculation of consumer price indices and retail prices and retail price indices in the province are collected through stratified random sampling. Large–scale shops, supermarkets, fairs and service outlets with wide variety of commodities in Xi'an are selected as survey points. Representative commodities and services are selected as sample commodities and services. Regular surveys are conducted to collect data on market prices. The data on the population are estimated on the basis of the sample.

4.The producer price indices for industrial producers, purchasing price indices for industrial producers and price indices for investment in fixed assetsare collected through stratified random sampling. The producer price indices for industrial producers and purchasing price indices for industrial producers are collected by online direct report of Xi'an industrial enterprises. Price indices for investment in fixed assetsare collected by quarterly report of Xi'an construction and installation enterprises. Selling price indices of residential buildings are collected by monthly data of online residential sales record.

Ⅱ.Major Indicators

		Increase over Preceding Year
Consumer Price Index(the price of preceding year=100)	102.7	0.8 percentage points
Retail Price Index(the price of preceding year=100)	102.1	–0.1 percentage points

7-1 主要年份各种价格指数

Price Indices in Representative Years

(以上年价格为100) (the price of preceding year= 100)

年 份 Year	居民消费价格指数 Consumer Price Index	商品零售价格指数 Retail Price Index	工业生产者出厂价格指数 Producer Price Indices (PPI) for Industrial Producers	工业生产者购进价格指数 Industrial Purchasing Indices （IPI）for Industrial Producers	固定资产投资价格指数 Price Index for Investment in Fixed Assets
1980	108.7	109.3			
1982	100.9	101.0			
1983	102.6	102.0			
1984	104.7	104.8			
1985	109.7	109.3			
1986	108.5	107.4			
1987	110.6	111.4			
1988	122.8	123.2			
1989	118.3	117.8			
1990	102.5	100.9			
1991	109.4	108.3			
1992	112.2	112.4			
1993	117.2	112.8	102.5	104.3	
1994	128.5	126.2	132.2	115.0	
1995	117.0	114.6	110.8	113.1	
1996	110.9	107.9	100.7	103.8	
1997	106.0	101.5	98.6	102.5	
1998	97.9	95.5	94.4	97.5	
1999	96.8	97.4	97.5	96.9	100.8
2000	100.2	98.7	99.4	102.4	102.1
2001	99.9	98.9	99.3	101.0	101.3
2002	98.6	98.5	98.2	98.4	101.2
2003	100.5	100.0	101.5	105.3	102.4
2004	102.3	101.9	102.7	110.4	103.3
2005	100.3	99.7	103.9	109.6	102.4
2006	101.6	101.5	103.2	106.1	102.0
2007	104.7	103.7	101.9	106.2	103.5
2008	106.0	105.4	103.7	108.5	110.5
2009	99.7	99.5	99.9	100.7	97.9
2010	103.5	102.7	102.3	106.3	103.8
2011	105.6	104.4	102.5	108.8	105.4
2012	102.8	102.3	100.5	97.2	101.9
2013	102.7	101.7	99.5	97.2	100.8
2014	101.4	100.7	99.5	99.5	100.8
2015	100.7	99.7	98.5	94.5	97.9
2016	100.9	100.1	97.8	97.6	100.0
2017	102.0	101.7	100.3	104.7	105.4
2018	101.9	102.2	101.1	102.7	104.7
2019	102.7	102.1	101.6	100.0	

注：本表数据来源国家统计局西安调查队。
本表2017年数据为西安原口径数据。下同。
本表2018年PPI、IPI、住宅销售价格指数和固定资产投资价格指数包含西咸地区，其他指标为西安原口径数据。下同。
2019年固定资产投资价格调查方案变动，2019年不出价格指数。2020年固投调查暂停。

7-2 居民消费价格指数（2019年）

Residents Consumer Price Indices（2019）

(以上年价格为100) (the price of preceding year=100)

指 标	Item	2019
居民消费价格指数	**Consumer Price Index**	**102.7**
非食品烟酒价格指数	Non-Food，Tobaccol and Liquor Price Index	102.1
服务价格指数	Price Index of Service	102.8
工业品价格指数	Industrial Price Index	101.5
鲜活食品价格指数	Price Index of Fresh Food	108.3
消费品价格指数	Price Index of Consumer Goods	102.6
能源价格指数	Energy Price Index	99.9
非食品价格指数	Non-foodstuff Price Index	102.2
扣除食品和能源价格指数	Price Index with Food And Energy Excluded	102.3
扣除鲜菜鲜果价格指数	Price Index with Fresh Vegetables Fruits Excluded	102.8
扣除自有住房价格指数	Price Index with Self-owned Housing Excluded	102.6
居住（扣自有住房）价格指数	Housing (Self-owned Housing Excluded) Price Index	101.9
一、食品和烟酒	**Food，To bacco and Liquor**	**104.1**
1. 食品	Food	104.9
（1）粮食	Grain	100.4
（2）薯类	Potato	98.8
（3）豆类	Beans	101.3
（4）食用油	Cooking Oil	99.3
（5）菜	Vegetables	101.2
（6）畜肉类	Livestock Meat	126.2
（7）禽肉类	Poultry Meat	113.1
（8）水产品	Aquatic Products	97.9
（9）蛋类	Eggs	107.3
（10）奶类	Milk	102.9
（11）干鲜瓜果类	Dried Fresh Melons and Fruits	98.7
（12）糖果糕点类	Sweets and Cakes	100.4
（13）调味品	Flavouring	102.0
（14）其他食品类	Other Food	102.2
2. 茶及饮料	Tea and Drinks	100.9
3. 烟酒	Tobacco and Liquor	100.5
（1）烟草	Tobacco	99.9
（2）酒类	Liquor	101.7
4. 在外用餐	Dining Out	103.3
二、衣着	**Clothing**	**103.1**
1. 服装	Garments	103.8
2. 服装材料	Clothing Material	100.0
3. 其他衣着及配件	Other Clothing And Accessories	102.1
4. 衣着加工服务费	Clothing Manufacturing Services	99.3
5. 鞋类	Footwear	101.5
三、居住	**Residence**	**102.6**
1. 租赁房房租	Rental Housing	104.2
2. 住房保养维修及管理	Housing Maintenance And Management	102.4
3. 水电燃料	Water,Electricity, Fuels	100.8
4. 自有住房	Private Housing	103.4

注：本表数据来源国家统计局西安调查队。

7-2 续表 continued

(以上年价格为100) (the price of preceding year= 100)

指 标	Item	2019
四、生活用品及服务	**Daily Necessities and Services**	**101.5**
1. 家具及室内装饰品	Furniture and Interior Decorations	100.0
2. 家用器具	Household Appliances	99.1
3. 家用纺织品	Home Textiles	105.2
4. 家庭日用杂品	Daily Use Household Articles	103.2
5. 个人护理用品	Personal Care Articles	99.5
6. 家庭服务	Home Services	105.6
五、交通和通信	**Transportation And Communication**	**99.3**
1. 交通	Transportation	98.8
（1）交通工具	Transportation Facility	99.6
（2）交通工具用燃料	Fuels For Vehicles	94.1
（3）交通工具使用和维修	Vehicles Use And Maintenance	101.3
（4）交通费	Traffic Fare	98.1
2. 通信	Communications	100.3
（1）通信工具	Telecommunication facility	100.9
（2）通信服务	Telecommunication Service	100.0
（3）邮递服务	Postal Service	100.0
六、教育文化和娱乐	**Education, Culture And Recreation**	**104.2**
1. 教育	Education	104.8
（1）教育用品	Educational Articles	101.1
（2）教育服务	Education Service	105.3
2. 文化娱乐	Culture And Recreation	103.5
（1）文娱耐用消费品	Durable Consumer Goods for Cultural and Recreational Use and Service	98.8
（2）其他文娱用品	Other Recreational Articles	103.5
（3）文化娱乐服务	Cultural And Recreational Services	101.6
（4）旅游	Touring	106.4
七、医疗保健	**Health Care**	**100.9**
1. 药品及医疗器具	Medical Instrument Articles	102.1
（1）中药	Traditional Chinese Medicine	103.4
（2）西药	Western Medicine	100.2
（3）滋补保健品	Health Care Articles	108.1
（4）医疗卫生器具	Medical Apparatus	100.0
（5）保健器具	Health Care Appliances	100.0
2. 医疗服务	Medical Service	100.0
八、其他用品和服务	**Other Supplies And Services**	**103.9**
1. 其他用品类	Other Supplies	104.1
（1）首饰手表	Jewelry and Watches	107.2
（2）其他杂项用品	Other Miscellaneous Articles	99.9
2. 其他服务类	Other Service	103.8

7-3 商品零售价格指数（2019年）

Retail Price Indices（2019）

(以上年价格为100) (the price of preceding year= 100)

指 标	Item	2019
商品零售价格指数	**Retail Price Indices**	**102.1**
一、食品	**Food**	**105.1**
1. 粮食	Grain	100.4
2. 薯类	Potato	98.8
3. 豆类	Beans	101.3
4. 食用油	Cooking Oil	99.7
5. 菜	Vegetables	101.2
6. 畜肉类	Livestock Meat	129.6
7. 禽肉类	Poultry Meat	113.1
8. 水产品	Aquatic Products	97.8
9. 蛋类	Eggs	107.3
10. 奶类	Milk	102.9
11. 干鲜瓜果类	Dried Fresh Melons and Fruits	98.7
12. 糖果糕点类	Sweets and Cakes	100.4
13. 调味品	Flavouring	102.0
14. 其他食品类	Other Food	102.2
15. 在外餐饮	Dining Out	103.3
二、饮料、烟酒	**Drinks, Tobacco and Liquor**	**100.8**
1. 茶及饮料	Tea and Drinks	100.9
2. 烟草	Tobacco	99.9
3. 酒类	Liquor	101.7
三、服装、鞋帽	**Garments, Shoes And Hats**	**103.1**
1. 服装	Garments	103.8
2. 鞋帽袜	Footwear and Hats	101.3
3. 其他衣着配件	Other Clothing Accessories	100.6
四、纺织品	**Textiles**	**105.5**
1. 服装材料	Cotton Cloth	100.0
2. 床上用品	Blend Cloth	106.2
五、家用电器及音像器材	**Household Appliances，Music and Video Equipment**	**98.4**
1. 家庭设备	Household Facility	99.0
2. 文娱用耐用消费品	Durable Consumer Goods for Cultural and Recreational Use	97.4
3. 专业音响器材	Music and Video Equipment	99.3

注：本表数据来源国家统计局西安调查队。

7-3 续表 continued

(以上年价格为100) (the price of preceding year= 100)

指　标	Item	2019
六、文化办公用品	**Cultural and Office Appliances**	**100.5**
七、日用品	**Articles for Daily Use**	**102.4**
1. 日用百货	General Merchandise for Daily Use	100.8
2. 厨具餐具茶具	Kitchenware, Tableware, Tea Set	105.2
3. 清洗用品	Daily Use Articles For Washing	103.4
4. 其他日用品	Other Daily Articles	99.7
八、体育娱乐用品	**Sports And Recreation Articles**	**101.1**
1. 体育户外用品	Sports Outdoor Articles	100.2
2. 娱乐用品	Recreation Articles	101.7
九、交通、通信用品	**Transportation And Communication Goods**	**99.8**
1. 交通运输机械	Transportation Machinery	99.7
2. 通信器材	Communication Equipment	100.4
十、家具	**Furniture**	**101.3**
十一、化妆品	**Cosmetics**	**99.9**
十二、金银饰品	**Gold , Silver and Jewelry**	**109.1**
十三、中西药品及医疗保健用品	**Traditional Chinese And Western Medicines And Health Care Articles**	**101.5**
1. 医疗卫生器具	Medical Apparatus	100.0
2. 中药	Traditional Chinese Medicine	103.4
3. 西药	Western Medicine	100.2
4. 保健器具及用品	Health Care Apparatus and Article	104.7
十四、书报杂志及电子出版物	**Books, Newspapers,Magazines And Electronic Publications**	**103.7**
1. 教材及参考书	Teaching Materials and Reference Books	101.1
2. 书报杂志	Books, Newspapers,Magazines	109.4
3. 计算机办公软件	Computer Office Software	100.1
十五、燃料	**Fuel**	**99.3**
1. 煤炭及制品	Coal and Its Products	105.2
2. 石油及制品	Oil and Its Products	97.7
十六、建筑材料及五金电料	**Building Materials And Hardware**	**102.0**
1. 建筑装潢材料	Building Decoration Materials	102.5
2. 五金水暖	Hardware Plumbing	99.7

7-4 主要年份工业生产者出厂价格指数

(上年价格=100)

类　别	Classify	1998	1999	2000	2001	2002	2003
工业生产者出厂价格指数	**Producer Price Index**	**94.4**	**97.5**	**99.4**	**99.3**	**98.2**	**101.5**
按轻重工业分	Grouped by Light Industry and Heavy Industry						
轻工业	Light Industry	91.1	95.9	97.8	99.6	98.4	101.3
以农产品为原料	Using Farm Products as Raw Materials	89.5	95.2	99.2	99.0	98.4	104.5
以非农产品为原料	Using Non-farm Products as Raw Materials	93.4	97.0	95.5	100.6	98.6	99.9
重工业	Heavy Industry	97.3	98.9	100.8	99.2	98.2	101.6
采掘	Mining & Quarrying	104.1	101.5	97.5	94.8	101.3	103.4
原料	Raw Materials	100.7	102.3	107.7	101.1	101.3	111.2
加工	Processing	95.6	98.0	98.4	98.5	97.7	100.1
按生产生活资料分	by means of production and livelihood						
生产资料	Means of Production	96.6	98.3	100.5	99.1	98.0	101.8
采掘	Mining & Quarrying	104.1	101.5	97.5	94.8	101.3	103.4
原料	Raw Materials	100.6	100.2	106.4	101.1	101.0	108.1
加工	Processing	94.7	97.6	98.7	98.5	97.4	100.9
生活资料	Consumer Goods	91.4	96.5	97.3	99.9	99.1	100.5
（1）食品	Food	97.8	95.8	94.4	99.6	101.2	101.0
（2）衣着	Clothing	83.9	95.2	101.6	99.4	100.8	99.4
（3）一般日用品	Articles for Daily Use	95.1	97.6	96.9	101.9	97.9	101.2
（4）耐用消费品	Durable Consumer Goods	95.4	98.0	95.9	97.0	98.1	97.2
按工业部门分	Grouped by Industrial Sector						
1. 冶金工业	Metallurgical Industry	97.5	91.2	98.2	97.2	98.7	103.8
2. 电力工业	Power Industry	111.2	109.3	109.6	102.4	100.0	103.2
3. 煤炭及炼焦工业	Coal and Coking Industry	98.5	96.3	100.5	110.3	106.7	136.8
4. 石油工业	Petroleum Industry		107.1	134.2	96.6	100.7	118.6
5. 化学工业	Chemical Industry	92.9	96.6	96.7	100.5	99.2	100.2
6. 机械工业	Machine Manufacturing Industry	94.6	98.1	98.0	98.3	97.6	99.8
7. 建筑材料工业	Building Materials Industry	99.3	96.7	98.5	100.6	99.6	99.7
8. 森林工业	Timber Industry	104.5	97.9	98.9	98.1	98.9	100.1
9. 食品工业	Food Industry	95.3	95.5	94.3	99.8	101.1	102.8
10. 纺织工业	Textiles Industry	82.6	93.7	103.4	97.5	94.9	117.3
11. 缝纫工业	Tailoring Industry	97.3	99.1	103.5	100.0	101.1	100.2
12. 皮革工业	Leather Industry	96.8	98.0	99.2	101.0	101.8	98.7
13. 造纸工业	Paper Industry		95.3	96.7	102.3	95.0	96.9
14. 文教艺术用品工业	Cultural,Educational & Handicrafts Articles		96.7	96.4	101.1	103.4	97.5
15. 其它工业	Other Industry	109.2	98.9	104.8	107.1	99.4	103.3

注：本表数据来源国家统计局西安调查队。

Producer Price Indices (PPI) for Industrial Producers in Representative Years

(the price of preceding year= 100)

2004	2005	2006	2007	2008	2009	2010	2011	2012	2013	2014	2015	2016	2017	2018	2019
102.7	**103.9**	**103.2**	**101.9**	**103.7**	**99.9**	**102.3**	**102.5**	**100.5**	**99.5**	**99.5**	**98.5**	**97.8**	**100.3**	**101.1**	**101.6**
103.4	99.9	100.2	101.8	103.7	100.6	102.5	107.0	100.4	100.7	100.9	100.3	98.5	100.5	102.5	101.3
108.7	97.3	100.1	103.3	106.0	98.9	104.0	109.3	100.3	101.0	100.8	99.1	97.8	100.9	103.0	101.2
100.8	101.2	100.2	100.8	102.1	101.8	101.4	100.9	100.5	99.9	101.3	103.3	100.1	99.7	101.3	101.5
101.9	107.9	105.5	101.9	103.8	99.3	102.2	101.6	100.5	99.2	99.2	98.2	97.6	100.3	100.7	101.8
140.5	107.9	100.6	111.6	122.3	90.0	150.2	102.6	101.8	100.6	100.6	99.8	99.8	106.0	107.1	110.3
109.0	114.2	111.8	104.9	110.8	99.5	108.9	111.2	108.6	95.1	97.6	90.4	91.4	103.4	106.1	103.6
100.6	106.7	104.2	101.2	101.9	99.4	100.8	100.1	99.2	99.9	99.5	99.3	98.3	99.8	100.0	101.5
102.7	105.3	104.2	101.3	103.4	99.3	102.2	101.9	100.3	99.2	99.5	98.3	97.4	100.7	101.7	101.7
140.5	107.9	100.6	111.6	122.3	90.0	150.2	102.6	101.8	100.6	100.6	99.8	99.8	106.0	107.1	110.3
106.6	111.3	111.6	104.8	110.2	99.7	109.0	111.3	108.7	95.2	97.7	90.5	91.2	102.7	106.0	103.6
102.0	104.3	103.0	100.6	102.0	99.3	101.0	100.3	98.9	99.9	99.7	99.6	98.3	100.3	101.0	101.4
102.5	100.4	100.4	103.5	104.7	101.4	102.5	104.5	100.8	100.4	99.7	99.4	98.6	99.7	100.1	101.5
103.6	100.3	100.4	105.3	106.6	100.3	103.3	109.5	101.6	100.9	101.2	100.1	97.7	100.3	102.5	101.9
102.7	102.0	103.3	104.6	105.1	102.7	101.2	111.9	99.4	100.4	99.1	96.0	100.2	101.3	100.4	100.2
101.2	101.3	100.8	100.1	102.7	102.6	101.2	101.5	101.5	99.1	101.3	102.1	98.9	99.6	96.8	99.9
98.3	99.1	99.4	100.7	100.7	103.9	101.9	99.5	99.0	100.9	95.9	95.6	99.5	98.5	101.3	103.3
107.1	103.9	106.5	103.2	104.8	92.0	105.8	116.3	100.7	97.5	97.5	96.5	95.2	104.9	107.3	104.3
104.1	110.6	107.9	105.5	110.0	109.0	101.2	104.7	111.2	100.6	99.4	98.9	92.3	99.4	102.3	95.5
131.4	97.1	95.4	106.8	104.8	101.7	110.6	109.3	101.5	100.0	100.0	100.0				
110.5	121.7	117.6	104.8	115.6	96.7	114.2	108.4	108.2	89.7	97.2	81.0	95.4	102.5	107.3	107.1
100.8	103.2	100.8	101.1	104.1	102.6	100.8	104.2	100.3	99.6	100.9	100.6	96.8	100.6	97.9	99.6
100.6	104.9	103.4	101.0	101.7	99.9	100.9	99.5	99.0	100.0	99.4	99.5	98.6	99.5	100.1	101.4
100.0	98.6	98.9	98.9	101.8	101.9	99.9	100.6	99.6	99.3	99.1	99.5	98.0	106.1	118.8	114.5
100.2	101.6	101.6	101.1	101.1	101.1	101.7	105.2	103.2	103.4	101.6	91.7	99.9	100.0	102.0	102.0
107.5	98.3	99.0	106.1	109.3	98.3	104.3	110.1	101.7	101.0	101.3	99.8	97.0	99.9	102.6	101.8
119.1	89.9	102.4	98.4	99.7	97.5	108.9	107.2	88.7	103.9	99.3	96.0	93.7	103.5	102.8	100.4
103.6	100.8	103.5	104.6	105.1	102.6	101.3	113.4	99.4	100.4	99.0	93.4	100.5	102.7	100.7	100.4
99.6	101.2	100.0	99.0	99.6	99.7	99.6	98.0	99.9	99.9	100.0	118.9	99.8	99.6	100.0	100.0
100.2	101.2	100.0	100.1	104.5	98.4	100.4	103.4	99.2	98.4	98.1	98.1	100.9	109.7	106.3	97.8
96.5	98.1	100.1	99.1	99.2	102.2	99.9	100.7	106.0	97.5	100.0	102.6	98.0	99.0	100.9	99.9
105.0	103.4	105.7	111.4	104.3	99.7	100.5	104.3	101.2	99.6	100.0	100.0	99.7	96.2	93.6	101.9

7–5 主要年份工业生产者购进价格指数

Industrial Purchasing Indices (IPI) for Industrial Producers in Representative Years

(上年价格=100) (the price of preceding year= 100)

指 标	Item	2000	2002	2003	2004	2005	2006	2007	2008	2009
工业生产者购进价格指数	**Industrial Producer Price Index**	**102.4**	**98.4**	**105.3**	**110.4**	**109.6**	**106.1**	**106.2**	**108.5**	**100.7**
燃料、动力类	Fuel and Power	105.0	100.9	105.7	109.4	123.5	112.6	107.0	109.8	105.1
黑色金属材料类	Ferrous Metals	102.7	98.5	107.4	117.4	107.6	99.2	104.8	111.3	99.2
#钢材	Steel	103.4	97.9	106.0	114.8	107.5	98.5	104.9	111.7	98.7
有色金属材料和电线类	Non-ferrous Metals and Electric Wires	105.2	96.8	105.8	114.1	107.8	116.5	110.7	99.1	93.9
化工原料类	Raw Chemical Materials	104.6	97.9	102.4	106.3	106.1	101.6	105.6	111.4	95.0
木材及纸浆类	Timber and Paper Pulp	101.2	99.4	101.2	100.3	108.2	111.7	105.9	106.5	102.6
建筑材料及非金属矿类	Building Materials and Non-metal ores	100.3	98.6	99.6	110.4	99.3	100.7	104.0	104.8	106.8
其它工业原材料及半成品类	Other Industrial Raw Materials and Semi-Products	98.8	98.9	102.5	111.2	106.1	104.3	108.8	110.6	101.4
农副产品类	Agricultural Products	100.4	98.2	113.7	112.7	100.9	107.2	107.2	108.9	99.6
纺织原料类	Textile Materials	98.0	90.6	103.4	103.9	97.6	101.5	100.5	99.8	97.6

注：本表数据来源国家统计局西安调查队。

7-5 续表 continued

(上年价格=100) (the price of preceding year= 100)

指 标	Item	2010	2011	2012	2013	2014	2015	2016	2017	2018	2019
工业生产者购进价格指数	**Industrial Producer Price Index**	**106.3**	**108.8**	**97.2**	**97.2**	**99.5**	**94.5**	**97.6**	**104.7**	**102.7**	**100.0**
燃料、动力类	Fuel and Power	108.6	113.5	102.3	96.8	98.2	95.3	98.3	101.6	99.8	101.7
黑色金属材料类	Ferrous Metals	103.1	102.9	93.4	98.0	97.9	91.6	96.0	109.0	104.1	99.4
#钢材	Steel	103.5	102.9	93.3	98.0	97.9	91.5	96.0	109.0	104.0	99.4
有色金属材料和电线类	Non-ferrous Metals and Electric Wires	113.6	118.9	93.0	94.5	96.6	96.3	99.3	117.7	115.1	104.0
化工原料类	Raw Chemical Materials	103.9	108.1	87.7	90.8	104.6	91.3	94.1	104.2	99.2	97.0
木材及纸浆类	Timber and Paper Pulp	101.1	105.4	100.9	99.2	100.7	101.0	98.7	107.3	103.9	95.6
建筑材料及非金属矿类	Building Materials and Non-metal ores	102.1	102.9	97.4	102.2	101.1	98.1	97.1	101.0	111.1	111.0
其它工业原材料及半成品类	Other Industrial Raw Materials and Semi-Products	108.1	109.4	100.3	98.9	100.9	99.1	98.9	100.8	100.4	99.7
农副产品类	Agricultural Products	106.5	107.4	103.4	100.5	98.8	92.8	100.4	101.0	102.3	101.2
纺织原料类	Textile Materials	104.6	107.0	89.1	97.6	99.3	89.7	94.1	102.7	99.4	99.3

7-6 住宅销售价格指数（2019年）

Selling Price Indices of Residential Buildings（2019）

(上年价格=100) (the price of preceding year= 100)

指　标	Item	2019
新建商品住宅	**New commodity residential house**	**121.1**
90平方米及以下	90 square meters and less	122.4
90-144平方米	90-144 square meters	121.1
144平方米以上	144 square meters and more	120.0
二手住宅	**used/second hand residential buildings**	**108.8**
90平方米及以下	90 square meters and the following	109.1
90-144平方米	90-144 square meters	107.5
144平方米以上	144 square meters and more	111.3

注：本表数据来源国家统计局西安调查队。

主要统计指标解释

居民消费价格指数 是反映一定时期内城乡居民所购买的生活消费品和服务项目价格变动趋势和程度的相对数，是对城市居民消费价格指数和农村居民消费价格指数进行综合汇总计算的结果。通过该指数可以观察和分析消费品的零售价格和服务项目价格变动对城乡居民实际生活费支出的影响程度。

商品零售价格指数 是反映一定时期内城乡商品零售价格变动趋势和程度的相对数。商品零售价格的变动与国家的财政收入、市场供需的平衡、消费与积累的比例关系有关。因此，该指数可以从一个侧面对上述经济活动进行观察和分析。

工业生产者价格指数 是反映工业产品价格变化趋势和变动幅度的统计指标，是工业企业的产品价格在不同的时间和空间条件下平均变动的相对数。工业生产者价格包括工业品第一次出售时的出厂价格和企业作为中间投入的原材料、燃料、动力购进价格，简称工业生产者出厂价格和工业生产者购进价格。工业生产者价格指数是进行国民经济核算和经济管理的主要依据。

住宅销售价格指数 是综合反映商品住宅价格水平总体变化趋势和变化辐度的相对数。

固定资产投资价格指数 是反映一定时期内固定资产投资品和取费项目价格的变动趋势和变动幅度的相对数。固定资产投资额是由建筑安装工程投资完成额、设备工器具购置投资完成额和其他费用投资完成额三部分组成的。编制固定资产投资价格指数应首先分别编制上述三部分投资的价格指数，然后采用加权算术平均法求出固定资产投资价格总指数。

该指数可以准确地反映固定资产投资中涉及的各类投资品和取费项目价格变动趋势和变动幅度，消除按现价计算的固定资产投资指标中的价格变动因素，真实地反映固定资产投资的规模、速度、结构和效益，为国家科学地制定、检查固定资产投资计划和进行国民经济核算提供科学的、可靠的依据。

Explanatory Notes on Main Statistical Indicators

Consumer Price Indices reflect the trend and degree of changes in prices of consumer goods and services purchased by urban and rural households during a given period. They are obtained by combining Consumer Price Indices of Urban Household and Consumer Price Indices of Rural Household. The Indices enable the observation and analysis of the degree of impact of the changes in the prices of retailed goods and services on the actual living expenses of urban and rural residents.

Retail Price Indices reflect the trend and degree of change in retail prices of commodities during a given period. The change in retail prices of commodities is related to government revenue, the equilibrium of market supply and demand, and the ratio of consumption to accumulation. Therefore, the retail price indices are useful from an oblique perspective for observing and analyzing the changes of the above economic activities.

Industrial Producer Price Index refelct the trend and degree of changes of industrial product price, which is the relative number of average change prices of industrial enterprises products under different condition of time and space. Including the first time of sale prices of industrial products and the price of raw materials, fuel and power as intermediate inputs, be called for short of PPI and IPI.

Industrial producer price Index is an important basis for national accounts and economic manegement.

Price Indices for Investment in Fixed Assets reflect the trend and degree of changes in prices of investment goods and projects in fixed assets during a given period. The investment in fixed assets consists of three components, namely the investment in construction and installation, the investment in purchases of equipment and instrument, and the investment in other items. Price indices for investment in fixed assets are calculated as the weighted arithmetic mean of the price indices for the three components of investment in fixed assets.

Removing the factor of price change in the aggregates of investment at current prices, this indicator shows the changes in the prices of commodities and fees involved in the investment of fixed assets, and can be used to observe the actual size, growth, structure, and efficiency of investment in fixed assets and provides reliable and scientific data for government planning and further improving the current national accounting .

8 人民生活

PEOPLE´S LIVELIHOOD

资料整理：张　磊　宋　洁
Data management：Zhang Lei Song Jie
数据审核：罗朝晖
Data audit：Luo Zhaohui

第八部分　人民生活

一、简要说明

1.本章资料反映我市城乡居民生活现状和变化情况，主要包括居民家庭基本情况及生活状况、收入及支出、住房等。

2.本章资料来源于国家统计局西安调查队城乡一体化住户收支与生活状况抽样调查。

3.统计资料范围及口径变化：①2014年西安开始实施城乡住户一体化改革，新老口径存在差距。②因2018年是分市、分省数据衔接年的基数年，衔接后西安各区县新口径与老口径数据相比，绝对额有所下降。③自2018年起本章调查资料包含13区、县及西咸新区城乡住户调查数据。

4.统计调查方法：住户收支与生活状况以各市（区）为总体，采用分层、多阶段、与人口规模大小成比例的概率抽样方法，随机抽选调查住宅，确定调查户。在全市抽选出调查小区，对抽中小区中的住户进行全面摸底调查，在此基础上随机等距选出调查户参与记账调查。定期对调查小区和调查住宅进行轮换。

二、主要指标

全体居民人均可支配收入（元）	34064	比上年增长	8.5%
城镇常住居民人均可支配收入（元）	41850	比上年增长	8.1%
城镇常住居民人均消费支出（元）	28140	比上年增长	8.4%
农村常住居民人均可支配收入（元）	14588	比上年增长	9.8%
农村常住居民人均消费支出（元）	12561	比上年增长	11.8%

8 PEOPLE'S LIVELIHOOD

Ⅰ.Brief Introduction

1.The data in this chapter reflects the people's living conditions and their changes in Xi'an, consisting of the basic conditions of all households, income, expenditure, the inhabit situation and etc.

2.The data are provided by NBS Survey Office in Xi'an, collected though sample survey.

3.The field of investigation and statistics range have been changed. ①In 2014, reformed household survey programme was used in Xi'an in order to produce aggregates with the same concepts and definitions for the urban and rural population. ② Since 2018 is the base year for the data convergence of cities and provinces, the absolute amount of new caliber data of Xi'an districts and counties has declined compared with the old caliber data. ③Since 2018, the data in this chapter consists of 13 Districts (Counties) and Xi'an new area.

4. Methodology on household survey. The household survey is conducted by selecting sampled houses randomly, deciding surveyed households, with all households in the city (district) as the population, with stratified sampling, multi-stage sampling, probability sampling in proportion scale. The households in selected communities are surveyed comprehensively, and then on the basis, randomly select some households for keeping diaries. Communities and households surveyed rotate regularly.

Ⅱ.Major Indicators

		Increase over Preceding Year
Per capita disposable income of all residents(yuan)	34064	8.5%
Per capita annual disposable income of Urban residents (yuan)	41850	8.1%
Per capita consumption expenditure of Urban residents (yuan)	28140	8.4%
Per capita annual disposable income of Rural residents (yuan)	14588	9.8%
Per capita consumption expenditure of Rural residents(yuan)	12561	11.8%

8-1 主要年份城乡居民人均收入及恩格尔系数

Per Capita Annual Income and Engel's Coefficient of Urban and Rural Households in Representative Years

年 份 Year	城镇居民人均可支配收入 Per Capita Annual Disposable Income of Urban		农村居民人均纯收入（可支配收入） Per Capita Annual Net Income of Rural （Disposable Income）		城镇居民家庭恩格尔系数（%） Engel's Coefficient of Urban Households（%）	农村居民家庭恩格尔系数（%） Engel's Coefficient of Rural Households（%）
	绝对数(元) Absolute number (yuan)	指数 1980年=100 Index year of 1980=100	绝对数(元) Absolute number (yuan)	指数 1978年=100 Index year of 1978=100		
1978			140	100.0		
1979						
1980	414	100.0	190	135.7	53.3	53.3
1985	719	173.5	351	250.7	49.5	48.5
1990	1518	366.5	610	435.7	53.1	49.5
1991	1619	390.9	707	505.0	51.6	46.7
1992	1992	481.0	783	559.3	52.5	50.9
1993	2661	642.5	870	621.4	46.4	46.0
1994	3517	849.1	1078	770.0	45.2	50.1
1995	4153	1002.5	1353	966.4	44.7	50.3
1996	5023	1212.6	1586	1132.9	42.6	49.9
1997	5344	1290.1	1846	1318.6	40.7	49.2
1998	5670	1368.7	2052	1465.7	39.8	42.4
1999	5999	1448.3	2203	1573.6	36.3	39.1
2000	6364	1536.5	2344	1674.3	36.5	36.6
2001	6705	1618.8	2490	1778.6	34.8	33.9
2002	7184	1734.3	2641	1886.4	34.4	31.1
2003	7748	1870.7	2838	2027.1	34.8	37.6
2004	8544	2062.8	3143	2245.0	36.1	35.7
2005	9628	2324.5	3460	2471.4	37.0	36.3
2006	10905	2632.9	3808	2720.0	34.4	36.8
2007	12662	3057.0	4399	3142.1	36.6	38.2
2008	15207	3671.4	5212	3722.9	36.4	37.0
2009	18963	4578.2	6275	4482.3	32.4	35.8
2010	22244	5370.4	7750	5535.7	31.3	32.5
2011	25981	6272.6	9788	6991.4	31.3	31.9
2012	29982	7238.5	11442	8172.9	32.5	33.8
2013	33100	7991.3	12930	9235.7	32.5	33.0
2014	30715	8718.5	12898	10334.7	32.3	34.2
2015	33188	9422.0	14072	11270.0	32.7	32.2
2016	35630	10119.2	15191	12171.6	29.3	26.9
2017	35837	10948.9	12190	13267.0	29.4	27.3
2018	38729	11835.8	13286	14461.0	27.1	24.4
2019	41850	12794.5	14588	15878.2	26.8	25.4

注：2014年实施城乡住户一体化调查后，统计口径发生变化，新老口径存在差异。本表2014年开始为新口径数据，“农村居民人均纯收入”改为“农村居民人均可支配收入”。2014-2015年恩格尔系数按新口径进行了修订。

本表2018年起数据包含西咸新区数据。下同。

8-1表中2017年城镇、农村居民人均可支配收入已依据2018年口径进行衔接，其他年份不可比。

8-2 主要年份城乡居民人民币储蓄存款

Savings Deposit of Urban and Rural Households in Representative Years

单位：亿元　　(100 million yuan)

年　份 Year	年末余额 Balance at Year-end	指数（上年＝100） Index(preceding year=100)
1978	2.57	
1979	3.30	128.4
1980	4.22	127.8
1981	4.90	116.0
1982	5.97	121.9
1983	7.35	123.1
1984	10.73	146.0
1985	14.26	132.9
1986	19.45	136.4
1987	33.95	174.6
1988	40.77	120.1
1989	56.65	138.9
1990	77.09	136.1
1991	97.42	126.4
1992	120.27	123.5
1993	158.28	131.6
1994	218.74	138.2
1995	291.46	133.2
1996	394.02	135.2
1997	433.56	110.0
1998	499.68	115.3
1999	586.40	117.4
2000	675.83	115.3
2001	800.86	118.5
2002	988.04	123.4
2003	1210.56	122.5
2004	1432.86	118.4
2005	1716.76	119.8
2006	1950.53	113.6
2007	2002.38	102.7
2008	2513.70	125.5
2009	3084.20	122.7
2010	3641.09	118.1
2011	4155.65	114.1
2012	4787.03	115.2
2013	5357.05	111.9
2014	5698.15	106.4
2015	6571.18	115.3
2016	7035.81	107.1
2017	7497.30	106.6
2018	8360.33	111.5
2019	9553.29	114.3

注：1.本表数据来源于人民银行西安分行营管部,对部分历史年份数据进行了修订，为西安原口径数据。
2.2015年以后“储蓄存款”为“住户存款”。

8-3 各区县城乡居民人均可支配收入

Per Capita Income of Urban and Rural Households by Region

区 县	Region	城镇居民人均可支配收入 Per Capita Disposable Income of Urban Households			农村居民人均可支配收入 Per Capita Disposable Income of Rural Households		
		绝对数（元） Absolute number(yuan)		2019年比2018年增长% Growth of 2019 than 2018（%）	绝对数（元） Absolute number(yuan)		2019年比2018年增长% Growth of 2019 than 2018（%）
		2018	2019		2018	2019	
全 市	**Total**	**38729**	**41850**	**8.1**	**13286**	**14588**	**9.8**
新城区	Xincheng	44637	48208	8.0			
碑林区	Beilin	44382	47977	8.1			
莲湖区	Lianhu	44440	47995	8.0			
灞桥区	Baqiao	37306	40328	8.1	16395	17969	9.6
未央区	Weiyang	41056	44628	8.7			
雁塔区	Yanta	44995	48685	8.2			
阎良区	Yanliang	37448	40631	8.5	14423	15808	9.6
临潼区	Lintong	28449	30810	8.3	13363	14659	9.7
长安区	Chang'an	38900	42051	8.1	14520	15928	9.7
高陵区	Gaoling	35788	38794	8.4	14936	16370	9.6
鄠邑区	Huyi	22909	24788	8.2	12415	13632	9.8
蓝田县	Lantian	22082	23893	8.2	13404	14731	9.9
周至县	Zhouzhi	20633	22407	8.6	11954	13137	9.9
西咸新区	Xixian	23333	25270	8.3	12775	14027	9.8

8-4 全市居民家庭基本情况

Basic Conditions of All Households

指标名称	Item	2018	2019
调查户数（户）	**Number of Households Surveyed (household)**	**2460**	**2410**
调查户人口（人）	**Residents Surveyed(person)**		
平均每户常住人口	Average Household Size	3.0	3.0
平均每户劳动力人数	Average Number of Employed Persons	2.2	2.2
平均每劳动力负担人口	Average Number of Persons Supported by a Laborer	1.4	1.4
人均可支配收入（元）	**Annual Per Capita Disposable Income(yuan）**	**31406.7**	**34064.3**
工资性收入	Wages Income	19251.7	20991.0
经营净收入	Net Income from Business	2444.7	2629.9
财产净收入	Net Income from Property	2847.8	3070.4
转移净收入	Net Income from Transfer	6862.5	7373.0
人均消费支出（元）	**Annual Per Capita Consumption Expenditure (yuan)**	**21722.6**	**23691.2**
食品烟酒	Food,Tobacco and Alcohol	5797.1	6300.5
衣着	Clothing	1653.9	1761.8
居住	Residence	4463.4	5050.9
生活用品及服务	Living Articles and Services	1701.2	1719.7
交通通信	Transport and Communication Services	2548.7	2807.6
教育文化娱乐	Recreation, Education and Culture Services	3003.9	3223.6
医疗保健	Medical and Health Care Services	2048.8	2210.9
其他用品和服务	Other Commodities and Services	505.6	616.2

8-5 全市居民人均可支配收入

Per Capita Annual Disposable Income of All Households

单位：元 (yuan)

指标名称	Item	2018	2019
可支配收入	**Disposable income**	**31406.7**	**34064.3**
一、工资性收入	**Wage income**	**19251.7**	**20991.0**
（一）工资	Wage	18355.1	19837.4
（二）实物福利	Benefits in kind	65.3	64.8
（三）其他	Others	831.3	1088.8
二、经营净收入	**Net Income from Business**	**2444.7**	**2629.9**
（一）第一产业经营净收入	Net Income from Primary Industry Business	401.4	424.3
（二）第二产业经营净收入	Net Income from Secondary Industry Business	205.6	188.5
（三）第三产业经营净收入	Net Income from Tertiary Industry Business	1837.7	2017.1
三、财产净收入	**Net Income from Properties**	**2847.8**	**3070.4**
#利息净收入	Net interest	81.3	124.4
红利收入	Bonus	497.1	364.0
转让承包土地经营权租金净收入	Net Rental from Transfer of Contracted Land Management Rights	36.6	43.7
出租房屋财产性收入	The Property Income by Renting House	1009.7	1066.0
出租机械、专利、版权等资产的收入	The Income by Renting Assets like Mechanical, Patents, Copyright ect.	15.0	56.9
四、转移净收入	**Net Income from Transfer**	**6862.5**	**7373.0**
（一）转移性收入	Net Income from Transfer	8297.6	8874.3
（二）转移性支出	Transfer Expenditure	1435.1	1501.3

8-6 全市居民年人均消费支出

Per Capita Living Expenditure of All Households

单位：元 (yuan)

指标名称	Item	2018	2019
消费支出	**Total Living Expenditure**	**21722.6**	**23691.2**
一、食品烟酒	**Food,Tobacco and Alcohol**	**5797.1**	**6300.5**
1.食品	food	3433.2	3568.8
2.烟酒	Alcohol and tobacco	513.5	542.7
3.饮料	Drink	160.2	168.8
4.饮食服务	Catering Services	1690.2	2020.2
二、衣着	**Clothing**	**1653.9**	**1761.8**
衣类	Garments	1297.6	1408.6
鞋类	Footwear	356.3	353.2
三、居住	**Residence**	**4463.4**	**5050.9**
#租赁房房租	Rental Housing Rent	287.7	353.2
住房维修及管理	Housing Repair and Management	445.6	691.1
水电燃料及其他	Water,Electric Power Fuel and Others	1101.2	1058.8
四、生活用品及服务	**Living Articles and Services**	**1701.2**	**1719.7**
家具及室内装饰品	Furniture and Interior Decorations	266.6	235.3
家用器具	Household Appliances	487.7	495.6
家用纺织品	Household textile	133.8	124.9
家庭日用杂品	Household Articles of Daily Use	375.9	345.2
个人用品	Personal Items	370.6	430.5
家庭服务	Household Services	66.6	88.2
五、交通通信	**Transportation and Communications**	**2548.7**	**2807.6**
交通	Transportation	1758.3	2016.7
通信	Communications	790.4	790.9
六、教育文化娱乐	**Recreation, Education and Culture Services**	**3003.9**	**3223.6**
教育	Education	1760.5	2041.6
文化娱乐	Recreation	1243.4	1182.0
七、医疗保健	**Medicine and Medical Services**	**2048.8**	**2210.9**
医疗器具及药品	Medical Instruments and Medicines	754.8	706.3
医疗服务	Medical Services	1294.0	1504.6
八、其他用品和服务	**Others**	**505.6**	**616.2**

8-7 全市居民家庭人均购买主要商品数量

Per Capita Annual Purchases of Major Commodities of All Households

单位：千克 (kg)

指标名称	Item	2018	2019
面粉	Flour	20.6	19.5
大米	Rice	16.0	14.3
薯类	Potato	13.8	16.7
豆类	Beans	10.6	11.4
食用植物油	Edible vegetable oil	10.7	9.5
鲜菜	Fresh vegetables	90.5	97.8
猪肉	Pork	10.8	9.7
牛肉	Beef	1.9	2.1
羊肉	Lamb	0.7	0.7
鸡	Chicken	2.5	2.8
鱼类	Fish	3.1	3.4
虾类	Shrimp	0.8	0.9
鲜蛋	Eggs	10.1	11.3
鲜奶	Milk	13.3	12.9
酸奶	Yogurt	6.8	7.4
奶粉	Milk	0.9	0.9
鲜瓜果	Fresh fruit	59.4	66.2
糕点	Cake	5.5	5.8
茶叶	Tea	0.5	0.4
卷烟（盒）	Cigarettes (box)	27.4	30.2
啤酒	Beer	3.3	3.1
白酒	Liquor	1.2	1.3
果酒	Wine	0.3	0.2
鞋（双）	Footwear (pair)	2.9	2.8
水（吨）	Water (tons)	28.8	29.5
电（度）	Electricity （kwh）	786.3	784.5
煤炭	Coal	23.7	13.9
管道天燃气（立方米）	Gas pipeline (cu.m)	98.0	74.8
罐装液化石油气	Bottled liquefied petroleum gas	4.0	2.7

8-8 全市居民家庭每百户年末耐用品拥有情况

Ownership of Major Durable Consumer Goods Every 100 Households

指标名称	Item	2018	2019
家用汽车（辆）	Automobile (unit)	38.6	36.3
摩托车（辆）	Motorcycles (unit)	14.4	10.2
助力车（台）	Strength-aid Cycle (unit)	43.9	46.0
洗衣机（台）	washing machine (unit)	99.0	98.5
电冰箱（柜）	Refrigerator (unit)	96.4	95.8
微波炉（台）	Microwave Oven (unit)	45.5	43.9
彩色电视机（台）	Color TV Set (unit)	107.9	107.0
#接入有线电视（台）	Cable TV Set(unit)	43.2	-
空调（台）	Air conditioning(unit)	156.3	160.0
热水器（台）	Water heaters(unit)	89.5	87.1
#太阳能热水器（台）	Solar water heaters (unit)	30.1	-
洗碗机（台）	Dishwasher (unit)	1.7	1.4
排油烟机（台）	Exhauster (unit)	73.7	73.1
固定电话（部）	Ordinary Telephone (unit)	21.5	11.4
移动电话（部）	Mobile phones (unit)	251.9	255.6
#接入互联网（部）	Access to the Internet(unit)	171.8	194.4
计算机（台）	Computer (a)	58.7	57.6
#接入互联网（台）	Access to the Internet(unit)	42.6	43.4
照相机（台）	Camera (unit)	19.6	18.9
中高档乐器（架）	High-end Instruments (unit)	6.3	7.3
健身器材（台）	Setting-up Apparatus (unit)	5.5	7.4
空气净化器（台）	Air-cleaner（unit）	9.7	12.4
吸尘器（台）	Vacuum Cleaner（unit）	9.4	11.3

8-9 城镇常住居民家庭基本情况

Basic Conditions of Urban Households

指标名称	Item	2018	2019
调查户数（户）	**Number of Households Surveyed (household)**	**1800**	**1770**
调查户人口（人）	**Residents Surveyed(person)**		
平均每户常住人口	Average Household Size	2.8	2.8
平均每户劳动力人数	Average Number of Employed Persons	2.1	2.1
平均每劳动力负担人口	Average Number of Persons Supported by a Laborer	1.3	1.3
人均可支配收入（元）	**Annual Per Capita Disposable Income(yuan)**	**38729.1**	**41850.0**
工资性收入	Wages Income	23797.3	25883.5
经营净收入	Household Business Income	2513.1	2715.5
财产净收入	Property Income	3879.4	4167.3
转移净收入	Transfer Income	8539.3	9083.7
人均消费支出（元）	**Annual Per Capita Consumption Expenditure (yuan)**	**25961.5**	**28140.4**
食品烟酒	Food,Tobacco and Alcohol	7030.5	7541.3
衣着	Clothing	2052.6	2152.4
居住	Residence	5195.7	5910.1
生活用品及服务	Living Articles and Services	2040.8	2044.4
交通通信	Transport and Communication Services	3047.2	3334.8
教育文化娱乐	Recreation, Education and Culture Services	3616.2	3851.7
医疗保健	Medical and Health Care Services	2329.8	2519.2
其他用品和服务	Other Commodities and Services	648.7	786.5

8-10 城镇常住居民人均消费支出

Per Capita Living Expenditure of Urban Households

单位：元 (yuan)

指标名称	Item	2018	2019
消费支出	**Total Living Expenditure**	**25961.5**	**28140.4**
一、食品烟酒	**Food,Tobacco and Alcohol**	**7030.5**	**7541.3**
1.食品	food	4054.8	4166.3
2.烟酒	Alcohol and tobacco	566.4	586.9
3.饮料	Drink	200.4	205.1
4.饮食服务	Catering Services	2208.9	2583.0
二、衣着	**Clothing**	**2052.6**	**2152.4**
衣类	Garments	1611.6	1725.8
鞋类	Footwear	441.0	426.6
三、居住	**Residence**	**5195.7**	**5910.1**
#租赁房房租	Rental Housing Rent	359.8	438.9
住房维修及管理	Housing Repair and Management	474.4	741.4
水电燃料及其他	Water,Electric Power Fuel and Others	1330.1	1276.1
四、生活用品及服务	**Living Articles and Services**	**2040.8**	**2044.4**
家具及室内装饰品	Furniture and Interior Decorations	326.0	281.2
家用器具	Household Appliances	548.1	576.0
家用纺织品	Household textile	163.3	147.7
家庭日用杂品	Household Articles of Daily Use	443.1	388.1
个人用品	Personal Items	474.5	547.6
家庭服务	Household Services	85.8	103.8
五、交通通信	**Transportation and Communications**	**3047.2**	**3334.8**
交通	Transportation	2109.4	2402.3
通信	Communications	937.8	932.5
六、教育文化娱乐	**Recreation, Education and Culture Services**	**3616.2**	**3851.7**
教育	Education	1979.1	2310.1
文化娱乐	Recreation	1637.1	1541.6
七、医疗保健	**Medicine and Medical Services**	**2329.8**	**2519.2**
医疗器具及药品	Medical Instruments and Medicines	917.7	853.3
医疗服务	Medical Services	1412.1	1665.9
八、其他用品和服务	**Others**	**648.7**	**786.5**

8-11 城镇常住居民家庭人均购买主要商品数量

Per Capita Annual Purchases of Major Commodities of Urban Households

单位：千克 (kg)

指标名称	Item	2018	2019
面粉	Flour	19.0	17.0
大米	Rice	17.7	15.1
薯类	Potato	14.9	17.0
豆类	Beans	11.3	11.6
食用植物油	Edible vegetable oil	10.1	8.5
鲜菜	Fresh vegetables	100.5	106.1
猪肉	Pork	11.9	10.6
牛肉	Beef	2.5	2.7
羊肉	Lamb	0.9	0.9
鸡	Chicken	3.2	3.4
鱼类	Fish	4.0	4.4
虾类	Shrimp	1.0	1.2
鲜蛋	Eggs	11.5	12.2
鲜奶	Milk	15.9	15.2
酸奶	Yogurt	8.7	9.5
奶粉	Milk	0.9	1.0
鲜瓜果	Fresh fruit	69.3	75.0
糕点	Cake	6.5	6.7
茶叶	Tea	0.6	0.5
卷烟（盒）	Cigarettes (box)	25.5	27.5
啤酒	Beer	3.3	3.1
白酒	Liquor	1.4	1.5
果酒	Wine	0.3	0.2
鞋（双）	Footwear (pair)	3.1	2.8
水（吨）	Water (tons)	34.8	33.2
电（度）	Electricity （kwh）	867.9	834.6
煤炭	Coal	9.6	6.3
管道天燃气（立方米）	Gas pipeline (cu.m)	136.0	102.1
罐装液化石油气	Bottled liquefied petroleum gas	2.5	1.8

8-12 城镇常住居民家庭每百户耐用品拥有情况

Ownership of Major Durable Consumer Goods Every 100 Urban Households

指标名称	Item	2018	2019
家用汽车（辆）	Automobile (unit)	40.2	37.5
摩托车（辆）	Motorcycles (unit)	5.4	2.9
助力车（台）	Strength-aid Cycle (unit)	33.1	33.4
洗衣机（台）	washing machine (unit)	99.3	97.9
电冰箱（柜）	Refrigerator (unit)	96.9	95.7
微波炉（台）	Microwave Oven (unit)	55.2	52.8
彩色电视机（台）	Color TV Set (unit)	104.2	102.7
# 接入有线电视（台）	The Number of Cable Television Accessed to Network (unit)	48.6	-
空调（台）	Air conditioning(unit)	168.8	173.4
热水器（台）	Water heaters(unit)	93.2	90.5
#太阳能热水器（台）	Solar water heaters (unit)	22.6	-
洗碗机（台）	Dishwasher (unit)	2.0	1.6
排油烟机（台）	Exhauster (unit)	87.1	85.2
固定电话（部）	Ordinary Telephone (unit)	24.3	13.6
移动电话（部）	Mobile phones (unit)	234.5	237.1
#接入互联网（部）	Access to the Internet(unit)	163.8	183.3
计算机（台）	Computer (a)	67.4	65.3
#接入互联网（台）	Access to the Internet(unit)	49.9	51.0
照相机（台）	Camera (unit)	24.8	23.7
中高档乐器（架）	High-end Instruments (unit)	7.6	9.2
健身器材（台）	Setting-up Apparatus (unit)	6.5	9.1
空气净化器（台）	Air-cleaner（unit）	12.5	15.9
吸尘器（台）	Vacuum Cleaner（unit）	12.1	14.4

8-13 城镇常住居民家庭居住情况

Housing Conditions of Urban Households

指标名称	Item	2018	2019
调查户数（户）	**Number of Households Surveyed (household)**	**1800**	**1770**
平均每户居住人口（人）	**Average Number of Resident Population (person)**	**2.8**	**2.8**
人均现住房建筑面积（平方米/人）	**The Average Floor Area Per Person (sq.m / person)**	**34.4**	**34.8**
一、按居住空间样式分（%）	**by Living space style（%）**	**100.0**	**100.0**
单栋楼房	Single building Room	10.9	8.4
单栋平房	Single-storey House	3.9	4.8
单元房	Apartment	80.2	79.7
筒子楼或连片平房	Tube-shaped Apartment or Lace Single-storey Houses	5.0	7.1
其他	Other		
二、按主要建筑材料分（%）	**by main construction materials（%）**	**100.0**	**100.0**
钢筋混凝土	Reinforced concrete soil	59.9	63.8
砖混材料	Brick and concrete material	39.5	35.6
砖瓦砖土	Tile and brick earth	0.5	0.5
其他	Others	0.1	0.1
三、按房屋来源分（%）	**by Source of Housing（%）**	**100.0**	**100.0**
租赁住房	Rental housing	10.9	14.8
自建住房	Self-establish Housing	14.6	15.2
购买商品房	Commercial Residential Housing	37.2	35.2
购买房改住房	Private Housing through Housing Reform	18.0	17.5
购买保障性住房	Indemnificatory Housing	4.7	3.2
拆迁安置房	Resettlement Housing	8.4	8.9
继承或获赠住房	Inheriting and Donation Housing	2.5	1.3
其他	Others	3.7	3.9
四、住房外道路为硬化路面的户比重（%）	**proportion of households which outer road is Hardened road（%）**	**99.7**	**99.9**
五、按住宅有管道供水情况分（%）	**By Piped Water Supply Condition（%）**	**100.0**	-
管道供水入户	Pipe water into People's Homes	98.3	-
管道供水至公共取水点	Pipe water to Public Watering Points	1.0	-
没有管道设施	No Pipeline Facilities	0.7	-
六、按住户主要饮水来源情况分（%）	**By Source of main Drinking Water（%）**	**100.0**	**100.0**
经过净化处理的自来水	Purified Tap Water	90.6	89.2
受保护的井水和泉水	Protected Wells and Springs	6.6	8.5
不受保护的井水和泉水	Unprotected Wells and Springs	1.3	0.9
江河湖泊水	Rivers and Lakes Water	0.8	0.6
其他饮用水来源	Others	0.7	0.8
七、按住宅内厕所类型分（%）	**By Household Lavatory Type (%)**	**100.0**	**100.0**
水冲式卫生厕所	Sanitary Water Closet	95.9	97.3
水冲式非卫生厕所	Insanitary Water Closet	1.2	1.0
卫生旱厕	Sanitary Latrine	1.2	1.6
普通旱厕	Latrine	1.4	0.1
无厕所	No Lavatory	0.3	
八、按主要炊用能源状况分（%）	**By Cooking Fuel Condition（%）**	**100.0**	**100.0**
天然气、煤气、液化石油气	Pipeline Natural Gas，Pipeline Gas，Pipeline Liquified Petroleum Gas	80.9	81.1
煤炭	Coal		
电	Electricity	17.3	17.9
沼气	Methane		
其他	Others	1.8	1.0

8-14 农村常住居民家庭基本情况

Basic Conditions of Rural Households

指标名称	Item	2018	2019
调查户数（户）	**Number of Households Surveyed (household)**	**660**	**640**
调查户人口（人）	**Residents Surveyed(person)**		
平均每户常住人口	Average Household Size	3.7	3.7
平均每户劳动力人数	Average Number of Employed Persons	2.4	2.3
平均每劳动力负担人口	Average Number of Persons Supported by a Laborer	1.5	1.6
人均可支配收入（元）	**Annual Per Capita Disposable Income(yuan）**	**13286.3**	**14588.0**
工资性收入	Wages Income	8000.8	8752.0
经营净收入	Household Business Income	2275.4	2415.9
财产净收入	Property Income	294.6	326.4
转移净收入	Transfer Income	2715.5	3093.7
人均消费支出（元）	**Annual Per Capita Consumption Expenditure (yuan)**	**11231.1**	**12561.4**
食品烟酒	Food,Tobacco and Alcohol	2744.5	3196.7
衣着	Clothing	667.1	784.8
居住	Residence	2650.9	2901.7
生活用品及服务	Living Articles and Services	860.6	907.4
交通通信	Transport and Communication Services	1314.8	1488.7
教育文化娱乐	Recreation, Education and Culture Services	1488.5	1652.2
医疗保健	Medical and Health Care Services	1353.3	1439.6
其他用品和服务	Other Commodities and Services	151.4	190.3

8-15 农村常住居民人均消费支出

Per Capita Living Expenditure of Rural Households

单位：元 (yuan)

指标名称	Item	2018	2019
消费支出	**Total Living Expenditure**	**11231.1**	**12561.4**
一、食品烟酒	**Food,Tobacco and Alcohol**	**2744.5**	**3196.7**
1.食品	food	1894.9	2074.3
2.烟酒	Alcohol and tobacco	382.6	432.1
3.饮料	Drink	60.6	78.0
4.饮食服务	Catering Services	406.4	612.3
二、衣着	**Clothing**	**667.1**	**784.8**
衣类	Garments	520.5	615.0
鞋类	Footwear	146.6	169.8
三、居住	**Residence**	**2650.9**	**2901.7**
#租赁房房租	Rental Housing Rent	109.2	138.7
住房维修及管理	Housing Repair and Management	374.5	565.3
水电燃料及其他	Water,Electric Power Fuel and Others	534.7	515.1
四、生活用品及服务	**Living Articles and Services**	**860.6**	**907.4**
家具及室内装饰品	Furniture and External Decorations	119.8	120.7
家用器具	Household Appliances	338.2	294.4
家用纺织品	Household textile	60.8	67.9
家庭日用杂品	Household Articles of Daily Use	209.5	237.6
个人用品	Personal Items	113.4	137.7
家庭服务	Household Services	18.9	49.1
五、交通通信	**Transportation and Communications**	**1314.8**	**1488.7**
交通	Transportation	889.3	1051.9
通信	Communications	425.5	436.8
六、教育文化娱乐	**Recreation, Education and Culture Services**	**1488.5**	**1652.2**
教育	Education	1219.5	1369.6
文化娱乐	Recreation	269.0	282.6
七、医疗保健	**Medicine and Medical Services**	**1353.3**	**1439.6**
医疗器具及药品	Medical Instruments and Medicines	351.7	338.5
医疗服务	Medical Services	1001.6	1101.1
八、其他用品和服务	**Others**	**151.4**	**190.3**

8-16 农村常住居民家庭人均购买主要商品数量

Per Capita Annual Purchases of Major Commodities of Rural Households

单位：千克 (kg)

指标名称	Item	2018	2019
面粉	Flour	24.5	25.6
大米	Rice	11.6	12.4
薯类	Potato	10.9	15.9
豆类	Beans	8.9	10.8
食用植物油	Edible vegetable oil	12.1	12.1
鲜菜	Fresh vegetables	65.7	77.2
猪肉	Pork	8.3	7.7
牛肉	Beef	0.4	0.6
羊肉	Lamb	0.1	0.3
鸡	Chicken	1.0	1.4
鱼类	Fish	0.8	1.1
虾类	Shrimp	0.1	0.1
鲜蛋	Eggs	6.8	9.1
鲜奶	Milk	6.7	7.1
酸奶	Yogurt	2.1	2.2
奶粉	Milk	0.8	0.7
鲜瓜果	Fresh fruit	34.8	44.0
糕点	Cake	3.1	3.6
茶叶	Tea	0.3	0.3
卷烟（盒）	Cigarettes (box)	32.3	36.9
啤酒	Beer	3.4	3.1
白酒	Liquor	0.7	0.9
果酒	Wine	0.3	0.2
鞋（双）	Footwear (pair)	2.3	2.7
水（吨）	Water (tons)	14.1	20.2
电（度）	Electricity （kwh）	584.4	659.3
煤炭	Coal	58.8	33.0
管道天燃气（立方米）	Gas pipeline （cu.m)	3.9	6.6
罐装液化石油气	Bottled liquefied petroleum gas	7.8	4.8

8-17 农村常住居民家庭平均每百户耐用品拥有情况

Ownership of Major Durable Consumer Goods Every 100 Rural Households

指标名称	Item	2018	2019
家用汽车（辆）	Automobile (unit)	33.2	32.3
摩托车（辆）	Motorcycles (unit)	43.5	34.1
助力车（台）	Strength-aid Cycle (unit)	78.9	87.6
洗衣机（台）	washing machine (unit)	98.1	100.2
电冰箱（柜）	Refrigerator (unit)	94.7	96.3
微波炉（台）	Microwave Oven (unit)	14.3	14.8
彩色电视机（台）	Color TV Set (unit)	119.9	121.0
#接入有线电视（台）	The Number of Cable Television Accessed to Network	25.7	-
空调（台）	Air conditioning(unit)	116.0	115.6
热水器（台）	Water heaters(unit)	77.8	75.6
#太阳能热水器（台）	Solar water heaters (unit)	54.4	-
洗碗机（台）	Dishwasher (unit)	0.7	0.5
排油烟机（台）	Exhauster (unit)	30.4	33.0
固定电话（部）	Ordinary Telephone (unit)	12.4	4.4
移动电话（部）	Mobile phones (unit)	308.0	316.7
#接入互联网（部）	Access to the Internet(unit)	197.8	231.2
计算机（台）	Computer (a)	30.6	32.2
#接入互联网（台）	Access to the Internet(unit)	19.1	18.4
照相机（台）	Camera (unit)	3.0	3.0
中高档乐器（架）	High-end Instruments (unit)	1.9	1.0
健身器材（台）	Setting-up Apparatus (unit)	2.3	2.1
空气净化器（台）	Air-cleaner（unit）	0.8	0.8
吸尘器（台）	Vacuum Cleaner（unit）	0.8	1.0

8-18 农村常住居民家庭居住情况

Housing Conditions of Rural Households

指标名称	Item	2018	2019
调查户数（户）	**Number of Households Surveyed (household)**	**660**	**640**
平均每户居住人口（人）	**Average Number of Resident Population (person)**	**3.7**	**3.7**
人均现住房建筑面积（平方米/人）	**The Average Floor Area Per Person (sq.m / person)**	**51.4**	**49.1**
一、按居住空间样式分（%）	**by Living space style（%）**	**100.0**	**100.0**
单栋楼房	Single building Room	49.4	51.4
单栋平房	Single-storey House	47.2	45.1
单元房	Apartment	1.6	2.6
筒子楼或连片平房	Tube-shaped Apartment or Lace Single-storey Houses	0.3	
其他	Other	1.5	0.9
二、按主要建筑材料分（%）	**by main construction materials（%）**	**100.0**	**100.0**
钢筋混凝土	Reinforced concrete soil	16.5	16.1
砖混材料	Brick and concrete material	76.5	78.5
砖瓦砖土	Tile and brick earth	5.9	4.5
竹草土坯	Bamboo grass mud	0.6	
其他	Others	0.5	0.9
三、按房屋来源分（%）	**by Source of Housing（%）**	**100.0**	**100.0**
租赁住房	Rental housing	0.6	3.0
自建住房	Self-establish Housing	97.7	95.2
购买商品房	Commercial Residential Housing	0.3	0.5
购买房改住房	Private Housing through Housing Reform		
购买保障性住房	Indemnificatory Housing		
拆迁安置房	Resettlement Housing	1.3	1.2
继承或获赠住房	Inheriting and Donation Housing		
其他	Others	0.1	0.1
四、住房外道路为硬化路面的户比重（%）	**proportion of households which outer road is Hardened road（%）**	**99.9**	**99.9**
五、按住宅有管道供水情况分（%）	**By Piped Water Supply Condition（%）**	**100.0**	
管道供水入户	Pipe water into People's Homes	93.1	-
管道供水至公共取水点	Pipe water to Public Watering Points	1.1	-
没有管道设施	No Pipeline Facilities	5.8	-
六、按住户主要饮水来源情况分（%）	**By Source of main Drinking Water（%）**	**100.0**	**100.0**
经过净化处理的自来水	Purified Tap Water	51.7	51.7
受保护的井水和泉水	Protected Wells and Springs	40.7	41.1
不受保护的井水和泉水	Unprotected Wells and Springs	4.6	6.7
江河湖泊水	Rivers and Lakes Water	0.7	0.2
其他饮用水来源	Others	2.3	0.3
七、按住宅内厕所类型分（%）	**By Household Lavatory Type (%)**	**100.0**	**100.0**
水冲式卫生厕所	Sanitary Water Closet	33.1	65.4
水冲式非卫生厕所	Insanitary Water Closet	8.3	20.0
卫生旱厕	Sanitary Latrine	29.3	14.2
普通旱厕	Latrine	29.0	0.4
无厕所	No Lavatory	0.3	
八、按主要炊用能源状况分（%）	**By Cooking Fuel Condition（%）**	**100.0**	**100.0**
天然气、煤气、液化石油气	Pipeline Natural Gas，Pipeline Gas，Pipeline Liquified Petroleum Gas	17.9	8.8
煤炭	Coal	2.1	0.7
电	Electricity	61.0	76.6
沼气	Methane	0.2	
其他	Others	18.8	13.9

主 要 统 计 指 标 解 释

住户 指居住在一个住宅内，共同分享生活开支或收入的一群人。居住在同一房间内、不共同分享生活开支的人群，每个人都视为一个住户。住家保姆、住家家庭帮工视为单独的住户。

常住成员指住户成员中，经常在家居住、或者调查期内居住时间超过一半的人员，以及本住户供养的学生。

可支配收入 指调查户在调查期内获得的、可用于最终消费支出和储蓄的总和，即调查户可以用来自由支配的收入。可支配收入既包括现金，也包括实物收入。按照收入的来源，可支配收入包含四项，分别为：工资性收入、经营净收入、财产净收入和转移净收入。计算公式为：

可支配收入 = 工资性收入 + 经营净收入 + 财产净收入 + 转移净收入

工资性收入 指就业人员通过各种途径得到的全部劳动报酬和各种福利，包括受雇于单位或个人、从事各种自由职业、兼职和零星劳动得到的全部劳动报酬和福利。

经营净收入 指住户或住户成员从事生产经营活动所获得的净收入，是全部经营收入中扣除经营费用、生产性固定资产折旧和生产税之后得到的净收入。计算公式具体为：

经营净收入 = 经营收入 – 经营费用 –生产性固定资产折旧–生产税

财产净收入 指住户或住户成员将其所拥有的金融资产、住房等非金融资产和自然资源交由其他机构单位、住户或个人支配而获得的回报并扣除相关的费用之后得到的净收入。

财产性净收入=财产性收入– 财产性支出

转移性收入 指国家、单位、社会团体对住户的各种经常性转移支付和住户之间的经常性收入转移。包括养老金或退休金、社会救济和补助、政策性生产补贴、政策性生活补贴、经常性捐赠和赔偿、报销医疗费、住户之间的赡养收入，以及本住户非常住成员寄回带回的收入等。计算公式为：

转移净收入 = 转移性收入 –转移性支出

消费支出 指住户用于满足家庭日常生活消费需要的全部支出，包括用于消费品的支出和用于服务性消费的支出。根据用途不同，消费支出可划分为食品烟酒、衣着、居住、生活用品及服务、交通通信、教育文化娱乐、医疗保健、其他用品及服务八大类。

农村居民人均纯收入（老口径） 指农村住户当年从各个来源得到的家庭总收入扣除相关费用性支出后，最终归农村居民所有的收入总和，按照农村住户人口平均的纯收入水平。计算公式为：

纯收入=总收入 –家庭经费费用支出–税费支出–生产性固定资产折旧–赠送农村内部亲友

Explanatory Notes on Main Statistical Indicators

Households refer to persons living and sharing economically together in one house. When people don`t share living expenses, every single person are deemed to be one household. Live-in Nanny and family helpers are deemed to be one household.

Usual Resident Population refers to persons staying at home regularly or for over half of time in survey period and students provided by the by the household.

Disposable Income of Households refers to the actual income of households for purpose of final expenditure and savings in survey period, households can use that at their disposable. It includes income both in cash and in kind. By sources of income, disposable income includes four categories: income from wages and salaries, net business income, net income from properties and net income from transfer. The formula is:

Disposable Income of Households = Income from Wages and Salaries + Net Business Income + Net Income from Properties + Net Income from Transfer

Income from Wages and Salaries refers to remuneration of labour and salaries from all kinds of sources, including those employed by other units or individuals, freelance work, part-time jobs, and sporadic labour.

Net Business Income refers to net income earned by households and their members engaged in production and business activities. It refers to the operating revenue minus operating costs, depreciation of productive fixed assets, and production tax. The formula is:

Net Business Income = Operating Revenue - Operating Costs - Depreciation of Productive Fixed Assets - Production Tax

Net Income from Properties refers to net income received as returns by households or members of financial assets, non-financial assets such as housing, to other institutions, households and individuals, and minus relevant costs. The formula is:

Net Income from Properties = Property Income – Property Expenditure

Income from Transfer refersto the regular transfer from country, institutions, social communities to households and between households. It includes old-age and retirement pension, regular donation and compensation, applying for medical fees, supporting income between households, income from non-usual-residing members of households, etc.

Net Income from Transfer The formula is:

Net Income from Transfer = Income from Transfer – Expenditure from Transfer

Consumption Expenditure of Households refers to all expenditure of households for living expenditure to satisfy family daily living. It includesexpenditure on eight categories: food tobacco and liquor; clothing; residence; household facilities, articles and services; transport and communications; education, cultural and recreational activities; health care and medical services, and miscellaneous goods and services.

The Average Per Capita Net Income of Rural Residents (the old range) refers to the total income of rural households from all sources minus all corresponding expenses. The formula is:

Net Income = Total Income –Household Operation Expenses – Taxes and Fees Paid – Taxes and Fees Depreciation of Fixed Assets for Production – Gifts to Non-rural Relatives

9 城市公用事业

URBAN PUBLIC UTILITIES

资料整理：郝　静
Data management：Hao Jing
数据审核：刘栋婷
Data audit：Liu Dongting

第九部分　城市公用事业

一、简要说明

本章资料主要包括城市供水、供燃气、供热、公共交通、市政设施、市政设施水平、城市规模及用地状况、园林绿地、环境卫生等情况，由西安市统计局服务业和社会科技处根据西安市建委、市交通局、市地铁办及市水务局提供的数据整理。

二、主要指标

人均公园绿地面积（平方米）	9.97	与上年	持平
人均城市道路面积（平方米）	18.34	比上年增加	0.37
供水普及率（%）	98.27	比上年提高	0.42个百分点
燃气普及率（%）	99.96	比上年提高	0.06个百分点

9　URBAN PUBLIC UTILITIES

Ⅰ.Brief Introduction

Data in this chapter reflects basic condition of urban public utilities of Xi'an City. Data on public utilities primarily consists of urban water supply, gas sales, urban heating, public transportation, municipal facilities, level of municipal construction, scale of the city, condition of land utilization, parks, greenbelt and environmental sanitation. Data in this chapter is compiled by Tertiary Industry and Social Science & Technology Division of Xi'an Bureau of Statistics according to the data provided by Committee of Urban Construction of Xi'an, Xi'an Burean of Transportation and Xi'an Metro Office.

Ⅱ.Major Indicators

		Increase over Preceding Year
Per Capita Public Green Areas (sq.m)	9.97	持平
Per Captia Area of Roads (sq.m)	18.34	0.37
Water-Consuming Popularization (%)	98.27	0.42 percenage points
Gas-Consuming Popularization (%)	99.96	0.06 percenage points

9-1 城市（县城）供水

Urban (County) Water Supply

指　标	Item	2010	2014	2015	2016	2017	2018	2019
年末水厂个数（个）	Number of Water Factory at Year-end (units)	9	16	22	22	24	22	28
供水综合生产能力（万立方米/日）	Total Volume of Water Supply (10 000 cu.m/day)	197.40	196.50	211.50	219.38	206.47	215.10	287.22
#地下水	Groundwater	55.80	51.33	62.86	64.61	65.11	89.86	86.64
年末供水管道总长度（公里）	Length of Water Supply Pipelines at Year-end (kms)	2416.00	3499.97	4371.05	4522.46	4899.56	4959.94	4977.08
全年供水总量（万立方米）	Total Annual Volume of Water Supply (10 000 cu.m)	41089.00	53798.99	56055.25	59953.03	89215.62	90394.45	75392.33
#生产运营用水	For Productive Use	6267.00	15680.53	16146.29	16567.21	43095.31	39453.60	22675.54
居民家庭用水	For Residential Use	20944.00	28497.40	30742.79	32182.87	34896.60	39078.56	39962.46
用水人口（万人）	Population with Access to Tap Water (10 000 persons)	410.90	452.57	463.05	475.00	506.26	589.90	642.91

注：本表数据来源于市建委和市住房和城乡建设局、市水务局。
本表2017年及以后年份数据含西咸新区。

9-2 城市（县城）供燃气

Gas Supply in Urban Area（County）

指　标	Item	2010	2014	2015	2016	2017	2018	2019
一、天然气	**Natural Gas**							
供气管道长度（公里）	Total Length of Gas Pipelines (km)	4488	6892.25	7465.73	8199.80	9174.87	10659.68	11928.62
供气总量（万立方米）	Total Gas Supply(10 000 cu.m)	109052	186259.15	196826.38	206068.05	231168.38	285215.47	320847.29
#销售气量	Volume of Gas Sales	104055	179536.78	189066.21	201078.36	224419.93	279030.23	311544.57
#家庭用量	Residential Households	20989	59057.38	65952.81	67024.75	105249.81	100959.64	103357.70
用气人口（万人）	Population with Access to Gas (10 000 persons)	333	425.72	437.96	452.11	477.01	588.40	646.89
二、液化石油气	**Liquefied Petroleum Gas**							
供气总量（吨）	Total Gas Supply (tons)	11469	5299.70	5030.30	4955.50	7607.20	31023.54	9965.79
#销售气量	Volume of Gas Sales	11441	5244.00	4950.00	4875.20	7478.90	30397.32	9865.50
#家庭用量	Residential Households	7376	4281.00	4064.00	4056.00	6081.47	8881.82	7241.36
用气人口（万人）	Population with Access to Gas (10 000 persons)	31.20	21.00	19.50	17.60	13.02	13.65	7.11

注：本表数据来源于市住房和城乡建设局。
本表2017年及以后年份数据含西咸新区。

9-3 城市（县城）集中供热

Heating in Urban Area（County）

指　标	Item	2010	2014	2015	2016	2017	2018	2019
供热能力	Heating Capacity							
蒸气（吨/小时）	Steam (tons/hour)	2235	2893	3013	3013	6200	4325	4425
热水（兆瓦）	Hot Water (megawatts)	3531	13967.00	17191.90	17765.90	14477.00	14465.47	15414.44
供热总量(万吉焦)	Volume Supplied (10 000 gigajoules)							
蒸气	Steam	1674	1743.87	1671.14	1789.13	2813.00	1972.08	2042.18
热水	Hot Water	2570	3726.89	4241.30	5032.84	6338.00	6532.89	7538.46
集中供热管道长度（公里）	Length of Centralized Heating Pipelines(km)	541	894.24	1054.41	1141.24	1842.00	1516.83	1739.61
集中供热面积（万平方米）	Heated Area (10 000sq.m)	6094	13492.55	16690.65	19566.81	29118.90	24922.93	27615.69
#住宅	Residential Buildings	5009	11828.59	14730.49	17282.39	17541.10	20751.73	22778.29

注：本表数据来源于市住房和城乡建设局。
本表2017年及以后年份数据包含西咸新区。

9-4 城市公共交通

Urban Public Traffic

指　标	Item	2010	2014	2015	2016	2017	2018	2019
运营车辆（辆）	Operating Vehicles (units)	7107	7769	7781	7829	7780	8743	10566
标准运营车辆（标台）	Standard Vehicles (units)	8139	9050	9061	9140	9243	10712	13092
公交客运总量（万人次）	Total of Bus Passenger(10 000 person-times)	162400	170960	161032	147089	133465	135919	145280
公交客运收入（万元）	Bus Passenger Transport Income (10 000 yuan)	129397	140914	137492	129132	165072	126590	159040
出租汽车数（辆）	Number of Taxis (units)	12786	14159	14459	14459	14509	14609	16832
地铁运营线路长度（公里）	Length of Subway Lines in Operation(km)		50.94	50.94	88.97	88.97	126.70	132.41
地铁客运量（万人次）	Total of Subway Passenger(10 000 person-times)		29953.07	34209.35	40815.75	60534.01	74624.64	94383.62

注：本表数据来源于市交通局和市轨道交通集团有限公司。
本表数据为西安原口径。

9-5 市政设施

Municipal Facilities

指　标	Item	2010	2014	2015	2016	2017	2018	2019
一、道路长度（公里）	**Length of Roads (km)**	**2662**	**3461.18**	**3570.58**	**3683.14**	**4398.83**	**4712.47**	**5141.85**
二、道路面积（万平方米）	**Area of Roads (10 000 sq.m)**	**5965**	**8144.22**	**8457.14**	**8618.93**	**10063.55**	**10834.70**	**11998.06**
三、人行道面积（万平方米）	**Area of Sidewalks (10 000 sq.m)**	**1834**	**2310.46**	**2381.20**	**2423.70**	**2814.31**	**2886.16**	**3105.42**
四、桥梁数（座）	**Number of Bridges (units)**	**347**	**437**	**448**	**449**	**491**	**502**	**439**
#立交桥	Overpasses	71	105	106	107	127	126	99
五、路灯盏数（盏）	**Number of Street Lights (units)**	**291754**	**337991**	**343465**	**349808**	**382979**	**383174**	**461408**
六、排水管道长度（公里）	**Length of Drainage Pipelines (km)**	**3765**	**4839.49**	**4984.94**	**5161.83**	**5802.36**	**6126.11**	**6445.80**
七、污水年排放量（万立方米）	**Annual Discharge Volume of Sewage (10 000 cu.m)**	**34706**	**51673**	**62092**	**56578**	**58303**	**70374**	**74617**
八、污水处理厂处理能力（万立方米/日）	**Daily Disposal Capacity of Sewage (10 000 cu.m/day)**	**106.5**	**153.1**	**200.6**	**212.1**	**147.6**	**225.1**	**229.7**
九、污水年处理量（万立方米）	**Yearly Disposal Capacity of Sewage Disposal Plant (10 000 cu.m)**	**25088**	**47907**	**57034**	**52011**	**54279**	**66048**	**71917**

注：本表数据来源于市住房和城乡建设局。
本表2017年及以后年份数据包含西咸新区。

9-6 城市（县城）设施水平

Urban（County）Municipal Facilities

指　标	Item	2010	2014	2015	2016	2017	2018	2019
一、人均日生活用水量（升）	**Per Capita Daily Consumption of Tap Water For Residential Use (liters)**	**186.20**	**178.45**	**187.79**	**191.35**	**199.09**	**189.56**	**176.07**
二、供水普及率（%）	**Water-Consuming Popularization(%)**	**98.8**	**100**	**100**	**100**	**99.25**	**97.85**	**98.27**
三、燃气普及率（%）	**Gas-Consuming Popularization(%)**	**97.0**	**98.71**	**98.79**	**98.89**	**96.07**	**99.90**	**99.96**
四、人均城市道路面积（平方米）	**Per Captia Area of Roads (sq.m)**	**15.4**	**18.00**	**18.26**	**18.15**	**19.73**	**17.97**	**18.34**
五、建成区排水管道密度（公里/平方公里）	**Density of Drainage Pipelines in Developed Areas (km/sq.km)**	**9.5**	**9.27**	**9.09**	**9.12**	**1.46**	**7.88**	**7.96**
六、污水处理率（%）	**Rate of Sewerage Disposal(%)**	**84.0**	**92.71**	**91.85**	**91.93**	**93.10**	**93.85**	**96.38**
七、园林绿化	**Afforestation and Parks and Gardens**							
人均公园绿地面积（平方米）	Per Capita Public Green Areas (sq.m)	9.1	11.22	11.47	11.61	12.04	9.97	9.97
建城区绿地率（%）	Rate of Green Areas in Developed Areas (%)	29.2	32.60	34.03	34.95	36.78	35.23	36.02
八、生活垃圾无害化处理率（%）	**Rate of No Harm Disposal of Garbage(%)**	**93.9**	**93.48**	**98.09**	**96.70**	**98.11**	**98.97**	**98.87**

注：本表数据来源于市住房和城乡建设局。
本表2017年及以后年份数据包含西咸新区。
本表供水普及率指标2016年及以前数据为用水普及率。

9–7 城市（县城）规模及用地情况

City（County）Scale and Land Use

单位：平方公里 (sq.km)

指 标	Item	2010	2014	2015	2016	2017	2018	2019
建成区面积	Area of the Constructed Regions	395	521.91	548.60	565.75	683.09	723.68	722.70
城市建设用地	Land use for Construction	336	507.66	536.10	553.29	646.54	679.35	722.53

注：本表数据来源于市住房和城乡建设局。
本表2017年及以后年份数据包含西咸新区。

9–8 城市（县城）园林绿化

Urban（County）Parks,Gardens and Green Areas in Cities

指 标	Item	2010	2014	2015	2016	2017	2018	2019
一、公园个数（个）	**Number of Parks (units)**	**68**	**85**	**91**	**95**	**103**	**104**	**117**
二、公园面积（公顷）	**Area of Parks (hectares)**	**1335**	**2483.83**	**2599.83**	**2647.40**	**3259.70**	**3272.70**	**3490.53**
三、绿地面积（公顷）	**Total Area of Parks,Gardens and Green Areas (hectares)**	**12140**	**18914.05**	**20582.44**	**22502.87**	**30703.66**	**31680.89**	**32586.46**
#公园绿地面积	Public Green Areas	3526	5075.85	5310.58	5517.08	6142.98	6010.08	6522.65
四、年末绿化覆盖面积（公顷）	**Coverage Space of Green Areas at year-end (hectares)**	**15646**	**23216.65**	**25639.88**	**27617.83**	**35936.49**	**35939.67**	**36885.61**
五、建成区绿化覆盖率（%）	**Coverage of Green Areas in Developed Areas (%)**	**37.50**	**40.76**	**42.04**	**42.57**	**40.79**	**38.53**	**39.32**

注：本表数据来源于市住房和城乡建设局。
本表2017年及以后年份数据包含西咸新区。

9-9 城市（县城）环境卫生

Urban（County）Environment Sanitation

指 标	Item	2010	2014	2015	2016	2017	2018	2019
清扫面积（万平方米）	Area Under Cleaning Program (10 000 sq.m)	6290	10110	9842	9137	12241	7790	10527
生活垃圾清运量（万吨）	Volume of Residential Garbage Disposal (10 000 tons)	237	359.37	359.16	371.51	422.25	430.68	396.78
公共厕所（座）	Number of Public Lavatories (units)	1257	2151	2239	2314	3274	4030	3551
市容环卫专用车辆设备总数（辆）	Special Vehicles of Environmental Sanitation (units)	1042	1990	2050	2000	2571	3305	2491

注：本表数据来源于市住房和城乡建设局。
本表2017年及以后年份数据含西咸新区。
按照住房和城乡建设部门意见，个别指标数据进行了修订。

9-10 市区及县供水（2019年）

Urban and County Water Supply (2019)

指 标	Item	西安 Xi'an	市区 City	蓝田 Lantian	周至 ZhouZhi
年末水厂个数（个）	Number of Water Factory at Year-end (units)	28	26	1	1
供水综合生产能力（万立方米/日）	Total Volume of Water Supply (10 000 cu.m/day)	287.22	280.67	2.54	4.01
#地下水	Groundwater	86.64	82.22	1.74	2.68
年末供水管道总长度（公里）	Length of Water Supply Pipelines at Year-end (km)	4977.08	4728.88	126.36	121.84
全年供水总量（万立方米）	Total Annual Volume of Water Supply (10 000 cu.m)	75392.33	74235.10	617.02	540.21
#生产运营用水	For Productive Use	22675.54	22334.86	265.58	75.10
居民家庭用水	For Residential Use	39962.46	39421.49	268.24	272.73
用水人口（万人）	Population with Access to Tap Water (10 000 persons)	642.91	627.08	8.13	7.70

注：本表数据来源于市住房和城乡建设局、市水务局。
本表数据含西咸新区。

9-11　市区及县供燃气（2019年）

Urban and County Gas Supply (2019)

指　标	Item	西安 Xi'an	市区 Urban	蓝田 Lantian	周至 ZhouZhi
一、天然气	**Natural Gas**				
管道长度（公里）	Total Length of Gas Pipelines (km)	11928.62	11695.89	124.73	108.00
供气总量（万立方米）	Total Gas Supply(10 000 cu.m)	320847.29	315237.91	2756.38	2853.00
#销售气量	Volume of Gas Sales	311544.57	306058.14	2635.43	2851.00
#家庭用量	Residential Households	103357.70	101352.70	1185.00	820.00
用气人口（万人）	Population with Access to Gas (10 000 persons)	646.89	632.76	7.23	6.90
二、液化石油气	**Liquefied Petroleum Gas**				
供气总量（吨）	Total Gas Supply (tons)	9965.79	7078.09	1087.50	1800.20
#销售气量	Volume of Gas Sales	9865.50	7010.50	1055.00	1800.00
#家庭用量	Residential Households	7241.36	4466.36	975.00	1800.00
用气人口（万人）	Population with Access to Gas (10 000 persons)	7.11	4.92	0.98	1.21

注：本表数据来源于市住房和城乡建设局。
本表数据含西咸新区。

9-12　市区及县集中供热（2019年）

Urban and County Heating (2019)

指　标	Item	西安 Xi'an	市区 Urban	蓝田 Lantian	周至 ZhouZhi
供热能力	Heating Capacity				
蒸气（吨/小时）	Steam (tons/hour)	4425.00	4425.00		
热水（兆瓦）	Hot Water (megawatts)	15414.44	15408.71		5.73
供热总量(万吉焦)	Volume Supplied(10 000 gigajoules)				
蒸气	Steam	2042.18	2042.18		
热水	Hot Water	7538.46	7532.43		6.03
集中供热管道长度（公里）	Length of Centralized Heating Pipelines(km)	1739.61	1739.61		
供热面积（万平方米）	Heated Area (10 000sq.m)	27615.69	27603.22		12.47
#住宅	Residential Buildings	22778.29	22767.89		10.40

注：本表数据来源于市住房和城乡建设局。
本表数据含西咸新区。

9-13 市区及县市政设施（2019年）

Urban and County Municipal Facilities (2019)

指 标	Item	西安 Xi'an	市区 Urban	蓝田 Lantian	周至 ZhouZhi
一、道路长度（公里）	**Length of Roads (km)**	**5141.85**	**5019.30**	**75.99**	**46.56**
二、道路面积（万平方米）	**Area of Roads (10 000 sq.m)**	**11998.06**	**11762.51**	**137.57**	**97.98**
三、人行道面积（万平方米）	**Area of Sidewalks (10 000 sq.m)**	**3105.42**	**3011.47**	**59.11**	**34.84**
四、桥梁数（座）	**Number of Bridges (units)**	**439**	**426**	**8**	**5**
#立交桥	Crossroads	99	99		
五、路灯盏数（盏）	**Number of Street Lights (units)**	**461408**	**453961**	**2232**	**5215**
六、排水管道长度（公里）	**Length of Drainage Pipelines (km)**	**6445.80**	**6290.73**	**94.67**	**60.40**
七、污水年排放量（万立方米）	**Annual Discharge Volume of Sewage (10 000 cu.m)**	**74617**	**73589**	**538**	**490**
八、污水处理厂处理能力（万立方米/日）	**Daily Disposal Capacity of Sewage (10 000 cu.m/day)**	**229.7**	**224.1**	**3.0**	**2.6**
九、污水年处理量（万立方米）	**Yearly Disposal Capacity of Sewage Disposal Plant (10 000 cu.m)**	**71917**	**71077**	**440**	**400**

注：本表数据来源于市住房和城乡建设局。
本表数据含西咸新区。

9-14 市区及县市政设施水平（2019年）

Urban and County Municipal Facilities Level (2019)

指 标	Item	西安 Xi'an	市区 Urban	蓝田 Lantian	周至 ZhouZhi
一、人均日生活用水量（升）	**Per Capita Daily Consumption of Tap Water For Residential Use (liters)**	**176.07**	**177.27**	**107.77**	**150.60**
二、供水普及率（%）	**Water-Consuming Popularization (%)**	**98.27**	**98.32**	**97.83**	**94.83**
三、燃气普及率（%）	**Gas-Consuming Popularization (%)**	**99.96**	**99.98**	**98.80**	**99.88**
四、人均城市道路面积（平方米）	**Per Captia Area of Roads (sq.m)**	**18.34**	**18.44**	**16.55**	**12.07**
五、建成区排水管道密度（公里/平方公里）	**Density of Drainage Pipelines (km/sq.km)**	**7.96**	**8.09**	**4.14**	**3.63**
六、污水处理率（%）	**Rate of Sewerage Disposal (%)**	**96.38**	**96.59**	**81.80**	**81.63**
七、园林绿化	**Afforestation and Parks and Gardens**				
人均公园绿地面积（平方米）	Per Capita Public Green Areas (sq.m)	9.97	9.98	9.30	10.10
建城区绿地率（%）	Rate of Green Areas in Developed Areas(%)	36.02	36.37	31.33	17.00
八、生活垃圾无害化处理率（%）	**Rate of No Harm Disposal of Garbage (%)**	**98.87**	**99.76**		**97.02**

注：本表数据来源于市住房和城乡建设局。
本表数据含西咸新区。

主 要 统 计 指 标 解 释

建成区面积 城市行政区内实际已成片开发建设、市政公用设施和公共设施基本具备的区域。对核心城市，它包括集中连片的部分以及分散的若干个已经成片建设起来，市政公用设施和公共设施基本具备的地区；对一城多镇来说，它包括由几个连片开发建设起来的，市政公用设施和公共设施基本具备的地区组成。因此建成区范围，一般是指建成区外轮廓线所能包括的地区，也就是这个城市实际建设用地所达到的范围。

供水综合生产能力 指按供水设施取水、净化、送水、出厂输水干管等环节设计能力计算的综合生产能力。包括在原设计能力的基础上，经挖、革、改增加的生产能力。计算时，以四个环节中最薄弱的环节为主确定能力。

供水管道长度 指从送水泵至用户水表之间所有管道的长度。不包括新安装尚未使用、水厂内以及用户建筑物内的管道。在同一条街道埋设两条或两条以上管道时，应按每条管道的长度计算。

供水总量 指报告期供水企业（单位）供出的全部水量。包括有效供水量和漏损水量。

用水普及率 指报告期末城区内用水人口与总人口的比率。计算公式:

$$用水普及率=\frac{用水人口（含暂住人口）}{人口+暂住人口}\times100\%$$

供气管道长度 指报告期末从气源厂压缩机的出口或门站出口至各类用户引入管之间的全部已经通气投入使用的管道长度。不包括煤气生产厂、输配站、液化气储存站、灌瓶站、储配站、气化站、混气站、供应站等厂（站）内的管道。

供气总量 指报告期燃气企业（单位）向用户供应的燃气数量。包括销售量和损失量。

燃气普及率 指报告期末城区内使用燃气的人口与总人口的比率。计算公式：

$$燃气普及率=\frac{用气人口（含暂住人口）}{人口+暂住人口}\times100\%$$

供热能力 指供热企业（单位）向城市热用户输送热能的设计能力。不是热电厂的生产能力。

供热总量 指在报告期供热企业（单位）向城市热用户输送全部蒸汽和热水的总热量。

供热管道长度 指从各类热源到热用户建筑物接入口之间的全部蒸汽和热水的管道长度。不包括各类热源厂内部的管道长度。

供热面积 指供热企业（单位）向城市各类房屋建筑物、构筑物及其附属设施供热的全部建筑面积。

道路长度 指道路长度和与道路相通的桥梁、隧道的长度，按车行道中心线计算。

道路面积 指道路实际铺装面积和与道路相通的广场、桥梁、隧道的铺装面积（统计时，将人行道面积单独统计）。

人行道面积按道路两侧面积相加计算，包括步行街和广场，不含人车混行的道路。

排水管道长度 指所有排水总管、干管、支管、检查井及连接井进出口等长度之和。计算时按单管计算，即在同一条街道上如有两条或两条以上并排的排水管道时，应按每条排水管道的长度相加计算。

绿化覆盖面积 指城市中的乔木、灌木、草坪等所有植被的垂直投影面积。包括公园绿地、防护绿地、生产绿地、附属绿地、其他绿地的绿化种植覆盖面积、屋顶绿化覆盖面积以及零散树木的覆盖面积，不含各类绿地中的水域面积以及没有被植被覆盖的面积（硬化道路、无屋顶绿化的建筑物等）。乔木树冠下重迭的灌木和草本植物不重复计算。

人均城市道路面积 指报告期末城区内平均每人拥有的城市道路面积。计算公式：

$$人均城市道路面积=\frac{城区道路面积}{城区人口+城区暂住人口}$$

建成区排水管道密度 指报告期末建成区排水管道分布的疏密程度，计算公式：

$$排水管道密度=\frac{排水管道长度}{建成区面积}$$

污水处理率 指报告期内污水处理总量与污水排放总量的比率。计算公式：

$$污水处理率=\frac{污水处理总量}{污水排放总量}\times100\%$$

人均公园绿地面积 指报告期末城区内平均每人拥有的公园绿地面积。计算公式：

$$人均公园绿地面积=\frac{城区公园绿地面积}{城区人口+城区暂住人口}$$

建成区绿地率 指报告期末建成区内绿地面积与建成区面积的比率。计算公式：

$$建成区绿地率=\frac{建成区绿地面积}{建成区面积}\times100\%$$

Explanatory Notes on Main Statistical Indicators

Area of the Constructed Regions refers to developed and built city administrative area where basic municipal utilities and public facilities complete constructed. To core city, it includes part of contiguous centralized and a number of decentralized part where basic municipal utilities and public facilities complete constructed. To a multi-city town, it consists of several contiguous developed and build area where municipal utilities and public facilities with basic composition. Therefore, the range of built-up area, generally refers to the built-up areas in the contour line, which is the actual construction site of the city achieved range.

Production Capacity of Water Supply refers to the designed overall production capacity of water facilities, covering the four segments of water collection, purification, conveyance, and out flow through trunk pipelines. Increased capacity through transformation and innovation projects is included as well. The capacity is determined mainly on the weakest of the above-mentioned four segments.

Length of Water Supply Pipelines at Year–end refers to the total length of all the pipelines between the water pumps and the user water meters, excluding pipelines newly installed but not used yet, pipeline in the water factory, and pipeline in the user's buildings.

Volume of Water Supply refers to the total volume of water supplied by water-works(units) during the reference period, including both the effective water supply and loss during the water supply.

Coverage Rate of Urban Population with Access to Tap Water refers to the ratio of the urban population with access to tap water to the total urban population . The formula is :

$$\text{Coverage of urban population with access to tap water} = \frac{\text{population with access to tap water}}{\text{population}} \times 100\%$$

Length of Gas Pipeline refers to the total length of pipelines in use between the outlet of the compressor of gas-work of outlet gas stations and the leading pipe of users , excluding pipelines within gasworks , delivery stations ,LPG storage stations ,refilling stations, gas-mixing stations and supply stations.

Volume of Gas Supply refers to the total volume of gas provided to users by gas-producing enterprises (units) in a year , including the volume sold and the volume lost .

Coverage Rate of Urban Population with Access to Gas refers to the ratio of the urban population with access to gas to the total urban population at the end of the reference period. The formula is :

$$\text{Coverage rate of urban population with access to gas} = \frac{\text{population with access to gas}}{\text{population}} \times 100\%$$

City Heating capacity in Urban Areas refers to the designed capacity of heating enterprises (units) in supplying heating energy to urban users during the reference period .

City Quantity of Heat Supplied in Urban Areas refers to the total quantity of heat from steam and hot water urban users by heating enterprises (units) during the reference period .

City Length of Urban Heating Pipelines refers to the total length of steam or hot water pipelines for sources of heat to the leading pipelines of the building of the users, excluding internal pipelines in heat generating enterprises .

Heated Area refers to the total structure area of heat supplied to urban constructions, structures and ancillary facilities by heating enterprises (units) during the reference period .

Length of Paved Roads refers to the length of roads with paved surface including bridges and tunnels connected with roads. Length of the roads is measured by the central lines .

Area of Paved Roads refers to the actual pavement area of roads and the actual pavement area of squares, bridges and tunnels connecting to the roads (the area of sidewalk pavements is calculated separately).

The area of sidewalk pavements is the sum of area of roads on sides of road, including pedestrian streets and squares, excluding roads for both pedestrians and vehicles .

Length of exhaust pipelines refers to the total length of all main drain piles, trunk pipes ,branch pipes, access manholes, and connector well entrances and exits, and so on . The whole length is calculated as of single pipes. Namely, if there are two or more drain pipes parallel on a street, the length of every pipe shall be summed.

Total area of green land refers to vertical projection area of all vegetation including trees, shrubs, lawns. Including parks, protective green space, production green space, green subsidiaries, green plants covering area, covering an area other green spaces, green roofs and covering area of scattered trees, excluding kinds of water area in kinds of green area and the area not covered by vegetation(hardened road, building of no green roof). shrubs and herbaceous plants overlap under the canopy of trees do not double counting.

Per Capita Area of Paved Roads refers to the area of urban roads per capita at the end of the reporting period. The formula is :

$$\text{Per capita area of paved roads} = \frac{\text{Area of urban roads}}{\text{Urban population+temporary resident population}}$$

Density of Drainage Pipelines refers to density of drainage pipelines in developed areas at the end of the reporting period .The formula is :

$$\text{Density of drainage pipelines} = \frac{\text{Length of drainage pipelines}}{\text{Ares of developed areas}}$$

Rate of Sewerage Disposal refers to the ratio of waste water disposed with the total discharge of waste water in the reporting period .The formula is:

$$\text{Rate of Sewerage Disposal} = \frac{\text{Waste Water Disposed}}{\text{Total Discharge of Waste Water}} \times 100\%$$

Per Capita Area of Public Green refers to the area of public green areas per capita at end of the reporting period .The formula is :

$$\text{Per capita area of public green} = \frac{\text{Area of public green areas}}{\text{Urban population+temporary resident population}}$$

Coverage of Green Areas in Developed Areas refers to the ratio of green areas in built-up areas with the area of developed areas at the end of reporting period . The formula is:

$$\text{Coverage of green land in developed areas} = \frac{\text{Area of green land in developed aresa}}{\text{Area of developed areas}} \times 100\%$$

10 环境保护

ENVIRONMENT PROTECTION

资料整理：张　育
Data management: Zhang Yu
数据审核：马建华
Data audit: Ma Jianhua

第十部分　环境保护

一、简要说明

本章资料反映环境保护、工业污染排放及处理利用情况、危险废物集中处置情况、生活及其他污染情况和工业污染治理项目建设情况，由西安市统计局能源与环境处根据西安市环保局提供的数据资料整理。本章数据不包含西咸新区。

二、主要指标

全年环境空气质量达标天数（天）	225	比上年增加	10
工业固体废物综合利用率（%）	87.5	比上年提高	28.0个百分点

10　ENVIRONMENT PROTECTION

Ⅰ.Brief Introduction

This chapter contains information that reflect environment protection, discharge and treatment of industrial pollutant, centralized treatment of dangerous wastes, domestic pollution and other pollution, construction of projects of industrial pollution treatment. Data in this chapter is compiled by General Division of the Xi'an Bureau of Statistics according to the reported data from Xi'an Environment Protection Bureau. Data from Xixian is not contained in this chapter from 2017.

Ⅱ.Major Indicators

		Increase over Preceding Year
Days of Air Quality up to the Standards（days）	225	10
Percentage of InduStrial Solid Waste Utilized（%）	87.5	28.0 percentage points

10-1 城市环境保护（2019年）

Urban Environmental Protection（2019）

指　标	Item	2019
一、饮用水环境	**Potable Water Environment**	
全市饮用水水质达标率（%）	Compliance Rate of the City's Potable Water Quality（%）	100
二、大气环境	**Atmospheric Environment**	
颗粒物（PM10）年平均浓度（微克/立方米）	Particulate matter (PM10) Annual average concentration (μg / m^3)	96
颗粒物（PM2.5）年平均浓度（微克/立方米）	Particulate matter (PM2.5) Annual average concentration (μg / m^3)	57
二氧化硫浓度年平均值（微克/立方米）	Annual Average Concentration of Sulphur Dioxide (μg / m^3)	9
二氧化氮浓度年平均值（微克/立方米）	Annual Average Concentration of Nitrogen Dioxide (μg / m^3)	48
一氧化碳第95百分位数（微克/立方米）	The 95th percentile of carbon monoxide (μg / m^3)	1.7
臭氧八小时第90百分位数（微克/立方米）	Ozone eight hours 90th percentile (μg / m^3)	166
全年环境空气质量达标天数(天)	Days of Air Quality up to the Standards(days)	225
全年环境空气质量达标率(%)	Annual compliance rate of Ambient Air Quality（%）	61.6
三、声环境	**Voice**	
1、功能区噪声平均值(昼/夜)	Average Noise Value of Functional Districts（day/night)	
0类区(dB(A)/dB(A))	Class 0(dB(A)/dB(A))	48/43
1类区(dB(A)/dB(A))	Class 1(dB(A)/dB(A))	51/45
2类区(dB(A)/dB(A))	Class 2(dB(A)/dB(A))	54/49
3类区(dB(A)/dB(A))	Class 3(dB(A)/dB(A))	59/54
4类区(dB(A)/dB(A))	Class 4(dB(A)/dB(A))	68/64
2、道路交通噪声平均值(dB(A))	Average Noise Value of Road Traffic(dB(A))	70.5
3、区域噪声平均值(dB(A))	Average Noise Value of Region(dB(A))	55.8
四、环境污染治理	**Environmental pollution treatment**	
当年完成环保验收项目环境保护投资（亿元）	Year Completed Investment in Environmental Protection Projects of Environmental acceptance(100 million yuan)	11.21

注：本表数据来源于市生态环境局。表中当年完成环保验收项目环境保护投资额包含市本级及区县、开发区。
本表不含西咸新区。下同。

10-2 主要年份工业“三废”排放及处理利用情况

指　标	Item	2000	2010
一、工业废水排放量（万吨）	**Volume of Waste Water Discharge (10 000 tons)**	**9145**	**13840**
工业废水处理量（万吨）	Volume of Industrial Wastewater Disposal (10 000 tons)		10673.52
废水治理设施数（套）	Number of Facilities for Treatment of Waste Water (sets)		267
二、工业废气排放量（亿立方米）	**Total Volume of Industrial Waste Gas Emission (100 million cu.m)**	**275.97**	**791.56**
废气治理设施数（套）	Number of Facilities for Treatment of Waste Gas(sets)		816
三、工业固体废物产生量（万吨）	**Volume of Industrial Solid Wastes Produced (10 000 tons)**	**107**	**267.29**
工业固体废物处置量（万吨）	Volume of Industrial Solid Wastes Treated (10 000 tons)	20	3.56
工业固体废物综合利用量（万吨）	Volume of Industrial Solid Waste Utilized (10 000 tons) in a Comprehensive Way	63	262
工业固体废物综合利用率（%）	Percentage of Volume of Industrial Solid Waste Utilized in a Comprehensive Way (%)	58.88	98.05
四、工业锅炉（台/蒸吨）	**Industrial Boilers (units/tons)**		

注：1.本表数据来源于市生态环境局。
2.2010年全国统一进行了污染源普查动态更新调查工作，“十二五”的环境统计体系与污染源普查体系相衔接，与“十一五”环境统计口径不同。
3.工业固体废物综合利用率依据环境统计口径计算。

Discharge and Treatment of Waste Gas, Water & Solid Wastes in Repersentative Years

2011	2012	2013	2014	2015	2016	2017	2018	2019
13148	**10223.73**	**8972.97**	**6339.85**	**5203.56**	**4029.83**	**4247.57**	**4163.40**	**3913.70**
12632.38	9089.04	6798.71	5818.27	4783.60	4264.99	4448.08	4091.10	3955.70
314	312	295	305	315	266	275	299	311
1018.46	**1043.31**	**844.11**	**901.23**	**1108.48**	**1034.46**	**1444.60**	**1040.40**	**1067.30**
745	649	661	740	801	834	1048	1225	1641
279	**259.14**	**255.78**	**252.66**	**238.53**	**195.99**	**190.30**	**198.70**	**206.66**
6	9.24	9.68	17.54	20.95	28.66	28.00	78.10	22.70
271	248.58	244.08	233.52	216.64	167.20	159.80	118.30	182.98
97.30	95.92	95.43	92.43	90.82	85.31	83.97	59.50	87.50
	503/8785	**576/13466**	**520/14177**	**501/18278**	**480/12791.8**	**457/14682.3**	**466/17078.2**	**478/16955.3**

10-3 工业污染排放及处理利用情况（2019年）

Discharge and Treatment of Industrial Pollution （2019）

指 标	Item	2019
一、被调查企业基本情况	**Basic condition of Enterprises investigated**	
1. 企业数（个）	Number of Enterprises (units)	581
2. 工业总产值（亿元）	Gross Industry Output Value (100 millian yuan)	3404.52
3. 工业锅炉数（台/蒸吨）	Industrial Boilers (units/tons)	478/16955.3
4. 工业炉窑数（座）	Number of Industrial Grates (items)	331
二、工业废水	**Industrial Waste Water**	
1. 工业取水量（万吨）	Industrial water intake (10000 tons)	8120.1
2. 废水治理设施数（套）	Number of Facilities for Treatment of Waste Water (sets)	311
3. 废水治理设施处理能力（万吨/日）	Disposal Capacity of Facilities for Treatment of Waste Water (10 000 tons/day)	24.8
4. 废水治理设施运行费用（万元）	Operating Expense of Facilities for Treatment of Waste Water (10 000 yuan)	32963.3
5. 工业废水排放量（万吨）	Volume of Industrial Waste Water Discharged (10 000 tons)	3913.7
三、工业废气	**Industrial Waste Gas**	
1. 煤炭消费量（万吨）	Total Coal Consumption (10 000 tons)	573.6
2. 燃料油消费量（不含车船用）（万吨）	Fuel Oil Consumption (10 000 tons)	0.2
3. 天然气消费量（亿立方米）	Natural Gas Consumption (100 millian cu.m)	8.1
4. 工业废气排放总量（亿立方米）	Total Volume of Industrial Waste Gas Emission (100 millian cu.m)	1067.3
5. 废气治理设施数（套）	Number of Facilities for Treatment of Waste Gas (sets)	1641
6. 废气治理设施处理能力（万立方米/时）	Disposal Capacity of Facilities for Treatment of Waste Gas (10 000 cu.m./h)	10936.7
7. 废气治理设施设备运行费用（万元）	Operating Expense of Facilities for Treatment of Waste gas(10 000 yuan)	31927.7
8. 二氧化硫产生量（吨）	Sulfur dioxide production (tons)	105756.2
9. 二氧化硫排放量（吨）	Volume of Sulphur Dioxide Emission (tons)	2078.6
10. 氮氧化物产生量（吨）	Production of nitrogen oxides(tons)	26546.9
11. 氮氧化物排放量（吨）	Nitrogen oxide emissions(tons)	3895.6
12. 烟（粉）尘产生量（吨）	Tobacco (powder) dust production(tons)	659751.5
13. 烟（粉）尘排放量（吨）	The smoke (powder) dust emissions(tons)	4489.9
四、工业固体废物	**Industrial Solid Waste**	
1. 工业固体废物产生量（万吨）	Volume of Industrial Solid Waste Produced (10 000tons)	206.65
2. 工业固体废物综合利用量（万吨）	Volume of Industrial Solid Waste Utilized (10 000tons)	182.98
3. 工业固体废物综合利用率（%）	Percentage of Industrial Solid Waste Utilized (%)	87.5
4. 工业固体废物贮存量（万吨）	Volume of Industrial Solid Waste Accumulated (10 000tons)	3.9
5. 工业固体废物处置量（万吨）	Volume of Industrial Solid Waste Treated (10 000tons)	22.7
6. 工业固体废物倾倒丢弃量（吨）	Volume of Industrial Solid Waste Discharged (tons)	11.24

注：本表数据来源于市生态环境局。

10–4 城市污水处理情况（2019年）

Urban Sewage Treatment（2019）

指　标	Item	2019
一、污水处理厂数（座）	**Number of Sewage Treatment Works(units)**	**39**
污水处理厂处理能力（万吨/日）	Daily Disposal Capacity of Sewage(10 000 tons/day)	275.9
二、污水处理	**Sewgae Disposal**	
污水实际处理量（万吨）	Volume of Sewgae Disposal(10 000 tons)	90283.76
生活污水处理量	Volume of Domestic Sewgae Disposal	87373.07
工业污水处理量	Volume of Industrial Sewage Disposal	2910.7
三、再生水（万吨）	**Utilization(10 000 tons)**	
生产量	Production	6370.38
利用量	Utilization	5328.96
四、化学需氧量去除量（吨）	**Volume of COD Removed (tons)**	**423516.97**
五、氨氮去除量（吨）	**Volume of Ammonia and Nitrogen Removed(tons)**	**31435.84**
六、总磷去除量（吨）	**Volume of Total Phosphorus Removed(tons)**	**6193.05**
七、污泥生产量（万吨）	**Volume of Sludge Produced(10 000 tons)**	**19.69**
八、污泥处置量（万吨）	**Volume of Sludge Disposal(10 000 tons)**	**19.69**
九、污泥倾倒丢弃量（吨）	**Dumping sludge discards (tons)**	
十、本年运行费用（万元）	**Operating Expense(10 000 yuan)**	**84373.28**

注：本表数据来源于市生态环境局。

10-5 危险废物（医疗废物）集中处理情况（2019年）

Condition of Concentrated Disposal of Dangerous Wastes (Medical Wastes) (2019)

指　标	Item	2019
一、危险废物集中处理（置）厂数（个）	**Number of Colleted Dangerous Wastes Treated Plants(items)**	**1**
二、医疗废物集中处理（置）厂数（个）	**The number of Manufacturing Plants of Medical waste treatment (units)**	**1**
三、危险废物设计处置能力（吨/日）	**Design hazardous waste disposal capacity (tons / day)**	**52**
四、实际处置危险废物量（吨）	**The actual amount of hazardous waste disposal (tons)**	**16032.2**
五、危险废物综合利用量（吨）	**Volume of Dangerous Wastes Utilized in a Comprehensive Way (tons)**	
六、焚烧残渣流向（千克）	**Flow Direction of Residuum after Burning (kg)**	
1. 焚烧残渣量	Volume of Residuum after Burning	703722.7
2. 焚烧残渣安全填埋处置量	Secure landfill disposal incineration residues	702762.7
3. 焚烧飞灰产生量	Fly ash production	78085.5
4. 焚烧飞灰安全填埋处置量	Fly ash landfill disposal safety	78084
七、当年运行费用（万元）	**Operating Expenses in Current year(10 000 yuan)**	**4422**

注：本表数据来源于市生态环境局。

10-6 生活及其他污染情况（2019年）

Domestic Pollution and Other Conditions (2019)

指　标	Item	2019
一、基本情况	**Basic Condition**	
1. 生活天然气消费量（万立方米）	Volume of Living natural gas consumption (10 000 cu.m)	109082
2. 生活用水总量（万吨）	Volume of Living water (10 000 tons)	110132
二、污染排放情况	**Discharge of Pollutant**	
1. 城镇生活污水排放量（万吨）	Volume of Urban Domestic Sewage Discharged(10 000 tons)	92689
2. 生活污水处理量（万吨）	Volume of Domestic Sewgae Disposal(10 000 tons)	89591
3. 生活CDD产生量（吨）	Volume of Life CDD production (tons)	432040
4. 生活CDD排放量（吨）	Volume of Life CDD emissions (tons)	22377
5. 生活氨氮产生量（吨）	Volume of Ammonia and Nitrogen in Urban Domestic Sewage Produced (tons)	33370
6. 生活氨氮排放量（吨）	Volume of Ammonia and Nitrogen in Urban Domestic Sewage Discharged (tons)	2064
7. 二氧化硫排放量（吨）	Volume of Domestic and Other Sulphur Dioxide Emission (tons)	31523
8. 氨氮化物排放量（吨）	Volume of Ammonia and Nitrogen in Urban Domestic Sewage Discharged (tons)	5508
9. 烟尘排放量（吨）	Volume of Soot Emission (tons)	18543

注：本表数据来源于市生态环境局。

10–7 工业污染治理项目建设情况（2019年）

Condition of Anti-Industrial-Pollution Projects（2019）

指　标	Item	2019
一、工业企业数（个）	**Number of Industrial Enterprises (units)**	**24**
二、老工业污染源项目治理本年施工总数（个）	**The total number of construction projects of Old industrial pollution sources control this year(units)**	**29**
#工业废水治理项目	Treatment of Waste Water	3
工业废气治理项目	Treatment of Waste Gas	24
工业固体废物治理项目	Treatmen of Solid Wastes	
三、老工业污染源项目治理本年竣工总数（个）	**The Total Number of Old Industrial Pollution Control Projects Completed this year(units)**	**26**
#工业废水治理项目	Treatment of Waste Water	2
工业废气治理项目	Treatment of Waste Gas	22
工业固体废物治理项目	Treatmen of Solid Wastes	
四、老工业污染源治理项目本年完成投资（万元）	**Investment completed in Old industrial pollution control projects this Year(10 000 yuan)**	**28428**
#废水治理项目	Treatment of Waste Water	839
废气治理项目	Treatment of Waste Gas	4249
固体废物治理项目	Treatmen of Solid Wastes	
五、老工业污染源治理项目本年投资来源（万元）	**Source of Investment in Old industrial pollution control projects this Year(10 000 yuan)**	**28428**
#政府其他补助	Other Government Subsidies	4921
企业自筹	Self-raising Funds	23507
银行贷款	Lonans	
六、“三同时”项目竣工验收数（个）	**Number of "Three simultaneous"project completion and acceptance (a)**	**847**
七、“三同时”竣工验收项目实际环保投资（万元）	**"Three simultaneous" actual environmental investment completed and accepted (10 000 yuan)**	**112076**
八、“三同时”项目废水治理新增处理能力（万吨/日）	**"Three simultaneous"Add processing capacity of wastewater treatment (10 000 tons / day)**	**0.04**
九、“三同时”项目废气治理新增处理能力（万立方米/时）	**"Three simultaneous"Add processing capacity of Exhaust treatment (10 000 cu.m/h)**	**8521**

注：本表数据来源于市生态环境局。

“三同时”指建设项目中防治污染的措施，必须与主体工程同时设计，同时施工，同时投产使用。

10-8　各区县、开发区环境保护基本情况（2019年）

区县、开发区	Region	本年完成环保验收项目环保投资额（万元）Investment Completed in accepted Environmental projects this year (10 000 yuan)	工业二氧化硫排放量（吨）Volume of Industrial Sulphur Dioxide Discharged (tons)
全　市	**Total**	**112076.0**	**2078.6**
新城区	Xincheng	4605.9	0.8
碑林区	Beilin	39.4	46.8
莲湖区	Lianhu	597.5	79.1
灞桥区	Baqiao	11352.5	266.8
未央区	Weiyang	7465.7	69.9
雁塔区	Yanta	3072.8	167.8
阎良区	Yanliang	1089.0	135.0
临潼区	Lintong	9304.5	37.2
长安区	Chang'an	755.4	275.4
高陵区	Gaoling	11941.3	73.6
鄠邑区	Huyi	1640.4	192.5
蓝田县	Lantian	3601.4	127.8
周至县	Zhouzhi	8133.9	1.3
高新开发区	Gaoxinkaifaqu	17779.4	242.0
经济开发区	Jingjikaifaqu	3575.4	168.9
航天基地	Hangtianjidi	6471.1	194.8

注：本表数据来源于市生态环境局。

环境统计中污水处理厂个数包含部分大学园区及部分大型小区的污水处理厂。

区县、开发区环保验收项目环保投资额未包括市本级完成数。

Condition of Environment Protection by Regions（2019）

工业化学需氧量排放量 （吨） Volume of COD Removed (tons)	垃圾处理站数 （座） Number of Rubbish Disposal Works (units)	污水处理厂数 （个） Number of Sewage Treatment Works (units)
1287.8	**2**	**39**
33.5		
146.2		2
34.6	1	3
48.0		6
73.1		2
39.9		2
82.5		2
37.6		5
49.3	1	1
433.1		3
5.0		3
7.7		2
155.7		6
93.8		2
47.9		

主要统计指标解释

工业用水 指工矿企业在生产过程中用于制造、加工、冷却、空调、净化、洗涤等方面的用水，按新水取用量计，不包括企业内部的重复利用水量。

工业废水排放量 指经过企业厂区所有排放口排到企业外部的工业废水量。包括生产废水、外排的直接冷却水、超标排放的矿井地下水和与工业废水混排的厂区生活污水，不包括外排的间接冷却水（清污不分流的间接冷却水应计算在内）。

直接排入海的 指经企业位于海边的排放口，直接排入海的废水量。直接排放指废水经过工厂的排污口直接排入海，而未经过城市下水道或其他中间体，也不受其他水体的影响。

工业废水排放达标量 指报告期内废水中各项污染物指标都达到国家或地方排放标准的外排工业废水量，包括未经处理外排达标的，经废水处理设施处理后达标排放的，以及经污水处理厂处理后达标排放的。

生活污水排放量 指城镇居民每年排放的生活污水。用人均系数法测算。测算公式为：

$$\text{生活污水排放量} = \text{城镇生活污水排放系数} \times \text{市镇非农业人口} \times 365$$

生活污水中化学需氧量（COD）排放量 指城镇居民每年排放的生活污水中的COD的量。用人均系数法测算。测算公式为：

$$\text{城镇生活污水中COD产生系数} = \text{城镇牛活污水中COD排放量} \times \text{市镇非农业人口} \times 365$$

化学需氧量（COD） 指用化学氧化剂氧化水中有机污染物时所需的氧量。COD值越高，表示水中有机污染物污染越重。

工业废气排放量 指报告期内企业厂区内燃料燃烧和生产工艺过程中产生的各种排入大气的含有污染物的气体的总量，以标准状态（273K，101325Pa）计算。测算公式为：

$$\text{工业废气排放量} = \text{燃料燃烧过程中废气排放量} + \text{生产工艺过程中废气排放量}$$

生活及其他SO_2排放量 以生活及其他煤炭消费量和其含硫量为基础，根据以下公式计算：

$$\text{生活及其他}SO_2\text{排放量} = \text{生活及其他煤炭消费量} \times \text{含硫量} \times 0.8 \times 2$$

工业SO_2排放量 指报告期内企业在燃料燃烧和生产工艺过程中排入大气的SO_2总量，计算公式为：

$$\text{工业}SO_2\text{排放量} = \text{燃料燃烧过程中}SO_2\text{排放量} + \text{生产工艺过程中}SO_2\text{排放量}$$

工业烟尘排放量 指企业厂区内燃料燃烧过程中产生的烟气中夹带的颗粒物排放量。

生活及其他烟尘排放量 指除工业生产活动以外的所有社会、经济活动及公共设施的经营活动中燃烧所排放的烟尘纯重量。以生活及其他煤炭消费量为基础进行测算。

工业粉尘排放量 指企业在生产工艺过程中排放的能在空气中悬浮一定时间的固体颗粒物排放量。如钢铁企业的耐火材料粉尘、焦化企业的筛焦系统粉尘、烧结机的粉尘、石灰窑的粉尘、建材企业的水泥粉尘等。不包括电厂排入大气的烟尘。

工业固体废物产生量 指报告期内企业在生产过程中产生的固体状、半固体状和高浓度液体状废弃物的总量，包括危险废物、冶炼废渣、粉煤灰、炉渣、煤矸石、尾矿、放射性废物和其他废物等；不包括矿山开采的剥离废石和掘进废石（煤矸石和呈酸性或碱性的废石除外）。酸性或碱性废石指采掘的废石其流经水、雨淋水的pH值小于4或pH值大于10.5者。

危险废物 指列入国家危险废物名录或根据国家规定的危险废物鉴别标准和鉴别方法认定的，具有爆炸性、易燃性、易氧化性、毒性、腐蚀性、易传染疾病等危险特性之一的废物。

工业固体废物综合利用量 指报告期内企业通过回收、加工、循环、交换等方式，从固体废物中提取或者使其转化为可以利用的资源、能源和其他原材料的固体废物量（包括当年利用往年的工业固体废物贮存量），如用作农业肥料、生产建筑材料、筑路等。综合利用量由原产生固体废物的单位统计。

工业固体废物综合利用率 指工业固体废物综合利用量占丁业固体废物产生量（包括综合利用往年贮存量）的百分率。计算公式为：

$$\text{工业固体废物综合利用率}=\frac{\text{工业固体废物综合利用量}}{\text{工业固体废物产生量}+\text{综合利用往年贮存量}}\times 100\%$$

工业固体废物贮存量 指报告期内企业以综合利用或处置为目的，将固体废物暂时贮存或堆存在专设的贮存设施或专设的集中堆存场所内的数量。专设的固体废物贮存场所或贮存设施必须有防扩散、防流失、防渗漏、防止污染大气、水体的措施。

工业固体废物处置量 指报告期内企业将固体废物焚烧或者最终置于符合环境保护规定要求的场所，并不再回取的工业固体废物量（包括当年处置往年的工业固体废物贮存量）。处置方式有填埋（其中危险废物应安全填埋）、焚烧、专业贮存场（库）封场处理、深层灌注、回填矿井及海洋处置（经海洋管理部门同意投海处置）等。

工业固体废物排放量 指报告期内企业将所产生的固体废物排到固体废物污染防治设施、场所以外的数量，不包括矿山开采的剥离废石和掘进废石（煤矸石和呈酸性或碱性的废石除外）。

“三废”综合利用产品产值 指报告期内利用“三废”作为主要原料生产的产品价值（现行价）；已经销售或准备销售的应计算产品价值，留作生产自用的不应计算产品价值。

生活垃圾清运量 指报告期内收集和运送到各生活垃圾处理厂（场）和生活垃圾最终消纳点的生活垃圾数量。生活垃圾指城市日常生活或为城市日常生活提供服务的活动中产生的固体废物以及法律行政规定的视为城市生活垃圾的固体废物。包括：居民生活垃圾、商业垃圾、集市贸易市场垃圾、街道清扫垃圾、公共场所垃圾和机关、学校、厂矿等单位的生活垃圾。

生活垃圾无害化处理率 指报告期生活垃圾无害化处理量与生活垃圾产生量的比率。在统计上，由于生活垃圾产生量不易取得，可用清运量代替。计算公式为：

$$\text{生活垃圾无害化处理率}=\frac{\text{生活垃圾无害化处理量}}{\text{生活垃圾产生量}}\times 100\%$$

Explanatory Notes on Main Statistical Indicators

Water Used by Industry refers to new withdrawals of water, excluding reuse of water within enterprises.

Waste Water Discharged by Industry refers to the volume of waste water discharged by industrial enterprises through all their outlets, including waste water from production process, directly cooled water, groundwater from mining wells which does not meet discharge standards and sewage from households mixed with waste water produced by industrial activities, but excluding indirectly cooled water discharged (It should be included if the discharge is not separated from waste water).

Waste Water Directly Discharged into Sea refers to the volume of waste water directly discharged into sea through outlets of enterprises situated by sea without going through municipal sewerage networks or any other intermediates or being affected by any other water bodies.

Industrial Waste Water Meeting Discharge Standards refers to volume of industrial waste water discharge which, with or without treatment, reaches national or local standards with regard to all pollutants.

Urban Non-industrial Waste Water Discharge refers to annual discharge of non-industrial waste water by urban households. It is estimated by per capita coefficient using the formula:

$$\text{Urban non-industrial waste water discharge} = \text{urban non-industrial waste water discharge coefficient} \times \text{urban non-alagricultur population} \times 365$$

Volume of Chemical Oxygen Demand (COD) Generated by Urban Non-industrial Waster Water refers to chemical oxygen demand generated through the annual discharge of non-industrial waste water by urban households. It is estimated as:

$$\text{Volume of chemical oxygen demand (cod) generated by urban non-industrial waster water} = \text{Coefficient of COD generated through urban non-industrial waste water} \times \text{urban non-agricultural population} \times 365$$

Chemical Oxygen Demand (COD) refers to the amount of oxygen required when chemical oxidants are used to oxidize organic pollutants in water. A higher value of COD corresponds to more serious pollution by organic pollutants.

Industrial Waste Air Emission refers to the discharge into atmosphere of waste air containing pollutants generated from fuel burning and production processes in enterprises within a given period of time. It is calculated at standard status (273K, 101325Pa) as:

$$\text{Industrial waste air emission} = \text{tnoissimehrough fuel burning} + \text{tnoissimehrough production process}$$

SO_2 Emission through Non-industrial and Other Activities is calculated on the basis of consumption of coal by households and other activities and the sulphur content of coal with the following formula:

$$SO_2 \text{ emission through non-industrial and other activities} = \text{of coalby households andother activities} \times \text{sulphur content} \times 0.8 \times 2$$

SO_2 Emission through Industrial Activities refers to volume of sulphur dioxide emission from fuel burning and production process by enterprises during a given period of time. It is calculated as:

$$SO_2 \text{ emission through industrial activities} = SO_2 \text{emission from fuel burning} + SO_2 \text{ emission from production process}$$

Industrial Soot Emission refers to the volume of soot in smoke emitted in the process of fuel burning in the premises of enterprises.

Soot Emission by Consumption and Others refers to the net volume of soot emitted by fuel burning from all social and economic activities and operations of public facilities other than industrial activities. It is calculated on the basis of coal consumption by households and others.

Industrial Dust Emission refers to volume of dust emitted by production process of enterprises and suspended in the air for a given period of time, including dust from refractory material of iron and steel works, dust from coke-screening systems and sintering machines of coke plants, dust from lime kilns and dust from cement production in building material enterprises, but excluding soot and dust emitted from power plants.

Industrial Solid Wastes Produced refers to total volume of solid, semi-solid and high concentration liquid residues produced by industrial enterprises from production process in a given period of time, including hazardous wastes, slag, coal ash, gangue, tailings, radioactive residues and other wastes, but excluding stones stripped or dug out in mining - gangue and acid or alkaline stones not included (a stone is acid or alkaline according to the pH value of the water being below 4 or above 10.5 when the stone is in, or soaked by water).

Hazardous Wastes refers to those included in the national hazardous wastes catalogue or specified as any one of the following properties in the national hazardous wastes identification standards: explosive, ignitable, oxidizable, toxic, corrosive or liable to cause infectious diseases or lead to other dangers.

Industrial Solid Wastes Utilized refers to volume of solid wastes from which useful materials can be extracted or which can be converted into usable resources, energy or other materials by means of reclamation, processing, recycling and exchange (including utilizing in the year the stocks of industrial solid wastes of the previous year). Examples of such utilizations include fertilizers, building materials and road materials. The information shall be collected by the producing units of the wastes.

Rate of Utilization of Industrial Solid Wastes refers to the percentage of industrial solid wastes utilized over industrial solid wastes produced (including stocks of the previous years). It is calculated as:

$$\text{Rate of utilization of industrial solid wastes} = \frac{\text{volume of industrial solid wastes utilized}}{\text{industrial solid wastesproduced+ stock of previous years}} \times 100\%$$

Stock of Industrial Solid Wastes refers to the volume of solid wastes placed in special facilities or special sites for purposes of utilization or disposal. The sites or facilities should take measures against dispersion, loss, seepage, and air and water contamination.

Industrial Solid Wastes Disposed refers to the quantity of industrial solid wastes which are burnt or placed ultimately in the sites meeting the requirements for environmental protection and not salvaged or recycled (including disposition in the year of those wastes of previous years). The disposition includes landfill (Safe landfills should be conducted for hazardous wastes), incineration, containment spaces, deep underground disposal, backfill in mining pits and disposal at sea.

Industrial Solid Wastes Discharged refers to the volume of industrial solid wastes discharged by producing enterprises to disposal facilities or to other sites. The wastes exclude stones stripped or dug from mining (gangue and acid or alkaline waste stones not included).

Output Value of Products Made from Waste Gas, Waste Water and Solid Wastes refers to the current value of products with waste gas, waste water and solid wastes as main materials of production. Products sold and ready to sell shall be included while those produced for own use shall not be included.

Consumption Wastes Transported refers to volume of consumption wastes collected and transported to disposal factories or sites. Consumption wastes are solid wastes produced from urban households or from service activities for urban households, and solid wastes regarded by laws and regulations as urban consumption wastes, including those from households, commercial activities, markets, cleaning of streets, public sites, offices, schools, factories, mining units and other sources.

Ratio of Consumption Wastes Treated refers to consumption wastes treated over that produced. In practical statistics, as it is difficult to estimate, the volume of consumption wastes produced is replaced with that transported. It is calculated as:

$$\text{Ratio of consumption wastes treated} = \frac{\text{consumption wastes treated}}{\text{consumption wastes produced}} \times 100\%$$

11 农 业

AGRICULTURE

资料整理：薛　丰　张喜兰　马秋娟　吴光卫
Data management：Xue Feng　Zhang Xilan　Ma Qiujuan　Wu guangwei
数据审核：马　琰
Data audit：Ma yan

第十一部分　农业

一、简要说明

1.本章资料反映西安农业生产和农村经济的基本情况。内容主要包括耕地、农林牧渔业产值、主要农产品产量、造林、水利水保、农业机械拥有量、农村经济效益主要指标、区县农业生产情况等方面统计资料。

2.农业统计范围包括主要涉农区县的农业生产经营活动。

3.涉及主要年份数据资料，按照《陕西省根据第三次全国农业普查结果核定和修订常规年报相关数据方案》要求，对2007–2017年数据进行了修订。其中，畜牧业中猪牛羊禽修订了2013–2017年数据。11–1、11–3、11–5、11–7表不做修订。

二、主要指标

年末常用耕地面积（万亩）	361.33	比上年下降	1.7%
农林牧渔业总产值（亿元）	499.32	比上年增长	4.3%
农作物播种面积（万亩）	537.90	比上年下降	1.7%
粮食产量（万吨）	139.89	比上年下降	1.6%

11 AGRICULTURE

Ⅰ.Brief Introduction

1. Data in this chapter reflects basic condition of agriculture production of Xi'an city. The mainly including cultivated land, output of agriculture, forestry, animal husbandry and fishery, output of major products, forestation, water conservancy and protection, quantity of agricultural machinery and agricultural base county.

2. Rural social and economic statistics cover social and economic activities in all townships except county towns.

3. Data related to major years, revised the data from 2007 to 2017 by Shanxi Province in accordance with the results of the third national agricultural census approved and revised the regular annual report data programmed. Among them, animal husbandry such as hog, cattle, sheep are revised the data from 2013 to 2017.

Ⅱ.Major Indicators

		Increase over Preceding Year
Cultivated Area Year–end(10 000 mu)	361.33	–1.7%
Gross Output Value of Farming, Forestry, Animal Husbandry and Fishery (100 mil. Yuan)	499.32	4.3%
Sown Area of Crops(10 000 mu)	537.90	–1.7%
Grain Output(10 000 tons)	139.89	–1.6%

11-1 主要年份乡村劳动力、从业人员及基础设施情况

Rural Labor Force、Employees and Basic Facilities in Representative Years

指 标	Item	2000	2005	2009	2010	2011	2012	2013
一、农村劳动力和从业人员情况	**Condition of Rural Population and Employment**							
1. 乡村劳动力资源总数（万人）	Total Rural Labor Force (10000 persons)	240.76	255.93	255.00	256.36	260.97	259.06	257.96
2. 乡村从业人员数（万人）	Number of Rural Workers (10000 persons)	212.65	223.30	223.13	225.04	230.56	226.92	222.67
#女性	Female	99.07	103.22	102.76	103.25	109.61	107.63	106.70
#农林牧渔业	Forestry Animal Husbandry and Fishery	146.07	137.69	121.78	116.58	116.15	113.29	108.48
二、自来水受益村数（个）	**The Number of Tap Water Villages (unit)**	**1527**	**1756**	**2058**	**2184**	**2400**	**2545**	**2650**
三、通有线电视村数（个）	**The Number of Villages connected with cable TV (unit)**							
四、通宽带村数（个）	**The Number of Villages connected to broadband (unit)**							

11-1 续表 continued

指 标	Item	2014	2015	2016	2017	2018	2019
一、农村劳动力和从业人员情况	**Condition of Rural Population and Employment**						
1. 乡村劳动力资源总数（万人）	Total Rural Labor Force (10000 persons)	252.40	230.21	230.62	262.44	259.06	261.74
2. 乡村从业人员数（万人）	Number of Rural Workers (10000 persons)	216.33	200.38	204.11	225.88	222.99	224.11
#女性	Female	104.03	96.46	98.10	107.16	105.88	105.89
#农林牧渔业	Forestry Animal Husbandry and Fishery	110.30	105.10	102.32	110.38	97.65	97.83
二、自来水受益村数（个）	**The Number of Tap Water Villages (unit)**	**2765**	**2718**	**2507**	**2706**	**2027**	**1966**
三、通有线电视村数（个）	**The Number of Villages connected with cable TV (unit)**			**2338**	**2328**	**1750**	**1637**
四、通宽带村数（个）	**The Number of Villages connected to broadband (unit)**			**2720**	**2694**	**2070**	**1964**

11-2 各区县乡村从业人员数（2019年）

Number of Rural Employees by Region（2019）

单位：万人 （10 000 persons）

区 县	Region	乡村劳动力资源总数 Total rural labor force	乡村从业人员数合计 Total number of employees in rural areas	女性从业人员 Female employees	农林牧渔业 Forestry Animal Husbandry and Fishery
全 市	**Total**	**261.74**	**224.11**	**105.89**	**97.83**
新城区	Xingcheng				
碑林区	Beilin				
莲湖区	Lianhu				
灞桥区	Baqiao	19.67	14.98	6.17	4.57
未央区	Weiyang	1.32	0.08	0.01	0.02
雁塔区	Yanta				
阎良区	Yanliang	11.48	10.24	4.74	6.53
临潼区	Lintong	36.61	32.15	15.06	19.57
长安区	Chang'an	35.95	38.81	17.61	9.79
高陵区	Gaoling	9.77	8.20	3.67	2.50
鄠邑区	Huyi	31.48	26.72	12.47	12.02
蓝田县	Lantian	31.03	29.32	18.57	12.25
周至县	Zhouzhi	40.56	32.64	13.77	17.79
西咸新区	Xixian	43.87	30.97	13.82	12.79

11-3 主要年份耕地面积

Area of Cultivated Land in Representative Years

单位：万亩 (10 000 mu)

年 份 Year	年末常用耕地面积 Cultivated Area Year-end	水田 Paddy Field	水浇地 Irrigable Land
1970	554.09	18.20	297.05
1975	538.35	20.34	349.13
1978	530.96	16.70	370.46
1980	526.29	17.45	372.96
1985	508.88	17.63	328.10
1990	495.32	17.97	311.91
1991	492.09	17.03	309.17
1992	485.30	16.44	298.19
1993	479.04	14.36	304.49
1994	471.44	13.98	299.58
1995	463.97	17.04	278.01
1996	451.50	14.21	283.76
1997	456.62	11.90	290.49
1998	455.15	11.18	282.23
1999	450.74	11.31	281.96
2000	443.37	10.26	284.04
2001	431.69	9.00	274.73
2002	424.46	7.98	275.96
2003	413.84	6.65	263.75
2004	404.87	6.59	254.04
2005	400.17	5.55	254.04
2006	395.79	5.33	263.75
2007	391.77	4.80	255.95
2008	390.77	4.64	255.36
2009	387.89	4.39	260.71
2010	383.32	4.03	257.43
2011	377.10	3.80	253.46
2012	369.91	3.32	248.97
2013	366.23	5.33	263.75
2014	360.73	2.42	237.26
2015	356.89	2.37	228.14
2016	346.80	0.96	223.91
2017	374.45	0.62	242.13
2018	367.61	0.53	236.02
2019	361.33	0.52	231.85

11-4 各区县耕地面积（2019年）

单位：万亩

区 县	Region	年末常用耕地面积 Cultivated Area Year-end	水田 Paddy Field	旱地 Dry Land	水浇地 Irrigable Land
全 市	**Total**	**361.33**	**0.52**	**360.81**	**231.85**
新城区	Xincheng				
碑林区	Beilin				
莲湖区	Lianhu				
灞桥区	Baqiao	5.57		5.57	3.73
未央区	Weiyang	0.16		0.16	0.16
雁塔区	Yanta				
阎良区	Yanliang	22.77		22.77	22.39
临潼区	Lintong	66.22		66.22	49.75
长安区	Chang'an	46.88	0.36	46.52	16.67
高陵区	Gaoling	22.15		22.15	20.30
鄠邑区	Huyi	50.47	0.05	50.42	43.69
蓝田县	Lantian	58.50	0.04	58.46	
周至县	Zhouzhi	48.94	0.07	48.87	37.20
西咸新区	Xixian	39.67		39.67	37.96

Area of Cultivated Land by Region (2019)

(10 000 mu)

当年增加的耕地面积 Area of Newly Increased Cultivated Land	新开荒地面积 Area of Newly Reclamation of Wasteland	当年减少的耕地面积 Decrease in Cultivated Area in the Year	国家基建占地 Capital Construction	退耕改果、茶、桑面积 Area for Change into Fruit, Tea and Mulberry	退耕造林面积 Area for Change into Woods
0.75	**0.03**	**10.74**	**4.65**	**1.40**	**0.47**
0.07	0.01	1.15	0.65	0.37	0.06
		0.02	0.02		
		0.06	0.06		
		1.77	0.19	0.10	
0.06	0.01	3.02	0.75		0.01
		0.06	0.06		
0.05		0.11	0.10		
		0.21			
0.51	0.01	1.89	0.86	0.86	
0.06		2.45	1.96	0.05	0.40

11-5 主要年份农业机械拥有量（年末数）

指　标	Item	2005	2009	2010
农业机械总动力（千瓦）	Total Power of Agricultural Machinery(kw)	2239001	2616053	2677334
大中型拖拉机（台）	Large and Medium Tractors(unit)	8415	11479	14675
小型拖拉机（台）	Mini-tractors(unit)	26326	18406	14194
拖拉机配套农具（台）	Number of Tactor Towing Farm Machinery(unit)	67217	55614	53608
农用水泵（台）	Agricultural Water Pump(unit)	77567	80174	77367
节水灌溉类机械（套）	Equipment in Water-saving Irrigation(set)	1290	1799	1710
联合收割机（台）	Combine Harvesters(unit)	4802	6155	6718
机动脱粒机（台）	Motorized Huller (unit)	13870	11960	13231

注：1.本表数据来源于市农业农村局，2017年西咸新区由西安代管，2017年、2018年数据不包含西咸新区。
2.2017年以前大中型拖拉机动力标准为14.7千瓦及以上，小型拖拉机动力标准为2.2–14.7千瓦，含2.2千瓦。2018年起大中型拖拉机动力标准为22.1千瓦以上，小型拖拉机动力标准为22.1千瓦及以下。

Possession of Agricultural Machinery in Representative Years (Number of year-end)

2011	2012	2013	2014	2015	2016	2017	2018	2019
2890247	2983979	3108354	3203302	3253733	2615435	2543023	2429137	2456028
12585	12987	12927	9946	9652	10177	9275	8580	8938
13008	11471	8971	7538	8447	9175	8501	8226	6009
65833	60035	58515	53257	54120	59805	50559	47582	45635
75426	80982	80575	79849	79695	79681	76916	70533	62397
1733	2106	2218	2562	2517	2476	2366	2135	1869
7854	8502	9114	7815	8144	8458	7656	7390	7685
13407	14493	14700	14749	14504	14272	14169	14074	12813

11-6 各区县农业机械拥有量（2019年）

指 标	Item	西安市 Xi' an	新城区 Xincheng	碑林区 Peilin	莲湖区 Lianhu	灞桥区 Baqiao
农业机械总动力（千瓦）	Total Power of Agricultural Machinery(kw)	2456028				118980
大中型拖拉机（台）	Large and Medium Tractors(unit)	8938				80
小型拖拉机（台）	Mini-tractors(unit)	6009				20
拖拉机配套农具（台）	Number of Tactor Towing Farm Machinery(unit)	45635				289
农用水泵（台）	Agricultural Water Pump(unit)	62397				1340
节水灌溉类机械（套）	Equipment in Water-saving Irrigation(set)	1869				43
联合收割机（台）	Combine Harvesters(unit)	7685				47
机动脱粒机（台）	Motorized Huller (unit)	12813				35

注：1.本表数据来源于市农业农村局。

2.2017年以前大中型拖拉机动力标准为14.7千瓦及以上，小型拖拉机动力标准为2.2-14.7千瓦，含2.2千瓦。2018年起大中型拖拉机动力标准为22.1千瓦以上，小型拖拉机动力标准为22.1千瓦及以下。

Possession of Agricultural Machinery by Region（2019）

未央区 Weiyang	雁塔区 Yanta	阎良区 Yanliang	临潼区 Lintong	长安区 Chang'an	高陵区 Gaoling	鄠邑区 Huyi	蓝田县 Lantian	周至县 Zhouzhi	西咸新区 Xixian
37550	40174	110650	422225	356114	231471	501694	247797	341683	47690
10	17	483	1178	1321	1573	1783	906	1243	344
0	12	264		916	142	1515	927	2012	201
67	56	2182	9952	4796	6450	9943	6212	4637	1051
400	350	4194	14460	9718	3760	12735	2486	12954	
90		225	142	936		149	63	221	
5	12	450	1799	1115	795	2518	374	328	242
6		1064	4948	792	545	2381	1815	1227	

11-7 主要年份农业机械化、化肥、水利情况

指　标	Item	2000	2005	2008
一、农业机械化水平（万亩）	**Statistics on Agricultural Machinery (10 000 mu)**			
当年机械耕地面积（实际）	Area Ploughed by Tractors	366.81	360.68	404.42
当年机械播种面积（作业）	Seeded Area by Tractors	482.74	485.62	539.81
当年机械收获面积（作业）	Harvest Area by Tractors	272.83	271.77	313.11
二、农用化肥施用量（吨）	**Use of Agricultural Fertilizers and Insecticides(ton)**			
1. 按实物量计算合计	Practicality Consumption	697243	749802	767980
氮肥	Nitrogenous Fertilizer	392366	411161	413397
磷肥	Phosphate Fertilizer	155480	161444	157145
钾肥	Potash Fertilizer	31841	34114	34149
复合肥	Compound Fertilizer	78620	115458	132481
2. 按折纯法计算合计	Standard Consumption	196343	211790	225949
氮肥	Nitrogenous Fertilizer	102982	107645	112000
磷肥	Phosphate Fertilizer	18658	19368	18855
钾肥	Potash Fertilizer	15921	17055	17077
复合肥	Compound Fertilizer	39313	57009	66247
三、农用塑料薄膜使用量（公斤）	**Plastic Sheet for Agricultural Use(kg)**	**1622198**	**1855383**	**2122310**
四、农用柴油使用量（吨）	**Diesel Oil for Agricultural Use (ton)**	**52706**	**50832**	**51097**
五、农药使用量（公斤）	**Pesticide (kg)**	**1559333**	**1427879**	**1465819**
六、农村水利化情况（万亩）	**Irrigation and Water Conservancy (10 000 mu)**			
有效灌溉面积	Effective Irrigation Area	335.97	280.1	274.48
旱涝保收面积	Stable-Harvesting Arable Land	294.06	255.37	249.31

注：1.本表第一部分数据来源于市农业农村局，第六部分数据来源于市水务局。
2.2017年西咸新区由西安代管，2017年、2018年第一部分和第六部分数据不含西咸新区，2019年第六部分不含西咸新区。

Agricultural Machinery,Chemical Fertilizers,Water Conservancy, in Representative Years

2009	2010	2011	2012	2013	2014	2015	2016	2017	2018	2019
413.70	367.32	427.03	425.40	425.21	549.07	533.21	518.07	498.57	465.25	417.01
544.86	548.28	507.55	529.99	523.15	509.58	492.90	499.36	532.61	501.27	469.46
342.82	403.50	413.93	428.28	443.57	466.21	474.10	488.85	470.66	456.27	393.97
776319	781072	785885	807900	794361	820315	810849	771144	800468	783707	742830
414481	397975	398395	414339	401140	412544	408396	374476	383467	374479	332950
153825	152943	151005	151967	152565	156662	157601	152278	153808	146521	127457
33069	37715	38195	43356	39630	42504	46284	46388	45866	45520	48494
142137	158062	163797	198238	201026	208605	198568	198002	217327	217187	233929
230299	235532	239497	243281	239701	251217	246284	242871	255267	252662	243916
112275	108868	110412	113662	109497	116055	108833	111150	115631	113745	103059
18457	18315	18026	18061	18023	18505	18584	18033	19072	18456	16797
16534	17997	18095	21267	18973	20110	21986	21779	21486	21228	20969
71042	78811	81764	90291	93208	96547	96881	91909	99078	99233	103091
2141969	**2450496**	**2533372**	**2683201**	**2678745**	**2657870**	**2770750**	**2880480**	**3157710**	**3380130**	**3350070**
51346	**61917**	**61637**	**57451**	**62563**	**74935**	**59360**	**55982**	**67510**	**67091**	**61141**
1325459	**1243105**	**1242773**	**1252490**	**1210060**	**1220638**	**1174883**	**1126305**	**1703736**	**1506859**	**1367993**
273.17	281.28	262.32	267.84	240.22	248.34	244.72	259.78	256.13	282.83	245.72
247.60	234.15	214.62	211.31	196.96	189.69	188.50	201.70	184.91	184.78	193.44

11-8 各区县农业机械化、化肥、水利情况（2019年）

指　标	Item	西安市 Xi'an	新城区 Xincheng	碑林区 Peilin	莲湖区 Lianhu
一、农业机械化水平（万亩）	**Statistics on Agricultural Machinery (10 000 mu)**				
当年机械耕地面积（实际）	Area Ploughed by Tractors	417.01			
当年机械播种面积（作业）	Seeded Area by Tractors	469.46			
当年机械收获面积（作业）	Harvest Area by Tractors	393.97			
二、农用化肥施用量（吨）	**Use of Agricultural Fertilizers and Insecticides(ton)**				
1. 按实物量计算合计	Practicality Consumption	742830			
氮肥	Nitrogenous Fertilizer	332950			
磷肥	Phosphate Fertilizer	127457			
钾肥	Potash Fertilizer	48494			
复合肥	Compound Fertilizer	233929			
2.按折纯法计算合计	Standard Consumption	243916			
氮肥	Nitrogenous Fertilizer	103059			
磷肥	Phosphate Fertilizer	16797			
钾肥	Potash Fertilizer	20969			
复合肥	Compound Fertilizer	103091			
三、农用塑料薄膜使用量（公斤）	**Plastic Sheet for Agricultural Use(kg)**	**3350070**			
四、农用柴油使用量（吨）	**Diesel Oil for Agricultural Use (ton)**	**61141**			
五、农药使用量（公斤）	**Pesticide (kg)**	**1367993**			
六、农村水利化情况（万亩）	**Irrigation and Water Conservancy (10 000 mu)**				
有效灌溉面积	Effective Irrigation Area	245.72			
旱涝保收面积	Stable-Harvesting Arable Land	193.44			

注：本表第一部分数据来源于市农业农村局，第六部分数据来源于市水务局。

Agricultural Machinery,Chemical Fertilizers,
Water Conservancy by Region（2019）

灞桥区 Baqiao	未央区 Weiyang	雁塔区 Yanta	阎良区 Yanliang	临潼区 Lintong	长安区 Chang'an	高陵区 Gaoling	鄠邑区 Huyi	蓝田县 Lantian	周至县 Zhouzhi	西咸新区 Xixian
8.49			35.46	93.02	45.59	33.48	38.55	57.39	42.28	62.74
9.39			25.60	102.06	55.98	26.70	60.93	66.60	47.60	74.60
7.30			24.56	95.80	46.73	24.40	53.17	54.00	33.51	15.21
8908	466		75288	138591	51601	55504	102035	119586	148893	41958
2814	135		32950	55681	22841	24463	56613	64312	61480	11661
1531	126		12793	31489	6977	14665	14351	25356	15862	4307
1593	83		5501	7024	6513	3365	5450	8356	9065	1544
2970	122		24044	44397	15270	13011	25621	21562	62486	24446
3389	169		30042	39222	15572	12802	30730	45932	52414	13644
1294	61		14488	15591	6618	4200	14104	28312	15099	3292
183	16		1659	4723	963	1828	1785	2899	1905	836
797	41		2805	2037	2852	1554	2359	3721	4450	353
1115	51		11090	16871	5139	5220	12482	11000	30960	9163
7320	**16000**		**1543700**	**204110**	**165440**	**34050**	**573000**	**379000**	**100200**	**327250**
209	**298**		**3427**	**8315**	**7284**	**1920**	**11176**	**9456**	**3309**	**15747**
7941	**280**		**187866**	**214836**	**62724**	**155660**	**59625**	**71568**	**165006**	**442487**
6.64			22.57	53.13	33.54	22.94	39.63	8.90	58.37	
			22.56	46.65	19.83	20.35	43.10	4.50	36.45	

11-9 主要年份农林牧渔业总产值及指数

Gross Output Value of Farming,Forestry,Animal Husbandry,Fishery, Service and Related Indices in Representative Years

单位：万元 (10 000 yuan)

年 份 Year	农林牧渔业总产值（现价） Gross Output Value (At current prices)	农业 Farming	林业 Forestry	牧业 Animal Husbandry	渔业 Fishery	农林牧渔专业及辅助性活动 Farming, Forestry, Animal Husbandry, Fishery and Auxiliary Activities	指数（上年=100）（可比价） Indices(preceding year= 100) (At cinstant prices)
1970	40617	35965	713	3896	43		111.2
1975	55322	47378	1509	6403	32		93.9
1978	65423	56519	1444	7427	33		104.7
1980	65322	54004	1177	10106	35		85.0
1985	134933	105888	2559	26186	300		106.4
1990	262073	191088	3134	65840	2011		102.5
1991	295620	208324	3362	81070	2864		108.6
1992	321155	219160	4225	94045	3725		108.6
1993	387068	261959	5031	115810	4268		112.8
1994	565056	359609	7819	192140	5488		102.4
1995	754597	513348	7185	228598	5466		106.8
1996	786003	552726	7573	219214	6490		102.1
1997	836201	585973	9226	233623	7379		110.3
1998	853279	625465	8146	212045	7623		107.5
1999	739905	530029	8883	194552	6441		100.7
2000	743712	514845	8482	212612	7773		104.3
2001	767511	527160	8427	223861	8063		102.8
2002	797444	539978	11378	238761	7327		103.0
2003	837857	551398	10550	269610	6299		101.5
2004	967946	580798	12773	314517	6728	53130	108.4
2005	1065437	657262	13086	329856	7340	57893	107.7
2006	1141484	686748	15188	346626	7017	85905	107.2
2007	1317442	790316	15845	395003	9147	107131	105.3
2008	1629892	943261	23365	521950	11348	129968	107.8
2009	1695468	1034208	22663	486142	11830	140625	106.5
2010	2124191	1389118	26787	538396	12830	157060	107.4
2011	2501236	1651250	34453	616943	14856	183734	106.6
2012	2785682	1827705	62291	643347	19877	232462	106.0
2013	3057732	2038346	80199	648800	22773	267614	104.9
2014	3232984	2196966	86889	633519	24030	291580	105.1
2015	3308141	2251512	97776	613417	19519	325917	105.1
2016	3467506	2357901	102222	621737	19640	366006	104.2
2017	4373298	3009278	135570	729219	22700	476531	104.8
2018	4612088	3230380	169157	679813	26268	506470	103.5
2019	4993219	3493828	184739	727047	21867	565738	104.3

注：本表2007-2017年数根据第三次全国农业普查结果进行了修订。

11-10 主要年份农林牧渔业总产值指数

Related Indices of Gross Output Value of Farming,Forestry,Animal Husbandry and Fishery in Representative Years

年 份 Year	农林牧渔业总产值指数（上年=100）（可比价） Gross Output Value Index of Farming, Forestry, Animal Husbandry and Fishery (preceding year = 100) (At constant prices)	农业 Farming	林业 Forestry	牧业 Animal Husbandry	渔业 Fishery	农林牧渔专业及辅助性活动 Farming, Forestry, Anima l Husbandry, Fishery and Auxiliary Activities
2005	107.7	108.0	98.7	107.3	112.6	108.0
2006	107.2	106.0	102.5	109.3	104.5	109.0
2007	105.3	106.4	101.3	102.4	106.3	109.0
2008	107.8	107.9	112.2	106.0	100.5	114.0
2009	106.5	105.4	121.3	106.8	107.4	110.2
2010	107.4	108.7	115.2	104.3	92.7	108.9
2011	106.6	108.2	105.7	102.9	102.1	107.8
2012	106.0	105.6	143.0	104.8	113.4	108.5
2013	104.9	104.3	131.3	104.0	110.1	105.9
2014	105.1	105.8	105.7	103.2	106.0	105.9
2015	105.1	106.7	113.8	100.2	71.2	106.2
2016	104.2	104.8	114.7	100.6	100.1	106.6
2017	104.8	105.0	111.0	103.0	104.3	106.2
2018	103.5	102.8	131.0	100.1	111.4	105.1
2019	104.3	104.7	120.1	98.0	86.4	105.5

11-11 主要年份农林牧渔业总产值构成

Gross Output Value and Its Composition of Farming, Forestry, Animal Husbandry and Fishery at Current Price in Representative Years

单位：% (%)

年 份 Year	农林牧渔业总产值（现价） Gross Output Value (At current prices)	农业 Farming	林业 Forestry	牧业 Animal Husbandry	渔业 Fishery	农林牧渔专业及辅助性活动 Farming, Forestry, Animal Husbandry, Fishery and Auxiliary Activities
2005	100.0	61.7	1.2	31.0	0.7	5.4
2006	100.0	60.9	1.3	31.5	0.6	5.7
2007	100.0	60.0	1.2	30.0	0.7	8.1
2008	100.0	57.9	1.4	32.0	0.7	8.0
2009	100.0	61.0	1.3	28.7	0.7	8.3
2010	100.0	65.4	1.3	25.3	0.6	7.4
2011	100.0	66.0	1.4	24.7	0.6	7.3
2012	100.0	65.6	2.2	23.1	0.7	8.4
2013	100.0	66.7	2.6	21.2	0.7	8.8
2014	100.0	68.0	2.7	19.6	0.7	9.0
2015	100.0	68.1	3.0	18.5	0.6	9.8
2016	100.0	68.0	2.9	17.9	0.6	10.6
2017	100.0	68.8	3.1	16.7	0.5	10.9
2018	100.0	70.0	3.7	14.7	0.6	11.0
2019	100.0	70.0	3.7	14.6	0.4	11.3

11-12 各区县农林牧渔业总产值（2019年）

Gross Output Value of Farming, Forestry, Animal Husbandry and Fishery by Region（2019）

单位：万元 (10 000 yuan)

区 县	Region	农林牧渔业总产值（现价）Gross Output Value (At current prices)	农业 Farming	林业 Forestry	牧业 Animal Husbandry	渔业 Fishery	农林牧渔专业及辅助性活动 Farming, Forestry, Animal Husbandry, Fishery and Auxiliary Activities
全 市	**Total**	**4993219**	**3493828**	**184739**	**727047**	**21867**	**565738**
新城区	Xincheng						
碑林区	Beilin						
莲湖区	Lianhu						
灞桥区	Baqiao	332266	256405	6490	23352	422	45597
未央区	Weiyang	6419	2186	1603	674		1956
雁塔区	Yanta						
阎良区	Yanliang	489024	383957	828	56204	298	47737
临潼区	Lintong	666124	432885	4141	147003	5348	76747
长安区	Chang'an	492276	341185	3644	78130	4881	64436
高陵区	Gaoling	528830	346616	6042	87589	1498	87085
鄠邑区	Huyi	483560	315058	27388	89014	2100	50000
蓝田县	Lantian	519089	313925	35566	113113	5251	51234
周至县	Zhouzhi	643428	425673	70522	79967	491	66775
西咸新区	Xixian	832203	675938	28515	52001	1578	74171

11-13 各区县农林牧渔业总产值指数和构成（2019年）

Gross Output Value and Its Composition of Farming, Forestry, Animal Husbandry and Fishery at Current Price by Region（2019）

单位：% （%）

区 县	Region	农林牧渔业总产值 Gross Output Value	农业 Farming	林业 Forestry	牧业 Animal Husbandry	渔业 Fishery	农林牧渔专业及辅助性活动 Farming, Forestry, Animal Husbandry, Fishery and Auxiliary Activities
全市指数	**Total**	**104.3**	**104.7**	**120.1**	**98.0**	**86.4**	**105.5**
新城区	Xincheng						
碑林区	Beilin						
莲湖区	Lianhu						
灞桥区	Baqiao	102.0	99.3	187.2	107.8	52.1	108.9
未央区	Weiyang	71.5	77.5	112.1	32.7		109.6
雁塔区	Yanta						
阎良区	Yanliang	105.0	106.5	44.2	97.9	92.5	104.6
临潼区	Lintong	105.5	108.0	109.6	98.0	110.6	105.6
长安区	Chang'an	104.0	107.2	53.6	95.4	87.7	106.5
高陵区	Gaoling	105.0	105.9	106.4	98.4	242.9	106.9
鄠邑区	Huyi	104.7	103.3	146.1	100.1	92.3	103.6
蓝田县	Lantian	102.7	103.9	108.0	98.9	85.1	102.3
周至县	Zhouzhi	106.7	106.9	114.9	99.1	67.7	105.4
西咸新区	Xixian	103.0	102.0	159.6	93.2	52.4	105.5
全市构成	**Total**	**100.0**	**70.0**	**3.7**	**14.6**	**0.4**	**11.3**
新城区	Xincheng						
碑林区	Beilin						
莲湖区	Lianhu						
灞桥区	Baqiao	100.0	77.2	2.0	7.0	0.1	13.7
未央区	Weiyang	100.0	34.1	25.0	10.5		30.5
雁塔区	Yanta						
阎良区	Yanliang	100.0	78.5	0.2	11.5	0.1	9.8
临潼区	Lintong	100.0	65.0	0.6	22.1	0.8	11.5
长安区	Chang'an	100.0	69.3	0.7	15.9	1.0	13.1
高陵区	Gaoling	100.0	65.5	1.1	16.6	0.3	16.5
鄠邑区	Huyi	100.0	65.2	5.7	18.4	0.4	10.3
蓝田县	Lantian	100.0	60.5	6.9	21.8	1.0	9.9
周至县	Zhouzhi	100.0	66.2	11.0	12.4	0.1	10.4
西咸新区	Xixian	100.0	81.2	3.4	6.2	0.2	8.9

注：1.总产值指数按可比价计算。
2.总产值构成按现价计算。

11-14 主要年份农林牧渔业增加值

Value-Added of Farming, Forestry, Animal Husbandry and Fishery in Representative Years

单位：万元 (10 000 yuan)

年 份 Year	农林牧渔业增加值（现价）Value-Added of Farming,Forestry,Animal Husbandry and Fishery (At current prices)	农业 Farming	林业 Forestry	牧业 Animal Husbandry	渔业 Fishery	农林牧渔专业及辅助性活动 Farming, Forestry, Animal Husbandry, Fishery and Auxiliary Activities
2017	2708351	1953733	78658	406750	11740	257470
2018	2861844	2097265	98148	379191	13586	273654
2019	3096776	2267013	107115	405837	11310	305501

注：本表2017年数根据第三次全国农业普查结果进行了修订。

11-15 主要年份农林牧渔业增加值指数

Indices of Value-Added of Farming, Forestry, Animal Husbandry and Fishery in Representative Years

年 份 Year	农林牧渔业增加值指数（上年=100）（可比价）Value-Added Index of Farming, Forestry, Animal Husbandry and Fishery (preceding year = 100) (At constant prices)	农业 Farming	林业 Forestry	牧业 Animal Husbandry	渔业 Fishery	农林牧渔专业及辅助性活动 Farming, Forestry, Animal Husbandry, Fishery and Auxiliary Activities
2008	107.6	107.6	112.0	105.8	100.0	114.0
2009	106.3	103.6	114.6	111.2	106.3	108.8
2010	106.9	107.9	108.7	104.3	94.0	108.9
2011	106.7	108.1	106.1	102.8	102.7	108.1
2012	106.0	105.6	142.8	104.8	113.4	108.5
2013	104.8	104.3	131.3	104.0	110.1	105.9
2014	105.2	105.8	104.1	103.2	106.0	105.9
2015	105.1	106.5	114.0	100.5	71.3	106.2
2016	104.1	104.5	112.6	100.5	100.3	106.9
2017	104.8	105.1	111.0	102.3	104.3	106.2
2018	103.5	102.8	131.0	100.1	111.4	105.1
2019	104.4	104.8	120.1	98.1	86.4	105.5

11-16 各区县农林牧渔业增加值（2019年）

Value-Added of Farming, Forestry, Animal Husbandry, Fishery and Service by Region（2019）

单位：万元 (10 000 yuan)

区 县	Region	农林牧渔业增加值（现价）Value-Added of Farming,Forestry,Animal Husbandry and Fishery (At current prices)	农业 Farming	林业 Forestry	牧业 Animal Husbandry	渔业 Fishery	农林牧渔专业及辅助性活动 Farming, Forestry, Animal Husbandry, Fishery and Auxiliary Activities
全 市	**Total**	**3096776**	**2267013**	**107115**	**405837**	**11310**	**305501**
新城区	Xincheng						
碑林区	Beilin						
莲湖区	Lianhu						
灞桥区	Baqiao	217211	174453	4461	13215	171	24911
未央区	Weiyang	3876	1531	866	352		1127
雁塔区	Yanta						
阎良区	Yanliang	314957	255391	453	32521	154	26438
临潼区	Lintong	405378	280142	2505	76958	2326	43447
长安区	Chang'an	321072	246598	2352	35083	3235	33804
高陵区	Gaoling	325491	216327	3602	51304	639	53619
鄠邑区	Huyi	300110	204572	15687	55573	1290	22988
蓝田县	Lantian	310156	192465	22037	66528	2402	26724
周至县	Zhouzhi	392638	274020	37743	46845	255	33775
西咸新区	Xixian	505887	421514	17409	27458	838	38668

11-17 各区县农林牧渔业增加值指数（2019年）

Indices of Value-Added of Farming, Forestry, Animal Husbandry and Fishery by Region（2019）

区 县 Region	农林牧渔业增加值指数（上年=100）（可比价）Value-Added Index of Farming, Forestry, Animal Husbandry and Fishery (preceding year = 100) (At constant prices)	农业 Farming	林业 Forestry	牧业 Animal Husbandry	渔业 Fishery	农林牧渔专业及辅助性活动 Farming, Forestry, Animal Husbandry, Fishery and Auxiliary Activities
全 市 Total	104.4	104.8	120.1	98.1	86.4	105.5
新城区 Xincheng						
碑林区 Beilin						
莲湖区 Lianhu						
灞桥区 Baqiao	102.1	99.6	187.3	107.2	51.2	108.9
未央区 Weiyang	76.2	77.6	112.2	32.6		111.9
雁塔区 Yanta						
阎良区 Yanliang	105.0	106.2	41.7	97.9	90.9	104.8
临潼区 Lintong	105.7	107.9	109.1	98.2	110.4	105.7
长安区 Chang'an	104.0	106.3	53.6	95.3	87.6	106.4
高陵区 Gaoling	105.0	106.0	105.8	98.3	241.9	107.0
鄠邑区 Huyi	104.8	103.8	147.0	99.9	91.8	103.5
蓝田县 Lantian	103.0	104.1	108.4	98.8	85.3	102.2
周至县 Zhouzhi	106.7	107.1	115.1	99.0	65.6	105.3
西咸新区 Xixian	103.0	102.1	156.0	92.8	52.5	104.4

11-18 主要年份农作物播种面积

Sown Areas of Farm Crops In Representative Years

单位：万亩 （10 000mu）

年 份 Year	总播种面积 Total Sown Area	粮食 Grain Crops	小麦 Wheat	玉米 Corn	油料 Oil-bearing Crops	蔬菜 Vegetables
1980	835.43	706.35	324.17	273.14	10.01	24.02
1985	795.41	704.36	378.20	271.14	8.01	45.03
1990	816.41	731.42	387.20	282.14	12.00	51.03
1991	820.41	731.37	389.19	283.14	13.01	47.03
1992	820.65	715.50	384.60	273.60	16.20	54.60
1993	821.63	713.49	380.40	273.69	14.84	63.90
1994	821.10	719.00	375.90	272.40	13.80	59.90
1995	784.74	690.63	370.41	259.55	18.57	57.59
1996	797.40	709.00	366.30	286.80	18.80	55.50
1997	755.78	670.83	367.71	248.79	15.53	59.36
1998	789.99	705.03	370.17	285.45	14.69	60.95
1999	793.08	709.95	371.94	294.00	12.74	60.68
2000	784.94	697.55	369.89	283.70	13.46	64.35
2001	763.16	678.05	359.19	278.57	11.87	61.77
2002	751.10	655.59	350.64	271.95	11.40	67.71
2003	737.06	632.55	336.05	261.89	11.04	69.44
2004	753.83	630.63	311.52	286.50	9.74	77.55
2005	757.91	642.75	325.10	287.87	9.51	83.33
2006	769.49	648.00	313.23	307.89	8.58	87.03
2007	753.54	646.06	296.48	327.93	7.18	75.31
2008	710.48	605.57	294.42	292.34	8.04	75.86
2009	684.56	578.01	285.73	273.35	7.75	77.23
2010	665.89	559.09	277.34	264.07	7.77	78.06
2011	631.45	525.12	259.98	240.74	7.40	78.98
2012	612.90	508.16	256.22	233.84	6.25	79.54
2013	569.95	465.64	236.98	211.66	5.93	80.82
2014	543.19	437.10	224.27	200.39	5.21	81.72
2015	520.78	413.31	215.61	189.60	4.86	82.50
2016	502.63	401.95	209.78	180.80	4.13	81.43
2017	548.50	424.14	228.89	180.39	4.28	104.64
2018	547.46	419.56	227.84	177.58	4.61	107.74
2019	537.90	409.71	221.62	174.43	4.66	107.72

注：本表2007-2017年数根据第三次全国农业普查结果进行了修订。

11-19 各区县主要农作物播种面积（2019年）

Sown Areas of Major Farm Crops by Region（2019）

单位：万亩 (10 000 mu)

区 县	Region	总播种面积 Total Sown Area	粮食 Grain Crops	小麦 Wheat	玉米 Corn	油料 Oil-bearing Crops	蔬菜 Vegetables	瓜果类 Fruits Class
全 市	**Total**	**537.90**	**409.71**	**221.62**	**174.43**	**4.66**	**107.72**	**14.73**
新城区	Xincheng							
碑林区	Beilin							
莲湖区	Lianhu							
灞桥区	Baqiao	11.46	7.07	4.41	2.56	0.19	4.02	0.12
未央区	Weiyang	0.06	0.02	0.02			0.02	0.01
雁塔区	Yanta							
阎良区	Yanliang	49.22	26.85	13.60	13.24	0.06	15.19	7.11
临潼区	Lintong	119.47	100.11	53.01	42.33	0.42	16.79	1.96
长安区	Chang'an	58.69	46.46	28.17	18.02	0.71	9.72	1.79
高陵区	Gaoling	40.53	26.35	13.18	11.94		14.03	0.15
鄠邑区	Huyi	66.36	55.81	28.62	26.08	0.24	8.76	1.55
蓝田县	Lantian	69.92	60.32	35.29	20.76	2.48	5.81	1.13
周至县	Zhouzhi	48.14	38.25	18.92	17.78	0.39	8.86	0.09
西咸新区	Xixian	74.05	48.47	26.40	21.72	0.17	24.52	0.82

11-20 主要年份农作物产品产量

Yield of Major Farm Crops in Representative Years

单位：万吨 (10 000 ton)

年份 Year	粮食作物 Grain Crops	夏粮 Summer Grain	小麦 Wheat	秋粮 Autumn Grain	稻谷 Rice	玉米 Corn	油料 Oil-bearing Crops	油菜籽 Rapeseeds	蔬菜 Vegetables
1978	132.80	64.20	58.20	68.60	5.10	55.80	0.09	0.07	45.66
1979	145.70	81.80	74.20	63.90	4.50	53.40	0.33	0.29	49.11
1980	114.40	56.60	52.20	57.80	4.70	47.70	0.54	0.50	40.13
1981	116.10	78.70	74.30	37.40	3.40	31.50	0.76	0.75	34.06
1982	148.90	85.60	82.20	63.30	4.90	55.50	0.51	0.49	53.71
1983	148.10	81.80	79.60	66.30	4.80	58.50	0.36	0.34	46.99
1984	157.60	82.40	81.00	75.20	5.00	66.50	0.46	0.29	75.47
1985	150.10	76.10	74.80	74.00	5.10	65.10	0.75	0.39	86.44
1986	162.40	91.70	90.10	70.70	4.80	61.80	1.25	0.82	85.84
1987	171.20	87.00	85.20	84.20	5.00	74.30	1.57	1.22	95.16
1988	158.00	86.80	84.60	71.10	3.80	61.40	0.89	0.51	113.50
1989	173.60	93.50	91.20	80.10	4.70	70.40	1.33	0.94	129.32
1990	172.40	91.70	89.70	80.70	5.50	70.40	1.35	0.94	119.32
1991	178.80	91.10	89.20	87.70	5.00	77.50	1.20	0.74	117.41
1992	183.40	101.70	99.60	81.70	4.70	72.30	1.49	0.87	128.12
1993	190.00	101.10	99.00	88.90	4.90	78.60	1.40	1.00	145.80
1994	157.40	86.90	84.90	70.50	4.50	61.40	1.08	0.78	135.26
1995	175.30	99.80	97.40	75.50	3.40	67.80	2.17	1.90	133.60
1996	187.50	80.10	78.40	107.40	3.40	95.60	1.83	1.55	138.01
1997	190.50	114.30	112.30	76.20	3.50	69.40	1.86	1.65	142.11
1998	212.70	104.40	104.00	108.30	3.20	99.10	1.67	1.36	148.87
1999	204.40	95.50	94.40	108.90	2.90	99.70	1.30	1.00	153.24
2000	201.90	92.60	91.60	109.30	3.10	100.50	1.34	0.95	162.14
2001	197.10	98.10	97.20	98.90	2.70	91.30	1.23	0.90	152.80
2002	192.40	94.50	93.50	97.90	2.10	91.60	1.22	0.84	169.74
2003	176.30	98.20	96.70	78.10	1.60	72.30	1.13	0.70	169.67
2004	195.80	97.80	96.00	98.00	1.70	91.60	1.14	0.84	180.96
2005	205.50	100.00	99.10	105.50	1.60	99.30	1.16	0.89	195.70
2006	193.50	86.00	85.40	107.40	1.40	101.20	1.08	0.87	189.30
2007	192.52	73.97	71.97	118.55	1.51	113.83	0.93	0.74	168.98
2008	185.48	87.95	87.36	97.53	0.80	94.02	1.08	0.86	180.60
2009	177.91	81.90	81.03	96.01	0.78	92.49	1.04	0.84	195.07
2010	174.51	81.29	80.71	93.22	0.56	89.47	1.01	0.84	207.11
2011	167.05	78.35	76.66	88.70	0.54	84.37	1.00	0.84	214.13
2012	167.67	79.69	79.02	87.98	0.44	84.18	0.83	0.74	227.96
2013	151.68	67.73	67.05	83.95	0.29	80.04	0.77	0.71	243.92
2014	140.77	68.72	68.15	72.05	0.16	69.99	0.71	0.59	257.86
2015	141.42	72.34	71.95	69.08		67.71	0.68	0.57	267.91
2016	135.39	68.86	68.45	66.53	0.07	64.09	0.58	0.50	268.87
2017	139.89	75.26	74.90	64.63	0.05	60.96	0.62	0.55	354.74
2018	142.14	74.28	73.86	67.86	0.06	64.36	0.67	0.57	373.69
2019	139.89	70.62	70.22	69.27	0.06	65.85	0.67	0.59	378.58

注：本表2007-2017年数根据第三次全国农业普查结果进行了修订。

11-21 各区县主要农作物产品产量（2019年）

Yield of Major Farm Crops by Region（2019）

单位：万吨 (10 000 tons)

区 县	Region	粮食作物 Grain Crops	夏粮 Summer Grain	小麦 Wheat	秋粮 Autumn Grain	稻谷 Rice	玉米 Corn
全 市	**Total**	**139.89**	**70.62**	**70.22**	**69.27**	**0.06**	**65.85**
新城区	Xincheng						
碑林区	Beilin						
莲湖区	Lianhu						
灞桥区	Baqiao	2.47	1.56	1.56	0.91		0.89
未央区	Weiyang						
雁塔区	Yanta						
阎良区	Yanliang	11.50	5.58	5.58	5.92		5.91
临潼区	Lintong	33.26	16.17	16.17	17.09		15.45
长安区	Chang'an	15.75	8.71	8.71	7.04	0.05	6.97
高陵区	Gaoling	12.29	5.63	5.63	6.66		6.12
鄠邑区	Huyi	19.59	9.68	9.48	9.91		9.85
蓝田县	Lantian	17.10	9.39	9.25	7.71	0.01	7.06
周至县	Zhouzhi	12.02	5.70	5.64	6.32		6.04
西咸新区	Xixian	15.91	8.20	8.20	7.71		7.56

11-21 续表 continued

单位：万吨 (10 000 tons)

区 县	Region	油料 Oil-bearing Crops	油菜籽 Rapeseeds	蔬菜 Vegetables	瓜果类 Fruits Class
全 市	**Total**	**0.67**	**0.59**	**378.58**	**52.44**
新城区	Xincheng				
碑林区	Beilin				
莲湖区	Lianhu				
灞桥区	Baqiao	0.03	0.02	12.28	0.19
未央区	Weiyang			0.07	0.01
雁塔区	Yanta				
阎良区	Yanliang	0.01	0.01	74.07	27.13
临潼区	Lintong	0.06	0.05	53.13	9.56
长安区	Chang'an	0.11	0.08	20.58	3.72
高陵区	Gaoling			62.33	1.09
鄠邑区	Huyi	0.05	0.02	28.65	4.88
蓝田县	Lantian	0.33	0.33	10.94	2.72
周至县	Zhouzhi	0.05	0.05	22.88	0.27
西咸新区	Xixian	0.02	0.02	93.65	2.87

11-22 主要年份农作物单位面积产量

Yield of Farm Crops Per Unit Area in Representative Years

单位：公斤/亩 (kg/mu)

年份 Year	粮食作物 Grain Crops	夏粮 Summer Grain	小麦 Wheat	秋粮 Autumn Grain	玉米 Corn	油料 Oil-bearing Crops	油菜籽 Rapeseeds	蔬菜 Vegetables
1990	236	232	232	241	249	103	101	2349
1991	245	229	229	264	274	94	89	2332
1992	256	259	259	253	264	92	101	2344
1993	266	260	260	274	287	94	107	2282
1994	219	226	226	211	225	79	84	2260
1995	254	263	263	243	261	117	128	2320
1996	265	214	214	321	333	86	100	2489
1997	284	305	306	257	279	76	129	2395
1998	302	278	279	328	347	114	121	2443
1999	288	253	254	327	339	102	106	2526
2000	289	247	248	338	354	102	112	2520
2001	291	270	271	314	328	104	113	2474
2002	293	266	267	326	337	107	115	2507
2003	279	287	288	269	276	102	110	2444
2004	310	308	308	313	320	117	129	2333
2005	320	304	305	336	345	121	132	2349
2006	299	273	273	323	329	125	135	2175
2007	298	247	246	342	347	130	131	2244
2008	306	297	297	315	322	134	137	2381
2009	308	284	284	331	338	134	130	2526
2010	312	292	291	333	339	130	130	2653
2011	318	297	295	340	350	135	133	2711
2012	330	309	308	352	360	133	129	2866
2013	326	284	283	370	378	129	122	3018
2014	322	304	304	342	349	136	129	3155
2015	342	333	334	352	357	139	132	3247
2016	337	326	326	349	354	141	132	3302
2017	330	325	327	333	338	144	138	3390
2018	339	324	324	357	362	146	137	3468
2019	341	317	317	371	378	144	135	3514

注：本表2007-2017年数据根据第三次全国农业普查结果进行了修订。

11-23 各区县主要农作物单位面积产量（2019年）

The Output of Main Crops Per Unit Area by Region（2019）

单位：公斤/亩 (kg/mu)

区 县	Region	粮食作物 Grain Crops	夏粮 Summer Grain	小麦 Wheat	秋粮 Autumn Grain	玉米 Corn
全 市	**Total**	**341**	**317**	**317**	**371**	**378**
新城区	Xincheng					
碑林区	Beilin					
莲湖区	Lianhu					
灞桥区	Baqiao	349	354	354	341	346
未央区	Weiyang	348	348	348	346	346
雁塔区	Yanta					
阎良区	Yanliang	428	410	410	447	447
临潼区	Lintong	332	305	305	363	365
长安区	Chang'an	339	309	309	385	387
高陵区	Gaoling	467	427	427	506	512
鄠邑区	Huyi	351	329	331	376	378
蓝田县	Lantian	284	263	262	313	340
周至县	Zhouzhi	314	297	298	331	340
西咸新区	Xixian	328	311	311	349	348

11-23 续表 continued

单位：公斤/亩 (kg/mu)

区 县	Region	油料 Oil-bearing Crops	油菜籽 Rapeseeds	蔬菜 Vegetables	瓜果类 Fruits Class
全 市	**Total**	**144**	**135**	**3514**	**3560**
新城区	Xincheng				
碑林区	Beilin				
莲湖区	Lianhu				
灞桥区	Baqiao	142	137	3059	1559
未央区	Weiyang			2960	842
雁塔区	Yanta				
阎良区	Yanliang	139	139	4876	3818
临潼区	Lintong	153	139	3164	4878
长安区	Chang'an	159	136	2117	2077
高陵区	Gaoling			4442	7072
鄠邑区	Huyi	199	128	3271	3141
蓝田县	Lantian	134	134	1884	2420
周至县	Zhouzhi	139	132	2581	2936
西咸新区	Xixian	137	137	3820	3538

11-24 设施农业生产情况（2019年）

Agricultural Production Facilities（2019）

指　标	Item	播种面积（亩）Seeded Area (mu)	产量（吨）output (ton)
一、蔬菜	**Vegetables**	**221430**	**1159463**
芹菜	Celery	75037	335464
油菜	Rape	9450	27634
菠菜	Spinach	24332	54151
生姜	Ginger	114	390
黄瓜	Cucumber	21291	108108
西葫芦	Squash	14795	92741
四季豆	Green Beans	7414	43617
茄子	Eggplant	17261	76858
辣椒	Chilli	14541	61559
西红柿	Tomato	23859	97739
其他蔬菜	Other Vegetables	13336	261202
二、瓜果类	**Fruits class**	**98863**	**355450**
其中：草莓	Strawberry	14356	29081
三、花卉苗木	**Flower seedling wood**	**13312**	
四、食用菌	**Edible Fungi**		**5214**
干品	Dry Product		775
鲜品	Fresh Product		4439
蘑菇	Mushroom		4256
五、其他作物	**Other Crops**	1464	
补充资料：设施数量数（个）	Number of Facilities (unit)		133143
设施占地面积（亩）	Area of Facilities(mu)	237267	

11-25 主要年份林业生产情况

Statistics on Forestry in Representative Years

指　标	Item	2000	2005	2010	2014	2015	2016	2017	2018	2019
一、营林情况	**Afforestation**									
当年造林面积合计（万亩）	Build Forestry Areas(10 000 mu)	27.47	16.56	16.10	14.70	8.28	4.51	4.07	3.56	3.83
封山育林面积（万亩）	Hill-closeure for Afforestation Areas(10 000 mu)	18.78	18.65	55.10	42.99	44.00	43.80	28.80	28.80	
零星（四旁）植树（万株）	Planting(10 000 plants)	731.0	1064.0	509.2	621.0	516.0	462.0	686.7	656.2	
育苗面积（万亩）	Raise Seedlings Areas(10 000 mu)	2.05	5.99	11.95	17.73	19.84	22.78	48.24	61.02	68.63
二、主要林产品产量（吨）	**Main Forestry Product(ton)**									
核桃	Walnuts	997	3351	7875	16531	24344	24097	36639	36970	38732
板栗	Chinese Chestnut	744	2076	7736	6922	8225	8223	8970	9282	9042
花椒	Pepper	140	525	1420	371	204	402	293	1044	937
三、村及村以下采伐木材（万立方米）	**Timber Harvested at or below Village Level (10 000 cu.m)**	1.62	1.87	3.30		0.07	0.28		0.37	

注：本表数据第一、三部分来源于市自然资源和规划局。

11-26 各区县林业生产情况（2019年）

Statistics On Forestry by Region（2019）

区 县 Region		当年造林面积（亩）Build Forestry Areasin in The Year(mu)	零星植树（万株）Planting (10 000 plants)	育苗面积（亩）Raise Seedlings Areas(mu)	核桃产量（吨）Output of Walnuts (ton)	板栗产量（吨）Output of Chinese Chestnut (ton)
全 市	**Total**	**38326**		**686280**	**38732**	**9042**
新城区	Xincheng					
碑林区	Beilin					
莲湖区	Lianhu					
灞桥区	Baqiao	1316		570	4549	117
未央区	Weiyang					
雁塔区	Yanta					
阎良区	Yanliang	954		4575		
临潼区	Lintong	5248		9795	6120	151
长安区	Chang'an	3355		58080	3072	946
高陵区	Gaoling	1550		53295		
鄠邑区	Huyi	3029		79590	546	21
蓝田县	Lantian	12154		186615	15680	5865
周至县	Zhouzhi	7287		190035	4880	1942
西咸新区	Xixian	3433		103725	3885	

注：本表前三项指标数据来源于市自然资源和规划局。

11-27 主要年份果业生产情况

Statistics on Fruits in Representative Years

指标	Item	2000	2005	2010	2014	2015	2016	2017	2018	2019
果园面积合计（万亩）	**Areas of Orchards (10 000 mu)**	**47.86**	**55.55**	**63.26**	**63.44**	**61.00**	**62.73**	**72.72**	**74.28**	**74.53**
苹果园	Apple Orchards	12.15	5.96	3.07	0.91	1.04	0.99	6.03	6.08	6.07
梨园	Pears Orchards	5.79	3.01	1.64	0.84	0.74	1.06	0.95	0.97	1.10
葡萄园	Grapes Orchards	1.89	3.02	6.42	10.78	10.94	11.65	12.55	12.61	11.98
桃园	Peach Orchards	3.47	8.66	7.68	5.85	5.33	5.82	5.99	6.19	5.96
猕猴桃园	Chinese Goosebeery Orchards	16.83	4.33	20.36	27.88	27.69	27.97	28.19	29.32	30.09
杏园	Apricot Orchards	0.62	2.50	2.21	1.49	1.31	1.25	1.63	1.74	1.95
柿子园	Presimmons Orchards	1.96	2.69	2.08	0.35	0.21	0.22	0.19	0.27	0.36
石榴园	Pomegranate Orchards			3.31	3.30	2.93	2.93	3.33	3.24	3.24
水果产量（万吨）	**Output of Fruits (10 000ton)**	**34.36**	**51.29**	**66.11**	**73.11**	**73.33**	**75.53**	**89.80**	**89.15**	**97.18**
苹果	Apple	8.94	5.34	2.96	1.49	1.71	1.70	6.93	6.91	7.07
梨	Pears	6.55	5.71	3.61	2.09	2.11	2.20	2.28	2.27	2.03
葡萄	Grapes	1.66	3.10	6.20	10.81	11.48	13.07	16.45	16.62	16.86
桃	Peach	2.70	8.98	9.85	7.52	7.76	8.61	9.92	10.51	11.02
猕猴桃	Chinese Goosebeery	9.66	13.79	24.87	35.10	35.30	35.47	36.84	35.83	42.45
杏	Apricot			3.71	3.02	2.57	2.53	2.57	2.45	2.61
柿子	Persimmon			3.01	1.11	0.81	0.26	0.33	0.40	0.41
石榴	Pomegranate			2.93	2.66	2.54	2.44	3.20	3.32	3.51

注：本表2007-2017年数根据第三次全国农业普查结果进行了修订。

11–28　各区县果业生产情况（2019年）

Area and Output of Fruits by Region (2019)

区　县	Region	果园（亩）Orchard (mu)	水果产量（吨）Output of Fruits(ton)
全　市	**Total**	**745330**	**971789**
新城区	Xincheng		
碑林区	Beilin		
莲湖区	Lianhu		
灞桥区	Baqiao	63875	78587
未央区	Weiyang	105	104
雁塔区	Yanta		
阎良区	Yanliang	18000	30992
临潼区	Lintong	66855	78317
长安区	Chang'an	34553	50474
高陵区	Gaoling	19556	27061
鄠邑区	Huyi	80241	103130
蓝田县	Lantian	64624	69407
周至县	Zhouzhi	305691	417744
西咸新区	Xixian	91830	115973

11-29 果品加工、销售及生产服务情况（2019年）

指标	Item	西安市 Xi' an	灞桥区 Baqiao	未央区 Weiyang
一、果品加工企业数（个）	**Number of Fruit Processing Enterprises(unit)**	**36**		
其中：苹果加工企业数量	Number of Apple Processing Enterprises			
猕猴桃加工企业数	Number of Kiwi Processing Enterprises	26		
二、果品加工企业果汁加工能力（吨）	**Processing Ability of Fruit Juice in Fruit Processing Enterprises (ton)**	**3400**		
其中：苹果汁加工能力	Processing Ability of Apple Juice			
三、当年果品加工企业鲜果消耗量（吨）	**Fresh Fruit Consumption of Fruit Processing Enterprise in the Year (ton)**	**77370**		
其中：加工消耗苹果数量	Number of Fresh Apple Consumption			
加工消耗猕猴桃数量	Number of Fresh Kiwi Consumption	60000		
四、仓储能力（吨）	**Storage Capacity(ton)**	**386072**	**200**	
其中：气调库	Gas Reservoir	61507	200	
机械库	Machine Shop	324565		
五、果业合作（个）	**Fruit Industry Cooperation(unit)**	**1331**	**71**	
六、果苗木繁育中心（个）	**Fruit Seedling Breeding Center(unit)**	**14**		
七、果业服务投入（万元）	**Service Investment in Fruit Industry(10000 yuan)**	**982**	**50**	**4**
1. 技术培训投入	Technical Training Investment	269	40	
2. 科研投入	Scientific Research Investment	176		4
3. 生产技术指导投入	Production Technology Guidance Investment	537	10	
八、果品销售方式（吨）	**Fruit Sales Mode(ton)**	**1167257**	**61202**	
1. 产品批发市场	Product Wholesale Market	554364	26800	
2. 采供商	Supplier	278098	13020	
3. 专卖、直销店	Franchised and Direct Outlets	16670		
4. 超级市场	Supermarket	35830	1382	
5. 电子商务	Electronic Commerce	94924	2800	
6. 农产品加工厂	Agricultural Product Processing Plant	67443		
7. 其它	Others	119928	17200	
九、按销售区域分（吨）	**By the Sales Area(ton)**	**1167257**	**61202**	
1. 国内市场	Domestic market	1057857	61202	
2. 国际市场	International Market	109400		
附记：累计建成绿色果园面积（亩）	Cumulative Green Orchard Area(mu)	3870		
建成有机果园面积面积（亩）	Construction of Organic Orchard Area(mu)	5580		

The Situation of Fruit Processing, Sales and Production Service（2019）

阎良区 Yanliang	临潼区 Lintong	长安区 Chang'an	高陵区 Gaoling	鄠邑区 Huyi	蓝田县 Lantian	周至县 Zhouzhi	西咸新区 Xixian
1	**4**			**2**	**3**	**26**	
						26	
	2600			**550**	**250**		
420	**2600**			**14000**	**350**	**60000**	
						60000	
17650	**3915**	**1000**	**5**	**6300**		**355500**	**1502**
17650	2650	1000	5	4200		35800	2
	1265			2100		319700	1500
22	**77**	**24**	**11**	**60**	**25**	**1015**	**26**
9				**1**		**3**	**1**
3	**445**		**13**	**243**	**3**	**10**	**211**
3	82		8	35		10	91
	74			50			48
	289		5	158	3		72
33000	**61550**	**47800**	**26957**	**113000**	**69400**	**565600**	**188748**
	12000	10280	8000	83770	55500	310650	47364
	11000	500	14000	14000	4900	94000	126678
	300	50	3600	3400		5200	4120
		50		6000		25400	2998
	12000	20	1000	2230	1400	70200	5274
	2000	100		3600	350	60150	1243
33000	24250	36800	357		7250		1071
33000	**61550**	**47800**	**26957**	**113000**	**69400**	**565600**	**188748**
33000	61550	47800	26957	113000		525600	188748
					69400	40000	
				1600	650	300	1320
		4500		240	600		240

11-30 主要年份畜牧业生产情况

Statistics on Livestock Husbandry in Representative Years

指标	Item	2013	2014	2015	2016	2017	2018	2019
一、活牲畜年末存栏（头）	**Live Animals in Stock at Year-end (head)**	**55619**	**58737**	**56100**	**61179**	**51075**	**50705**	**51704**
#役畜	Draught Animals	7748	7235	6730	6203	578	555	419
1. 牛	Cattle	54900	58100	55900	61000	50900	50556	51567
#肉牛	Farm Cattle	15673	17317	18465	23736	21509	21325	23258
奶牛	Dairy Cattle	31479	33887	30705	31061	28819	28681	27895
2. 马（匹）	Horses	220	219	200	176	175	149	137
3. 驴	Donkeys	52	59					
4. 骡	Mules	447	359		3			
二、猪年末存栏（头）	**Pigs in Stock at Year-end (head)**	**377300**	**377100**	**366800**	**363000**	**335700**	**312882**	**296612**
#能繁殖的母猪	Female Hogs of Reprductive Ability	60900	58700	56300	55600	51800	44304	41317
三、羊年末存栏（只）	**Sheep and Goats in Stock at Year-end (head)**	**84100**	**101700**	**107600**	**109800**	**75200**	**74200**	**71900**
1. 山羊	Goats	82145	98974	104033	107260	73769	72942	71198
#奶山羊	Milch Goats	68370	69093	65180	66388	62120	60619	69052
2. 绵羊	Sheeps	1955	2726	3567	2540	1431	1258	702
四、家禽年末存栏（万只）	**Poultry in Stock at Year-end (10 000 heads)**	**663.37**	**663.05**	**702.69**	**702.42**	**642.73**	**625.83**	**643.67**
五、年末养蜂箱数（箱）	**Honey (box)**	**23346**	**22485**	**19536**	**21420**	**20377**	**19129**	**23033**

注：本表2013-2017年数根据第三次全国农业普查结果进行了修订。

11-31 各区县畜牧业生产情况（2019年）

Statistics On Livestock, Animal Husbandry by Region（2019）

区 县	Region	活牲畜年末存栏（头） Live Animals In Stock at Year-end (head)	役畜 Draught Animals	牛 Cattle	奶牛 Dairy Cattle	肉牛 Beef cattle	马（匹） Horses (head)	驴 Donkeys	骡 Mutes
全 市	**Total**	**51704**	**419**	**51567**	**27895**	**23258**	**137**		
新城区	Xincheng								
碑林区	Beilin								
莲湖区	Lianhu								
灞桥区	Baqiao	1146		1078	1062	15	68		
未央区	Weiyang	21		21	21				
雁塔区	Yanta								
阎良区	Yanliang	6242		6242	5962	280			
临潼区	Lintong	13852		13852	11584	2268			
长安区	Chang'an	2780		2720	1048	1672	60		
高陵区	Gaoling	5872		5872	4187	1685			
鄠邑区	Huyi	4215		4215	1108	3107			
蓝田县	Lantian	10305	370	10305	1182	8753			
周至县	Zhouzhi	6221	49	6212	1074	5095	9		
西咸新区	Xixian	1050		1050	667	383			

11-31 续表 continued

区 县	Region	猪年末存栏（头） Swine (head)	能繁殖的母猪 breeding sows	羊年末存栏（只） Sheep and Goats (head)	山羊 Goats	奶山羊 Milch Goats	家禽年末存栏（万只） Poultry (10 000 head)	蜂（箱） Honey (box)
全 市	**Total**	**296612**	**41317**	**71900**	**71198**	**69052**	**643.67**	**23033**
新城区	Xincheng							
碑林区	Beilin							
莲湖区	Lianhu							
灞桥区	Baqiao	5067	522	862	862	862	6.2	305
未央区	Weiyang							
雁塔区	Yanta							
阎良区	Yanliang	14253	2600	9102	9102	9102	38.4	760
临潼区	Lintong	60417	6731	21307	21307	21307	163.53	1906
长安区	Chang'an	21954	2844	3718	3712	2721	95.22	2630
高陵区	Gaoling	21188	3064	5050	4790	4790	90	
鄠邑区	Huyi	55712	7981	6157	6157	6157	75.85	6910
蓝田县	Lantian	35786	5325	21568	21452	21452	97	3800
周至县	Zhouzhi	62208	9069	2140	2104	949	56.27	6682
西咸新区	Xixian	20027	3181	1996	1712	1712	21.2	40

11-32 主要年份畜产品和水产品产量

单位：吨

年 份 Year	肉类总产量 Output of Meat	猪 肉 Pork	牛 肉 Beef	羊 肉 Mutton	禽 肉 Poultry
2013	66100	43900	4000	3300	13100
2014	70900	47400	4400	3700	13400
2015	72100	47100	4400	4100	14500
2016	68700	44200	3700	4400	14600
2017	58708	36900	4600	3300	12300
2018	54496	35932	3439	989	12473
2019	51437	33531	3329	927	12257

注：1.2010年起，根据统计制度要求，水产品产量及养殖面积统计数据取自市水务局，2019年取自市农业农村局。
2.2013-2017年数根据第三次全国农业普查结果进行了修订。

Output of Livestock Products and Aquatic Products in Representative Years

(ton)

奶类产量 Output of Milk	牛奶 Cow Milk	禽蛋 Poultry Eggs	蜂蜜（公斤） Honey(kg)	水产品 Output of Aquatic Products	养殖面积（万亩） Water Raise Areas (10 000 mu)
73834	41700	48700	380000	14200	2.19
80961	42200	47900	376800	14218	2.31
76779	40800	51000	351582	14190	2.26
79281	43100	62900	371409	13449	1.96
116491	83300	52785	404337	13832	2.24
115200	80446	52610	308015	13528	2.23
123711	80060	53874	322965	13614	1.82

11-33 各区县主要畜产品和水产品产量（2019年）

Output of Major Livestock Products and Aquatic Products by Region（2019）

单位：吨　　　　(ton)

区 县	Region	肉类总产量 Output of Meat	猪 肉 Pork	牛 肉 Beef	羊 肉 Mutton	禽 肉 Poultry
全 市	**Total**	**51437**	**33531**	**3329**	**927**	**12257**
新城区	Xincheng					
碑林区	Beilin					
莲湖区	Lianhu					
灞桥区	Baqiao	1788	1230	65	19	467
未央区	Weiyang					
雁塔区	Yanta					
阎良区	Yanliang	2297	956	488	145	707
临潼区	Lintong	15932	12212	396	116	2538
长安区	Chang'an	4832	2835	186	73	1705
高陵区	Gaoling	3676	1683	172	90	1246
鄠邑区	Huyi	5830	3677	380	91	1537
蓝田县	Lantian	8488	4389	1056	343	2675
周至县	Zhouzhi	6759	5243	385	18	1108
西咸新区	Xixian	1835	1306	201	32	274

11-33 续表 continued

区 县	Region	奶类产量 Output of Milk	牛 奶 Cow Milk	禽 蛋 Poultry Eggs	蜂蜜（公斤） Honey(kg)	水产品 Output of Aquatic Products	养殖面积（公顷） Water Raise Areas (hectare)
全 市	**Total**	**123711**	**80060**	**53874**	**322965**	**13614**	**1213**
新城区	Xincheng						
碑林区	Beilin						
莲湖区	Lianhu						
灞桥区	Baqiao	3449	2878	795	7686	700	83
未央区	Weiyang	41	41			500	26
雁塔区	Yanta						
阎良区	Yanliang	20771	15378	3214	18904	225	12
临潼区	Lintong	51948	34208	12512	14690	3300	331
长安区	Chang'an	6244	4112	9900	67900	5425	270
高陵区	Gaoling	12605	9570	8365		235	12
鄠邑区	Huyi	7287	3462	6635	60800	1101	28
蓝田县	Lantian	14317	5441	6859	98124	1340	247
周至县	Zhouzhi	3349	3035	4431	54532	500	154
西咸新区	Xixian	3700	1935	1163	329	288	50

注：水产品产量及养殖面积统计数据取自市农业农村局。

11-34 农业科技、教育情况（2019年）

Agricultural Science and Technology Education（2019）

指标	Item	2019
农业研究开发机构（个）	Agricultural research and development institutions (unit)	225
农业科技人员（人）	Agricultural scientific and technical personnel(persons)	2744
农业科研成果（个）	Agricultural scientific research achievements (unit)	
农民技能培训人数（万人）	The number of peasants skills training(10000 persons)	16.5
良种推广面积（万亩）	Thoroughbred promotion area (10000 mu)	580.76
农业信息站（个）	Information station of Agricultural (unit)	2822

注：本表数据来源于市农业农村局。

11-35 主要年份农产品人均占有量

Per Capita Output of Major Farm Products in Representative Years

单位：公斤/人 (kg/ person)

年份 Year	粮食 Grain	油料 Oil-bearing Crops	猪牛羊肉 Pork Beef and Mutton	禽蛋 Poultry Eggs	奶类 Milk	水果 Fruits	蔬菜 Vegetables
1978	266.7	0.2	5.4	0.9	3.3	6.8	91.7
1979	288.6	0.6	6.7	1.0	4.0	5.1	97.3
1980	223.5	1.1	5.9	1.2	4.1	6.9	78.4
1985	271.4	1.4	6.8	5.7	10.2	7.6	156.3
1990	298.7	2.1	9.4	9.2	14.2	11.5	196.0
1995	270.4	3.4	15.7	21.8	20.5	37.5	206.1
2000	293.5	1.9	17.9	20.1	35.7	49.9	235.7
2005	277.1	1.6	21.1	15.9	56.9	69.1	263.8
2010	206.4	1.2	13.8	14.6	74.8	78.2	245.0
2013	177.0	0.9	6.0	5.7	8.6	83.9	284.6
2014	163.5	0.8	6.4	5.6	9.4	84.9	299.6
2015	163.2	0.8	6.4	5.9	8.9	84.6	309.1
2016	154.4	0.7	6.0	7.2	9.0	86.1	306.6
2017	151.7	0.7	4.7	5.5	12.1	97.4	368.9
2018	144.9	0.7	4.1	5.4	11.6	90.9	380.9
2019	138.5	0.7	3.7	5.3	12.2	96.2	374.7

11–36 主要年份农村经济效益指标

Main Indicators of Rural Economic Benefit in Representative Years

年份	每一劳动力创造的 Average Labor Force Production			每亩耕地种植业总产值（元）	每百元物耗生产的总产值（元）
Year	农林牧渔业总产值（元） Gross Output Value of Farming,Forestry, Animal Husbandry, Fishery (yuan)	粮食（公斤） Grain Crops(kg)	油料（公斤） Oil-bearing Crops(kg)	Output of Each Unit of Area Planting(yuan)	Output per 100-Yuan of Material Consumed(yuan)
1978	504.7	1024.6	0.7	104.3	
1979	549.0	1096.5	2.3	116.0	
1980	483.1	846.1	4.0	99.2	
1981	502.8	840.5	5.5	105.4	
1982	631.5	1058.9	3.6	139.3	
1983	606.5	1053.2	2.6	124.1	
1984	850.7	1154.2	3.4	163.6	
1985	1020.1	1134.6	5.6	183.1	
1986	1132.2	1236.4	9.5	204.6	
1987	1280.3	1277.2	11.7	231.5	
1988	1558.4	1148.0	6.5	273.2	
1989	1605.3	1231.9	9.5	295.0	
1990	1766.3	1279.1	10.0	343.4	233.3
1991	1958.8	1326.6	8.9	380.4	238.4
1992	2093.7	1360.7	11.1	451.6	241.8
1993	2528.9	1409.7	10.4	546.8	240.1
1994	3705.0	1167.8	8.0	762.8	227.6
1995	4953.0	1300.6	16.1	1106.5	225.9
1996	5154.8	1391.2	13.6	1224.2	234.5
1997	5493.0	1413.4	13.8	1283.3	239.2
1998	5615.9	1578.1	12.4	1374.3	247.0
1999	4826.5	1516.6	9.7	1175.9	251.7
2000	5091.5	1498.0	9.9	1161.1	250.2
2001	5328.5	1462.4	9.1	1221.1	248.6
2002	5617.4	1427.5	9.1	1272.0	265.9
2003	5761.2	1308.1	8.4	1332.4	254.3
2004	6885.4	1452.7	8.5	1434.6	261.7
2005	7737.9	1524.7	8.6	1642.3	262.9
2006	8415.5	1435.7	8.0	1756.9	263.1
2007	9983.6	1458.9	7.0	2017.3	259.6
2008	12888.6	1466.7	8.5	2413.9	257.7
2009	13922.4	1460.9	8.5	2666.2	259.7
2010	18220.9	1496.9	8.7	3623.9	258.7
2011	21534.5	1438.2	8.6	4378.8	271.0
2012	24588.9	1480.0	7.3	4940.9	269.8
2013	28187.1	1398.2	7.1	5565.8	269.9
2014	29310.8	1276.2	6.4	6090.3	270.3
2015	31476.1	1345.6	6.5	6308.7	268.3
2016	33888.8	1323.2	5.7	6799.0	265.9
2017	39620.4	1267.3	5.6	8036.5	262.7
2018	47231.8	1455.6	6.9	8787.5	263.5
2019	51037.4	1429.9	6.8	9669.4	263.3

主要统计指标解释

农林牧渔业总产值 指以货币表现的农、林、牧、渔业全部产品和对农林牧渔业生产活动进行的各种支持性服务活动的价值总量，它反映一定时期内农林牧渔业生产总规模和总成果。1957年以前的农林牧渔业总产值中包括了厩肥和农民自给性手工业（如农民自制衣服、鞋、袜，自己从事粮食初步加工等）。1958年及以后，林业中增加了村及村以下竹木采伐产值；牧业中取消了厩肥产值；副业中取消了农民自给性手工业产值，增加了村及村以下办的工业产值；渔业中增加了海洋捕捞水产品产值。1980年及以后，在副业中增加了农民家庭兼营工业商品部分的产值。从1984年起村及村以下工业产值划归工业。从1993年起取消副业，将野生动物的捕猎划入牧业，野生植物采集和农民家庭兼营商品性工业划归农业。从2003年起，执行新的国民经济行业分类标准，农林牧渔业总产值中包括了农林牧渔服务业产值。林业中增加了森林采运业产值。农业中取消了家庭兼营商品性工业产值，将野生林产品的采集划归林业。第三次农业普查以后，由于主要农产品年报数据与普查数据之间存在一定的差距，根据农业普查结果对主要农产品年报数据进行了修正，并对产值进行了相应修正。

农林牧渔业总产值的计算方法通常是按农、林、牧、渔业产品及其副产品的产量分别乘以各自单位产品价格求得；少数生产周期较长，当年没有产品或产品产量不易统计的，则采用间接方法匡算其产值；然后将四业产品产值及农林牧渔服务业产值相加即为农林牧渔业总产值。

粮食产量 指全社会的产量。包括国有经济经营的、集体统一经营的和农民家庭经营的粮食产量，还包括工矿企业办的农场和其他生产单位的产量。粮食除包括稻谷、小麦、玉米、高粱、谷子及其他杂粮外，还包括薯类和豆类。其产量计算方法，豆类按去豆荚后的干豆计算；薯类（包括甘薯和马铃薯，不包括芋头和木薯）1963年以前按每4公斤鲜薯折1公斤粮食计算，从1964年开始改为按5公斤鲜薯折1公斤粮食计算。城市郊区作为蔬菜的薯类（如马铃薯等）按鲜品计算，并且不作粮食统计。其他粮食一律按脱粒后的原粮计算。1989年以前全国粮食产量数据主要靠全面报表取得，1989年开始使用抽样调查数据。

棉花产量 指全社会的产量。包括春播棉和夏播棉。产量按皮棉计算。不包括木棉。

油料产量 指全部油料作物的生产量。包括花生、油菜籽、芝麻、向日葵籽、胡麻籽（亚麻籽）和其他油料。不包括大豆、木本油料和野生油料。花生以带壳干花生计算。

水产品产量 指人工养殖的水产品和天然生长的水产品的捕捞量。包括海水的鱼类、虾蟹类、贝类和藻类以及内陆水域的鱼类、虾蟹类和贝类，不包括淡水生植物。水产品产量是通过各级水产和统计部门逐级上报取得数据。1995年及以前，贝类中牡蛎按鲜肉计算；蚶、蛤、蛏按5斤鲜品折1斤计算。1996年以后则统一按鲜品计算。

猪、牛、羊肉产量 指当年出栏并已屠宰、除去头蹄下水后带骨肉（即胴体重）的重量。包括全社会范围内的产量。1996年前为各级逐级上报数据。1996年第一次农业普查以后，由于畜牧业产品年报数据与普查数据之间存在一定的差距，根据普查结果对畜牧业年报数据进行了修正。1999年以后，国家统计局在部分地区开展了猪、牛、羊、禽等主要畜禽品种的抽样调查，并用抽样数据作为国家定案数据使用。未开展抽样调查的地区和品种，仍使用各级统计部门逐级上报数据。2008年，根据第二次农业普查结果，对2006年2007年畜牧业年报数据进行了修正。2019年，根据第三次农业普查结果，对2013年—2017年畜牧业年报数据进行了修正。

畜禽存栏头（只）数 指报告期末农村各种合作经济组织和国营农场、农民个人、机关、团体、学校、工矿企业、部队等单位以及城镇居民饲养的大牲畜、猪、羊、家禽等畜禽的存栏数。

常用耕地 是指耕地总资源中专门种植农作物并经常进行耕种、能够正常收获的土地。包括当年实际耕种的熟地；弃耕、休闲不满三年，随时可以复耕的地；开荒利用三年以上的地。不包括临时种植农作物的坡度在25度以上的陡坡地；在河套、湖畔、库区临时开发的成片或零星土地；也不包括已列为国家和省（区、市）退耕计划但临时耕种的土地。

农作物播种面积 指实际播种或移植有农作物的面积。凡是实际种植有农作物的面积，不论种植在耕地上还是种植在非耕地上，均包括在农作物播种面积中。在播种季节基本结束后，因遭灾而重新改种和补种的农作物面积，也包括在内。它是反映我国耕地面积利用情况的一个重要指标。目前，农作物播种面积主要包括粮食、棉花、油料、糖料、麻类、烟叶、蔬菜和瓜类、药材和其他农作物九大类。

有效灌溉面积 指具有一定的水源，地块比较平整，灌溉工程或设备已经配套，在一般年景下，当年能够进行正常灌溉的耕地面积。在一般情况下，有效灌溉面积应等于灌溉工程或设备已经配备，能够进行正常灌溉的水田和水浇地面积之和。它是反映我国耕地抗旱能力的一个重要指标。

农用化肥施用量 指本年内实际用于农业生产的化肥数量，包括氮肥、磷肥、钾肥和复合肥。化肥施用量要求按折纯量计算数量。折纯量是指把氮肥、磷肥、钾肥分别按含氮、含五氧化二磷、含氧化钾的百分之百成份进行折算后的数量。复合肥按其所含主要成分折算。公式为：

折纯量=实物量×某种化肥有效成份含量的百分比

农业机械总动力 指主要用于农、林、牧、渔业的各种动力机械的动力总和。包括耕作机械、排灌机械、收获机械、农用运输机械、植物保护机械、牧业机械、林业机械、渔业机械和其他农业机械【内燃机按引擎马力折成瓦（特）计算、电动机按功率折成瓦（特）计算】。不包括专门用于乡、镇、村、组办工业、基本建设、非农业运输、科学试验和教学等非农业生产方面用的动力机械与作业机械。这个指标的统计数据主要来源于农机部门。

Explanatory Notes on Main Statistical Indicators

Gross Output Value of Agriculture, Forestry, Animal Husbandry and Fishery refers to the total value of products of agriculture, forestry, animal husbandry and fishery, and total value of services in support of agriculture, forestry, animal husbandry and fishery activities. It reflects the total scale and results of agricultural production during a given period. Prior to 1957, China's gross agricultural output value included barnyard manure and handicraft products for self- consumption (clothes, shoes, stockings, and initial grain processing undertaken by peasants). Since 1958, cutting and felling of bamboo and trees by villages and other cooperative organizations under villages have been included in forestry; value of barnyard manure has been excluded from animal husbandry; self consumed handicrafts have not been included from sideline occupations, while the output value of industries run by villages and cooperative organizations under village has been included in sideline occupations; and the output value of fish catches by motor fishing boats has been added to fishery. Since 1980, the value of handicraft products made for sale by individuals in households has been added to sideline occupations. Since 1984, industries run by villages and under villages have been included in the sector of industry. Since 1993, the subdivision of sideline occupations has been cancelled, and the hunting of wild animals has been classified into animal husbandry, and the gathering of wild plants and commodity industry run by rural household have been included in farming. A new industrial classification of economic activities was introduced in 2003. Under the new classification, value of services to agriculture, forestry, animal husbandry and fishery is included in the gross output value of agriculture, value of wood felling and transport is included in forestry, value of industrial output by rural households is not included in agriculture, and the collection of wild forest products is taken from agriculture and included in forestry. The third Agriculture Census of China revealed some discrepancy between the main agricultural products from the annual reports and that from the census. According to the result of the First Agriculture census, efforts were made to adjust the output value of main agricultural to make the figures from the annual reports consistent with the census data.

Gross output value of agrieulture is obtained by multiplying the output of each product or by-product by its price, resulting in the output value of each single item. For a small number of products, annual output of which is not available or difficult to get due to the long production (growing) process involved, the output value is estimated through an indirect approach. The sum of output values of all products of agriculture, forestry, animal husbandry and fishery and services in support to those industries is then equal to the gross output value of agriculture.

Grain Output refers to the total output in the whole country including grains produced by State farms, collective units, rural households, as well as by farms affiliated to industrial and mining enterprises and other production units. Grain includes rice, wheat, corn, sorghum, millet and other miscellaneous grains as well as tubers and beans. Output of beans refers to dry beans without pods. The output of tubers (sweet potatoes and potatoes, not including taros and cassava) are converted into that of grain at the ratio 4:1, i.e. 4 kilograms of fresh tubers were equivalent to 1 kilogram of grain up to 1963. Since 1964 the ratio for conversion has been 5:1. Tubers supplied as vegetables (such as potatoes) in cities and suburbs are calculated as fresh vegetables and their output is not included in the output of grain. Output of all other grains refers to husked grain. Data on grain production before 1989 were obtained through the Comprehensive Statistical Reporting System. Since 1989, data from sample surveys are used.

Cotton Output refers to cotton production in the whole country including cotton planted in spring and in autumn. Output is measured as the weight of ginned cotton. Ceiba is not included.

Output of Oil–bearing Crops refers to the total production of oil-bearing crops of various kinds, including peanuts (dry, in shell), rapeseeds, sesame, sunflower seeds, flax seeds, and other oil-bearing crops. Soybeans, oil-bearing woody plants, and wild oil-bearing crops are not included.

Output of Aquatic Products refers to catches of both artificially cultured and naturally grown aquatic products, including fish, shrimps, crabs and shellfish in sea and inland water as well as seaweed. Freshwater plants are not included. Data on output of aquatic products are reported by aquatic product and statistical agencies level by level. Before 1995, among the shellfish, oyster was counted as fresh meat; 5 kilograms of ark shell, clams and frogs are equivalent to 1 kilogram of fresh aquatic products; they have all been counted as flesh aquatic products since 1996.

Output of Pork, Beef, and Mutton refers to the meat of slaughtered hogs, cattle, sheep and goats with head, feet, and offal taken away. Data refers to the production of the whole country. The First Agricultural Census of China in 1996 revealed some discrepancy between the production of animal products from the annual reports and that from the census. Efforts were made to adjust the output value of animal husbandry to make the figures from the annual reports consistent with the census data. Since 1999, the NBS conducted sample surveys for the major animal husbandry products, such as hogs, cattle, sheep and goats and fowls, and the data from sample surveys are used as national finalized data. Those products, which are not covered by the sample survey, are still reported by statistical agencies level by level. In 2007. the data on animal husbandry from 2000 to 2006 were revised according to the results of the Second Agriculture Census of China. In 2008, A Monitoring and Survey Program was set up on main livestock, the data on the main livestock such as hog, cattle, sheep and poultry became the official data based on the sampling survey. In 2019, data from the annual husbandry report 2013-2017 were revised based on the results of the third agricatural census.

Number of Livestock or Poultry in Stock at Beginning (or End) of Period refers to the total number of large animals, pigs, sheep, fowls, etc. raised by rural cooperative organizations, State farms, rural individuals, government agencies, schools, industrial and mining enterprises, army, and urban residents at the beginning (or end) of the reference period.

Regularly Cultivated Land refers to farmland among the total land resources which is exclusively used for farming and is under regular cultivation with harvest in normal years. Included are currently cultivated land, land that has been abandoned or put in idle for less than 3 years and could be re-used for cultivation at any time, and new-claimed land that has been put into cultivation for more than 3 years. Excluded under this category are steep slope land over 25 degrees under temporary cultivation, land (large or small plots) that is claimed along river bends, lake sides or banks of reservoirs, as well as land that has been designated under the "Green for Grain" programmes of the state and provincial governments but is still temporarily under cultivation.

Sown Area of Crops refers to area of transplanted with crops regardless of being land sown or in cultivated area or non-cultivated area. Area of land re-sown due to lso included. This is an important indicator that can reflect the utilization condition of the cultivated land in China. At present, the sown area of crops mainly include the following 9 categories of crops: grain, cotton, oil-bearing crops, sugar crops, flax crops, tobacco, vegetables and melons, medicinal materials and other farm crops.natural disasters is also included. This is an important indicator that can reflect the utilization condition of the cultivated land in China. At present, the sown area of crops mainly include the following 9 categories of crops: grain, cotton, oil-bearing crops, sugar crops, flax crops, tobacco, vegetables and melons, medicinal materials and other farm crops.

Irrigated Area refers to area of land that are effectively irrigated, i.e. relatively level land, where there are water sources or complete sets of irrigation facilities to lift and move adequate water for irrigation purpose under normal conditions. Under normal situations, irrigated area is the sum of watered fields and irrigated fields where irrigation systems or equipment have been installed for regular irrigation purpose. This important indicator reflects drought resistance capacity of the cultivated land in China.

Consumption of Chemical Fertilizers in Agriculture refers to the quantity of chemical fertilizers applied in agriculture in the year, including nitrogenous fertilizer, phosphate fertilizer, potash fertilizer, and compound fertilizer. The consumption of chemical fertilizers is calculated in terms of volume of effective components by means of converting the gross weight of the respective fertilizers into weight containing effective component (e.g. nitrogen content in nitrogenous fertilizer, phosphorous pentoxide contents in phosphate fertilizer, and potassium oxide contents in potash fertilizer). Compound fertilizer is converted in regard to its major components. The formula is:

Volume of effective component= physical quantity × effective component of certain chemical fertilizer (%)

Total Power of Agricultural Machinery refers to total mechanical power of machinery used in agriculture, forestry, animal husbandry and fishery, including machinery for ploughing, irrigation and drainage, harvesting, transport, plant protection, animal husbandry, forestry and fishery and other agricultural machineries. (For the power of internal combustion engines, it is converted from its horsepower into watts while for electric motors the output power is converted into watts.) Machinery employed for non-agricultural purposes, such as the machines used in township-run and village-run industry, construction, non-agricultural transport, scientific experiments and teaching, are not included. Data are mainly from agricultural machinery agencies.

12 工 业

INDUSTRY

资料整理：罗延庆 陈小兵 李 玫 沈佳慧 张思敏 王 玥
Data management：Luo Yanqing Chen Xiaobing Li Mei Shen Jiahui Zhang Simin Wang Yue
数据审核：丁抗玲
Data audit：Ding Kangling

第十二部分　工业

一、简要说明

1.本章资料反映西安市工业经济方面的基本情况。

2.本章资料包括规模以上工业企业按企业登记类型、轻重工业、企业规模、工业行业大类分组的主要经济指标和经济效益指标，主要工业产品产量，主要产品生产能力。

3.规模以上工业企业统计范围。

1998年至2006年为全部国有及年主营业务收入在500万元及以上非国有工业企业。

2007年至2010年为年主营业务收入在500万元及以上工业企业。

2011年起提高到年主营业务收入在2000万元及以上工业企业。

4.数据来源。

根据国家统计局制定的《企业一套表统计调查制度》和《工业统计报表制度》，对规模以上工业法人单位采用全面调查的方法，从国家一套表平台采集。

5.数据说明。

2018年规模以上工业数据为第四次全国经济普查上报数。

二、主要指标

规模以上工业企业单位数（个）	1631	比上年增长	10.7%
规模以上工业增加值（快报数）	–	比上年增长	6.9%
规模以上工业出口交货值（亿元）（快报数）	703.11	比上年增长	16.7%

12 INDUSTRY

Ⅰ.Brief Introduction

1. This chapter reflects the basic conditions of the industrial sector.

2. This chapter mainly including economic indicators of industrial enterprises above designated size; as well as their economic indicators, efficiency indicators, output and production capacity of key industrial products classified by type of registration by light and heavy industries, by size of enterprise, by branch of industry.

3. The Scopes of Industrial Statistics

The scopes of industrial statistics are all State-owned industrial enterprises and non-State-owned industrial enterprises with revenue from principal business over 5 million yuan from 1998 to 2006.

The scopes of industrial statistics are all industrial enterprises with revenue from principal business over 5 million yuan from 2007 to 2010.

The scopes of industrial statistics are raised to all industrial enterprises with revenue from principal business over 20 million yuan from 2011.

4.Sources of Data

According to the A set of table survey system for enterprises and System of industrial statistical report forms by the National Bureau of Statistics, the method of comprehensive investigation shall be adopted for industrial legal entities above the designated size, collected from a set of table platforms by the National Bureau of Statistics.

5. Data Collection

The industrial data in 2018 is the fourth economic census.

Ⅱ.Major Indicators

		Increase over Preceding Year
Number of industrial Enterprises Gross Output Above Designated Size(item)	1631	10.7%
Industrial added value above designated size	–	6.9%
Export delivery value above designated size （100million yuan）	703.11	16.7%

12-1 主要年份各区县规模以上工业总产值

Gross Output Value of Industry above Designated Size in Representative Years

单位：亿元 (100 million yuan)

区 县	Region	1998	1999	2000	2001	2002	2003	2004	2005	2006	2007	2008
合 计	**Total**	**350.38**	**366.59**	**417.97**	**482.61**	**544.78**	**638.66**	**830.06**	**981.02**	**1187.74**	**1577.05**	**2007.85**
新城区	Xincheng	67.19	71.36	78.25	89.87	105.92	137.46	145.61	196.00	135.14	157.18	147.54
碑林区	Beilin	20.57	19.48	21.50	23.15	30.32	22.22	15.92	20.13	18.31	19.10	48.99
莲湖区	Lianhu	63.24	65.92	75.68	93.78	106.33	124.24	157.67	185.86	200.75	281.57	356.90
灞桥区	Baqiao	19.55	19.95	21.35	20.56	22.99	28.80	37.25	42.29	57.11	80.01	123.34
未央区	Weiyang	53.31	52.84	61.41	73.63	80.14	93.23	145.63	170.16	220.08	265.93	327.65
雁塔区	Yanta	65.00	75.88	94.38	102.58	107.75	113.99	151.61	144.51	167.58	204.70	262.32
阎良区	Yanliang	26.54	26.06	27.56	36.22	40.04	40.98	55.86	68.10	75.84	95.29	109.43
临潼区	Lintong	8.90	7.55	7.64	9.36	14.14	34.67	53.49	66.91	85.96	114.09	130.93
长安区	Chang'an	7.92	7.70	8.70	8.42	9.96	10.81	19.40	26.43	67.19	101.61	154.74
高陵区	Gaoling	1.60	1.83	2.58	3.28	3.97	7.09	14.89	16.50	97.94	177.65	256.55
鄠邑区	Huyi	12.75	13.24	13.07	15.27	16.58	18.74	24.48	35.28	49.55	61.28	65.09
蓝田县	Lantian	2.58	2.37	3.81	4.76	5.12	5.00	5.34	5.69	8.35	13.13	17.62
周至县	Zhouzhi	1.24	2.41	2.05	1.73	1.51	1.45	2.92	3.16	3.94	5.52	6.76
西咸新区	Xixian											

注：2013年数据为第三次全国经济普查数据。2018年数据为第四次全国经济普查上报数据。下同。

12-1 续表 continued

单位：亿元 (100 million yuan)

区 县	Region	2009	2010	2011	2012	2013	2014	2015	2016	2017	2018	2019
合 计	**Total**	**2468.27**	**3130.15**	**3552.21**	**4066.31**	**4436.58**	**4961.12**	**4924.57**	**5266.25**	**6018.79**	**6396.28**	**6846.16**
新城区	Xincheng	195.45	272.13	323.64	307.67	344.30	372.75	398.68	401.62	394.86	248.69	320.28
碑林区	Beilin	58.60	108.14	138.72	18.46	23.48	27.66	29.59	31.91	31.15	17.60	16.70
莲湖区	Lianhu	399.83	458.30	457.96	459.41	419.81	407.16	402.62	405.48	471.67	531.29	429.36
灞桥区	Baqiao	178.82	242.15	280.52	278.37	308.04	300.73	175.89	181.17	137.52	123.92	151.91
未央区	Weiyang	393.22	499.88	510.39	684.55	733.75	858.40	839.29	959.84	1014.93	1083.72	1101.03
雁塔区	Yanta	249.69	286.19	367.97	587.65	624.55	694.34	677.00	648.80	721.42	663.32	733.17
阎良区	Yanliang	128.99	163.55	176.67	219.31	276.71	300.25	321.23	342.53	316.66	350.69	366.14
临潼区	Lintong	165.77	222.01	277.75	341.01	404.45	418.75	263.29	204.22	181.43	209.65	242.48
长安区	Chang'an	277.98	334.89	350.68	354.65	383.41	546.35	720.87	956.32	1001.19	1401.03	1554.18
高陵区	Gaoling	305.94	402.98	516.33	662.99	741.34	854.73	869.60	835.74	939.03	1214.57	1075.02
鄠邑区	Huyi	81.54	96.89	100.42	93.55	101.40	104.68	135.94	189.31	359.94	126.00	376.83
蓝田县	Lantian	23.40	31.93	35.87	41.60	49.33	46.22	49.32	55.47	74.43	73.47	64.32
周至县	Zhouzhi	9.03	11.11	15.29	17.08	26.01	29.10	41.25	53.84	65.64	44.26	38.68
西咸新区	Xixian										308.08	376.06

12-2 各区县规模以上工业企业工业总产值（2019年）

单位：亿元

区 县	Region	单位数（个） Number of Enterprises (unit)	工业总产值 Gross Industrial Output Value	国有经济 State-owned Enterprises	集体经济 Collective-owned Enterprises	其他经济类型 Enterprises of Other Ownership
新城区	Xincheng	12	320.28	288.76	0.58	30.94
碑林区	Beilin	6	16.70	4.89	0.00	11.81
莲湖区	Lianhu	28	429.36	407.83	1.33	20.21
灞桥区	Baqiao	89	151.91	80.32	3.49	68.10
未央区	Weiyang	199	1101.03	357.01	1.05	742.97
雁塔区	Yanta	269	733.17	414.14	1.15	317.88
阎良区	Yanliang	120	366.14	236.88	4.45	124.80
临潼区	Lintong	85	242.48	120.45	0.46	121.58
长安区	Chang'an	193	1554.18	227.60	10.07	1316.51
高陵区	Gaoling	186	1075.02	820.01	0.66	254.35
鄠邑区	Huyi	132	376.83	39.79	0.91	336.13
蓝田县	Lantian	57	64.32	5.18		59.14
周至县	Zhouzhi	46	38.68	3.63	0.37	34.68
西咸新区	Xixian	209	376.06	161.20	0.48	214.38

Gross Output Value of Industrial Enterprises above Designated Size by Region (2019)

(100 million yuan)

轻工业 Light Industry	重工业 Heavy Industry	大型工业 Large-size Industry Enterprises	中型工业 Medium-size Industry Enterprises	小型工业 Small-size Industry Enterprises	微型工业 Micro Enterprises
29.43	290.85	288.76	28.64	2.88	
13.15	3.54	10.01	4.89	1.80	
31.10	398.27	375.32	38.90	14.94	0.21
30.42	121.49	47.37	27.69	75.16	1.70
318.59	782.44	443.55	214.00	435.08	8.39
162.94	570.23	266.17	225.34	234.57	7.08
56.86	309.28	196.18	35.22	133.87	0.87
95.92	146.56	96.15	78.57	66.31	1.46
94.27	1459.91	1171.24	160.88	221.09	0.97
50.96	1024.06	605.48	256.36	200.78	12.40
154.01	222.81	250.19	38.86	85.16	2.62
29.55	34.77		4.97	58.84	0.51
23.96	14.72	3.63		34.22	0.83
51.06	325.01	94.14	124.24	153.62	4.07

12-3 主要年份规模以上工业企业主要经济指标

单位：亿元

年份 Year	企业单位数（个） Number of Enterprises (unit)	工业总产值（当年价格） Gross Industrial Output Value (At Current Prices)	平均用工人数（万人） Average Number of Employed Persons (10 000person)
1998	793	350.38	51.71
1999	770	366.59	45.64
2000	816	417.97	43.25
2001	785	482.61	40.12
2002	771	544.78	38.48
2003	735	638.66	36.55
2004	1066	830.06	38.08
2005	902	981.02	37.92
2006	904	1187.74	37.94
2007	937	1577.05	38.55
2008	1032	2007.85	40.17
2009	1131	2468.27	43.42
2010	1126	3130.15	47.11
2011	891	3552.21	50.42
2012	970	4066.31	49.23
2013	1056	4436.58	48.36
2014	1146	4961.12	49.65
2015	1150	4924.57	50.59
2016	1220	5266.25	49.54
2017	1403	6018.79	51.11
2018	1474	6396.28	51.40
2019	1631	6846.16	49.75

Major Economic Indicators of Industrial Enterprises above Designated Size in Representative Years

(100 million yuan)

资产总计 Total Assets	负债合计 Total Liabilites	所有者权益合计 Owners' Equities	主营业务收入 Revenue from Principal Business	利润总额 Total Profits	利税总额 Total Pre-tax Profits
810.56	548.68	261.88	346.84	-1.26	14.82
853.90	577.94	275.96	346.26	8.26	27.30
958.05	622.46	323.72	420.42	16.11	36.29
1054.36	657.88	384.65	451.62	17.97	40.84
1065.76	643.78	412.27	541.64	25.43	51.31
1195.69	733.04	460.97	645.53	33.82	64.99
1333.91	869.30	464.60	812.46	38.57	74.23
1503.85	977.42	508.82	980.97	28.72	67.25
1651.67	1062.11	578.33	1183.51	61.46	110.23
1940.52	1254.01	686.51	1561.25	106.22	168.54
2426.13	1518.86	907.27	1928.05	84.89	168.63
2913.56	1779.38	1130.76	2384.52	177.20	280.68
3592.13	2069.29	1515.65	3011.19	245.37	373.56
3975.38	2295.49	1678.19	3381.27	172.94	312.78
4775.92	2835.55	1926.72	3758.56	167.77	320.57
5127.69	3049.36	2071.72	4171.21	211.26	392.14
6048.34	3607.62	2436.06	4566.20	226.17	401.20
6740.26	3860.55	2926.55	4374.11	206.88	341.40
7473.07	4158.75	3302.36	5028.28	290.96	438.59
7862.59	4162.97	3595.73	5710.70	367.77	532.35
8294.08	4522.64	3771.44	6021.12	402.44	570.81
9449.95	5096.70	4349.39	6483.80	325.60	465.42

12-4 各区县规模以上工业企业主要经济指标（2019年）

单位：亿元

区 县	Region	企业单位数（个）Number of Enterprises (unit)	平均用工人数（万人）Average Number of Employed Persons (10 000 persons)	资产合计 Total Assets
新城区	Xingcheng	12	2.97	527.85
碑林区	Beilin	6	0.34	78.81
莲湖区	Lianhu	28	4.50	844.02
灞桥区	Baqiao	89	2.04	256.33
未央区	Weiyang	199	6.56	1104.74
雁塔区	Yanta	269	8.20	1455.26
阎良区	Yanliang	120	3.36	656.10
临潼区	Lintong	85	1.75	385.75
长安区	Chang'an	193	7.41	2232.79
高陵区	Gaoling	186	4.49	776.79
鄠邑区	Huyi	132	3.48	398.97
蓝田县	Lantian	57	0.61	73.89
周至县	Zhouzhi	46	0.36	35.66
西咸新区	Xixian	209	3.67	622.99

Major Economic Indicators of Industrial Enterprises above Designated Size by Region（2019）

(100 million yuan)

负债合计 Total Liabilites	所有者权益合计 Total Owners' Equities	营业收入 Revenue	利润总额 Total Profits	利税总额 Total Pre-tax Profits
330.06	197.80	370.55	11.57	19.97
53.52	25.29	30.25	3.57	4.69
398.40	445.62	416.63	25.43	38.73
163.04	93.01	167.44	5.59	9.74
584.83	518.83	1051.13	42.94	58.37
761.13	692.40	762.16	47.78	69.69
332.63	323.47	314.77	17.27	21.52
229.07	156.24	233.83	9.34	15.47
955.82	1276.74	1378.92	112.21	133.14
531.63	245.16	1044.79	33.08	49.29
255.42	143.55	387.40	13.38	26.52
53.58	20.31	62.16	2.72	4.48
12.81	22.85	36.83	2.20	3.18
434.76	188.15	368.80	-1.49	10.64

12-5 规模以上工业企业主要工业产品产量（2019年）

Major Output of Industrial Enterprises above Designated Size（2019）

产品名称	Name of Products	2019	比上年增长(%) Increase over Preceding Year (%)
自来水生产量(亿立方米)	Tap Water Production (100 million cu.m)	6.52	7.0
大米(万吨)	Rice (10 000 ton)	1.95	10.7
小麦粉(万吨)	Wheat Flour (10 000 ton)	44.01	-20.8
精制食用植物油(万吨)	Edible Vegetable Oil (10 000 ton)	20.28	16.7
鲜、冷藏肉（万吨）	Fresh/Frozen Meat(10 000 ton)	7.83	-22.5
饲料（万吨）	Mixed Feed(10 000 ton)	74.28	-7.2
#配合饲料	Compound feed	15.91	-14.2
混合饲料	Mixed feed	57.43	-4.3
方便面(万吨)	Instant Noodle(10 000 ton)	15.20	12.6
乳制品(万吨)	Dairy Products (10 000 ton)	72.64	-3.0
液体乳	Milk	57.58	-6.6
固体及半固体乳制品	Solid and semi-solid dairy products	15.06	13.8
饮料酒(万千升)	Beverage Wine (10 000 kiloliter)	36.03	-9.3
#白酒（折65度，商品量）	Liquor (as 65 degree, amount of goods)	0.01	-66.0
啤酒	Beer	35.46	-8.6
葡萄酒	Wine	0.46	-35.5
饮料(万吨)	Beverage (10 000 ton)	207.59	22.7
#碳酸饮料类（汽水）	Carbonated Beverage	43.07	22.0
果汁和蔬菜汁饮料	Juice and Fruit Beverage	17.67	-37.9
包装饮用水类	Canned Drinking Water	101.82	90.4
纱(万吨)	Yarn (10 000 ton)	2.80	-4.6
棉纱	Cotton Yarn	1.12	-12.5
棉混纺纱	Blend Fabric	0.59	-5.8
化学纤维纱	Pure Chemical-Fibre Yarn	1.09	6.1
布(亿米)	Cloth (100 million m)	1.21	-4.7

12-5 续表1 continued1

产品名称	Name of Products	2019	比上年增长(%) Increase over Preceding Year (%)
棉布	Cotton Cloth	0.50	-8.4
棉混纺布	Blend Fabric	0.30	2.5
化学纤维短纤布	Chemical Fiber short fiber Cloth	0.41	-4.8
人造板（万立方米）	Artificial Board (10 000 cu.m)	11.14	10.7
纤维板	Fibre Board	11.14	10.7
家具（万件）	Furniture (10 000unit)	49.54	10.5
#木质家具	Wooden Furniture	34.23	41.7
软体家具	Soft Furniture	5.53	-46.2
机制纸及纸板（外购原纸加工除外）（万吨）	Machine Made Paper(not including processing of procured base paper)(10 000 ton)	11.38	-26.0
纸制品（万吨）	Paper-Made Products (10 000 ton)	12.45	-20.9
#瓦楞纸箱	Corrugated Paper	9.68	-25.9
单色印刷（万令）	Monochrom Printed products(10 000 ream)	102.81	-1.8
多色印刷品（万对开色令）	Colored Printed products(10 000 ream)	1081.06	3.2
化学农药原药(折有效成分100%)(万吨)	Chemical Pesticide(100% effective content)(10 000 ton)	0.08	-39.8
涂料（万吨）	Construction Paint(10 000 ton)	1.35	-14.7
合成洗涤剂（万吨）	Synthetic Detergents (10 000 ton)	6.35	36.3
#合成洗衣粉	Washing Power	1.07	27.3
液体洗涤剂	Liquid detergent	3.19	-0.7
化学原料药（万吨）	Chemical Medicine (10 000 ton)	0.07	108.7
中成药（万吨）	Traditional Chinese Medicine (10 000 ton)	1.25	16.7
化学纤维（万吨）	Chemical Fiber (10 000 ton)	4.30	15.0
#人造纤维（纤维素纤维）	Man-made Fiber	3.98	19.6
塑料制品（万吨）	Plastic Product (10 000 ton)	27.57	16.2
水泥（万吨）	Cement (10 000 ton)	199.80	-6.7

12-5 续表2 continued2

产品名称	Name of Products	2019	比上年增长(%) Increase over Preceding Year (%)
硅酸盐水泥熟料（万吨）	Portland Cement Clinker (10 000 ton)	76.65	0.9
水泥混凝土电杆（万根）	Cement Pole(10 000 unit)	0.93	-2.8
商品混凝土(万立方米)	Ready-mixed Concrete (10 000 cu.m)	3851.27	14.8
沥青和改性沥青防水卷材（万平方米）	Asphalt and Modified Bitumen Membrane(10 000 sq.m)	1400.41	-16.0
钢化玻璃(万平方米)	Toughened Glass(10 000 sq.m)	459.24	-18.2
日用玻璃制品（万吨）	Glassware(10 000 ton)	0.00	0.0
钢材（万吨）	Rolled-steel Final Products (10 000 ton)	31.47	17.5
#线材（盘条）	Wire Rod	14.85	58.4
其他钢材	Other steel	12.06	-19.6
铝材(万吨)	Aluminum Material (10 000 ton)	2.11	-17.2
单晶硅（万千克）	Monocrystalline Silicon (10 000kg)	176.36	225.3
多晶硅（万千克）	Polycrystalline Silicon(10 000kg)	1030.20	200.2
工业锅炉（蒸发量吨）	Industrial Boiler steam(ton)	1448.80	-48.8
发动机（万千瓦）	Engine (10 000 kw)	389.41	1.6
#汽车发动机	Motor Engine	389.41	1.6
金属切削机床(万台)	Metal-cutting Machines (10 000 unit)	0.34	-31.1
泵(万台)	Pump (Liquid pump)(10 000 unit)	0.35	-6.2
风机（万台）	Fan(10 000 unit)	0.70	-4.7
气体压缩机（万台）	Gas Compressor(10 000 unit)	77.34	11.9
阀门（万吨）	Valves (10 000 ton)	0.13	-17.3
铸铁件（万吨）	Iron Castings (10 000 ton)	1.72	-2.1
铸钢件（万吨）	Steel Castings (10 000 ton)	0.17	-86.7
锻件（万吨）	Forgings (10 000 ton)	0.98	-0.4
矿山专用设备（万吨）	Mining Equipment (10 000 ton)	1.57	-6.0
炼油、化工生产专用设备（万吨）	Oil Refining and Chemical industry Machine(10 000 ton)	0.43	0.1

12-5 续表3 continued3

产品名称	Name of Products	2019	比上年增长(%) Increase over Preceding Year (%)
金属冶炼设备（吨）	Metal Smelting Equipments(ton)	4096.70	15.0
金属轧制设备（吨）	Metal-rolling Machine(ton)	32562.50	-66.9
印刷专用设备（吨）	Printing Equipment(ton)	183.00	47.6
环境污染防治专用设备(台/套)	Special Equipment for Environment Protection（sets）	10644.00	-19.0
#大气污染防治设备	Equipment for Preventing Atmospheric Pollution	9187.00	-26.4
汽车（万辆）	Motor Vehicle(10 000unit)	42.63	-1.7
其中：基本型乘用车（轿车）	Basic Type Passenger Vehicles(car)	14.14	-21.8
#轿车（排量≤1升）	Car0L-1.0L Gas Displacement(1.0L included)	6.80	19.5
轿车（1升＜排量≤1.6升）	Car1.0L-1.6L Gas Displacement(1.6L included)	7.34	-40.8
运动型多用途乘用车（SUV）	Sports Utility Vehicle (SUV)	9.26	33.5
载货汽车	Trucks	19.23	5.0
其中：新能源汽车	New Energy Vehicles	9.35	-32.5
改装汽车（万辆）	Refit Trucks (10 000 unit)	1.40	-9.3
铁路货车（万辆）	Freight(10 000 unit)	0.44	5.5
电动机（万千瓦）	Electric motor(10 000 kilowatts)	295.34	3.3
#直流电动机	DC motors	34.02	32.3
交流电动机	Alternating Current Motor	261.32	0.5
变压器（万千伏安）	Transformer(10 000KVA)	17365.29	31.2
高压开关板（万面）	High-voltage Switch Panel(10 000 unit)	0.89	10.0
低压开关板（万面）	Low-voltage Switch Panel(10 000 unit)	0.77	-45.8
电力电缆(万千米)	Electric Power Cables(10 000 km)	14.09	-39.6
通信及电子网络用电缆(万对千米)	Communication Cables(10 000 pair km)	3.60	6.2
光缆（万芯千米）	Cable (10 000 Core.km)	676.75	-22.5
绝缘制品(吨)	Insulating Products(ton)	41408.00	18.1

12-5 续表4 continued 4

产品名称	Name of Products	2019	比上年增长(%) Increase over Preceding Year (%)
电子元件（亿只）	Electronic Components(100 million unit)	45.84	-10.4
工业自动化调节仪表与控制系统（万台/套）	Automatization meter and system (10 000 unit)	7.38	63.7
分析仪器及装置（万台/套）	Analysis instruments and Apparatus (10 000 unit)		-99.8
化学试剂（万吨）	Chemicals Reagents(10000 ton)	63.62	17.8
起重机（吨）	Crane (ton)	625.00	-8.9
减速机（台）	Reducer (unit)	18322.00	29.4
模具（万套）	Molds (10 000set)	0.45	60.9
电动自行车（万辆）	Electric bicycle (10 000car)	52.72	-40.6
电力电容器（万千乏）	Power capacitors (10 000KW)	6684.82	25.9
高压开关设备（11万伏以上）（万台）	High Voltage Switchgear (above 110,000 volt) (10 000unit)	1.34	3.7
灯具及照明装置（万套/台/个）	Lamps and lighting equipment (10 000set /unit)	10.82	21.2
半导体分立器件（亿只）	Discrete semiconductor devices (100million unit)	51.73	-10.7
光电子器件（万只/片）	Optoelectronic devices (10 000unit)	427.20	22.8
工业仪表（万台/个）	Industrial Instrumentation (10 000unit)	67.20	8.1
环境监测专用仪器仪表（台）	Special equipment for prevention and control of environmental pollution(unit)	10432.00	79.5
集成电路圆片（万片）	Integrated circuit wafer (10 000 pieces)	143.30	-4.5
锂离子电池（万只）	Lithium ion battery (10 000unit)	1761.04	17.1
太阳能电池（万千瓦）	Solar cell (10 000 KW)	856.69	16.6
智能手机（万台）	Smart phones (10 000 sets)	1141.21	-31.1
发电量（亿千瓦小时）	Power generation(100 million kilowatt-hours)	155.00	-10.5
火力发电量	Thermal power generation	147.58	-11.8
水力发电量	Hydropower	0.87	6.0
太阳能发电量	Solar energy generation	6.55	34.0

12-6 主要年份规模以上工业企业经济效益指标

Indicators of Economic Performance of Industrial Enterprises above Designated Size in Representative Years

年 份 Year	总资产贡献率（%） Ratio of Total Assets to Industrial Output Value（%）	资产负债率（%） Assets-Liability Ratio（%）	流动资产周转次数（次/年） Rate of Annual Turnover Working Capitals (times/year)	成本费用利润率（%） Ratio of Profits to Cost（%）	全员劳动生产率（元/人·年） Overall Labor Productivity (yuan/person · ear)	产品销售率（%） Proportion of Industrial Products Sold（%）
1998		67.7	0.9	-266.1	19185	95.3
1999		67.7	0.9	2.5	22878	95.9
2000		65.0	1.0	4.2	29496	97.1
2001	5.8	62.4	0.9	4.1	38267	96.7
2002	6.2	60.4	1.1	5.1	46940	96.7
2003	7.0	61.3	1.1	5.7	58801	96.3
2004	6.9	65.2	1.2	5.0	66752	97.9
2005	8.4	65.0	1.3	3.1	82815	97.5
2006	7.8	64.3	1.4	5.5	97561	98.2
2007	10.2	64.6	1.6	7.3	129706	96.8
2008	8.6	62.6	1.5	4.6	150641	96.1
2009	11.3	61.1	1.7	8.1	161289	97.6
2010	12.2	57.6	1.7	8.8	188483	97.1
2011	8.6	57.7	1.5	5.2	194105	97.4
2012	7.7	59.4	1.5	4.5	230032	96.7
2013	8.5	59.5	1.5	5.2	264324	95.7
2014	7.4	59.7	1.4	5.2	266789	94.9
2015	5.7	57.3	1.3	4.8	268182	94.5
2016	6.4	55.7	1.3	6.0	277240	96.0
2017	7.2	53.0	1.4	6.6	294393	97.3
2018	7.3	54.5	1.3	6.8		96.2
2019	5.4	53.9	1.2	5.1		94.0

注：产品销售率2019年数据为快报数。

12-7 规模以上工业企业主要经济指标（2019年）

单位：万元

分 组	Classify	企业单位数（个）Number of Enterprises (unit)	亏损企业 Loss Making Enterprises	工业总产值（当年价格）Gross Industrial Output Value (At Current Prices)
总计	**Total**	**1631**	**272**	**68461605**
#亏损企业	Deficit Enterprises	272	272	3497415
按隶属关系分	**Grouped by Jurisdiction of Management**			
#中央企业	Central Enterprises	113	17	14477494
地方企业	Local Enterprises	182	40	19305898
按登记注册类型分组	**Grouped by Registion Status**			
内资企业	Domestic Investment Enterprises	1517	251	54880757
国有	State-owned Enterprises	23	1	4538406
集体	Collective-owned Enterprises	4		32448
股份合作	Share-holding Corperative	4	1	13073
联营	Joint Ownership Enterprises			
有限责任公司	Limited Liability Corporations	633	123	32474022
股份有限公司	Share-holding Corperation Ltd.	122	26	6915190
私营	Private Enterprises	730	100	10904610
其他	Other Domestic Funded Enterprises	1		3007
港澳台商投资	Enterprises with Funds from Hong Kong,Macao and Taiwan	22	4	2909295
外商投资	Foreign Funded Enterprises	92	17	10671553
按轻重工业分	**Grouped by Light Industry and Heavy Industry**			
轻工业	Light Industry	385	79	11422363
重工业	Heavy Industry	1246	193	57039242
按企业规模分	**Grouped by Size of Enterprises**			
大型企业	Large-size	68	9	38481834
中型企业	Medium-size	181	30	12385590
小型企业	Small-size	1308	211	17183202
微型企业	Microenterprise	74	22	410979
按控股情况分	**Grouped by Cast strand**			
国有控股	State owned shares	305	61	31676836

Major Economic Indicators of Industrial Enterprises above Designated Size（2019）

(10 000yuan)

平均用工人数（人） Average Number of Employed Persons (person)	资产总计 Total Assets	流动资产合计 Total Working Capitals	固定资产原价 Origing Value of Fixed Assets	累计折旧 Accumulative Total Depreciation
497460	**94499505**	**53300537**	**40484936**	**20939580**
54374	9270802	4174112	3536487	1321565
153303	26808533	15105959	13926708	7196822
96805	25378734	14543877	7512904	3496200
429314	77858965	46745120	28338987	13197066
52104	9359842	4209638	6591137	3187976
509	10682	6218	15605	11635
232	22341	18751	6175	3586
258217	45313652	28613416	16263452	7552266
43665	13601531	7233540	2989151	1472095
74545	9550326	6663090	2472705	969158
42	592	467	762	351
28671	2762371	1413316	1183844	505154
39475	13878169	5142101	10962105	7237359
87415	10980026	6511938	4422714	1872979
410045	83519479	46788598	36062222	19066601
266099	56879379	30451804	28072513	16091640
98806	17562532	10580751	5664013	2378751
130702	19623341	11924114	6691375	2451065
1853	434253	343869	57035	18124
264782	52080983	30166562	22395411	11053175

12-7 续表1

单位：万元

分 组	Classify	负债合计 Total Liabilites	流动负债合计 Total Working Liabilities
总计	**Total**	**50966962**	**42070874**
#亏损企业	Deficit Enterprises	7095105	5517595
按隶属关系分	**Grouped by Jurisdiction of Management**		
#中央企业	Central Enterprises	14095880	11742600
地方企业	Local Enterprises	15271744	13447306
按登记注册类型分组	**Grouped by Registion Status**		
内资企业	Domestic Investment Enterprises	43992132	36904635
国有	State-owned Enterprises	6015921	4690909
集体	Collective-owned Enterprises	2595	2381
股份合作	Share-holding Corperative	8050	6807
联营	Joint Ownership Enterprises		
有限责任公司	Limited Liability Corporations	26608234	22805460
股份有限公司	Share-holding Corperation Ltd.	5908755	4715517
私营	Private Enterprises	5448527	4683561
其他	Other Domestic Funded Enterprises	50	
港澳台商投资	Enterprises with Funds from Hong Kong,Macao and Taiwan	1791443	1492624
外商投资	Foreign Funded Enterprises	5183386	3673615
按轻重工业分	**Grouped by Light Industry and Heavy Industry**		
轻工业	Light Industry	6455037	4995774
重工业	Heavy Industry	44511925	37075100
按企业规模分	**Grouped by Size of Enterprises**		
大型企业	Large-size	29661305	24424520
中型企业	Medium-size	9620122	7724229
小型企业	Small-size	11411553	9777797
微型企业	Microenterprise	273982	144328
按控股情况分	**Grouped by Cast strand**		
国有控股	State owned shares	30270742	25573751

continued1

(10 000yuan)

所有者权益合计 Total Owners' Equities	实收资本 Total Capital Hold	营业收入 Total Revenue	主营业务收入 Revenue from Principal Business	营业成本 Total Cost	税金及附加 Taxs and Other Changes
43493950	**18411047**	**66256734**	**64838006**	**57031519**	**384756**
2161336	2557126	3488225	3417443	3089804	27806
12704384	5510443	14627498	14327797	12977998	86067
10092587	3460780	19476201	18922791	17067846	79840
33828240	13508041	54384770	53218877	46663001	286602
3343920	1419125	5249844	5149656	4583210	25080
8086	4427	29858	29758	26170	98
14291	6475	12414	12414	10564	75
18678709	8188109	31916899	30997010	27683574	177216
7692775	2052489	6683341	6607246	5483646	37911
4089917	1837266	10489408	10419795	8874216	46141
542	152	3007	2999	1620	82
970928	272368	2919692	2788570	2980212	53220
8694782	4630639	8952272	8830559	7388307	44933
4507439	1878228	11148873	10985670	8473368	70928
38986510	16532820	55107861	53852336	48558151	313828
27218075	10244862	36695533	35786657	32706468	221713
7942408	3563928	12439386	12203337	10067908	70041
8211774	4506884	16703979	16433005	13879191	91303
121693	95374	417835	415006	377952	1699
21787569	9112534	32181518	31279469	28551973	175493

12-7 续表2

单位：万元

分 组	Classify	销售费用 Expenses for Sales	管理费用 Expenses for Management	研发费用 R&D Expenses
总计	**Total**	**2510122**	**2678346**	**1203752**
#亏损企业	Deficit Enterprises	195527	283107	76742
按隶属关系分	**Grouped by Jurisdiction of Management**			
#中央企业	Central Enterprises	268223	788411	338137
地方企业	Local Enterprises	727163	568329	228368
按登记注册类型分组	**Grouped by Registion Status**			
内资企业	Domestic Investment Enterprises	1971115	2263962	995192
国有	State-owned Enterprises	36100	259462	110848
集体	Collective-owned Enterprises	1273	626	3
股份合作	Share-holding Corperative	264	874	159
联营	Joint Ownership Enterprises			
有限责任公司	Limited Liability Corporations	1197753	1309714	567087
股份有限公司	Share-holding Corperation Ltd.	288721	254857	132569
私营	Private Enterprises	446844	438249	184527
其他	Other Domestic Funded Enterprises	160	181	
港澳台商投资	Enterprises with Funds from Hong Kong,Macao and Taiwan	65887	117261	28468
外商投资	Foreign Funded Enterprises	473121	297123	180092
按轻重工业分	**Grouped by Light Industry and Heavy Industry**			
轻工业	Light Industry	1282292	540326	89054
重工业	Heavy Industry	1227830	2138020	1114698
按企业规模分	**Grouped by Size of Enterprises**			
大型企业	Large-size	1081712	1299018	635910
中型企业	Medium-size	754293	528743	283669
小型企业	Small-size	668086	836125	280186
微型企业	Microenterprise	6031	14460	3986
按控股情况分	**Grouped by Cast strand**			
国有控股	State owned shares	689185	1349184	615887

continued2

(10 000yuan)

财务费用 Financial cost	营业利润 Operating Profit	利润总额 Total Profits	亏损企业亏损总额 Total Loss of Deficit Enterprises	利税总额 Total Pre-tax Profits	应付职工薪酬 Salary Payable	本年应交增值税 Value Added Tax Payable
373149	**3126335**	**3256004**	**532691**	**4654247**	**6477384**	**1013487**
115399	-531450	-532691	532691	-457955	486768	46930
61049	422417	415621	271102	736851	2338228	235163
101712	922636	962793	76532	1318667	1570735	276033
353117	2352819	2440642	498202	3618177	5535566	890933
55588	208492	199183	564	323291	807485	99027
62	1600	1710		2374	1860	565
9	587	630	25	1142	849	437
156248	1200351	1267853	394579	1971486	3469998	526417
79691	518156	528983	71125	679614	470103	112720
61356	422832	441482	31910	639366	784898	151743
163	801	801		906	372	23
18738	51081	52985	972	122352	265056	16147
1294	722435	762377	33516	913718	676763	106408
119374	566744	629114	49906	958417	905185	258375
253775	2559591	2626890	482785	3695831	5572200	755113
83124	1788091	1825852	100297	2504090	4226748	456525
124058	530668	555877	261307	860268	1180885	234351
162164	799242	865393	164632	1274402	1063488	317706
3804	8334	8883	6455	15488	6263	4906
174348	1033800	1059338	412102	1733422	4004823	498591

12-7 续表3

单位：万元

分 组	Classify	企业单位数（个） Number of Enterprises (unit)	亏损企业 Loss Making Enterprises	工业总产值（当年价格） Gross Industrial Output Value (At Current Prices)
集体控股	Collective shares	18	5	249873
私人控股	Private holdings	1170	180	25448030
港澳台控股	Hong Kong and Macao Holdings	14	1	434586
外商投资	Foreign Investment	58	8	9166039
其他	Others	66	17	1486240
按工业行业大类分	**Grouped by Sector**			
煤炭开采和洗选业	Mining and Washing of Coal			
石油和天然气开采业	Extraction of Petroleum and Natural Gas			
黑色金属矿采选业	Mining and Processing of Ferrous Metal Ores			
有色金属矿采选业	Mining and Processing of Non-ferrous Metal Ores			
非金属矿采选业	Mining and Processing of Nonmetal Ores			
开采专业及辅助性活动	Mining Professional and Auxiliary Activity	7	1	1080247
其他采矿业	Mining of other Ores			
农副食品加工业	Processing of Food from Agricultural Porducts	46	7	1552498
食品制造业	Manufacture of Foods	53	13	1823229
酒、饮料和精制茶制造业	Manufacture of Alcohol,Beverages and Tea	22	6	777518
烟草制品业	Manufacture of Tobacco	1		9472
纺织业	Manufacture of Textile	15	5	176595
纺织服装、服饰业	Textile, apparel industry	4	1	63448
皮革、毛皮、羽毛及其制品和制鞋业	Manufacture of Leather, Fur, Feather and Related Products, and Shoes	2	1	23567
木材加工和木、竹、藤、棕、草制品业	Processing of Timber, Manufacture of Wood,Plam and Straw Products	3	2	29583
家具制造业	Manufacture of Furniture	18	2	174741
造纸和纸制品业	Manufacture of Paper and Paper Products	24	4	186359
印刷和记录媒介复制业	Printing,Reproduction of Recording Media	32	9	1079689

continued3

(10 000yuan)

平均用工人数（人） Average Number of Employed Persons (person)	资产总计 Total Assets	流动资产合计 Total Working Capitals	固定资产原价 Origing Value of Fixed Assets	累计折旧 Accumulative Total Depreciation
2895	350864	230755	120193	66626
182169	27435026	17434369	6532034	2456185
3915	330797	208695	183006	106487
30648	12213530	4215880	10215973	6937850
13051	2088306	1044276	1038319	319258
13318	1296351	923019	743086	505625
6717	985760	667627	346871	163056
16782	866436	416830	555038	274898
6440	1136679	613205	515548	284425
497	37171	21696	32579	17179
6005	317486	140458	225548	85805
1167	101862	82771	19079	5798
799	61234	41256	9429	5577
416	108291	51454	40371	9946
2082	131853	76433	45863	8944
2264	150637	96154	44289	14021
7334	862576	493964	565764	355030

12-7 续表4

单位：万元

分组	Classify	负债合计 Total Liabilites	流动负债合计 Total Working Liabilities
集体控股	Collective shares	162540	141528
私人控股	Private holdings	15043268	12587295
港澳台控股	Hong Kong and Macao Holdings	126579	120688
外商投资	Foreign Investment	4221200	2771642
其他	Others	1142632	875970
按工业行业大类分	**Grouped by Sector**		
煤炭开采和洗选业	Mining and Washing of Coal		
石油和天然气开采业	Extraction of Petroleum and Natural Gas		
黑色金属矿采选业	Mining and Processing of Ferrous Metal Ores		
有色金属矿采选业	Mining and Processing of Non-ferrous Metal Ores		
非金属矿采选业	Mining and Processing of Nonmetal Ores		
开采专业及辅助性活动	Mining Professional and Auxiliary Activity	513278	502674
其他采矿业	Mining of other Ores		
农副食品加工业	Processing of Food from Agricultural Porducts	683472	614487
食品制造业	Manufacture of Foods	438088	386256
酒、饮料和精制茶制造业	Manufacture of Alcohol,Beverages and Tea	654619	550930
烟草制品业	Manufacture of Tobacco	2320	2320
纺织业	Manufacture of Textile	192944	98795
纺织服装、服饰业	Textile, apparel industry	56641	55651
皮革、毛皮、羽毛及其制品和制鞋业	Manufacture of Leather, Fur, Feather and Related Products, and Shoes	20115	13688
木材加工和木、竹、藤、棕、草制品业	Processing of Timber, Manufacture of Wood,Plam and Straw Products	49197	13144
家具制造业	Manufacture of Furniture	64645	48520
造纸和纸制品业	Manufacture of Paper and Paper Products	72983	65645
印刷和记录媒介复制业	Printing,Reproduction of Recording Media	371872	287160

continued4

(10 000yuan)

所有者权益合计 Total Owners' Equities	实收资本 Total Capital Hold	营业收入 Total Revenue	主营业务收入 Revenue from Principal Business	营业成本 Total Cost	税金及附加 Taxs and Other Changes
188324	94454	236505	234229	192513	1291
12375837	4392749	24638873	24223025	20841135	153813
204217	133306	407890	402525	293616	8124
7992330	4165180	7454704	7396535	6026969	39361
945673	512824	1337244	1302223	1125314	6675
783073	474606	919078	905442	828640	6184
299688	134019	1565210	1515714	1436082	2605
428347	222576	1589164	1571767	1275062	12725
482060	148279	981165	967775	729839	14048
34851	27400	9619	9472	4620	397
124542	48179	198574	187803	186536	1641
45221	33109	45814	45667	36817	456
41119	38000	29349	29349	24947	92
59094	13668	23679	23287	21476	59
67208	26795	158537	158406	137346	1049
77653	29590	192742	192000	178394	544
490703	233506	1182275	1166227	986095	5208

12-7 续表5

单位：万元

分　组	Classify	销售费用 Expenses for Sales	管理费用 Expenses for Management	研发费用 R&D Expenses
集体控股	Collective shares	14044	12659	5134
私人控股	Private holdings	1296695	999176	385725
港澳台控股	Hong Kong and Macao Holdings	46886	20855	9569
外商投资	Foreign Investment	435630	246812	158950
其他	Others	27683	49661	28487
按工业行业大类分	**Grouped by Sector**			
煤炭开采和洗选业	Mining and Washing of Coal			
石油和天然气开采业	Extraction of Petroleum and Natural Gas			
黑色金属矿采选业	Mining and Processing of Ferrous Metal Ores			
有色金属矿采选业	Mining and Processing of Non-ferrous Metal Ores			
非金属矿采选业	Mining and Processing of Nonmetal Ores			
开采专业及辅助性活动	Mining Professional and Auxiliary Activity	4252	25868	29310
其他采矿业	Mining of other Ores			
农副食品加工业	Processing of Food from Agricultural Porducts	43989	36811	2398
食品制造业	Manufacture of Foods	146256	64136	3255
酒、饮料和精制茶制造业	Manufacture of Alcohol,Beverages and Tea	163595	27943	1247
烟草制品业	Manufacture of Tobacco	950	2758	
纺织业	Manufacture of Textile	3666	7921	4059
纺织服装、服饰业	Textile, apparel industry	2794	4448	
皮革、毛皮、羽毛及其制品和制鞋业	Manufacture of Leather, Fur, Feather and Related Products, and Shoes	732	724	1253
木材加工和木、竹、藤、棕、草制品业	Processing of Timber, Manufacture of Wood,Plam and Straw Products	612	3514	
家具制造业	Manufacture of Furniture	4863	7260	16
造纸和纸制品业	Manufacture of Paper and Paper Products	3256	5264	
印刷和记录媒介复制业	Printing,Reproduction of Recording Media	46055	75481	7657

continued5

(10 000yuan)

财务费用 Financial cost	营业利润 Operating Profit	利润总额 Total Profits	亏损企业亏损总额 Total Loss of Deficit Enterprises	利税总额 Total Pre-tax Profits	应付职工薪酬 Salary Payable	本年应交增值税 Value Added Tax Payable
997	8175	9496	2941	15924	24910	5138
183720	1317513	1374851	88362	1926102	1720672	397438
1734	27418	28301	9	42046	48152	5622
-4682	643264	681786	11909	812837	557970	91690
17033	96166	102233	17367	123917	120859	15009
-5743	39166	37575	41	48943	281932	5185
11599	43026	49624	2205	61089	51556	8861
3386	86141	99017	6160	147120	153150	35378
5205	39565	57556	3049	97378	77394	25773
-285	1183	1200		2756	3397	1160
829	-5340	-4571	10886	-868	34726	2062
574	872	1233	15	3670	6706	1981
107	1629	2023	43	2398	3760	283
1672	-3253	-2748	2942	-2513	1716	176
626	7369	7632	13	10444	14366	1764
1730	3384	4446	584	7513	10875	2523
9518	53083	56918	2897	84400	119144	22275

12-7 续表6

单位：万元

分 组	Classify	企业单位数（个） Number of Enterprises (unit)	亏损企业 Loss Making Enterprises	工业总产值（当年价格） Gross Industrial Output Value (At Current Prices)
文教、工美、体育和娱乐用品制造业	Manufacture of Articles For Cultural,Educational and Sports Activities	9	3	265559
石油、煤炭及其他燃料加工业	Petroleum, coal and other fuel processing industries	6	2	35176
化学原料和化学制品制造业	Manufacture of Raw Chemical Materials and Chemical Products	78	9	1846104
医药制造业	Manufacture of Medicines	66	14	2618641
化学纤维制造业	Manufacture of Chemical Fibers	4	1	256854
橡胶和塑料制品业	Manufacture of Rubber and Plastics	49	5	1178543
非金属矿物制品业	Manufacture of Non-metallic Mineral Products	185	19	3416504
黑色金属冶炼和压延加工业	Smelting and Pressing of Ferrous Metals	11	1	280167
有色金属冶炼和压延加工业	Smelting and Pressing of Non-ferrous Metals	45	6	1182641
金属制品业	Manufacture of Metal Products	112	17	1429344
通用设备制造业	Manufacture of General Purpose Machinery	98	14	2020414
专用设备制造业	Manufacture of Special Equipment	146	30	2909722
汽车制造业	Manufacture of Motor Vehicle	67	9	11611916
铁路、船舶、航空航天和其他运输设备制造业	Railways,Shipbuilding,Aerospace and Other Transportation Equipment Manufacturing Industry	97	10	5940789
电气机械和器材制造业	Manufacture of Electric Equipment and Machinery	158	23	7621335
计算机、通讯和其他电子设备制造业	Manufacture of Communication Equipment, Computers and other Electronic Equipment	123	26	11736716
仪器仪表制造业	Manufacture of Measuring Instruments and Machinery	71	12	1959019
其他制造业	Manufacture of Other Manufacturing	7	1	45390
废弃资源综合利用业	Recycling and Disposal of Waste	4		128377
金属制品、机械和设备修理业	Metal Products,Machinery and Equipment Repair Industry	9	2	62709
电力、热力生产和供应业	Production and Supply of Electric Power and Heat Power	26	8	2888446
燃气生产和供应业	Gas Mining and Supplying Industry	18	2	1861184
水的生产和供应业	Production and Supply of Water	15	7	189113

continued6

(10 000yuan)

平均用工人数（人）Average Number of Employed Persons (person)	资产总计 Total Assets	流动资产合计 Total Working Capitals	固定资产原价 Origing Value of Fixed Assets	累计折旧 Accumulative Total Depreciation
854	47348	33477	13301	5005
693	87348	46529	16751	6791
16856	2918888	1618706	1579154	715590
20225	2678755	1612906	834296	280266
830	164662	89925	160356	82155
10403	2182578	1329756	734937	180105
19106	3160273	2227061	1110701	467440
1707	243128	177602	119393	51032
7929	2731316	1310213	639441	215205
21863	2275273	1313546	1015031	447462
20130	4447634	3442476	903352	426278
28740	4890443	3305757	1106907	446649
57441	8718524	6214027	2379133	1174979
66844	12205737	7436784	3612539	1734490
47825	10647330	7277662	2982624	1234460
60787	18937457	7916586	10021026	6834364
16700	2941144	2077551	770505	339128
904	79282	50806	31703	11356
200	43706	29168	10876	1542
1224	114285	64953	24485	8487
20278	5581633	1219045	7321740	3753082
7797	2309487	536158	1244987	539241
4303	1036942	344975	708235	254171

12-7 续表7

单位：万元

分组	Classify	负债合计 Total Liabilites	流动负债合计 Total Working Liabilities
文教、工美、体育和娱乐用品制造业	Manufacture of Articles For Cultural,Educational and Sports Activities	13724	8025
石油、煤炭及其他燃料加工业	Petroleum, coal and other fuel processing industries	52271	51196
化学原料和化学制品制造业	Manufacture of Raw Chemical Materials and Chemical Products	1869223	1203654
医药制造业	Manufacture of Medicines	1261250	1043333
化学纤维制造业	Manufacture of Chemical Fibers	76077	61817
橡胶和塑料制品业	Manufacture of Rubber and Plastics	1532236	1136082
非金属矿物制品业	Manufacture of Non-metallic Mineral Products	2128842	1860876
黑色金属冶炼和压延加工业	Smelting and Pressing of Ferrous Metals	140969	135292
有色金属冶炼和压延加工业	Smelting and Pressing of Non-ferrous Metals	869938	695369
金属制品业	Manufacture of Metal Products	1720727	1314203
通用设备制造业	Manufacture of General Purpose Machinery	2574828	2406378
专用设备制造业	Manufacture of Special Equipment	2494198	2026924
汽车制造业	Manufacture of Motor Vehicle	5679751	5178279
铁路、船舶、航空航天和其他运输设备制造业	Railways,Shipbuilding,Aerospace and Other Transportation Equipment Manufacturing Industry	5844491	5012679
电气机械和器材制造业	Manufacture of Electric Equipment and Machinery	5564845	4978654
计算机、通讯和其他电子设备制造业	Manufacture of Communication Equipment, Computers and other Electronic Equipment	8063644	6077540
仪器仪表制造业	Manufacture of Measuring Instruments and Machinery	1566341	1459842
其他制造业	Manufacture of Other Manufacturing	41311	34876
废弃资源综合利用业	Recycling and Disposal of Waste	28761	27670
金属制品、机械和设备修理业	Metal Products,Machinery and Equipment Repair Industry	36297	34945
电力、热力生产和供应业	Production and Supply of Electric Power and Heat Power	4199078	3035034
燃气生产和供应业	Gas Mining and Supplying Industry	1295724	1138691
水的生产和供应业	Production and Supply of Water	792264	510250

continued7

(10 000yuan)

所有者权益合计 Total Owners' Equities	实收资本 Total Capital Hold	营业收入 Total Revenue	主营业务收入 Revenue from Principal Business	营业成本 Total Cost	税金及附加 Taxs and Other Changes
33079	14533	265386	265369	256718	360
35077	50601	62354	32919	58195	455
1049663	651404	1850581	1811637	1455263	11142
1417505	328151	2423148	2418586	1224151	22214
88585	85552	214902	213159	182109	1330
650341	455754	1015977	983972	865070	5395
1022401	530838	3436653	3406011	2992578	18504
102158	82933	556565	552192	526403	1589
1861378	506484	1019150	978795	854780	5014
553757	553270	1699316	1670326	1486130	11906
1872804	465849	2152154	2038520	1759224	13359
2387977	961064	2748439	2723528	2152577	18029
3038772	911488	11202843	10816932	10572944	75860
6361244	2408421	5655556	5553101	4780255	27069
5068082	1996677	7059495	6903246	6249417	38277
10870865	4823057	10190731	10081582	8800907	47972
1374804	398439	1977637	1961634	1559887	8664
37971	21520	44531	42815	33300	346
14944	12011	128366	127659	124485	1982
77987	60725	69277	67169	52777	446
1382555	1085288	3448693	3364339	3203514	20034
1013762	396798	1932374	1862085	1816725	6144
244679	180468	207401	189522	178257	3662

12-7 续表8

单位：万元

分 组	Classify	销售费用 Expenses for Sales	管理费用 Expenses for Management	研发费用 R&D Expenses
文教、工美、体育和娱乐用品制造业	Manufacture of Articles For Cultural,Educational and Sports Activities	2488	3180	62
石油、煤炭及其他燃料加工业	Petroleum, coal and other fuel processing industries	1043	2458	167
化学原料和化学制品制造业	Manufacture of Raw Chemical Materials and Chemical Products	49786	122070	52197
医药制造业	Manufacture of Medicines	711910	203787	40205
化学纤维制造业	Manufacture of Chemical Fibers	1132	7003	1910
橡胶和塑料制品业	Manufacture of Rubber and Plastics	34742	35068	12016
非金属矿物制品业	Manufacture of Non-metallic Mineral Products	104104	110168	19932
黑色金属冶炼和压延加工业	Smelting and Pressing of Ferrous Metals	8806	8633	972
有色金属冶炼和压延加工业	Smelting and Pressing of Non-ferrous Metals	12927	45592	43499
金属制品业	Manufacture of Metal Products	24019	92023	37817
通用设备制造业	Manufacture of General Purpose Machinery	68174	133569	55968
专用设备制造业	Manufacture of Special Equipment	145764	165438	96773
汽车制造业	Manufacture of Motor Vehicle	236844	232366	126384
铁路、船舶、航空航天和其他运输设备制造业	Railways,Shipbuilding,Aerospace and Other Transportation Equipment Manufacturing Industry	94152	316917	120567
电气机械和器材制造业	Manufacture of Electric Equipment and Machinery	375983	369938	129128
计算机、通讯和其他电子设备制造业	Manufacture of Communication Equipment, Computers and other Electronic Equipment	100789	285912	328430
仪器仪表制造业	Manufacture of Measuring Instruments and Machinery	57094	117191	71899
其他制造业	Manufacture of Other Manufacturing	2031	4103	2922
废弃资源综合利用业	Recycling and Disposal of Waste	1537	1722	
金属制品、机械和设备修理业	Metal Products,Machinery and Equipment Repair Industry	1515	9084	2795
电力、热力生产和供应业	Production and Supply of Electric Power and Heat Power	7544	89639	6275
燃气生产和供应业	Gas Mining and Supplying Industry	40186	39432	3989
水的生产和供应业	Production and Supply of Water	6535	20928	654

continued8

(10 000yuan)

财务费用 Financial cost	营业利润 Operating Profit	利润总额 Total Profits	亏损企业亏损总额 Total Loss of Deficit Enterprises	利税总额 Total Pre-tax Profits	应付职工薪酬 Salary Payable	本年应交增值税 Value Added Tax Payable
575	2004	1660	61	3092	4772	1072
264	126	252	88	1548	4343	841
43775	10547	20708	152309	65102	175825	33252
23175	167847	181658	5866	333120	287355	129248
1461	13429	13799	106	17696	10171	2566
28376	36615	37692	1817	62033	77246	18947
24589	165415	168340	10969	277679	127447	90836
2236	4989	5271	212	11481	18063	4622
5853	60768	62784	5275	85748	106276	17950
16308	8950	3040	60153	30943	220479	15998
14638	123616	127536	10736	191974	225022	51079
33974	142456	155653	61464	234554	315296	60872
-1026	349831	357644	3353	561930	985474	128425
9849	356034	369576	12025	469223	902276	72578
26491	211063	217883	80949	323055	757912	66896
13563	863739	876607	31087	1003929	688211	79350
-214	173245	180317	9360	222385	249192	33404
1416	603	2363	9	4198	7517	1489
2126	1673	1659		4591	1583	951
175	2873	3058	2109	5862	19096	2358
58789	80876	71995	32300	168518	376007	76489
19769	101030	98078	2106	118101	104153	13879
17769	-18219	-11474	21502	-4845	54949	2967

12-8 规模以上国有及国有控股工业企业主要经济指标（2019年）

单位：万元

分 组	Classify	企业单位数（个） Number of Enterprises (unit)	亏损企业 Loss Making Enterprises	工业总产值（当年价格） Gross Industrial Output Value (At Current Prices)
总计	**Total**	**305**	**61**	**31676836**
#亏损企业	Deficit Enterprises	61	61	1422416
按隶属关系分	**Grouped by Jurisdiction of Management**			
#中央企业	Central Enterprises	108	17	14447817
地方企业	Local Enterprises	107	22	13079089
按轻重工业分	**Grouped by Light Industry and Heavy Industry**			
轻工业	Light Industry	33	6	1861627
重工业	Heavy Industry	272	55	29815209
按企业规模分	**Grouped by Size of Enterprises**			
大型企业	Large-size	46	5	22735493
中型企业	Medium-size	86	18	5511178
小型企业	Small-size	169	36	3392003
微型企业	Microenterprise	4	2	38162
按工业行业大类分	**Grouped by Sector**			
煤炭开采和洗选业	Mining and Washing of Coal			
石油和天然气开采业	Extraction of Petroleum and Natural Gas			
黑色金属矿采选业	Mining and Processing of Ferrous Metal Ores			
有色金属矿采选业	Mining and Processing of Non-ferrous Metal Ores			
非金属矿采选业	Mining and Processing of Nonmetal Ores			
开采专业及辅助性活动	Mining Professional and Auxiliary Activity	2		1019320
其他采矿业	Mining of Other Ores			
农副食品加工业	Processing of Food from Agricultural Porducts	2	2	19268
食品制造业	Manufacture of Foods	8		234487
酒、饮料和精制茶制造业	Manufacture of Alcohol,Beverages and Tea	1		111912
烟草制品业	Manufacture of Tobacco	1		9472
纺织业	Manufacture of Textile	4	2	87430
纺织服装、服饰业	Textile, apparel industry			
皮革、毛皮、羽毛及其制品和制鞋业	Leather fur feathers and its products and footwear	1		20697
木材加工和木、竹、藤、棕、草制品业	Processing of Timber, Manufacture of Wood,Plato and Straw Products			

Major Economic Indicators of State-owned and State-holding Share Industrial Enterprises above Designated Size (2019)

(10 000yuan)

平均用工人数（人） Average Number of Employed Persons (person)	资产总计 Total Assets	流动资产合计 Total Working Capitals	固定资产原价 Origing Value of Fixed Assets	累计折旧 Accumulative Total Depreciation
264782	**52080983**	**30166562**	**22395411**	**11053175**
25320	5095706	1933711	2229196	828618
152995	26779485	15086465	13905727	7183476
73783	18786098	10728317	6460477	3149160
21958	2925400	1893367	1353832	625499
242824	49155583	28273195	21041579	10427676
189883	37101737	22013615	17110976	8907679
51150	9334500	5248970	3285061	1503489
23489	5586782	2860922	1999014	641858
260	57965	43056	360	148
12489	1202458	847866	711886	484792
466	54781	31253	38792	21587
3067	123600	80798	74692	37537
1293	227950	157675	49626	35168
497	37171	21696	32579	17179
4894	245067	87737	208330	77950
630	51967	32404	8761	5252

12-8 续表1

单位：万元

分组	Classify	负债合计 Total Liabilites	流动负债合计 Total Working Liabilities
总计	**Total**	**30270742**	**25573751**
#亏损企业	Deficit Enterprises	4380860	3563207
按隶属关系分	**Grouped by Jurisdiction of Management**		
#中央企业	Central Enterprises	14081514	11729649
地方企业	Local Enterprises	11832946	10331980
按轻重工业分	**Grouped by Light Industry and Heavy Industry**		
轻工业	Light Industry	1890596	1358399
重工业	Heavy Industry	28380145	24215352
按企业规模分	**Grouped by Size of Enterprises**		
大型企业	Large-size	21340859	18055155
中型企业	Medium-size	4976259	4044023
小型企业	Small-size	3918359	3471945
微型企业	Microenterprise	35265	2628
按工业行业大类分	**Grouped by Sector**		
煤炭开采和洗选业	Mining and Washing of Coal		
石油和天然气开采业	Extraction of Petroleum and Natural Gas		
黑色金属矿采选业	Mining and Processing of Ferrous Metal Ores		
有色金属矿采选业	Mining and Processing of Non-ferrous Metal Ores		
非金属矿采选业	Mining and Processing of Nonmetal Ores		
开采专业及辅助性活动	Mining Professional and Auxiliary Activity	490366	480023
其他采矿业	Mining of Other Ores		
农副食品加工业	Processing of Food from Agricultural Porducts	86725	85119
食品制造业	Manufacture of Foods	61286	60370
酒、饮料和精制茶制造业	Manufacture of Alcohol,Beverages and Tea	140045	92086
烟草制品业	Manufacture of Tobacco	2320	2320
纺织业	Manufacture of Textile	157515	65353
纺织服装、服饰业	Textile, apparel industry		
皮革、毛皮、羽毛及其制品和制鞋业	Leather fur feathers and its products and footwear	17004	10577
木材加工和木、竹、藤、棕、草制品业	Processing of Timber, Manufacture of Wood,Plato and Straw Products		

continued1

(10 000yuan)

所有者权益合计 Total Owners' Equities	实收资本 Total Capital Hold	营业收入 Total Revenue	主营业务收入 Revenue from Principal Business	营业成本 Total Cost	税金及附加 Taxs and Other Changes
21787569	**9112534**	**32181518**	**31279469**	**28551973**	**175493**
706578	1594826	1433291	1406625	1333477	13992
12689702	5505049	14597822	14298120	12950952	85798
6938749	2544193	13237532	12757043	11876080	57627
1020401	505459	1954839	1905359	1595950	19498
20767167	8607075	30226679	29374110	26956023	155995
15760877	5762273	23133174	22416268	20637349	129396
4358240	2177641	5484758	5375827	4789436	28020
1668422	1170921	3529985	3453774	3096253	18053
30	1700	33601	33601	28936	24
712092	459650	863906	851161	782936	5705
-31944	9100	16860	16462	13414	41
62314	30100	236891	232711	189907	1127
87906	28790	262998	262835	192818	8985
34851	27400	9619	9472	4620	397
87552	20814	118442	107670	115993	1322
34963	31500	22373	22373	18593	68

12-8 续表2

单位：万元

分组	Classify	销售费用 Expenses for Sales	管理费用 Expenses for Management	研发费用 R&D Expenses
总计	**Total**	**689185**	**1349184**	**615887**
#亏损企业	Deficit Enterprises	39462	141219	28005
按隶属关系分	**Grouped by Jurisdiction of Management**			
#中央企业	Central Enterprises	268221	788080	338137
地方企业	Local Enterprises	292146	385023	187409
按轻重工业分	**Grouped by Light Industry and Heavy Industry**			
轻工业	Light Industry	81610	89905	25085
重工业	Heavy Industry	607575	1259279	590802
按企业规模分	**Grouped by Size of Enterprises**			
大型企业	Large-size	514232	941635	422842
中型企业	Medium-size	110552	251338	117132
小型企业	Small-size	63901	154878	75131
微型企业	Microenterprise	500	1333	783
按工业行业大类分	**Grouped by Sector**			
煤炭开采和洗选业	Mining and Washing of Coal			
石油和天然气开采业	Extraction of Petroleum and Natural Gas			
黑色金属矿采选业	Mining and Processing of Ferrous Metal Ores			
有色金属矿采选业	Mining and Processing of Non-ferrous Metal Ores			
非金属矿采选业	Mining and Processing of Nonmetal Ores			
开采专业及辅助性活动	Mining Professional and Auxiliary Activity	3507	21391	29206
其他采矿业	Mining of Other Ores			
农副食品加工业	Processing of Food from Agricultural Porducts	3414	2211	
食品制造业	Manufacture of Foods	11325	17077	
酒、饮料和精制茶制造业	Manufacture of Alcohol,Beverages and Tea	28653	3307	
烟草制品业	Manufacture of Tobacco	950	2758	
纺织业	Manufacture of Textile	1396	5581	2857
纺织服装、服饰业	Textile, apparel industry			
皮革、毛皮、羽毛及其制品和制鞋业	Leather fur feathers and its products and footwear	443	416	1253
木材加工和木、竹、藤、棕、草制品业	Processing of Timber, Manufacture of Wood,Plato and Straw Products			

continued2

(10 000yuan)

财务费用 Financial cost	营业利润 Operating Profit	利润总额 Total Profits	亏损企业亏损总额 Total Loss of Deficit Enterprises	利税总额 Total Pre-tax Profits	应付职工薪酬 Salary Payable	本年应交增值税 Value Added Tax Payable
174348	**1033800**	**1059338**	**412102**	**1733422**	**4004823**	**498591**
58283	-409155	-412102	412102	-385670	238694	12440
61047	420352	413680	271102	734606	2333614	235128
65082	477091	501612	68342	747526	1249837	188287
20913	121525	123625	15232	190129	225076	47006
153435	912275	935713	396870	1543293	3779746	451585
81353	932427	934330	85164	1421578	3108348	357853
46841	16639	25616	252311	131491	641872	77856
44508	85669	100302	72917	181848	254340	63494
1646	-936	-910	1710	-1496	263	-611
-5839	35619	34029		42767	273570	3033
26	-2202	-1900	1900	-1850	2448	9
-22	17862	17766		24308	27660	5415
-2499	32488	32870		51710	18836	9855
-285	1183	1200		2756	3397	1160
154	-8036	-7559	10567	-5591	29648	646
51	1685	2066		2245	2995	111

12-8 续表3

单位：万元

分　组	Classify	企业单位数（个）Number of Enterprises (unit)	亏损企业 Loss Making Enterprises	工业总产值（当年价格）Gross Industrial Output Value (At Current Prices)
家具制造业	Manufacture of Furniture			
造纸和纸制品业	Manufacture of Paper and Paper Products			
印刷和记录媒介复制业	Printing,Reproduction of Recording Media	5	1	346962
文教、工美、体育和娱乐用品制造业	Manufacture of Articles For Cultural,Educational and Sports Activities	1		2583
石油、煤炭及其他燃料加工业	Petroleum, coal and other fuel processing industries			
化学原料和化学制品制造业	Manufacture of Raw Chemical Materials and Chemical Products	19	4	947450
医药制造业	Manufacture of Medicines	3		76293
化学纤维制造业	Manufacture of Chemical Fibers	2		170848
橡胶和塑料制品业	Manufacture of Rubber and Plastics	5		906825
非金属矿物制品业	Manufacture of Non-metallic Mineral Products	13		412564
黑色金属冶炼和压延加工业	Smelting and Pressing of Ferrous Metals	2		188972
有色金属冶炼和压延加工业	Smelting and Pressing of Non-ferrous Metals	15	3	844105
金属制品业	Manufacture of Metal Products	13	3	456320
通用设备制造业	Manufacture of General Purpose Machinery	22	5	1334917
专用设备制造业	Manufacture of Special Equipment	31	7	1050686
汽车制造业	Manufacture of Motor Vehicle	19	3	8491181
铁路、船舶、航空航天和其他运输设备制造业	Railways,Shipbuilding,Aerospace and Other Transportation Equipment Manufacturing Industry	35	4	5052872
电气机械和器材制造业	Manufacture of Electric Equipment and Machinery	22	6	3093864
计算机、通讯和其他电子设备制造业	Manufacture of Communication Equipment, Computers and other Electronic Equipment	31	6	1157293
仪器仪表制造业	Manufacture of Measuring Instruments and Machinery	11	3	1100275
其他制造业	Manufacture of Other Manufacturing			
废弃资源综合利用业	Recycling and Disposal of Waste	1		6750
金属制品、机械和设备修理业	Metal Products,Machinery and Equipment Repair Industry	2		22603
电力、热力生产和供应业	Production and Supply of Electric Power and Heat Power	16	5	2764714
燃气生产和供应业	Gas Mining and Supplying Industry	8	2	1583801
水的生产和供应业	Production and Supply of Water	10	5	162375

continued3

(10 000yuan)

平均用工人数（人） Average Number of Employed Persons (person)	资产总计 Total Assets	流动资产合计 Total Working Capitals	固定资产原价 Origing Value of Fixed Assets	累计折旧 Accumulative Total Depreciation
3775	506520	315156	370084	245394
110	2367	2010	363	173
11815	1320253	691267	1011778	518298
949	106519	69622	50281	19255
524	78192	55979	82252	53604
7305	1927030	1172598	642186	145632
2515	525046	376950	161359	53121
896	182099	133441	104414	46337
4670	2364927	1059314	523584	175450
13020	1506647	804274	765373	359758
11006	3655133	2861284	661861	293215
13795	2420688	1632866	593298	277891
26654	5524396	4519011	1150968	693313
59248	11039211	6693899	3295994	1635816
24424	5259164	3815270	1658660	849705
21225	4193910	1932691	890895	346947
9268	1812982	1189469	561407	255557
102	13406	1581	9419	819
737	44748	27071	5192	2118
19217	4739494	805573	6874027	3653467
6282	2048153	429006	1150805	493964
3909	867107	318805	706546	253877

12-8 续表4

单位：万元

分组	Classify	负债合计 Total Liabilites	流动负债合计 Total Working Liabilities
家具制造业	Manufacture of Furniture		
造纸和纸制品业	Manufacture of Paper and Paper Products		
印刷和记录媒介复制业	Printing,Reproduction of Recording Media	163285	156710
文教、工美、体育和娱乐用品制造业	Manufacture of Articles For Cultural,Educational and Sports Activities	443	443
石油、煤炭及其他燃料加工业	Petroleum, coal and other fuel processing industries		
化学原料和化学制品制造业	Manufacture of Raw Chemical Materials and Chemical Products	1011471	772597
医药制造业	Manufacture of Medicines	39053	38996
化学纤维制造业	Manufacture of Chemical Fibers	9781	9511
橡胶和塑料制品业	Manufacture of Rubber and Plastics	1391216	1018549
非金属矿物制品业	Manufacture of Non-metallic Mineral Products	357411	337190
黑色金属冶炼和压延加工业	Smelting and Pressing of Ferrous Metals	111709	109115
有色金属冶炼和压延加工业	Smelting and Pressing of Non-ferrous Metals	655926	521851
金属制品业	Manufacture of Metal Products	1186328	821669
通用设备制造业	Manufacture of General Purpose Machinery	2198547	2063154
专用设备制造业	Manufacture of Special Equipment	1217133	992111
汽车制造业	Manufacture of Motor Vehicle	3628660	3486483
铁路、船舶、航空航天和其他运输设备制造业	Railways,Shipbuilding,Aerospace and Other Transportation Equipment Manufacturing Industry	5449077	4662429
电气机械和器材制造业	Manufacture of Electric Equipment and Machinery	2320608	2064620
计算机、通讯和其他电子设备制造业	Manufacture of Communication Equipment, Computers and other Electronic Equipment	3175486	2652098
仪器仪表制造业	Manufacture of Measuring Instruments and Machinery	1004941	925629
其他制造业	Manufacture of Other Manufacturing		
废弃资源综合利用业	Recycling and Disposal of Waste	7904	7904
金属制品、机械和设备修理业	Metal Products,Machinery and Equipment Repair Industry	14912	14659
电力、热力生产和供应业	Production and Supply of Electric Power and Heat Power	3504343	2612144
燃气生产和供应业	Gas Mining and Supplying Industry	1166907	1024582
水的生产和供应业	Production and Supply of Water	700340	485458

continued4

(10 000yuan)

所有者权益合计 Total Owners' Equities	实收资本 Total Capital Hold	营业收入 Total Revenue	主营业务收入 Revenue from Principal Business	营业成本 Total Cost	税金及附加 Taxs and Other Changes
343235	167462	412439	408774	322945	3182
1924	200	2842	2842	1825	31
308782	310735	876681	857201	743657	6258
67466	19590	74687	74621	50652	704
68411	64052	136755	135476	115565	645
535814	384025	784845	753471	674944	4359
167635	124744	364287	363005	324819	1850
70390	64049	423178	418896	400541	1322
1709001	432872	686559	661380	565472	3613
320319	375188	711557	688929	603129	3570
1456586	217666	1538431	1428315	1288187	9462
1195287	540558	1047121	1035010	869361	8393
1895735	604123	8106424	7862475	7421911	27158
5590133	2125602	5002808	4905305	4320344	22601
2924153	903779	2860532	2742996	2693521	23044
1018423	511892	1344240	1331410	1063590	9449
808041	202552	1167150	1155128	970607	3906
5501	5000	6756	6750	3217	159
29836	12044	22564	22564	18338	177
1235151	1007993	3269532	3185211	3081649	19383
881246	323297	1632738	1576098	1546092	5341
166766	107759	178305	160929	153326	3241

12-8 续表5

单位：万元

分 组	Classify	销售费用 Expenses for Sales	管理费用 Expenses for Management	研发费用 R&D Expenses
家具制造业	Manufacture of Furniture			
造纸和纸制品业	Manufacture of Paper and Paper Products			
印刷和记录媒介复制业	Printing,Reproduction of Recording Media	10185	32328	5809
文教、工美、体育和娱乐用品制造业	Manufacture of Articles For Cultural,Educational and Sports Activities		531	
石油、煤炭及其他燃料加工业	Petroleum, coal and other fuel processing industries			
化学原料和化学制品制造业	Manufacture of Raw Chemical Materials and Chemical Products	18557	76588	28021
医药制造业	Manufacture of Medicines	6440	4283	1731
化学纤维制造业	Manufacture of Chemical Fibers	607	4096	1910
橡胶和塑料制品业	Manufacture of Rubber and Plastics	25947	22935	11055
非金属矿物制品业	Manufacture of Non-metallic Mineral Products	3003	9643	5852
黑色金属冶炼和压延加工业	Smelting and Pressing of Ferrous Metals	6410	5732	386
有色金属冶炼和压延加工业	Smelting and Pressing of Non-ferrous Metals	6459	31867	36897
金属制品业	Manufacture of Metal Products	4640	51272	30709
通用设备制造业	Manufacture of General Purpose Machinery	38825	89696	39643
专用设备制造业	Manufacture of Special Equipment	43788	67401	45971
汽车制造业	Manufacture of Motor Vehicle	186936	107430	94786
铁路、船舶、航空航天和其他运输设备制造业	Railways,Shipbuilding,Aerospace and Other Transportation Equipment Manufacturing Industry	71371	260453	95994
电气机械和器材制造业	Manufacture of Electric Equipment and Machinery	138027	201356	78324
计算机、通讯和其他电子设备制造业	Manufacture of Communication Equipment, Computers and other Electronic Equipment	28191	129482	48208
仪器仪表制造业	Manufacture of Measuring Instruments and Machinery	11323	68892	47749
其他制造业	Manufacture of Other Manufacturing			
废弃资源综合利用业	Recycling and Disposal of Waste	469	1246	
金属制品、机械和设备修理业	Metal Products,Machinery and Equipment Repair Industry	14	3710	
电力、热力生产和供应业	Production and Supply of Electric Power and Heat Power	760	76790	5640
燃气生产和供应业	Gas Mining and Supplying Industry	31283	31109	3889
水的生产和供应业	Production and Supply of Water	6267	19601	

continued5

(10 000yuan)

财务费用 Financial cost	营业利润 Operating Profit	利润总额 Total Profits	亏损企业亏损总额 Total Loss of Deficit Enterprises	利税总额 Total Pre-tax Profits	应付职工薪酬 Salary Payable	本年应交增值税 Value Added Tax Payable
1350	36810	36693	382	55571	75443	15696
	455	280		557	815	247
21064	-118637	-111307	151462	-85617	130087	19432
-60	10960	11071		15280	8476	3506
-71	11722	11671		14080	6840	1764
25270	21654	22360		41788	62172	15069
5251	14026	13148		25426	26205	10427
1648	4205	4280		8952	13630	3350
1307	48232	48930	3499	67204	79524	14661
10084	-13296	-19612	50269	-11603	159655	4439
7840	82679	85083	6364	128944	153542	34400
10806	-8949	696	42997	29907	171305	20817
-22574	283131	288026	1579	416993	718743	101810
3717	274780	284241	10672	358520	825355	51679
2205	79282	80292	61083	160531	327995	57195
39700	22039	32010	20351	62553	198717	21094
-1150	74762	77196	3614	92916	164664	11813
636	1031	1028		2128	989	941
-26	520	663		2123	12678	1282
44992	57937	39531	27870	135803	366646	76889
17161	89426	85433	2106	101285	90026	10510
13616	-17565	-10846	17389	-6261	52761	1344

12-9 规模以上外商及港澳台商投资工业企业主要经济指标（2019年）

单位：万元

分 组	Classify	企业单位数（个） Number of Enterprises (unit)	亏损企业 Loss Making Enterprises	工业总产值（当年价格） Gross Industrial Output Value (At Current Prices)
总计	**Total**	**114**	**21**	**13580848**
#亏损企业	Deficit Enterprises	21	21	399921
按登记注册类型分组	**Grouped by Type of Registration**			
港澳台商投资	Enterprises with Funds from Hong Kong, Macao &Taiwan	22	4	2909295
与港澳台商合资经营	Cooperative Enterprises	13	3	2527046
与港澳台商合作经营	Joint-venture Enterprises	1	1	2361
港澳台商独资	Enterprises with Sole Investment	7		357755
港澳台商投资股份有限公司	Share-holding Corporations Ltd. With their Investment			
其他港澳台投资	Other	1		22132
外商投资	Foreign Funded Enterprises	92	17	10671553
中外合资经营	Joint-venture Enterprises	52	11	2751321
中外合作经营	Cooperation Enterprises			
外资企业	Foreign Funded Enterprises	38	6	7070053
外商投资股份有限公司	Share-holding Corporations Ltd. With Foreign Funds	1		842128
其他外商投资	Other	1		8051
按轻重工业分	**Grouped by Light Industry and Heavy Industry**			
轻工业	Light Industry	27	5	3032196
重工业	Heavy Industry	87	16	10548652
按企业规模分	**Grouped by Size of Enterprises**			
大型企业	Large-size	12	1	9833763
中型企业	Medium-size	26	3	1975488
小型企业	Small-size	73	17	1736640
微型企业	Microenterprise	3		34957
按工业行业大类分	**Grouped by Sector**			
煤炭开采和洗选业	Mining and Washing of Coal			
石油和天然气开采业	Extraction of Petroleum and Natural Gas			
黑色金属矿采选业	Mining and Processing of Ferrous Metal Ores			
有色金属矿采选业	Mining and Processing of Non-ferrous Metal Ores			
非金属矿采选业	Mining and Processing of Nonmetal Ores			
开采专业及辅助性活动	Mining Professional and Auxiliary Activity			
其他采矿业	Mining of Other Ores			

Major Economic Indicators of Foreign,Hong Kong,Macao and Taiwan Invested Industrial Enterprises above Designated Size (2019)

(10 000 yuan)

平均用工人数（人） Average Number of Employed Persons (person)	资产总计 Total Assets	流动资产合计 Total Working Capitals	固定资产原价 Origing Value of Fixed Assets	累计折旧 Accumulative Total Depreciation
68146	**16640540**	**6555417**	**12145949**	**7742514**
5018	536677	278558	316124	161214
28671	2762371	1413316	1183844	505154
25416	2522464	1258307	1029713	412163
59	1637	1440	928	731
2940	199464	130527	131597	78084
256	38806	23043	21607	14177
39475	13878169	5142101	10962105	7237359
15950	3361849	1949339	1497962	637152
20497	9825554	2798328	9195316	6560516
2898	659689	373835	257260	36713
130	31077	20599	11568	2979
15862	2732379	1394848	1463548	583014
52284	13908162	5160569	10682401	7159499
45135	12742141	4135068	10158313	6854321
13790	1892102	1289843	829431	387258
9181	1997356	1121737	1157832	500804
40	8941	8769	373	130

12-9 续表1

单位：万元

分组	Classify	负债合计 Total Liabilites	流动负债合计 Total Working Liabilities
总计	**Total**	**6974830**	**5166239**
#亏损企业	Deficit Enterprises	356977	321485
按登记注册类型分组	**Grouped by Type of Registration**		
港澳台商投资	Enterprises with Funds from Hong Kong, Macao &Taiwan	1791443	1492624
与港澳台商合资经营	Cooperative Enterprises	1693034	1397826
与港澳台商合作经营	Joint-venture Enterprises	134	134
港澳台商独资	Enterprises with Sole Investment	87206	83594
港澳台商投资股份有限公司	Share-holding Corporations Ltd. With their Investment		
其他港澳台投资	Other	11070	11070
外商投资	Foreign Funded Enterprises	5183386	3673615
中外合资经营	Joint-venture Enterprises	2023577	1856631
中外合作经营	Cooperation Enterprises		
外资企业	Foreign Funded Enterprises	2775716	1489017
外商投资股份有限公司	Share-holding Corporations Ltd. With Foreign Funds	372437	316312
其他外商投资	Other	11656	11656
按轻重工业分	**Grouped by Light Industry and Heavy Industry**		
轻工业	Light Industry	1776667	1548899
重工业	Heavy Industry	5198163	3617340
按企业规模分	**Grouped by Size of Enterprises**		
大型企业	Large-size	4934320	3415098
中型企业	Medium-size	998702	927360
小型企业	Small-size	1036300	818273
微型企业	Microenterprise	5507	5507
按工业行业大类分	**Grouped by Sector**		
煤炭开采和洗选业	Mining and Washing of Coal		
石油和天然气开采业	Extraction of Petroleum and Natural Gas		
黑色金属矿采选业	Mining and Processing of Ferrous Metal Ores		
有色金属矿采选业	Mining and Processing of Non-ferrous Metal Ores		
非金属矿采选业	Mining and Processing of Nonmetal Ores		
开采专业及辅助性活动	Mining Professional and Auxiliary Activity		
其他采矿业	Mining of Other Ores		

continued 1

(10 000 yuan)

所有者权益合计 Total Owners' Equities	实收资本 Total Capital Hold	营业收入 Total Revenue	主营业务收入 Revenue from Principal Business	营业成本 Total Cost	税金及附加 Taxs and Other Changes
9665710	**4903006**	**11871963**	**11619129**	**10368518**	**98154**
179700	327340	374643	364955	311573	3150
970928	272368	2919692	2788570	2980212	53220
829429	185606	2559596	2433299	2717078	45343
1503	714	2172	2165	1946	9
112259	59510	339137	334319	246081	7630
27736	26539	18787	18787	15106	238
8694782	4630639	8952272	8830559	7388307	44933
1338271	793647	2832143	2741114	2378092	10707
7049838	3806002	5149804	5119464	4384007	29273
287252	28432	962275	962275	621761	4944
19421	2559	8051	7707	4447	9
955712	475890	3159800	3135396	2367873	19763
8709998	4427116	8712163	8483733	8000645	78391
7807821	3663237	8103257	7887585	7330539	74485
893400	552382	1936432	1911461	1523536	14779
961055	684715	1799375	1787184	1484529	8844
3434	2672	32900	32900	29916	46

12-9 续表2

单位：万元

分 组	Classify	销售费用 Expenses for Sales	管理费用 Expenses for Management	研发费用 R&D Expenses
总计	**Total**	**539008**	**414383**	**208559**
#亏损企业	Deficit Enterprises	45361	25027	7290
按登记注册类型分组	**Grouped by Type of Registration**			
港澳台商投资	Enterprises with Funds from Hong Kong, Macao &Taiwan	65887	117261	28468
与港澳台商合资经营	Cooperative Enterprises	21291	101841	23784
与港澳台商合作经营	Joint-venture Enterprises	105	131	
港澳台商独资	Enterprises with Sole Investment	43470	14651	3844
港澳台商投资股份有限公司	Share-holding Corporations Ltd. With their Investment			
其他港澳台投资	Other	1022	637	840
外商投资	Foreign Funded Enterprises	473121	297123	180092
中外合资经营	Joint-venture Enterprises	193946	98815	30035
中外合作经营	Cooperation Enterprises			
外资企业	Foreign Funded Enterprises	116527	117725	149237
外商投资股份有限公司	Share-holding Corporations Ltd. With Foreign Funds	162608	79869	
其他外商投资	Other	40	715	819
按轻重工业分	**Grouped by Light Industry and Heavy Industry**			
轻工业	Light Industry	423008	151839	6487
重工业	Heavy Industry	116000	262545	202073
按企业规模分	**Grouped by Size of Enterprises**			
大型企业	Large-size	327472	261653	160081
中型企业	Medium-size	143660	68547	28814
小型企业	Small-size	67161	83031	19470
微型企业	Microenterprise	716	1152	195
按工业行业大类分	**Grouped by Sector**			
煤炭开采和洗选业	Mining and Washing of Coal			
石油和天然气开采业	Extraction of Petroleum and Natural Gas			
黑色金属矿采选业	Mining and Processing of Ferrous Metal Ores			
有色金属矿采选业	Mining and Processing of Non-ferrous Metal Ores			
非金属矿采选业	Mining and Processing of Nonmetal Ores			
开采专业及辅助性活动	Mining Professional and Auxiliary Activity			
其他采矿业	Mining of Other Ores			

continued 2

(10 000 yuan)

财务费用 Financial cost	营业利润 Operating Profit	利润总额 Total Profits	亏损企业亏损总额 Total Loss of Deficit Enterprises	利税总额 Total Pre-tax Profits	应付职工薪酬 Salary Payable	本年应交增值税 Value Added Tax Payable
20032	**773516**	**815362**	**34489**	**1036070**	**941819**	**122555**
7503	-34191	-34489	34489	-23083	58065	8256
18738	51081	52985	972	122352	265056	16147
17634	27431	29196	963	85014	225039	10476
-10	-9	-9	9	62	424	62
636	22775	22886		35732	36890	5216
479	885	912		1544	2704	393
1294	722435	762377	33516	913718	676763	106408
20327	177426	195637	23303	245353	209710	39010
-31566	499251	510365	10213	573478	339723	33840
12438	43783	54343		92739	126454	33452
95	1975	2032		2148	876	106
38834	124519	167930	6937	259176	274969	71483
-18802	648997	647432	27552	776894	666850	51072
-5628	499127	534150	1617	676355	647256	67721
11149	166545	166637	4903	206895	182263	25479
14406	107074	113785	27968	151985	112027	29356
105	770	790		836	272	

12-9 续表3

单位：万元

分　组	Classify	企业单位数（个） Number of Enterprises (unit)	亏损企业 Loss Making Enterprises	工业总产值（当年价格） Gross Industrial Output Value (At Current Prices)
农副食品加工业	Processing of Food from Agricultural Porducts			
食品制造业	Manufacture of Foods	7	2	784759
酒、饮料和精制茶制造业	Manufacture of Alcohol,Beverages and Tea	6	1	441600
烟草制品业	Manufacture of Tobacco			
纺织业	Manufacture of Textile			
纺织服装、服饰业	Textile, apparel industry			
皮革、毛皮、羽毛及其制品和制鞋业	Leather fur feathers and its products and footwear			
木材加工和木、竹、藤、棕、草制品业	Processing of Timber,Manufacture of Wood,Plam and Straw Products			
家具制造业	Manufacture of Furniture			
造纸和纸制品业	Manufacture of Paper and Paper Products	1		12392
印刷和记录媒介复制业	Printing,Reproduction of Recording Media	2		125915
文教、工美、体育和娱乐用品制造业	Manufacture of Articles For Cultural,Educational and Sports Activities			
石油、煤炭及其他燃料加工业	Petroleum, coal and other fuel processing industries	1		9882
化学原料和化学制品制造业	Manufacture of Raw Chemical Materials and Chemical Products	7	1	148621
医药制造业	Manufacture of Medicines	4	1	930521
化学纤维制造业	Manufacture of Chemical Fibers	2		153838
橡胶和塑料制品业	Manufacture of Rubber and Plastics	1	1	1072
非金属矿物制品业	Manufacture of Non-metallic Mineral Products	7	2	189086
黑色金属冶炼和压延加工业	Smelting and Pressing of Ferrous Metals	1		4610
有色金属冶炼和压延加工业	Smelting and Pressing of Non-ferrous Metals	5	2	39738
金属制品业	Manufacture of Metal Products	4	1	56909
通用设备制造业	Manufacture of General Purpose Machinery	7	2	146506
专用设备制造业	Manufacture of Special Equipment	9		222063
汽车制造业	Manufacture of Motor Vehicle	10	2	2902274
铁路、船舶、航空航天和其他运输设备制造业	Railways,Shipbuilding,Aerospace and Other Transportation Equipment Manufacturing Industry	9		188681
电气机械和器材制造业	Manufacture of Electric Equipment and Machinery	9	3	897591
计算机、通讯和其他电子设备制造业	Manufacture of Communication Equipment, Computers and other Electronic Equipment	14		5777875
仪器仪表制造业	Manufacture of Measuring Instruments and Machinery	3	1	100665
其他制造业	Manufacture of Other Manufacturing	1	1	2361
废弃资源综合利用业	Recycling and Disposal of Waste			
金属制品、机械和设备修理业	Metal Products,Machinery and Equipment Repair Industry	3	1	14479
电力、热力生产和供应业	Production and Supply of Electric Power and Heat Power			
燃气生产和供应业	Gas Mining and Supplying Industry	1		429412
水的生产和供应业	Production and Supply of Water			

continued 3

(10 000 yuan)

平均用工人数（人）Average Number of Employed Persons (person)	资产总计 Total Assets	流动资产合计 Total Working Capitals	固定资产原价 Origing Value of Fixed Assets	累计折旧 Accumulative Total Depreciation
5112	347900	169806	211243	93564
3458	703508	354417	365530	212368
179	8560	4941	4876	1898
158	32990	10967	14706	5631
396	45456	14767	2047	951
501	427251	125529	407466	137924
5020	871686	451372	364439	78505
380	125654	62878	136869	78465
165	6632	2947	2217	1544
1382	296247	184927	183170	96563
11	4399	4350	79	32
466	88955	50925	37314	10392
749	78837	44639	56639	25844
1342	146094	104683	78642	56511
1973	325850	248680	96180	50298
26773	2794283	1450521	1167731	464335
1675	297602	260117	59820	43215
2955	934534	573964	426800	155401
11985	8314748	2096757	8146309	6119343
705	159056	144759	24961	15755
59	1637	1440	928	731
168	23607	13860	9742	3416
2534	605056	178171	348244	89828

12-9 续表4

单位：万元

分　组	Classify	负债合计 Total Liabilites	流动负债合计 Total Working Liabilities
农副食品加工业	Processing of Food from Agricultural Porducts		
食品制造业	Manufacture of Foods	206007	199242
酒、饮料和精制茶制造业	Manufacture of Alcohol,Beverages and Tea	454306	410274
烟草制品业	Manufacture of Tobacco		
纺织业	Manufacture of Textile		
纺织服装、服饰业	Textile, apparel industry		
皮革、毛皮、羽毛及其制品和制鞋业	Leather fur feathers and its products and footwear		
木材加工和木、竹、藤、棕、草制品业	Processing of Timber,Manufacture of Wood,Plam and Straw Products		
家具制造业	Manufacture of Furniture		
造纸和纸制品业	Manufacture of Paper and Paper Products	4440	4269
印刷和记录媒介复制业	Printing,Reproduction of Recording Media	20399	20399
文教、工美、体育和娱乐用品制造业	Manufacture of Articles For Cultural,Educational and Sports Activities		
石油、煤炭及其他燃料加工业	Petroleum, coal and other fuel processing industries	25228	25198
化学原料和化学制品制造业	Manufacture of Raw Chemical Materials and Chemical Products	206257	78055
医药制造业	Manufacture of Medicines	501246	389545
化学纤维制造业	Manufacture of Chemical Fibers	72276	58286
橡胶和塑料制品业	Manufacture of Rubber and Plastics	5076	3223
非金属矿物制品业	Manufacture of Non-metallic Mineral Products	178765	154491
黑色金属冶炼和压延加工业	Smelting and Pressing of Ferrous Metals	2224	2224
有色金属冶炼和压延加工业	Smelting and Pressing of Non-ferrous Metals	60374	38759
金属制品业	Manufacture of Metal Products	57682	57614
通用设备制造业	Manufacture of General Purpose Machinery	38296	38289
专用设备制造业	Manufacture of Special Equipment	123893	111292
汽车制造业	Manufacture of Motor Vehicle	1828396	1517588
铁路、船舶、航空航天和其他运输设备制造业	Railways,Shipbuilding,Aerospace and Other Transportation Equipment Manufacturing Industry	97615	95303
电气机械和器材制造业	Manufacture of Electric Equipment and Machinery	665732	606818
计算机、通讯和其他电子设备制造业	Manufacture of Communication Equipment, Computers and other Electronic Equipment	1921737	864600
仪器仪表制造业	Manufacture of Measuring Instruments and Machinery	42297	41697
其他制造业	Manufacture of Other Manufacturing	134	134
废弃资源综合利用业	Recycling and Disposal of Waste		
金属制品、机械和设备修理业	Metal Products,Machinery and Equipment Repair Industry	7198	6849
电力、热力生产和供应业	Production and Supply of Electric Power and Heat Power		
燃气生产和供应业	Gas Mining and Supplying Industry	455251	442090
水的生产和供应业	Production and Supply of Water		

continued 4

(10 000 yuan)

所有者权益合计 Total Owners' Equities	实收资本 Total Capital Hold	营业收入 Total Revenue	主营业务收入 Revenue from Principal Business	营业成本 Total Cost	税金及附加 Taxs and Other Changes
141893	82817	672784	664696	534435	9286
249202	85521	513789	501567	387873	2593
4119	2000	10903	10802	9771	21
12591	4660	123017	122885	118982	102
20228	33660	8599	8270	7898	312
220994	171349	209258	209255	162775	1324
370440	76747	1034239	1030843	656173	6375
53378	45800	136414	135950	110074	770
1556	1030	2302	2302	1729	20
117481	54255	191705	188112	151303	1358
2174	1266	4610	4610	4101	4
28581	33732	38149	36951	34500	224
21155	22137	81081	80717	72607	768
107798	92332	140705	140477	121712	798
201957	73455	236634	234863	184100	1500
965887	263550	2927674	2784487	3015159	47405
199986	61608	165554	164827	121973	1325
268802	332887	934805	932959	769774	2239
6393011	3325597	3852715	3835939	3354530	19548
116759	14538	100636	99253	59829	799
1503	714	2172	2165	1946	9
16410	23354	18753	16645	15193	52
149805	100000	465468	410556	472084	1325

12-9 续表5

单位：万元

分 组	Classify	销售费用 Expenses for Sales	管理费用 Expenses for Management	研发费用 R&D Expenses
农副食品加工业	Processing of Food from Agricultural Porducts			
食品制造业	Manufacture of Foods	66623	22103	575
酒、饮料和精制茶制造业	Manufacture of Alcohol,Beverages and Tea	106233	14591	
烟草制品业	Manufacture of Tobacco			
纺织业	Manufacture of Textile			
纺织服装、服饰业	Textile, apparel industry			
皮革、毛皮、羽毛及其制品和制鞋业	Leather fur feathers and its products and footwear			
木材加工和木、竹、藤、棕、草制品业	Processing of Timber,Manufacture of Wood,Plam and Straw Products			
家具制造业	Manufacture of Furniture			
造纸和纸制品业	Manufacture of Paper and Paper Products	232	225	
印刷和记录媒介复制业	Printing,Reproduction of Recording Media	1695	853	
文教、工美、体育和娱乐用品制造业	Manufacture of Articles For Cultural,Educational and Sports Activities			
石油、煤炭及其他燃料加工业	Petroleum, coal and other fuel processing industries	77	92	
化学原料和化学制品制造业	Manufacture of Raw Chemical Materials and Chemical Products	5182	8203	1100
医药制造业	Manufacture of Medicines	180535	91684	1267
化学纤维制造业	Manufacture of Chemical Fibers	816	5409	
橡胶和塑料制品业	Manufacture of Rubber and Plastics	179	431	
非金属矿物制品业	Manufacture of Non-metallic Mineral Products	996	7992	3243
黑色金属冶炼和压延加工业	Smelting and Pressing of Ferrous Metals	90	98	
有色金属冶炼和压延加工业	Smelting and Pressing of Non-ferrous Metals	1591	3197	1012
金属制品业	Manufacture of Metal Products	840	4538	647
通用设备制造业	Manufacture of General Purpose Machinery	6396	5223	2824
专用设备制造业	Manufacture of Special Equipment	7612	16884	6357
汽车制造业	Manufacture of Motor Vehicle	41820	108120	26945
铁路、船舶、航空航天和其他运输设备制造业	Railways,Shipbuilding,Aerospace and Other Transportation Equipment Manufacturing Industry	5513	8864	8022
电气机械和器材制造业	Manufacture of Electric Equipment and Machinery	81335	35341	5632
计算机、通讯和其他电子设备制造业	Manufacture of Communication Equipment, Computers and other Electronic Equipment	7146	56440	149604
仪器仪表制造业	Manufacture of Measuring Instruments and Machinery	6940	4873	87
其他制造业	Manufacture of Other Manufacturing	105	131	
废弃资源综合利用业	Recycling and Disposal of Waste			
金属制品、机械和设备修理业	Metal Products,Machinery and Equipment Repair Industry		2327	1247
电力、热力生产和供应业	Production and Supply of Electric Power and Heat Power			
燃气生产和供应业	Gas Mining and Supplying Industry	17053	16763	
水的生产和供应业	Production and Supply of Water			

continued 5

(10 000 yuan)

财务费用 Financial cost	营业利润 Operating Profit	利润总额 Total Profits	亏损企业亏损总额 Total Loss of Deficit Enterprises	利税总额 Total Pre-tax Profits	应付职工薪酬 Salary Payable	本年应交增值税 Value Added Tax Payable
1513	39025	51031	1925	78273	61721	17957
6993	-4605	12504	532	27975	41972	12878
97	523	523		661	1018	118
956	1198	4855		5727	2208	770
24	195	195		697	2173	190
4602	25630	26104	72	32245	9405	4817
14647	47032	56596	1611	100210	140165	37240
1462	11386	11454		14180	5041	1956
176	-233	-232	232	-155	450	57
2794	23869	25863	3789	33664	9929	6443
36	282	286		290	74	
804	-1984	-1942	3116	-1570	4307	148
1219	496	563	2868	3330	9137	2000
63	4121	4174	575	6081	16256	1110
432	25343	25793		28791	25618	1498
18252	63707	65492	1548	134018	242274	21122
614	19354	19340		25512	28882	4847
12040	35057	35917	15884	44693	48608	6537
-42676	417558	411738		431471	239529	185
-3547	31634	31640	358	34461	10568	2021
-10	-9	-9	9	62	424	62
139	-163	-149	1969	-50	2550	47
-597	34104	33628		35506	39512	554

12-10 规模以上大中型工业企业主要经济指标（2019年）

单位：万元

分 组	Classify	企业单位数（个） Number of Enterprises (unit)	亏损企业 Loss Making Enterprises	工业总产值（当年价格） Gross Industrial Output Value (At Current Prices)
总计	**Total**	**249**	**39**	**50867424**
#亏损企业	Deficit Enterprises	39	39	1716700
按隶属关系分	**Grouped by Jurisdiction of Management**			
#中央企业	Central Enterprises	63	7	13479093
地方企业	Local Enterprises	54	7	17488394
按登记注册类型分组	**Grouped by Registion Status**			
内资企业	Domestic Investment Enterprises	211	35	39058173
国有	State-owned Enterprises	17	1	4488356
集体	Collective-owned Enterprises			
股份合作	Share-holding Corperative			
联营	Joint Ownership Enterprises			
有限责任公司	Limited Liability Corporations	131	21	25105614
股份有限公司	Share-holding Corperation Ltd.	44	11	5528275
私营	Private Enterprises	19	2	3935928
其他	Other Domestic Funded Enterprises			
港澳台商投资	Enterprises with Funds from Hong Kong,Macao and Taiwan	7		2811406
外商投资	Foreign Funded Enterprises	31	4	8997846
按轻重工业分	**Grouped by Light Industry and Heavy Industry**			
轻工业	Light Industry	61	10	6623843
重工业	Heavy Industry	188	29	44243581
按企业规模分	**Grouped by Size of Enterprises**			
大型企业	Large-size	68	9	38481834
中型企业	Medium-size	181	30	12385590

Major Economic Indicators of Large and Medium-sized Industrial Enterprises above Designated Size（2019）

(10 000 yuan)

平均用工人数（人） Average Number of Employed Persons (person)	资产总计 Total Assets	流动资产合计 Total Working Capitals	固定资产原价 Origing Value of Fixed Assets	累计折旧 Accumulative Total Depreciation
364905	**74441911**	**41032554**	**33736526**	**18470391**
31319	4877910	2278870	1820977	821316
146565	25436609	14235541	13574772	7024339
80526	21816942	12927446	6162897	3097739
305980	59807668	35607644	22748782	11228812
50828	9233445	4135013	6544934	3165792
204783	35853016	23233167	13147478	6561581
32549	11068109	5626780	2349709	1228889
17820	3653099	2612684	706662	272550
27179	2577206	1294001	1129472	476502
31746	12057037	4130910	9858273	6765078
54334	7594556	4518483	3035255	1276084
310571	66847355	36514072	30701271	17194308
266099	56879379	30451804	28072513	16091640
98806	17562532	10580751	5664013	2378751

12-10 续表1

单位：万元

分　组	Classify	负债合计 Total Liabilites	流动负债合计 Total Working Liabilities
总计	**Total**	**39281427**	**32148749**
#亏损企业	Deficit Enterprises	3836881	2682739
按隶属关系分	**Grouped by Jurisdiction of Management**		
#中央企业	Central Enterprises	13387902	11107570
地方企业	Local Enterprises	12663933	11158747
按登记注册类型分组	**Grouped by Registion Status**		
内资企业	Domestic Investment Enterprises	33348405	27806291
国有	State-owned Enterprises	5954848	4643404
集体	Collective-owned Enterprises		
股份合作	Share-holding Corperative		
联营	Joint Ownership Enterprises		
有限责任公司	Limited Liability Corporations	20387278	17434015
股份有限公司	Share-holding Corperation Ltd.	4815320	3796013
私营	Private Enterprises	2190959	1932858
其他	Other Domestic Funded Enterprises		
港澳台商投资	Enterprises with Funds from Hong Kong,Macao and Taiwan	1725264	1429676
外商投资	Foreign Funded Enterprises	4207759	2912782
按轻重工业分	**Grouped by Light Industry and Heavy Industry**		
轻工业	Light Industry	4791456	3541799
重工业	Heavy Industry	34489971	28606950
按企业规模分	**Grouped by Size of Enterprises**		
大型企业	Large-size	29661305	24424520
中型企业	Medium-size	9620122	7724229

continued 1

(10 000 yuan)

所有者权益合计 Total Owners' Equities	实收资本 Total Capital Hold	营业收入 Total Revenue	主营业务收入 Revenue from Principal Business	营业成本 Total Cost	税金及附加 Taxs and Other Changes
35160482	**13808790**	**49134919**	**47989995**	**42774375**	**291753**
1041028	1541288	1679604	1629749	1458083	14199
12048706	5133696	13417041	13123314	11897133	80379
9153009	2778823	17703030	17224080	15590445	70395
26459262	9593171	39095230	38190949	33920301	202490
3278597	1390276	5198118	5098980	4543401	24606
15465737	6274032	24584414	23853995	21481265	137991
6252788	1481792	5453392	5396008	4563703	29212
1462139	447071	3859307	3841967	3331933	10681
851942	193370	2813991	2683674	2901034	52786
7849279	4022250	7225698	7115372	5953040	36478
2803100	1045179	6637512	6531882	4820149	49702
32357382	12763611	42497407	41458113	37954226	242052
27218075	10244862	36695533	35786657	32706468	221713
7942408	3563928	12439386	12203337	10067908	70041

12-10 续表2

单位：万元

分 组	Classify	销售费用 Expenses for Sales	管理费用 Expenses for Management	研发费用 R&D Expenses
总计	**Total**	**1836005**	**1827761**	**919579**
#亏损企业	Deficit Enterprises	109202	136258	41844
按隶属关系分	**Grouped by Jurisdiction of Management**			
#中央企业	Central Enterprises	254713	744169	314645
地方企业	Local Enterprises	660898	462134	187958
按登记注册类型分组	**Grouped by Registion Status**			
内资企业	Domestic Investment Enterprises	1364873	1497561	730684
国有	State-owned Enterprises	34044	251219	108270
集体	Collective-owned Enterprises			
股份合作	Share-holding Corperative			
联营	Joint Ownership Enterprises			
有限责任公司	Limited Liability Corporations	944488	971027	432758
股份有限公司	Share-holding Corperation Ltd.	219647	178850	96186
私营	Private Enterprises	166695	96465	93470
其他	Other Domestic Funded Enterprises			
港澳台商投资	Enterprises with Funds from Hong Kong,Macao and Taiwan	61492	109129	22539
外商投资	Foreign Funded Enterprises	409640	221071	166355
按轻重工业分	**Grouped by Light Industry and Heavy Industry**			
轻工业	Light Industry	962759	332175	52464
重工业	Heavy Industry	873246	1495585	867115
按企业规模分	**Grouped by Size of Enterprises**			
大型企业	Large-size	1081712	1299018	635910
中型企业	Medium-size	754293	528743	283669

continued 2

(10 000 yuan)

财务费用 Financial cost	营业利润 Operating Profit	利润总额 Total Profits	亏损企业亏损总额 Total Loss of Deficit Enterprises	利税总额 Total Pre-tax Profits	应付职工薪酬 Salary Payable	本年应交增值税 Value Added Tax Payable
207182	**2318759**	**2381728**	**361604**	**3364357**	**5407633**	**690876**
65484	-357552	-361604	361604	-322289	313500	25116
51054	391114	380024	250644	677767	2255948	217364
70016	872234	902227	33962	1217591	1424028	244969
201661	1653087	1680942	355083	2481108	4578114	597676
55555	208169	196582	564	318097	795484	96910
76834	910120	943875	295925	1477479	3003029	395613
60441	402078	406986	56720	516910	358524	80711
8831	132721	133498	1875	168622	421077	24443
17508	44847	45956		114448	252271	15706
-11986	620825	654831	6520	768802	577248	77493
86237	329621	379484	27084	622787	668292	193602
120945	1989138	2002244	334520	2741570	4739341	497274
83124	1788091	1825852	100297	2504090	4226748	456525
124058	530668	555877	261307	860268	1180885	234351

12-10 续表3

单位：万元

分组	Classify	企业单位数（个） Number of Enterprises (unit)	亏损企业 Loss Making Enterprises	工业总产值（当年价格） Gross Industrial Output Value (At Current Prices)
按控股情况分	**Grouped by Cast strand**			
国有控股	State owned shares	132	23	28246671
集体控股	Collective shares	2		135621
私人控股	Private holdings	81	12	13472655
港澳台控股	Hong Kong and Macao Holdings	4		337234
外商投资	Foreign Investment	24	3	8132942
其他	Others	6	1	542301
按工业行业大类分	**Grouped by Sector**			
煤炭开采和洗选业	Mining and Washing of Coal			
石油和天然气开采业	Extraction of Petroleum and Natural Gas			
黑色金属矿采选业	Mining and Processing of Ferrous Metal Ores			
有色金属矿采选业	Mining and Processing of Non-ferrous Metal Ores			
非金属矿采选业	Mining and Processing of Nonmetal Ores			
开采专业及辅助性活动	Mining Professional and Auxiliary Activity	2		1053534
其他采矿业	Mining of other Ores			
农副食品加工业	Processing of Food from Agricultural Porducts	7	1	755837
食品制造业	Manufacture of Foods	13	3	1056397
酒、饮料和精制茶制造业	Manufacture of Alcohol,Beverages and Tea	6		431890
烟草制品业	Manufacture of Tobacco	1		9472
纺织业	Manufacture of Textile	3	2	74265
纺织服装、服饰业	Textile, apparel industry	1		36585
皮革、毛皮、羽毛及其制品和制鞋业	Manufacture of Leather, Fur, Feather and Related Products, and Shoes	1		20697
木材加工和木、竹、藤、棕、草制品业	Processing of Timber, Manufacture of Wood,Plam and Straw Products			
家具制造业	Manufacture of Furniture	2		42454
造纸和纸制品业	Manufacture of Paper and Paper Products			
印刷和记录媒介复制业	Printing,Reproduction of Recording Media	5	1	553384

continued 3

(10 000 yuan)

平均用工人数（人） Average Number of Employed Persons (person)	资产总计 Total Assets	流动资产合计 Total Working Capitals	固定资产原价 Origing Value of Fixed Assets	累计折旧 Accumulative Total Depreciation
241033	46436236	27262584	20396037	10411168
1029	136117	102327	49737	26259
86943	15966568	9622658	3299088	1217139
2841	177592	117347	125079	74960
26307	11047318	3643805	9379447	6597751
6752	678081	283832	487138	143114
13030	1261457	899445	733169	501624
3492	628163	460306	201338	109148
11848	494700	241030	318370	142729
4828	913497	530536	377239	236379
497	37171	21696	32579	17179
4711	225321	68526	205760	75689
808	62845	50352	12088	3286
630	51967	32404	8761	5252
820	29368	9237	16449	5495
4211	584511	342380	406620	269913

12-10 续表4

单位：万元

分 组	Classify	负债合计 Total Liabilites	流动负债合计 Total Working Liabilities
按控股情况分	**Grouped by Cast strand**		
国有控股	State owned shares	26317118	22099178
集体控股	Collective shares	80961	77689
私人控股	Private holdings	8876722	7347419
港澳台控股	Hong Kong and Macao Holdings	78955	75343
外商投资	Foreign Investment	3565730	2287003
其他	Others	361942	262118
按工业行业大类分	**Grouped by Sector**		
煤炭开采和洗选业	Mining and Washing of Coal		
石油和天然气开采业	Extraction of Petroleum and Natural Gas		
黑色金属矿采选业	Mining and Processing of Ferrous Metal Ores		
有色金属矿采选业	Mining and Processing of Non-ferrous Metal Ores		
非金属矿采选业	Mining and Processing of Nonmetal Ores		
开采专业及辅助性活动	Mining Professional and Auxiliary Activity	501941	491336
其他采矿业	Mining of other Ores		
农副食品加工业	Processing of Food from Agricultural Porducts	484449	424955
食品制造业	Manufacture of Foods	272115	261766
酒、饮料和精制茶制造业	Manufacture of Alcohol,Beverages and Tea	565276	473297
烟草制品业	Manufacture of Tobacco	2320	2320
纺织业	Manufacture of Textile	146661	54955
纺织服装、服饰业	Textile, apparel industry	42302	42302
皮革、毛皮、羽毛及其制品和制鞋业	Manufacture of Leather, Fur, Feather and Related Products, and Shoes	17004	10577
木材加工和木、竹、藤、棕、草制品业	Processing of Timber, Manufacture of Wood,Plam and Straw Products		
家具制造业	Manufacture of Furniture	16098	9631
造纸和纸制品业	Manufacture of Paper and Paper Products		
印刷和记录媒介复制业	Printing,Reproduction of Recording Media	234188	156033

continued 4

(10 000 yuan)

所有者权益合计 Total Owners' Equities	实收资本 Total Capital Hold	营业收入 Total Revenue	主营业务收入 Revenue from Principal Business	营业成本 Total Cost	税金及附加 Taxs and Other Changes
20119117	7939914	28617932	27792094	25426785	157416
55156	32725	117718	117191	94717	641
7089845	1819197	13224246	12968498	11473847	90688
98637	54359	309780	304962	220281	7627
7481588	3800645	6365506	6313086	5134844	33237
316139	161950	499737	494163	423903	2145
759516	460760	893504	879867	807703	5986
143714	54512	769763	765309	712798	1116
222585	99906	901506	888084	662360	10934
348221	104961	653009	641230	472592	11384
34851	27400	9619	9472	4620	397
78660	17624	101362	90591	105327	1270
20543	7500	23050	22903	17212	271
34963	31500	22373	22373	18593	68
13270	6060	41475	41475	35573	104
350323	165898	631103	618803	513410	3223

12-10 续表5

单位：万元

分　组	Classify	销售费用 Expenses for Sales	管理费用 Expenses for Management	研发费用 R&D Expenses
按控股情况分	**Grouped by Cast strand**			
国有控股	State owned shares	624784	1192973	539974
集体控股	Collective shares	6733	4455	3137
私人控股	Private holdings	763985	406710	203874
港澳台控股	Hong Kong and Macao Holdings	43307	13407	3844
外商投资	Foreign Investment	383855	196700	155258
其他	Others	13341	13516	13493
按工业行业大类分	**Grouped by Sector**			
煤炭开采和洗选业	Mining and Washing of Coal			
石油和天然气开采业	Extraction of Petroleum and Natural Gas			
黑色金属矿采选业	Mining and Processing of Ferrous Metal Ores			
有色金属矿采选业	Mining and Processing of Non-ferrous Metal Ores			
非金属矿采选业	Mining and Processing of Nonmetal Ores			
开采专业及辅助性活动	Mining Professional and Auxiliary Activity	3494	23847	29310
其他采矿业	Mining of other Ores			
农副食品加工业	Processing of Food from Agricultural Porducts	21880	15383	21
食品制造业	Manufacture of Foods	124171	44357	1158
酒、饮料和精制茶制造业	Manufacture of Alcohol,Beverages and Tea	112680	18731	1008
烟草制品业	Manufacture of Tobacco	950	2758	
纺织业	Manufacture of Textile	568	4869	
纺织服装、服饰业	Textile, apparel industry	2000	3119	
皮革、毛皮、羽毛及其制品和制鞋业	Manufacture of Leather, Fur, Feather and Related Products, and Shoes	443	416	1253
木材加工和木、竹、藤、棕、草制品业	Processing of Timber, Manufacture of Wood,Plam and Straw Products			
家具制造业	Manufacture of Furniture	2008	2531	
造纸和纸制品业	Manufacture of Paper and Paper Products			
印刷和记录媒介复制业	Printing,Reproduction of Recording Media	17787	39780	5555

continued 5

(10 000 yuan)

财务费用 Financial cost	营业利润 Operating Profit	利润总额 Total Profits	亏损企业亏损总额 Total Loss of Deficit Enterprises	利税总额 Total Pre-tax Profits	应付职工薪酬 Salary Payable	本年应交增值税 Value Added Tax Payable
128193	949066	959946	337476	1553070	3750220	435708
1012	5959	6859		10637	13071	3137
89361	735906	753385	17902	1017358	1052274	173286
618	20645	20783		33626	35949	5216
-14962	572380	606207	5086	710013	492043	70570
2959	34803	34548	1139	39653	64077	2959
-5863	37697	36117		45984	280356	3881
9705	15305	20327	560	28847	29090	7405
1249	59034	71096	4631	109635	124378	27605
3874	33499	51421		86570	56741	23764
-285	1183	1200		2756	3397	1160
163	-9904	-9878	10567	-8208	27806	400
498	97	452		1896	5286	1172
51	1685	2066		2245	2995	111
285	986	1048		1860	6100	708
6693	44826	44673	536	63544	86737	15648

12-10 续表6

单位：万元

分　组	Classify	企业单位数（个） Number of Enterprises (unit)	亏损企业 Loss Making Enterprises	工业总产值（当年价格） Gross Industrial Output Value (At Current Prices)
文教、工美、体育和娱乐用品制造业	Manufacture of Articles For Cultural,Educational and Sports Activities			
石油、煤炭及其他燃料加工业	Petroleum, coal and other fuel processing industries			
化学原料和化学制品制造业	Manufacture of Raw Chemical Materials and Chemical Products	10	4	774512
医药制造业	Manufacture of Medicines	15		2149924
化学纤维制造业	Manufacture of Chemical Fibers	1		100827
橡胶和塑料制品业	Manufacture of Rubber and Plastics	3		898791
非金属矿物制品业	Manufacture of Non-metallic Mineral Products	7		502919
黑色金属冶炼和压延加工业	Smelting and Pressing of Ferrous Metals	1		117647
有色金属冶炼和压延加工业	Smelting and Pressing of Non-ferrous Metals	7	1	739503
金属制品业	Manufacture of Metal Products	9	1	480062
通用设备制造业	Manufacture of General Purpose Machinery	8	3	1119681
专用设备制造业	Manufacture of Special Equipment	25	6	1833514
汽车制造业	Manufacture of Motor Vehicle	16	1	11100731
铁路、船舶、航空航天和其他运输设备制造业	Railways,Shipbuilding,Aerospace and Other Transportation Equipment Manufacturing Industry	26	3	4641203
电气机械和器材制造业	Manufacture of Electric Equipment and Machinery	20	5	5641803
计算机、通讯和其他电子设备制造业	Manufacture of Communication Equipment, Computers and other Electronic Equipment	36	5	10816977
仪器仪表制造业	Manufacture of Measuring Instruments and Machinery	7		1499550
其他制造业	Manufacture of Other Manufacturing			
废弃资源综合利用业	Recycling and Disposal of Waste			
金属制品、机械和设备修理业	Metal Products,Machinery and Equipment Repair Industry	1		15940
电力、热力生产和供应业	Production and Supply of Electric Power and Heat Power	8	2	2657578
燃气生产和供应业	Gas Mining and Supplying Industry	6	1	1616330
水的生产和供应业	Production and Supply of Water	1		115537

continued 6

(10 000 yuan)

平均用工人数（人） Average Number of Employed Persons (person)	资产总计 Total Assets	流动资产合计 Total Working Capitals	固定资产原价 Origing Value of Fixed Assets	累计折旧 Accumulative Total Depreciation
396	45456	14767	2047	951
11413	1567137	866917	978030	510820
13945	1976304	1188624	613290	190617
340	36014	24698	22207	3054
7212	1921018	1167635	641370	145246
2810	519055	353629	130354	59737
680	105213	77443	79878	36148
4743	2204323	939341	482721	167226
13248	1527342	807679	772075	349490
11121	3403109	2666779	675322	320480
17979	3195865	2128144	842604	344084
51916	8109561	5799818	2186332	1109135
59021	11042718	6701060	3237738	1596587
36485	8695232	5825209	2639564	1093159
50723	16930829	6982036	9549646	6661433
9917	2051655	1419038	629711	278557
629	19747	18763	791	95
18468	4280145	671664	6490883	3536627
6465	2061602	450171	1141555	506106
2519	460588	273229	308037	194147

12-10 续表7

单位：万元

分 组	Classify	负债合计 Total Liabilites	流动负债合计 Total Working Liabilities
文教、工美、体育和娱乐用品制造业	Manufacture of Articles For Cultural,Educational and Sports Activities		
石油、煤炭及其他燃料加工业	Petroleum, coal and other fuel processing industries	25228	25198
化学原料和化学制品制造业	Manufacture of Raw Chemical Materials and Chemical Products	1194214	738358
医药制造业	Manufacture of Medicines	898292	706420
化学纤维制造业	Manufacture of Chemical Fibers	2155	1885
橡胶和塑料制品业	Manufacture of Rubber and Plastics	1389101	1016434
非金属矿物制品业	Manufacture of Non-metallic Mineral Products	299857	284453
黑色金属冶炼和压延加工业	Smelting and Pressing of Ferrous Metals	57419	56290
有色金属冶炼和压延加工业	Smelting and Pressing of Non-ferrous Metals	519456	391860
金属制品业	Manufacture of Metal Products	1213049	857520
通用设备制造业	Manufacture of General Purpose Machinery	2038491	1905641
专用设备制造业	Manufacture of Special Equipment	1684071	1300286
汽车制造业	Manufacture of Motor Vehicle	5309391	4849373
铁路、船舶、航空航天和其他运输设备制造业	Railways,Shipbuilding,Aerospace and Other Transportation Equipment Manufacturing Industry	5404603	4615899
电气机械和器材制造业	Manufacture of Electric Equipment and Machinery	4534204	4017700
计算机、通讯和其他电子设备制造业	Manufacture of Communication Equipment, Computers and other Electronic Equipment	6805768	4896518
仪器仪表制造业	Manufacture of Measuring Instruments and Machinery	1042240	989632
其他制造业	Manufacture of Other Manufacturing		
废弃资源综合利用业	Recycling and Disposal of Waste		
金属制品、机械和设备修理业	Metal Products,Machinery and Equipment Repair Industry	11497	11497
电力、热力生产和供应业	Production and Supply of Electric Power and Heat Power	3067325	2342132
燃气生产和供应业	Gas Mining and Supplying Industry	1176892	1045164
水的生产和供应业	Production and Supply of Water	325821	169321

continued 7

(10 000 yuan)

所有者权益合计 Total Owners' Equities	实收资本 Total Capital Hold	营业收入 Total Revenue	主营业务收入 Revenue from Principal Business	营业成本 Total Cost	税金及附加 Taxs and Other Changes
20228	33660	8599	8270	7898	312
372924	279003	806342	776806	646727	5726
1078011	165415	2021429	2017888	1027460	17345
33859	39252	76441	75162	70029	364
531917	381625	775016	744971	665955	4342
219198	75199	543480	521696	431016	3112
47794	48549	119025	114745	104552	735
1684866	400380	625437	590163	518254	3297
314293	337321	754191	730785	634719	3016
1364618	172474	1339285	1231458	1106286	8989
1511795	591708	1758459	1747152	1436199	11943
2800170	791604	10692243	10311136	10153050	72628
5638115	2103767	4535400	4464795	3857770	21889
4161028	1485528	5193002	5044750	4699101	28714
10125060	4366549	9393967	9344461	8180802	43872
1009415	230539	1516899	1506700	1248296	4901
8250	10000	15940	15940	13862	153
1212820	959401	3120515	3049165	2941440	18550
884710	321694	1662460	1598310	1570365	5220
134768	39000	130029	115537	110406	1890

12-10 续表8

单位：万元

分　组	Classify	销售费用 Expenses for Sales	管理费用 Expenses for Management	研发费用 R&D Expenses
文教、工美、体育和娱乐用品制造业	Manufacture of Articles For Cultural,Educational and Sports Activities			
石油、煤炭及其他燃料加工业	Petroleum, coal and other fuel processing industries	77	92	
化学原料和化学制品制造业	Manufacture of Raw Chemical Materials and Chemical Products	20447	78014	24957
医药制造业	Manufacture of Medicines	595451	166574	26663
化学纤维制造业	Manufacture of Chemical Fibers	315	1369	1910
橡胶和塑料制品业	Manufacture of Rubber and Plastics	25730	22583	11055
非金属矿物制品业	Manufacture of Non-metallic Mineral Products	36203	15549	5775
黑色金属冶炼和压延加工业	Smelting and Pressing of Ferrous Metals	5810	4632	386
有色金属冶炼和压延加工业	Smelting and Pressing of Non-ferrous Metals	5480	27608	31282
金属制品业	Manufacture of Metal Products	8412	50807	31431
通用设备制造业	Manufacture of General Purpose Machinery	39690	86494	36035
专用设备制造业	Manufacture of Special Equipment	87104	88748	47965
汽车制造业	Manufacture of Motor Vehicle	217239	200177	119238
铁路、船舶、航空航天和其他运输设备制造业	Railways,Shipbuilding,Aerospace and Other Transportation Equipment Manufacturing Industry	71291	257019	95877
电气机械和器材制造业	Manufacture of Electric Equipment and Machinery	302184	266656	103467
计算机、通讯和其他电子设备制造业	Manufacture of Communication Equipment, Computers and other Electronic Equipment	77227	218887	288517
仪器仪表制造业	Manufacture of Measuring Instruments and Machinery	22237	68809	47289
其他制造业	Manufacture of Other Manufacturing			
废弃资源综合利用业	Recycling and Disposal of Waste			
金属制品、机械和设备修理业	Metal Products,Machinery and Equipment Repair Industry		2113	
电力、热力生产和供应业	Production and Supply of Electric Power and Heat Power	534	72016	5640
燃气生产和供应业	Gas Mining and Supplying Industry	29456	32311	3789
水的生产和供应业	Production and Supply of Water	5142	11510	

continued 8

(10 000 yuan)

财务费用 Financial cost	营业利润 Operating Profit	利润总额 Total Profits	亏损企业亏损总额 Total Loss of Deficit Enterprises	利税总额 Total Pre-tax Profits	应付职工薪酬 Salary Payable	本年应交增值税 Value Added Tax Payable
24	195	195		697	2173	190
33681	-111338	-109831	150099	-87176	123619	16929
17675	140379	153496		276463	247038	105621
-33	2457	2451		3425	4778	610
25269	21489	22151		41459	61593	14966
3094	47543	47847		69547	28149	18588
355	1102	1193		3079	11623	1152
1989	44621	44692	1614	61914	75401	13926
7675	-4093	-11569	47895	-5224	159803	3329
7263	70083	71753	4786	113564	154056	32823
22897	66113	71615	43068	121367	212897	37809
-4854	323650	329490	1434	514914	948184	112797
4156	273361	283689	8175	344992	825038	39415
11741	141824	145163	61884	212283	652951	38405
6003	823423	829232	8248	936994	595791	63890
-5156	144248	146698		167475	180026	15876
-20	14	14		1391	11092	1224
38709	60777	44721	18091	138486	356661	75216
17370	90791	86629	16	104643	95029	12793
2975	-2284	3579		8935	38847	3466

12-11 规模以上高技术产业工业企业主要经济指标（2019年）

单位：万元

行业	Sector	企业单位数（个）Number of Enterprises (unit)	亏损企业 Loss Making Enterprises
总计	**Total**	**358**	**66**
一、医药制造业	**Pharmaceutical Manufacturing**	**66**	**14**
（一）化学药品制造	Chemical manufacturing	25	5
化学药品原料药制造	Chemical raw materials Medicine manufacturing	8	2
化学药品制剂制造	Chemical preparations manufacturing	17	3
（二）中药饮片加工	Chinese medicine Pieces processing	1	
（三）中成药生产	Chinese medicine production	26	6
（四）兽用药品制造	Veterinary pharmaceutical manufacturing	4	2
（五）生物药品制造	Biopharmaceutical manufacturing	5	1
（六）卫生材料及医药用品制造	Sanitary materials and medical supplies manufacturing	1	
（七）药用辅料及包装材料	Pharmaceutical Excipients and Packaging Materials	4	
二、航空、航天及设备制造业	**Aviation, Aerospace and Equipment Manufacturing Industry**	**70**	**6**
（一）飞机制造	Aircraft Manufacturing	17	1
（二）航天器及运载火箭制造	Spacecraft and Launch Vehicles Manufacturing	3	
（三）航空、航天相关设备制造	Aviation and aerospace-related equipment manufacturing	40	3
（四）其他航空航天器制造	Other aerospace manufacturing	6	
（五）航空航天器修理	Aerospace vehicle repair	4	2
三、电子及通讯设备制造业	**Electronic and communication equipment manufacturing**	**131**	**27**
（一）电子工业专用设备制造	Electronic equipment manufacturing	8	1
（二）光纤、光缆及锂离子电池制造	Optical Fiber, Cable and Lithium-ion Battery Manufacturing	4	2
（三）通信设备、雷达及配套设备制造	Communications Equipment, Radar and Ancillary Equipments	26	5
（四）广播电视设备制造	Broadcasting and TV Equipment	2	1
（五）非专业视听设备制造	Non-professional audiovisual equipment manufacturing	1	
（六）电子器件制造	Electronic device manufacturing	36	7
（七）电子元件及电子专用材料制造	Electronic components and electronic materials manufacturing	40	7
（八）智能消费设备制造	Smart consumer device manufacturing	3	2
（九）其他电子设备制造	Other electronic equipment manufacturing	11	2
四、计算机及办公设备制造业	**Computer and office equipment manufacturing**	**4**	**2**
（一）计算机整机制造	Computer machine manufacturing		
（二）计算机零部件制造	Computer parts manufacturing	1	1
（三）计算机外围设备制造	Computer peripheral equipment manufacturing	1	
（四）工业控制计算机及系统制造	Industrial Control Computer and System Manufacturing	2	1
（五）信息安全设备制造	Information Security Equipment Manufacturing		
（六）其他计算机制造	Other computer manufacturing		
（七）办公设备制造	Office Equipment manufacturing		
五、医疗设备及仪器仪表制造业	**Medical equipment and instrumentation manufacturing**	**86**	**16**
（一）医疗仪器设备及器械制造	Medical equipment and device manufacturing	17	4
（二）通用仪器仪表制造	General Measuring Instruments and Machinery Manufacturing	39	9
（三）专用仪器仪表制造	Special Measuring Instruments and Machinery Manufacturing	18	2
（四）光学仪器制造	Optical Instruments Manufacturing	6	1
（五）其他仪器仪表制造业	Other instrumentation manufacturing	6	
六、信息化学品制造业	**Information chemicals manufacturing**	**1**	**1**
信息化学品制造	Information Chemical Manufacturing	1	1

Major Economic Indicators of High Technology Industry

Industrial Enterprises above Designated Size（2019）

(10 000 yuan)

工业总产值（当年价格） Gross Industrial Output Value (At Current Prices)	平均用工人数（人） Average Number of Employed Persons (person)	资产总计 Total Assets	流动资产合计 Total Working Capitals	固定资产原价 Origing Value of Fixed Assets	累计折旧 Accumulative Total Depreciation
22117735	**161164**	**36843740**	**18879549**	**15350877**	**9187837**
2618641	**20225**	**2678755**	**1612906**	**834296**	**280266**
1602482	9609	1466254	876748	535865	147267
210468	1057	193274	143247	40267	15218
1392015	8552	1272980	733501	495598	132048
8632	80	13492	7842	1166	162
769884	8151	814534	511325	156697	67696
10611	374	59002	53673	10894	5056
194489	1480	288666	145949	117540	54805
3851	46	2832	1700	1339	331
28693	485	33975	15668	10795	4949
4919199	**58015**	**11010020**	**6580996**	**3263073**	**1590106**
3329249	43545	8453903	5116533	2431780	1241093
423767	4574	1063230	437650	410029	162212
1061820	8503	1226090	854344	376265	171631
76697	1085	213501	145517	31726	10693
27666	308	53296	26952	13272	4478
12413435	**64071**	**19834558**	**8324485**	**10441888**	**6960512**
40969	831	80633	64647	18285	5493
685347	2888	902389	412128	412678	122380
2404895	19673	2261869	1573525	691726	345414
28369	242	24549	21892	2561	1740
5300	60	6995	2963	280	
6397474	20604	9822123	2993150	8678289	6249490
2746114	17947	6504623	3091142	599887	217299
19186	910	89936	47410	26783	12853
85780	916	141443	117626	11399	5843
49598	**435**	**85920**	**68877**	**10102**	**1725**
5653	45	5132	4200	1014	135
33175	222	71795	56675	8927	1495
10770	168	8993	8002	161	96
2105590	**18246**	**3158472**	**2252446**	**789645**	**349544**
179489	1895	255823	197376	38683	15959
791343	4892	847374	645995	149504	61369
208729	3007	531671	425348	58626	33019
866455	7564	1426862	928696	516496	230450
59574	888	96741	55031	26336	8747
11274	**172**	**76015**	**39839**	**11874**	**5684**
11274	172	76015	39839	11874	5684

12-11 续表1

单位：万元

行　业	Sector	负债合计 Total Liabilites	流动负债合计 Total Working Liabilities
总计	**Total**	**17163167**	**13899570**
一、医药制造业	**Pharmaceutical Manufacturing**	**1261250**	**1043333**
（一）化学药品制造	Chemical manufacturing	662565	533719
化学药品原料药制造	Chemical raw materials Medicine manufacturing	62566	53745
化学药品制剂制造	Chemical preparations manufacturing	599999	479974
（二）中药饮片加工	Chinese medicine Pieces processing	4361	4361
（三）中成药生产	Chinese medicine production	489502	406828
（四）兽用药品制造	Veterinary pharmaceutical manufacturing	24422	24413
（五）生物药品制造	Biopharmaceutical manufacturing	61289	55803
（六）卫生材料及医药用品制造	Sanitary materials and medical supplies manufacturing	1759	1759
（七）药用辅料及包装材料	Pharmaceutical Excipients and Packaging Materials	17351	16451
二、航空、航天及设备制造业	**Aviation, Aerospace and Equipment Manufacturing Industry**	**5342730**	**4538346**
（一）飞机制造	Aircraft Manufacturing	4132335	3598923
（二）航天器及运载火箭制造	Spacecraft and Launch Vehicles Manufacturing	513042	332514
（三）航空、航天相关设备制造	Aviation and aerospace-related equipment manufacturing	608574	520815
（四）其他航空航天器制造	Other aerospace manufacturing	72845	70911
（五）航空航天器修理	Aerospace vehicle repair	15935	15185
三、电子及通讯设备制造业	**Electronic and communication equipment manufacturing**	**8800344**	**6681127**
（一）电子工业专用设备制造	Electronic equipment manufacturing	41334	37997
（二）光纤、光缆及锂离子电池制造	Optical Fiber, Cable and Lithium-ion Battery Manufacturing	721985	590812
（三）通信设备、雷达及配套设备制造	Communications Equipment, Radar and Ancillary Equipments	1190417	999145
（四）广播电视设备制造	Broadcasting and TV Equipment	16244	13101
（五）非专业视听设备制造	Non-professional audiovisual equipment manufacturing	2308	2308
（六）电子器件制造	Electronic device manufacturing	2788966	1467923
（七）电子元件及电子专用材料制造	Electronic components and electronic materials manufacturing	3953147	3488811
（八）智能消费设备制造	Smart consumer device manufacturing	19241	18409
（九）其他电子设备制造	Other electronic equipment manufacturing	66702	62621
四、计算机及办公设备制造业	**Computer and office equipment manufacturing**	**26620**	**25222**
（一）计算机整机制造	Computer machine manufacturing		
（二）计算机零部件制造	Computer parts manufacturing	4314	3316
（三）计算机外围设备制造	Computer peripheral equipment manufacturing	16305	16205
（四）工业控制计算机及系统制造	Industrial Control Computer and System Manufacturing	6001	5701
（五）信息安全设备制造	Information Security Equipment Manufacturing		
（六）其他计算机制造	Other computer manufacturing		
（七）办公设备制造	Office Equipment manufacturing		
五、医疗设备及仪器仪表制造业	**Medical equipment and instrumentation manufacturing**	**1650451**	**1529769**
（一）医疗仪器设备及器械制造	Medical equipment and device manufacturing	104237	89877
（二）通用仪器仪表制造	General Measuring Instruments and Machinery Manufacturing	579156	532659
（三）专用仪器仪表制造	Special Measuring Instruments and Machinery Manufacturing	223038	211545
（四）光学仪器制造	Optical Instruments Manufacturing	707179	660332
（五）其他仪器仪表制造业	Other instrumentation manufacturing	36842	35356
六、信息化学品制造业	**Information chemicals manufacturing**	**81773**	**81773**
信息化学品制造	Information Chemical Manufacturing	81773	81773

continued 1

(10 000 yuan)

所有者权益合计 Total Owners' Equities	实收资本 Total Capital Hold	营业收入 Total Revenue	主营业务收入 Revenue from Principal Business	营业成本 Total Cost	税金及附加 Taxs and Other Changes
19677624	**7951109**	**20217371**	**20008381**	**16327690**	**100558**
1417505	**328151**	**2423148**	**2418586**	**1224151**	**22214**
803689	160731	1596178	1592719	887047	13087
130708	27240	131565	131552	97436	1144
672981	133491	1464613	1461168	789611	11943
9131	3000	4344	4344	2954	7
325032	93265	664016	663350	272382	6955
34580	7468	7983	7983	5478	68
227376	52307	119040	118950	37518	1828
1073	500	3960	3960	1615	31
16624	10880	27627	27281	17156	238
5667289	**2113313**	**4670198**	**4601357**	**3993339**	**19585**
4321568	1672295	3241080	3185344	2861436	14634
550188	79547	437928	431596	340713	501
617516	285327	866907	862261	708160	3572
140656	32548	90010	89990	56906	689
37362	43596	34273	32165	26124	188
11031267	**5038054**	**10955396**	**10869319**	**9465627**	**48675**
39298	16420	43950	41047	32899	386
180404	228825	774092	766678	666474	583
1068505	295489	2479851	2465161	2244541	7032
8305	3808	29478	29234	21750	143
4687	290	5236	5236	4469	
7033156	3670160	4741045	4702579	4030550	24512
2551476	771913	2780974	2759793	2389693	15351
70695	10797	13748	13733	10691	85
74741	40352	87022	85857	64560	583
59301	**30249**	**53377**	**19988**	**34653**	**267**
818	338	5460	5460	5406	2
55490	27600	36966	3578	21593	217
2992	2311	10951	10951	7654	48
1508021	**437343**	**2095491**	**2079368**	**1590014**	**9693**
151586	52403	151535	151416	54525	1190
268219	157817	731557	727614	593701	3657
308633	58470	250339	246564	150733	2689
719683	148287	898959	891348	743377	1830
59900	20366	63102	62426	47679	327
-5758	**4000**	**19762**	**19762**	**19907**	**125**
-5758	4000	19762	19762	19907	125

12-11 续表2

单位：万元

行 业	Sector	销售费用 Expenses for Sales	管理费用 Expenses for Management
总计	**Total**	**1030700**	**893833**
一、医药制造业	**Pharmaceutical Manufacturing**	**711910**	**203787**
（一）化学药品制造	Chemical manufacturing	382938	129518
化学药品原料药制造	Chemical raw materials Medicine manufacturing	8441	3947
化学药品制剂制造	Chemical preparations manufacturing	374498	125571
（二）中药饮片加工	Chinese medicine Pieces processing	383	390
（三）中成药生产	Chinese medicine production	266791	60321
（四）兽用药品制造	Veterinary pharmaceutical manufacturing	779	561
（五）生物药品制造	Biopharmaceutical manufacturing	57706	10064
（六）卫生材料及医药用品制造	Sanitary materials and medical supplies manufacturing	496	803
（七）药用辅料及包装材料	Pharmaceutical Excipients and Packaging Materials	2817	2130
二、航空、航天及设备制造业	**Aviation, Aerospace and Equipment Manufacturing Industry**	**69078**	**255143**
（一）飞机制造	Aircraft Manufacturing	52785	166304
（二）航天器及运载火箭制造	Spacecraft and Launch Vehicles Manufacturing	1027	22216
（三）航空、航天相关设备制造	Aviation and aerospace-related equipment manufacturing	11155	51666
（四）其他航空航天器制造	Other aerospace manufacturing	2807	10647
（五）航空航天器修理	Aerospace vehicle repair	1303	4310
三、电子及通讯设备制造业	**Electronic and communication equipment manufacturing**	**170594**	**301818**
（一）电子工业专用设备制造	Electronic equipment manufacturing	2277	3031
（二）光纤、光缆及锂离子电池制造	Optical Fiber, Cable and Lithium-ion Battery Manufacturing	69121	15715
（三）通信设备、雷达及配套设备制造	Communications Equipment, Radar and Ancillary Equipments	11399	64162
（四）广播电视设备制造	Broadcasting and TV Equipment	2350	1632
（五）非专业视听设备制造	Non-professional audiovisual equipment manufacturing	73	63
（六）电子器件制造	Electronic device manufacturing	46943	92864
（七）电子元件及电子专用材料制造	Electronic components and electronic materials manufacturing	33634	115755
（八）智能消费设备制造	Smart consumer device manufacturing	536	1417
（九）其他电子设备制造	Other electronic equipment manufacturing	4260	7179
四、计算机及办公设备制造业	**Computer and office equipment manufacturing**	**1594**	**2840**
（一）计算机整机制造	Computer machine manufacturing		
（二）计算机零部件制造	Computer parts manufacturing	100	170
（三）计算机外围设备制造	Computer peripheral equipment manufacturing	698	1619
（四）工业控制计算机及系统制造	Industrial Control Computer and System Manufacturing	796	1051
（五）信息安全设备制造	Information Security Equipment Manufacturing		
（六）其他计算机制造	Other computer manufacturing		
（七）办公设备制造	Office Equipment manufacturing		
五、医疗设备及仪器仪表制造业	**Medical equipment and instrumentation manufacturing**	**77324**	**129447**
（一）医疗仪器设备及器械制造	Medical equipment and device manufacturing	23483	14993
（二）通用仪器仪表制造	General Measuring Instruments and Machinery Manufacturing	27735	30007
（三）专用仪器仪表制造	Special Measuring Instruments and Machinery Manufacturing	18980	24281
（四）光学仪器制造	Optical Instruments Manufacturing	2369	55457
（五）其他仪器仪表制造业	Other instrumentation manufacturing	4758	4710
六、信息化学品制造业	**Information chemicals manufacturing**	**200**	**799**
信息化学品制造	Information Chemical Manufacturing	200	799

continued 2

(10 000 yuan)

研发费用 R&D Expenses	财务费用 Financial cost	营业利润 Operating Profit	利润总额 Total Profits	亏损企业亏损总额 Total Loss of Deficit Enterprises	利税总额 Total Pre-tax Profits	应付职工薪酬 Salary Payable	本年应交增值税 Value Added Tax Payable
547912	**55602**	**1566505**	**1609882**	**69133**	**1999666**	**2059413**	**289225**
40205	**23175**	**167847**	**181658**	**5866**	**333120**	**287355**	**129248**
24678	19322	104567	114749	3997	204343	176260	76508
7208	2691	11653	12049	85	15483	7605	2291
17469	16631	92914	102700	3912	188860	168655	74217
213	99	298	313		372	314	52
8829	2321	49427	52022	1573	102343	90497	43366
241	523	334	416	248	583	1872	100
4665	533	8844	9266	48	18722	14472	7628
230		817	835		1194	279	328
1349	377	3560	4058		5564	3661	1267
93139	**6650**	**291319**	**299177**	**10290**	**358750**	**777725**	**39989**
32504	-851	166408	166844	1936	193790	541220	12312
28110	891	49939	50855		51914	94339	557
22493	5914	62899	68675	6245	94007	124359	21760
7539	555	12142	12850		18155	13648	4615
2493	142	-69	-48	2109	885	4159	745
332233	**25245**	**879918**	**894104**	**39775**	**1023833**	**723199**	**81055**
3223	551	2103	2377	447	3866	8620	1103
3560	11827	24060	25160	8992	27163	31020	1420
38628	8261	130330	133651	2861	168225	187245	27543
918	172	2643	2647	10	4364	2982	1575
	2	630	630		630	330	
242083	-28155	452270	453986	4886	501281	320323	22783
37115	32244	263212	270687	19183	310494	152933	24457
2205		-814	-769	2113	-495	10707	189
4500	343	5484	5736	1283	8305	9039	1987
2981	**696**	**9984**	**10040**	**751**	**11125**	**4652**	**818**
	213	-431	-390	390	-388	26	
1689	238	10385	10400		11082	2837	465
1293	245	29	30	361	431	1789	353
79096	**-247**	**218914**	**226380**	**10975**	**274062**	**264962**	**37989**
7897	943	47310	47738	1615	54360	18490	5432
15685	1811	55942	57682	7083	77192	58110	15853
10169	-1108	55379	57502	2181	70142	36669	9951
43579	-2334	56652	59015	96	65935	144081	5090
1766	442	3630	4443		6434	7612	1664
260	**83**	**-1477**	**-1477**	**1477**	**-1226**	**1520**	**126**
260	83	-1477	-1477	1477	-1226	1520	126

12-12 规模以上工业企业主要经济效益指标（2019年）

行 业	Sector	总资产贡献率（%） Ratio of Total Assets to Industrial Output Value (%)	资产负债率(%) Assets-Liability Ratio (%)
总计	**Total**	**5.4**	**53.9**
按工业行业大类分	**Grouped by Sector**		
煤炭开采和洗选业	Mining and Washing of Coal		
石油和天然气开采业	Extraction of Petroleum and Natural Gas		
黑色金属矿采选业	Mining and Processing of Ferrous Metal Ores		
有色金属矿采选业	Mining and Processing of Non-ferrous Metal Ores		
非金属矿采选业	Mining and Processing of Nonmetal Ores		
开采专业及辅助性活动	Mining Professional and Auxiliary Activity	3.4	39.6
其他采矿业	Mining of Other Ores		
农副食品加工业	Processing of Food from Agricultural Porducts	7.1	69.3
食品制造业	Manufacture of Foods	17.2	50.6
酒、饮料和精制茶制造业	Manufacture of Alcohol,Beverages and Tea	9.0	57.6
烟草制品业	Manufacture of Tobacco	6.7	6.2
纺织业	Manufacture of Textile	-0.1	60.8
纺织服装、服饰业	Textile, Garments industry	4.1	55.6
皮革、毛皮、羽毛及其制品和制鞋业	Manufacture of Leather, Fur, Feather and Related Products	3.9	32.9
木材加工和木、竹、藤、棕、草制品业	Processing of Timber, Manufacture of Wood,Plam and Straw Products	-0.8	45.4
家具制造业	Manufacture of Furniture	8.3	49.0
造纸和纸制品业	Manufacture of Paper and Paper Products	5.5	48.5
印刷和记录媒介复制业	Printing,Reproduction of Recording Media	10.9	43.1
文教、工美、体育和娱乐用品制造业	Manufacture of Articles For Cultural,Educational and Sports Activities	7.1	29.0

Major Indicators of Economic Performance of Industrial Enterprises above Designated Size (2019)

流动资产周转率（次/年）Rate of Annual Turnover Working Capitals (times/year)	成本费用利润率（%）Ratio of Profits to Cost (%)	营业收入利润率（%）Profit Margin of Operating Income (%)	每百元资产实现营业收入（元）Operating Income per 100 yuan of Assets (yuan)
1.2	**5.1**	**4.9**	**70**
1.0	4.3	4.1	71
2.3	3.2	3.2	159
3.8	6.6	6.2	183
1.6	6.2	5.9	86
0.4	14.9	12.5	26
1.4	-2.3	-2.3	63
0.6	2.8	2.7	45
0.7	7.3	6.9	48
0.5	-10.1	-11.6	22
2.1	5.1	4.8	120
2.0	2.4	2.3	128
2.4	5.1	4.8	137
7.9	0.6	0.6	561

12-12 续表1

行 业	Sector	总资产贡献率（%） Ratio of Total Assets to Industrial Output Value (%)	资产负债率(%) Assets-Liability Ratio (%)
石油、煤炭及其他燃料加工业	Petroleum, coal and other fuel processing industries	1.8	59.8
化学原料和化学制品制造业	Manufacture of Raw Chemical Materials and Chemical Products	3.4	64.0
医药制造业	Manufacture of Medicines	12.8	47.1
化学纤维制造业	Manufacture of Chemical Fibers	11.6	46.2
橡胶和塑料制品业	Manufacture of Rubber and Plastics	4.0	70.2
非金属矿物制品业	Manufacture of Non-metallic Mineral Products	9.4	67.4
黑色金属冶炼和压延加工业	Smelting and Pressing of Ferrous Metals	5.5	58.0
有色金属冶炼和压延加工业	Smelting and Pressing of Non-ferrous Metals	3.3	31.9
金属制品业	Manufacture of Metal Products	2.0	75.6
通用设备制造业	Manufacture of General Purpose Machinery	4.6	57.9
专用设备制造业	Manufacture of Special Equipment	5.5	51.0
汽车制造业	Manufacture of Motor Vehicle	6.4	65.2
铁路、船舶、航空航天和其他运输设备制造业	Railways, Shipbuilding,Aerospace and Other Transportation Equipment Manufacturing Industry	3.9	47.9
电气机械和器材制造业	Manufacture of Electric Equipment and Machinery	3.3	52.3
计算机、通讯和其他电子设备制造业	Manufacture of Communication Equipment, Computers and other Electronic Equipment	6.0	42.6
仪器仪表制造业	Manufacture of Measuring Instruments and Machinery	7.6	53.3
其他制造业	Manufacture of Other Manufacturing	5.9	52.1
废弃资源综合利用业	Recycling and Disposal of Waste	15.1	65.8
金属制品、机械和设备修理业	Metal Products,Machinery and Equipment Repair Industry	5.1	31.8
电力、热力生产和供应业	Production and Supply of Electric Power and Heat Power	4.0	75.2
燃气生产和供应业	Gas Mining and Supplying Industry	5.9	56.1
水的生产和供应业	Production and Supply of Water	1.3	76.4

continued 1

流动资产周转率 （次/年） Rate of Annual Turnover Working Capitals (times/year)	成本费用利润率 （%） Ratio of Profits to Cost （%）	营业收入利润率 （%） Profit Margin of Operating Income （%）	每百元资产实现营业收入（元） Operating Income per 100 yuan of Assets (yuan)
1.3	0.4	0.4	71
1.1	1.2	1.1	63
1.5	8.3	7.5	90
2.4	7.1	6.4	131
0.8	3.9	3.7	47
1.5	5.2	4.9	109
3.1	1.0	1.0	229
0.8	6.5	6.2	37
1.3	0.2	0.2	75
0.6	6.3	5.9	48
0.8	6.0	5.7	56
1.8	3.2	3.2	128
0.8	6.9	6.5	46
1.0	3.1	3.1	66
1.3	9.2	8.6	54
1.0	10.0	9.1	67
0.9	5.4	5.3	56
4.4	1.3	1.3	294
1.1	4.6	4.4	61
2.8	2.1	2.1	62
3.6	5.1	5.1	84
0.6	-5.1	-5.5	20

12-13 规模以上大中型工业企业主要经济效益指标（2019年）

行　业	Sector	总资产贡献率（%）Ratio of Total Assets to Industrial Output Value (%)	资产负债率(%) Assets-Liability Ratio (%)
总计	**Total**	**4.9**	**52.8**
按国民经济行业分	**Grouped by Sector**		
煤炭开采和洗选业	Mining and Washing of Coal		
石油和天然气开采业	Extraction of Petroleum and Natural Gas		
黑色金属矿采选业	Mining and Processing of Ferrous Metal Ores		
有色金属矿采选业	Mining and Processing of Non-ferrous Metal Ores		
非金属矿采选业	Mining and Processing of Nonmetal Ores		
开采专业及辅助性活动	Mining Professional and Auxiliary Activity	3.2	39.8
其他采矿业	Mining of other Ores		
农副食品加工业	Processing of Food from Agricultural Porducts	5.9	77.1
食品制造业	Manufacture of Foods	22.3	55.0
酒、饮料和精制茶制造业	Manufacture of Alcohol,Beverages and Tea	9.9	61.9
烟草制品业	Manufacture of Tobacco	6.7	6.2
纺织业	Manufacture of Textile	-3.6	65.1
纺织服装、服饰业	Textile, apparel industry	3.8	67.3
皮革、毛皮、羽毛及其制品和制鞋业	Leather fur feathers and its products and footwear	4.3	32.7
木材加工和木、竹、藤、棕、草制品业	Processing of Timber,Manufacture of Wood,Plam and Straw Products		
家具制造业	Manufacture of Furniture	7.3	54.8
造纸和纸制品业	Manufacture of Paper and Paper Products		
印刷和记录媒介复制业	Printing,Reproduction of Recording Media	12.0	40.1
文教、工美、体育和娱乐用品制造业	Manufacture of Articles For Cultural,Educational and Sports Activities		

Major Economic Indicators of Large and Medium-sized Industrial Enterprises above Designated Size（2019）

流动资产周转率（次/年）Rate of Annual Turnover Working Capitals (times/year)	成本费用利润率（%）Ratio of Profits to Cost (%)	营业收入利润率（%）Profit Margin of Operating Income (%)	每百元资产实现营业收入（元）Operating Income per 100 yuan of Assets (yuan)
1.2	**5.0**	**4.9**	**66.0**
1.0	4.2	4.0	70.8
1.7	2.7	2.6	122.5
3.7	8.5	7.9	182.2
1.2	8.5	7.9	71.5
0.4	14.9	12.5	25.9
1.5	-8.9	-9.8	45.0
0.5	2.0	2.0	36.7
0.7	10.0	9.2	43.1
4.5	2.6	2.5	141.2
1.8	7.7	7.1	108.0

12-13 续表1

行 业	Sector	总资产贡献率（%） Ratio of Total Assets to Industrial Output Value（%）	资产负债率（%） Assets-Liability Ratio（%）
石油、煤炭及其他燃料加工业	Petroleum, coal and other fuel processing industries	1.5	55.5
化学原料和化学制品制造业	Manufacture of Raw Chemical Materials and Chemical Products	-3.9	76.2
医药制造业	Manufacture of Medicines	14.2	45.5
化学纤维制造业	Manufacture of Chemical Fibers	9.4	6.0
橡胶和塑料制品业	Manufacture of Rubber and Plastics	3.3	72.3
非金属矿物制品业	Manufacture of Non-metallic Mineral Products	14.1	57.8
黑色金属冶炼和压延加工业	Smelting and Pressing of Ferrous Metais	3.3	54.6
有色金属冶炼和压延加工业	Smelting and Pressing of Non-ferrous Metals	2.9	23.6
金属制品业	Manufacture of Metal Products	0.2	79.4
通用设备制造业	Manufacture of General Purpose Machinery	3.6	59.9
专用设备制造业	Manufacture of Special Equipment	4.6	52.7
汽车制造业	Manufacture of Motor Vehicle	6.3	65.5
铁路、船舶、航空航天和其他运输设备制造业	Railways,Shipbuilding,Aerospace and Other Transportation Equipment Manufacturing Industry	3.2	48.9
电气机械和器材制造业	Manufacture of Electric Equipment and Machinery	2.7	52.2
计算机、通信和其他电子设备制造业	Manufacture of Communication Equipment, Computers and other Electronic Equipment	6.3	40.2
仪器仪表制造业	Manufacture of Measuring Instruments and Machinery	7.9	50.8
其他制造业	Manufacture of Other Manufacturing		
废弃资源综合利用	Recycling and Disposal of Waste		
金属制品、机械和设备修理业	Metal Products,Machinery and Equipment Repair Industry	6.9	58.2
电力、热力生产和供应业	Production and Supply of Electric Power and Heat Power	4.0	71.7
燃气生产和供应业	Gas Mining and Supplying Industry	5.8	57.1
水的生产和供应业	Production and Supply of Water	2.8	70.7

continued 1

流动资产周转率（次/年）Rate of Annual Turnover Working Capitals (times/year)	成本费用利润率（%）Ratio of Profits to Cost (%)	营业收入利润率（%）Profit Margin of Operating Income (%)	每百元资产实现营业收入（元）Operating Income per 100 yuan of Assets (yuan)
0.6	2.4	2.3	18.9
0.9	-13.7	-13.6	51.5
1.7	8.4	7.6	102.3
3.1	3.3	3.2	212.3
0.7	3.0	2.9	40.3
1.5	9.7	8.8	104.7
1.5	1.0	1.0	113.1
0.7	7.6	7.2	28.4
0.9	-1.6	-1.5	49.4
0.5	5.6	5.4	39.4
0.8	4.3	4.1	55.0
1.8	3.1	3.1	131.9
0.7	6.6	6.3	41.1
0.9	2.7	2.8	59.7
1.4	9.5	8.8	55.5
1.1	10.6	9.7	73.9
0.9	0.1	0.1	80.7
4.7	1.5	1.4	72.9
3.7	5.2	5.2	80.6
0.5	2.8	2.8	28.2

12-14 规模以上工业主要产品生产能力（2019年）

Production Capacity of Major Products of Industrial Enterprises above Designated Size (2019)

指 标	Item	2019
棉纺锭/纺纱量（锭/吨）	Cotton spindles / spinning volume(ingot/ton)	203281
气流纺锭/纺纱量（头/吨）	Rotor spinning / spinning volume(head/ton)	1056
棉布织机（台）	Cotton Loom（unit）	6132
化学纤维（吨）	Chemical Fibre (ton)	44000
硅酸盐水泥熟料（吨）	Portland Cement Clinker (ton)	766454
水泥（吨）	Cement(ton)	2793341
平板玻璃（重量箱）	Plate Glass(weight case)	6370000
钢材（吨）	Rolled Steel (ton)	611807
铁合金（吨）	Ferroalloy (ton)	
金属切削机床（台）	Metal-cutting Machine Tools（unit）	7186
汽车（辆）	Motor Vehicles（unit）	540000
其中：基本型乘用车	Basic Passenger Vehicles（unit）	300000
新能源乘用车	New energy passenger car(unit)	130000
商用汽车	Commercial vehicle(unit)	240000
太阳能电池（千瓦）	Solar cell （KW）	8900000
房间空气调节器（台）	Room Air Conditioner (set)	2000350
移动通信手持机（台）	Mobile Handset（unit）	20084000
彩色电视机（台）	Color TV Set（unit）	400000
发电设备容量总计/发电量（万千瓦/万千瓦小时）	Total capacity of power generation equipment / generation capacity (10000 KW/10000 KWh)	353
其中：火电设备容量	Thermal Power	351
水电设备容量	Hydropower	2
风电设备容量	Wind Power	

主 要 统 计 指 标 解 释

工业 指从事自然资源的开采，对采掘品和农产品进行加工和再加工的物质生产部门。具体包括：（1）对自然资源的开采，如采矿、晒盐等（但不包括禽兽捕猎和水产捕捞）；（2）对农副产品的加工、再加工，如粮油加工、食品加工、缫丝、纺织、制革等；（3）对采掘品的加工、再加工，如炼铁、炼钢、化工生产、石油加工、机器制造、木材加工等，以及电力、自来水、煤气的生产和供应等；（4）对工业品的修理、翻新，如机器设备的修理、交通运输工具（如汽车）的修理等。

工业统计调查单位为独立核算法人工业企业。

独立核算法人工业企业指从事工业生产经营活动的单位。独立核算法人工业企业应同时具备以下条件：①依法成立，有自己的名称、组织机构和场所，能够承担民事责任；②独立拥有和使用资产，承担负债，有权与其他单位签订合同；③独立核算盈亏，并能够编制资产负债表。

国有及国有控股企业 指国有企业加上国有控股企业。国有企业（即原全民所有制工业或国营工业）指企业全部资产归国家所有，并按《中华人民共和国企业法人登记管理条例》规定登记注册的非公司制的经济组织。包括国有企业、国有独资公司和国有联营企业。1957年以前的公私合营和私营工业，后均改造为国营工业，1992年改为国有工业，这部分工业的资料不单独分列时，均包括在国有企业内。国有控股企业是对混合所有制经济的企业进行的"国有控股"分类。它是指这些企业的全部资产中国有资产（股份）相对其他所有者中的任何一个所有者占资（股）最多的企业。该分组反映了国有经济控股情况。

本篇涉及的其他企业登记注册类型的解释详见综合篇。

轻工业 指主要提供生活消费品和制作手工工具的工业。按其所使用的原料不同，可分为两大类：（1）以农产品为原料的轻工业，是指直接或间接以农产品为基本原料的轻工业。主要包括食品制造、饮料制造、烟草加工、纺织、缝纫、皮革和毛皮制作、造纸以及印刷等工业；（2）以非农产品为原料的轻工业，是指以工业品为原料的轻工业。主要包括文教体育用品、化学药品制造、合成纤维制造、日用化学制品、日用玻璃制品、日用金属制品、手工工具制造、医疗器械制造、文化和办公用机械制造等工业。

重工业 指为国民经济各部门提供物质技术基础的主要生产资料的工业。按其生产性质和产品用途，可以分为下列三类：（1）采掘（伐）工业，是指对自然资源的开采，包括石油开采、煤炭开采、金属矿开采、非金属矿开采等工业；（2）原材料工业，指向国民经济各部门提供基本材料、动力和燃料的工业。包括金属冶炼及加工、炼焦及焦炭、化学、化工：原料、水泥、人造板以及电力、石油和煤炭加工等工业；（3）加工工业，是指对工业原材料进行再加工制造的工业。包括装备国民经济各部门的机械设备制造工业、金属结构、水泥制品等工业，以及为农业提供的生产资料如化肥、农药等工业。

根据上述划分原则，修理业中以重工业产品为修理作业对象的划为重工业，反之划为轻工业。

工业总产值

（1）定义：

工业总产值是工业企业在一定时期内生产的以货币形式表现的工业最终产品和提供工业性劳务活动的总价值量。它反映一定时间内工业生产的总规模和总水平。

（2）计算原则：

工业生产的原则，即凡是企业在报告期生产的经检验合格的产品，不管是否在报告期销售，均包括在内。

最终产品的原则，即凡是计入工业总产值的产品，必须是本企业生产的经检验合格的，不需要再进行任何加工的最终产品。如果企业有中间产品（半成品）对外销售，则对外销售的中间产品应视为企业的最终产品。

工厂法原则，即工业总产值是以工业企业作为基本计算（核算）单位，即按企业的最终产品计算工业总产值。按这种方法计算的工业总产值，不允许同一产品价值在企业内部重复计算，不能把企业内部各个车间（分厂）生产的成果相加，但允许企业间的重复计算。

（3）内容及计算方法：

1995年全国工业普查对工业总产值（原规定）的内容及计算原则和方法做了某些修订，修订后的工业总产值（新规定）包括三项内容：即本期生产成品价值、对外加工费收入、在制品半成品期末期初差额价值三部分。

本期生产成品价值指企业本期生产，并在报告期内不再进行加工，经检验、包装入库的全部工业成品（半成品）价值合计，包括企业生产的自制设备及提供给本企业在建工程、其他非工业部门和福利部门等单位使用的成品价值。本期生产成品价值为按自备原材料生产的产品的数量乘以本期不含增值税（销项税额）的产品实际销售平均单价计算；会计核算中按成本价格转账的自制设备和自产自用的成品，按成本价格计算生产成品价值。生产成品价值中不包括用订货者来料加工的成品（半成品）价值。

对外加工费收入指企业在报告期内完成的对外承接的工业品加工（包括用订货者来料加工生产）的加工费收入和对外工业修理作业所取得的加工费收入。对外加工费收入按不含增值税（销项税额）的价格计算，可根据会计“产品销售收入”科目的有关资料取得。

对于本企业对内非工业部门提供的加工修理、设备安装的劳务收入，如果企业会计核算基础较好，能取得这部分资料，而且这部分价值所占比重较大，应包括在对外加工费收入中。

自制半成品在制品期末期初差额价值指企业报告期自制半成品在制品期末减期初的差额价值，本指标一般可以从会计核算资料中取得。如果会计产品成本核算中不计算半成品、在制品的成本，则总产值中也不包括这部分价值,反之则包括。

（4）工业总产值统计范围变化和计算方法修订情况：

1984年以前工业总产值不包括村办工业，村办工业总产值划归农业。1984年以后工业总产值包括村办工业。

1995年工业普查对工业总产值计算方法做了修订，即从1995年始按新修订（新规定）方法计算工业总产值。新规定与原规定的区别如下：

全价与加工费的计算原则不同：新规定为凡自备原材料，不论其生产繁简程度如何，一律按全价计算工业总产值；凡来料加工，允许按加工费计算工业总产值。原规定则视生产加工的繁简程度不同，规定哪些行业按全价，哪些行业按加工费计算工业总产值。

自制半成品、在产品期末期初差额价值的计算原则不同：新规定要求，凡会计产品成本核算时计算了成本的差额价值，总产值中就应包括，否则可不包括；原规定则按生产周期六个月的界限区分，凡生产周期六个月以上的企业，总产值计算中应包括这部分差额价值，否则可不包括。

计算价格不同：新规定按不含增值税（销项税额）的价格计算；原规定则按含增值税（销项税额）的价格计算。

工业增加值 指工业企业在报告期内以货币表现的工业生产活动的最终成果。

工业增加值有两种计算方法：一是生产法，即工业总产出减去工业中间投入加上应交增值税；二是收入法，即从收入的角度出发，根据生产要素在生产过程中应得到的收入份额计算，具体构成项目有固定资产折旧、劳动者报酬、生产税净额、营业盈余，这种方法也称要素分配法。本年鉴中的工业增加值是以收入法计算的。

生产法工业增加值的计算方法为：

工业增加值＝工业总产出-工业中间投入+应交增值税

（1）工业总产出：指工业企业在一定时期内工业生产活动的总成果。工业总产出包括：成品生产价值，对外加工费收入，自制半成品、在产品期末期初差额价值。1995年后用新规定计算的工业总产值代替。

（2）工业中间投入：指工业企业在工业生产活动中消耗的外购物质产品和对外支付的服务费用。服务费用包括支付给物质生产部门（工业、农业、批发零售贸易业、建筑业、运输邮电业）的服务费用和支付给非物质生产部门（如保险、金融、文化教育、科学研究、医疗卫生、行政管理等）的服务费用。工业中间投入的确定须遵循以下原则：必须从外部购入的，并已计入工业总产出的产品和服务价值；必须是本期投入生产，并一次性消耗掉（包括本期摊销的低值易耗品等）的产品和服务价值。

工业中间投入包括直接材料费用、制造费用中的工业中间投入、管理费用中的工业中间投入、销售费用中的工业中间投入和利息支出五部分。

资产总计 指企业拥有或控制的能以货币计量的经济资源，包括各种财产、债权和其他权利。资产按流动性分为流动资产、长期投资、固定资产、无形资产、递延资产和其他资产。该指标根据企业会计“资产负债表”中“资产总计”项目的期末数增列。

流动资产 指企业可以在一年内或者超过一年的一个生产周期内变现或者耗用的资产，包括现金及各种存款、短期投资，应收及预付款项、存货等。

固定资产原价 指企业在建造、购置、安装、改建、扩建、技术改造某项固定资产时所支出的全部货币总额。它一般包括买价、包装费、运杂费和安装费等。

固定资产净值 指固定资产原价减去历年已提折旧额后的净额。计算公式为：

固定资产净值=固定资产原价-累计折旧

负债合计 指企业所承担的能以货币计量，将以资产或劳务偿付的债务，偿还形式包括货币、资产或提供劳务。负债一般按偿还期长短分为流动负债和长期负债。根据会计“资产负债表”中“负债合计”的年末数填列。

所有者权益合计 指企业投资人对企业净资产的所有权。企业净资产为企业全部资产与企业全部负债的差额，包括实收资本、资本公积、盈余公积、未分配利润等。根据会计“资产负债表”中“所有者权益”项的期末数填列。

营业收入 指企业从事销售商品、提供劳务和让渡资产使用权等生产经营活动形成的经济利益流入。包括“主营业务收入”和“其他业务收入”。根据会计“利润表”中“营业收入”项目的本年累计数填报。

主营业务收入 指会计“利润表”中对应指标的本年累计数。未执行2001年《企业会计制度》的企业，用“产品销售收入”的本期累计数代替。

营业成本 指企业从事销售商品、提供劳务和让渡资产使用权等生产经营活动发生的实际成本。“营业成本”应当与“营业收入”进行配比。包括“主营业务成本”和“其他业务成本”。根据会计“利润表”中“营业成本”项目的本年累计数填报。

税金及附加 指企业因从事生产 经营 活动按税法规定应缴纳的消费税、城市维护建设税、资源税、环境保护税、教育附加及房产税、土地使用税、车船使用税、印花税等相关税费。根据会计“利润表”中“税金及附加”项目的本年累计数填报。

销售费用 指企业在销售商品和材料、提供劳务的过程中发生的各种费用，包括保险费、包装费、展览费和广告费、商品维修费、预计产品质量保证损失、运输费、装卸费等以及为销售本企业商品而专设的销售机构（含销售网点、售后服务网点等）的职工薪酬、业务费、折旧费等经营费用。

管理费用 指企业为组织和管理企业生产经营所发生的费用，包括企业在筹建期间内发生的开办费、董事会和行政管理部门在企业经营管理中发生的，或者应当由企业统一负担的公司经费等，不包含“研发费用”。执行企业会计准则的企业，根据会计“利润表”中“管理费用”项目的本年累计数填报。执行《小企业会计准则》的企业，应将会计“利润表”中“管理费用”项目本年累计数减“研发费用”项目本年累计数后填报。执行其他企业会计制度的企业以及未执行财政部《关于修订印发2019年度一般企业财务报表格式的通知》（财会[2019]6号）的企业，在会计“利润表”中“管理费用”项目的本年累计数的基础上，根据会计“管理费用”科目下和“研究费用”明细科目，将“研发费用”剔除后填报。

研发费用 指企业在新知识、新技术、新产品、新工艺等的研究与开发过程中发生的费用化支出，以及计入“管理费用”会计科目的企业自行开发无形资产的摊销。费用化支出主要包括研发活动的人工费用、直接投入费用、用于研发活动的仪器、设备的折旧费、用于研发活动的软件、专利权、非专利技术的摊销费用、新产品设计费、新工艺规程制定费以及其他研发活动相关费用。执行企业会计准则的企业，根据会计“利润表”中“研发费用”项目的本年累计数填报。执行《小企业会计准则》的企业，根据会计“利润表”中“研发费用”项目的本年累计数填报。执行其他企业会计制度的企业以及会计“利润表”未列示“研发费用”或“研究费用”的企业，根据会计“管理费用”科目下“研究费用”明细科目的本期发生额，以及“管理费用”科目下“无形资产摊销”明细科目的本期发生额分析填报。

财务费用 指企业为筹集生产经营所需资金等而发生的筹资费用，包括企业生产经营期间发生的利息支出（减利息收入）、汇兑损失（减汇兑收益）以及相关的手续费等。根据会计“利润表”中“财务费用”项目的本年累计数填报。

利润总额 指企业在生产经营过程中各种收入扣除各种耗费后的盈余，反映企业在报告期内实现的盈亏总额，包括营业利润、补贴收入、投资净收益和营业外收支净额。根据会计“利润表”中的对应指标的本期累计数填列。

本年应交增值税 指企业按税法规定，从事货物销售或提供加工、修理修配劳务等增加货物价值的活动本期应交纳的税金。指企业在报告期应交增值税额。计算公式为：

本年应交增值税=销项税额-（进项税额-进项税额转出）-出口抵减内销产品应纳税额-减免税款+出口退税

本年进项税额 指工业企业在报告期内购入货物或接受应税劳务而支付的、准予从销项税额中抵扣的增值税额。

本年销项税额 指工业企业在报告期内销售货物或

提供应税劳务应收取的增值税额。

总资产贡献率 反映企业全部资产的获利能力，是企业经营业绩和管理水平的集中体现，是评价和考核企业盈利能力的核心指标。计算公式为：

总资产贡献率（%）=（利润总额+税金总额+利息支出）/平均资产总额×100%

公式中：税金总额为产品销售税金及附加与应交增值税之和；平均资产总额为期初期末资产之和的算术平均值。

资产负债率 该指标既反映企业经营风险的大小，也反映企业利用债权人提供的资金从事经营活动的能力。计算公式为：

资产负债率（%）=负债总额/资产总额×100%

资产与负债均为报告期期末数。

流动资产周转次数 指一定时期内流动资产完成的周转次数，反映投入工业企业流动资金的周转速度。计算公式为：

流动资产周转次数=产品销售收入/全部流动资产平均余额

公式中：全部流动资产平均余额为期初和期末的流动资产之和的算术平均值。

成本费用利润率 反映企业投入的生产成本及费用的经济效益，同时也反映企业降低成本所取得的经济效益。计算公式为：

成本费用利润率（%）=利润总额/成本费用总额×100%

公式中：成本费用总额为产品销售成本、销售费用、管理费用、财务费用之和。

产品销售率 该指标反映工业产品已实现销售的程度，是分析工业产销衔接情况，研究工业产品满足社会需求的指标。计算公式为：

产品销售率（%）=工业销售产值/工业总产值（现价）×100%

Explanatory Notes on Main Statistical Indicators

Industry refers to the material production sector which is engaged in the extraction of natural resources and processing and reprocessing of minerals and agricultural products, including (1) extraction of natural resources, such as mining, salt production (but not including hunting and fishing); (2) processing and reprocessing of farm and sideline produces, such as rice husking, flour milling, wine making, oil pressing, silk reeling, spinning and weaving, and leather making; (3) manufacture of industrial products, such as steel making, iron smelting, chemicals manufacturing, petroleum processing, machine building, timber processing; water and gas production and electricity generation and supply; (4)repairing of industrial products such as the repairing of machinery and means of transport (including cars).

In industrial statistics surveys, the units of enquiry are corporate industrial enterprises with independent accounting systems.

Corporate industrial enterprises with independent accounting systems refer to enterprises engaging in industrial production activities, which meet the following requirements: (1) They are established legally, having their own names, organizations, location and able to take civil liability; (2) They possess and use their assets independently, assume liabilities and are entitled to sign contracts with other units; (3) They are financially independent and compile their own balance sheets.

State-owned and State-holding Enterprises refer to state-owned enterprises plus State-holding enterprises. State-owned enterprises (originally known as State-run enterprises with ownership by the whole society) are non-corporate economic entities registered in accordance with the Regulation of the People's Republic of China on the Management of Registration of Legal Enterprises, where all assets are owned by the State. Included in this category are State-owned enterprises, State-funded corporations and State-owned joint-operation enterprises. Joint State- private industries and private industries, which existed before 1957, were transformed into state-run industries since 1957, and into State-owned industries after 1992. Statistics on those enterprises are included in the State- owned industries instead of being grouped them separately. State-holding enterprises are a sub- classification of enterprises with mixed ownership, referring to enterprises where the percentage of State assets (or shares by the State) is larger than any other single share holder of the same enterprise. This sub- classification illustrates the control of the State over a particular industry.

For explanation of enterprises of other types of registration covered in this chapter, please refer to General Survey.

Light Industry refers to the industry that produces consumer goods and hand tools. It consists of two categories, depending on the materials used:

(1) Industries using farm products as raw materials. These are the branches of light industry which directly or indirectly use farm products as basic raw materials, including the manufacture of food and beverages, tobacco processing, textile, clothing, fur and leather manufacturing, paper making, printing, etc.

(2) Industries using non-farm products as raw materials. These are the branches of light industry which use manufactured goods as raw materials, including the manufacture of cultural, educational articles and sports goods, chemicals, synthetic fibre, chemical products for daily use, glass products for daily use, metal products for daily use, hand tools, medical apparatus and instruments, and the manufacture of cultural and office machinery.

Heavy Industry refers to the industry which produces capital goods, and provides various sectors of the national economy with necessary material and technical basis for production. It consists of the following three branches according to the purpose of production or the use of products:

(1) Mining, quarrying and logging industry, which refers to the industry that extracts natural resources, including extraction of petroleum, coal, metal and non-metal ores.

(2) Raw materials industry refers to the industry that provides various sectors of the national economy with raw materials, fuels and power. It includes smelting and processing of metals, coking and coke chemistry, chemical materials and building materials such as cement, plywood, and power, petroleum refining and coal dressing

(3) Manufacturing industry which refers to the industry that processes raw materials. It includes machine-building industries which equip sectors of the national economy; industries producing metal structure and cement products; and industries producing means of agricultural production, such as chemical fertilizers and pesticides.

In accordance with the above principles of classification, the repairing trades, which are engaged primarily in repairing products of heavy industry, are classified as heavy industry while those which are engaged in repairing products of light industry are classified as light industry.

Gross Industrial Output Value

(1) Definition: Gross industrial output value is the total volume of final industrial products produced and industrial services provided during a given period in monetary terms. It reflects the total achievements and overall scale of industrial production during a given period.

(2) Principles for calculation:

Statistics on industrial production follow the principle that all products produced by the enterprises and accepted through quality check during the reference period are to be included no matter whether they are sold or not during the reference period.

Determination of final products follows the principle that all products that are included in the calculation of gross industrial output value are the final products of the enterprise which have been accepted through quality check and require no further processing. If an enterprise has intermediate (semi-finished) products to sell, these intermediate products are considered as the final products of the enterprise.

Gross industrial output value is calculated following the principle of factory approach, i.e. industrial enterprise is used as the basic accounting unit in calculating the gross industrial output value. By this approach, value of the same product is not to be double-counted, and the output value of different workshops (branch factories) within the enterprise should not be added. However, this approach allows the possibility of double counting between enterprises.

(3) Content and method of calculation: The old definition of gross industrial output value was modified during the 1995 National Industrial Census. The revised (new) definition of gross industrial output value consists of 3 components: value of the finished products during the reference period, income from processing for external parties, and value of change in semi-finished products between the end and the beginning of the reference period.

Value of finished products during the reference period: refers to the value of all finished (semi-finished) industrial products that are produced during the reference period without the need for further processing, checked for acceptance, packed and put into the warehouse of the enterprise, including the value of own-produced equipment and the value of products provided to the projects under construction of the enterprise, and to other non-industrial or welfare units. Value of finished products during the reference period is calculated by the quantity of products produced using own materials multiplied by the average unit prices at which products are sold (excluding value-added tax). Own-produced equipment and products produced for own use are valued at cost prices as in the case of enterprise accounting. Value of finished products does not include the value of finished products (semi-finished products) that are produced using the materials from the clients who place the orders.

Income from external processing: refers to income from contracted external processing of industrial products (including processing of industrial products using materials from the clients), and the income from industrial repairing work provided to other parties. Income from external processing is calculated using information from the item "products sales income" in the enterprise accounting at the prices with value-added tax excluded.

For income from services such as processing, repairing and installation of equipment provided to non- industrial units within the enterprise, if the accounting work of the enterprise is good enough to separate it from other records, and the share of such services is significant, it should also be included in the income from external processing.

Value of change in semi-finished products between the end and the beginning of the reference period: refers to the value of change in semi-finished products between the end and the beginning of the reference period, which generally can be obtained from accounting records of enterprises. If the enterprise accounting excludes the cost of semi-finished products, then it should not be included in the gross industrial output value, and the reverse if otherwise.

(4) Changes in the scope and method of calculation of the gross industrial output value

Prior to 1984, the value of rural industry run by villages was classified into agriculture instead of industry Since 1984, it has been included in the gross industrial output value. Method of calculation for the gross industrial output value was modified in the industriaLcensus in 1995. The difference in the new method as compared with the old one is outlined below:

Principle in using full value vs. processing fee: The new method stipulates that all products produced using own materials are to be calculated with full value in reporting the gross industrial output value irrespective of the complexity of production, and for external processing, it allows calculation using processing fee. In the old method, however, the use of full value or processing fee was determined by the degree of complexity of production in different branches of industries.

Principle in determining the value of change in semi-finished products: The new method requires that value of change in semi-finished products should be included in the gross industrial output value if it is included in the accounting record of the enterprise, otherwise it should not be included. In the old method, it is determined by the type of enterprises in terms of production cycle. If the production cycle is over 6 months, the value of change in semi-finished products is included in the gross industrial output value, otherwise it is not.

Difference in prices: The new method uses prices excluding value-added tax in the calculation of gross industrial output value, while the old method used prices including value-added tax.

Value–added of Industry refers to the final results of industrial production of industrial enterprises in money terms during the reference period.

Industrial value-added can be calculated by two approaches: the production approach, i.e. gross industrial output value minus intermediate input plus value-added tax, and the income approach, i.e. income for various factors used in the course of production, including depreciation of fixed assets, remuneration of labourers, net of production tax, and operating surplus. Value-added of industry in the Yearbook is calculated by the income approach as follows:

Value-added of industry = gross industrial output - industrial intermediate input + value-added tax

(1) Gross industrial output: refers to the total achievements of industrial production activities during a given period. Gross industrial output includes value of finished products, income from external processing, and value of change in semi-finished products between the end and the beginning of the reference period. Since 1995, the gross industrial output value obtained by the new method is used in the calculation.

(2) Industrial intermediate input: refers to purchased goods and paid services consumed during the industrial production of enterprises. Fees paid for services include fees paid for the services provided by material production sectors (industry, agriculture, wholesale and retail trade, construction, transport, post and telecommunications) and by non-material production sectors (insurance, banking, culture, education, scientific research, health and medical care, public administration, etc.). The determination of industrial intermediate input follows the principle that the goods and services must be purchased from outside and included in the gross industrial output, and that the goods and services are inputted into production and consumed (include low-value consumables) during the reference period.

Industrial intermediate input includes 5 components, namely direct consumption of materials, industrial intermediate input in manufacturing cost, industrial intermediate input in management cost, industrial intermediate input in marketing cost and expenditure on interest.

Total Assets refer to all economic resources, in monetary term, these are owned or controlled by enterprises, including properties, creditor's equity and other economic rights of all forms. Classified by the degree of liquidity, total assets include working capitals, long-term investment, fixed assets, intangible assets, deferred assets and other assets. Data on this indicator can be obtained by the year-end figures of total assets in the Assets and Liability Table of accounting records of enterprises.

Working Capital refers to capital that an enterprise can cash or use during one year or one production cycle that may exceed one year, including cash and savings deposits of various forms, short-term investment, money receivable and prepaid money, inventories, etc.

Original Value of Fixed Assets refers to the total value, in monetary terms, that an enterprise spent on fixed assets, through construction, purchase, installation, transformation, expansion or technical upgrading. Generally, it covers cost of purchase, packing, transportation and installation, etc.

Net Value of Fixed Assets refers to the original value of fixed assets minus depreciation over the years, i.e.:

Net value of fixed assets = original value of fixed assets - cumulative depreciation

Total Liabilities refer to payable liabilities of enterprises that have to be repaid in terms of money, assets or labour services. In terms of payment, it can be divided into liquid liabilities and long-term liabilities. Data on this item is obtained from the ending figures on total liabilities from the Assets and Liability Table from the enterprises.

Total Equity refers to the ownership of net assets of enterprise by its investors. Net assets equal total assets minus total liabilities of the enterprise, including the paid-in capital, accumulation of capital and operating surplus and non-distributed profits. Data are obtained from the ending figures on "total equity" from the "balance sheets" .

Operating Income It refers to the inflow of economic interests generated by an enterprise's production and operation activities such as selling goods, providing labor services and transferring the right to use assets. Operating income includes "main business income" and "other business income". The current year's cumulative counting is reported according to the item of "Operating income" in the accounting "income statement".

Revenue from Principal Business refers to the annual accumulation of the corresponding item in the "profit table" of the accountant. For enterprises that do not follow the 2001 Enterprise Accounting Standards, the year-end accumulation of revenue from the sales of products is used as a substitute.

Operating Cost It refers to the actual cost incurred by an enterprise in such production and operation activities as selling goods, providing labor services and transferring the right to use assets. "Operating cost" shall be matched with "operating revenue". Include "main business cost" and "other business cost". The current year's cumulative counting is reported according to the operating cost item in the accounting "income statement".

Taxes and Surcharges It refers to the consumption tax payable in accordance with the tax law for an enterprise engaged in production and business activities, including urban maintenance and construction tax, resource tax, environmental protection tax, education surcharge, property tax, land use tax, vehicle and vessel use tax, stamp tax and other related taxes. It is filled according to the cumulative number of taxes and additional items in the accounting income statement for this year.

Sales Cost It refers to the enterprises in the process of selling goods and materials to provide services of all kinds of costs, including insurance premium package exhibition and advertising goods maintenance product quality assurance is expected loss freight handling charge and so on and designed for sales of the enterprise products sales organizations (including sales outlets after-sales service network, etc.) of business expenses such as depreciation of employee compensation fees.

Cost management It refers to the enterprise for the cost of production in which the enterprise organization and management, including enterprise organization expenses the board of directors in the preparation period and the administrative departments in the enterprise management, or shall be borne by the enterprise unified company funds, etc., does not include the development costs, perform the enterprise accounting standard for business enterprises according to the management of project cost accounting profit statement this year accumulative fill in the implementation of accounting standards for small business enterprises, should be to reduce the management cost accounting profit statement project this year accumulative R&D projects this year accumulative after fill in Perform other enterprise accounting system of enterprises and not issued by the Ministry of Finance on revising the 2019 annual general enterprise financial report format to inform (finance and accounting) [2019] 6 enterprises, management of project cost in accounting profit this year accumulative frequency, on the basis of administrative subjects and research expenses according to the accounting detail course, will cost out the development is allowed.

R & D Expenses It refer to the expenses incurred by enterprises in the research and development process of new knowledge, new technology, new products and new processes. It mainly includes the labor cost of research and development activities, direct input cost, depreciation cost of instruments and equipment used in research and development activities, amortization cost of software, patent right and non-patent technology used in research and development activities, new product design fee, new process procedure formulation fee and other related costs of research and development activities. An enterprise implementing the accounting standards for business enterprises shall fill in the current year's cumulative count of the items of "Research and development expenses" in the accounting "income statement". The enterprises implementing the Accounting Standards for Small Enterprises shall fill in the current year's accumulations according to the items of "research expenses" in the accounting "income statement". Enterprises implementing accounting systems of other enterprises and enterprises that do not list "RESEARCH and development expenses" or "research expenses" in the accounting "income statement" shall fill in the amount incurred in the current period according to the relevant items of "Research expenses" under the accounting "administrative expenses".

Total Profits refers to the balance of various incomes minus various spendings in the course of operation, reflecting the total profits and losses of enterprises in reporting period. It includes: operating profits, income from subsidies, net investment income and net income from activities other than operation. Data are obtained from the annual accumulation of the corresponding item in the "profit table" of the accountant.

Value-added Tax Payable in the Current Year refers to the payable tax of enterprises which engaged in selling of goods or providing services that bring added value to the goods, such as processing, repairing, fitting and other activities should be paid according to Tax Law. It refers to the amount of the value-added tax which should be paid by the enterprises during the reference period. The formula is as tollows:

Value-added Tax Payable in the Current Year = tax on sales-(tax on purchase-transferred tax on purchase)- exports deduct tax payable on domestic sales-tax relief+the export tax rebate.

Tax on Purchase in Current Year refers to goods purchased by industrial enterprises or value added tax that should be paid but being granted the right to deduct from the tax on sales.

Tax on Sales in Current Year refers to value added tax on industrial enterprises from sales of goods or taxable services that should be charged value added tax.

Ratio of Profits, Taxes and Interests to Average Assets reflects the profit-making capability of all assets of the enterprise and is a key indicator manifesting the performance and management and evaluating the profit-making potential of the enterprise. It is calculated as

$$\text{Ratio of Profits, Taxes and Interests to Average Assets(\%)} = \frac{\text{otal profits+ total taxes+ interest payment}}{\text{average assets}} \times 100\%$$

In the above formula, total taxes is the sum of tax and extra charges on the sales of products and value-added tax payable; and average assets is the arithmetic mean of the sum of beginning assets and ending assets.

Ratio of Debts to Assets reflects both the operation risk and the capability of the enterprise in making use of the capital from the creditors. It is calculated as follows:

$$\text{Ratio of Debts toAssets(\%)} = \frac{\text{total debts}}{\text{total assets}} \times 100\%$$

Both assets and debts are figures at the end of the reference period.

Turnover of Working Capital refers to the number of times of turnover of working capital in a given period of time, which reflects the speed of the turnover of working capital of industrial enterprises, and is calculated as follows:

$$\text{Turnover of Working Capital} = \frac{\text{sales revenue of products}}{\text{average balance of total working capital}}$$

In the above formula, average balance of total working capital refers to the arithmetic mean of the sum of working capital at the beginning and at the end of the reference period.

Ratio of Profits to Total Industrial Costs refers to the ratio of profits realized in a given period to the total costs in the same period, which reflects the economic efficiency of input cost and is calculated as follows:

$$\text{Ratio of Profits to Total Industrial Cost (\%)} = \frac{\text{total profits}}{\text{total costs}} \times 100\%$$

Total costs in the above formula are the sum of cost of products sold, marketing cost, management cost and financial cost.

Sales Ratio of Products is an indicator reflecting the actual sale of industrial products, analyzing the production-selling and supply-demand relations. It is calculated as:

$$\text{Sales Ratio of Products (\%)} = \frac{\text{value of industrial sales}}{\text{gross industrial output value (current prices)}} \times 100\%$$

13 能 源

ENERGY

资料整理：于元英　张　育　李　婷
Data management：Yu Yuanying　Zhang Yu　Li Ting
数据审核：马建华
Data audit：Ma Jianhua

第十三部分　能源

一、简要说明

本章资料包括规模以上工业能源购销存情况、全市单位GDP能耗、规模以上工业企业用水情况等，由西安市统计局能源与环境处提供。

二、主要指标

规模以上工业综合能源消费量（万吨标准煤）	634.77	比上年下降	8.4%
单位GDP能耗（吨标准煤/万元）	0.324	比上年下降	4.78%

13　ENERGY

Ⅰ.Brief Introduction

Data in this chapter reflects energy purchases consumption and inventory of industrial enterprises above designated size,energy consumption per unit of GDP in whole city, and statistics on water use of industrial enterprises above designated size. data in this chapter are provided and compiled by Energy and Environment Division of the Xi'an Bureau of Statistics.

Ⅱ.Major Indicators

		Increase over Preceding Year
Comprehensive Energy Consumption Above Designated Size(10 000 Tons of Standard Coal)	634.77	-8.4%
Energy Consumption of GDP per Unit (Tons of Standard Coal /10 000 yuan)	0.324	-4.78%

13-1 全市及各区县单位GDP能耗增长率

Grouth Rates of Energy Consumption per Unit of GDP by Region

单位：% （%）

区 县	Region	2010	2011	2012	2013	2014	2015	2016	2017	2018	2019
西安市	**Xi'an**	**-2.06**	**-3.56**	**-3.51**	**-3.57**	**-5.89**	**-3.20**	**-3.83**	**-4.61**	**-5.99**	**-4.78**
新城区	Xincheng	-1.15	-3.51	-3.50	-3.50	-5.39	-3.27	-3.58	-3.27	-4.72	-4.19
碑林区	Beilin	-0.91	-3.89	-3.50	-3.50	-6.06	-3.20	-3.66	-3.65	-5.42	-4.37
莲湖区	Lianhu	-3.58	-3.84	-3.60	-3.61	-7.76	-3.14	-3.58	-5.93	-6.12	-3.50
灞桥区	Baqiao	-4.20	-3.81	-3.62	-3.64	-5.20	-3.30	-3.75	-6.95	-8.25	-3.98
未央区	Weiyang	-1.31	-3.60	-3.60	-3.60	-7.60	-4.16	-3.86	-4.49	-4.48	-2.95
雁塔区	Yanta	-4.18	-3.61	-3.61	-3.60	-3.89	-3.58	-3.55	-6.36	-6.54	-5.86
阎良区	Yanliang	-0.61	-3.38	-3.50	-3.50	-7.59	-3.00	-3.46	-3.99	-4.32	-2.91
临潼区	Lintong	-4.81	-3.52	-3.51	-3.51	-8.07	-3.00	-3.46	-6.29	-5.71	-5.18
长安区	Chang'an	-2.08	-3.60	-3.63	-3.63	-3.40	-4.10	-3.56	-5.10	-4.56	-2.95
高陵区	Gaoling	-3.82	-3.93	-3.52	-3.54	-7.32	-3.00	-3.52	-4.00	-5.88	-2.90
鄠邑区	Huyi	-2.99	-3.85	-3.60	-3.62	-3.40	-3.82	-3.84	-3.89	-5.86	-4.13
蓝田县	Lantian	-2.06	-3.39	-3.40	-3.30	-5.48	-3.17	-3.84	-3.27	-5.21	-3.35
周至县	Zhouzhi	-2.06	-3.30	-3.30	-3.30	-7.63	-2.90	-3.50	-3.64	-5.59	-2.96
西咸新区	Xixian									-12.51	-12.31

注：单位GDP能耗中GDP按可比价计算；2018年数据根据第四次经济普查结果进行了调整。

13-2 主要年份全社会用电量

单位：万千瓦时

行　业	Sector	2000	2007	2008	2009
总　计	**Total**	**732373**	**1482896**	**1605089**	**1724067**
A、全行业用电量合计	Total of Industry of Electricity	599855	1215799	1293574	1358483
1. 第一产业	Primary Industry	77579	120134	127054	99083
2. 第二产业	Secondary Industry	354245	700026	724852	766029
3. 第三产业	Tertiary Industry	168031	395639	441668	493371
B、城乡居民生活用电	Electricity Consumption of and Rural ResidentsUrban	132518	267097	311515	365585
1. 乡村	Rural	31281	38395	63072	99941
2. 城市	City	101237	228702	248443	265644
一、农、林、牧、渔业	Agriculture,Forestry,Animal Husbandry and Fishery	77579	120134	127054	99083
二、工业	Industry	345175	674990	696291	724920
三、建筑业	Construction	9070	25036	28561	41108
四、交通运输、仓储及邮政业	Traffic,Transport, Storage and Post	22904	53825	56614	62031
五、信息传输、软件和信息技术服务业	Information Transmission,Computer Services and Software		21938	26680	29328
六、批发和零售业	Wholesale and Retail Trades		107343	111676	122203
七、住宿和餐饮业	Hotels and Catering Services				
八、金融业	Financial Intermediation		67674	81674	102400
九、房地产业	Real Estate				
十、租赁和商务服务业	Leasing and Business Services				
十一、公共事业及管理组织	Public Utilities and Management Organization		144859	165024	177409

注：1.本表数据来源于国网陕西省供电公司西安供电公司和国网陕西电力公司西咸供电公司。
2.2017年及以后为包含西咸新区数据。
3.2018年采用新行业分类标准，所以2017年及之前的农、林、牧、渔业、批发和零售业、住宿和餐饮业、金融业、房地产业、租赁和商务服务业无法分类，故2017年及之前农、林、牧、渔业为农、林、牧、渔、水利业合计，批发和零售业为商业、住宿和餐饮业合计，金融业为金融、房地产、商务及居民服务业合计。

Electricity Consumption of the Whole Society in Representative Years

(10 000 kw. h)

2010	2011	2012	2013	2014	2015	2016	2017	2018	2019
1993751	**2167453**	**2352571**	**2554679**	**2753213**	**2844836**	**3120582**	**3613693**	**3967465**	**4184997**
1499903	1590486	1706859	1854696	2002503	2049492	2216797	2586468	2821250	3031213
108720	117984	109086	110405	95997	89970	87825	102033	28998	26057
883259	910360	932622	991202	1086105	1088866	1147294	1388903	1430389	1470195
507924	562142	665151	753089	820401	870656	981678	1095531	1361863	1534962
493848	576966	645713	699982	750710	795344	903785	1027226	1146216	1153784
142059	169898	197937	216148	235938	241920	263871	288571	321715	347306
351789	407068	447776	483834	514773	553424	639914	738655	824501	806478
108720	117984	109086	110405	95997	89970	87825	102033	100432	75902
838317	859796	875018	920024	998132	997115	1062188	1287836	1326060	1345516
44942	50564	57605	71179	87973	91750	85106	101068	110600	131824
58509	66684	69633	78722	88805	90914	109911	128970	149353	174658
30760	33191	37444	39551	42662	46203	61950	77104	90433	105752
148418	166558	199970	228117	253199	277248	301414	334387	302014	371987
								94270	98522
116163	131236	150832	165833	180824	185329	212666	232317	13599	13908
								180942	214133
								25860	30222
154074	164473	207271	240866	254911	270962	295737	322753	427688	468790

13–3 规模以上工业企业能源购进、消费及库存（2019年）

能源名称	Name	年初库存量 Stock (year-beginning)	购进量/实物量 Purchases	其中：购自省外 Wherein: purchased from outside the province
原煤(吨)	Raw Coal (ton)	762171	10438720	
洗精煤(吨)	Washed Coal(ton)			
其他洗煤(吨)	Other Washed Coals(ton)	114230	230933	1975
煤制品（吨）	Briquettes(ton)			
焦炭(吨)	Coke(ton)		370	370
其他焦化产品(吨)	Other Coking Products(ton)			
焦炉煤气(万立方米)	Coke Oven Gas(10000 cu.m)			
高炉煤气(万立方米)	Blast Furnace Gas(10000 cu.m)			
转炉煤气(万立方米)	Converter Gas(10000 cu.m)			
发生炉煤气(万立方米)	Producer Gas(10000 cu.m)			
天然气（气态）（万立方米）	Natural Gas(10 000cu.m)	908	83230	
液化天然气（液态）（吨）	Liquefied Natural Gas (Liquid)(ton)	40	8124	
煤层气(万立方米)	Voalbed Gas(10000 cu.m)			
原油(吨)	Crude Oil(ton)			
汽油(吨)	Gasoline(ton)	66	16111	496
煤油(吨)	Kerosene(ton)	40	203	
柴油(吨)	Diesel Oil(ton)	1130	80131	381
燃料油(吨)	Fuel Oil(ton)		511	117
液化石油气(吨)	LPG(ton)	1	18209	
炼厂干气(吨)	Refinery Gas(ton)			
石脑油(吨)	Naphtha(ton)			
润滑油（吨）	Lubricating Oil (ton)		1249	
石蜡(吨)	Paraffin(ton)			
溶剂油（吨）	Solvent Oil (ton)	1	74	
石油焦(吨)	Petrol Coke(ton)			
石油沥青(吨)	Petroleum Asphalt(ton)	760		
其它石油制品(吨)	Other Petroleum Products(ton)	72	2227	
热力(百万千焦)	Heat (1 million kilo-joule)		4520443	
电力(万千瓦时)	Electricity(10 000kwh)		828595	
煤矸石(用于燃料)(吨)	Coal Gangue(used for fuel)(ton)		660	
城市生活垃圾(用于燃料)(吨)	City Domestic Waste(used for fuel)(ton)			
生物燃料（吨标准煤）	Biofuel(tons of SCE)	852	11710	5161
余热余压（百万千焦）	Residual Heat and Pressure(million of KJ)		512515	
工业废料(用于燃料)（吨）	Industrial Waste(used for fuel)(ton)			
其他燃料（吨标准煤）	Other Fuels(ton of SCE)	168	2794	
能源合计(吨标准煤)	Total Energy(ton of SCE)			

Energy Purchases, Consumption and Inventory of Industrial Enterprises above Designated Size (2019)

消费量 合计 Consumption Total	工业 生产消费 Industrial Production Consume	用于 原材料 as Raw Material	非工业 生产消费 Non-industrial Production Consume	期末库存量 Stock (year-end)
10281371	10276692	1063511	4679	914901
253933	253933			86591
360	360			
82885	82223	1155	662	607
8133	8124		9	29
16237	13587	21	2650	33
206	206			37
79701	77694	380	2007	1221
461	456		5	50
18212	18060	17650	152	
1254	1254	1		
75	75	8		
211	211			
2227	2227			71
6429118	6395823		33295	
970862	963816		7046	
660	660			
5	5			
11920	11770		150	543
512519	512519			
2022	1988		34	
10168746	10139938		28808	

13-4 规模以上工业企业分行业主要能源品种消费量（2019年）

Major Energy Consumption above Designated Size by Industry（2019）

行 业	Sector	原煤 (吨) Raw Coal (ton)	天然气 (万立方米) Natural Gas(10 000 cu.m)
总 计	**Total**	**10281371**	**82885**
煤炭开采和洗选业	Mining and Washing of Coal		
石油和天然气开采业	Extraction of Petroleum and Natural Gas		
黑色金属矿采选业	Mining and Processing of Ferrous Metal Ores		
有色金属矿采选业	Mining and Processing of Non-ferrous Metal Ores		
非金属矿采选业	Mining and Processing of Nonmetal Ores		
开采专业及辅助性活动	Mining Professional and Auxiliary Activity		402
其他采矿业	Mining of other Ores		
农副食品加工业	Processing of Food from Agricultural Porducts	210369	1741
食品制造业	Manufacture of Foods		3796
酒、饮料和精制茶制造业	Manufacture of Alcohol,Beverages and Tea		1657
烟草制品业	Manufacture of Tobacco		
纺织业	Manufacture of Textile		246
纺织服装、服饰业	Textile, apparel industry		46
皮革、毛皮、羽毛及其制品和制鞋业	Manufacture of Leather, Fur, Feather and Related Products, and Shoes		
木材加工和木、竹、藤、棕、草制品业	Processing of Timber, Manufacture of Wood,Plam and Straw Products		
家具制造业	Manufacture of Furniture		111
造纸和纸制品业	Manufacture of Paper and Paper Products		809
印刷和记录媒介复制业	Printing,Reproduction of Recording Media		541
文教、工美、体育和娱乐用品制造业	Manufacture of Articles For Cultural,Educational and Sports Activities		
石油、煤炭及其他燃料加工业	Processing of Petroleum, Cokeing,Processing of Nuclear and Nuclear Fuel		203
化学原料和化学制品制造业	Manufacture of Raw Chemical Materials and Chemical	1368727	3146
医药制造业	Manufacture of Medicines		2416
化学纤维制造业	Manufacture of Chemical Fibers		30
橡胶和塑料制品业	Manufacture of Rubber and Plastics	42901	11799
非金属矿物制品业	Manufacture of Non-metallic Mineral Products	111756	2273
黑色金属冶炼和压延加工业	Smelting and Pressing of Ferrous Metals		180
有色金属冶炼和压延加工业	Smelting and Pressing of Non-ferrous Metals		973
金属制品业	Manufacture of Metal Products		483
通用设备制造业	Manufacture of General Purpose Machinery		416
专用设备制造业	Manufacture of Special Equipment		427
汽车制造业	Manufacture of Motor Vehicle		4808
铁路、船舶、航空航天和其他运输设备制造业	Railways,Shipbuilding,Aerospace and Other Transportation Equipment Manufacturing Industry		183
电气机械和器材制造业	Manufacture of Electric Equipment and Machinery		2998
计算机、通信和其他电子设备制造业	Manufacture of Communication Equipment, Computers and other Electronic Equipment		3754
仪器仪表制造业	Manufacture of Measuring Instruments and Machinery		33
其他制造业	Manufacture of Other Manufacturing		19
废弃资源综合利用业	Recycling and Disposal of Waste		
金属制品、机械和设备修理业	Metal Products,Machinery and Equipment Repair Industry		7
电力、热力生产和供应业	Production and Supply of Electric Power and Heat Power	8547618	35790
燃气生产和供应业	Gas Mining and Supplying Industry		3429
水的生产和供应业	Production and Supply of Water		169

13-4 续表 continued

行 业	Sector	汽油 (吨) Gasoline (ton)	柴油 (吨) Diesel Oil (ton)	热力 (百万千焦) Heat (million kilo joule)	电力 (万千瓦时) Electricity (10 000 kwh)
总 计	**Total**	**16237**	**79701**	**6429118**	**970862**
煤炭开采和洗选业	Mining and Washing of Coal				
石油和天然气开采业	Extraction of Petroleum and Natural Gas				
黑色金属矿采选业	Mining and Processing of Ferrous Metal Ores				
有色金属矿采选业	Mining and Processing of Non-ferrous Metal Ores				
非金属矿采选业	Mining and Processing of Nonmetal Ores				
开采专业及辅助性活动	Mining Professional and Auxiliary Activity	1406	13387		3541
其他采矿业	Mining of other Ores				
农副食品加工业	Processing of Food from Agricultural Porducts	897	578	1970332	18794
食品制造业	Manufacture of Foods	451	1432	435215	18378
酒、饮料和精制茶制造业	Manufacture of Alcohol,Beverages and Tea	59	68	142056	13475
烟草制品业	Manufacture of Tobacco	10	24	92690	549
纺织业	Manufacture of Textile	60	4	96038	20984
纺织服装、服饰业	Textile, apparel industry	34	15		153
皮革、毛皮、羽毛及其制品和制鞋业	Manufacture of Leather, Fur, Feather and Related Products, and Shoes	32		10117	203
木材加工和木、竹、藤、棕、草制品业	Processing of Timber, Manufacture of Wood,Plam and Straw Products	19			1835
家具制造业	Manufacture of Furniture	150	125		2734
造纸和纸制品业	Manufacture of Paper and Paper Products	85	115	50610	4463
印刷和记录媒介复制业	Printing,Reproduction of Recording Media	276	199	75871	12191
文教、工美、体育和娱乐用品制造业	Manufacture of Articles For Cultural,Educational and Sports Activities	191	967		1033
石油、煤炭及其他燃料加工业	Processing of Petroleum, Cokeing,Processing of Nuclear and Nuclear Fuel	314	429		621
化学原料和化学制品制造业	Manufacture of Raw Chemical Materials and Chemical	555	1556	485744	86656
医药制造业	Manufacture of Medicines	785	143	212491	14497
化学纤维制造业	Manufacture of Chemical Fibers			1390084	6386
橡胶和塑料制品业	Manufacture of Rubber and Plastics	178	3103	2205	26763
非金属矿物制品业	Manufacture of Non-metallic Mineral Products	939	47641	2902	52527
黑色金属冶炼和压延加工业	Smelting and Pressing of Ferrous Metals	13	9		5257
有色金属冶炼和压延加工业	Smelting and Pressing of Non-ferrous Metals	521	163	24222	29003
金属制品业	Manufacture of Metal Products	1075	294	7508	16281
通用设备制造业	Manufacture of General Purpose Machinery	618	270	310	12037
专用设备制造业	Manufacture of Special Equipment	1502	991	59517	15715
汽车制造业	Manufacture of Motor Vehicle	1975	5676	361277	116105
铁路、船舶、航空航天和其他运输设备制造业	Railways,Shipbuilding,Aerospace and Other Transportation Equipment Manufacturing Industry	675	335	52954	16255
电气机械和器材制造业	Manufacture of Electric Equipment and Machinery	1162	700	829521	68329
计算机、通讯和其他电子设备制造业	Manufacture of Communication Equipment, Computers and other Electronic Equipment	410	69	121231	228363
仪器仪表制造业	Manufacture of Measuring Instruments and Machinery	655	26	4174	2424
其他制造业	Manufacture of Other Manufacturing	61	42		587
废弃资源综合利用业	Recycling and Disposal of Waste		220		752
金属制品、机械和设备修理业	Metal Products,Machinery and Equipment Repair Industry	27			138
电力、热力生产和供应业	Production and Supply of Electric Power and Heat Power	101	1001	2049	148428
燃气生产和供应业	Gas Mining and Supplying Industry	456	82		7323
水的生产和供应业	Production and Supply of Water	545	37		18082

13-5 规模以上工业企业分行业综合能源消费量（2019年）

Comprehensive Energy Consumption by Sector above Designated Size（2019）

单位：吨标准煤 (ton of SCE)

行 业	Scetor	2019	比上年增长(%) Increase over Preceding Year (%)
总 计	**Total**	**6347671**	**-8.4**
煤炭开采和洗选业	Mining and Washing of Coal		
石油和天然气开采业	Extraction of Petroleum and Natural Gas		
黑色金属矿采选业	Mining and Processing of Ferrous Metal Ores		
有色金属矿采选业	Mining and Processing of Non-ferrous Metal Ores		
非金属矿采选业	Mining and Processing of Nonmetal Ores		
开采专业及辅助性活动	Mining Professional and Auxiliary Activity	31375	2.0
其他采矿业	Mining of other Ores		
农副食品加工业	Processing of Food from Agricultural Porducts	175354	0.7
食品制造业	Manufacture of Foods	88815	-9.0
酒、饮料和精制茶制造业	Manufacture of Alcohol,Beverages and Tea	41327	-47.7
烟草制品业	Manufacture of Tobacco	3886	
纺织业	Manufacture of Textile	29593	-10.0
纺织服装、服饰业	Textile, apparel industry	827	-4.2
皮革、毛皮、羽毛及其制品和制鞋业	Manufacture of Leather, Fur, Feather and Related Products, and Shoes	641	-16.9
木材加工和木、竹、藤、棕、草制品业	Processing of Timber, Manufacture of Wood,Plam and Straw Products	5352	7.7
家具制造业	Manufacture of Furniture	4964	17.5
造纸和纸制品业	Manufacture of Paper and Paper Products	19602	10.0
印刷和记录媒介复制业	Printing,Reproduction of Recording Media	25392	3.0
文教、工美、体育和娱乐用品制造业	Manufacture of Articles For Cultural,Educational and Sports Activities	2404	-18.3
石油、煤炭及其他燃料加工业	Processing of Petroleum, Cokeing,Processing of Nuclear and Nuclear Fuel	5202	-62.7
化学原料和化学制品制造业	Manufacture of Raw Chemical Materials and Chemical Products	1139503	-8.1
医药制造业	Manufacture of Medicines	58640	7.4
化学纤维制造业	Manufacture of Chemical Fibers	55601	12.1
橡胶和塑料制品业	Manufacture of Rubber and Plastics	89479	-0.3
非金属矿物制品业	Manufacture of Non-metallic Mineral Products	291377	-22.1
黑色金属冶炼和压延加工业	Smelting and Pressing of Ferrous Metals	17972	96.4
有色金属冶炼和压延加工业	Smelting and Pressing of Non-ferrous Metals	50194	1.7
金属制品业	Manufacture of Metal Products	28666	-4.5
通用设备制造业	Manufacture of General Purpose Machinery	19505	1.3
专用设备制造业	Manufacture of Special Equipment	28256	-3.2
汽车制造业	Manufacture of Motor Vehicle	192307	-4.9
铁路、船舶、航空航天和其他运输设备制造业	Railways,Shipbuilding,Aerospace and Other Transportation Equipment Manufacturing Industry	24110	22.8
电气机械和器材制造业	Manufacture of Electric Equipment and Machinery	154296	8.6
计算机、通信和其他电子设备制造业	Manufacture of Communication Equipment, Computers and other Electronic Equipment	333921	6.5
仪器仪表制造业	Manufacture of Measuring Instruments and Machinery	4410	-2.8
其他制造业	Manufacture of Other Manufacturing	958	-28.5
废弃资源综合利用业	Recycling and Disposal of Waste	1245	73.9
金属制品、机械和设备修理业	Metal Products,Machinery and Equipment Repair Industry	295	2.0
电力、热力生产和供应业	Production and Supply of Electric Power and Heat Power	3352128	-10.9
燃气生产和供应业	Gas Mining and Supplying Industry	46611	37.2
水的生产和供应业	Production and Supply of Water	23463	15.8

13-6 规模以上工业企业用水情况（2019年）

Statistics on Water Use of Industrial Enterprises above Designated Size（2019）

指 标	Item	取水量（万立方米）Water Use (10 000 cu.m)	外供水量（万立方米）Outward Water Supply (10 000 cu.m)
合 计	**Total**	**88914**	**73291**
地表淡水	Surface fresh water	54272	122
地下淡水	Underground fresh water	16071	1180
自来水	Tap Water	17430	71989
陆地苦咸水	Land lake Salt water	1	
矿井水	Mine Water	83	
雨水	Rain Water	25	
再生水	Reclaimed Water	1031	
其他水	Other Water	1	
外排水量	Efflux capacity	15734	
重复用水量	Repeated water consumption	133326	

13-7 规模以上工业企业分行业用水情况（2019年）

Volume of Water Use of Industrial Enterprises above Designated Size by Industry (2019)

行业	Sector	取水量（万立方米） Water Use (10 000 cu.m)
总计	**Total**	**88914**
煤炭开采和洗选业	Mining and Washing of Coal	
石油和天然气开采业	Extraction of Petroleum and Natural Gas	
黑色金属矿采选业	Mining and Processing of Ferrous Metal Ores	
有色金属矿采选业	Mining and Processing of Non-ferrous Metal Ores	
非金属矿采选业	Mining and Processing of Nonmetal Ores	
开采专业及辅助性活动	Mining Professional and Auxiliary Activity	138
其他采矿业	Mining of other Ores	
农副食品加工业	Processing of Food from Agricultural Porducts	252
食品制造业	Manufacture of Foods	445
酒、饮料和精制茶制造业	Manufacture of Alcohol,Beverages and Tea	553
烟草制品业	Manufacture of Tobacco	2
纺织业	Manufacture of Textile	75
纺织服装、服饰业	Textile, apparel industry	17
皮革、毛皮、羽毛及其制品和制鞋业	Manufacture of Leather, Fur, Feather and Related Products, and Shoes	1
木材加工和木、竹、藤、棕、草制品业	Processing of Timber, Manufacture of Wood,Plam and Straw Products	2
家具制造业	Manufacture of Furniture	12
造纸和纸制品业	Manufacture of Paper and Paper Products	14
印刷和记录媒介复制业	Printing,Reproduction of Recording Media	58
文教、工美、体育和娱乐用品制造业	Manufacture of Articles For Cultural,Educational and Sports Activities	5
石油、煤炭及其他燃料加工业	Processing of Petroleum, Cokeing,Processing of Nuclear and Nuclear Fuel	79
化学原料和化学制品制造业	Manufacture of Raw Chemical Materials and Chemical Products	3775
医药制造业	Manufacture of Medicines	329
化学纤维制造业	Manufacture of Chemical Fibers	56
橡胶和塑料制品业	Manufacture of Rubber and Plastics	197
非金属矿物制品业	Manufacture of Non-metallic Mineral Products	630
黑色金属冶炼和压延加工业	Smelting and Pressing of Ferrous Metals	4
有色金属冶炼和压延加工业	Smelting and Pressing of Non-ferrous Metals	136
金属制品业	Manufacture of Metal Products	248
通用设备制造业	Manufacture of General Purpose Machinery	67
专用设备制造业	Manufacture of Special Equipment	145
汽车制造业	Manufacture of Motor Vehicle	719
铁路、船舶、航空航天和其他运输设备制造业	Railways,Shipbuilding,Aerospace and Other Transportation Equipment Manufacturing Industry	104
电气机械和器材制造业	Manufacture of Electric Equipment and Machinery	665
计算机、通信和其他电子设备制造业	Manufacture of Communication Equipment, Computers and other Electronic Equipment	1573
仪器仪表制造业	Manufacture of Measuring Instruments and Machinery	39
其他制造业	Manufacture of Other Manufacturing	4
废弃资源综合利用业	Recycling and Disposal of Waste	6
金属制品、机械和设备修理业	Metal Products,Machinery and Equipment Repair Industry	6
电力、热力生产和供应业	Production and Supply of Electric Power and Heat Power	4122
燃气生产和供应业	Gas Mining and Supplying Industry	27
水的生产和供应业	Production and Supply of Water	74409

13-7 续表 continude

行　业	Sector	外供水量（万立方米）Outward Water Supply (10 000 cu.m)
总　计	**Total**	**73291**
煤炭开采和洗选业	Mining and Washing of Coal	
石油和天然气开采业	Extraction of Petroleum and Natural Gas	
黑色金属矿采选业	Mining and Processing of Ferrous Metal Ores	
有色金属矿采选业	Mining and Processing of Non-ferrous Metal Ores	
非金属矿采选业	Mining and Processing of Nonmetal Ores	
开采专业及辅助性活动	Mining Professional and Auxiliary Activity	
其他采矿业	Mining of other Ores	
农副食品加工业	Processing of Food from Agricultural Porducts	
食品制造业	Manufacture of Foods	
酒、饮料和精制茶制造业	Manufacture of Alcohol,Beverages and Tea	
烟草制品业	Manufacture of Tobacco	
纺织业	Manufacture of Textile	
纺织服装、服饰业	Textile, apparel industry	
皮革、毛皮、羽毛及其制品和制鞋业	Manufacture of Leather, Fur, Feather and Related Products, and Shoes	
木材加工和木、竹、藤、棕、草制品业	Processing of Timber, Manufacture of Wood,Plam and Straw Products	
家具制造业	Manufacture of Furniture	
造纸和纸制品业	Manufacture of Paper and Paper Products	
印刷和记录媒介复制业	Printing,Reproduction of Recording Media	
文教、工美、体育和娱乐用品制造业	Manufacture of Articles For Cultural,Educational and Sports Activities	
石油、煤炭及其他燃料加工业	Processing of Petroleum, Cokeing,Processing of Nuclear and Nuclear Fuel	
化学原料和化学制品制造业	Manufacture of Raw Chemical Materials and Chemical Products	
医药制造业	Manufacture of Medicines	
化学纤维制造业	Manufacture of Chemical Fibers	
橡胶和塑料制品业	Manufacture of Rubber and Plastics	
非金属矿物制品业	Manufacture of Non-metallic Mineral Products	
黑色金属冶炼和压延加工业	Smelting and Pressing of Ferrous Metals	
有色金属冶炼和压延加工业	Smelting and Pressing of Non-ferrous Metals	
金属制品业	Manufacture of Metal Products	
通用设备制造业	Manufacture of General Purpose Machinery	2
专用设备制造业	Manufacture of Special Equipment	3
汽车制造业	Manufacture of Motor Vehicle	
铁路、船舶、航空航天和其他运输设备制造业	Railways,Shipbuilding,Aerospace and Other Transportation Equipment Manufacturing Industry	
电气机械和器材制造业	Manufacture of Electric Equipment and Machinery	
计算机、通信和其他电子设备制造业	Manufacture of Communication Equipment, Computers and other Electronic Equipment	
仪器仪表制造业	Manufacture of Measuring Instruments and Machinery	
其他制造业	Manufacture of Other Manufacturing	
废弃资源综合利用业	Recycling and Disposal of Waste	
金属制品、机械和设备修理业	Metal Products,Machinery and Equipment Repair Industry	
电力、热力生产和供应业	Production and Supply of Electric Power and Heat Power	74
燃气生产和供应业	Gas Mining and Supplying Industry	
水的生产和供应业	Production and Supply of Water	73212

13-8 分区县规模以上工业企业综合能源消费量（2019年）

Comprehensive Energy Consumption above Designated Size by Region（2019）

单位：吨标准煤 (ton of SCE)

区 县	Region	综合能源消费量 Comprehensive Energy Consumption	增速（%） Growth Rate（%）
全 市	**Total**	**6347671**	**-8.4**
新城区	Xincheng	375137	2.9
碑林区	Beilin	88001	14.9
莲湖区	Lianhu	178926	4.1
灞桥区	Baqiao	759081	-7.5
未央区	Weiyang	254093	-0.8
雁塔区	Yanta	238480	-6.4
阎良区	Yanliang	38491	-0.5
临潼区	Lintong	71392	-8.7
长安区	Chang'an	519634	-1.8
高陵区	Gaoling	179568	-1.6
鄠邑区	Huyi	761855	-5.1
蓝田县	Lantian	110567	-3.1
周至县	Zhouzhi	17351	10.7
西咸新区	Xixian	2755095	-14.6

主要统计指标解释

单位生产总值能耗 指一定时期内，一个国家或地区每生产一个单位的生产总值所消耗的能源。计算公式为：

单位生产总值能耗=能源消费总量/生产总值

工业企业能源消费量 指工业企业在工业生产活动和非工业生产活动中消费的能源，包括工业生产活动中作为燃料、动力、原料、辅助材料使用的能源，生产工艺中使用的能源，用于能源加工转换的能源；非工业生产活动中使用的能源。具体包括：

（1）用于本企业产品生产、工业性作业和其他生产性活动的能源；

（2）用于技术更新改造措施、新技术研究和新产品试制以及科学试验等方面的能源；

（3）用于经营维修、建筑及设备大修理、机电设备和交通运输工具等方面的能源；

（4）用于劳动保护的能源；

（5）生产交通运输工具的企业（如造船厂、汽车制造厂），向成品轮船、汽车中添加动力用油，应算作企业的能源消费，但不作为工业生产消费，应作为非工业生产消费和交通运输工具消费。

（6）其他非生产消费的能源。

工业生产能源消费量 指工业企业为进行工业生产活动所消费的能源。主要包括：

（1）用于本企业产品生产、工业性作业的能源，包括用作原料、材料、燃料、动力的能源；作为能源加工转换企业，还包括用作加工转换的能源（这部分能源不能理解为用作原材料，用作原材料的概念见后面的解释）；

（2）产品生产过程中作为辅助材料使用的能源；

（3）生产工艺过程使用的能源；

（4）新技术研究、新产品试制、科学试验使用的能源；

（5）为了工业生产活动而在进行的各种修理过程中使用的能源；

（6）生产区内的劳动保护用能等。

用于原材料的能源消费量 指能源产品不作能源使用，即不作燃料、动力使用，而作为生产另外一种产品（非能源产品）的原料或作为辅助材料使用，作原料使用时通常构成这种产品的实体。它与用作加工转换的区别是：用作加工转换，投入的是能源，产出的主要产品还是能源（或产出的产品属于加工转换过程中产生的不作能源使用的其他副产品和联产品）。而用作原材料时，投入的是能源，产出的主要产品是能源范畴以外的产品，包括产出的某种产品在广义上可以用作能源（比如可以燃烧以提供热量），但通常意义上不作能源使用的产品。

非工业生产能源消费量 指在工业企业能源消费中，除“工业生产能源消费”以外的能源消费，即非工业生产用能和工业企业附属的不从事工业生产活动的非独立核算单位用能。比如本企业施工单位进行技术更新改造、维修等过程用能，非生产区的劳动保护用能，科研单位、农场、车队、学校、医院、食堂、托儿所等单位用能。但是必须注意，上述单位如果是独立核算的，其用能既不能包括在“工业企业能源消费”中，亦不能包括在“非工业生产能源消费”中。

生产交通运输工具的企业（如造船厂、汽车制造厂），向成品轮船、汽车中添加动力用油，应算作企业的非工业生产消费。

综合能源消费量 指企业（单位）在报告期内工业生产实际消费的各种能源（扣除能源加工转换和能源回收利用等重复因素）的总和。计算综合能源消费量时，需要将各种能源品种的消费量换算成按照标准计量单位（如：吨标准煤）计量的消费量。

取水量 指企业从各种水源直接提取或者从市场购买的用于厂区、办公区内工业生产活动的水量，以实际获得的新水量为准。

外供水量 指企业外供给其他单位的水或水产品的量，以离厂水量为准。包括外供给其他企业或市场的原水、自来水、海水淡化水、矿泉水、纯净水等。不包括直流冷却水量、再生水（中水）、未利用直接排放的矿井水和雨水量、北方地区供暖企业供给城镇热力网内循环的热水量、进入城镇污水管网和直接排到自然环境中的水量。

Explanatory Notes on Main Statistical Indicators

Energy Consumption per Unit of GDP refers to the energy consumption per unit of Gross Domestic Product in a country or the Gross Regional Product in a region in the same reference period. The formula is:

Energy Consumption per Unit of GDP= Total Energy Consumption/Gross Domestic Product

Energy Consumption of Industrial Enterprises refers to the energy consumed by industrial enterprises in industrial production activities and non-industrial production activities, including energy used as fuel, power, raw materials and auxiliary materials in industrial production activities, energy used in production processes, energy for processing and conversion, and energy in the course of use of non-industrial production activities. Specifically, it includes:

(1)Energy used for the production, industrial operation and other productive activities of the enterprise;

(2)Energy for technological upgrading, new technology research and trial production of new products and scientific experiments.

(3) Energy for maintenance, construction and equipment repair, electrical and mechanical equipment and transportation.

(4) Energy for labor protection;

(5)Enterprises manufactured means of conveyance (such as making shipyards and automobile manufacturers), adding power oil to the finished product ships and cars, should be used as the energy consumption of the enterprises, but not as industrial production and consumption, it should be included in the consumption of non-industrial production and transportation means.

(6)Other non-productive energy sources.

Energy Consumption of Industrial Production refers to the energy consumed by industrial enterprises in industrial production activities. It mainly includes:

(1)Energy for the production and industrial operation of the products of the enterprise, including energy for raw materials, materials, fuel and power; as energy processing and conversion enterprises, including energy for processing and conversion (this part of the energy cannot be understood as raw materials, the concept of raw material is explained later)

(2)Energy used as auxiliary material during the production of products;

(3)Energy used in the production process;

(4)Energy for new technology research, trial production of new products and scientific test;

(5)Energy used in various repair processes for industrial production activities;

(6)Labor protection energy in the production area.

Energy Consumption for Raw Materials refers the energy products are not used for energy use, that is, not to be used as fuel and power, but as raw materials for the production of another product (non-energy products) or as auxiliary materials, which usually constitute the entity of this product when used as a raw material. The difference between it and the conversion of processing is that it is used as a process conversion, which is invested in energy, the main product of the output still is energy (or the produced product belongs to other by-products and associated products that are not used for energy use in the process of processing and conversion). When used as raw materials, energy is invested, and the main product is beyond the energy category, including a product that can be used as a source of energy in the broad sense (for example, to be burned to provide heat), but in general, it is not used for energy use.

Non-industry Consumption Energy refers to the energy consumed by industrial enterprises except for industrial production activities, means that energy consumed by non-industry production and it is not independent accounting units which was engaged in industrial production activities affiliated to industrial enterprises. For example, the energy consumption of technical renovation, maintenance and other processes carried out by construction units of this enterprise, labor protection for non-production areas, energy consumption of scientific research units, farms, motorcade, schools, hospitals, canteens, nursery schools and other units. However, it must be noted that if the above-mentioned units are independently accounted, their use can neither be included in the "industrial energy consumption" nor in the "non-industrial production energy consumption".

Enterprises manufactured means of conveyance(such as making shipyards and automobile manufacturers) adding power oil to finished ships and cars, should be regarded as non-industrial production and consumption of enterprises.

Comprehensive Energy Consumption refers to the sum of the various energy sources for the actual consumption of industrial production during the reporting period (the repeating factors of the conversion of energy processing and energy recovery and utilizationhave been deducted). When calculating the comprehensive energy consumption, it is necessary to convert the consumption of various types of energy into the consumption measured in accordance with the standard unit of measurement (e.g. tons of standard coal).

Water Intake refers to the amount of water directly extracted from a variety of water sources or purchased from the market for industrial production activities in the factory and office areas, which is based on the actual new amount of water.

External Water Supply refers to the quantity of water or aquatic products supplied to other units by the enterprises, taking the quantity of water away from the plant as the criterion. It includes raw water, tap water, desalination water, mineral water, purified water, etc., which are supplied to other enterprises or markets. Direct current cooling water, reclaimed water (water), unused mine water and rain water, the hot water in the urban heat network supplied by the heating enterprises in the north are not included.

14 建筑业

CONSTRUCTION

资料整理：杨雪峰
Data management: Yang Xuefeng
数据审核：陈　英
Data audit: Chen Ying

第十四部分　建筑业

一、简要说明

1.本章资料反映我市建筑业概况和发展情况。包括建筑业企业基本情况和生产经营情况。主要指标有企业个数、签订合同额、本年新签合同额、建筑业总产值、从事建筑业活动的平均人数、房屋施工面积、营业利润、应交增值税、劳动生产率等。

2.本章资料统计范围，根据建筑业发展的实际情况，建筑业统计范围从2002年年报起由原具有建筑业资质等级四级及四级以上的独立核算的建筑业企业调整为具有建筑业资质的独立核算建筑业企业。

3.本章建筑业企业统计数据是根据国家统计局制定的《建筑业统计报表制度》整理汇总的。资质以内建筑业统计报表由国家统计局根据企业实际情况采取全面调查的方法布置、收集，2011年年报开始由资质内建筑业企业通过联网直报系统上报。

4.2018年资质以内建筑业数据为四经普一套表单位上报数据。

5.2019年年报取消劳务分包建筑业企业生产经营情况表。

二、主要指标

企业个数（个）	1288	比上年增长	6.5%
#国有及国有控股企业	180	比上年增长	7.1%
建筑业总产值（亿元）	4514.38	比上年增长	15.0%
#国有及国有控股企业	3467.90	比上年增长	12.5%
房屋建筑竣工面积（万平方米）	2726.28	比上年下降	1.1%
房屋建筑面积竣工率（%）	15.9	比上年下降	1.5个百分点

14 CONSTRUCTION

I. Brief Introduction

1.Main Contents:Data in this chapter show the general situation and the development of the construction industry in Xi'an. They cover the situation of production and management of the construction enterprises, including the number of enterprises; total contract value; newly signed contract value; gross output value of the construction industry; the average number of employed persons engage in the activities of construction enterprises; floor space of building completed in construction enterprises; profits of construction enterprises; value-added tax payable; labour productivity and etc.

2.Scope of Statistics:In view of the development of the construction industry, starting from 2002 the scope of construction statistics has been adjusted to include all the construction enterprises of various types of ownership with qualification certificates and independent accounting systems, replacing the previous criteria that required construction enterprises of various types of ownership to have qualification certificates at or above Class 4 with independent accounting systems.

3.Sources of Data and Methods of Survey:Data on construction enterprises are collected in accordance with the Statistical Reporting System of Constructionby the National Bureau of Statistics. The construction statistical reports are deployed and collected through comprehensive survey by National Bureau of Statistics in accordance with the real conditions of the enterprises. Since 2011,construction enterprises with qualification certificates reported through internet.

4.The construction industry data within the 2018 qualification shall be reported as a set of forms for the fourth economic census.

Ⅱ.Major Indicators.

		Increase over Preceding Year
Number of Enterprises(item)	1288	6.5%
#State-owned or State Holding Majority Shares	180	7.1%
Total Output Value of Construction(100 mil. yuan)	4514.38	15.0%
State-owned or State Holding Majority Shares	3467.90	12.5%
Floor Space of Buildings Completed(10 000 sq.m)	2726.28	-1.1%
Rate of Floor Space of Buildings Completed(%)	15.9	-1.5 percentage points

14-1 主要年份建筑业总产值

Total Output Value of Construction in Representative Years

单位：亿元 (100 million yuan)

年份 Year	单位数（个） Number of Enterprises (unit)	建筑业总产值 Total Output Value of Construction	国有及国有控股 State-owned or State Holding Majority Shares	集体企业 Collective-owned Enterprises
2000	184	105.93	78.87	14.87
2001	205	114.81	91.82	15.47
2002	223	133.47	85.03	15.35
2003	204	177.11	119.99	13.40
2004	244	244.42	201.68	16.59
2005	235	326.65	276.68	19.61
2006	217	416.48	348.20	23.65
2007	279	604.75	432.63	32.67
2008	328	915.12	676.12	460.14
2009	326	1074.55	875.19	47.15
2010	324	1334.00	1034.04	58.39
2011	336	1619.09	1278.33	79.42
2012	396	1874.23	1364.70	96.83
2013	420	2228.41	1702.08	154.87
2014	539	2586.33	1981.24	95.02
2015	706	2650.41	2044.05	69.73
2016	893	2897.55	2288.23	63.35
2017	1055	3304.54	2588.18	70.56
2018	1209	3925.72	3083.48	52.99
2019	1288	4514.38	3467.90	47.48

注：1.1996年以后建筑业年报统计范围由往年的县及县以上（含县级建制镇）各种经济类型的建筑企业，改为具有建筑业资质等级三级及三级以上的各种经济类型的建筑施工企业；2002年改为具有建筑业资质等级的各种经济类型的建筑施工企业。

2.本表资料含劳务分包企业。

3.由于统计口径变化，对部分年份建筑业总产值相关数据进行了修订。

14-2 全市建筑施工总承包企业基本情况（2019年）

Basic Situation of Construction General Contracting Contractors in Whole City（2019）

指　　标	Item	合计 Total	国有及国有控股 State-owned or State Holding Majority Shares
企业单位数（个）	Number of Enterprises (unit)	840	142
#二级以上企业	Special and First and Second Class Enterprise	659	123
计算劳动生产率的平均人数（万人）	Average Number of Employed Persons in Calculation of Labor Productivity (10 000 persons)	89.38	65.75
#二级以上企业	Special and First and Second Class Enterprise	86.41	64.58
建筑业总产值（亿元）	Total Output Value of Construction(100 million yuan)	4175.74	3313.85
#二级以上企业	Special and First and Second Class Enterprise	4041.43	3235.83
全员劳动生产率	Overall Labor Productivity	46.72	50.40
按总产值计算（万元/人）	Calculated by Total Output Value(10 000yuan/person)		

14-3 施工总承包和专业承包建筑企业生产情况（2019年）

分 组	Classify	签订的合同额（万元） Contract Value (10 000 yuan)	上年结转合同额（万元） Contract Value Carried Over from 2017 (10 000 yuan)	本年新签合同额（万元） Contract Value Signed in 2018 (10 000 yuan)
总计	**Total**	**126694512**	**62040472**	**64654040**
#国有及国有控股	State-owned and State Holding Majority Shares	106990996	53578572	53412424
一、按登记注册类型分	**Grouped by Registion Status**			
内资	Domestic Investment Enterprises	125839967	61883044	63956924
国有企业	State-owned Enterprises	3805354	2622992	1182363
集体企业	Collective-owned Enterprises	784350	194385	589965
股份合作企业	Share-holding Corperative Enterprises	4919		4919
联营企业	Joint Ownership Enterprises	27264	5944	21321
国有独资公司	State-owned Company	21837067	10880298	10956769
其他有限责任公司	Limited Liability Corporations	83971289	41639880	42331409
股份有限公司	Share-holding Corperation Ltd.	1503243	916245	586998
私营企业	Private Enterprises	13906481	5623301	8283180
其他企业	Others			
港澳台商投资企业	Enterprises with Funds from Hong Kong,Macao and Taiwan	39100	100	39000
外商投资企业	Enterprises with Foreign Investment	815445	157329	658116
二、按国民经济行业分	**Grouped by Sector**			
房屋建筑业	Building Engineering Construction	44981785	17677974	27303812
土木工程建筑业	Civil Engineering Construction	76179440	42902464	33276976
建筑安装业	Installation of Construction	3879299	987085	2892214
建筑装饰、装修和其他建筑业	Architectural Decoration and Other Construction	1653988	472949	1181039
三、按隶属关系分	**Grouped by Administrative Relationship**			
中央	Central	73148776	41998246	31150530
地方	Region	53545736	20042226	33503511
四、按企业资质等级分	**Grouped by Class of Enterprises**			
1. 施工总承包	Overall Contractor for Construction	121178627	60297959	60880668
#特级	Special Class	71280217	35537940	35742277
一级	First Class	34150330	17077206	17073125
二级	Second Class	11130533	5697525	5433008
2. 专业承包	Special Contractor	5515886	1742514	3773372
#一级以上	First Class	3872423	1216631	2655792
二级	Second Class	787937	224203	563734

Main Indicators on General Constructing Contractors and Professional Contractors (2019)

建筑业总产值（万元） Total Output Value of Constrution (10 000 yuan)					竣工产值（万元） Completed Output Value (10 000 yuan)	房屋建筑施工面积（平方米） Number of Projects under Constrution (sq.m)	
	在外省完成的产值 Output Value in Other Provinces	建筑工程产值 Output Value of Constrution	安装工程产值 Output Value of Installation	其他产值 Others			本年新开工 Beginning Projects in This Year
45143850	**20081479**	**40219643**	**3417472**	**1506735**	**13074489**	**171740453**	**48271466**
34679035	18367702	32110288	1709031	859716	9914735	136108019	36992041
45120588	20072349	40202850	3411002	1506735	13073889	171308410	48271443
1389314	709270	1160921	183555	44839	509308	453451	73980
474764	950	362278	57993	54493	287420	3139578	1948122
4806		4806			3918		
21440		21440			15840	13526	13526
8047539	3410083	7636520	240466	170553	2092791	27504452	7794201
26657210	13958453	24201752	1803149	652308	7211513	110934912	29099694
690875	391645	647117	43735	23	342650	4364434	597214
7834640	1601949	6168017	1082103	584519	2610448	24898057	8744706
9129	9129	7379	1750			50	23
14133		9413	4720		600	431993	
17986201	4596660	16271499	1343191	371512	7006543	150660524	42512900
23836975	14337589	22123369	899676	813930	5130472	14452858	4182427
2162752	790961	871181	1071715	219857	434205	5506046	1029226
1157921	356270	953594	102890	101436	503269	1121025	546913
20782929	15442168	20003157	456037	323735	4586254	44152069	10574509
24360921	4639311	20216486	2961436	1183000	8488235	127588384	37696957
41757408	19314755	37672064	2741193	1344151	11498045	168238642	46345593
21334192	11747414	19820899	1238119	275174	6402178	106051697	26503464
13621257	6663675	12418765	762246	440247	2967663	42120995	12492399
5458868	666527	4527906	671816	259147	1891602	18628958	6957475
3386442	766724	2547579	676279	162584	1576444	3501811	1925873
2304485	588638	1751499	451073	101913	1193345	1722915	946882
619742	84534	430872	152408	36461	264627	652613	398629

14-3 续表

分 组	Classify	房屋建筑竣工面积（平方米）Floor Space of Buildings Completed (sq.m)	房屋竣工价值（万元）Housing Completion Value (10 000 yuan)
总计	**Total**	**27262836**	**6268046**
#国有及国有控股	State-owned and State Holding Majority Shares	18060212	4673266
一、按登记注册类型分	**Grouped by Registion Status**		
内资	Domestic Investment Enterprises	27262836	6268046
国有企业	State-owned Enterprises	47594	10583
集体企业	Collective-owned Enterprises	1597815	228026
股份合作企业	Share-holding Corperative Enterprises		
联营企业	Joint Ownership Enterprises	12420	1042
国有独资公司	State-owned Company	3376973	945788
其他有限责任公司	Limited Liability Corporations	14283403	3638011
股份有限公司	Share-holding Corperation Ltd.	1265280	197004
私营企业	Private Enterprises	6679351	1247593
其他企业	Others		
港澳台商投资企业	Enterprises with Funds from Hong Kong,Macao and Taiwan		
外商投资企业	Enterprises with Foreign Investment		
二、按国民经济行业分	**Grouped by Sector**		
房屋建筑业	Building Engineering Construction	24517518	5760593
土木工程建筑业	Civil Engineering Construction	1591032	394168
建筑安装业	Installation of Construction	629344	88679
建筑装饰、装修和其他建筑业	Architectural Decoration and Other Construction	524942	24605
三、按隶属关系分	**Grouped by Administrative Relationship**		
中央	Central	3966783	995273
地方	Region	23296053	5272773
四、按企业资质等级分	**Grouped by Class of Enterprises**		
1. 施工总承包	Overall Contractor for Construction	25443776	6108886
#特级	Special Class	13755862	3669661
一级	First Class	8454095	1549449
二级	Second Class	2792639	818928
2. 专业承包	Special Contractor	1819060	159161
#一级以上	First Class	988738	63445
二级	Second Class	616287	53387

continued

从事建筑业活动的平均人数（人） Average Number of Employed Persons in Construction Enterprises Productivity(person)	建筑业企业期末从业人员数（人） The Number of Employees in Construction Enterprises at the end of Period (person)	工程技术人员 Technical Personnel	自有机械设备年末净值（万元） The Net Value of Machinery and Equipment Owned at the end of the Year (10 000 yuan)	自有机械设备年末总台数（台） The Total Number of Machinery and Equipment Owned owned (stand)	自有机械设备年末总功率（千瓦） Total Power of Machinery and Equipment Owned at the end of the Year (kw)	企业总产值（万元） Gross Output Value of Enterprises (10 000 yuan)
1004128	**835995**	**125322**	**665802**	**63189**	**3280254**	**50540509**
689125	572373	78465	484543	40625	2694599	39162613
1003305	834362	124911	665802	63189	3280254	50199619
51529	50464	4727	22518	5005	123570	1389324
17565	16627	2943	8733	3060	27204	500204
219	248	33	1285	46	4460	4806
983	992	282	6375	34	2039	21440
140884	105175	26385	106563	10127	738358	8177913
513053	407230	49694	376326	27601	1922980	31020590
27697	29245	2160	1263	227	5201	693165
251375	224381	38687	142739	17089	456442	8392176
210	1020	91				9129
613	613	320				331761
436579	345210	47562	125736	19352	527643	18643552
471727	412072	66911	516461	36657	2602663	28364181
45063	31016	5932	6733	4409	60857	2278636
50759	47697	4917	16872	2771	89091	1254141
430578	393917	48414	416863	28485	2332038	25084656
573550	442078	76908	248939	34704	948216	25455853
893755	747731	109215	626333	57871	3135502	46826498
374962	263329	36217	270562	23960	1604060	25632870
346970	333698	39901	234410	16795	1035009	13806836
142193	122189	23807	96908	14065	423962	5626516
110373	88264	16107	39469	5318	144752	3714011
73312	56497	7895	17953	3190	88251	2461156
17028	15505	3563	15051	1668	38426	724612

14-4 施工总承包和专业承包建筑业企业主要指标（2019年）

指　标	Item	企业数（个）Number of Enterprises (unit)	总产值（万元）Total Output Value (10 000 yuan)	从事建筑业活动的平均人数（人）Average Number of Employed Persons in Construction Enterprises (person)
总计	**Total**	**1286**	**45143850**	**1004128**
#国有及国有控股	State-owned and State Holding Majority Shares	180	34679035	689125
一、按登记注册类型分	**Grouped by Registion Status**			
内资	Domestic Investment Enterprises	1279	45120588	1003305
国有企业	State-owned Enterprises	22	1389314	51529
集体企业	Collective-owned Enterprises	41	474764	17565
股份合作企业	Share-holding Corperative Enterprises	1	4806	219
联营企业	Joint Ownership Enterprises	2	21440	983
国有独资公司	State-owned Company	53	8047539	140884
有限责任公司	Limited Liability Corporations	139	26657210	513053
股份有限公司	Share-holding Corperation Ltd.	8	690875	27697
私营企业	Private Enterprises	1013	7834640	251375
其他企业	Others			
港澳台商投资企业	Enterprises with Funds from Hong Kong,Macao and Taiwan	1	9129	210
外商投资企业	Enterprises with Foreign Investment	6	14133	613
二、按国民经济行业分	**Grouped by Sector**			
房屋建筑业	Building Engineering Construction	486	17986201	436579
土木工程建筑业	Civil Engineering Construction	408	23836975	471727
建筑安装业	Installation of Construction	188	2162752	45063
建筑装饰、装修和其他建筑业	Architectural Decoration and Other Construction	204	1157921	50759
三、按隶属关系分	**Grouped by Administrative Relationship**			
中央	Central	59	20782929	430578
地方	Region	1227	24360921	573550
四、按企业资质等级分	**Grouped by Class of Enterprises**			
1. 施工总承包	Overall Contractor for Construction	840	41757408	893755
#特级	Special Class	24	21334192	374962
一级	First Class	175	13621257	346970
二级	Second Class	460	5458868	142193
2. 专业承包	Special Contractor	446	3386442	110373
#一级以上	First Class	168	2304485	73312
二级	Second Class	194	619742	17028

Major Indicators of General Construction Contractors and Professional Contractors (2019)

建筑业企业期末从业人员数（人）The Number of Employees in Construction Enterprises at the End of Period (person)	利润总额（万元）Total Profit (10000 yuan)	利税总额（万元）Total Profits and Taxes (10000 yuan)	按总产值计算劳动生产率（万元/人）Productivity by Gross Output Value (10000 yuan/person)	产值利润率（%）Profit Rate of Output Value（%）	产值利税率（%）Profit and Tax Rate of Output Value（%）	资产总计（万元）Total Assets (10000 yuan)	负债总计（万元）Total Liabilities (10000 yuan)	资产负债率（%）Asset Liability Ratio（%）
835995	**1140952**	**2075374**	**44.96**	**2.5**	**4.6**	**62411078**	**48386464**	**77.5**
572373	860094	1479764	50.32	2.5	4.3	48653862	39678122	81.6
834362	1114550	2037435	44.97	2.5	4.5	61938847	48000155	77.5
50464	12379	40617	26.96	0.9	2.9	842717	648193	76.9
16627	12090	29955	27.03	2.5	6.3	500228	273094	54.6
248	156	415	21.95	3.2	8.6	9841	8283	84.2
992	265	1057	21.81	1.2	4.9	53905	28863	53.5
105175	239709	397035	57.12	3.0	4.9	12483435	9765233	78.2
407230	624968	1082183	51.96	2.3	4.1	36723467	30436433	82.9
29245	7248	23377	24.94	1.0	3.4	692810	561022	81.0
224381	217734	462797	31.17	2.8	5.9	10632445	6279034	59.1
1020	5439	7716	43.47	59.6	84.5	64945	53813	82.9
613	20963	30222	23.06	148.3	213.8	407286	332496	81.6
345210	397701	811806	41.20	2.2	4.5	22756332	17631154	77.5
412072	643944	1078462	50.53	2.7	4.5	35281716	27562073	78.1
31016	78344	130236	47.99	3.6	6.0	3193777	2407644	75.4
47697	20962	54868	22.81	1.8	4.7	1179253	785593	66.6
393917	497296	777055	48.27	2.4	3.7	27427648	22496044	82.0
442078	643656	1298319	42.47	2.6	5.3	34983430	25890419	74.0
747731	1044359	1847418	46.72	2.5	4.4	57988563	45223682	78.0
263329	559165	905328	56.90	2.6	4.2	32807574	26751718	81.5
333698	257243	507404	39.26	1.9	3.7	15572926	12426406	79.8
122189	153551	315238	38.39	2.8	5.8	7362524	4716470	64.1
88264	96593	227957	30.68	2.9	6.7	4422515	3162781	71.5
56497	63084	142942	31.43	2.7	6.2	2649846	1933470	73.0
15505	21466	45990	36.40	3.5	7.4	1076379	712228	66.2

14-5 施工总承包和专业承包建筑业企业财务状况（2019年）

单位：万元

指　标	Item	资产总计 Total Assets	流动资产合计 Total Current Assets
总计	**Total**	**62411078**	**51510152**
#国有及国有控股	State-Owned and State Holding Majority Shares	48653862	39441514
一、按登记注册类型分	**Grouped by Registion Status**		
内资	Domestic Investment Enterprises	61938847	51039687
国有企业	State-owned Enterprises	842717	756922
集体企业	Collective-owned Enterprises	500228	434974
股份合作企业	Share-holding Corperative Enterprises	9841	9485
联营企业	Joint Ownership Enterprises	53905	16508
国有独资公司	State-owned Company	12483435	9897257
有限责任公司	Limited Liability Corporations	36723467	30099377
股份有限公司	Share-holding Corperation Ltd.	692810	564862
私营企业	Private Enterprises	10632445	9260302
其他企业	Others		
港澳台商投资企业	Enterprises with Funds from Hong Kong, Macao and Taiwan	64945	64918
外商投资企业	Enterprises with Foreign Investment	407286	405548
二、按国民经济行业分	**Grouped by Sector**		
房屋建筑业	Building Engineering Construction	22756332	20394715
土木工程建筑业	Civil Engineering Construction	35281716	27303319
建筑安装业	Installation of Construction	3193777	2785721
建筑装饰、装修和其他建筑业	Architectural Decoration and Other Construction	1179253	1026397
三、按隶属关系分	**Grouped by Administrative Relationship**		
中央	Central	27427648	20669059
地方	Region	34983430	30841093
四、按企业资质等级分	**Grouped by Class of Enterprises**		
1. 施工总承包	Overall Contractor for Construction	57988563	47614082
#特级	Special Class	32807574	25773761
一级	First Class	15572926	13810717
二级	Second Class	7362524	6310483
2. 专业承包	Special Contractor	4422515	3896070
#一级	First Class	2649846	2386683
二级	Second Class	1076379	919004

Financial Status of General Constructing Contractors and Professional Contractors (2019)

(10 000yuan)

固定资产原价 Original Value of Fixed Assets	累计折旧 Accumulated Depreciation	本年折旧 Depreciation of This Year	负债合计 Total Liabilities	流动负债合计 Total Current Liabilities	非流动负债 Non Current Liabilities	所有者权益合计 Total Owners' Equity	实收资本 Paid in Capital
4471380	**2476128**	**464425**	**48386464**	**45361449**	**2677025**	**14024615**	**14115728**
3406494	1979414	390815	39678122	37272539	2381940	8975741	5133213
4469544	2475573	464028	48000155	44975140	2677025	13938693	14105628
100242	45987	6266	648193	610372	35900	194524	133570
64488	27858	3797	273094	227196	9332	227134	201718
1378	1214	4	8283	8112	171	1558	847
1221	1005	147	28863	13137		25042	14362
1125776	771034	165016	9765233	8878628	882019	2718201	1559013
2252414	1201455	231019	30436433	28960611	1458391	6287034	3603250
30469	9561	2030	561022	540677	20344	131789	66946
893556	417458	55750	6279034	5736406	270868	4353411	8525921
49	22	7	53813	53813		11132	5500
1787	534	390	332496	332496		74790	4600
855213	386368	57161	17631154	16467510	965255	5125178	8185578
3372372	1983173	391785	27562073	25844194	1598574	7719642	5112058
153920	66358	9319	2407644	2295264	96119	786133	494641
89875	40230	6161	785593	754480	17077	393661	323451
2773304	1733008	352742	22496044	21283846	1212022	4931604	2928836
1698075	743121	111684	25890419	24077603	1465003	9093011	11186892
4162406	2323013	442326	45223682	42393447	2540820	12764881	13275405
1814334	1062573	192471	26751718	25081791	1669751	6055855	2981316
1365016	821849	151305	12426406	11850341	505178	3146520	7522110
646599	292474	68906	4716470	4226174	291165	2646054	2205328
308974	153115	22099	3162781	2968002	136205	1259734	840323
184856	100722	12552	1933470	1871055	39973	716377	480097
83833	39148	5764	712228	665997	22954	364151	266455

14-5 续表

单位：万元

指 标	Item	营业收入 Total Revenue	主营业务收入 Main Business Income
总计	**Total**	**51370719**	**48019269**
#国有及国有控股	State-owned and State Holding Majority Shares	39694619	37248128
一、按登记注册类型分	**Grouped by Registion Status**		
内资	Domestic Investment Enterprises	50698044	47388118
国有企业	State-owned Enterprises	941184	880203
集体企业	Collective-owned Enterprises	466543	427363
股份合作企业	Share-holding Corperative Enterprises	5329	5060
联营企业	Joint Ownership Enterprises	14564	12972
国有独资公司	State-owned Company	8772712	8041356
其他有限责任公司	Limited Liability Corporations	31169479	29438064
股份有限公司	Share-holding Corperation Ltd.	674332	627121
私营企业	Private Enterprises	8653901	7955979
其他企业	Others		
港澳台商投资企业	Enterprises with Funds from Hong Kong, Macao and Taiwan	88585	82194
外商投资企业	Enterprises with Foreign Investment	584090	548958
二、按国民经济行业分	**Grouped by Sector**		
房屋建筑业	Building Engineering Construction	18673598	17572004
土木工程建筑业	Civil Engineering Construction	28896049	27012371
建筑安装业	Installation of Construction	2536047	2282811
建筑装饰、装修和其他建筑业	Architectural Decoration and Other Construction	1265026	1152083
三、按隶属关系分	**Grouped by Administrative Relationship**		
中央	Central	25370889	24019336
地方	Region	25999831	23999934
四、按企业资质等级分	**Grouped by Class of Enterprises**		
1. 施工总承包	Overall Contractor for Construction	47349323	44365139
#特级	Special Class	26693910	25282127
一级	First Class	13159607	12211629
二级	Second Class	5702364	5252993
2. 专业承包	Special Contractor	4021396	3654131
#一级	First Class	2618810	2400806
二级	Second Class	735436	644293

continued 1

(10 000yuan)

营业成本 Total Cost	主营业务成本 Main Business Costs	税金及附加 Taxs and Other Charges	主营业务税金及附加 The Main Business Tax and Surcharges	管理费用 Management Costs	营业利润 Operating Profit	利润总额 Total Profit	应付职工薪酬 Payable to Employees	应交增值税 Value Added Tax Payable
48411121	**48019269**	**168142**	**165494**	**1222325**	**1117638**	**1140952**	**7353176**	**766280**
37493198	37248128	103505	101486	757398	826720	860094	5784930	516165
47779935	47388118	166627	163980	1207097	1091311	1114550	7302128	756258
880855	880203	5846	5739	37704	11415	12379	195093	22392
428083	427363	4665	4648	16048	12355	12090	67349	13200
5060	5060	53	53	62	153	156	954	206
12972	12972	93	93	905	276	265	1464	699
8124082	8041356	31770	30951	202424	232454	239709	1388281	125556
29604339	29438064	72612	71505	579866	598681	624968	4342079	384603
627513	627121	1518	1518	17774	7037	7248	151049	14611
8097030	7955979	50072	49473	352315	228939	217734	1155860	194991
82194	82194	432	432	712	5401	5439	5688	1845
548993	548958	1082	1082	14516	20926	20963	45360	8177
17704504	17572004	68712	67794	328643	402024	397701	3131908	345393
27246093	27012371	84170	82862	727473	614631	643944	3754890	350348
2296769	2282811	8492	8268	104491	78793	78344	295085	43400
1163755	1152083	6767	6570	61718	22190	20962	171293	27139
24171547	24019336	54092	52774	479751	463655	497296	3664929	225667
24239574	23999934	114050	112720	742573	653983	643656	3688247	540613
44741286	44365139	146906	144348	1040266	1015529	1044359	6887908	656153
25409583	25282127	56705	56136	444735	529247	559165	3774330	289458
12328870	12211629	43792	43149	274190	256800	257243	2116028	206369
5373608	5252993	38633	37515	253692	154620	153551	786202	123054
3669835	3654131	21236	21147	182059	102109	96593	465268	110128
2413683	2400806	13364	13359	103120	63276	63084	279183	66494
646190	644293	3714	3637	49846	21446	21466	93653	20810

14-6 各区县建筑业主要经济指标（2019年）

Major Indicators of Construction Enterprises by Region（2019）

区 县	Region	企业个数（个）Number of Enterprises (unit)	总产值（亿元）Total Output Value (100 million yuan)	从事建筑业活动的平均人数（万人）Average Number of Employed Persons in Construction Enterprises Labor Productivity(10 000person)	全员劳动生产率（万元/人）Overall Labor Productivity (10 000 yuan/person)	利税总额（亿元）Total Pre-tax Profits (100 million yuan)
全 市	**Total**	**1286**	**4514.38**	**100.41**	**44.96**	**207.54**
新城区	Xincheng	67	335.25	4.68	71.63	11.00
碑林区	Beilin	151	900.85	19.08	47.21	40.65
莲湖区	Lianhu	96	328.81	7.17	45.86	18.76
灞桥区	Baqiao	53	261.17	4.35	60.04	10.24
未央区	Weiyang	255	961.48	28.50	33.74	32.08
雁塔区	Yanta	407	1082.29	22.29	48.55	65.08
阎良区	Yanliang	31	22.98	0.76	30.24	1.58
临潼区	Lintong	36	11.63	0.57	20.40	0.98
长安区	Chang'an	62	242.54	4.91	49.40	10.80
高陵区	Gaoling	20	36.42	1.96	18.58	1.80
鄠邑区	Huyi	15	14.53	0.56	25.95	0.98
蓝田县	Lantian	13	15.72	0.52	30.23	1.56
周至县	Zhouzhi	13	6.05	0.25	24.20	0.55
西咸新区	Xixian	67	294.66	4.80	61.39	11.47

注：本表数据依据施工总承包和专业承包企业数据加工整理。

14-7 各区县建筑业房屋施工及竣工面积（2019年）

Floor Space of Buildings under Construction & Completed by Region（2019）

区 县	Region	房屋建筑施工面积（万平方米）Floor Space under Construction (10 000sq.m)	本年新开工面积 Newly Started This Year	房屋建筑竣工面积（万平方米）Floor Space of Buildings Completed (10 000sq.m)	竣工房屋价值（亿元）Value of Buildings Completed (100 million yuan)
全 市	**Total**	**17174.05**	**4827.15**	**2726.28**	**626.80**
新城区	Xincheng	337.14	81.21	69.54	12.11
碑林区	Beilin	5082.11	1341.57	825.27	205.12
莲湖区	Lianhu	2460.93	750.10	318.36	94.32
灞桥区	Baqiao	399.96	163.61	3.70	0.93
未央区	Weiyang	4057.41	1101.61	590.01	140.18
雁塔区	Yanta	3058.76	841.97	437.24	95.39
阎良区	Yanliang	43.49	17.68	17.92	2.94
临潼区	Lintong	71.46	27.43	14.72	2.80
长安区	Chang'an	202.14	32.45	35.19	6.08
高陵区	Gaoling	111.60	54.65	67.98	9.65
鄠邑区	Huyi	63.47	31.03	32.63	7.49
蓝田县	Lantian	102.24	63.34	82.78	9.73
周至县	Zhouzhi	21.86	4.48	7.75	1.14
西咸新区	Xixian	1161.47	316.01	223.22	38.92

14-8 各区县建筑业企业主要经济效益指标（2019年）

Major Economic Performance Indicators on Construction Enterprises by Region（2019）

区 县	Region	人均利润总额（元/人） Per Profit (yuan/person)	人均利税（元/人） Per Pre-Tax Profits (yuan/person)	人均竣工产值（元/人） Per Output Value of Buildings Completed (yuan/person)	人均施工面积（平方米/人） Per Floor Space of Buildings Under Construcyion (sq.m/person)	人均竣工面积（平方米/人） Per Floor Space of Buildings Completed (sq.m/person)
全 市	**Total**	**11363**	**20668**	**130207**	**171**	**27**
新城区	Xincheng	12672	23486	142662	72	15
碑林区	Beilin	12424	21305	167775	266	43
莲湖区	Lianhu	11048	26151	227718	343	44
灞桥区	Baqiao	12368	23513	366144	92	1
未央区	Weiyang	6545	11257	82779	142	21
雁塔区	Yanta	16903	29198	102096	137	20
阎良区	Yanliang	7809	20741	156571	57	23
临潼区	Lintong	4551	17288	69136	126	26
长安区	Chang'an	10558	22000	52788	41	7
高陵区	Gaoling	4023	9171	56302	57	35
鄠邑区	Huyi	6029	17654	155238	114	59
蓝田县	Lantian	14712	29879	230276	196	158
周至县	Zhouzhi	3399	22056	98551	88	31
西咸新区	Xixian	14150	23877	121394	242	46

14-8 续表 continued

区 县	Region	产值利润率（%） Ratio of Profits to Output Value (%)	产值利税率（%） Ratio of Pre-tax Profits to Output Value (%)	资产利润率（%） Ratio of Profits to Assets (%)	资产利税率（%） Ratio of Pre-tax Profits to Assets (%)	资产负债率（%） Ratio of Debts to Assets (%)
全 市	**Total**	**2.5**	**4.6**	**1.8**	**3.3**	**77.5**
新城区	Xincheng	1.8	3.3	1.8	3.4	87.7
碑林区	Beilin	2.6	4.5	1.9	3.2	83.8
莲湖区	Lianhu	2.4	5.7	1.2	2.8	78.5
灞桥区	Baqiao	2.1	3.9	1.6	3.1	72.2
未央区	Weiyang	1.9	3.3	1.5	2.5	79.2
雁塔区	Yanta	3.5	6.0	2.1	3.7	74.0
阎良区	Yanliang	2.6	6.9	1.9	5.1	54.5
临潼区	Lintong	2.2	8.4	0.4	1.5	35.9
长安区	Chang'an	2.1	4.5	2.2	4.5	74.4
高陵区	Gaoling	2.2	4.9	1.4	3.2	44.7
鄠邑区	Huyi	2.3	6.7	2.3	6.7	63.7
蓝田县	Lantian	4.9	9.9	12.7	25.8	45.3
周至县	Zhouzhi	1.4	9.1	1.5	10.0	53.8
西咸新区	Xixian	2.3	3.9	3.5	5.9	80.4

主 要 统 计 指 标 解 释

建筑业统计单位 指从事房屋、构筑物建造和设备安装活动的法人企业。建筑业法人企业应具有建筑业资质并能够独立核算，同时其应具备以下条件：①依法成立，有自己的名称、组织机构和场所，能够承担民事责任；②独立拥有和使用资产，承担负债，有权与其他单位签订合同；③独立核算盈亏，能够编制资产负债表。

建筑业总产值 是以货币形式表现的建筑业企业在一定时期内生产的建筑业产品和提供的服务的总和。建筑业总产值包括：

（1）建筑工程产值：指列入建筑工程预算内的各种工程价值。

（2）安装工程产值：指设备安装工程价值，不包括被安装设备本身的价值。

（3）其他产值：建筑业总产值中除建筑工程、安装工程以外的产值。包括房屋构筑物修理产值、非标准设备制造产值、总包企业向分包企业收取的管理费以及不能明确划分的施工活动所完成的产值。

a. 房屋构筑物修理产值：指房屋和构筑物修理所完成的产值，但不包括被修理房屋、构筑物本身价值和生产设备的修理价值。

b. 非标准设备制造产值：指加工制造没有定型的非标准生产设备的加工费和原材料价值（如化工厂、炼油厂用的各种罐、槽，矿井生产统一使用的各种漏斗、三角槽、阀门等）以及附属加工厂为本企业承建工程制作的非标准设备的价值。

建筑业增加值 指建筑业企业在报告期内以货币形式表现的建筑业生产经营活动的最终成果。

从2004年第一次全国经济普查开始，建筑业现价增加值按生产法和分配法（收入法）两种方法计算，以收入法的计算结果为准，即从收入的角度出发，根据生产要素在生产过程中应得的收入份额计算。具体计算方法：经济普查年度建筑业增加值按照《经济普查年度GDP核算方案》计算，非经济普查年度建筑业增加值按照非经济普查年度GDP核算方案》计算。

房屋建筑施工面积 指在报告期内施过工的全部房屋建筑面积，包括本期新开工的房屋面积、上期施工跨入本期继续施工的房屋面积、上期停缓建在本期恢复施工的房屋面积、本期竣工的房屋面积及本期施工后又停缓建的房屋面积。

房屋建筑竣工面积 指在报告期内房屋建筑按照设计要求全部完工，达到了使用条件，经验收鉴定合格，正式移交使用单位的房屋建筑面积。

Explanatory Notes on Main Statistical Indicators

Statistical Unit in the Construction Industry refers to a corporate enterprise engaged in the construction of buildings and structures and in the installation of equipment. A corporate construction enterprise should have qualification certificates with independent accounting system, and should meet the following 3 requirements: a) being set up in line with relevant legal basis, having its full name, organization and location, and capable of taking civil liabilities; b) independently possessing and using its assets and assuming its liabilities, and entitled to sign contracts with other institutions; and c) making independent accounts of its profits and losses, and capable of compiling its own balance sheet.

Gross Output Value of Construction refers to total of construction products and services, expressed in money terms, produced or rendered by construction and installation enterprises during a given period of time. It includes:

(1)Output value of construction projects: the value of projects covered by the project budgets;

(2) Output value of installation projects: the value of the installation of equipment, (excluding the value of the equipment to be installed);

(3)Other output values: the output value of construction industry apart from that of construction projects and installation projects. It includes: output value of repair of buildings and structures; output value of non-standard equipment manufacturing; overhead expenses received by contracted enterprises from the sub-contracted enterprises and the completed output value of construction activities for which there is no clear definition.

a. Output value of repair of buildings and structures: the value created through the repairs of buildings or structures. It does not include the value of buildings or structures being repaired and the value of the repair of production equipment;

b. Output value of manufactured non-standard equipment: the value of non-standard production equipment, including raw materials and manufacturing cost, made for the construction project (i.e., chemical plant; kettles or tanks used by refineries; various fillers, triangle tanks, valves used by mines). It also includes the output value of equipment manufactured by subsidiary workshops.

Value-added of Construction refers to the final result of the activities of production and operation of enterprises of the construction industry in monetary terms during the reference period.

Starting from the 2004 economic census, value-added of construction is calculated by both production approach and income approach, with the figures from the income approach as the final figures. Under the income approach, calculation starts from the perspective of income and is based on the share of income derived from the production process by the relevant factors of production. Specifically, value-added of construction for the Census years is calculated in accordance with the Programme of Compilation of GDP and National Accounts for the Year of Economic Census, and value-added of construction for other years is calculated in accordance with the Programme of Compilation of GDP and National Accounts for the Non Economic Census Years.

Floor Space of Buildings Under Construction refers to floor space of buildings under construction during the reference period, including the floor space of buildings for which construction has newly started; buildings for which construction has started earlier and is continuing during the reference period; and buildings for which construction has been suspended earlier but has restarted during the reference period; buildings completed during the reference period; and buildings under construction but construction has subsequently been during the reference period.

Floor Space of Buildings Completed refers to the floor space of buildings that are completed in the reference period in accordance with the requirements of the design, up to the standard for being put into use, and having been checked and accepted by departments concerned as qualified ones.

15 运输邮电和信息化

TRANSPORT,POSTAL TELECOMMUNICATION SERVICE AND INFORMATIZATION

资料整理：王家峰　刘志杰
Data management：Wang Jiafeng　Liu Zhijie
数据审核：刘栋婷
Data audit：Liu Dongting

第十五部分　运输邮电和信息化

一、简要说明

本章资料包括交通运输业和邮电通信业的基本情况，主要是交通运输工具、货物和旅客运输量、邮电业务、邮政局所及服务点等基本情况，以及一套表单位信息化情况。运输邮电资料由西安市统计局服务业和社会科技处根据有关部门提供资料整理。信息化资料主要根据国家统计联网直报平台一套表单位的信息化统计数据整理。2017年起运输邮电数据为西安原口径数据，信息化数据为包含西咸新区数据。

二、主要指标

邮电业务总量（亿元）	1421.70	比上年增长	92.2%
全社会车辆数（万辆）	359.42	比上年增长	10.4%
#民用小轿车	204.05	比上年增长	11.2%

15　TRANSPORT,POSTAL TELECOMMUNICATION SERVICES AND INFORMATIZATION

Ⅰ.Brief Introduction

Data in this chapter consists of primarily basic condition of transportation, postal service and communication, mainly including transportation facility amount of goods and passenger transportation, basic data of postal service, post offices and service establishments of Xi'an City. Data on transportation industry in this chapter is compiled by Tertiary Industry and Social&Science and Technology Division of the Xi'an Bureau of Statistics according to the data provided by department concerned of the municipal government. Data on informationization are obtained from data in “Five Top” Units of National Statistical Networking Platrform. Since 2017, the range of data on transportation, post and communication industry is the original range in Xi'an and data on informationization includes data in XiXian.

Ⅱ.Major Indicators

		Increase over Preceding Year
Amount of Postal and Telecommunication Service(100 mil. yuan)	1421.70	92.2%
Number of Vehides in the whole Sciety(10 000 unit)	359.42	10.4%
Civil Car	204.05	11.2%

15-1 主要年份各种交通线路和桥梁

Transportation Routes and Bridges in Representative Years

年 份 Year	公路里程 （公里） Length of Highways (km)	桥 梁 （座） Bridges (seat)	桥梁长度 （米） Length of Bridge (m)
1989	2563		
1990	2586		
1991	2785		
1992	2786		
1993	2801		
1994	2830		
1995	2852		
1996	2877		
1997	3026		
1998	3047		
1999	2789		
2000	3010		
2001	3298		
2002	7862	629	29799
2003	8360	629	29799
2004	8360	629	29799
2005	8500	634	46973
2006	9530	634	46973
2007	9672	1319	91412
2008	11895	1710	151996
2009	12378	1856	154866
2010	12378	1856	154866
2011	12599	1863	149743
2012	13127	2190	214978
2013	13135	2213	224962
2014	13251	2213	224949
2015	13328	2323	250910
2016	13356	2423	256058
2017	13383	2435	286841
2018	14722	2413	292710
2019	13386	2436	300939

注：1.本表数据来自市交通局。
2.民航通航里程2013年统计口径发生较大变化，从2018年起此数据不再统计。
3.2018年桥梁数和桥梁长度重新进行了修订。
4.本表数据为西安原口径数据。

15-1 续表 continued

年 份 Year	永久式桥梁 （座） Permanent Bridges (seat)	永久式桥梁长度 （米） Length of Permanent Bridges (m)	民航通航里程 （重复航线）（公里） Length of Total Civil Aviation Routes(km)
1989			
1990			
1991			
1992			65007
1993			83215
1994			100800
1995			119753
1996			126433
1997			173010
1998			180000
1999			141284
2000			139764
2001			154614
2002	629	29799	211000
2003	629	29799	381800
2004	629	29799	386953
2005	632	46915	485749
2006	632	46915	418852
2007	1275	90716	553355
2008	1657	150980	515524
2009	1803	153850	587904
2010	1803	153850	742375
2011	1811	148810	898628
2012	2138	213985	981450
2013	2161	223970	70643568
2014	2171	224165	78626210
2015	2286	250175	93375419
2016	2386	255322	92561215
2017	2399	286164	113501600
2018	2438	292960	
2019	2414	300416	

15-2 各种交通线路里程和桥梁数（2019年）

Length of Transportation Routes and Number of Bridges (2019)

指　标	Item	2019
公路里程（公里）	**Length of Highways (km)**	**13386**
等级公路	Expressways and Class I to IV Highways	13040
高速	Expressway	652
一级	First Class	404
二级	Second Class	1334
三级	Third Class	1100
四级	Forth Class	9550
等外公路	Highways below Class IV	346
桥梁	**Bridges**	
永久式桥梁	Permanent	
座（座）	Seat (seat)	2414
长度（米）	Length (m)	300416
民航通航里程（公里）（重复航线）	**Length of Total Civil Aviation Routes(km)**	
国际航线（公里）	International routes(km)	
民航航线条数（条）	**Length of Civil Aviation routes(Article)**	**370**
国际航线（条）	International routes(Article)	88

注：1.本表数据来自市交通局，为西安原口径数据。
　　2.民航通航里程从2018年起此数据不再统计。

15-3 主要年份全社会车辆数

Possession of Civil Vehicles in Representative Years

单位：辆、台 (unit)

年 份	合计	汽车			摩托车	拖拉机
			载客汽车	载货汽车		
Year	Total	Motor	Passenget Vehicles	Ordinary Trucks	Motorcycles	Tractors
1999	**279335**	133192	63772	44348		38023
2000	**310252**	138318	89783	44974		37177
2001	**369988**	172436	110744	55453		31355
2002	**454998**	206653	134527	64623	176960	36083
2003	**516719**	242599	163872	70781	191834	34733
2004	**512802**	276012	195524	74557	156709	34755
2005	**544586**	377628	240923	82463	131440	34741
2006	**608155**	393778	296078	89772	131449	33236
2007	**840376**	522616	360081	97614	284594	32028
2008	**875005**	595735	430472	89093	247079	30176
2009	**1012937**	754803	567326	113430	224121	31347
2010	**1253461**	961283	739038	145740	259239	29151
2011	**1445811**	1174874	928669	171649	241132	25600
2012	**1633257**	1380125	1123105	186412	224279	24458
2013	**1862063**	1634885	1372371	207058	200419	21898
2014	**2139024**	1926012	1658714	224409	190625	17484
2015	**2394052**	2191023	1929195	224322	179619	18099
2016	**2588479**	2444000	2191862	226915	119771	19352
2017	**2885557**	2716361	2451906	243998	145207	17776
2018	**3256344**	3098008	2804240	272474	134264	16808
2019	**3594233**	3427557	3137323	269155	158203	

注：本表数据来自市车管所，为西安原口径数据。

15-4 全社会车辆数（2019年）

Possession of Civil Vehicles（2019）

单位：辆 (unit)

指　标	Item	2019
合计	**Total (unit)**	**3594233**
民用汽车	Motor(unit)	3427557
#私人汽车拥有量	Possession of Private Vehicles	3082649
载客汽车	Passenger Vehicles	3137323
#大　型	Large	21533
轿　车	Car	2040532
普通载货汽车	Ordinary Trucks	269155
#重、中型	Heavy and Medium	64853
其他汽车	Others	21079
#三　轮	Three Wheelers	2344
摩托车	Motorcycle (unit)	158203
普通摩托车	Bicycle Motor	153062
挂车	Articulated Trailers (unit)	8473
其他类型车	Others (unit)	

注：本表数据来自市车管所，为西安原口径数据。

15-5 主要年份交通运输量及周转量

Passenger Traffic and Kilometers and Freight Traffic and Ton-kilometers in Representative Years

年 份 Year	客运量 （万人次） Passenger Traffic (10 000 person-times)	旅客周转量 （万人公里） Passenger-Km (10 000 person-Km)	货运量 （万吨） Freight Traffic (10 000 tons)	货物周转量 （万吨公里） Freight Ton-Km (10 000 ton-Km)
1978	1334		3723	
1979	1420		3919	
1980	1508		3655	
1981	1839		3379	
1982	2340		4067	
1983	3054		4225	
1984	2899		4966	
1985	2404		5681	
1986	2186		5409	
1987	3781		6294	
1988	5721		6968	
1989	6092		8742	
1990	5748		6980	
1991	4193		3389	
1992	4368		8233	
1993	8036		8406	
1994	8321		8754	
1995	9069		9590	
1996	9854		10577	
1997	8922		9358	
1998	9223		9429	
1999	10311	2130383	9766	3452383
2000	8068	2507896	6999	3691963
2001	9078	2658037	7728	4229430
2002	12399	2524444	9482	4544040
2003	11413	2596402	9392	5037684
2004	10832	3112374	14845	5850029
2005	10479	1607568	12051	1249525
2006	11245	1721217	11832	1354318
2007	12466	1753464	15124	1473182
2008	26501	2529007	27560	3490707
2009	28693	2582025	30606	3766806
2010	30294	2942957	34323	4301680
2011	33375	3223544	39239	5212010
2012	36154	3387448	44924	5958742
2013	38289	3634915	50119	6471497
2014	25719	3091147	42039	6234128
2015	26904	3241463	46270	6430083
2016	23671	2909172	23888	5521252
2017	24287	3267158	25497	5979131
2018	26057	3624193	26219	5188953
2019	26315	3875080	27426	5190086

注：1.本表数据由市交通局、西安铁路局、咸阳机场、长安航空公司、东方航空公司西北分公司提供，2018年起铁路数据为西铁局西安辖区数据，与以前年度不可比。
2.2016年陕西省公路运输统计计算系数变化，因此与往年数据不可比。
3.本表数据为西安原口径数据。

15-6 交通运输量及运输周转量（2019年）

Passenger Traffic and Kilometers and Freight Traffic and Ton-kilometers（2019）

指　标	Item	2018	2019
一、客运量合计（万人次）	**Passenger Traffic(10 000 person-times)**	**26057**	**26315**
铁路	Railway	6037	6332
公路	Highway	15555	15261
民航	Civil Aviation	4465	4722
二、旅客周转量合计（万人公里）	**Passenger-Km (10 000 person-Km)**	**3624193**	**3875080**
铁路	Railway	787488	819035
公路	Highway	899071	877786
民航	Civil Aviation	1937634	2178259
三、货运量合计（万吨）	**Freight Traffic(l0 000 tons)**	**26219**	**27426**
铁路	Railway	497	487
公路	Highway	25691	26901
民航	Civil Aviation	31	38
四、货物周转量（万吨公里）	**Freight Ton-Kin (10 000 ton-Km)**	**5188953**	**5190086**
铁路	Railway	1371910	1242489
公路	Highway	3805312	3934603
民航	Civil Aviation	11731	12994

注：1.本表数据由市交通局、西安铁路局、咸阳机场、长安航空公司、东方航空公司西北分公司提供，2018年起铁路数据为西铁局西安口径数据。
2.本表数据为西安原口径数据。

15-7　主要年份邮政电信情况

年份 Year	邮电业务总量（万元） Business Volume of Postal and Telecommunication Services(10 000 yuan)	电信业务总量 Business Volume of Telecommunication Services	邮政业务总量 Business Volume of Postal Services
1978	1420		
1979	1616		
1980	1640		
1981	1713		
1982	2154		
1983	2250		
1984	2484		
1985	2972		
1986	3244		
1987	3911		
1988	5327		
1989	5973		
1990	7843		
1991	5700		
1992	6610		
1993	36581		
1994	54034		
1995	76450		
1996	104566		
1997	124601		
1998	204927		
1999	306457		
2000	461628		
2001	367620		
2002	515259	470492	44767
2003	820943	770673	50270
2004	1027415	975045	52370
2005	1320447	1261033	59414
2006	1867560	1796533	71027
2007	2267633	2191250	76383
2008	2646662	2564524	82138
2009	2989246	2900836	88410
2010	3231059	3167750	63309
2011	2005025	1944329	60696
2012	2162035	2098273	63762
2013	2479430	2313630	165800
2014	2922011	2695332	226679
2015	3315324	2983024	332300
2016	3831119	3299859	531260
2017	4398547	3728783	669764
2018	7395253	6621776	773477
2019	14217000	13096111	1120889

注：1.2002年及以后，邮政电信机构分离；2001−2010年邮电业务总量按2000年不变价格计算；2011年后邮电业务总量按2010年不变价格计算，故与以往年份不可比。
2.本表数据为西安原口径数据。
3.本表数据由市邮政管理局、市邮政局，中国联通、中国电信、中国移动等西安分公司提供。

Basic Statistic on Postal and Telecommunication Service in Representative Years

固定电话年末用户数（户） Number of Immobile Telephone at Year-end (subscriber)	农村电话用户数 Number of Telephone in Rural Areas at Year-end	移动电话用户年末数（户） Number of Mobile Phone at Year-end (subscriber)	互联网年末宽带用户数（户） Number of Broad Band Net User (subscriber)
12828	1062		
13487	1052		
14024	1086		
14497	1125		
15357	1129		
16922	1156		
18611	1203		
21624	1239		
26373	1235		
30200	1290		
34265	1357		
39506	1498		
45267	1668		
49516	2479		
60727	2613		
101327	2671		
197398	5067		
299485	8386		
430270	13654		
573244	21202		
736998	37863		
874586	74761		
1242637	170199		
1711500	259374	1277400	17183
2095230	358803	1964200	35230
2538393	415593	2412392	160900
2934424	480276	3500900	243448
3214806	500847	4199570	339280
3159639	467526	5510720	508775
3145819	419446	6645863	586213
3068807	383869	7377575	813987
2891009	358238	11200566	1167916
2617691	335048	14230800	1461804
2703640	320189	16141463	1841027
3110176	335864	18035397	2023059
3191112	330602	21606662	2670473
3066575	372823	20253157	2779458
2920773	306336	17669953	2899714
2843336	314457	17395026	3358343
2732174	294055	18542137	3467859
2622787	244984	18580879	3924786
2500807	206246	17113569	4386532

15-8 邮政业务及服务网点

Postal Service and Branch Post Office

指 标	Item	2010	2011	2012	2013	2014	2015	2016	2017	2018	2019
一、邮政业务总量（万元）	**Business Volume of Postal Services(10 000 yuan)**	**63309**	**60696**	**63077**	**165800**	**226679**	**332300**	**531260**	**669764**	**773477**	**1120889**
二、邮政业务收入（万元）	**Gross Income of Post Services (10 000 yuan)**	**58831**	**65174**	**71778**	**177100**	**213893**	**307008**	**439867**	**544555**	**616823**	**794417**
#快递业务收入（万元）	Express Delivery Business Income (10 000 yuan)				97100	134306	207451	331605	413699	475783	624260
三、函件（万件）	**Number of Letters (10 000 pcs)**	**8176**	**3061**	**2769**	**2856**	**2112**	**1707**	**1367**	**1360**	**1081**	**1028**
四、包件（万件）	**Parcels (10 000 pcs)**	**59**	**91**	**50**	**89**	**71**	**69**	**51**	**48**	**49**	**31**
五、汇票（万张）	**Money Order (10 000 pcs)**	**123**	**112**	**90**	**148**	**81**	**48**	**17**	**15**	**11**	**16**
六、报纸订销累计份数（万份）	**Accumulated Newspaper Prescribing and Sales Volume (10 000 pcs)**	**11724**	**12603**	**13052**	**14495**	**14338**	**14457**	**14395**	**14744**	**14915**	**14749**
七、杂志订销累计份数（万份）	**Accumulated Magazine Prescribing and Sales Volume (10 000 pcs)**	**550**	**564**	**613**	**1628**	**1572**	**1285**	**1155**	**956**	**1059**	**760**
八、特快专递类业务（万件）	**Express Mail Service Volume (10 000 pcs)**	**582**	**1901**	**129**	**138**	**107**	**61**	**63**	**63**	**63**	**1182**
九、集邮业务量（万枚）	**Stamps For Collection (10 000 pcs)**	**860**	**1060**	**2312**	**1431**	**1477**	**1920**	**1607**	**1687**	**1135**	**51**
十、邮政营销网点（处）	**Number of Post Office Branch Establishments (unit)**	**305**	**277**	**279**	**269**	**280**	**299**	**297**	**297**	**297**	**297**
#设在农村的局所	In it: Number of Post Offices in Rural Area	20	50	115	110	123	140	149	149	148	148
十一、邮政信筒信箱（个）	**Number of Mailboxes(unit)**	**1108**	**1108**	**1108**	**1108**	**1170**	**1170**	**422**	**422**	**290**	**417**

注：1.本表数据来自市邮政管理局和邮政局，2013年邮政数据统计口径变化。
2.本表数据为西安原口径数据。

15–9 电信业务情况

Telecommunication Service

指 标	Item	2010	2011	2012	2013	2014	2015	2016	2017	2018	2019
一、电信业务总量（万元）	**Business Volume of Telecommunication Services (10 000 yuan)**	**3167750**	**1944329**	**2098273**	**2313630**	**2695332**	**2983024**	**3299859**	**3728783**	**6621776**	**13096111**
二、电信业务总收入（万元）	**Gross Income of Telecommunication Services (10 000 yuan)**	**1038865**	**1029629**	**1162257**	**1316435**	**1356705**	**1338203**	**1420708**	**1451625**	**1495207**	**1465283**
三、固定电话年末用户数（万户）	**Number of Immobile Telephone at Year-end(10 000 subscribers)**	**261.77**	**270.36**	**311.02**	**319.11**	**306.66**	**292.08**	**284.33**	**273.22**	**262.28**	**250.08**
#农村电话年末户数	Number of Telephone in Rural Areas at Year-end	33.50	32.02	33.59	33.06	37.28	30.63	31.45	29.41	24.50	20.62
四、电话交换机总容量（万门）	**Capacity (number) of Telephone Switchboard (10 000 lines)**	**449.05**	**441.49**	**420.38**	**378.02**	**230.01**	**145.08**	**75.92**			
五、移动电话用户年末数（万户）	**Number of Mobile Phone at Year-end (10 000 subscribers)**	**1423.08**	**1614.15**	**1803.54**	**2160.67**	**2025.32**	**1767.00**	**1739.50**	**1854.21**	**1858.09**	**1711.36**
#4G电话用户数	4G Mobile Phone Subscribers							1113.03	1369.00	1499.18	1439.45
六、互联网年末用户数（万户）	**Number of Broad Band Net User (10 000 subscribers)**	**146.18**	**184.10**	**202.31**	**267.05**	**277.95**	**289.97**	**335.83**	**346.79**	**392.48**	**438.65**

注：本表数据由中国联通、中国电信、中国移动等西安分公司提供，为西安原口径数据。

15-10 一套表单位信息化基本情况（2019年）

单位：个

指　标	Item	企业数 Number of Enterprises
总计	**Total**	**8489**
按国民经济门类分	**According To the Categories of National Economy**	
采矿业	Mining Industry	7
制造业	Manufacturing Industry	1514
电力、热力、燃气及水生产和供应业	Electricity, Heat, Gas and Water Production and Supply	59
建筑业	Construction Business	1258
批发和零售业	Wholesale and Retail Trade	1821
交通运输、仓储和邮政业	Transportation, Warehousing and Postal Services	234
住宿和餐饮业	Accommodation and Catering Industry	728
信息传输、软件和信息技术服务业	Information Transmission, Software and Information Technology	286
房地产业	Estate	1327
租赁和商务服务业	Leasing and Business Services	399
科学研究和技术服务业	Scientific Eesearch and Eechnical Services	375
水利、环境和公共设施管理业	Management of Water Wonservancy, Environment and Public Facilities	67
居民服务、修理和其他服务业	Services of Households, Repairs and Other Services	73
教育	Education	25
卫生和社会工作	Health and Social Service	74
文化、体育和娱乐业	Culture, Sports and Entertainment	242

注：一套表单位包括规模以上工业企业、限额以上批零住餐企业、资质以内建筑业企业、规模以上服务业企业、房地产开发经营企业。

Basic Statistics on Informatization of "One Sheet" Units (2019)

(unit)

使用计算机的企业 Computer-used Enterprise	有信息技术人员的企业 Enterprises with Information Technology Personnel	有局域网的企业 LAN Enterprises	使用信息化管理的企业 Enterprises Managed by Information Technology	有信息化投入的企业 Enterprises with Informatization Input
8466	**6395**	**6472**	**8231**	**6711**
7	5	7	7	6
1514	1343	1288	1481	1344
59	48	51	58	49
1257	973	913	1224	1011
1819	1226	1341	1751	1326
234	147	166	223	162
728	539	534	701	573
286	282	264	282	269
1315	889	968	1290	996
394	277	293	385	295
374	305	287	363	309
66	50	48	63	53
73	52	46	70	58
25	24	19	25	25
74	70	65	74	64
241	165	182	234	171

15-11　一套表单位信息化设施及投入情况（2019年）

指　标	Item	期末使用计算机数量（台）Computers Used at the End of Period（unit）
总计	**Total**	**713085**
按国民经济门类分	**According To the Categories of National Economy**	
采矿业	Mining Industry	9048
制造业	Manufacturing Industry	168100
电力、热力、燃气及水生产和供应业	Electricity, Heat, Gas and Water Production and Supply	7755
建筑业	Construction Business	85708
批发和零售业	Wholesale and Retail Trade	70938
交通运输、仓储和邮政业	Transportation, Warehousing and Postal Services	31751
住宿和餐饮业	Accommodation and Catering Industry	17825
信息传输、软件和信息技术服务业	Information Transmission, Software and Information Technology	159693
房地产业	Estate	44973
租赁和商务服务业	Leasing and Business Services	19186
科学研究和技术服务业	Scientific Eesearch and Eechnical Services	63136
水利、环境和公共设施管理业	Management of Water Wonservancy, Environment and Public Facilities	5412
居民服务、修理和其他服务业	Services of Households, Repairs and Other Services	1494
教育	Education	5537
卫生和社会工作	Health and Social Service	11537
文化、体育和娱乐业	Culture, Sports and Entertainment	10992

注：一套表单位包括规模以上工业企业、限额以上批零住餐企业、资质以内建筑业企业、规模以上服务业企业、房地产开发经营企业。

Information Technology Facilities and Investment of "One Sheet" Units (2019)

信息技术人员 （人） Information Technology Personnel （Person）	拥有网站个数 （个） Number of Websites Owned （unit）
33300	**5322**
65	6
8189	1386
382	35
4047	741
3782	831
1165	110
1170	295
6905	342
2247	626
940	283
3016	319
244	47
133	45
172	27
322	76
521	153

15-12 一套表单位信息化管理情况（2019年）

单位：个

指　标	Item	企业数 Number of Enterprises	使用信息化管理的企业 Number of Enterprises Managed by Information Technology
总计	**Total**	**8489**	**8231**
按国民经济门类分	**According To the Categories of National Economy**		
采矿业	Mining Industry	7	7
制造业	Manufacturing Industry	1514	1481
电力、燃气及水的生产供应业	Electricity, Heat, Gas and Water Production and Supply	59	58
建筑业	Construction Business	1258	1224
批发和零售业	Wholesale and Retail Trade	1821	1751
交通运输、仓储和邮政业	Transportation, Warehousing and Postal Services	234	223
住宿和餐饮业	Accommodation and Catering Industry	728	701
信息传输、软件和信息技术服务业	Information Transmission, Software and Information Technology	286	282
房地产业	Estate	1327	1290
租赁和商务服务业	Leasing and Business Services	399	385
科学研究和技术服务业	Scientific Eesearch and Eechnical Services	375	363
水利、环境和公共设施管理业	Management of Water Wonservancy, Environment and Public Facilities	67	63
居民服务、修理和其他服务业	Services of Households, Repairs and Other Services	73	70
教育	Education	25	25
卫生和社会工作	Health and Social Service	74	74
文化、体育和娱乐业	Culture, Sports and Entertainment	242	234

注：一套表单位包括规模以上工业企业、限额以上批零住餐企业、资质以内建筑业企业、规模以上服务业企业、房地产开发经营企业。

Information Management Situation of "One Sheet" Units (2019)

(unit)

财务管理 Financial Management	购销存管理 Purchase and Sale Management	生产制造管理 Manufacturing Management	物流配送管理 Logistics Distribution Management	客户关系管理 Customer Relationship Management	人力资源管理 Human Resource Management	其他 Others
7476	**3698**	**1270**	**894**	**2646**	**3234**	**1270**
7	3	1		1	4	3
1383	971	716	273	464	556	150
55	24	27	5	13	30	6
1129	248	118	40	260	497	204
1513	1287	117	384	672	484	215
199	59	20	82	53	79	44
602	343	36	29	226	210	137
262	118	47	18	125	170	49
1198	321	87	24	455	654	219
357	57	13	10	141	172	69
341	83	54	10	102	186	86
60	16	4		7	23	13
59	34	2	4	25	34	13
25	5	1		10	9	9
66	58	4	3	25	31	12
220	71	23	12	67	95	41

15-13 一套表单位电子商务交易情况（2019年）

指 标	Item	企业数（个）Number of Enterprises (unit)
总计	**Total**	**8489**
按国民经济门类分	**According To the Categories of National Economy**	
采矿业	Mining Industry	7
制造业	Manufacturing Industry	1514
电力、燃气及水的生产供应业	Electricity, Heat, Gas and Water Production and Supply	59
建筑业	Construction Business	1258
批发和零售业	Wholesale and Retail Trade	1821
交通运输、仓储和邮政业	Transportation, Warehousing and Postal Services	234
住宿和餐饮业	Accommodation and Catering Industry	728
信息传输、软件和信息技术服务业	Information Transmission, Software and Information Technology	286
房地产业	Estate	1327
租赁和商务服务业	Leasing and Business Services	399
科学研究和技术服务业	Scientific Eesearch and Eechnical Services	375
水利、环境和公共设施管理业	Management of Water Wonservancy, Environment and Public Facilities	67
居民服务、修理和其他服务业	Services of Households, Repairs and Other Services	73
教育	Education	25
卫生和社会工作	Health and Social Service	74
文化、体育和娱乐业	Culture, Sports and Entertainment	242

注：一套表单位包括规模以上工业企业、限额以上批零住餐企业、资质以内建筑业企业、规模以上服务业企业、房地产开发经营企业。

E-commerce Transactions of “One Sheet” Units（2019）

有电子商务交易的企业（个）Enterprises with Ecommerce Transactions（unit）	有电子商务销售的企业 Ecommerce Sales Enterprises	有电子商务采购的企业 E-Commerce Purchases Enterprises	拥有电子商务交易平台的企业（个）With Ecommerce Trading Platform Enterprises（unit）	全年电子商务销售金额（万元）Sales of Ecommerce (10 000 yuan)	全年电子商务采购金额（万元）Purchases of Ecommerce (10 000 yuan)
1025	**812**	**447**	**107**	**9869644**	**5708539**
144	91	87	9	220334	279863
2	1	2	1	2924	1037
62	6	57	1	327	1598493
310	291	123	55	8252569	3301333
13	7	9	6	156232	20591
296	290	59	4	187540	1662
53	29	33	15	734022	384884
24	2	22		732	2192
33	27	14	10	165876	58056
21	9	16	1	60281	58955
10	9	4		6113	127
6	3	5	1	67	62
3	3	3		47230	571
7	5	3	1	1919	76
41	39	10	3	33478	637

主要统计指标解释

公路里程 指在一定时期内实际达到《公路工程技术标准JTJ01-88》规定的等级公路，并经公路主管部门正式验收交付使用的公路里程数。包括大中城市的郊区公路以及通过小城镇街道部分的公路里程和桥梁、隧道渡口的长度，不包括大中城市的街道、厂矿、林区生产用道和农业生产用道的里程。两条或多条公路共同经由同一路段，只计算一次，不得重复计算里程长度。它是反映公路建设发展规模的重要指标，也是计算运输网密度等指标的基础资料。

民用航空航线里程 指民航运输定期班机飞行的航线长度的总和。航线长度按机场之间的距离计算，通常有两种计算方法：一是将每条航线长度相加称为重复计算航线里程；一是将两线或两条以上航线经过同一区段里程，只计算一次航线长度称为不重复计算航线里程。一般常用的是后者，它能确切反映民航运输网的规模，是表明民航事业为国民经济服务和方便人民生活程度的主要指标。

货（客）运量 指在一定时期内，各种运输工具实际运送的货物（旅客）数量。它是反映运输业为国民经济和人民生活服务的数量指标，也是制定和检查运输生产计划、研究运输发展规模和速度的重要指标。货运按吨计算，客运按人计算。货物不论运输距离长短、货物类别，均按实际重量统计。旅客不论行程远近或票价多少，均按一人一次客运量统计；半价票、小孩票也按一人统计。

货物（旅客）周转量 指在一定时期内，由各种运输工具运送的货物（旅客）数量与其相应运输距离的乘积之总和。它是反映运输业生产总成果的重要指标，也是编制和检查运输生产计划，计算运输效率、劳动生产率以及核算运输单位成本的主要基础资料。计算货物周转量通常按发出站与到达站之间的最短距离，也就是计费距离计算。计算公式为：

货物（旅客）周转量=∑货物（旅客）运输量×运输距离

民用汽车拥有量 指报告期末，在公安交通管理部门按照《机动车注册登记工作规范》，已注册登记领有民用车辆牌照的全部汽车数量。汽车拥有量统计的主要分类：根据汽车结构分为载客汽车、载货汽车及其他汽车；根据汽车所有者不同分为个人（私人）汽车、单位汽车；根据汽车的使用性质分为营运汽车、非营运汽车；根据汽车大小规格不同载客汽车分为大型、中型、小型和微型，载货汽车分为重型、中型、轻型和微型。

邮电业务总量 指以价值量形式表现的邮电通信企业为社会提供各类邮电通信服务的总数量。邮电业务量按专业分类包括函件、包件、汇票、报刊发行、邮政快件、特快专递、邮政储蓄、集邮、公众电报、用户电报、传真、长途电话、出租电路、无线寻呼、移动电话、分组交换数据通信、出租代维等。计算方法为各类产品乘以相应的平均单价（不变价）之和，再加上出租电路和设备、代用户维护电话交换机和线路等的服务收入。它综合反映了一定时期邮电业务发展的总成果，是研究邮电业务量构成和发展趋势的重要指标。计算公式为：

邮电业务总量=∑（各类邮电业务量×不变单价）+出租代维及其他业务收入

移动电话用户 是指通过移动电话交换机进入移动电话网、占用移动电话号码的电话用户。用户数量以报告期末在移动电话营业部门实际办理登记手续进入移动电话网的户数进行计算，一部移动电话统计为一户。

电话用户 指接入国家公众固定电话网，并按固定电话业务进行经营管理的电话用户。1997年以前，电话用户分为市内电话用户和农村电话用户。“市内电话用户”是指接入县城及县以上城市的电话网上的电话用户；“农村电话用户”是指接入县邮电局农话台及县以下农村电话交换点，以县城为中心（除市活用户外）联通县、乡（镇）、行政村、村民小组的用户。从1997年起，电话用户数分组调整为以用户所在区域划分为“城市电话用户”和“乡村电话用户”，与过去的按市内电话和农村电话划分方法不同。而电话用户总数、电话机总部数统计范围不变。

农村电话用户 指县城关区以下的集镇和农村接入局用交换机的电话用户数。

局用交换机容量 是指安装在本地电信运营商内用于接续本地固定电话的电话交换机容量，有倍增设备按倍增后的数量计数。包括现用和备用的人工或自动交换机的全部容量。

计算机数 指报告期末企业（单位）使用的计算机数量，包括台式机、笔记本电脑和平板电脑。

信息技术人员 指专职从事信息技术系统的制定、设计、开发、安装、操作、维护、管理和评估的人员。

信息化投入 包括企业（单位）一次性投入和运

营维护投入。

一次性投入 包括企业（单位）购置各类硬件和软件的实际支出。

运营维护投入 包括企业（单位）更新维护各类信息通信硬件和软件的实际支出。

互联网 指在世界范围内的公共计算机网络。它提供一系列通信服务（包括万维网）的接入，并传送电子邮件、新闻、娱乐和数据文件等。

全年电子商务销售金额 指报告期内企业（单位）借助网络订单而销售的商品和服务总额。借助网络订单指通过网络接受订单，付款和配送可以不借助于网络。

全年电子商务采购金额 指报告期内企业（单位）借助网络订单而采购的商品和服务总额。借助网络订单指通过网络发送订单，付款和配送可以不借助于网络。

Explanatory Notes on Main Statistical Indicators

Length of Highways refers to the length of highways which are built in conformity with the grades specified by the highway engineering standard formulated by the Ministry of Communications, and have been formally checked and accepted by the departments of highways and put into use. The length of highways includes that of the suburb highways at large and medium- sized cities,highways passing through streets at small cities and towns,and also the length of bridges, tunnel and ferries. It does not include the length of streets in big and medium-sized cities and highways built for the production purpose at factories, mines, forest areas and agricultural areas. If two or more highways go the same section of the way, the length of the section is only calculated for once and no duplication is allowed. The length of highways is an important indicator to show the development of the highway construction and to provide essential information to calculate the transport network density.

Length of Civil Aviation Routes refers to the length of all routes for regular civil aviation flights. There are usually two ways to calculate the distance between airports connected by the route length: one is to put the length of all air routes together, called duplicated calculation of the length of the routes; the other is not to allow the duplication in calculation when two or more routes passing the same section of aviation routes. The latter is usually used, as it can precisely show the size of the civil aviation network and indicate the extent of civil aviation serving the national economy and the people.

Freight (Passenger) Traffic refers to the volume of freight (passenger) transported with various means. Freight transport is calculated in tons and passenger traffic is calculated in the number of persons. Despite the type of freight and travelling distance, the freight transport is calculated in the actual weight of the goods: and despite the travelling distance and ticket price, the passenger traffic is calculated by the principle that one person can be counted only once in one travel. The passenger who travel with a half price ticket or a child ticket is also calculated as one person. The freight (passenger) traffic provides a quantitative measure to show how the transport industry serves the national economy and people, and is also an important indicator for planning the transport industry and for studying the development scale and speed of the transport industry.

Freight Ton–kilometers(Passenger–kilometers) refer to the sum of the products of the volume of transported cargo (passengers) multiplying by the transport distance, usually using ton-kilometer and passenger-kilometer as units for measurement. Normally, the shortest distance between the departure station and the destination station (i.e., the payable distance) is the basis to calculate the freight ton-kilometers. This is an important indicator to show the total results of the transport industry, to prepare and examine the transport plan and to measure the efficiency, the labour productivity and the unit cost of transport.

The formula is as follows:

Freight Ton-kilometers(Passenger-kilometers)=Σ {Freight (Passenger) Traffic × Distance of Transportation }

Measuring unit: ton-kilometer (person-kilometer)

Possession of Civil Motor Vehicles refer to the total numbers of vehicles that are registered and received vehicles license tags according to the Work Standard for Motor Vehicles Registration formulated by the Transport Management Office under the department of public security at the end of the reference period. They are divided into categories. According to the structure of motor vehicles, they are divided into passenger vehicles, trucks and others; according to ownership into private vehicles and vehicles for the unit' s use; according to kind of usage into working vehicles and non-working vehicles; and according to size of vehicles into large passenger vehicles, medium-sized passenger vehicles, small passenger vehicles and mini passenger vehicles, heavytrucks, light-heavy trucks, light trucks and mini-trucks.

Business Volume of Post and Telecommunications refers to the total amount of post and telecommunications services, expressed in value terms, provided by the post and telecommunications departments for the society. Post and telecommunication services can be classified asletters, parcels, remittance, issue of newspapers and magazines, fast mail service, express mail service, savings deposits, stamps for collection, public and individual telegraph service, facsimiles, long-distance telephone service,leasing of telephone lines, urban paging service, mobile telephone service, data transfer and transmission, etc. The accounting approach is to multiply the service products of all types with their average unit price (constant price) to get sum of business value, plus income from other services such as leasing of telephone lines and equipment, maintenance of telephone switchboards and lines on behalf of customers. This indicator reflects the overall results of post and telecommunications service during a given period, and is important to study the composition of business service and the development of post and telecommunications service.

The formula is as follows:

Business Volume of Post and Telecommunications=Σ (Transaction of Post and Telecommunication Service x Constant Price) + Income from Leasing, Maintenance and other Services

Mobile Telephone Subscribers refer to the persons who own mobile telephone numbers and are connected with the mobile telephone communication network through the mobile telephone switchboards. The number of subscribers is calculated by the subscribers who have completed registration at mobile communication business centers and entered into the mobile telephone network. One mobile telephone is taken as a subscriber.

Telephone Subscribers refer to subscribers that are connected to the public line telephone network provided with telephone services. Before 1997, telephone subscribers were classified as city subscribers and village subscribers. City subscribers referred to those connected to city telephone networks in county towns and cities, while village subscribers referred to those connected to village telephone stations at and below counties. Since 1997, the classification of telephone subscribers was modified on the basis of physical location of the subscribers as Urban telephone subscribers and rural telephone subscribers , which is different from the previous classification of categorizing local telephones and rural telephones , while the definition of total subscribers and total number of telephones remain unchanged.

Rural Telephone Subscribers refer to telephone subscribers, located at towns under county town and country, that are connected to the public line telephone network.

Capacity of Office Telephone Exchanges refers to the capacity (measured in gate) of telephone exchanges installed in the offices of local telecommunication service providers for communication between fixed telephones. It includes the capacity of both manual and automatic exchanges in use and for stand-by purpose. Equipment with expansion function is to be counted by the expanded capacity.

The number of computer srefers to the number of computers used in an enterprise or a company at the end of the reporting period, including desktops, laptops, and tablet computers.

Information technology personnel refers topeople who is engaged in the formulation, design, development, installation, operation, maintenance, management and evaluation of an information technology system.

Informatization Input includes the One-time investment input and operation maintenance investment of an enterprise or a company.

One-time Investment Input includes the actual expenditure in purchasing all kinds of hardware and software of an enterprise or a company.

Operation and Maintenance Input includesthe actual expenditure inupdating and maintenance of all kinds of information communication hardware and software of anenterprise or a company.

The Internet refers to the public computer network around the world. It provides access to a range of communications services including the world wide web, and transmits e-mail, news, entertainment, and data files,etc.

The amount of E-commerce sales during the whole year the total amount of goods and services sold by means of network orders of an enterprise or a company during the reporting period.By means of network ordersmeans that the orders are received over the network, but the payment and distribution can be made without the network.

The amount of E-commerce purchases during the whole year refers to the total amount of goods and services purchased by means of network orders of an enterprise or a company during the reporting period.

By means of network orders means that the orders are sent over the network, but the payment and distribution can be made without the network.

16 国内贸易

DOMESTIC TRADE

资料整理：杨　骏　左　宇　赵琳瑛　胡树建　李鹏涛
Data management: Yang Jun Zuo Yu Zhao Linying Hu Shujian Li Pengtao
数据审核：赵　晖
Data audit: Zhao Hui

第十六部分　国内贸易

一、简要说明

1.本章资料反映西安市批发和零售业、住宿和餐饮业的发展与经营状况，主要内容包括：社会消费品零售总额，限额以上批发和零售业、住宿和餐饮业基本情况、连锁经营情况，重点交易市场情况等。

2.限额以上企业指年主营业务收入2000万元及以上的批发企业（单位）；500万元及以上的零售业企业（单位）；200万元及以上的住宿和餐饮业企业（单位）。

3.批发业、零售业、住宿业、餐饮业大中小微型企业划分按照《统计上大中小微型企业划分办法（2017）》标准执行。

4.社会消费品零售总额和增速根据第四次经济普查结果进行了修订。

二、主要指标

社会消费品零售总额（亿元）	5140.93	比上年增长	6.0%

16　DOMESTIC TRADE

I.Brief Introduction

1.This chapter reflects the management and development of wholesale and retail trades, hotels and catering services in Xi'an , mainly including: total retail sales of consumer goods, the basic conditions enterprises above designated size in wholesale and retail trades, hotels and catering services, the conditions of chain stores,focus on transaction markets, etc.

2.Enterprises above designated size cover wholesale enterprises with revenue from principal business over 20 million yuan, retail enterprises with revenue from principal business over 5 million yuan, hotel and catering services enterprises with revenue from principal business over 2 million yuan.

3.The division standard of large/medium/small/mini sized enterprises of wholesale, retail trades, hotels and catering services is based on the division standard of large/medium/small/mini sized enterprises in 2017.

4.According to the results of the fourth economic census, the total retail sales of consumer goods and the growth rate were revised.

Ⅱ .Maior Indicators

		Increase over Preceding Year
Total Retail Sales of Consumer Goods (100 mil. yuan)	5140.93	6.0%

16-1 主要年份社会消费品零售额

Total Retail Sales of Consumer Goods in Representative Years

单位：亿元 (100 million yuan)

年 份 Year	社会消费品零售总额 Total Retail Sales of Consumer Goods	城镇 Urban	乡村 Village	批发零售贸易业 Wholesale Trades and Retail Trades	住宿餐饮业 Accommodation and Catering Trade	其他行业 Others
1978	12.70	8.82	3.88	11.01	0.53	0.21
1980	15.88	11.53	4.35	13.05	0.80	0.20
1985	32.92	26.09	6.83	25.04	1.69	0.48
1986	37.50	29.25	8.25	28.88	1.97	0.64
1987	43.86	34.62	9.24	33.32	2.50	0.49
1988	59.65	47.74	11.91	44.84	2.97	0.78
1989	68.05	54.60	13.45	54.41	2.98	0.76
1990	72.77	59.42	13.35	57.46	3.79	0.90
1991	81.04	66.93	14.11	60.35	4.43	1.26
1992	100.84	89.17	11.67	71.86	6.13	2.30
1993	117.10	105.97	11.13	77.12	7.60	2.75
1994	148.95	135.48	13.47	92.46	9.39	3.53
1995	188.35	167.54	20.81	116.54	12.08	3.76
1996	225.71	200.65	25.06	146.85	16.03	4.07
1997	268.49	241.79	26.70	171.65	22.46	4.23
1998	296.71	262.04	34.67	186.74	31.53	4.35
1999	330.13	289.24	40.89	212.31	35.51	4.95
2000	368.96	324.63	44.33	238.41	42.40	5.56
2001	416.95	368.46	48.49	272.26	50.16	6.01
2002	473.12	421.77	51.35	318.35	52.91	6.64
2003	518.67	463.95	54.72	454.32	55.00	9.36
2004	601.12	541.21	59.91	529.43	59.09	12.60
2005	698.37	629.71	68.66	617.36	66.23	14.79
2006	819.32	739.33	80.00	724.42	78.04	16.86
2007	979.18	884.40	94.78	866.67	93.42	19.10
2008	1233.44	1115.35	118.09	1082.92	128.84	21.68
2009	1469.37	1404.26	65.11	1313.89	155.47	
2010	1765.42	1694.79	70.63	1575.73	189.69	
2011	2146.43	2071.87	74.55	1921.76	224.67	
2012	2530.95	2453.11	77.84	2273.52	257.43	

年 份 Year	社会消费品零售总额 Total Retail Sales of Consumer Goods	按销售单位所在地分 By Location of Establishments 城镇零售额 Urban Areas	城区 Urban District	乡村零售额 Rural Areas	按消费形态分By Consumption Patterns 商品零售 Retail Sales	餐饮收入 Catering income
2013	2898.62	2808.37	2245.35	90.25	2669.52	229.10
2014	3277.33	3174.09	2749.92	103.24	3034.94	242.39
2015	3620.90	3501.23	3011.94	119.67	3345.59	275.32
2016	4012.44	3876.23	3479.35	136.20	3713.16	299.28
2017	4422.72	4264.73	3667.72	157.99	4075.53	347.18
2018	4854.70	4759.97	4067.48	94.73	4476.48	378.22
2019	5140.93	5039.17	4280.42	101.76	4733.65	407.28

注：本表1993年到2018年数据根据第四次经济普查结果进行了修订。

16-2 社会消费品零售总额（2019年）

Total Retail Sales of Consumer Goods (2019)

单位：亿元 (100 million yuan)

分　组	Classify	2018	2019
社会消费品零售总额	**Total Retail Sales of Consumer Goods**	**4854.70**	**5140.93**
（一）按销售单位所在地分	Grouped by Region		
（1）城镇	Urban	4759.97	5039.17
#城区	District	4067.48	4280.42
（2）乡村	Village	94.73	101.76
（二）按消费形态分	Grouped by Consumption Patterns		
（1）商品零售	Retail Sales	4476.48	4733.65
（2）餐饮收入	Catering Income	378.22	407.28

注：本表数据根据第四次经济普查结果进行了修订。

16–3 各区县社会消费品零售总额

Total Retail Sales of Consumer Goods by Region

单位：亿元 (100 million yuan)

区 县	Region	2005	2009	2010	2011	2012	2013	2014	2015	2016	2017	2018	2019
全 市	**Toatl**	**698.37**	**1469.37**	**1765.42**	**2146.43**	**2530.95**	**2898.62**	**3277.33**	**3620.90**	**4012.44**	**4422.72**	**4854.70**	**5140.93**
新城区	Xincheng	58.12	103.74	121.94	145.61	167.61	187.08	209.82	235.49	255.50	259.80	292.82	293.11
碑林区	Beilin	130.35	228.89	269.18	321.45	368.06	412.03	468.74	523.35	566.28	568.99	584.86	622.29
莲湖区	Lianhu	124.47	202.03	238.27	284.80	326.71	367.14	411.75	453.14	490.72	493.16	507.10	553.76
灞桥区	Baqiao	32.63	63.04	86.80	117.08	163.08	224.57	262.22	296.24	341.66	366.32	417.48	448.66
未央区	Weiyang	103.08	306.07	372.62	454.94	542.65	631.55	717.33	773.27	875.42	772.86	865.32	904.20
雁塔区	Yanta	156.02	386.23	462.69	563.77	659.18	739.97	826.95	915.51	991.33	1006.54	1107.71	1162.36
阎良区	Yanliang	6.55	12.41	14.80	17.90	20.72	23.17	25.83	28.19	30.51	31.27	34.81	38.33
临潼区	Lintong	13.25	21.26	25.26	30.52	35.19	38.80	44.02	47.55	51.36	54.25	61.57	64.77
长安区	Chang'an	39.55	77.50	92.22	111.30	129.03	142.84	161.78	181.97	199.95	211.78	240.51	251.33
高陵区	Gaoling	11.68	26.98	32.86	40.68	51.68	57.26	65.08	73.15	102.17	110.09	127.80	142.11
鄠邑区	Huyi	8.21	15.07	17.92	21.52	24.67	27.47	31.03	34.58	37.79	38.91	44.05	46.78
蓝田县	Lantian	8.15	14.35	16.96	20.26	23.24	25.64	28.94	31.84	34.88	36.67	42.91	47.63
周至县	Zhouzhi	6.31	11.79	13.91	16.61	19.15	21.11	23.83	26.63	34.88	36.44	40.77	40.85
西咸新区	Xixian										435.65	487.00	524.74

注：本表数据根据第四次经济普查结果进行了修订。

16-4 限额以上批发零售贸易企业财务状况（2019年）

单位：万元

分组	Classify	单位数（个）Number (unit)	资产总计 Total Assets	流动资产合计 Circulating Funds
总计	**Total**	**1870**	**35444607.1**	**28187039.7**
一、批发企业	**Wholesale Enterprises**	**956**	**23519101.2**	**20034896.0**
1. 按登记注册类型分	Grouped by Category of Commodities			
内资企业	Domestic Funded Enterprises	931	18277328.2	15412282.7
国有	State-owned Enterprises	13	599373.2	509340.8
集体	Collective-owned Enterprises	2	3492.4	3409.4
股份合作	Corperative Enterprises			
联营	Joint Ownership Enterprises			
国有联营	State Joint Ownership Enterprises			
集体联营	Collective Joint Ownership Enterprises			
国有与集体联营	Joint State-collective Enterprises			
其他联营	Others Joint Ownership Enterprises			
有限责任公司	Limited Liability Corporations	302	11655985.4	9777548.1
国有独资公司	State Funded Corporations	23	2046911.3	1687435.7
其他有限责任公司	Other Limited Liability Corporations	279	9609074.1	8090112.4
股份有限公司	Share-holding Corporations Ltd.	19	1713251.7	1354661.7
私营	Private Enterprises	592	4303439.5	3766622.9
私营独资	Private-funded Enterprises	2	1902.6	1722.6
私营合伙	Private Partnership Enterprises			
私营有限责任公司	Private Limited Liability Corporations	580	4143714.3	3633291.2
私营股份有限公司	Private Share-holding Corporations Ltd.	10	157822.6	131609.1
其他	Other Enterprises	3	1786.0	699.8
港澳台商投资	Enterprises with Funds from Hong Kong, Macao &Taiwan	4	75454.2	64950.6
外商投资	Foreign Funded Enterprises	21	5166318.8	4557662.7
2. 按国民经济行业分	Grouped by Sector			

Financial Status of Wholesale and Retail Enterprises above Designated Size (2019)

(10 000 yuan)

固定资产原价 Original Value of Fixed Assets	累计折旧 Accumulated Depreciation	负债合计 Total Liabilities	流动负债合计 Circulating Liabilities	所有者权益合计 Total Owners' Equities	实收资本 Paid in Capital	营业收入 Total Revenue	主营业务收入 Revenue from Principal Business
3114021.1	**1025259.9**	**26464354.5**	**23957673.2**	**8974634.8**	**7294047.3**	**85862557.4**	**85289322.7**
924533.6	**363370.4**	**17876345.2**	**16410938.6**	**5637845.6**	**4759735.1**	**65537053.0**	**65313216.7**
828575.6	346215.8	13123534.6	11950531.5	5148883.2	4519925.3	51264236.1	51042210.4
119679.6	64141.6	173448.1	169405.6	425925.1	32064.2	1461988.0	1460681.0
109.5	27.5	3121.3	1599.6	371.1		9079.9	9079.9
367112.0	135136.1	8101085.7	7424705.6	3553519.3	2607578.6	33402340.0	33270047.0
28808.7	15308.8	1207807.2	878010.8	838678.1	559765.7	5460632.0	5446729.0
338303.3	119827.3	6893278.5	6546694.8	2714841.2	2047812.9	27941708.0	27823318.0
114768.6	47681.0	1457508.9	1121209.6	254876.0	201613.8	4975247.2	4945222.3
224953.5	98308.3	3388050.6	3233306.1	912725.7	1677501.2	11394438.9	11336038.1
313.2	133.3	1367.6	1348.9	535.0	550.0	7431.2	7371.5
213470.0	93460.0	3290225.2	3142954.7	850825.9	1630844.6	11254317.9	11198204.1
11170.3	4715.0	96457.8	89002.5	61364.8	46106.6	132689.8	130462.5
1952.4	921.3	320.0	305.0	1466.0	1167.5	21142.1	21142.1
12211.3	3308.7	60039.0	58824.4	15415.2	6321.7	117077.1	117077.1
83746.7	13845.9	4692771.6	4401582.7	473547.2	233488.1	14155739.8	14153929.2

16-4 续表1

单位：万元

分 组	Classify	营业成本 Total Cost	税金及附加 Taxs and Other Changes
总计	**Total**	**80878582.2**	**315380.8**
一、批发企业	**Wholesale Enterprises**	**63089792.4**	**232134.0**
1. 按登记注册类型分	Grouped by Category of Commodities		
内资企业	Domestic Funded Enterprises	49094416.7	225586.0
国有	State-owned Enterprises	1069137.1	175950.4
集体	Collective-owned Enterprises	8894.6	9.4
股份合作	Corperative Enterprises		
联营	Joint Ownership Enterprises		
国有联营	State Joint Ownership Enterprises		
集体联营	Collective Joint Ownership Enterprises		
国有与集体联营	Joint State-collective Enterprises		
其他联营	Others Joint Ownership Enterprises		
有限责任公司	Limited Liability Corporations	32528080.5	32499.0
国有独资公司	State Funded Corporations	5415115.1	4232.4
其他有限责任公司	Other Limited Liability Corporations	27112965.4	28266.6
股份有限公司	Share-holding Corporations Ltd.	4836404.0	3104.8
私营	Private Enterprises	10633375.5	14022.4
私营独资	Private-funded Enterprises	6811.8	8.2
私营合伙	Private Partnership Enterprises		
私营有限责任公司	Private Limited Liability Corporations	10505437.3	13773.3
私营股份有限公司	Private Share-holding Corporations Ltd.	121126.4	240.9
其他	Other Enterprises	18525.0	
港澳台商投资	Enterprises with Funds from Hong Kong, Macao &Taiwan	79610.2	666.6
外商投资	Foreign Funded Enterprises	13915765.5	5881.4
2. 按国民经济行业分	Grouped by Sector		

continued 1

(10 000 yuan)

销售费用 Sale Expenses	管理费用 Management Expenses	财务费用 Financial Expenses	营业利润 Business Profits	利润总额 Total Profits	应付职工薪酬 Salary Payable	所得税费用 Income Tax Expenses	应交增值税 Value Added Tax Payable
2568010.9	**1017396.2**	**339891.0**	**989080.7**	**1030045.3**	**1178308.0**	**227418.7**	**484543.2**
955993.7	**473117.8**	**225895.3**	**750221.2**	**768496.8**	**510416.4**	**149560.1**	**239646.7**
893885.0	439978.7	124081.4	656776.6	673113.1	450843.9	133236.7	227044.9
39884.5	29793.4	-768.9	149203.5	152712.4	72564.6	39009.7	50636.7
61.7	77.5	17.8	18.9	18.9	135.0	8.7	12.2
379592.6	212418.6	87580.0	309466.1	317864.5	212492.8	64353.8	97322.5
39180.9	29352.1	5310.0	76872.8	77374.7	36686.1	11635.9	19126.7
340411.7	183066.5	82270.0	232593.3	240489.8	175806.7	52717.9	78195.8
116775.1	8450.9	5349.3	4208.5	4111.7	51354.6	5130.7	5368.6
357394.6	189088.8	31829.9	191580.5	195704.5	113618.2	24733.8	73704.9
61.5	468.3	28.3	53.1	53.1	150.2	11.9	69.6
352372.7	185372.0	30772.0	190853.0	195349.9	111345.6	24585.4	72108.3
4960.4	3248.5	1029.6	674.4	301.5	2122.4	136.5	1527.0
176.5	149.5	73.3	2299.1	2701.1	678.7		
22452.0	10333.5	217.4	3852.9	3824.9	16605.4	-134.2	4041.9
39656.7	22805.6	101596.5	89591.7	91558.8	42967.1	16457.6	8559.9

16-4 续表2

单位：万元

分　组	Classify	单位数（个）Number (unit)	资产总计 Total Assets	流动资产合　计 Circulating Funds
农、林、牧产品批发	Wholesale of Agricultural,Forestry and Animal Husbandry Products	6	77745.8	32409.0
食品、饮料及烟草制品批发	Wholesale of food Beverages and Tobaccos	98	1553143.5	1268024.8
纺织、服装及家庭服务器批发	Wholesale of Textiles, Garments and Daily Articles	49	580783.5	543322.1
文化、体育用品及器材批发	Wholesale of Culture, Sports Appliances and Equipments	40	389546.0	307476.7
医药及医疗器材批发	Wholesale of Medicines and Medical Appliances	148	3359599.3	3176915.2
矿产品、建材及化工产品批发	Wholesale of Mineral Products, Building Materials and Chemical Products	373	13891665.2	11336854.5
机械设备、五金产品及电子产品批发	Wholesale of Machinery, Hardware, and Electronic Equipment	215	3473312.3	3194360.6
贸易经纪与代理	Trade Broker and Agency	5	86790.0	84757.4
其他批发	Other wholesale not Classified Elsewhere	22	106515.6	90775.7
二、零售企业	**Retail Trade**	**914**	**11925505.9**	**8152143.7**
1. 按登记注册类型分	Grouped by Category of Commodities			
内资	Domestic Funded Enterprises	858	8176647.5	5788508.7
国有	State-owned Enterprises	5	380895.1	325711.3
集体	Collective-owned Enterprises	15	12302.7	5750.2
股份合作	Corperative Enterprises			
联营	Joint Ownership Enterprises			
国有联营	State Joint Ownership Enterprises			
集体联营	Collective Joint Ownership Enterprises			
国有与集体联营	Joint State-collective Enterprises			
其他联营	Others Joint Ownership Enterprises			
有限责任公司	Limited Liability Corporations	289	4356567.1	2860526.3
国有独资公司	State Funded Corporations	10	208872.9	135401.6

continued 2

(10 000 yuan)

固定资产原价 Original Value of Fixed Assets	累计折旧 Accumulated Depreciation	负债合计 Total Liabilities	流动负债合计 Circulating Liabilities	所有者权益合计 Total Owners' Equities	实收资本 Paid in Capital	营业收入 Total Revenue	主营业务收入 Revenue from Principal Business
18646.1	5166.1	64988.9	36756.0	11917.1	2757.0	47693.9	47238.6
218043.5	83046.5	717942.7	665489.0	834334.0	158323.0	3169886.2	3147291.5
22112.5	13036.0	502731.2	494571.4	78052.3	53706.6	1224856.8	1200811.8
22423.9	11902.4	254448.7	233290.1	134142.9	1048157.6	863921.0	861883.4
115872.8	48274.1	2800320.5	2606364.3	559278.8	376251.1	4590649.0	4579126.6
397567.1	147561.4	10554271.8	9452783.5	3335359.7	2691185.9	49474824.0	49327050.2
119845.8	49187.6	2817405.1	2758047.0	655691.5	405672.7	5776390.2	5761948.2
1231.4	401.3	78783.3	78436.9	8006.7	5481.3	196560.9	196170.0
8790.5	4795.0	85453.0	85200.4	21062.6	18199.9	192271.0	191696.4
2189487.5	**661889.5**	**8588009.3**	**7546734.6**	**3336789.2**	**2534312.2**	**20325504.4**	**19976106.0**
1168225.6	400654.8	5983246.0	5128171.0	2192694.1	1990843.3	11988644.5	11759605.8
52698.8	21484.0	250440.0	247287.0	130455.1	3416.7	652424.0	646549.7
5311.6	834.4	7930.7	7064.5	4372.0	1270.0	26385.0	26268.3
727940.6	225006.6	3076861.5	2610970.9	1286553.6	764411.5	5850686.9	5711266.7
83333.0	22841.4	153639.0	143118.9	55233.9	22230.1	249099.6	244746.7

16-4 续表3

单位：万元

分组	Classify	营业成本 Total Cost	税金及附加 Taxs and Other Changes
农、林、牧产品批发	Wholesale of Agricultural,Forestry and Animal Husbandry Products	45926.7	29.4
食品、饮料及烟草制品批发	Wholesale of food Beverages and Tobaccos	2578099.7	178845.0
纺织、服装及家庭服务器批发	Wholesale of Textiles, Garments and Daily Articles	1098061.5	2048.2
文化、体育用品及器材批发	Wholesale of Culture, Sports Appliances and Equipments	803365.9	888.0
医药及医疗器材批发	Wholesale of Medicines and Medical Appliances	4188499.3	9542.1
矿产品、建材及化工产品批发	Wholesale of Mineral Products, Building Materials and Chemical Products	48535074.1	33663.5
机械设备、五金产品及电子产品批发	Wholesale of Machinery, Hardware, and Electronic Equipment	5476804.4	6325.5
贸易经纪与代理	Trade Broker and Agency	182544.6	112.9
其他批发	Other wholesale not Classified Elsewhere	181416.2	679.4
二、零售企业	**Retail Trade**	**17788789.8**	**83246.8**
1. 按登记注册类型分	Grouped by Category of Commodities		
内资	Domestic Funded Enterprises	10625867.5	52334.7
国有	State-owned Enterprises	608483.2	1734.4
集体	Collective-owned Enterprises	22767.6	173.0
股份合作	Corperative Enterprises		
联营	Joint Ownership Enterprises		
国有联营	State Joint Ownership Enterprises		
集体联营	Collective Joint Ownership Enterprises		
国有与集体联营	Joint State-collective Enterprises		
其他联营	Others Joint Ownership Enterprises		
有限责任公司	Limited Liability Corporations	5220197.2	21022.0
国有独资公司	State Funded Corporations	221274.7	607.3

continued 3

(10 000 yuan)

销售费用 Sale Expenses	管理费用 Management Expenses	财务费用 Financial Expenses	营业利润 Business Profits	利润总额 Total Profits	应付职工薪酬 Salary Payable	所得税费用 Income Tax Expenses	应交增值税 Value Added Tax Payable
589.7	1917.8	262.3	-1090.8	-571.3	1443.4	11.4	78.9
136963.0	70635.8	3978.5	228783.7	234886.4	123933.6	54410.3	65473.2
72862.8	28644.9	-317.7	25127.4	25760.9	36254.0	5639.1	15335.4
25425.8	25673.0	569.1	9519.8	9926.2	21543.3	1288.1	1876.9
167249.5	94877.6	60029.3	73418.5	75328.4	93146.7	17012.9	55351.3
419840.2	164417.9	158439.5	272157.0	275853.4	155547.6	42516.9	76592.0
120723.7	79403.3	2491.9	138025.0	141751.5	74087.9	28119.6	22330.0
8806.0	3036.4	-180.1	2670.2	3052.2	1669.9	370.9	74.8
3533.0	4511.1	622.5	1610.4	2509.1	2790.0	190.9	2534.2
1612017.2	**544278.4**	**113995.7**	**238859.5**	**261548.5**	**667891.6**	**77858.6**	**244896.5**
863548.1	380401.4	90816.9	47870.0	62836.1	450034.9	26070.6	150802.3
29898.1	15025.4	2077.4	18542.5	19139.4	26269.2	2754.1	8472.4
1074.0	1845.4	72.7	455.0	476.1	1611.4	24.2	418.1
353310.5	160787.7	35607.7	44435.4	52162.5	200091.1	15372.7	35400.7
20155.8	11465.4	1236.9	3024.3	5933.1	18609.8	710.2	5753.7

16-4 续表4

单位：万元

分 组	Classify	单位数（个）Number (unit)	资产总计 Total Assets	流动资产合计 Circulating Funds
其他有限责任公司	Other Limited Liability Corporations	279	4147694.2	2725124.7
股份有限公司	Share-holding Corporations Ltd.	11	772461.7	481962.5
私营	Private Enterprises	534	2650819.8	2113286.8
私营独资	Private-funded Enterprises	15	13311.5	10654.6
私营合伙	Private Partnership Enterprises	1	401.5	315.0
私营有限责任公司	Private Limited Liability Corporations	513	2617532.2	2087220.1
私营股份有限公司	Private Share-holding Corporations Ltd.	5	19574.6	15097.1
其他	Other Enterprises	4	3601.1	1271.6
港澳台商投资	Enterprises with Funds from Hong Kong, Macao &Taiwan	27	1867626.9	1418983.9
外商投资	Foreign Funded Enterprises	29	1881231.5	944651.1
2. 按国民经济行业分组	Grouped by Sector			
综合零售	Integrated Retail	122	3663176.3	2223332.7
食品、饮料及烟草制品专门零售	Food, Beverages and Tobaccos Special Retail Trade	80	215787.7	161060.0
纺织、服装及日用品专门零售	Special Retail of Textiles,Garments and Daily Consumer Articles	65	1151826.3	723939.4
文化、体育用品及器材专门零售	Retail of Culture,Sports Appliances and Equipments	57	368510.3	251921.0
医药及医疗器材专门零售	Retail of Medicines and Medical Appliances	44	433898.2	351503.4
汽车、摩托车、零配件和燃料及其他动力销售	Retail of automobiles, motorcycles, spare parts and fuel and other power	324	4327873.5	3021047.2
家用电器及电子产品专门零售	Special Retail of Household Electric Appliances and Electronic Products	100	609988.2	559136.7
五金、家具及室内装饰材料专门零售	Special Retail of Hardware,Furniture and Decoration Materials	36	357834.9	245909.4
货摊、无店铺及其他零售业	Non-shop and Other Retail	86	796610.5	614293.9

continued 4

(10 000 yuan)

固定资产原价 Original Value of Fixed Assets	累计折旧 Accumulated Depreciation	负债合计 Total Liabilities	流动负债合计 Circulating Liabilities	所有者权益合计 Total Owners' Equities	实收资本 Paid in Capital	营业收入 Total Revenue	主营业务收入 Revenue from Principal Business
644607.6	202165.2	2923222.5	2467852.0	1231319.7	742181.4	5601587.3	5466520.0
70842.3	35840.6	377058.3	335225.1	395403.4	329694.3	366890.9	360724.6
308816.2	116883.3	2269412.9	1926629.1	373851.5	889997.8	5078169.5	5000708.4
2528.4	698.7	8928.4	8811.3	4258.2	6627.2	51452.7	51452.7
104.1	3.8	266.8	266.8	134.7	100.0	3804.0	3804.0
298951.1	113420.3	2243092.4	1907714.3	367009.3	880970.6	4964476.4	4887614.3
7232.6	2760.5	17125.3	9836.7	2449.3	2300.0	58436.4	57837.4
2616.1	605.9	1542.6	994.4	2058.5	2053.0	14088.2	14088.1
510582.6	111705.5	1317162.1	1281986.6	550464.8	179624.6	2617602.2	2528579.2
510679.3	149529.2	1287601.2	1136577.0	593630.3	363844.3	5719257.7	5687921.0
1145639.6	278047.1	2574015.6	2289571.4	1089160.7	842832.3	3799317.7	3596187.2
44074.7	25383.6	184392.4	154969.0	31295.4	57988.9	301772.6	295077.2
74049.4	47248.0	552058.8	451927.0	599767.5	150985.3	1383898.6	1360237.4
110494.9	26649.6	310207.4	226938.8	55335.1	52831.0	271138.5	266509.4
37535.3	16525.4	335816.0	313849.1	98032.2	46914.5	615300.3	611290.9
645863.6	234148.0	3248170.0	2875443.5	1082652.3	1143000.5	8781054.2	8711299.2
12054.3	7723.3	420030.8	373525.1	189420.1	90506.1	1146920.1	1127635.1
52025.9	14003.6	329787.4	272557.4	28046.3	76745.0	345125.8	332502.1
67749.8	12160.9	633530.9	587953.3	163079.6	72508.6	3680976.6	3675367.5

16-4 续表5

单位：万元

分 组	Classify	营业成本 Total Cost	税金及附加 Taxs and Other Changes
其他有限责任公司	Other Limited Liability Corporations	4998922.5	20414.7
股份有限公司	Share-holding Corporations Ltd.	320993.9	927.7
私营	Private Enterprises	4439954.1	28412.6
私营独资	Private-funded Enterprises	48038.7	212.3
私营合伙	Private Partnership Enterprises	2608.1	23.5
私营有限责任公司	Private Limited Liability Corporations	4331009.1	27915.9
私营股份有限公司	Private Share-holding Corporations Ltd.	58298.2	260.9
其他	Other Enterprises	13471.5	65.0
港澳台商投资	Enterprises with Funds from Hong Kong, Macao &Taiwan	2176116.7	10329.8
外商投资	Foreign Funded Enterprises	4986805.6	20582.3
2. 按国民经济行业分组	Grouped by Sector		
综合零售	Integrated Retail	3101412.4	22641.3
食品、饮料及烟草制品专门零售	Food, Beverages and Tobaccos Special Retail Trade	254151.7	5557.4
纺织、服装及日用品专门零售	Special Retail of Textiles,Garments and Daily Consumer Articles	1085654.1	5845.3
文化、体育用品及器材专门零售	Retail of Culture,Sports Appliances and Equipments	217754.5	1450.4
医药及医疗器材专门零售	Retail of Medicines and Medical Appliances	467986.2	2361.0
汽车、摩托车、零配件和燃料及其他动力销售	Retail of automobiles, motorcycles, spare parts and fuel and other power	8081697.2	23630.8
家用电器及电子产品专门零售	Special Retail of Household Electric Appliances and Electronic Products	1002736.2	4869.1
五金、家具及室内装饰材料专门零售	Special Retail of Hardware,Furniture and Decoration Materials	256190.9	8707.9
货摊、无店铺及其他零售业	Non-shop and Other Retail	3321206.6	8183.6

continued 5

(10 000 yuan)

销售费用 Sale Expenses	管理费用 Management Expenses	财务费用 Financial Expenses	营业利润 Business Profits	利润总额 Total Profits	应付职工薪酬 Salary Payable	所得税费用 Income Tax Expenses	应交增值税 Value Added Tax Payable
333154.7	149322.3	34370.8	41411.1	46229.4	181481.3	14662.5	29647.0
34084.1	21756.4	1711.6	-6737.3	-4961.9	18584.5	1136.2	2123.0
444869.9	180722.4	51340.7	-8794.9	-3949.3	203148.8	6782.6	103874.3
1548.8	1720.0	36.0	-112.6	-112.6	1259.3	43.9	395.2
623.6	538.8	0.2	9.9	10.4	224.0	0.3	11.5
441608.1	177379.0	51137.0	-8440.8	-3797.7	200715.6	6738.4	103381.8
1089.4	1084.6	167.5	-251.4	-49.4	949.9		85.8
311.5	264.1	6.8	-30.7	-30.7	329.9	0.8	513.8
258818.2	76559.8	7094.2	71978.9	75105.8	129913.9	13262.5	40377.5
489650.9	87317.2	16084.6	119010.6	123606.6	87942.8	38525.5	53716.7
440689.5	159772.9	20146.1	29288.1	36058.3	193943.9	21419.4	32216.6
42684.8	14821.9	1495.3	-12792.3	-12960.9	24570.6	2307.5	8965.9
175665.8	58565.3	5156.1	61002.3	63080.3	90880.0	9699.8	27271.2
27387.8	28774.7	3414.6	845.6	4600.9	25669.6	204.4	3538.2
109307.9	21123.3	5249.4	13235.2	14552.0	58005.4	1779.3	15633.6
353714.9	143812.0	52297.1	132966.0	136939.5	192313.7	39314.1	94995.0
105240.9	33295.9	2986.1	959.9	1701.8	48324.1	514.9	37290.9
55919.0	40209.5	22007.9	7610.2	8851.1	6913.2	1194.5	5171.9
301406.6	43902.9	1243.1	5744.5	8725.5	27271.1	1424.7	19813.2

16-5 限额以上住宿和餐饮企业财务状况（2019年）

单位：万元

分组	Classify	单位数（个） Number (unit)	资产总计 Total Assets	流动资产合计 Circulating Funds
总计	**Total**	**792**	**3788593.4**	**1599404.7**
一、住宿业	**Hotel Services**	**415**	**3032915.1**	**1213548.3**
1.按登记注册类型分	Grouped by Type of Registration			
内资	Domestic Funded Enterprises	401	2344267.4	930276.8
国有	State-owned Enterprises	16	73086.9	16215.2
集体	Collective-owned Enterprises	2	267.9	257.5
股份合作	Cooperative Enterprises			
联营	Joint Ownership Enterprises			
国有联营	State Joint Ownership Enterprises			
集体联营	Collective Joint Ownership Enterprises			
国有与集体联营	Joint State-collective Enterprises			
其他联营	Others Joint Ownership Enterprises			
有限责任公司	Limited Liability Corporations	142	1649721.9	635292.6
国有独资公司	State Sole Funded Corporations	9	54895.2	23568.7
其他有限责任公司	Other Limited Liability Corporations	133	1594826.7	611723.9
股份有限公司	Share-holding Corporations Ltd.	2	10243.3	943.4
私营	Private Enterprises	239	610947.4	277568.1
私营独资	Private-funded Enterprises	5	3014.5	1935.2
私营合伙	Private Partnership Enterprises			
私营有限责任公司	Private Limited Liability Corporations	231	603639.9	272275.2
私营股份有限公司	Private Share-holding Corporations Ltd.	3	4293.0	3357.7
其他	Other Enterprises			
港澳台商投资	Enterprises with Funds from Hong Kong, Macao &Taiwan	7	199818.0	85092.6
外商投资	Foreign Funded Enterprises	7	488829.7	198178.9
2.按国民经济行业分	Grouped by Sector			
旅游饭店	Tourist Hotel	174	2555276.5	993025.2
一般旅馆	Normal Hotel	221	408951.6	208159.4
民宿服务	Home and Lodging Services	5	1705.4	935.0
露营地服务	Campsite Services	1	6453.7	1051.2
其他住宿业	Others	14	60527.9	10377.5

注：本表统计范围为法人单位。

Finacial Status of Hotels and Catering Enterprises above Designated Size (2019)

(10 000 yuan)

固定资产原价 Original Value of Fixed Assets	累计折旧 Accumulated Depreciation	负债合计 Total Liabilities	流动负债合计 Circulating Liabilities	所有者权益合计 Total Owners' Equities	实收资本 Paid in Capital	营业收入 Total Revenue	主营业务收入 Revenue from Principal Business
2317597.8	**928704.3**	**3151936.8**	**2205027.2**	**621381.9**	**1206680.5**	**1611145.6**	**1591746.6**
2084488.0	**811876.0**	**2646701.3**	**1766915.4**	**377139.6**	**909119.9**	**742344.5**	**733664.8**
1600705.4	662190.3	1994876.0	1223722.7	340317.2	743435.5	649145.2	640095.9
62436.0	30215.7	44268.6	36760.8	28818.3	27924.3	30196.3	29462.0
264.8	254.5	173.1	173.1	94.8	70.0	534.1	534.1
1179223.8	492315.8	1451091.7	766251.4	188224.7	488775.7	355084.2	351580.3
71603.9	51322.7	102920.5	44890.7	-48025.3	33360.7	33015.8	32848.1
1107619.9	440993.1	1348171.2	721360.7	236250.0	455415.0	322068.4	318732.2
17191.7	7892.5	4543.3	4226.8	5700.0	5700.0	3149.4	3149.4
341589.1	131511.8	494799.3	416310.6	117479.4	220965.5	260181.2	255370.1
1415.9	640.1	2655.2	2655.2	359.3	280.0	2221.6	2221.6
339218.3	130542.3	488057.6	410105.5	116913.6	219685.5	254476.1	249665.0
954.9	329.4	4086.5	3549.9	206.5	1000.0	3483.5	3483.5
194922.7	101520.0	169150.6	71053.5	30667.4	107184.4	46092.9	46729.0
288859.9	48165.7	482674.7	472139.2	6155.0	58500.0	47106.4	46839.9
1897247.3	736003.3	2316924.0	1501057.4	235989.1	732179.3	530084.5	525189.7
150197.0	66656.7	299864.3	241462.7	100717.2	164236.5	185787.9	182439.8
751.8	132.6	762.8	762.8	942.6	916.1	1270.0	1269.8
5671.1	272.0	2807.4	192.6	3646.3	5000.0	1120.2	1120.2
30620.8	8811.4	26342.8	23439.9	35844.4	6788.0	24081.9	23645.3

16-5 续表1

单位：万元

分 组	Classify	营业成本 Total Cost	税金及附加 Taxs and Other Changes
总计	**Total**	**735315.3**	**18376.7**
一、住宿业	**Hotel Services**	**293756.7**	**13551.3**
1.按登记注册类型分	Grouped by Type of Registration		
内资	Domestic Funded Enterprises	253215.9	9553.6
国有	State-owned Enterprises	14057.3	639.3
集体	Collective-owned Enterprises	331.3	1.5
股份合作	Cooperative Enterprises		
联营	Joint Ownership Enterprises		
国有联营	State Joint Ownership Enterprises		
集体联营	Collective Joint Ownership Enterprises		
国有与集体联营	Joint State-collective Enterprises		
其他联营	Others Joint Ownership Enterprises		
有限责任公司	Limited Liability Corporations	143644.6	6150.2
国有独资公司	State Sole Funded Corporations	8347.7	375.2
其他有限责任公司	Other Limited Liability Corporations	135296.9	5775.0
股份有限公司	Share-holding Corporations Ltd.	2070.1	275.0
私营	Private Enterprises	93112.6	2487.6
私营独资	Private-funded Enterprises	710.4	23.4
私营合伙	Private Partnership Enterprises		
私营有限责任公司	Private Limited Liability Corporations	91064.4	2453.5
私营股份有限公司	Private Share-holding Corporations Ltd.	1337.8	10.7
其他	Other Enterprises		
港澳台商投资	Enterprises with Funds from Hong Kong, Macao &Taiwan	15881.7	1666.0
外商投资	Foreign Funded Enterprises	24659.1	2331.7
2.按国民经济行业分	Grouped by Sector		
旅游饭店	Tourist Hotel	219284.5	11554.8
一般旅馆	Normal Hotel	68443.0	1255.7
民宿服务	Home and Lodging Services	677.8	403.4
露营地服务	Campsite Services	757.6	0.1
其他住宿业	Others	4593.8	337.3

continued 1

(10 000 yuan)

销售费用 Sale Expenses	管理费用 Management Expenses	财务费用 Financial Expenses	营业利润 Business Profits	利润总额 Total Profits	应付职工薪酬 Salary Payable	所得税费用 Income Tax Expenses	应交增值税 Value Added Tax Payable
544123.2	**335844.6**	**51149.7**	**-41753.2**	**-39388.4**	**412234.2**	**14831.3**	**29861.9**
236817.1	**231647.3**	**34334.9**	**-62747.6**	**-61679.3**	**206822.3**	**3566.1**	**18636.1**
213944.3	206076.0	22612.6	-51526.6	-47861.9	183771.9	1686.6	17095.2
9191.8	6055.5	496.2	-494.2	-595.6	9375.6	108.4	944.9
55.0	145.4	0.2	0.7	0.7	181.6	1.0	16.0
113141.0	115259.5	16289.7	-32305.1	-31433.1	112750.7	1201.8	9761.1
12515.2	7461.0	447.7	3902.0	4022.9	11223.7		520.2
100625.8	107798.5	15842.0	-36207.1	-35456.0	101527.0	1201.8	9240.9
1072.6	2.2	1.0	-272.3	-275.7	1481.0		167.2
90483.9	84613.4	5825.5	-18455.7	-15558.2	59983.0	375.4	6206.0
1074.3	416.4	3.9	0.7	-2.0	651.3	2.8	81.7
88099.4	83316.4	5816.1	-18395.1	-15498.0	58587.5	370.8	5979.3
1310.2	880.6	5.5	-61.3	-58.2	744.2	1.8	145.0
12678.1	15433.7	1603.1	-1025.8	-3772.9	12877.2	1190.3	944.0
10194.7	10137.6	10119.2	-10195.2	-10044.5	10173.2	689.2	596.9
158905.0	165783.5	28297.4	-49308.7	-48546.5	162036.1	2488.8	14067.6
67705.3	55496.7	5762.8	-12073.0	-11734.6	38972.7	1042.4	3894.2
547.7	47.5	2.1	-8.2	-8.2	159.0	3.8	33.3
141.6	572.4	167.2	-518.9	-518.5	384.7		-58.8
9517.5	9747.2	105.4	-838.8	-871.5	5269.8	31.1	699.8

16-5 续表2

单位：万元

分 组	Classify	单位数（个）Number (unit)	资产总计 Total Assets	流动资产合计 Circulating Funds
二、餐饮业	**Catering Trade**	**377**	**755678.3**	**385856.4**
1.按登记注册类型分	Grouped by Type of Registration			
内资	Domestic Funded Enterprises	365	620292.6	324088.4
国有	State-owned Enterprises	3	4467.4	1618.3
集体	Collective-owned Enterprises			
股份合作	Cooperative Enterprises			
联营	Joint Ownership Enterprises			
国有联营	State Joint Ownership Enterprises			
集体联营	Collective Joint Ownership Enterprises			
国有与集体联营	Joint State-collective Enterprises			
其他联营	Others Joint Ownership Enterprises			
有限责任公司	Limited Liability Corporations	115	168194.0	97355.6
国有独资公司	State Sole Funded Corporations	3	12880.1	3840.1
其他有限责任公司	Other Limited Liability Corporations	112	155313.9	93515.5
股份有限公司	Share-holding Corporations Ltd.	3	190156.4	80292.1
私营	Private Enterprises	244	257474.8	144822.4
私营独资	Private-funded Enterprises	11	3713.3	1898.6
私营合伙	Private Partnership Enterprises			
私营有限责任公司	Private Limited Liability Corporations	231	253371.3	142547.6
私营股份有限公司	Private Share-holding Corporations Ltd.	2	390.2	376.2
其他	Other Enterprises			
港澳台商投资	Enterprises with Funds from Hong Kong, Macao &Taiwan	6	73559.9	34212.5
外商投资	Foreign Funded Enterprises	6	61825.8	27555.5
2.按国民经济行业分	Grouped by Sdctor			
正餐服务	Dinner	354	605914.4	318112.5
快餐服务	Fast Food	10	90783.7	31921.3
饮料及冷饮服务	Beverages and Cold Drinks	9	54222.1	33419.7
餐饮配送及外卖送餐服务	Catering Distribution and Takeaway Servic	1	997.9	957.4
其他餐饮业	Other Catering Services	3	3760.2	1445.5

continued 2

(10 000 yuan)

固定资产原价 Original Value of Fixed Assets	累计折旧 Accumulated Depreciation	负债合计 Total Liabilities	流动负债合计 Circulating Liabilities	所有者权益合计 Total Owners' Equities	实收资本 Paid in Capital	营业收入 Total Revenue	主营业务收入 Revenue from Principal Business
233109.8	**116828.3**	**505235.5**	**438111.8**	**244242.3**	**297560.6**	**868801.1**	**858081.8**
183081.5	89823.1	439672.7	388202.8	174149.0	278257.6	639888.6	637437.1
4733.3	1985.4	1447.8	1447.8	3019.6	3384.1	7469.3	7469.3
64764.1	33230.6	147553.6	127677.9	16296.4	52501.8	179289.1	177749.0
15675.1	7538.5	9736.9	9388.5	2676.0	4731.2	13438.9	13264.0
49089.0	25692.1	137816.7	118289.4	13620.4	47770.6	165850.2	164485.0
40811.1	18068.2	82440.1	69962.5	107716.3	60705.6	92960.1	92835.7
72773.0	36538.9	208231.2	189114.6	47116.7	161666.1	360170.1	359383.1
2073.1	822.5	1653.4	1600.6	1751.4	954.9	5675.8	5644.8
70506.2	35536.6	206214.3	187150.5	45338.6	160601.2	353744.8	352988.8
193.7	179.8	363.5	363.5	26.7	110.0	749.5	749.5
21549.5	10801.9	39771.7	31716.0	33788.2	5345.4	82601.6	82601.6
28478.8	16203.3	25791.1	18193.0	36305.1	13957.6	146310.9	138043.1
179218.4	89517.6	431235.6	379433.8	168708.5	278096.3	598758.4	596166.1
42110.3	21862.9	49045.3	34200.5	41738.4	16035.8	185531.1	177404.1
8949.6	3413.5	22147.0	21871.3	31844.9	3008.7	76174.5	76174.5
31.2	19.3	166.6		831.3		2351.1	2351.1
2800.3	2015.0	2641.0	2606.2	1119.2	419.8	5986.0	5986.0

16-5 续表3

单位：万元

分　组	Classify	营业成本 Total Cost	税金及附加 Taxs and Other Changes
二、餐饮业	**Catering Trade**	**441558.6**	**4825.4**
1.按登记注册类型分	Grouped by Type of Registration		
内资	Domestic Funded Enterprises	339610.0	4604.7
国有	State-owned Enterprises	5931.6	355.5
集体	Collective-owned Enterprises		
股份合作	Cooperative Enterprises		
联营	Joint Ownership Enterprises		
国有联营	State Joint Ownership Enterprises		
集体联营	Collective Joint Ownership Enterprises		
国有与集体联营	Joint State-collective Enterprises		
其他联营	Others Joint Ownership Enterprises		
有限责任公司	Limited Liability Corporations	102446.0	1018.5
国有独资公司	State Sole Funded Corporations	8837.4	270.5
其他有限责任公司	Other Limited Liability Corporations	93608.6	748.0
股份有限公司	Share-holding Corporations Ltd.	47435.0	612.6
私营	Private Enterprises	183797.4	2618.1
私营独资	Private-funded Enterprises	3508.9	89.8
私营合伙	Private Partnership Enterprises		
私营有限责任公司	Private Limited Liability Corporations	179980.2	2524.5
私营股份有限公司	Private Share-holding Corporations Ltd.	308.3	3.8
其他	Other Enterprises		
港澳台商投资	Enterprises with Funds from Hong Kong, Macao &Taiwan	25826.7	77.4
外商投资	Foreign Funded Enterprises	76121.9	143.3
2.按国民经济行业分	Grouped by Sdctor		
正餐服务	Dinner	310484.9	4161.1
快餐服务	Fast Food	92681.4	219.2
饮料及冷饮服务	Beverages and Cold Drinks	34020.1	48.8
餐饮配送及外卖送餐服务	Catering Distribution and Takeaway Servic	759.7	2.4
其他餐饮业	Other Catering Services	3612.5	393.9

continued 3

(10 000 yuan)

销售费用 Sale Expenses	管理费用 Management Expenses	财务费用 Financial Expenses	营业利润 Business Profits	利润总额 Total Profits	应付职工薪酬 Salary Payable	所得税费用 Income Tax Expenses	应交增值税 Value Added Tax Payable
307306.1	**104197.3**	**16814.8**	**20994.4**	**22290.9**	**205411.9**	**11265.2**	**11225.8**
227262.9	84343.5	16773.5	-6406.0	-5141.1	162061.5	4384.2	10678.9
694.2	540.6	3.6	-56.4	-54.1	734.7	48.8	363.1
54789.0	24558.2	12240.4	-7127.3	-6722.8	41352.8	1013.7	2671.0
1455.3	1799.7	169.2	907.3	952.5	2848.2	171.6	216.4
53333.7	22758.5	12071.2	-8034.6	-7675.3	38504.6	842.1	2454.6
34676.7	8360.4	1113.8	1009.9	1545.6	36624.4	765.4	1018.1
137103.0	50884.3	3415.7	-232.2	90.2	83349.6	2556.3	6626.7
1072.1	680.1	27.1	314.8	320.2	1331.2	20.1	154.4
135701.3	50112.9	3387.0	-561.9	-245.1	81830.9	2534.6	6442.6
329.6	91.3	1.6	14.9	15.1	187.5	1.6	29.7
41563.3	3232.9	337.9	11602.8	11836.6	19829.7	3198.0	354.6
38479.9	16620.9	-296.6	15797.6	15595.4	23520.7	3683.0	192.3
217389.4	80320.0	16589.7	-3868.8	-2561.2	156259.8	4130.5	10392.8
57045.9	18925.0	164.5	17073.3	16778.0	34591.6	3997.4	542.9
31252.6	3804.9	42.0	7005.6	7275.8	14027.4	2939.8	123.8
980.4		4.9	603.6	612.4	118.1	153.1	6.6
637.8	1147.4	13.7	180.7	185.9	415.0	44.4	159.7

16-6 限额以上批发零售贸易业商品购进、销售、库存总额（2019年）

单位：万元

分　组	Classify	单位数（个）Number (unit)	商品购进额 Total Purchases	进口 Imports
总计	**Total**	**1891**	**93462323.8**	**7131414.5**
一、批发企业	**Wholesale Enterprises**	**960**	**74753166.4**	**6689279.0**
1.按登记注册类型分	Grouped by Type of Registration			
内资企业	Domestic Funded Enterprises	931	59342422.6	999112.2
国有	State-owned Enterprises	13	1197383.8	1102.7
集体	Collective-owned Enterprises	2	9309.3	
有限责任公司	Limited Liability Corporations	302	37151361.0	941814.0
国有独资公司	State Sole Funded Corporations	23	6984897.4	
其他有限责任公司	Other Limited Liability Corporations	279	30166463.6	941814.0
股份有限公司	Share-holding Corporations Ltd.	19	9722582.4	234.6
私营	Private Enterprises	592	11242325.1	55960.9
私营独资	Private-funded Enterprises	2	7479.7	
私营合伙	Private Partnership Enterprises			
私营有限责任公司	Private Limited Liability Corporations	580	11116071.5	55960.9
私营股份有限公司	Private Share-holding Corporations Ltd.	10	118773.9	
其他	Other Enterprises	3	19461.0	
港澳台商投资	Enterprises with Funds from Hong Kong, Macao &Taiwan	4	84901.7	
外商投资	Foreign Funded Enterprises	21	15078129.1	5690166.8
个体经营户	Individusl Enterprises	4	247713.0	
2.按国民经济行业分	Grouped by Economic Sector			
农、林、牧产品批发	Wholesale of Agricultural,Forestry and Animal Husbandry Products	6	47015.8	
食品、饮料及烟草制品批发	Wholesale of Food, Beverages and Tobacco Products	99	2531450.6	259.0
纺织、服装及家庭服务器批发	Wholesale of Textiles, Garments and Daily Articles	50	1229700.5	361.0
文化、体育用品及器材批发	Wholesale of Culture, Sports Articles and Equipments	40	862805.1	
医药及医疗器材批发	Wholesale of Medicines and Medical Appliances	148	4435480.3	15471.2
矿产品、建材及化工产品批发	Wholesale of Mineral Products, Building Materials and Chemical Products	374	59524903.6	4113488.0

Total Purchases,Sales and Inventories of Wholesale and Retail Enterprises above Designated Size （2019）

(10 000 yuan)

商品销售额 Sales Value	公共网络商品销售额 Public Network Sales	批发额 Wholesale Trade	出口 Exports	零售额 Retail Trade	期末商品库存额 Value of Stock at Final goods
101596702.9	**11405417.5**	**77859399.9**	**7055791.0**	**23662493.5**	**3858410.1**
78608499.0	**6838850.0**	**76983699.9**	**7054940.5**	**1551957.6**	**2068352.1**
62959517.1	6836192.0	61527822.0	1299554.2	1358853.6	1844689.0
1653369.0	1447506.1	1650354.4	35783.4	3014.6	54759.3
9627.3		9627.3			748.8
38671273.9	793760.0	38288816.5	608832.0	342267.3	1030769.2
7127614.5	183454.7	7087292.3	726.4	132.1	101708.2
31543659.4	610305.3	31201524.2	608105.6	342135.2	929061.0
10033339.1	4378936.3	9374795.9	446664.2	656522.9	86271.2
12569253.7	215989.6	12184871.6	208274.6	353751.0	672060.2
8149.8		7300.9		848.9	182.4
12417943.1	214679.6	12035492.7	208274.6	351819.3	659794.9
143160.8	1310.0	142078.0		1082.8	12082.9
22654.1		19356.3		3297.8	80.3
131548.1		73379.2		58168.9	31643.5
15249007.1	2658.0	15114994.0	5755386.3	134013.1	188852.4
268426.7		267504.7		922.0	3167.2
51107.7		51057.3			1619.3
3469898.0	1476455.5	3343612.3	9662.8	124265.4	213438.9
1362142.6	12026.0	1271607.4	154165.2	90535.2	249693.0
945334.8	198075.1	923403.1	3996.8	21931.7	62332.3
5237769.9	22402.0	4971434.1	8934.7	266335.8	464520.4
60923916.2	5040807.3	59921808.3	3534950.7	937155.0	852306.2

16-6 续表1

单位：万元

分　组	Classify	单位数（个）Number (unit)	商品购进额 Total Purchases	进口 Imports
机械设备、五金产品及电子产品批发	Wholesale of Machinery, Hardwares, Transport Means and Electronic Products	216	5761972.7	2533127.2
贸易经纪与代理	Trade Manage and Agent	5	179209.4	26572.6
其他批发	Other Wholesales	22	180628.4	
3.按经营形式分	Grouped by Means of Operation			
独立门店	Independent Shop	564	44795648.0	6409488.0
连锁总店	Headquarter of Chain Store	1	84139.9	
连锁门店	Chain Store	1	2641.7	
其他	Other	394	29870736.8	279791.0
二、零售企业	**Retail Trade**	**931**	**18709157.4**	**442135.5**
1.按登记注册类型分	Grouped by Registration Status			
内资	Domestic Funded Enterprises	858	10675207.9	249029.2
国有	State-owned Enterprises	5	649884.7	
集体	Collective-owned Enterprises	15	26399.6	
有限责任公司	Limited Liability Corporations	289	4930751.8	198420.0
国有独资公司	State Sole Funded Corporations	10	248130.2	9052.2
其他有限责任公司	Other Limited Liability Corporations	279	4682621.6	189367.8
股份有限公司	Share-holding Corporations Ltd.	11	291162.7	
私营	Private Enterprises	534	4766847.0	50609.2
私营独资	Private-funded Enterprises	15	53175.8	
私营合伙	Private Partnership Enterprises	1	4342.3	
私营有限责任公司	Private Limited Liability Corporations	513	4648070.1	28770.2
私营股份有限公司	Private Share-holding Corporations Ltd.	5	61258.8	21839.0
其他	Other Enterprises	4	10162.1	
港澳台商投资	Enterprises with Funds from Hong Kong, Macao &Taiwan	27	2679603.7	83295.5
外商投资	Foreign Funded Enterprises	29	5267944.7	105440.5
个体经营户	Individusl Enterprises	17	86401.1	4370.3
2.按国民经济行业分	Grouped by Registered Kind			
综合零售	General Retail Sales Trade	133	2808143.8	4370.3
食品、饮料及烟草制品专门零售	Retail of Food, Beverage and Tobaccos	81	243069.2	6481.0
纺织、服装及日用品专门零售	Retail of Textiles, Garments and Daily Articles	65	1400661.1	982.2
文化、体育用品及器材专门零售	Retail of Culture, Sports Articles and Equipments	58	279886.0	9052.2

continued 1

(10 000 yuan)

商品销售额 Sales Value	公共网络商品销售额 Public Network Sales	批发额 Wholesale Trade	出口 Exports	零售额 Retail Trade	期末商品库存额 Value of Stock at Final goods
6200248.7	39969.9	6084758.1	3192548.9	109672.7	207627.9
203646.4	7803.0	202940.6	150681.4	705.8	9882.5
214434.7	41311.2	213078.7		1356.0	6931.6
46424861.5	299819.5	45183834.3	6449327.0	1209003.0	1172612.6
84846.8		84846.8			407.9
2931.9		2931.9			268.1
32095858.8	6539030.5	31712086.9	605613.5	342954.6	895063.5
22988203.9	**4566567.5**	**875700.0**	**850.5**	**22110535.9**	**1790058.0**
13462606.5	960250.9	574380.5	850.5	12886258.0	1281985.8
702443.4		176231.0		526212.4	54524.7
28462.6		611.7		27850.9	2575.1
6748901.5	259344.1	248720.8	850.5	6500059.2	583986.4
265768.2	122.0	8283.1	850.5	257485.1	47791.3
6483133.3	259222.1	240437.7		6242574.1	536195.1
398429.7	59030.8			398429.7	64614.1
5570131.4	641876.0	148717.0		5419567.9	576193.0
57249.8	2902.4			57249.8	2695.1
4298.5				4298.5	45.0
5443936.5	625553.1	135297.0		5306793.0	569146.4
64646.6	13420.5	13420.0		51226.6	4306.5
14237.9		100.0		14137.9	92.5
2918969.5	120561.4	261341.3		2657628.2	409053.7
6503599.8	3480309.4	39948.9		6463650.9	88297.9
103028.1	5445.8	29.3		102998.8	10720.6
4392746.0	98641.3	2113.7		4390632.3	303256.4
332740.6	21024.8	22750.8		309989.8	55556.9
1635871.4	3511.6	272358.9		1363512.5	323452.4
328641.8	8999.0	34547.2	850.5	294094.6	75261.1

16-6 续表2

单位：万元

分 组	Classify	单位数（个）Number (unit)	商品购进额 Total Purchases	进口 Imports
医药及医疗器材专门零售	Retail of Medicines and Medical Appliances	44	427458.7	
汽车、摩托车、零配件和燃料及其他动力销售	Sales of automobiles, motorcycles, spare parts and fuel and other power	326	8711785.1	420523.5
家用电器及电子产品专门零售	Retail of Household Electronic Equipments and Products	100	817853.1	
五金、家具及室内装饰材料专门零售	Retail of Hardwares, Furniture and Room Decorative Building	37	276400.8	31.0
货摊、无店铺及其他零售业	No Fixed Stores and Other Retails	87	3743899.6	695.3
3.按经营形式分	Grouped by Means of Operation			
独立门店	Independent Shop	703	12060489.4	431678.2
连锁总店	Headquarter of Chain Store	44	998296.1	
连锁门店	Chain Store	21	262681.1	
其他	Other	163	5387690.8	10457.3
4.按零售业态分	Grouped by Retail Size			
有店铺	Retail of Shop	808	14848294.6	431678.2
食杂店	Grocery Store	4	23327.9	
便利店	Convenience Store	20	122539.1	
折扣店	Dime Store			
超市	Supermarket	74	589904.3	
大型超市	Larget Supermarket	13	1317735.6	
仓储会员店	Warehouse Club	6	18584.5	
百货店	Department Store	61	886639.7	
专业店	Special Store	296	5504208.3	111273.4
专卖店	Monopoly Store	282	5981479.5	316003.5
家居建材商店	Home-building Material Store	18	184354.5	31.0
购物中心	Shopping Center	14	87039.5	4370.3
厂家直销中心	Factory Outlet Center	20	132481.7	
无店铺零售	Retail of No-shop	123	3860862.8	10457.3
电视购物	TV Shopping	1	87017.2	
邮购	Mail Order			
网上商店	Online Stores	77	3596967.7	695.3
自动售货亭	Vending Machine	1	2205.5	
电话购物	Tele Shopping			
其他	Others	44	174672.4	9762.0

continued 2

(10 000 yuan)

商品销售额 Sales Value	公共网络商品销售额 Public Network Sales	批发额 Wholesale Trade	出口 Exports	零售额 Retail Trade	期末商品库存额 Value of Stock at Final goods
690725.1	17336.5	52380.3		638223.3	105714.5
9819226.8	225884.6	315671.9		9503554.9	819178.9
1285731.0	124987.5	123246.5		1161013.0	56303.2
375823.4	5779.2	23321.3		352502.1	15219.5
4126697.8	4060403.0	29309.4		4097013.4	36115.1
15141453.1	500774.8	402226.2		14738730.4	1242841.4
1383035.7	75616.1	2257.7		1380778.0	214590.4
671892.4	105832.4	50661.7		621230.7	27856.2
5791822.7	3884344.2	420554.4	850.5	5369796.8	304770.0
18698516.6	497671.0	833344.0		17863579.6	1712094.6
28610.9	95.4			28610.9	1849.3
145350.4	6895.5	12350.9		132999.5	15800.5
697560.9	68558.7	7597.5		689963.4	64772.5
1304701.9	9957.9			1304701.9	159122.4
19107.7		30.9		19076.8	4839.8
2129574.1	18322.7	1788.7		2127785.4	67249.6
6888653.6	145106.7	342066.8		6546586.8	569585.1
6533928.3	239197.6	441667.1		6092139.7	755785.0
208135.2	2126.8	12917.5		195217.7	7218.6
580896.5	4830.5	1825.9		577599.1	21129.8
161997.1	2579.2	13098.7		148898.4	44742.0
4289687.3	4068896.5	42356.0	850.5	4246956.3	77963.4
87921.1	87921.1			87921.1	2168.8
3978297.9	3961418.2	20832.1		3957090.8	31456.4
2590.9		490.9		2100.0	174.3
220877.4	19557.2	21033.0	850.5	199844.4	44163.9

16–7　限额以上住宿和餐饮业经营情况（2019年）

单位：万元

分　组	Classify	单位数（个）Number (unit)	营业额 Business Revenue
总计	**Total**	**873**	**1922601.6**
一、住宿业	**Lodging Services**	**436**	**921455.2**
1. 按国民经济行业分	Grouped by Economic Sector		
旅游饭店	Tour Restaurant	189	679432.9
一般旅馆	Common Hotel	227	212606.3
民宿服务	Home and Lodging Services	5	1306.3
露营地服务	Campsite Services	1	1167.3
其他住宿业	Others	14	26942.4
2. 按登记注册类型分	Grouped by Registration Status		
内资企业	Domestic Funded Enterprises	420	810744.0
国有	State-owned Enterprises	21	50442.1
集体	Collective-owned Enterprises	10	82953.0
股份合作	Corperative Enterprises		
联营	Joint Ownership Enterprises		
有限责任公司	Limited Liability Corporations	150	452602.4
国有独资公司	State-funded Corporations	9	34873.3
其他有限责任公司	Other Limited Liability Corporations	141	417729.0
股份有限公司	Stock Limited Corporation	4	23069.8
私营	Private Enterprises	242	282686.4
私营独资	Private-funded Enterprises	5	2281.1
私营合伙	Private Partnership Enterprises		
私营有限责任公司	Private Limited Liability Corporations	234	276850.0
私营股份有限公司	Private Share Holding Corporations	3	3555.3
其他	Others	1	1393.2
港澳台商投资	Enterprises Funded by Hong Kong, Macao and Taiwan	8	68257.4

注：此表统计范围为法人企业、大个体及产业活动单位。

Statistic on Hotel Services and Catering Services above Designed Size (2019)

(10 000 yuan)

客房收入 From Hotel Room	公共网络客房收入 Public Network Room Revenue	餐费收入 From Meals	公共网络餐费收入 Public Network Catering Revenue	商品销售额 Merchandis
550419.1	**112246.7**	**1203993.6**	**92404.9**	**68840.5**
513859.4	**107280.1**	**321328.9**	**20431.7**	**20527.8**
336173.4	63020.0	270349.9	18802.6	16853.0
161801.6	42971.1	39979.3	1582.5	2065.2
1187.4	633.5	110.2	42.5	8.7
1010.4		149.1		7.8
13686.6	655.5	10740.4	4.1	1593.1
459267.5	99344.0	277620.9	16497.4	19490.4
23478.1	2037.9	20862.8	99.8	1148.4
42381.0	2601.4	36278.9	2573.6	705.6
232716.6	39226.1	177526.6	12481.7	4976.1
16170.8	3928.2	16158.5	4153.0	391.4
216546.0	35298.0	161368.0	8329.0	4585.0
4945.3	78.1	5173.6		9510.7
196453.7	57963.6	73803.8	3915.9	3839.8
1620.0	27.9	291.2	0.2	37.2
192923.3	57791.7	71867.7	3885.6	3802.6
1910.4	144.0	1644.9	30.1	
1123.7	28.6	254.1		15.4
34346.9	3660.7	26575.8	216.4	228.9

16-7 续表1

单位：万元

分　组	Classify	单位数（个）Number (unit)	营业额 Business Revenue
外商投资	Foreign Funded Enterprises	7	41990.7
个体经营	Individual Enterprises	1	463.1
二、餐饮业	**Catering Trade**	**437**	**1001146.4**
1. 按国民经济行业分	Grouped by Economic Sector		
正餐服务	Dinner Services	412	714292.4
快餐服务	Fast Food Services	11	196769.4
饮料及冷饮服务	Beverages and Cold Drinks	9	81409.2
餐饮配送及外卖送餐服务	Catering Distribution and Takeaway Servic	1	2351.1
其他餐饮业	Other Catering Services	4	6324.3
2. 按登记注册类型分	Grouped by Registration Status		
内资	Domestic Funded Enterprises	375	729131.8
国有	State-owned Enterprises	6	14991.9
集体	Collective-owned Enterprises		
股份合作	Corperative Enterprises		
联营	Joint Ownership Enterprises		
有限责任公司	Limited Liability Corporations	121	223167.1
国有独资公司	State-funded Corporations	3	13996.7
其他有限责任公司	Other Limited Liability Corporations	118	209170.4
股份有限公司	Stock Limited Corporation	3	100696.4
私营	Private Enterprises	244	378128.3
私营独资	Private-funded Enterprises	11	5847.4
私营合伙	Private Partnership Enterprises		
私营有限责任公司	Private Limited Liability Corporations	231	371494.6
私营股份有限公司	Private Share Holding Corporations	2	786.3
其他	Others	1	12148.1
港澳台商投资	Enterprises Funded by Hong Kong, Macao and Taiwan	6	87931.7
外商投资	Foreign Funded Enterprises	6	155185.9
个体经营	Individual Enterprises	50	28897.0

continued 1

(10 000 yuan)

客房收入 From Hotel Room	公共网络客房收入 Public Network Room Revenue	餐费收入 From Meals	公共网络餐费收入 Public Network Catering Revenue	商品销售额 Merchandis
19781.9	4275.4	17132.2	3717.9	808.5
463.1				
36559.7	**4966.6**	**882664.7**	**71973.2**	**48312.7**
36559.7	4966.6	611417.1	49118.6	41975.8
		187521.5	10711.9	443.7
		75050.7	12142.7	5893.2
		2351.1		
		6324.3		
36211.0	4966.6	626810.4	60166.3	42256.8
1395.2		11218.6	1198.1	1723.1
21405.4	3149.8	183559.4	19697.2	7543.4
370.1		8439.7		1217.0
21035.3	3149.8	175119.7	19697.2	6326.4
2529.3	264.3	70097.1	9583.2	22690.1
5186.3	1552.5	355846.6	29687.8	10300.2
157.6		5590.6	1.1	99.2
5028.7	1552.5	349484.7	29662.2	10186.0
		771.3	24.5	15.0
5694.8		6088.7		
293.7		81974.2	7905.8	4676.7
		146395.7	3390.2	72.6
55.0		27484.4	510.9	1306.6

16-8 限额以上批发和零售业主要商品分类销售额（2019年）

Sale Values of Wholesale and Retail Enterprises above Designated Size by Category of Main Commodities（2019）

单位：万元 (10 000 yuan)

分组	Classify	销售合计 Total Sales Value	批发 Wholesale Value	零售 Retail Value
总计	**Total**	93667631.5	70789866.0	22877765.5
其中：通过公共网络实现的商品销售	Sales Achieved through the Public Network	10714705.8	6521683.1	4193022.7
粮油、食品类	Cereals, Oils and Foodstuffs	2857590.5	1035180.2	1822410.3
粮油类	Grain and Oil	851698.3	248371.0	603327.3
肉禽蛋类	Meat, Poultry and Eggs	266250.1	57795.2	208454.9
水产品类	Aquatic Products	101636.1	32314.7	69321.4
蔬菜类	Vegetables	635733.4	537281.3	98452.1
干鲜果品类	Fresh and Dried Fruit Category	279128.7	47034.0	232094.7
饮料类	Beverages	388398.2	196192.3	192205.9
烟酒类	Tobacco and Liquor	2397976.2	2011308.3	386667.9
服装、鞋帽、针纺织品类	Clothing, Shoes, Hats and Textiles	3177410.5	253777.9	2923632.6
#服装类	Clothing	2480360.6	73602.0	2406758.6
鞋帽类	Shoes and Hats	549945.3	138585.2	411360.1
针纺织品类	Knitwear and Textiles	147104.6	41590.7	105513.9
化妆品类	Cosmetics	808138.7	45715.5	762423.2
金银珠宝类	Gold,Silver and Jewelry	855539.6	398911.3	456628.3
日用品类	Articles for Daily Use	1071956.9	132248.4	939708.5
#可穿戴智能设备	Wearable intelligent device	8999.4	1210.8	7788.6
五金、电料类	Hardwear and Electrical Materials	168986.0	130906.7	38079.3
体育、娱乐用品类	Sports and Recreation Articles	293611.2	16431.3	277179.9
#照相器材类	Photography Equipment	110268.9		110268.9
书报杂志类	Newspapers and Magazines	397455.3	219222.7	178232.6
电子出版物及音像制品类	E-journal and Video Products	30218.4	1655.6	28562.8
家用电器和音像器材类	Household Appliances and Video Products	2308004.0	756410.9	1551593.1
中西药品类	Traditional Chinese and Western Medicine	5483325.8	4872183.3	611142.5
#西药	Western Medicine	4644352.2	4209566.6	434785.6
中草药及中成药	Chinese Herbal Medicine and Traditional Chinese Medicine	198793.7	126908.0	71885.7
文化办公用品类	Cultural and Official Goods	870919.5	309180.7	561738.8
#计算机及其配套产品	Among Them： Computers and Ancillary Products	494402.1	151020.6	343381.5
家具类	Furniture	306460.6	9175.1	297285.5
通讯器材类	Communication Appliances	1009394.5	124971.2	884423.3
煤炭及制品类	Coal and Related Products	6262947.2	6262947.2	
木材及制品类	Wood and Wooden Products	56656.9	56656.9	
石油及制品类	Petroleum and Related Products	15721151.5	13033565.2	2687586.3
化工材料及制品类	Raw Chemical Materials	4450864.5	4442597.4	8267.1
#化肥类	Chemical Fertilizers	150337.0	149312.9	1024.1
金属材料类	Metal Materials	29493149.0	29479503.4	13645.6
建筑及装潢材料类	Buildings and Decoration Materials	520424.4	396894.6	123529.8
机电产品及设备类	Mechanical and Electrical Products	3900349.4	3892272.9	8076.5
#农机类	Agricultural Machinery	4313.8	4313.8	
汽车类	Automobile	8698512.5	1047321.6	7651190.9
种子饲料类	Seeds and Feedstuff	9406.5	9395.5	11.0
棉麻类	Cotton,Hemp	26299.5	26287.5	12.0
其他类	Others	2102484.2	1628952.4	473531.8

注：本表为定期季度报表数据。

16-9 亿元以上商品交易市场成交情况（2019年）

Basic Statistics on Commodity Exchange Markets of Transaction Value over 100 Million Yuan（2019）

分　组	Classify	年末出租摊位数（个）Number of Rental Booths at Year-end (unit)	成交额（万元）Turnover (10 000 yuan)
1. 粮油、食品类	Cereals, Oils and Foodstuffs	7878	4188397
#粮油类	Grain and Oil	337	430491
肉禽蛋类	Meat, Poultry and Eggs	787	391432
水产品类	Aquatic Products	1039	562543
蔬菜类	Vegetables	2099	944904
干鲜果品类	Fresh and Dried Fruit Category	3601	1858937
2. 饮料类	Beverages	342	18440
3. 烟酒类	Tobacco and Liquor	154	14125
4. 服装、鞋帽、针纺织品类	Clothing, Shoes, Hats and Textiles	6027	1150495
#服装类	Clothing	3111	586449
鞋帽类	Shoes and Hats	1939	486049
针纺织品类	Knitwear and Textiles	977	77997
5. 化妆品类	Cosmetics	122	9571
6. 金银珠宝类	Gold,Silver and Jewelry	21	6713
7. 日用品类	Articles for Daily Use	753	143993
#可穿戴智能设备	Wearable intelligent device		
8. 五金、电料类	Hardwear and Electrical Materials	552	68970
9. 体育、娱乐用品类	Sports and Recreation Articles	363	24830
10. 书报杂志类	Newspapers and Magazines		
11. 电子出版物及音像制品类	E-journal and Video Products	3	30
12. 家用电器和音像器材类	Household Appliances and Video Products	146	18359
13. 中西药品类	Traditional Chinese and Western Medicine		
#西药	Western Medicine		
中草药及中成药	Chinese Herbal Medicine and Traditional Chinese Medicine		
14. 文化办公用品类	Cultural and Official Goods	1066	66314
#计算机及其配套产品	Computer and Related Products	997	54110
15. 家具类	Furniture	2314	796771
16. 通讯器材类	Communication Appliances	1006	43757
17. 煤炭及制品类	Coal and Related Products		
18. 木材及制品类	Wood and Wooden Products		
19. 石油及制品类	Petroleum and Related Products		
20. 化工材料及制品类	Raw Chemical Materials	231	155310
#化肥类	Chemical Fertilizers		
21. 金属材料类	Metal Materials	80	298500
22. 建筑及装潢材料类	Buildings and Decoration Materials	6303	834347
23. 机电产品及设备类	Mechanical and Electrical Products	635	101915
#农机类	Agricultural Machinery		
24. 汽车类	Automobile	1597	190700
25. 种子饲料类	Seeds and Feedstuff		
26. 棉麻类	Cotton,Hemp	6	30
27. 其他类	Others	220	21959

16-10 批发和零售业连锁经营情况（2019年）

Basic Statistics on Chain Business of Wholesale and Retail Trades（2019）

指　标	Item	本年合计 Total	上年合计 Total Last Year	本年直营店 Regular Chain
一、门店总数（个）	**Number of Stores(unit)**	**2746**	**2837**	**2484**
二、年末从业人员数（人）	**Employees at Year-end(person)**	**24323**	**25878**	**23187**
三、年末零售营业面积（平方米）	**Operating Area of Retail at Year-end(sq.m)**	**898636**	**947753**	**880865**
四、连锁门店商品购进额（万元）	**Purchases Value of Chain Stores(10 000 yuan)**	**3094927**	**3370582**	**3062098**
其中：统一配送商品购进额	Centralized Purchases and Delivery	2734313	2910085	2702477
其中：自有配送中心配送商品购进额	Self Centralized Purchases and Delivery	2372789	2594394	2372785
非自有配送中心配送商品购进额	Non-self Centralized Purchases and Delivery	256580	220245	256580
五、连锁门店商品销售额（万元）	**Sales Value of Chain Store(10 000 yuan)**	**3932523**	**4036866**	**3894215**
其中：零售额	Retail Value	1864366	1780652	1826095

注：上年同期数为本年在库企业加报数据。

16-10 续表 continued

指　标	Item	上年直营店 Regular Chain Last Year	本年加盟店 Franchise	上年加盟店 Franchise Last Year
一、门店总数（个）	**Number of Stores(unit)**	**2632**	**262**	**205**
二、年末从业人员数（人）	**Employees at Year-end(person)**	**24949**	**1136**	**929**
三、年末零售营业面积（平方米）	**Operating Area of Retail at Year-end(sq.m)**	**936703**	**17771**	**11050**
四、连锁门店商品购进额（万元）	**Purchases Value of Chain Stores(10 000 yuan)**	**3348899**	**32829**	**21683**
其中：统一配送商品购进额	Centralized Purchases and Delivery	2888402	31836	21683
其中：自有配送中心配送商品购进额	Self Centralized Purchases and Delivery	2589164	4	5230
非自有配送中心配送商品购进额	Non-self Centralized Purchases and Delivery	220245		
五、连锁门店商品销售额（万元）	**Sales Value of Chain Store(10 000 yuan)**	**4006724**	**38308**	**30142**
其中：零售额	Retail Value	1750510	38271	30142

16-11 住宿和餐饮业连锁经营情况（2019年）

Basic Statistics on Chain Business of Hotels and Catering Services（2019）

指 标	Item	本年合计 Total	上年合计 Total Last Year
一、门店总数（个）	**Number of Stores(unit)**	**488**	**413**
二、年末从业人员数（人）	**Employees at Year-end(person)**	**15920**	**13303**
三、年末餐饮营业面积（平方米）	**Operating Area of Retail at Year-end(sq.m)**	**161223**	**146570**
四、客房总数（间）	**Guest Rooms(room)**		
五、床位数（张）	**Guest Beds(bed)**		
六、餐位数（位）	**Dining Seats(set)**	**89194**	**84987**
七、连锁门店商品购进额（万元）	**Operating Area of Catering Services at Year end(room)(10 000yuan)**	**105666**	**97068**
其中：统一配送商品购进额	Centralized Purchases and Delivery	103016	92719
其中：自有配送中心配送商品购进额	Self Centralized Purchases and Delivery	75594	65328
非自有配送中心配送商品购进额	Non-self Centralized Purchases and Delivery	18083	16261
八、连锁门店商品营业额（万元）	**Sales Value of Chain Store(10 000 yuan)**	**301093**	**262999**
其中：餐费收入	Catering Revenues	292834	257930
商品销售额	Sales Value	8095	5019

16-11 续表 continued

指 标	Item	本年直营店 Regular Chain	上年直营店 Regular Chain Last Year
一、门店总数（个）	**Number of Stores(unit)**	**481**	**406**
二、年末从业人员数（人）	**Employees at Year-end(person)**	**15771**	**13136**
三、年末餐饮营业面积（平方米）	**Operating Area of Retail at Year-end(sq.m)**	**159873**	**145220**
四、客房总数（间）	**Guest Rooms(room)**		
五、床位数（张）	**Guest Beds(bed)**		
六、餐位数（位）	**Dining Seats(set)**	**88926**	**84719**
七、连锁门店商品购进额（万元）	**Operating Area of Catering Services at Year end(room)(10 000yuan)**	**104588**	**95770**
其中：统一配送商品购进额	Centralized Purchases and Delivery	103016	92719
其中：自有配送中心配送商品购进额	Self Centralized Purchases and Delivery	75594	65328
非自有配送中心配送商品购进额	Non-self Centralized Purchases and Delivery	18083	16261
八、连锁门店商品营业额（万元）	**Sales Value of Chain Store(10 000 yuan)**	**298409**	**259766**
其中：餐费收入	Catering Revenues	290150	254696
商品销售额	Sales Value	8095	5019

16-12 近年限额以上住宿和餐饮业经营情况

单位：个、亿元

分 组	Classify	2016	
		单位数 Number of Enterprises	营业额 Business Revenue
总计	**Total**	**604**	**127.52**
一、住宿业	**Lodging Services**	**258**	**60.07**
1. 按登记注册类型分	Grouped by Registration Status		
内资企业	Domestic Funded Enterprises	242	50.55
国有	State-owned Enterprises	30	6.45
集体	Collective-owned Enterprises	1	0.04
股份合作	Cooperative Enterprises		
联营	Joint Ownership Enterprises		
国有联营	State Joint Ownership Enterprises		
集体联营	Collective Joint Ownership Enterprises		
国有与集体联营	Joint State-collective Ownership Enterprises		
其他联营	Other Joint Ownership Enterprises		
有限责任公司	Limited Liability Corporations	126	31.67
国有独资公司	State-funded Corporations	7	2.84
其他有限责任公司	Other Limited Liability Corporations	119	28.83
股份有限公司	Stock Limited Corporation	4	1.72
私营	Private Enterprises	81	10.67
私营独资	Private-funded Enterprises	3	0.18
私营合伙	Private Partnership Enterprises		
私营有限责任公司	Private Limited Liability	77	10.45
	Corporations	1	0.04
私营股份有限公司	Private Share Holding Corporations		
其他	Others		
港澳台商投资	Enterprises Funded by Hong Kong, Macao and Taiwan	7	4.25
外商投资	Foreign Funded Enterprises	9	5.27
个体经营	Individual Enterprises		
2. 按国民经济行业分	Grouped by Economic Sector		
旅游饭店	Tour Restaurant	184	50.88
一般旅馆	Common Hotel	65	7.34
民宿服务	Home and Lodging Services		
露营地服务	Campsite Services		
其他住宿业	Others	9	1.85

注：本表统计范围为法人、个体及产业活动单位。

Statistic on Hotel Services and Catering Services above Designed Size

(unit，100 million yuan)

2017		2018		2019	
单位数 Number of Enterprises	营业额 Business Revenue	单位数 Number of Enterprises	营业额 Business Revenue	单位数 Number of Enterprises	营业额 Business Revenue
716	**142.38**	**742**	**166.64**	**873**	**192.26**
319	**68.04**	**353**	**81.53**	**436**	**92.15**
301	57.61	337	70.84	420	81.07
25	5.77	21	5.07	21	5.04
1	0.04	1	0.03	10	8.30
138	35.02	134	40.03	150	45.26
8	3.87	6	3.01	9	3.49
130	31.15	128	37.02	141	41.77
4	1.92	5	2.24	4	2.31
133	14.86	175	23.30	242	28.27
2	0.10	4	0.13	5	0.23
129	14.68	168	22.53	234	27.69
2	0.08	3	0.64	3	0.36
		1	0.17	1	0.14
7	5.21	7	5.62	8	6.83
9	5.14	8	5.05	7	4.20
2	0.08	1	0.02	1	0.05
193	54.26	184	61.97	189	67.94
116	11.61	154	16.78	227	21.26
		2	0.10	5	0.13
				1	0.12
10	2.17	13	2.68	14	2.69

16-12 续表1

单位：个、亿元

分 类	Classify	2016	
		单位数 Number of Enterprises	营业额 Business Revenue
二、餐饮业	**Catering Trade**	**346**	**67.45**
1. 按登记注册类型分	Grouped by Registration Status		
内资	Domestic Funded Enterprises	321	49.87
国有	State-owned Enterprises	4	1.06
集体	Collective-owned Enterprises		
股份合作	Cooperative Enterprises		
联营	Joint Ownership Enterprises		
国有联营	State Joint Ownership Enterprises		
集体联营	Collective Joint Ownership Enterprises		
国有与集体联营	Joint State-collective Ownership Enterprises		
其他联营	Other Joint Ownership Enterprises		
有限责任公司	Limited Liability Corporations	166	26.02
国有独资公司	State-funded Corporations	1	0.11
其他有限责任公司	Other Limited Liability Corporations	165	25.91
股份有限公司	Stock Limited Corporation	2	6.22
私营	Private Enterprises	146	15.49
私营独资	Private-funded Enterprises	12	0.56
私营合伙	Private Partnership Enterprises		
私营有限责任公司	Private Limited Liability Corporations	131	14.73
私营股份有限公司	Private Share Holding Corporations	3	0.20
其他	Others	3	1.08
港澳台商投资	Enterprises Funded by Hong Kong, Macao and Taiwan	6	3.97
外商投资	Foreign Funded Enterprises	5	10.13
个体经营	Individual Enterprises	14	3.48
2. 按国民经济行业分	Grouped by Economic Sector		
正餐服务	Dinner Services	335	61.68
快餐服务	Fast Food Services	8	4.82
饮料及冷饮服务	Beverage and Cold Beverage Services		
餐饮配送及外卖送餐服务	Catering Distribution and Takeaway Servic		
其他餐饮业	Other Catering Services	3	0.95

continued 1

(unit，100 million yuan)

2017		2018		2019	
单位数 Number of Enterprises	营业额 Business Revenue	单位数 Number of Enterprises	营业额 Business Revenue	单位数 Number of Enterprises	营业额 Business Revenue
397	**74.34**	**389**	**85.11**	**437**	**100.11**
364	56.40	360	61.16	375	72.91
4	1.03	6	1.31	6	1.50
144	22.36	136	22.48	121	22.32
2	0.67	4	1.32	3	1.40
142	21.69	132	21.16	118	20.92
5	8.58	4	9.48	3	10.07
208	23.31	213	26.67	244	37.81
13	0.65	11	0.64	11	0.58
192	22.49	201	25.97	231	37.15
3	0.17	1	0.06	2	0.08
3	1.12	1	1.22	1	1.21
7	3.97	6	7.65	6	8.79
5	11.66	6	13.93	6	15.52
21	2.31	17	2.37	50	2.89
384	58.74	369	63.17	412	71.43
10	15.25	11	17.43	11	19.68
		4	3.83	9	8.14
		1	0.26	1	0.24
3	0.35	4	0.42	4	0.63

主要统计指标解释

批发业 指批发商向批发、零售单位及其他企事业、机关单位批量销售生活用品和生产资料的活动，以及从事进出口贸易和贸易经纪与代理的活动。批发商可以对所批发的货物拥有所有权，并以本单位、公司的名义进行交易活动；也可以不拥有货物的所有权，而以中介身份做代理销售商。还包括各类商品批发市场中固定摊位的批发活动。

零售业 指百货商店、超级市场、专门零售商店、品牌专卖店、售货摊等主要面向最终消费者（如居民等）的销售活动。包括以互联网、邮政、电话、售货机等方式的销售活动，还包括在同地点，后面加工生产，前面销售的店铺（如前店后厂的面包房）。不包括：谷物、种子、饲料、牲畜、矿产品、生产用原料、化工原料、农用化工产品、机械设备(乘用车、计算机及通信设备等除外）等生产资料的销售（批发业）；非零售单位附带的零售活动（如汽车修理单位销售汽车零件）；商业零售单位所在商厦的物业管理（物业管理）；商业零售单位所在的商品市场、商业大厦的市场管理活动（市场管理）。

住宿业 指有偿为顾客提供临时住宿的服务活动，不包括提供长期住宿场所的活动（如出租房屋、公寓等）。

餐饮业 指在一定场所，对食物进行现场烹饪、调制，并出售给顾客主要供现场消费的服务活动。

社会消费品零售总额 指批发和零售业、餐饮业、新闻出版业、邮政业和其他服务业等，售予城乡居民用于生活消费的商品和社会集团用于公共消费的商品之总量。社会消费品零售总额包括：

一、批发和零售业企业（单位）售予城乡居民用于生活消费和社会集团用于公共消费的商品。包括：

1. 售予城乡居民的各种生活消费品；

2. 售予入境旅游的外国人、华侨、港澳台同胞的各类商品；

3. 售予行政事业单位、社会团体、军队和武警等机构的商品，以及以零售方式售予各类企业的商品。具体包括：用于非生产和社会交往的办公用品，如通讯设备、计算器具和设备、电讯网络设备、文印设备、音像视听器材和设备、纸张、本册、文具及装订文印材料、家具、日用电器、针纺织品、清洁卫生用品、文体用品、奖品、纪念品、礼品等；供内部人员乘坐的交通工具和燃料；用于办公设施修缮的各类配件、材料、工具等；用于取暖和防暑降温的设备、燃料、材料及食品等；专用于教学的用品和设备；非营利医疗机构的中、西药品、中药材和医疗设备器材；非专用的劳动保护用品；不对外营业的内部食堂用的餐具、炊具、设备、清洁卫生工具和食品、燃料等；军队、武警用于其人员生活的衣着品和个人用品；其他各类非生产性设备和用品。

二、餐饮业出售的主食、菜肴、烟酒饮料和其他商品。

三、新闻出版业、邮政业售予城乡居民、企事业单位、军队和武警等机构的书报杂志、音像制品、邮品等。

四、其他服务业出售的食品、烟酒饮料、服装鞋帽、日常生活用品、医药保健用品、艺术品、工艺美术品、玩具、殡葬用品以及其他消费品。

批发和零售业商品购进、销售、库存总额 指各种登记注册类型的批发和零售业企业（单位）以本企业（单位）为总体的，从国内、国外市场购进的商品总量，销售和出口的商品总量，库存的商品总量等情况。该指标可以反映商品流转过程中商品的购进、销售、库存之间的比例关系和存在的问题。

购进总额 指从本企业（单位）以外的单位和个人购进（包括从境外直接进口）作为转卖或加工后转卖的商品总额。它反映批发和零售业从国内、国外市场上购进商品的总量。商品购进包括：（1）从工农业生产者购进的商品；（2）从出版社、报社的出版发行部门购进的图书、杂志和报纸；（3）从各种登记注册类型的批发和零售业企业（单位）购进的商品；（4）从其他单位购进的商品，如从机关、团体、企业等单位购进的剩余物资，从住宿和餐饮业、其他服务业购进的商品，从海关、市场管理部门购进的缉私和没收的商品，从居民手中收购的废旧商品等；（5）从国（境）外直接进口的商品。不包括企业（单位）为自身经营用和未通过买卖行为而收入的商品以及销售退回、商品升溢等。

销售总额 指对本企业（单位）以外的单位和个人出售（包括对境外直接出口）的商品总额。它反映批发和零售业在国内市场上销售商品以及出口商品的总量。商品销售包括：（1）售给城乡居民和社会集团消费用的商品；（2）售给工业、农业、建筑业、运输邮电业、批发和零售业、住宿和餐饮业、其他服务业等作为生产、经营使用的商品；（3）售给批发和零售业作为转卖或加工后转卖的商品；（4）对国（境）外直接出口的商品。不包括出售本企业（单位）自用的废旧包装用品，未通过买卖行为付出的商品，经本单位介绍、由买卖双方直接结算、本单位只收取手续费的业务，购货退出的商品以及商品损耗和损失等。

库存总额 指报告期末各种登记注册类型的批发和零售业企业（单位）已取得所有权的商品。它反映批发和零售业企业（单位）的商品库存情况和对市场商品供应的保证程度。商品库存包括：（1）存放在批发和零售业经营单位（如门市部、批发站、经营处）仓库、货场、货柜和货架中的商品；（2）挑选、整理、包装中的商品；（3）已记入购进而尚未运到本单位的商品，即发货单或银行承兑凭证已到而货未到的商品；（4）寄放他处的商品，如因购货方拒绝承付而暂时存放在购货方的商品和已办完加工成品收回手续而未提回的商品；（5）委托其他单位代销（未做销售货调出）尚未售出的商品；（6）代其他单位购进尚未交付的商品。不包括所有权不属于本单位的商品、委托外单位加工生产尚未收回成品的商品、外贸企业代理其他单位从国外进口尚未付给订货单位的商品、代国家物资储备部门保管的商品等。

住宿和餐饮业营业额 指住宿和餐饮业法人企业（单位）在经营活动中因提供服务或销售商品等取得的收入。包括：客房收入、餐费收入、商品销售额和其他收入。客房收入指住宿和餐饮业法人企业（单位）在经营活动中因提供住宿服务取得的收入。餐费收入指住宿和餐饮业法人企业（单位）因为顾客提供就餐服务取得的收入，包括经烹饪、调制加工后出售的各种食品，如主食、炒菜、凉拌菜等的收入。商品销售额指住宿和餐饮业法人企业（单位）伴随服务而出售商品所取得的收入（含增值税）。其他收入指营业收入中除客房收入、餐费收入、商品销售额以外的其他收入，包括娱乐、健身和商务服务等。

连锁企业（或称连锁店、连锁公司） 指在核心企业或总店的领导下，由分散的、经营同类商品或服务的企业或活动单位，采取共同方针，实行集中采购和分散销售的有机结合，通过规范化经营，实现规模效益的经济联合组织形式。一般连锁店应由若干个分店组成。其经营特征：（1）经营同类商品；（2）使用统一商号；（3）统一采购配送，采购与销售相分离（部分商品可根据物流合理和保质保鲜原则，由供应商直接送货到门店，其余均由总部统一配送）。

连锁门店的形式分为直营连锁和加盟连锁。

直营连锁也叫正规连锁。指连锁门店均由总部独资或控股开设，在总部的直接领导下统一经营。总部采取纵深式的管理方式，直接下令掌管所有的零售门店，零售门店也必须完全接受总部指挥。这是大型垄断商业资本通过吞并、兼并或独资、控股等途径，发展壮大自身实力和规模的一种形式。

加盟连锁包括特许连锁和自由连锁两种形式。

特许连锁指各连锁门店（被特许人）通过合同形式，取得使用总部（特许人）商标、商号、经营技术和销售总部开发的商品的特许权，各加盟连锁门店为独立法人，在总部指导下统一经营。

自由连锁也称自愿连锁。指连锁公司的门店均为独立法人，各自的资产所有权关系不变，在公司总部的指导下共同经营。各成员店使用共同的店名，与总部订阅有关购、销、宣传等方面的合同，并按合同开展经营活动。在合同规定的范围之外，各成员店可以自由活动。根据自愿原则，各成员店可自由加入连锁体系，也可自由退出。

Explanatory Notes on Main Statistical Indicators

Wholesale Trade refers to the activities of wholesaler selling at wholesale commodities for daily use and capital goods to enterprises of wholesale and retail trades and other enterprises, institutions and government offices, including the activities of wholesaler engaged in import and export and acting as a trade agent. The wholesaler may have the right of ownership over the commodities of wholesale and trade in the name of its own or a company, the wholesaler may not have the right of ownership, only acts an agent. The wholesale trade also include the activities of wholesaler at the fixed stalls of the wholesale market of different commodities.

Retail Trade refers to the activities of department store,supermarket, franchised store, brand store, retail stall and on-the-spot-making-selling store selling commodities to the final consumers (citizens) by any means including internet, post, telephone, sales machine. Retail trade excludes the activities of sales of capital goods such a grain, seed, feed, livestock, mineral products, raw material for production, industrial chemicals, chemical products for farm, machine and equipment (vehicle, computer and communication equipment), and the activities of supplementary sales of non-retailer such as the sales of spare parts of car repair business

Hotel Services refer to the activities of enterprises providing paid services of lodging to the customer, excluding the activities of providing long period of services of lodging (such as leased house and apartments).

Catering Services refer to the activities of enterprises providing on-the-spot services of selling food cooked and prepared to the customer in certain sites

Total Retail Sales of Consumer Goods refer to the sum of retail sales of commodities sold by wholesale and retail trades, catering services, publishing, post and telecommunications and other service industries to urban and rural households for household consumption and to social institutions for public consumption. Retail sales of consumer goods include:

1) Sales sold by wholesale and retail trades to urban~thA and rural households for household consumption and to social institutions for public consumption.

a) of commodities to urban and rural households;

b) of commodities to foreigners, overseas Chinese and Chinese compatriots from Hong Kong, Macao and Taiwan visiting China;

c) of commodities to government agencies, institutions, social organizations, military and armed police units, and commodities to enterprises in the form of retail sales. More specifically, they include: office facilities and articles for non-production purposes such as communications equipment, computing equipment and instruments, TV and network equipment, printing and copying equipment, audio-visual equipment and instruments, paper, notebooks, stationeries, furniture, electric appliances, knitwear, sanitation and cleaning articles, cultural and sport articles, articles for prizes, souvenirs, etc.; transport vehicles and fuels for employees; materials, spare parts and tools for the maintenance of office facilities; equipment, fuels, materials and food for winter heating or summer cooling purposes; articles and equipment for teaching purpose; Chinese and western medicines and medical equipment and facilities purchased by non profit-making medical institutes; non- specialized work safety articles; cooking utensils, tableware, equipment, cleaning articles, food and fuels purchased by in-house cafeterias; clothes and personal articles purchased by military or armed police units for their officials and soldiers; and other equipment and articles for non-production purposes.

2) Sales of stable food, cooked dishes, beverages, tobaccos and other articles by catering units.

3) Sales of books, newspapers, magazines, audio-visual products and post products by publishing, post and telecommunications departments to urban and rural households and to enterprises, institutions, military and armed police units.

4) Sales of food, beverages, tobaccos, clothing, hats, footwear, articles for daily use, medicines, medical and health articles, work of art, handicrafts, toys, funeral articles and other articles by other service industries.

Purchase, Sales and Stock of Commodities by Wholesale and Retail Trades refer to the total volume of commodities purchased, total volume of sales and exports, and the stock of commodities by wholesale and retail enterprises (establishments) of different status of registration from domestic and overseas markets. This indicator reflects the relationship among purchase, sales and stock of commodities in the circulation of goods and reveals the existing problems.

Total Purchases of Commodities refer to the total value of purchases of commodities by enterprises (establishments)from other establishments or individuals (including direct import from abroad) for the purpose of re-selling, either with or without further processing of the commodities purchased. The commodities include: (1) commodities purchased from agricultural and industrial producer, wholesaler, retailer, publishing house and other service business; (2) commodities purchased from institutions and government departments; (3) confiscated goods purchased from the customs authorities or market management agencies; (4) second-hand goods and wastes purchased from residents; The commodities exclude 1 commodities purchased by enterprises (establishments) for use in their own business operation, commodities obtained without buying or selling procedures such as materials, consumable goods of low value, office appliances, etc. 2 received goods without trading, such as goods handed over from others, borrowed goods, preserved goods for others, donated goods from others, processed and retrieved goods, etc. 3. goods of direct settlement between buyer and seller with handling fees introduced by others, 4. goods returned or refused to pay by the buyer, 5. excessive goods.

Total Sales of Commodities refer to value of commodities sold by the establishments to other establishments and individuals (including goods sold for self consumption, including the value-added tax). The commodities include: (1) commodities sold to urban and rural residents and social groups for their consumption; (2) commodities sold to establishments in all industries for their production and operation, including agriculture, industry, construction, transportation, post and telecommunications, catering services, and public utility including commodities sold to wholesale and retail establishments for re-selling, with or without further processing; and (3) commodities for direct export to abroad.Excluded are (1) extended commodities without trading, such as goods handed over to other enterprises and institutions because of the change of organizations, lent goods, returned goods preserved for others, extended processing materials and samples donated to others, (2) goods of direct settlement between buyer and seller with handling fees introduced by others, (3)goods returned after purchase, (4) damaged and spoiled goods, (5) waste and used goods of selfuse,

Total Stock of Commodities refers to total commodities possessed by wholesaler and retailer of various types of registration status at the end of the reference period, reflecting the commodity stock level of various wholesaler and retailer and the potential for market supply. It includes: (1) commodities located in storage, garages, counters, and shelves of operating places (such as sale stores, wholesale centres, and operating offices) ; (2) commodities in the process of being selected, sorted, and packed; (3) commodities not arrived but recorded as purchase in the account, i.e. commodities not arrived but payment receipts for the commodities from the sellers or the banks arrived; (4) commodities deposited in other places rather than places mentioned above, for instance: commodities in the hold of purchasers temporarily due to the refusal of payment and commodities not taken back after going through the formalities; (5) commodities entrusted to other units to sell but not sold yet; (6) commodities purchased for other units but not delivered yet. Commodities not included as stock are those not owned by the enterprises (units), commodities on commission for processing but not yet delivered, imported commodities of agency of foreign trade enterprise but not yet delivered to ordering units and finally those put in stock on behalf of the state material reserves units.

Business Revenue of Hotels and Catering Services refers to revenue received from providing services or selling commodities by corporate enterprises and establishments engaged in hotels and catering services, including income from hotels, from catering services, from selling of commodities and from other services. Income from hotels refers to income of corporate enterprises and establishments engaged in hotels and catering services by providing lodging services. Income from catering services refers to income of corporate enterprises and establishments engaged in hotels and catering services by providing catering services, including selling of cooked or prepared foods such as staple food, cooked dishes or cold dishes. Income from selling of commodities refers to income of corporate enterprises and establishments engaged in hotels and catering services by selling commodities (including value-added tax) that accompany the services they provide. Income from other activities refers to income received other than income from hotels, catering services or selling of commodities, such as income from providing recreation, fitness or business services.

Chain Head Stores (headquarter) refer to the core leading stores responsible for development, allocation, administration and utilization of resources (name of stores, brand of stores, operation model, service standard, management way, ect.) of chain stores. Chain stores refers to the stores engaged in providing homogeneous commodities or services, with the central leadership of head store and guided by common policies, conduct centralized purchase and distributed selling of commodities, in order to gain better efficiency through standardized operation. The chain stores include regular chain stores, franchise chain stores and voluntary chain stores.

Regular Chain store refers to chain stores that are invested or controlled by the headquarters. They operate under direct and unified management from the headquarters.

Franchise chain store refers to the chain stores (franchisees) which are franchised with operation resources such as trade marks, names, patent and operation know-how by the franchisors in form of contract and pay the operation fees to the franchisors.

Voluntary chain store refers the stores operate jointly on the voluntary bases while maintaining their status of independent legal entities with full ownership of their assets. They sell goods of same brand from same channel of resource to the consumers.

17 对外经济贸易和旅游

FOREIGN TRADE AND ECONOMIC COOPERATION TOURISM

资料整理：李鹏涛
Data management: Li Pengtao
数据审核：赵　晖
Data audit: Zhao Hui

第十七部分　对外经济贸易和旅游

一、简要说明

本章资料包括对外经济贸易、利用外资和旅游等方面资料，由西安市统计局贸易外经处根据西安市商务局、投资合作局、文旅局和西安海关提供资料整理。

二、主要指标

进出口总值（亿元）	3242.52	比上年下降	1.8%
#出　口	1730.28	比上年下降	11.6%
实际利用外资（亿美元）	70.57	比上年增长	11.1%

17　FOREIGN TRADE AND ECONOMIC COOPERATION,TOURISM

Ⅰ.Brief Introduction

Data in this chapter consists of data on foreign trade, using of foreign capital and fund and tourism. Data on foreign economy and trade and tourism are compiled and provided by Foreign Economy Division of the Xi'an Bureau of Statistics according to the data from Xi'an Municipal Bureau of Commerce, Xi'an Municipal Bureau of Investment Cooperation. Xi'an Customs District and Xi'an Municipal Administration of Culture and Tourism Committee.

Ⅱ.Major Indicators

		Increase over Preceding Year
Total Imports and Exports (100 mil.yuan)	3242.52	-1.8%
#Exports	1730.28	-11.6%
Actual Utilized Foreign Investments (USD 100 mil.)	70.57	11.1%

17-1 主要年份外资、外贸基本情况

Main Indicators on Foreign Investments and International Trading in Representative Years

指 标	Item	1990	2000	2005	2010	2014*
一、新设立外商投资企业（个）	**Number of New Foreign-Invested Enterprises (unit)**	**11**	**135**	**157**	**82**	**103**
合同外资（万美元）	Contracted Foreign Investments (USD 10 000)	415	54123	121499	119689	255321
实际利用外资（万美元）	Actual Utilized Foreign Investments (USD 10 000)	1154	15633	57113	156653	370310
二、进出口总值（万美元）	**Total Imports and Exports (USD 10 000)**	**38229**	**173696**	**390146**	**1039273**	**15321514**
进口总值	Total Imports	9939	67634	126705	507544	7974693
出口总值	Total Exports	28290	106062	263441	531729	7346822
进出口差额(出口-进口)	Balance of Imports and Exports	18351	38428	136736	24185	-627871
三、国际旅游者人数总计（万人次）	**Total Number of International Tourists (10 000 person-times)**	**25.88**	**65.03**	**77.56**	**84.18**	
#外国人	Foreigners	15.40	54.65	65.86	73.21	
港、澳、台同胞	Chinese Compatriot From Hong Kong, Macao and Taiwan	10.07	10.38	11.70	10.97	
四、国际旅游者人天数总计（万人天）	**Total Number of Days of International Tourists (10 000 person/day)**	**55.03**	**162.69**	**224.93**	**241.67**	
#外国人	Foreigners	33.48	131.44	190.99	211.48	
港、澳、台同胞	Chinese Compatriot From Hong Kong, Macao and Taiwan	21.55	31.15	33.94	30.19	
五、国际旅游收入（亿元）	**Earning of International Tourism (100 millon yuan)**	**1.96**	**22.41**	**33.54**	**42.40**	
#商品收入	Income from Mercantile	0.44	7.71	11.25	11.87	
劳务收入	Income from Labour Service	1.52	14.70	22.29	30.53	
六、国际旅游者在西安人均停留天数（天）	**Number of Days of Average Tourists Staying in Xi'an (day)**	**2.1**	**2.5**	**2.9**	**2.9**	

注：1.2014年起市文化和旅游局未发布国际旅游统计数据。
2.本表来源于市商务局、西安海关、市文化和旅游局、市投资合作局。2018年及以后利用外资包含西咸新区。进出口总值为西安原口径数据。
3.本表2019年利用外资签定协议项目修改为“新设立外商投资企业”，合同外资2016年前名称为“利用外资签订协议金额”，实际利用外资2016年前名称为“外商实际直接投资额”。下同。
4.*号表示2014年及以后进出口数据计量单位为“万元”。下同。

17-1 续表 continued

指 标	Item	2015*	2016*	2017*	2018*	2019*
一、新设立外商投资企业（个）	**Number of New Foreign-Invested Enterprises (unit)**	**73**	**72**	**143**	**219**	**237**
合同外资（万美元）	Contracted Foreign Investments (USD 10 000)	193684	102103	464954	475508	196410
实际利用外资（万美元）	Actual Utilized Foreign Investments (USD 10 000)	400833	450466	530680	635370	705738
二、进出口总值（万美元）	**Total Imports and Exports (USD 10 000)**	**17616896**	**18299476**	**25450843**	**33032389**	**32425181**
进口总值	Total Imports	9418142	8826392	9928641	13460734	15122342
出口总值	Total Exports	8198754	9473084	15522202	19571655	17302839
进出口差额(出口-进口)	Balance of Imports and Exports	-1219388	646692	5593561	6110921	2180497
三、国际旅游者人数总计（万人次）	**Total Number of International Tourists (10 000 person-times)**					
#外国人	Foreigners					
港、澳、台同胞	Chinese Compatriot From Hong Kong, Macao and Taiwan					
四、国际旅游者人天数总计（万人天）	**Total Number of Days of International Tourists (10 000 person/day)**					
#外国人	Foreigners					
港、澳、台同胞	Chinese Compatriot From Hong Kong, Macao and Taiwan					
五、国际旅游收入（亿元）	**Earning of International Tourism (100 millon yuan)**					
#商品收入	Income from Mercantile					
劳务收入	Income from Labour Service					
六、国际旅游者在西安人均停留天数（天）	**Number of Days of Average Tourists Staying in Xi'an (day)**					

17–2 主要年份利用外资情况

Utilization of Foreign Capital in Representative Years

单位：万美元 (USD 10 000)

年 份 Year	合同外资 Contracted Foreign Investments	实际利用外资 Actual Utilized Foreign Investments
1983	3500	800
1985	8361	1106
1986	19919	4010
1987	3218	5552
1988	2423	6758
1989	1645	11632
1990	415	1154
1991	591	1094
1992	24165	5200
1993	57289	8996
1994	20321	15240
1995	28956	18653
1996	35978	20510
1997	27214	22057
1998	40034	22286
1999	40390	13801
2000	54123	15633
2001	60736	17687
2002	70692	20281
2003	96380	25557
2004	78312	27595
2005	121499	57113
2006	182525	82463
2007	143978	111567
2008	118230	114738
2009	60027	121872
2010	119689	156653
2011	120083	200522
2012	360264	247800
2013	251874	312994
2014	255321	370310
2015	193684	400833
2016	102103	450466
2017	464954	530680
2018	475508	635370
2019	196410	705738

注：本表数据来源于市投资合作局。2018年及以后数据包含西咸新区。

17-3 外国和港澳台地区在西安投资情况（2019年）

Foreign, Hong Kong, Macao and Taiwan Investment Situation in Xi'an (2019)

单位：万美元 (USD 10 000)

指　标	Item	新设立外商投资企业（个） Number of New Foreign-Invested Enterprises(unit)	合同外资 Contracted Foreign Investments	实际利用外资 Actual Utilized Foreign Investments
合计数	**Total**	**237**	**196410**	**705738**
一、按企业类别分组	By Enterprise Category			
1. 中外合资经营企业	Joint-venture Enterprises	81	37133	69041
2. 中外合作经营企业	Cooperation Enterprises			
3. 外资企业	Wholly Foreign-owned Enterprises	156	159277	179481
4. 外商投资股份制	FDI Shareholding Inc.			1119
5. 外方股东留存收益	Retained earnings of foreign shareholders			
6. 境外融资	Overseas Financing			456097
二、按国民经济行业分组	Grouped by Sector			
（一）农、林、牧、渔业	Agriculture, Forestry, Animal Husbandry and Fishery			
（二）采矿业	Mining			84790
（三）制造业	Manufacturing	22	86897	450291
（四）电力、燃气及水的生产供应业	Generation and Supply of Electricity, Production and Supply of Gas and Water	1	91	
（五）建筑业	Construction	6	10296	10620
（六）批发和零售业	Wholesale and Retail Trades	23	15090	37798
（七）交通运输、仓储和邮政业	Transportation, Storage and Post	30	3845	5433
（八）住宿和餐饮业	Hotels and Catering Services	55	536	1746
（九）信息传输、软件和信息技术服务业	Information Transmission, Computer Service and Software	18	10385	4233
（十）金融业	Financial Intermediation	11	310	4098
（十一）房地产业	Real Estate	33	23	62774
（十二）租赁和商务服务业	Leasing and Business Services	21	12937	9242
（十三）科学研究和技术服务业	Scientific Research and Technical Service	6	5401	775
（十四）水利、环境和公共设施管理业	Management of Water Conservancy, Environment and Public Facilities	2	131	2730

注：本表数据来源于市投资合作局。本表数据包含西咸新区。“新设立外商投资企业”2018年为“项目数”。

17-3 续表1

单位：万美元 (USD 10 000)

指 标	Item	新设立外商投资企业（个） Number of New Foreign-Invested Enterprises(unit)	合同外资 Contracted Foreign Investments	实际利用外资 Actual Utilized Foreign Investments
（十五）居民服务、修理和其他服务业	Services to Households, repairs and other services	1	403	25510
（十六）教育	Education	1	14	
（十七）卫生和社会工作	Health and social work	2	1	322
（十八）文化、体育和娱乐业	Culture, Sports and Entertainment	5	50050	5376
（十九）公共管理、社会保障和社会组织	Public administration, social security and social organizations			
（二十）国际组织	International Organizations			
三、按投资国别、地区分组	By Country(Region)			
香港	Hong Kong	75	135622	204941
澳门	Macao	1	1275	7756
台湾地区	Taiwan	9	7884	108392
日本	Japan	2	626	35731
马来西亚	Malaysia	1	251	
新加坡	Singapore	7	7936	40641
韩国	Korea Rep.	23	12306	235218
德国	Germany	4	-209	1330
意大利	Italy	1	45	
法国	France	1	33	10891
英国	United Kingdom	4	1233	326
瑞士	Switzerland			225
丹麦	Denmark			
加拿大	Canada	4	391	
美国	United States	12	619	19514
澳大利亚	Australia	5	1858	182
维尔京群岛	Virgin Is.(E)	2	1052	3440
其它	Others	86	25488	37151

17-4 各区县、开发区实际利用外资

Actual Utilized Investment by Foreign Entrepreneurs by Region and Development Zone

单位：万美元 (USD 10 000)

区县及开发区	Region and Economic Zone	2010	2011	2012	2013	2014	2015	2016	2017	2018	2019
区县合计	**Sum of Region**	**38855**	**49726**	**58119**	**45164**	**51423**	**59765**	**67874**	**72527**	**119635**	**129183**
新城区	Xincheng	4900	6765	7800	5012	6500	7775	8768	10340	11947	11609
碑林区	Beilin	5150	6273	7800	5103	5871	6873	9360	9941	10570	11450
莲湖区	Lianhu	5471	7405	7800	5100	5843	6873	7532	8656	9392	9820
灞桥区	Baqiao	5215	6001	7397	6124	6933	8148	9056	9601	10570	11450
未央区	Weiyang	5023	6202	7800	6000	6834	7870	8614	9433	10380	11260
雁塔区	Yanta	5488	6912	8190	6179	6847	8074	8907	9843	10772	11450
阎良区	Yanliang	1208	2070	2200	2200	2346	2555	2801	3000	3200	3360
临潼区	Lintong	1200	2000	2400	2400	2504	2765	3031	1102	4094	3680
长安区	Chang'an	1680	2300	2768	3003	3360	3961	4440	4762	5200	5620
高陵区	Gaoling	950	1089	1100	1100	1182	1478	1621	1740	1860	1960
鄠邑区	Huyi	1050	1060	1115	1173	1288	1339	1479	1700	1666	1600
蓝田县	Lantian	550	600	650	660	707	1283	1401	1490	1862	3185
周至县	Zhouzhi	970	1050	1100	1110	1210	773	864	920	920	
西咸新区	Xixian									37202	42739
开发区合计	**Sum of Development Zones**	**117798**	**150797**	**189681**	**267830**	**318887**	**311265**	**381023**	**458153**	**515513**	**576495**
高新区	GaoXin	51130	64935	81776	132632	149387	167112	203870	260293	287000	321383
经开区	JingKai	42608	54201	68202	81423	103009	114538	129186	145000	167000	186900
曲江新区	Qujiang	17187	21002	26433	33870	41436		20588	24212	26500	29600
浐灞生态区	Chanba Eco-District	3070	3856	4837	7266	8453	9800	10833	12402	13600	15000
航空基地	Aviation Industry Base	1239	1701	2072	2640	3082	3636	4186	2045	5250	6000
航天基地	Aerospace Base	1554	2030	2403	3000	3501	3980	4567	5117	6100	6599
国际港务区	International Trade&Logistic Park	1010	1571	2082	3469	5050	6429	7793	9083	10063	11013
其它	**Others**									222	60

注：1.本表数据来源于市投资合作局。2018年及以后数据包含西咸新区。
2.2011—2015年开发区合计含沣东新城。

17-5 主要年份进出口总值

Total Imports and Exports in Representative Years

单位：万美元 (USD 10 000)

年 份 Year	进出口总值 Total Imports and Exports	出口总值 Total Exports	进口总值 Total Imports
1987	13596	7540	6056
1990	38229	28290	9939
1991	55356	41511	13845
1992	70467	53060	17407
1993	93330	62393	30937
1994	104752	76897	27855
1995	137510	110163	27347
1996	143187	91745	51442
1997	150668	107753	42915
1998	180589	100492	80097
1999	172919	94495	78424
2000	173696	106062	67634
2001	169914	87948	81966
2002	186966	112479	74487
2003	230932	140327	90605
2004	309295	203539	105756
2005	390146	263441	126705
2006	415403	272862	142541
2007	536162	347133	189029
2008	704029	447113	256916
2009	724618	333114	391504
2010	1039273	531729	507544
2011	1260179	582662	677517
2012	1301446	729878	571568
2013	1798534	847819	950715
2014*	15321514	7346822	7974692
2015*	17616896	8198754	9418142
2016*	18299476	9473084	8826392
2017*	25450843	15522202	9928641
2018*	33032390	19571656	13460734
2019*	32425181	17302839	15122342

注：本表数据来源于西安海关。2014年及以后数据计量单位为万元。本表数据为西安原口径数据。

17-6 外贸商品进出口总值分国别和地区（2019年）

Total Value of Imports and Exports by Country and Region（2019）

单位：万元 (10 000 yuan)

国别和地区	Country and Region	进出口总值 Total Imports and Exports	出口 Exports
亚洲	**Asia**	**23598037**	**11918282**
#香港	Hong kong	3389475	3386149
台湾地区	Taiwan	7721039	2001080
日本	Japan	1811086	394675
菲律宾	Phiilippines	102312	75727
马来西亚	Malaysia	822529	660829
韩国	Korea	7139947	3498293
非洲	**Africa**	**581848**	**511068**
#埃及	Egypt	133843	133579
突尼斯	Tunisia	4086	3754
埃塞俄比亚	Ethiopia	2636	2636
博茨瓦纳	Botswana	10	10
南非	South Africa	116512	83180
欧洲	**Europe**	**3821988**	**2608937**
#德意志联邦国	Germany	969448	639515
法国	France	541556	455337
意大利	Italy	142084	64967
荷兰	Netherland	619780	427421
英国	England	177357	116216
瑞士	Switzerland	85671	11404
西班牙	Spain	125879	116689
俄罗斯联邦	Russia	237806	136467
拉丁美洲	**Latin America**	**1093490**	**667858**
#哥伦比亚	Colombia	32009	32005
巴西	Brazil	163229	50767
阿根廷	Argentina	38723	37365
北美洲	**North America**	**2813643**	**1476762**
#加拿大	Canada	218220	50874
美国	America	2595422	1425886
大洋洲及太平洋岛屿	**Oceanic and Pacific Islands**	**492553**	**119932**
#澳大利亚	Australia	479262	111743
新西兰	New Zealand	10091	5915

注：本表数据来源于西安海关，为西安原口径数据。

17-7 主要商品分大类出口金额

Export Value of Major Merchandise by Type

单位：万美元 (USD 10 000)

商品分类	HS Section and Division	2000	2005
食用蔬菜、根及块茎	Edible Vegetables, Certain,Roots amd Tubers	1095	1190
蔬菜、水果、坚果或植物其他部分的制品	Vegetables, Fruits, Nuts, or Products Made of Other Parts of Plants	2076	10531
矿砂、矿渣及矿灰	Ores,Slags and Ash	4083	63247
无机化学品；贵金属、稀土金属、放射性元素及其同位素的有机及无机化合物	Inorganic Chemicals,Organic or Inorganic Compounds of Precious Metals,of Rare Earth Metals,of Radioactive Elements or of Isotopes	3714	10997
有机化学品	Organic Chemicals	2367	8569
羊毛、动物细毛或粗毛、马毛纱线及其机织物	Wool ,Fine or Coarse Animal Hair; Horsehair Yarn and Woven Fabric	810	903
棉花	Cotton	3197	3240
化学纤维短纤	Short Staple Chemical' Fibers	5061	1471
针织或钩编的服装及衣着附件	Articles of Apparel and Clothing Accessories, Knitted or Crocheted	6753	5736
非针织或非钩编的服装及衣着附件	Articles of Apparel and Clothing Accessories, not Knitted or Crocheted	7269	5068
其它纺织制成品；成套物品；旧衣着及旧纺织品	Other Made Up Textile Articles;Sets;Worn Clothing and Worn Textile Articles;Rags Articles	1649	3000
鞋靴、护膝和类似品及其零件	Footwear,Gaiters and The Like;Parts of Such Articles Headgear and Parts Thereof	1347	1368
玻璃及其制品	Glass and Glassware	3376	8576
钢铁	Iron and Steel	3534	5314
钢铁制品	Articles of Iron or Steel	5535	13959
铅及制品	Lead Areticles Thereof	1371	12
锌及制品	Zinc Areticles Thereof	4031	135
其他贱金属、金属陶瓷及其制品	Other Base Metals,Germets;Areticles Thereof	1066	11233
贱金属工具、器具、利口器、餐匙、餐叉及其零件	Tools,Implements,Cutlery,Spons and Forks, of Base Metal;Parts Thereof of Base Metal	2933	3052
核反应堆、锅炉、机器、机械器具及其零件	Nuclear Reactors ,Boilers, Machinery and Mechanical Appliances; and Parts Thereof	10915	30832
电机、电气设备及其零件；录音机及放声机、电视图象、声音的录制和重放设备及其零件、附件	Electrical Machinery and Equipment and Parts Thereof;Sound Recorders and Repreducers, Television Image and Sound Recordes and Repreducers, and Parts and Accessories of Such Articles	8339	23605
光学、照相、电影、计量、检验、医疗或外科仪器及设备、精密仪器及设备；上述物品的零配件、附件	Optical,Photographic,Cinematographic,Measuring, Checking,Precision Medical or Surgical Instruments and Apparatus;Parts and Accessories Thereof	2020	2341
家具、寝具、褥垫、弹簧床垫、软床垫及类似的填充制品；未列名灯具及照明装置；发光标志、发光名牌及类似品；活动房屋	Mattresses,Mattress Supports,Cushions and Similar Stuffed Furnishings;Lamps and Lighting Fittings, not Elsewhere Spcified or Included;Illumihated Signs,Illuminated	2587	4773

注：1.本表数据来源于西安海关。2014年及以后数据计量单位为万元。本表数据为西安原口径数据。
2.个别年份数据根据海关最新提供数据进行了修正。

17-7 续表1

单位：万美元

商品分类	HS Section and Division	2006	2007
食用蔬菜、根及块茎	Edible Vegetables, Certain,Roots amd Tubers	1136	1232
蔬菜、水果、坚果或植物其他部分的制品	Vegetables, Fruits, Nuts, or Products Made of Other Parts of Plants	15374	37426
矿砂、矿渣及矿灰	Ores,Slags and Ash	52046	47378
无机化学品；贵金属、稀土金属、放射性元素及其同位素的有机及无机化合物	Inorganic Chemicals,Organic or Inorganic Compounds of Precious Metals,of Rare Earth Metals,of Radioactive Elements or of Isotopes	10916	16508
有机化学品	Organic Chemicals	11923	11182
羊毛、动物细毛或粗毛、马毛纱线及其机织物	Wool ,Fine or Coarse Animal Hair; Horsehair Yarn and Woven Fabric	1400	1065
棉花	Cotton	3808	3255
化学纤维短纤	Short Staple Chemical' Fibers	1556	1767
针织或钩编的服装及衣着附件	Articles of Apparel and Clothing Accessories, Knitted or Crocheted	5332	5345
非针织或非钩编的服装及衣着附件	Articles of Apparel and Clothing Accessories, not Knitted or Crocheted	4078	3875
其它纺织制成品；成套物品；旧衣着及旧纺织品	Other Made Up Textile Articles;Sets;Worn Clothing and Worn Textile Articles;Rags Articles	3342	3090
鞋靴、护膝和类似品及其零件	Footwear,Gaiters and The Like;Parts of Such Articles Headgear and Parts Thereof	216	348
玻璃及其制品	Glass and Glassware	8272	6246
钢铁	Iron and Steel	4900	11366
钢铁制品	Articles of Iron or Steel	16903	17329
铅及制品	Lead Areticles Thereof	158	1650
锌及制品	Zinc Areticles Thereof	4119	2470
其他贱金属、金属陶瓷及其制品	Other Base Metals,Germets;Areticles Thereof	17695	23414
贱金属工具、器具、利口器、餐匙、餐叉及其零件	Tools,Implements,Cutlery,Spons and Forks, of Base Metal;Parts Thereof of Base Metal	3607	3917
核反应堆、锅炉、机器、机械器具及其零件	Nuclear Reactors ,Boilers, Machinery and Mechanical Appliances; and Parts Thereof	36174	47381
电机、电气设备及其零件；录音机及放声机、电视图象、声音的录制和重放设备及其零件、附件	Electrical Machinery and Equipment and Parts Thereof;Sound Recorders and Repreducers, Television Image and Sound Recordes and Repreducers, and Parts and Accessories of Such Articles	22801	33393
光学、照相、电影、计量、检验、医疗或外科仪器及设备、精密仪器及设备；上述物品的零配件、附件	Optical,Photographic,Cinematographic,Measuring, Checking,Precision Medical or Surgical Instruments and Apparatus;Parts and Accessories Thereof	3521	4230
家具、寝具、褥垫、弹簧床垫、软床垫及类似的填充制品；未列名灯具及照明装置；发光标志、发光名牌及类似品；活动房屋	Mattresses,Mattress Supports,Cushions and Similar Stuffed Furnishings;Lamps and Lighting Fittings, not Elsewhere Spcified or Included;Illumihated Signs,Illuminated	5086	8301

continued 1

(USD 10 000)

2008	2009	2010	2011	2012	2013	2014*	2015*	2016*	2017*	2018*	2019*
1374	803	2633	2016	1961	2699	2686	2039	2555	1129	659	1337
29270	21920	22189	36763	2576	49361	132663	112701	102768	149311	131711	79123
40502	6141	5247	4709	1679	1686	14977	96	178	346	25	2
15882	9774	13645	11735	8911	12588	67764	44508	49950	52192	52289	61278
13954	16294	18881	20067	17890	28694	109986	109654	117162	148719	176287	185794
720	460	923	796	562	2433	15782	3005	5648	3153	5680	5731
3213	2346	3277	2628	2185	5827	9252	14309	6429	5301	5531	9583
1181	2217	1951	2586	2375	8245	13685	11581	11178	14502	12923	14903
4371	3617	3830	3366	12316	6491	29551	37030	31646	36441	30570	15335
3623	2919	3134	3262	7050	4861	33872	23610	19393	40633	52971	22579
3187	2813	3170	2838	4412	4471	18906	15677	15187	26219	19425	37534
380	367	544	1003	5252	6293	20186	5032	2292	18614	18514	19469
6538	5574	6691	8073	10995	13856	54453	45991	46764	46059	49904	44400
11966	4254	9622	16681	8407	6730	31854	20390	27589	28467	34424	26844
26568	11943	12149	25319	24259	33546	102720	88740	100956	164963	151403	132817
2	1	2	2	4913	16	3		26	19	1	12
46	78	10	10	11	59	109	93	20	334	48	83
27576	11276	20723	28092	21397	24030	106691	95442	83309	103608	115801	122230
4083	2777	3374	3641	5176	5992	30653	25321	24868	33582	41004	38312
75911	52372	102893	99631	127795	211009	1929864	2744726	3431041	6147739	8252801	4882165
56758	53355	118140	137105	183536	327931	3113155	3625079	4264312	7044093	8971300	10051890
6348	5255	9489	11066	14908	17879	112646	119117	107892	108613	149348	170976
8296	4769	4992	3860	25644	23595	52352	42140	40142	77439	83975	26295

17-8 主要商品分大类进口金额

Import Value of Major Merchandise by Type

单位：万美元 (USD 10 000)

商品分类	HS Section and Division	2000	2005	2010	2013	2014*
无机化学品；贵金属、稀土金属、放射性元素及其同位素的有机及无机化合物	Inorganic Chemicals,Organic or Inorganic Compounds of Precious Metals,of Rare Earth Metals,of Radioactive Elements or of Isotopes	1467	317	7513	11869	166549
有机化学品	Organic Chemicals	7257	15237	13949	12504	98293
塑料及其制品	Plastic and Articles Thereof	2559	4317	4091	8014	37082
钢铁	Iron and Steel	2467	752	10949	1802	11893
铜及制品	Copper and Articles Thereof	2367	689	43343	65170	169061
铝及制品	Aluminium and Articles Thereof	2652	3627	3116	11758	45295
核反应堆、锅炉、机器、机械器具及其零件	Nuclear Reactors ,Boilers, Machinery and Mechanical Appliances; and Parts Thereof	12990	38050	134753	186974	2017587
电机、电气设备及其零件；录音机及放声机、电视图象、声音的录制和重放设备及其零件、附件	Electrical Machinery and Equipment and Parts Thereof;Sound Recorders and Repreducers, Television Image and Sound Recordes and Repreducers,and Parts and Accessories of Such Articles	5911	23337	207937	444407	3919650
车辆及其零件、附件、铁道及电车道车辆除外	Vehicles Other Than Railway or Tramway Rolling-and Rarts and Accessories Thereof	1530	1387	3109	2966	17521
航空器、航天器及其零配件	Aircraft, Spacecraft and Parts Thereof	10443	8800	3620	9179	43191
光学、照相、电影、计量、检验、医疗或外科仪器及设备、精密仪器及设备；上述物品的零配件、附件	Optical,Photographic,Cinematographic,Measuring, Checking,Precision Medical or Surgical	3673	10424	37414	61727	452559

17-8 续表 continued

单位：万美元 (USD 10 000)

商品分类	HS Section and Division	2015*	2016*	2017*	2018*	2019*
无机化学品；贵金属、稀土金属、放射性元素及其同位素的有机及无机化合物	Inorganic Chemicals,Organic or Inorganic Compounds of Precious Metals,of Rare Earth Metals,of Radioactive Elements or of Isotopes	185175	299328	246352	371885	346091
有机化学品	Organic Chemicals	86359	154656	123439	148022	114497
塑料及其制品	Plastic and Articles Thereof	54103	76182	103008	157809	198420
钢铁	Iron and Steel	17403	16093	16567	18717	21793
铜及制品	Copper and Articles Thereof	484480	224287	240188	571455	652623
铝及制品	Aluminium and Articles Thereof	43935	34384	32032	71631	100994
核反应堆、锅炉、机器、机械器具及其零件	Nuclear Reactors ,Boilers, Machinery and Mechanical Appliances; and Parts Thereof	2021311	990108	926081	1056642	2881715
电机、电气设备及其零件；录音机及放声机、电视图象、声音的录制和重放设备及其零件、附件	Electrical Machinery and Equipment and Parts Thereof;Sound Recorders and Repreducers, Television Image and Sound Recordes and Repreducers,and Parts and Accessories of Such Articles	5011437	5272203	6510729	9406713	8561929
车辆及其零件、附件、铁道及电车道车辆除外	Vehicles Other Than Railway or Tramway Rolling-and Rarts and Accessories Thereof	19700	22697	26662	22430	23238
航空器、航天器及其零配件	Aircraft, Spacecraft and Parts Thereof	35164	31933	101247	31940	28326
光学、照相、电影、计量、检验、医疗或外科仪器及设备、精密仪器及设备；上述物品的零配件、附件	Optical,Photographic,Cinematographic,Measuring, Checking,Precision Medical or Surgical	542812	521411	307404	341141	580507

注：本表数据来源于西安海关。2014年及以后数据计量单位为万元。本表数据为西安原口径数据。

17-9 按贸易方式分出口总值

Total Value of Exports in Foreign Trade by Type of Trade

单位：万元 (10 000 yuan)

指 标	Item	2019	2019年比2018年增长（%） Growth Rate in 2019 over 2018（%）
出口总值	**Total Exports**	**17302839**	**-11.6**
1.一般贸易	General Trade	3778678	8.3
2.国家间、国际组织无偿援助	Between Countries, International Organizations	6968	-4.4
和赠送的物资	Aid and Donated Materials		
3.其他捐赠物资	Other Donated Materials	6	
4.来料加工装配贸易	Assembly Processing Trade	7036946	-26.9
5.进料加工贸易	Processing With Imported Trade	3587179	26.7
6.对外承包工程出口货物	Exports Contracted Projects	86790	-68.9
7.租赁贸易	Lease Trade	1327	4004.4
8.易货贸易	Barter		
9.出料加工贸易	Material Processing	93	54.2
10.保税监管场所进出境货物	Inward and Outward Goods of Free	196	73.9
（保税仓库进出境货物）	(Trade Storehouse)		
11.海关特殊监管区域物流货物	Re-export Goods of Free Trade Zone	2785700	-16.5
12.其他	Others	18956	119.9

注：本表数据来源于西安海关。本表数据为西安原口径数据。

17-10 按贸易方式分进口总值

Total Value of Imports in Foreign Trade by Type of Trade

单位：万元 (10 000 yuan)

指 标	Item	2019	2019年 比2018年增（%） Growth Rate in 2019 over 2018 (%)
进口总值	**Total Imports**	**15122342**	**12.3**
1.一般贸易	General Trade	2789579	9.5
2.国家间、国际组织无偿援助和赠送的物资	Between Countries, Internationals Organization Aid and Donated Materials		
3.华侨、港澳台同胞、外籍华人捐赠物资	The overseas Chinese, Hong Kong, Macao, Taiwan,Chinese of foreign Donated Materials		
4.来料加工装配贸易	Assembly Processing Trade	6448855	2.5
5.进料加工贸易	Processing With Imported Trade	3235821	-0.9
6.来料加工装配进口的设备	Assembly Processing Trade Equipment	44	-94.6
7.租赁贸易	Lease Trade	77	
8.外商投资企业作为投资进口的设备、物品	Foreign-invested Enterprises as the Import Investment of Equipment, Goods		-100.0
9.出料加工贸易	Material Processing	334	110.7
10.易货贸易	Barter		
11.保税监管场所进出境货物（保税仓库进出境货物）	Inward and Outward Goods of Free (Trade Storehouse)	77472	115.4
12.海关特殊监管区域物流货物（保税区仓储转口货物）	Re-export Goods of Free Trade Zone (Re-exports)	801703	148.6
13.海关特殊监管区域进口设备（出口加工区进口设备）	Export Processing Zones Imported (Equipment)	1653141	72.7
14.其他	Other	115316	428.6

注：本表数据来源于西安海关。本表数据为西安原口径数据。

17-11 主要年份旅游人数及收入

Number of Tourists and Tourism Earnings in Representative Years

年份 Year	接待旅游者人数（万人次） Number of Tourists (10 000 person-times)	#国际旅游人数 Number of International Tourists	旅游总收入（万元） Total Tourism Earnings (10 000 yuan)	#国际旅游收入 Earning of International Tourists	国际旅游者在西安人均停留天数（天） Number of Days of Average International Tourists Staying in Xi'an(day)
1980	4.00	4.00	1757	1757	3.8
1985	21.15	21.15	7029	7029	2.2
1990	25.88	25.88	19628	19628	2.1
1995	791.35	41.35	440000	103818	2.0
1997	1010.53	48.53	510000	166359	2.6
1998	1105.80	47.98	560000	160244	2.6
1999	1260.40	55.41	830000	186282	2.5
2000	1567.00	65.03	1050000	224100	2.5
2001	1752.20	67.20	1130000	240700	2.4
2002	1984.13	74.13	1310000	260000	2.2
2003	1647.67	33.66	1064200	121200	2.5
2004	2149.03	65.03	1544000	273900	2.9
2005	2423.60	77.56	1785000	335380	2.9
2006	2738.70	86.73	2043000	378270	2.9
2007	3118.01	100.01	2372000	424263	2.9
2008	3232.20	63.20	2435200	287200	2.6
2009	3929.29	67.29	2974000	310500	2.9
2010	5285.18	84.18	4051800	424000	2.9
2011	6653.23	100.23	5301500	512800	2.9
2012	7978.35	115.35	6543900	598900	2.9
2013	10130.00	121.11	8114400	641600	2.9
2014	12000.00		9500000		
2015	13600.80		10736900		
2016	15012.56		12138100		
2017	18093.14		16333000		
2018	24738.75		25548100		
2019	30110.43		31460500		

注：1.本表数据来源于市文化和旅游局。2014年以后市文化和旅游局未发布国际旅游统计数据。2018年及以后数据包含西咸新区。
2.1980-1994年因未开展国内旅游统计，接待旅游者人数和旅游总收入为国际旅游统计。

17-12 主要年份旅行社及A级景点

Statistics of Travel Agencies and Level-A Scenic Spots in Representative Years

项目	Item	2005	2010	2012	2013	2014	2015	2016	2017	2018	2019
旅行社数（个）	Number of Travel Agencies (unit)	221	334	344	360	385	353	410	452	583	574
旅行社营业收入（亿元）	Revenue of Travel Agencies (100 million yuan)	17.82	31.22	49.49	57.93	45.70	59.54	66.68	79.39	93.93	103.14
旅游A级景点数（个）	Number of Level-A Scenic Spots(unit)	18	34	55	61	67	74	72	77	77	77
旅游A级景点年接待游客人次（万人次）	Number of Tourists Received at Level-A Scenic Spots (10 000 person times)	930	2726	5306	7163	7462	8553	10454	18120	24506	22596

注：本表数据来源于市文化和旅游局。2018年旅行社数、旅行社管理收入来源于第四次经济普查583家有营业收入的企业数据。
2018年及以后旅游A级景点数及接待游客不包含西咸新区。

主要统计指标解释

进出口总额 指实际进出我国国境的货物总金额。包括对外贸易实际进出口货物，来料加工装配进出口货物，国家间、联合国及国际组织无偿援助物资和赠送品，华侨、港澳台同胞和外籍华人捐赠品，租赁期满归承租人所有的租赁货物，进料加工进出口货物，边境地方贸易及边境地区小额贸易进出口货物（边民互市贸易除外），中外合资企业、中外合作经营企业、外商独资经营企业进出口货物和公用物品，到、离岸价格在规定限额以上的进出口货样和广告品（无商业价值、无使用价值和免费提供出口的除外），从保税仓库提取在中国境内销售的进口货物，以及其他进出口货物。该指标可以观察一个国家在对外贸易方面的总规模。我国规定出口货物按离岸价格统计，进口货物按到岸价格统计。

商品经营单位所在地进、出口额 指在所在地海关注册登记的有进出口经营权的企业实际进、出口额。

商品目的地进口额和商品货源地出口额 目的地进口额指进口货物的消费、使用或最终抵运地的实际进口额；货源地出口额指出口货物的产地或原始发货地的实际出口额。

利用外资 指我国各级政府、部门、企业和其他经济组织通过对外借款、吸收外商直接投资以及用其他方式筹措的境外现汇、设备、技术等。

外商直接投资 指外国企业和经济组织或个人（包括华侨、港澳台胞以及我国在境外注册的企业）按我国有关政策、法规，用现汇、实物、技术等在我国境内开办外商独资企业、与我国境内的企业或经济组织共同举办中外合资经营企业、合作经营企业或合作开发资源的投资（包括外商投资收益的再投资），以及经政府有关部门批准的项目投资总额内企业从境外借入的资金。

旅游人数：

（1）入境旅游人数：指报告期内来我国观光、度假、探亲访友、就医疗养、购物、参加会议或从事经济、文化、体育、宗教活动的外国人、港澳台同胞、入境游客。统计时，外国人、港澳台同胞每入境一次统计1人次。

（2）出境人数：指中国（大陆）居民因公或因私出境前往其他国家、中国香港特别行政区、澳门特别行政区和台湾省观光、度假、探亲访友、就医疗养、购物、参加会议或从事经济、文化、体育、宗教活动的人数，即出境游客。统计时，按每出境一次统计1人次。

（3）国内旅游人数：指在报告期内在中国（大陆）观光游览、度假、探亲访友、就医疗养、购物、参加会议或从事经济、文化、体育、宗教活动的中国（大陆）居民人数，其出游的目的不是通过所从事的活动谋取报酬。统计时，国内游客按每出游一次统计1人次。

国际旅游（外汇）收入 指入境游客在中国（大陆）境内旅行、游览过程中用于交通、参观游览、住宿、餐饮、购物、娱乐等全部花费。

国内旅游收入 又称旅游总花费指国内游客在国内旅行、游览过程中用于交通、参观游览、住宿、餐饮、购物、娱乐等全部花费。

国际旅行社 指经营业务范围包括入境旅游业务、出境旅游业务和国内旅游业务的旅行社。

国内旅行社 指经营范围仅限于国内旅游业务的旅行社。

星级饭店 指设备、设施、服务符合《旅游饭店星级的划分与评定》（GB／T14308—2003），通过相关旅游管理部门评定，并取得星级饭店称号的饭店（含预备星级饭店）。

Explanatory Notes on Main Statistical Indicators

Total Imports and Exports at Customs refer to the real value of commodities imported and exported across the border of China. They include the actual imports and exports through foreign trade, imported and exported goods under the processing and assembling trades and materials, supplies and gifts as aid given gratis between governments and by the United Nations and other international organizations, and contributions donated by overseas Chinese, compatriots in Hong Kong and Macao and Chinese with foreign citizenship, leasing commodities owned by tenant at the expiration of leasing period, the imported and exported commodities processed with imported materials, commodities trading in border areas (excluding mutual exchange goods), the imported and exported commodities and articles for public use of the Sino-foreign joint ventures, cooperative enterprises and ventures with sole foreign investment. Also included is import or export of samples and advertising goods for which CIF or FOB value are beyond the permitted ceiling (excluding goods of no trading or use value and free commodities for export), imported goods sold in China from bonded warehouses and other imported or exported goods. The indicator of the total imports and exports at customs can be used to observe the total size of external trade in a country. In accordance with the stipulation of the Chinese government, imports are calculated at CIF, while exports are calculated at FOB.

Import Export Value by Location of China's Foreign Trade Managing Units refers to actual value of imports and exports carried out by corporations which have been registered by the local Customs house and are vested with right to run import export business.

Import Value of Commodities by Place of Destination and Export Value of Commodities by Place of Origin in China The former indicator refers to the value of import commodities of the places of their consumption, utilization or the places of their final destination. The latter indicator refers to the value of export commodities of the places of their origin or the places of the commodities dispatched.

Utilization of Foreign Capitals refers to remittance, equipment and technology financed from abroad, by loans, foreign direct investment and other forms undertaken by the Chinese governments at all levels, by various departments, enterprises and other economic units.

Foreign Direct Investment refers to the investments inside China by foreign enterprises and economic organizations or individuals (including overseas Chinese, compatriots from Hong Kong, Macao and Taiwan, and Chinese enterprises registered abroad), following the relevant policies and laws of China, for the establishment of ventures exclusively with foreign own investment, Sino-foreign joint ventures and cooperative enterprises or for co-operative exploration of resources with enterprises or economic organizations in China.

Number of Tourists

(1) Visitor arrivals refer to the number of foreigners,Chinese compatriots from Hong Kong, Macao and Taiwan Chinese (mainland) who come to China (mainland) for sight-seeing,vacation,visiting relatives, medical treatment, shopping, attending conference, or to engage in economic, cultural, sports and religious activities. In compiling statistics, each time of entering China is counted as one person-time.

(2) Number of Chinese residents going abroad refer to the number of Chinese (mainland) residents going to other countries, Hong Kong Special Administrative region, Macao Special Administrative region and Taiwan for on official or private purposes, for sight-seeing, vacation, visiting relatives, medical treatment, shopping, attending conference, or to engage in economic, cultural, sports and religious activities. In compiling statistics, each time of leaving is counted as one person-time.

(3) Number of domestic tourists refers to the number of Chinese (mainland) residents who travel within China (mainland) for sight-seeing, vacation, visiting relatives, medical treatment, shopping, attending conference, or to engage in economic, cultural, sports and religious activities. In compiling

statistics, each time of travelling is counted as one person-time.

Foreign Exchange Earnings from International Tourism refer to the total expenditure of foreigners, overseas Chinese,Chinese compatriots from Hong Kong,Macao and Taiwan during their stay in the mainland of China on transportation,sighting,accommodation, food,shopping and entertainment.

Income from Domestic Tourism refer to expenditure of domestic tourists on transportation,sighting, accommodation, food, shopping and entertainment while they travel.

International Travel Agencies refer to travel agencies engaged in tourism entering China, Chinese residents going abroad and domestic tourism.

Domestic Travel Agencies refer to travel agencies only engaged in domestic tourism.

Star–rated Hotels refer to hotels rated with stars as assessed by the relevant tourism authorities according to GB/T14308-2003 standard with reference to their infrastructure, facilities and service levels.

18 规模以上服务业

SERVICE INDUSTRY OBOVE DESIGNATED SIZE

资料整理：冯　乐　杜　晖
Data management：Feng Le　Du Hui
数据审核：刘栋婷
Data audit：Liu Dongting

第十八部分　规模以上服务业

一、简要说明

1.本章主要包括规模以上服务业（九个门类、四个中类）单位个数及主要经济指标，由西安市统计局服务业与社会科技统计处提供。

2.统计范围：辖区内年营业收入2000万元及以上服务业法人单位。包括：交通运输、仓储和邮政业，信息传输、软件和信息技术服务业，水利、环境和公共设施管理业三个门类和卫生行业大类。

辖区内年营业收入1000万元及以上服务业法人单位。包括：租赁和商务服务业，科学研究和技术服务业，教育三个门类，以及物业管理、房地产中介服务、房地产租赁经营和其他房地产业四个行业中类。

辖区内年营业收入500万元及以上服务业法人单位。包括：居民服务、修理和其他服务业，文化、体育和娱乐业两个门类，以及社会工作行业大类。

二、主要指标

规模以上服务业单位个数（个）	2075		
规模以上服务业资产总计（亿元）	10419.63	比上年增长	9.3%
规模以上服务业营业收入（亿元）	3084.80	比上年增长	11.2%
规模以上服务业利润总额（亿元）	205.24	比上年增长	25.5%

18 SERVICE INDUSTRY OBOVE DESIGNATED SIZE

Ⅰ.Brief Introduction

1.The data in this chapter consists of the number of service units and main economic indicators of Service enterprises above designated size (Including mine categories, four Class), data in this chapter is provided by Tertiary Industry and Social Science&Technology Division of Xi'an Bureau of Statistics.

2.Scope of statistics:The annual operating income of the service enterprise within the jurisdiction is 20 million yuan or more. It includes transportation, storage and postal services, information transmission, software and information technology services, water conservancy, environment and public facilities management, and health services. The annual operating income of the service enterprise within the jurisdiction is 10 million yuan or more. It includes: leasing and business services, scientific research and technology services, three categories of education, and property management, real estate intermediary services, real estate leasing and other real estate industry.

The annual operating income within the jurisdiction is 5 million yuan or more. Including: residential services, repair and other services, culture, sports and entertainment two categories, and social work industry categories.

Ⅱ. Major Indicators

		Increase over Preceding Year
Number of Units for services and Enterprises above the Designated Size(units)	2075	
Total Assets for services and Enterprises above the Designated Size(100 mil.yuan)	10419.63	9.3%
Operating Income for services and Enterprises above the Designated Size(100 mil.yuan)	3084.80	11.2%
The total Profit for services and Enterprises above the Designated Size(100 mil.yuan)	205.24	25.5%

18-1 规模以上服务业按登记注册类型分主要经济指标（2019年）

Main Economic Indicators for Services above the Designated Size grouped by Registration Type（2019）

单位：万元　　　　(10 000 yuan)

指　标	Item	企业单位数（个）Number of Enterprises (unit)	资产总计 Total Assets	固定资产原价 Original Value of Fixed Assets
总计	**Total**	**2075**	**104196300.9**	**52484267.4**
按登记注册类型分组	**Grouped by Registration Type**			
内资企业	Domestic Funded Enterprises	1999	102321633.7	51165724.9
国有	State-owned Enterprises	76	3045970.1	2127643.3
集体	Collective-owned Enterprises	14	54531.5	16459.2
股份合作	Corperative Enterprises	4	13050.8	3551.5
联营	Joint Ownership Enterprises	1	7158.5	542.5
国有联营	State Joint Ownership Enterprises			
集体联营	Collective Joint Ownership Enterprises			
国有与集体联营	Joint State-collective Enterprises			
其他联营	Others Joint Ownership Enterprises	1	7158.5	542.5
有限责任公司	Limited Liability Corporrations	965	87975371.2	42962950.4
国有独资公司	State Funded Corporations	113	38615478.1	22803030.5
其他有限责任公司	Other Limited Liability Corporrations	852	49359893.1	20159919.9
股份有限公司	Other Limited Liability Corporrations	63	5115919.6	4317905.1
私营	Other Limited Liability Corporrations	855	5885230.5	1637927.5
私营独资	Private-funded Enterprises	14	16525.6	4657.4
私营合伙	Private Partnership Enterprises	9	75301.6	43201.5
私营有限责任公司	Private Limited Liability Corporations	791	5358198.8	1540897.3
私营股份有限公司	Private Share-holding Corporations Ltd.	41	435204.5	49171.3
其他	Other Enterprises	21	224401.5	98745.4
港澳台商投资	Enterprises with Funds from Hong Kong, Macao &Taiwan	27	730056.7	957782.3
与港澳台商合资经营	Joint Ventures	6	183467.2	135231.4
与港澳台商合作经营	Cooperation Enterprises	1	21431.0	4578.4
港澳台商独资	Enterprises with Sole Investment from Hong Kong Macau and Taiwan	18	497229.7	808895.8
港澳台商投资股份有限公司	Share-holding Corporations Ltd. with funds from Hong Kong, Macao & Taiwan			
其他港澳台投资	Other Hong Kong, Macao and Taiwan Investment	2	27928.8	9076.7
外商投资	Foreign Funded Enterprises	49	1144610.5	360760.2
中外合资经营	Sino-foreign Joint Ventures Enterprises	13	288265.9	187961.9
中外合作经营	Sino-Foreign Cooperation Enterprises	1	4570.7	4424.9
外资企业	Foreign Owned Enterprises	29	389077.9	154492.3
外商投资股份有限公司	Limited Company Funded by Foreign Investment	2	425635.1	1051.0
其他外商投资	Other Foreign Funded Enterprises	4	37060.9	12830.1

18-1 续表1

单位：万元

指 标	Item	负债合计 Total Liabilities	所有者权益合计 Total Owners' Equities	营业收入 Paid in Capital
总计	**Total**	**61769819.9**	**42426481.0**	**30847961.6**
按登记注册类型分组	**Grouped by Registration Type**			
内资企业	Domestic Funded Enterprises	60705324.0	41616309.7	29852973.3
国有	State-owned Enterprises	2098047.4	947922.7	1590444.3
集体	Collective-owned Enterprises	31545.5	22986.0	48423.2
股份合作	Corperative Enterprises	7176.7	5874.1	4093.1
联营	Joint Ownership Enterprises	8479.1	-1320.6	0.1
国有联营	State Joint Ownership Enterprises			
集体联营	Collective Joint Ownership Enterprises			
国有与集体联营	Joint State-collective Enterprises			
其他联营	Others Joint Ownership Enterprises	8479.1	-1320.6	0.1
有限责任公司	Limited Liability Corporrations	53047643.7	34927727.5	20693770.5
国有独资公司	State Funded Corporations	22975250.8	15640227.3	3935338.9
其他有限责任公司	Other Limited Liability Corporrations	30072392.9	19287500.2	16758431.6
股份有限公司	Other Limited Liability Corporrations	1019464.2	4096455.4	2499603.3
私营	Other Limited Liability Corporrations	4341249.9	1543980.6	4779414.4
私营独资	Private-funded Enterprises	12566.3	3959.3	20077.4
私营合伙	Private Partnership Enterprises	40368.1	34933.5	90690.9
私营有限责任公司	Private Limited Liability Corporations	4108470.2	1249728.6	4323862.2
私营股份有限公司	Private Share-holding Corporations Ltd.	179845.3	255359.2	344783.9
其他	Other Enterprises	151717.5	72684.0	237224.4
港澳台商投资	Enterprises with Funds from Hong Kong, Macao &Taiwan	505380.2	224676.5	569894.1
与港澳台商合资经营	Joint Ventures	69769.9	113697.3	85613.2
与港澳台商合作经营	Cooperation Enterprises	18471.9	2959.1	8167.8
港澳台商独资	Enterprises with Sole Investment from Hong Kong Macau and Taiwan	399714.6	97515.1	429952.7
港澳台商投资股份有限公司	Share-holding Corporations Ltd. with funds from Hong Kong, Macao & Taiwan			
其他港澳台投资	Other Hong Kong, Macao and Taiwan Investment	17423.8	10505.0	46160.4
外商投资	Foreign Funded Enterprises	559115.7	585494.8	425094.2
中外合资经营	Sino-foreign Joint Ventures Enterprises	151131.3	137134.6	78315.7
中外合作经营	Sino-Foreign Cooperation Enterprises	263.6	4307.1	2660.5
外资企业	Foreign Owned Enterprises	168566.6	220511.3	304771.6
外商投资股份有限公司	Limited Company Funded by Foreign Investment	212886.8	212748.3	3871.6
其他外商投资	Other Foreign Funded Enterprises	26267.4	10793.5	35474.8

continued1

(10 000 yuan)

营业成本 Total Cost	销售费用 Sale Expenses	管理费用 Management Expenses	研发费用 R&D Expenditure
23565609.4	**1361655.9**	**2354924.6**	**660652.9**
22984505.1	1276861.4	2240595.3	630880.7
1527635.8	23976.8	224607.0	10769.2
17937.3	8838.9	19250.0	482.1
472.8	133.1	1934.8	1485.6
55.5		216.0	
55.5		216.0	
15821170.9	874279.7	1275517.0	478130.8
2672436.9	113416.8	239062.6	35346.3
13148734.0	760862.9	1036454.4	442784.5
1831019.3	142988.5	147099.4	17735.7
3610896.4	214646.8	539445.3	122271.5
15078.3	1053.2	4111.4	
52564.5	1100.4	19097.2	932.5
3340255.4	180969.6	480930.3	95206.1
202998.2	31523.6	35306.4	26132.9
175317.1	11997.6	32525.8	5.8
314460.4	72272.5	53622.8	4206.2
58396.0	1051.5	10481.6	1266.8
4128.8		1212.9	
231045.0	69573.5	40541.4	2939.4
20890.6	1647.5	1386.9	
266643.9	12522.0	60706.5	25566.0
48519.7	4877.7	9171.7	4661.5
674.9		280.3	
187541.6	6910.5	48094.1	20904.5
1598.8	39.1	973.6	
28308.9	694.7	2186.8	

18-1 续表2

单位：万元

指 标	Item	财务费用 Financial Expenses	投资收益 Investment Income
总计	**Total**	**1403795.5**	**282996.3**
按登记注册类型分组	**Grouped by Registration Type**		
内资企业	Domestic Funded Enterprises	1377229.5	282849.0
国有	State-owned Enterprises	18205.2	9911.9
集体	Collective-owned Enterprises	-324.2	197.4
股份合作	Corperative Enterprises	-115.6	503.7
联营	Joint Ownership Enterprises	742.2	
国有联营	State Joint Ownership Enterprises		
集体联营	Collective Joint Ownership Enterprises		
国有与集体联营	Joint State-collective Enterprises		
其他联营	Others Joint Ownership Enterprises	742.2	
有限责任公司	Limited Liability Corporrations	1270371.7	244728.0
国有独资公司	State Funded Corporations	882685.6	114036.1
其他有限责任公司	Other Limited Liability Corporrations	387686.1	130691.9
股份有限公司	Other Limited Liability Corporations	29795.4	13137.2
私营	Other Limited Liability Corporrations	52943.9	14353.8
私营独资	Private-funded Enterprises	130.0	
私营合伙	Private Partnership Enterprises	773.5	0.3
私营有限责任公司	Private Limited Liability Corporations	51726.2	13620.8
私营股份有限公司	Private Share-holding Corporations Ltd.	314.2	732.7
其他	Other Enterprises	5610.9	17.0
港澳台商投资	Enterprises with Funds from Hong Kong, Macao &Taiwan	14771.0	106.8
与港澳台商合资经营	Joint Ventures	-473.4	83.1
与港澳台商合作经营	Cooperation Enterprises	842.1	
港澳台商独资	Enterprises with Sole Investment from Hong Kong Macau and Taiwan	14037.0	23.7
港澳台商投资股份有限公司	Share-holding Corporations Ltd. with funds from Hong Kong, Macao & Taiwan		
其他港澳台投资	Other Hong Kong, Macao and Taiwan Investment	365.3	
外商投资	Foreign Funded Enterprises	11795.0	40.5
中外合资经营	Sino-foreign Joint Ventures Enterprises	6401.6	38.3
中外合作经营	Sino-Foreign Cooperation Enterprises	-25.3	
外资企业	Foreign Owned Enterprises	2495.9	2.2
外商投资股份有限公司	Limited Company Funded by Foreign Investment	2971.7	
其他外商投资	Other Foreign Funded Enterprises	-48.9	

continued2

(10 000 yuan)

营业利润 Business Profits	利润总额 Total Profits	应付职工薪酬 Salary Payable	平均用工人数（人） Annual Average Employed Persons (person)
1967982.6	**2052358.0**	**6346279.9**	**532203**
1829936.1	1912870.9	6092795.6	517239
-3417.1	-18096.2	515544.9	50911
2167.1	2137.9	25248.9	5411
573.6	709.3	1556.5	287
-1013.6	-1013.6	185.8	38
-1013.6	-1013.6	185.8	38
1232899.5	1310349.1	4014504.1	276753
182150.7	203605.3	712914.7	58978
1050748.8	1106743.8	3301589.4	217775
357076.8	362124.9	370061.9	31284
230613.5	244621.7	1103057.3	145493
-341.6	-260.9	7265.0	1489
15838.3	15789.2	24770.6	2454
168538.0	179504.7	984556.1	132491
46578.8	49588.7	86465.6	9059
11036.3	12037.8	62636.2	7062
95782.0	97385.2	78346.9	5536
13007.0	12809.5	18999.9	1835
1930.2	1960.3	94.5	7
59068.5	60843.8	57349.2	3450
21776.3	21771.6	1903.3	244
42264.5	42101.9	175137.4	9428
2616.8	1916.7	19282.1	1298
1703.8	1689.3	596.9	67
36576.9	37086.4	134983.1	6668
-1762.0	-1712.0	636.8	83
3129.0	3121.5	19638.5	1312

18-2 规模以上服务业按规模分主要经济指标（2019年）

单位：万元

指标	Item	企业单位数（个） Number of Enterprises (unit)	资产总计 Total Assets	固定资产原价 Original Value of Fixed Assets
总计	**Total**	**2075**	**104196300.9**	**52484267.4**
按企业规模分组	**Grouped by Size of Enterprises**			
大型企业	Large-size	185	54755793.5	43974079.8
中型企业	Medium-size	399	17054392.9	4653217.7
小型企业	Small-size	1125	23671347.5	3124415.1
微型企业	Microenterprise	366	8714767.0	732554.8

18-2 续表1

单位：万元

指标	Item	管理费用 Management Expenses	研发费用 R&D Expenditure	财务费用 Financial Expenses
总计	**Total**	**2354924.6**	**660652.9**	**1403795.5**
按企业规模分组	**Grouped by Size of Enterprises**			
大型企业	Large-size	1085701.9	442216.1	991175.6
中型企业	Medium-size	530955.6	123720.4	167458.8
小型企业	Small-size	608070.2	72107.6	188402.7
微型企业	Microenterprise	130196.9	22608.8	56758.4

Main Economic Indicators for Services above the Designated Size grouped by Size of Enterprises (2019)

(10 000 yuan)

负债合计 Total Liabilities	所有者权益合计 Total Owners' Equities	营业收入 Paid in Capital	营业成本 Total Cost	销售费用 Sale Expenses
61769819.9	**42426481.0**	**30847961.6**	**23565609.4**	**1361655.9**
31295265.7	23460527.8	16477502.7	12196103.5	771795.1
9809843.8	7244549.1	6033891.6	4694061.0	310476.9
14985983.4	8685364.1	6447192.0	5099662.4	248444.6
5678727.0	3036040.0	1889375.3	1575782.5	30939.3

continued 1

(10 000 yuan)

投资收益 Investment Income	营业利润 Business Profits	利润总额 Total Profits	应付职工薪酬 Salary Payable	平均用工人数（人） Annual Average Employed Persons (person)
282996.3	**1967982.6**	**2052358.0**	**6346279.9**	**532203**
100292.1	1169688.9	1175876.6	4228788.2	272572
88926.8	324537.8	346984.3	1046837.1	109640
84443.1	306632.3	346971.2	935272.0	126744
9334.3	167123.6	182525.9	135382.6	23247

18-3 规模以上服务业按行业分主要经济指标（2019年）

单位：万元

行业	Sector	企业单位数（个） Number of Enterprises (unit)	资产总计 Total Assets	固定资产原价 Original Value of Fixed Assets
总计	**Total**	**2075**	**104196300.9**	**52484267.4**
按国民经济行业大类分组	**Grouped by sector categories**			
铁路运输业	Railway transport industry	3	4215896.1	4818159.0
道路运输业	The road transport industry	147	30867901.1	23024747.0
水上运输业	Water transportation			
航空运输业	The air transport industry	12	3784171.5	2047200.8
管道运输业	Pipeline transportation	1	122507.6	16920.7
多式联运和运输代理业	Multimodal Transport and Transport Agent Industry	33	863833.5	119316.3
装卸搬运和仓储业	Loading, Unloading, Forwarding and Storage Industry	34	1092501.5	254356.6
邮政业	The postal service	10	778633.7	1096474.6
电信、广播电视和卫星传输服务	Telecommunication, broadcasting and satellite transmission services	23	8889552.3	14043504.2
互联网和相关服务	The Internet and related services	52	559196.0	36837.7
软件和信息技术服务业	Software and information technology services	215	3801438.8	733585.1
物业管理	Property management	187	1674577.8	437115.8
房地产中介服务	Real estate intermediary service	15	41174.4	5109.1
房地产租赁经营	Owned Real Estate Business Activities	51	1967566.8	527014.5
其他房地产业	Other Real Estate	1	1341.9	
租赁业	Leasing industry	15	177639.8	60937.4
商务服务业	Business services	393	18387005.7	1527804.9
研究和试验发展	Research and development	32	1344371.3	359641.1
专业技术服务业	Professional and technical services	323	8948657.2	966242.0
科技推广和应用服务业	Promotion and application of science and technology services	22	479944.0	112278.7
水利管理业	Water resources management industry	4	6416.9	1469.2
生态保护和环境治理业	Ecological protection and environmental control industries	8	141403.5	84117.2
公共设施管理业	Public facilities management industry	49	1532545.7	367049.4
土地管理业	Land Administration Industry	6	10106515.2	129651.4
居民服务业	Resident services	29	157682.7	92028.5
机动车、电子产品和日用产品修理业	Motor vehicles, electronics and household goods-repairing	23	171989.4	20167.3
其他服务业	Other service industries	24	47063.0	9549.6
教育	Education	26	196883.2	41101.2
卫生	Health	79	1285409.3	769350.2
社会工作	Social work	1	822.0	4.2
新闻出版业	Press and publishing industry	34	518265.2	112420.8
广播、电视、电影和影视录音制作业	Radio, television, film and video recordings	101	756730.8	102158.1
文化艺术业	Culture and arts	53	567628.9	343313.9
体育	Physical education	13	36243.1	28238.1
娱乐业	The entertainment industry	56	672791.0	196402.8

Main Economic Indicators for Services above the Designated Size grouped by Industry（2019）

（10 000 yuan）

负债合计 Total Liabilities	所有者权益合计 Total Owners' Equities	营业收入 Paid in Capital	营业成本 Total Cost	销售费用 Sale Expenses	管理费用 Management Expenses
61769819.9	**42426481.0**	**30847961.6**	**23565609.4**	**1361655.9**	**2354924.6**
2794603.0	1421293.1	751232.2	660700.6	128.0	6714.1
18832117.7	12035783.4	2716854.2	2044325.6	19040.2	152303.3
1395165.1	2389006.4	542251.7	495714.3	10516.4	52182.1
104278.6	18229.0	76028.6	54546.5		1396.5
605358.2	258475.3	489653.6	442265.4	2952.2	21612.5
793799.8	298701.7	390852.1	340929.2	13481.1	26255.8
547691.7	230942.0	963204.1	812034.3	5218.4	123256.5
2959331.2	5930221.1	4787518.4	3281030.8	490715.7	271301.6
276395.7	282800.3	950896.5	685078.9	119648.8	47984.1
2026112.3	1775326.5	3986597.3	2777455.2	145126.9	283913.9
1233734.1	440843.7	1062109.8	852172.9	11837.9	123229.5
19541.3	21633.1	52489.9	19735.6	15842.8	10601.2
1591280.7	376286.1	289901.7	114200.5	21028.6	65071.3
546.4	795.5	906.7	238.7	0.5	480.7
155052.6	22587.2	147899.4	136558.8	4299.7	7103.9
11785492.5	6601513.2	3856158.6	3237558.1	136708.5	290700.1
437898.8	906472.5	528212.8	386634.0	6657.3	55360.3
5295417.2	3653240.0	5717165.1	4666456.3	111377.0	395832.4
289122.1	190821.9	185387.0	144326.2	3897.2	12351.3
5297.9	1119.0	10183.6	8714.9	65.6	1106.8
67995.6	73407.9	53432.1	35278.5	7654.9	4475.6
1006071.5	526474.2	470401.2	353218.5	19517.4	66393.2
6686616.9	3419898.3	629075.2	423417.0	4437.3	20824.4
157896.2	-213.5	56834.3	28740.7	10248.9	18869.8
140766.3	31223.1	40288.2	31461.8	3111.0	4643.4
25131.6	21931.4	56914.7	44773.2	1478.9	7774.6
110829.6	86053.6	246658.4	160312.5	19081.3	33707.5
839575.9	445833.4	571731.7	409509.9	46856.6	97777.7
2267.4	-1445.4	1363.3	1146.6		277.1
254398.8	263866.4	339362.8	258422.3	26750.2	44674.0
455500.2	301230.6	304032.1	224904.2	37526.7	44684.7
327609.2	240019.7	197145.6	101076.3	44849.4	39415.7
39976.2	-3733.1	14666.2	5911.6	5661.9	2506.8
506947.6	165843.4	360552.5	326759.5	15938.6	20142.2

18-3 续表1

单位：万元

行 业	Sector	研发费用 R&D Expenditure	财务费用 Financial Expenses
总计	**Total**	**660652.9**	**1403795.5**
按国民经济行业大类分组	**Grouped by sector categories**		
铁路运输业	Railway transport industry	604.7	119053.8
道路运输业	The road transport industry	683.7	783804.8
水上运输业	Water transportation		
航空运输业	The air transport industry	69.6	20699.9
管道运输业	Pipeline transportation	75.0	-15.0
多式联运和运输代理业	Multimodal Transport and Transport Agent Industry		7060.4
装卸搬运和仓储业	Loading, Unloading, Forwarding and Storage Industry		18433.0
邮政业	The postal service		2562.4
电信、广播电视和卫星传输服务	Telecommunication, broadcasting and satellite transmission services	2881.1	76637.7
互联网和相关服务	The Internet and related services	20506.1	1572.8
软件和信息技术服务业	Software and information technology services	460168.7	13797.6
物业管理	Property management		14290.1
房地产中介服务	Real estate intermediary service		-36.3
房地产租赁经营	Owned Real Estate Business Activities	83.1	33564.6
其他房地产业	Other Real Estate		-1.8
租赁业	Leasing industry		1233.1
商务服务业	Business services	4981.9	149722.9
研究和试验发展	Research and development	35874.7	1104.4
专业技术服务业	Professional and technical services	128522.2	-120.6
科技推广和应用服务业	Promotion and application of science and technology services	3309.4	4262.5
水利管理业	Water resources management industry		5.0
生态保护和环境治理业	Ecological protection and environmental control industries	97.6	763.0
公共设施管理业	Public facilities management industry	134.8	8364.9
土地管理业	Land Administration Industry		102715.7
居民服务业	Resident services		578.4
机动车、电子产品和日用产品修理业	Motor vehicles, electronics and household goods-repairing		2112.6
其他服务业	Other service industries	157.2	172.5
教育	Education	774.2	247.2
卫生	Health	379.1	14276.7
社会工作	Social work		0.8
新闻出版业	Press and publishing industry	384.1	-1278.8
广播、电视、电影和影视录音制作业	Radio, television, film and video recordings	459.1	7807.8
文化艺术业	Culture and arts	407.8	7338.1
体育	Physical education		637.2
娱乐业	The entertainment industry	98.8	12428.1

continued 1

(10 000 yuan)

投资收益 Investment Income	营业利润 Business Profits	利润总额 Total Profits	应付职工薪酬 Salary Payable	平均用工人数（人） Annual Average Employed Persons (person)
282996.3	**1967982.6**	**2052358.0**	**6346279.9**	**532203**
	-36982.2	-41943.9	5475.1	210
25555.5	6715.9	18628.1	637923.5	63591
23341.7	6879.3	12550.7	175014.2	9833
	19098.8	19256.4	9821.1	576
6878.5	77203.3	77588.1	36476.4	4058
623.1	6920.5	15616.5	23231.9	2999
-183.5	15824.8	-8155.6	301222.0	32940
6288.8	592117.5	577436.6	708295.5	45048
1784.5	81489.0	86022.0	59043.4	4395
13062.5	341101.1	359397.1	1746508.4	79729
2494.7	74390.1	75662.7	288919.0	51285
865.2	5911.1	5994.2	23342.1	2400
8887.2	35933.2	37754.1	38999.3	3083
	182.6	182.6		1
	-1238.0	-1580.9	9095.6	1011
77714.3	100737.2	111773.2	618190.8	89716
10822.6	50928.3	58125.0	140240.0	6729
35410.3	423651.8	444202.4	902167.1	59334
1346.1	13440.6	13073.7	13828.6	980
	285.6	359.2	1071.1	157
61.3	5745.4	6893.6	9699.4	1011
550.6	19352.4	23039.5	111536.7	15266
43500.9	76182.0	76314.8	18465.1	1097
1440.9	-758.1	-593.5	17646.0	3992
2185.2	1002.2	524.2	5859.3	921
85.3	2140.7	2560.4	26854.6	6345
-674.3	30716.4	30543.2	59129.4	6982
1536.5	1668.7	3253.2	185228.5	20080
	-63.3	85.2	256.1	43
1659.2	10768.2	15157.1	60005.6	4673
17611.4	10052.3	13415.2	31013.8	3972
130.1	12814.4	21568.7	56520.5	6190
-290.3	-781.7	-4849.4	4204.9	689
308.0	-15447.5	2503.6	20994.9	2867

18–4 规模以上服务业按隶属关系分主要经济指标（2019年）

单位：万元

指标	Item	企业单位数（个） Number of Enterprises (unit)	资产总计 Total Assets	固定资产原价 Original Value of Fixed Assets
总计	**Total**	**2075**	**104196300.9**	**52484267.4**
按隶属关系分	**Grouped by affiliation**			
中央	Central	93	16027042.6	13965086.9
地方	Region	85	6884367.6	868819.5
其他	Others	1897	81284890.7	37650361.0

18–4 续表1

单位：万元

指标	Item	管理费用 Management Expenses	研发费用 R&D Expenditure	财务费用 Financial Expenses
总计	**Total**	**2354924.6**	**660652.9**	**1403795.5**
按隶属关系分	**Grouped by affiliation**			
中央	Central	468896.6	116552.0	162412.0
地方	Region	88248.6	12293.5	7109.1
其他	Others	1797779.4	531807.4	1234274.4

Main Economic Indicators for Services above the Designated Size grouped by Affiliation (2019)

(10 000 yuan)

负债合计 Total Liabilities	所有者权益合计 Total Owners' Equities	营业收入 Paid in Capital	营业成本 Total Cost	销售费用 Sale Expenses
61769819.9	**42426481.0**	**30847961.6**	**23565609.4**	**1361655.9**
8003137.7	8023904.9	8371117.9	6622924.7	406756.5
3402140.8	3482226.8	937882.1	731440.5	34287.9
50364541.4	30920349.3	21538961.6	16211244.2	920611.5

continued 1

(10 000 yuan)

投资收益 Investment Income	营业利润 Business Profits	利润总额 Total Profits	应付职工薪酬 Salary Payable	平均用工人数（人） Annual Average Employed Persons (person)
282996.3	**1967982.6**	**2052358.0**	**6346279.9**	**532203**
37024.0	574124.3	562641.4	1253612.3	77780
11519.5	59706.5	66437.2	158719.4	17135
234452.8	1334151.8	1423279.4	4933948.2	437288

主要统计指标解释

国家统计局规模以上服务业单位统计标准：辖区内年营业收入2000万元及以上服务业法人单位。包括：交通运输、仓储和邮政业，信息传输、软件和信息技术服务业，水利、环境和公共设施管理业三个门类和卫生行业大类。

辖区内年营业收入1000万元及以上服务业法人单位。包括：租赁和商务服务业，科学研究和技术服务业，教育三个门类，以及物业管理、房地产中介服务、房地产租赁经营和其他房地产业四个行业中类。

辖区内年营业收入500万元及以上服务业法人单位。包括：居民服务、修理和其他服务业，文化、体育和娱乐业两个门类，以及社会工作行业大类。

固定资产原价 指固定资产的成本，包括企业在购置、自行建造、安装、改建、扩建、技术改造某项固定资产时所发生的全部支出总额。根据会计“固定资产”科目的期末借方余额填报。

资产总计 指企业过去的交易或者事项形成的、由企业拥有或者控制的、预期会给企业带来经济利益的资源。包括企业拥有的土地、办公楼、厂房、机器、运输工具、存货等实物资产和现金、存款、应收账款和预付账款等金融资产。资产一般按流动性（资产的变现或耗用时间长短）分为流动资产和非流动资产。其中流动资产可分为货币资金、交易性金融资产、应收票据、应收账款、预付款项、其他应收款、存货等；非流动资产可分为长期股权投资、固定资产、无形资产及其他非流动资产等。根据会计“资产负债表”中“资产总计”项目的期末余额数填报。

负债合计 指企业过去的交易或者事项形成的，预期会导致经济利益流出企业的现时义务。包括银行贷款、借款、应付账款、应付职工工资、应付职工福利费、应交税金等企业负有偿还责任的债务。根据会计“资产负债表”中“负债合计”项目的期末余额数填报。

负债一般按偿还期长短分为流动负债和非流动负债。根据会计资产负债表中“负债合计”项目的期末余额数填报。执行企业会计准则或《小企业会计准则》的企业：负债合计=流动负债合计+非流动负债合计；执行其他企业会计制度的企业负债包括流动负债和长期负债。

所有者权益合计 指企业资产扣除负债后由所有者享有的剩余权益。公司的所有者权益又称股东权益。包括实收资本、资本公积、盈余公积、未分配利润等。根据会计“资产负债表”中“所有者权益合计”项目的期末余额数填报。

营业收入 指企业从事销售商品、提供劳务和让渡资产使用权等生产经营活动形成的经济利益流入。营业收入包括“主营业务收入”和“其他业务收入”。根据会计“利润表”中“营业收入”项目的本年累计数填报。

营业成本 指企业从事销售商品、提供劳务和让渡资产使用权等生产经营活动发生的实际成本。“营业成本”应当与“营业收入”进行配比。包括“主营业务成本”和“其他业务成本”。根据会计“利润表”中“营业成本”项目的本年累计数填报。

销售费用 指企业在销售商品和材料、提供劳务的过程中发生的各种费用，包括保险费、包装费、展览费和广告费、商品维修费、预计产品质量保证损失、运输费、装卸费等以及为销售本企业商品而专设的销售机构（含销售网点、售后服务网点等）的职工薪酬、业务费、折旧费等经营费用。建筑业企业销售费用指企业从事施工生产活动过程中发生的各项费用，包括应由企业负担的运输费、装卸费、包装费、保险费、维修费、展览费、差旅费、广告费和其他经费。房地产企业销售费用指企业在从事主要经营业务过程中所发生的各项销售费用，包括转让、销售、结算和出租开发产品等。执行企业会计准则或《小企业会计准则》的企业,根据会计“利润表”中“销售费用”项目的本年累计数填报。执行其他企业会计制度的企业，根据会计“利润表”中“营业费用（或经营费用）”项目的本年累计数填报。

管理费用 指企业为组织和管理企业生产经营所发生的费用，包括企业在筹建期间内发生的开办费、董事会和行政管理部门在企业经营管理中发生的，或者应当由企业统一负担的公司经费等。为了与财政部《关于修订印发2019年度一般企业财务报表格式的通知》（财会〔2019〕6号）保持一致，“管理费用”不包含“研发费用”。执行企业会计准则的企业,根据会计“利润表”中“管理费用”项目的本年累计数填报。执行《小企业会计准则》的企业,应将会计“利润表”中“管理费用”项目本年累计数减“研究费用”项目本年累计数后填报。执行其他企业会计制度的企业以及未执行财政部《关于修订印发2019年度一般企业财务报表格式的通知》（财会〔2019〕6号）的企业，在会计“利润表”中“管理费用”项目的本年累计数的基础上，根据会计“管理费用”科目下的“研究费用”相关明细科目，将“研发费用”剔除后填报。

研发费用 指企业在新知识、新技术、新产品、新工艺等的研究与开发过程中发生的费用化支出。主要包括研发活动的人工费用、直接投入费用、用于研发活动的仪器、设备的折旧费、用于研发活动的软件、专利权、非专利技术的摊销费用、新产品设计费、新工艺规程制定费以及其他研发活动相关费用。执行企业会计准则的企业,根据会计“利润表”中“研发费用”项目的本年累计数填报。执行《小企业会计准则》的企业,根据会计“利润表”中“研究费用”项目的本年累计数填报。执行其他企业会计制度的企业以及会计“利润表”未列示“研发费用”或“研究费用”的企业，根据会计“管理费用”科目下“研究费用”相关科目的本期发生额填报。

财务费用 指企业为筹集生产经营所需资金等而发生的筹资费用，包括企业生产经营期间发生的利息支出（减利息收入）、汇兑损失（减汇兑收益）以及相关的手续费等。根据会计“利润表”中“财务费用”项目的本年累计数填报。

投资收益 指企业确认的投资收益或投资损失，反映企业以各种方式对外投资所取得的收益。根据会计“利润表”中“投资收益”项目的本年累计数填报。如为投资损失以“–”号记。

营业利润 指企业从事生产经营活动所取得的利润。执行《企业会计准则》或《小企业会计准则》的企业，营业利润为营业收入减去营业成本、税金及附加、销售费用、管理费用、财务费用、研发费用、资产减值损失、信用减值损失，再加上公允价值变动收益、资产处置收益、投资收益、净敞口套期收益和其他收益。执行其他企业会计制度的企业，营业利润为营业收入减去营业成本、税金及附加，加上其他业务利润后，再减去销售费用、管理费用、财务费用、研发费用后的金额，应符合以下逻辑关系：营业利润等于营业收入减去营业成本、税金及附加、销售费用、管理费用、财务费用、研发费用。根据会计“利润表”中“营业利润”项目的本年累计数填报。

利润总额 指企业在一定会计期间的经营成果，是生产经营过程中各种收入扣除各种耗费后的盈余，反映企业在报告期内实现的盈亏总额。根据会计“利润表”中“利润总额”项目的本年累计数填报。执行《企业会计准则》或《小企业会计准则》的企业，利润总额为营业利润加上营业外收入，减去营业外支出后的金额；执行其他企业会计制度的企业，利润总额为营业利润加上投资收益、营业外收入，再减去营业外支出后的金额。

应付职工薪酬（本年贷方累计发生额） 指企业为获得职工提供的服务或解除劳动关系而给予的各种形式的报酬或补偿。包括职工工资、奖金、津贴和补贴，职工福利费，医疗保险费、养老保险费、失业保险费、工伤保险费和生育保险费等社会保险费，住房公积金，工会经费和职工教育经费，带薪缺勤，利润分享计划，非货币性福利，辞退福利和其他为获得职工提供的服务而给予的报酬或补偿。如果企业财务报告附注中包含“应付职工薪酬”项目，则根据其“应付职工薪酬列示”部分的合计项的本期增加额填报。或者，执行企业会计准则或《小企业会计准则》的企业，根据会计“应付职工薪酬”科目的本年贷方累计发生额填报；执行其他企业会计制度的企业，应将本年上述职工薪酬包含的项目归并填报。

如果企业“应付职工薪酬”会计科目的核算范围不包含“劳务派遣人员薪酬”，则应加“劳务派遣人员薪酬”后填报；如果企业“应付职工薪酬”会计科目的核算范围已包含“劳务派遣人员薪酬”，但不设置明细科目单独核算，则不对“应付职工薪酬”指标作特殊处理，避免“劳务派遣人员薪酬”重复计入。

平均用工人数 指报告期内（年度、月度）企业平均拥有的从事服务业活动的人员数。按“谁用工，谁统计”的原则实施统计，包括参加企业服务业活动的正式人员，劳务派遣人员和临时聘用人员。不包括在本企业领取工资、股息、红利、未参加服务业活动的人员。

Explanatory Notes on Main Statistical Indicators

Statistical standard of the services unit above the designated size of the National Bureau of Statistics: The legal entities of the area whoseannual revenues are10 million yuan and above, or at the end of the service sector whose employees are more than 50 people.Including: transportation, storage and postal services, information transmission, software and information technology services, leasing and business services, scientific research and technological services, water conservancy, environment and public facilities management industry, education, health and social work as well as property management and real estate services industries.The legal entitiesof the area whoseannual revenues are 5 million yuan and above, or at the end of the service sector whose employees are more than 50 people.Including: service, repair and other services, cultural, sports and entertainment.

Original value of fixed assets: It refers to the cost of fixed assets, including the enterprise itself costs on the acquisition, construction, installation, alteration, expansion, technological innovation of an asset for all expenditure. Depending on the "fixed assets" account debit balance at the end of filling.

Total assets: It refers to the resourcesformed by past transactions or events, that the enterprise owns or controls, is expected to bring economic benefits to the enterprise. Asset is classified into current assets and non-current assets by its liquidity (realization of assets or spent time). Current assets can be divided into currency, tradable financial assets, notes receivable, accounts receivable, prepayments, other receivables and inventory; and non-current assets can be classified as equity investments, fixed assets, intangible assets and other non-current assets. It depends on the "balance sheet" of "total assets" closing balance number of items.

For business enterprisesthat implemented the 2006 accounting standard: total assets= total current assets +total non-current assets; for those who didn't implement the accounting standards, assets for business enterprises include current assets, long-term investments, fixed assets, intangible assets and other assets.

Total liabilities: It refers tothe present obligations of the enterprise that formed by past transactions or events and are expected to lead to an outflow of economic benefits. Liability is divided into current and non-current liabilities according to the length of the repayment period. It depends onthe "balance sheets" in the "total" closing balance number of items.

For business enterprises that implemented the 2006 accounting standard: total liabilities = total current liabilities+ total non-current liabilities; for those who didn't implement the accounting standards, liabilities include current liabilities and long-term liabilities.

Totalowners ' equity: It refers to the residual rights and interests enjoyed by the owner after deducting the liabilities of an enterprise. The owner of the company is also called the shareholder's right. It includes the paid in capital, capital reserves, surplus reserves, undistributed profit and so on. According to the accounting "balance sheet", "the owner's equity total", the final balance of the project is reported.

Operating income: It refers to the total revenue recognized by the business and other business operations of the enterprise. Total operating income includes "main business income" and "other business income". It's reported according to the "business income" project of the "business income" in the accounting "profit statement".

The main business income: It refers to the income of the business of the main business, such as the sale of goods, services, etc..It's reported in accordance with the final credit balance of the accounts of the subject's "main business income" (before the transfer). For business enterprises that didn't implement the accounting standard, if not set up the subject, should fill the forms instead of the "operating income".

Operating cost: It refers to the total cost incurred by the business and other business of the enterprise. It includes a variety of costs of enterprises (units) in the reporting period to engage in sales of goods, services and other daily activities provided.It includes"the main business costs" and "other business costs". According to the "operating cost" of the "business cost" of the project in accordance with the accounting statement.

The main business cost: It refers to the total cost of the main business. It's reported in accordance with the final debit balance of the subject of accounting "main business cost". For business enterprises that didn't implement the accounting standard, if not set up the subject, should fill the forms instead of the "operating costs".

Selling expenses: It refers to the expenses of the enterprisein sales of goods and materials and providing services, including insurance, packing, exhibition fees and advertising fees, maintenance of commodity, expected to ensure product quality loss, transportation, loading and unloading charges and sales of the enterprise products and dedicated sales organizations (including sales network and after-sales service network) employee compensation, business expenses, depreciation charges and operating expenses. Construction enterprises selling expenses refers to expenses occurring in the process of production enterprises engaged in construction activities, including transportation fee shall be borne by the enterprise, handling, packing, insurance, maintenance, exhibition fees, poor travel costs, advertising costs and other expenses. Real estate enterprise sales cost refers to the business in the main business process of the sales costs, including transfer, sales, settlement and rental development products, etc.. According to the "sales expense" in accounting "profit statement", the amount of the item in this period of the project is reported. For business enterprises that didn't implement the 2006 accounting standard, according to the number of "operating expenses (or operating expenses)" of the project in accordance with the "profit statement".

Management expenses: It refers to the expenses for the organization and management of enterprise production and management of the enterprises, including costs in construction occurred during the start-up costs, the board of directors and administrative departments in enterprise management, or shall be made by the enterprise unified burden of company funds. According to the "management fee" in the accounting "profit table", the amount of this period of the project is reported.

Financial expenses: It refers to the costs of the enterprise to raise the production and business operation required capital and funding, including occurred during the production and operation of enterprises interest payments (a reduction in interest income), exchange loss (less exchange gains) and related fees. It is reported according to the amount of the "financial expense" in the project of "financial expense" in the accounting "profit statement".

Investment income: It refers to the enterprise confirming the investment income or investment losses, reflecting the foreign investment income of the enterprise in various ways. According to the "investment income" in the accounting "profit statement", the amount of this period of the project is reported. Such as investment losses to "-".

Operating profit: It refers tothe profits made by the enterprises in the production and operation activities. For business enterprises that implemented the 2006 accounting standard, operating profit is revenues minus operating costs, business taxes and surcharges, sales, management costs, financial costs, asset impairment loss and plus fair value changes in income and investment income. Without executing the "accounting standards for business enterprises" enterprises, operating profit equals the main business income minus the cost of major business, main business tax and surcharges, and plus profit from other operations, then minus the cost of sales and management costs, financial costs. It is reported according to the number of "operating profit" items in the accounting "profit table".

Total profit: It refers to the business results of the enterprise in a certain accounting period, and it is the production and operation of various kinds of income after deducting the cost of earnings, reflecting the enterprise in the reporting period to achieve total profit and loss. According to the amount of the total amount of the total profit of the project in accordance with the accounting profit table. For business enterprises that implemented the 2006 accounting standard, the total profit is operating profit plus operating income, andminus operating expenses; while who didn't execute the " accounting standards for business enterprises", a total profit is operating profit plus return on investment, income subsidies, camp outside the industry income, andminus operating expenses.

Employee compensation: It refers tovarious forms of remuneration and other related expenses paid by the company for the services provided by the staff and workers. It includes wages, bonuses, allowances and subsidies, employee welfare benefit expenses, medical insurance, endowment insurance, unemployment insurance, work-related injury insurance premiums and maternity insurance fees social insurance, housing provident fund, the trade union funds and employee education funds, non-monetary benefits, for the solution in addition to give labor relations and workers compensation, and obtain a worker to provide other services related expenditure. For business enterprises that implemented the accounting standard, according to accounting subjects "to deal with workers' compensation" this year, the accumulated credits is filled; those who didn't execute the "accounting standards for business enterprises", it should be the employee compensation including the amalgamative course reportingthis year.

Average number of persons engaged in service

activities: It refers to the number of persons engaged in the service industry in the reporting period (annual, monthly). The principles of statistics is implemented according to the principle that "who labor, who statistics," including the official personnel, labor sent contingent personnel and temporaryemployeeswho take part in the enterprise service activities. And it don't include employees who receive wages, dividends, bonusas well as not participate in the service activities of the enterprise.

19 金融业

FINANCIAL INTERMEDIATION

资料整理：孟　刚
Data management:Meng Gang
数据审核：刘　婷
Data audit：Liu Ting

第十九部分　金融业

一、简要说明

本章资料包括金融、证券和保险业情况，由西安市统计局综合处根据人民银行西安分行营业管理部和市金融工作局提供资料整理。本部分银行、保险类为西安原口径数据，证券类含西咸新区。

二、主要指标

金融机构人民币（含外资）存款余额（亿元）	23066.85	比上年增长	10.1%
金融机构人民币（含外资）贷款余额（亿元）	22264.12	比上年增长	12.8%
保费收入（亿元）	522.85	比上年增长	9.3%

19　FINANCIAL INTERMEDIATION

Ⅰ.Brief Introduction

This chapter includes information of the financial, securities and insurance, compiled by Integration Division of the Xi'an Bureau of Statistics, according to data from Xi'an Branch Management Department of the People's Bank of China, Provincial Banking Bureau and Xi'an Financial Office. Data in this chapter is based on original range.

Ⅱ.Major Indicators

		Increase over Preceding Year
Deposits in Financial Institution(100 mil. yuan)	23066.85	10.1%
Loans in Financial Institutions(100 mil.yuan)	22264.12	12.8%
Premiums(100 mil. yuan)	522.85	9.3%

19-1 西安银行系统机构、人员数

Number of Institution and Employed Person in Finance System in Xi'an

机构名称	Name of Institution	2018 机构数（个）Number of Institution (unit)	2018 年末人数（人）Number of Staff and Workers (person)	2019 机构数（个）Number of Institution (unit)	2019 年末人数（人）Number of Staff and Workers (person)
合计	**Total**	**2111**	**39172**	**2106**	**38962**
1. 人民银行西安分行营业管理部	Management Department of the People's Bank of China Xi'an Branch	1	355	1	357
2. 国家开发银行	National Development Bank	1	205	1	211
3. 中国进出口银行	Export Import Bank of China	1	77	1	76
4. 中国工商银行	Industrial and Commercial Bank of China	183	4562	181	4472
5. 中国农业银行	Agricultural Bank of China	166	3093	164	3093
6. 中国银行	Bank of China	129	3438	132	3335
7. 中国建设银行	Construction Bank of China	204	4374	203	4443
8. 交通银行	Bank of Communication	59	1191	59	1202
9. 中国邮政储蓄银行	The Postal Savings Bank of China	270	866	268	982
10. 中国农业发展银行	Agricultural Development Bank of China	11	280	11	280
11. 中信银行	CITIC Bank	29	852	29	861
12. 中国光大银行	China Everbright Bank	45	915	42	943
13. 华夏银行	China Huaxia Bank	24	797	25	747
14. 广发银行	China Guangfa Bank	9	206	11	218
15. 平安银行	Pingan Bank	12	404	16	427
16. 招商银行	China Merchants Bank	55	1535	55	1552
17. 上海浦东发展银行	Pufa Bank	35	665	31	703
18. 兴业银行	Fujian Industrial Bank	60	825	56	819
19. 中国民生银行	China Minsheng Banking	22	1086	22	1066
20. 恒丰银行	Evergrowing Bank	17	417	17	467
21. 浙商银行	China Zheshang Bank	10	490	10	487
22. 渤海银行	China Bohai Bank	2	133	2	125
23. 北京银行	Bank of Beijing	24	813	25	799
24. 齐商银行	Qi Commercial Bank	8	221	8	214
25. 成都银行	Bank of Chengdu	6	177	6	173
26. 重庆银行	Bank of Chongqing	6	290	7	283
27. 宁夏银行	Bank of Ningxia	7	230	7	204
28. 昆仑银行	Bank of Kunlun	15	447	16	465
29. 西安银行	Bank of Xi'an	144	2596	144	2581
30. 长安银行	Bank of Changan	59	710	59	673
31. 农村商业银行	Rural Commercial Bank	406	5503	406	5321
其中：秦农银行	Qinnong Bank	298	4380	298	4264
32. 农村信用社	Rural Credit Cooperatives	67	841	67	810
33. 村镇银行	Village Bank	11	248	12	259
34. 香港汇丰银行	Huifeng Bank of Hong Kong	3	40	2	40
35. 香港东亚银行	Dongya Bank of Hong Kong	6	177	6	157
36. 新加坡星展银行	DBS Bank	1	15	1	15
37. 英国标准渣打银行	British Standard Chartered Bank	1	34	1	31
38. 韩亚银行	Hana Bank	1	37	1	40
39. 富邦华一银行	Fubon Bank	1	27	1	31

注：本表数据来源于人民银行西安分行营管部，为西安原口径数据（下同，除证券类）。

19-2 金融机构（含外资）本外币存贷款年末余额（2019年）

Deposits and Loans of Local Currency and Foreign Currency in Financial Institution (Including Foreign-Funded Institution)at Year-end（2019）

单位：万元　　　　(10 000 yuan)

指　标	Item	2019	比年初增减额 Increase or Decrease Compared with The Beginning of The Year
一、各项存款	**All Deposits**	**233408354**	**20700807**
（一）境内存款	Domestic Deposits	233129538	20674987
1. 住户存款	Household Deposits	96532904	11845218
（1）活期存款	Demand Deposits	35494436	2798118
（2）定期及其他存款	Time and Other Deposits	61038468	9047100
2. 非金融企业存款	Non Financial Enterprises Deposits	89127014	5953892
（1）活期存款	Demand Deposits	45693244	1554544
（2）定期及其他存款	Time and Other Deposits	43433770	4399348
3. 机关团体存款	Institution Deposits	36364142	613565
4. 财政性存款	Fiscal Deposits	1958869	447444
5. 非银行业金融机构存款	Non Banking Financial Institution Deposits	9146609	1814868
（二）境外存款	Foreign Deposits	278816	25820
二、各项贷款	**All Loans**	**224366472**	**25206600**
（一）境内贷款	Domestic Loans	224176334	25222649
1. 住户贷款	Household loans	63135518	10804526
（1）短期贷款	Short-term Loans	8286883	2189299
消费贷款	Consumer loans	5745225	1838879
经营贷款	Business loans	2541658	350420
（2）中长期贷款	Medium-term and Long-term loans	54848635	8615227
消费贷款	Consumer loans	50481568	7896313
经营贷款	Business loans	4367067	718913
2. 非金融企业及机关团体贷款	Non Financial Enterprises and Institution Loans	161038958	14418123
（1）短期贷款	Short-term Loans	31292722	2895863
（2）中长期贷款	Medium-term and Long-term loans	117140179	9305313
（3）票据融资	Bill Financing	12451027	2322282
（4）融资租赁	Financial Leasing	989	-6107
（5）各项垫款	Various Advance Funds	154042	-99227
3. 非银行业金融机构贷款	Non Banking Financial Institution Loans	1857	
（二）境外贷款	Foreign Loans	190138	-16049

注：本表数据来源于人民银行西安分行营管部。

19-3 金融机构（不含外资）本外币存贷款年末余额（2019年）

Deposits and Loans Domestic Funded Financial Institution of Local Currency and Foreign Currency at Year-end（2019）

单位：万元 (10 000 yuan)

指 标	Item	2019	比年初增减额 Increase or Decrease Compared with The Beginning of The Year
一、各项存款	**All Deposits**	**231506700**	**20365162**
（一）境内存款	Domestic Deposits	231256142	20341304
1. 住户存款	Household Deposits	96340171	11858651
（1）活期存款	Demand Deposits	35433501	2794519
（2）定期及其他存款	Time and Other Deposits	60906670	9064131
2. 非金融企业存款	Non Financial Enterprises Deposits	87446902	5584214
（1）活期存款	Demand Deposits	45464652	1619043
（2）定期及其他存款	Time and Other Deposits	41982250	3965171
3. 机关团体存款	Institution Deposits	36363590	616127
4. 财政性存款	Fiscal Deposits	1958869	447444
5. 非银行业金融机构存款	Non Banking Financial Institution Deposits	9146609	1834868
（二）境外存款	Foreign Deposits	250558	23858
二、各项贷款	**All Loans**	**223038756**	**25101750**
（一）境内贷款	Domestic Loans	222875940	25117505
1. 住户贷款	Household loans	63058395	10811916
（1）短期贷款	Short-term Loans	8286473	2188889
消费贷款	Consumer loans	5745225	1838879
经营贷款	Business loans	2541248	350010
（2）中长期贷款	Medium-term and Long-term loans	54771922	8623026
消费贷款	Consumer loans	50416665	7900433
经营贷款	Business loans	4355257	722593
2. 非金融企业及机关团体贷款	Non Financial Enterprises and Institution Loans	159815688	14305589
（1）短期贷款	Short-term Loans	30847347	2654826
（2）中长期贷款	Medium-term and Long-term loans	116367686	9421071
（3）票据融资	Bill Financing	12445625	2335004
（4）融资租赁	Financial Leasing	989	-6107
（5）各项垫款	Various Advance Funds	154042	-99205
3. 非银行业金融机构贷款	Non Banking Financial Institution Loans	1857	
（二）境外贷款	Foreign Loans	162816	-15755

注：本表数据来源于人民银行西安分行营管部。

19-4 主要年份金融机构（含外资）人民币存贷款年末余额

Deposits and Loans in Financial Institutions (Including Foreign-funded) in Representative Years

单位：亿元 (100million yuan)

年 份 Year	存款年末余额 Balance of Deposit at Year-end	非金融企业存款 Non Financial Enterprises Deposits	住户存款 Household Deposits	贷款年末余额 Balance of Loan at Year-end
1978	11.66		2.57	21.72
1980	17.02		4.22	23.08
1985	40.64		14.26	49.08
1990	146.17	31.10	77.09	152.77
1995	471.89	114.54	291.46	403.16
1996	619.98	199.85	394.02	477.97
1997	686.72	227.61	433.56	503.32
1998	799.54	245.44	499.68	597.34
1999	1014.27	347.49	586.40	786.20
2000	1335.63	540.19	675.83	972.51
2001	1629.72	674.49	800.86	1185.97
2002	2191.47	884.69	988.04	1598.42
2003	2665.87	1041.43	1210.56	1954.18
2004	3061.66	1159.98	1432.86	2052.33
2005	3599.70	1237.37	1716.76	2158.10
2006	4066.16	1374.91	1950.53	2344.77
2007	4582.71	1702.12	2002.38	2683.77
2008	5749.37	2213.67	2513.70	3275.12
2009	7522.08	3077.99	3084.20	4482.63
2010	8933.23	3556.78	3641.09	6482.28
2011	10430.27	5997.60	4155.65	7564.93
2012	12125.53	6927.84	4787.03	8635.22
2013	13763.19	7759.61	5357.05	10023.63
2014	15166.78	8604.03	5698.15	11668.14
2015	17796.38	7031.75	6571.18	13714.02
2016	19073.96	7788.07	7035.81	15282.65
2017	20047.62	8203.27	7497.30	16954.81
2018	20948.18	8125.23	8360.33	19729.82
2019	23066.85	8756.48	9553.29	22264.12

注：本表数据来源于人民银行西安分行营管部，对部分历史年份数据进行了修订。

19-5　金融机构（含外资）人民币存贷款年末余额（2019年）

Year-end Balance of RMB Deposits and Loans in Financial Institutions（Including Foreign-funded）(2019)

单位：万元　　(10 000 yuan)

指　标	Item	2019	比年初增减额 Increase or Decrease Compared with The Beginning of The Year
一、各项存款	**All Deposits**	**230668531**	**21147218**
（一）境内存款	Domestic Deposits	230533432	21141232
1. 住户存款	Household Deposits	95532902	11897765
（1）活期存款	Demand Deposits	34973532	2835511
（2）定期及其他存款	Time and Other Deposits	60559371	9062254
2. 非金融企业存款	Non Financial Enterprises Deposits	87564763	6322393
（1）活期存款	Demand Deposits	44990794	1767213
（2）定期及其他存款	Time and Other Deposits	42573969	4555180
3. 机关团体存款	Institution Deposits	36334590	610041
4. 财政性存款	Fiscal Deposits	1958869	447444
5. 非银行业金融机构存款	Non Banking Financial Institution Deposits	9142307	1863589
（二）境外存款	Foreign Deposits	135099	5986
二、各项贷款	**All Loans**	**222641217**	**25100443**
（一）境内贷款	Domestic Loans	222634751	25106559
1. 住户贷款	Household loans	63132490	10804491
（1）短期贷款	Short-term Loans	8283955	2189318
消费贷款	Consumer loans	5742297	1838897
经营贷款	Business loans	2541658	350420
（2）中长期贷款	Medium-term and Long-term loans	54848535	8615173
消费贷款	Consumer loans	50481468	7896260
经营贷款	Business loans	4367067	718913
2. 非金融企业及机关团体贷款	Non Financial Enterprises and Institution Loans	159500404	14302068
（1）短期贷款	Short-term Loans	30325902	2737342
（2）中长期贷款	Medium-term and Long-term loans	116569289	9347647
（3）票据融资	Bill Financing	12451027	2322282
（4）融资租赁	Financial Leasing	989	-6107
（5）各项垫款	Various Advance Funds	153198	-99095
3. 非银行业金融机构贷款	Non Banking Financial Institution Loans	1857	
（二）境外贷款	Foreign Loans	6466	-6116

注：本表数据来源于人民银行西安分行营管部。

19-6 金融机构（不含外资）人民币存贷款年末余额（2019年）

Year-end Balance of RMB Deposits and Loans in Financial Institutions (Not Including Foreign-funded)（2019）

单位：万元 (10 000 yuan)

指 标	Item	2019	比年初增减额 Increase or Decrease Compared with The Beginning of The Year
一、各项存款	**All Deposits**	**228918845**	**20759799**
（一）境内存款	Domestic Deposits	228792660	20754967
1. 住户存款	Household Deposits	95389007	11911034
（1）活期存款	Demand Deposits	34933274	2834336
（2）定期及其他存款	Time and Other Deposits	60455733	9076698
2. 非金融企业存款	Non Financial Enterprises Deposits	85968439	5900297
（1）活期存款	Demand Deposits	44802634	1759548
（2）定期及其他存款	Time and Other Deposits	41165805	4140749
3. 机关团体存款	Institution Deposits	36334038	612603
4. 财政性存款	Fiscal Deposits	1958869	447444
5. 非银行业金融机构存款	Non Banking Financial Institution Deposits	9142307	1883589
（二）境外存款	Foreign Deposits	126185	4832
二、各项贷款	**All Loans**	**221352301**	**25000978**
（一）境内贷款	Domestic Loans	221346284	25006855
1. 住户贷款	Household loans	63055366	10811880
（1）短期贷款	Short-term Loans	8283545	2188908
消费贷款	Consumer loans	5742297	1838897
经营贷款	Business loans	2541248	350010
（2）中长期贷款	Medium-term and Long-term loans	54771821	8622972
消费贷款	Consumer loans	50416564	7900380
经营贷款	Business loans	4355257	722593
2. 非金融企业及机关团体贷款	Non Financial Enterprises and Institution Loans	158289060	14194975
（1）短期贷款	Short-term Loans	29892453	2501746
（2）中长期贷款	Medium-term and Long-term loans	115796795	9463406
（3）票据融资	Bill Financing	12445625	2335004
（4）融资租赁	Financial Leasing	989	-6107
（5）各项垫款	Various Advance Funds	153198	-99074
3. 非银行业金融机构贷款	Non Banking Financial Institution Loans	1857	
（二）境外贷款	Foreign Loans	6017	-5877

注：本表数据来源于人民银行西安分行营管部。

19-7 保险业务情况

Indicators of Insurance Business

单位：万元 (10 000 yuan)

指　标	Item	2015	2016	2017	2018	2019
保费收入	**Premiums**	**2630158**	**3458459**	**4211039**	**4785554**	**5228513**
一、财产险	**Property Insurance**	**835526**	**933181**	**1037060**	**1125618**	**1062003**
（一）财产保险	Property Insurance	746317	833296	916524	959618	868183
1. 机动车辆及第三者责任	Motor Vehicle and Outside Person Liability	674555	738965	821186	862137	759314
2. 企业财产险	Enterprise Property Insurance	49949	64568	62226	65716	73996
3. 货物运输险	Freight Transport Insurance	5497	4814	5314	6777	7230
4. 家庭财产险	Family Property Insurance	754	981	1385	1772	1436
5. 建工及安工保险及其责任险	Construction and Installation Projects Insurance and Related Liability Insurance	12325	18368	20001	17174	17067
6. 其他	Others	3237	5600	6412	6042	9140
（二）责任保险	Liability Insurance	23096	26922	32136	38508	54267
（三）信用保险	Export Credit Insurance	10449	17563	14733	10114	9128
（四）保证保险	Guarantee Insurance	45472	42665	60814	100393	112277
（五）农业保险	Agriculture Insurance	10192	12735	12853	16985	18148
二、人身险	**Personnel Insurance**	**1794632**	**2525278**	**3173979**	**3659936**	**4166510**
（一）人寿保险	Life Insurance	1506062	2158260	2625509	3023129	3313934
1. 普通寿险	General Life Insurance	681952	1261138	1554807	1355990	1653013
2. 分红保险	Dividend Insurance	810889	882110	1055099	1651416	1645508
3. 投资连接保险	Insurance Connection Insurance	286	236	217	212	280
4. 万能保险	Universal Insurance	12935	14776	15386	15512	15133
（二）意外伤害险	Unforeseen Injury Insurance	63450	71888	84603	112382	145991
（三）健康保险	Health Insurance	225120	295130	463867	524426	706585
赔款支出和各项给付	**Indemnity and Other Expenditure**	**876182**	**1159143**	**1187057**	**1308241**	**1414228**
一、财产险	**Property Insurance**	**406530**	**422765**	**489353**	**553641**	**617430**
（一）财产保险	Property Insurance	375449	393905	452892	497773	537006
1. 机动车辆及第三者责任	Motor Vehicle and Outside Person Liability	348185	359288	393011	459840	487263
2. 企业财产险	Enterprise Property Insurance	16753	22038	30811	20020	23175
3. 家庭财产保险	Family Property Insurance	112	324	757	4565	3255
4. 货物运输保险	Freight Transport Insurance	999	1341	2427	1376	864
5. 建工及安工保险及其责任险	Construction and Installation Projects Insurance and Related Liability Insurance	8023	9741	12471	9663	8136
6. 其他	Others	1377	1173	13414	2309	14314
（二）责任保险	Liability Insurance	6300	11030	12703	14948	20710
（三）信用保险	Export Credit Insurance	7884	3287	3346	5273	3384
（四）保证保险	Guarantee Insurance	13129	10690	11597	23608	48247
（五）农业保险	Agriculture Insurance	3768	3853	8816	12039	8082
二、人身险	**Personnel Insurance**	**469652**	**736378**	**697704**	**754600**	**796798**
（一）人寿保险	Life Insurance	379370	637444	557798	581062	565089
1. 普通寿险	General Life Insurance	56908	82635	136279	138591	136772
2. 分红保险	Dividend Insurance	318993	551206	418013	438997	424665
3. 投资连接保险	Insurance Connection Insurance	48	485	162	35	4
4. 万能保险	Universal Insurance	3421	3118	3344	3438	3647
（二）意外伤害险	Unforeseen Injury Insurance	16796	15577	19939	23621	30778
（三）健康保险	Health Insurance	73486	83357	119967	149917	200930
退保金	**Withdrawal**	**433227**	**482983**	**682534**	**762277**	**617446**
#人寿保险	Life Insurance	414260	459733	659965	751597	588932
1. 普通寿险	General Life Insurance	195551	276544	524211	582955	368570
2. 分红保险	Dividend Insurance	218693	183191	135723	168632	220354
3. 投资连接保险	Insurance Connection Insurance					
4. 万能保险	Universal Insurance	16	-2	31	11	7

注：本表数据来源于市金融工作局。

19-8 西安地区证券期货系统机构、人员数（2019年）

Number of Institution and Employed Person in Securities and Futures System in Xi'an (2019)

机构名称	Name of Institution	2018		2019	
		机构数（个）Number of Institution (unit)	年末人数（人）Number of Staff and Workers (person)	机构数（个）Number of Institution (unit)	年末人数（人）Number of Staff and Workers (person)
一、证券经营机构总数	**Number of Securities Operating Institutions**	**403**	**8718**	**400**	**8688**
1、证券公司机构总数	Number of Securities Companies	225	5102	206	5093
西部证券股份有限公司	Western Securities Company Ltd.	116	2568	115	2375
开源证券股份有限公司	KaiYuan Securities Company Ltd.	75	1838	49	1932
中邮证券有限责任公司	China Post Securities	34	696	42	786
2、外地驻我市证券机构总数	Number of Non-Local Securities Institutions In the City	178	3616	194	3595
二、期货公司机构总数	**Number of Futures Companies**	**34**	**552**	**33**	**551**
迈科期货股份有限公司	Maike Futures Company Ltd.	11	214	12	210
长安期货有限公司	ChangAn Company Ltd.	11	193	10	154
西部期货有限公司	Western Futures Brokerage Co., Ltd.	12	145	11	187

注：1.本表数据来源于市金融工作局。
2.证券公司包括三家公司及其在西安和外地的营业部。
3.中邮证券有限责任公司原为西安华弘证券经纪有限责任公司。

19-9 证券期货市场基本情况（2019年）

Basic Facts on Securities and Futures Markets（2019）

指　标	Item	2019
一、上市公司情况	**Listed Securities Companies**	
拥有境内上市股份公司（个）	Number of Domestic Listed Joint-Stock Companies(unit)	37
上市股份公司总股本（亿股）	Total Capital of Listed Share-holding Companies (100 millon shares)	615.18
#流通股(亿股)	Negotiable Shares(100 million shares)	508.42
总市值（亿元）	Total Market Capitalization(100 million yuan)	5667.12
累计证券市场筹措资金（亿元）	Accumulated Securities Market Financing(100 millon yuan)	1864.18
二、证券经营机构情况	**Securities Trading Organizations**	
拥有证券公司（个）	Number of Securities Companies(unit)	3
证券经营机构（个）	Number of Securities Trading Institutions (unit)	400
投资者开户数（万户）	Number of Investors Who have Opened an Account(10 000 accounts)	399.72
证券交易总额（亿元）	Total Turnover(100 million yuan)	45228.64
三、期货市场情况	**Futures Market**	
拥有期货经纪公司（个）	Number of Futures Business Management Companies(unit)	3
期货营业部（个）	Futures Business Department (unit)	33
期货代理交易额（亿元）	Total Transaction Value in Futures Commissioning (100 million yuan)	35797.42
每个经纪公司平均拥有注册资金（亿元）	Average Registered Capital of Each Business Management Company(100 million yuan)	3.93

注：本表数据来源于市金融工作局，期货分支机构、代理交易额数据为西安本市和外地公司在西安市口径数据。

主要统计指标解释

存款 指企业、机关、团体或居民根据资金必须收回的原则，把货币资金存入银行或其他信贷机构保管并取得一定利息的一种信用活动形式。根据存款对象或性质的不同可划分为企业存款、财政存款、机关团体存款、住户存款、信托及委托类存款、其他存款等科目。它是银行信贷资金的主要来源。

贷款 指银行或其他信贷机构根据资金必须归还的原则，按一定利率，为企业、个人等提供资金的一种信用活动形式。我国银行贷款分为短期贷款、中长期贷款、融资租赁、票据融资等。

保险金额 指保险人承担赔偿或者给付保险金责任的最高限额。

保费 指投保人为取得保险人在约定范围内所承担赔偿责任而支付给保险人的费用。

赔款 指保险人根据保险合同的规定，向被保险人支付的赔偿保险责任损失的金额。

给付 包括死伤医疗给付和满期给付。死伤医疗给付是指保险人根据人寿保险及长期健康保险合同的规定，因被保险人在保险期内发生保险责任范围内的保险事故支付给被保险人（或受益人）的金额。满期给付是指被保险人生存期满，保险人按人寿保险合同规定支付给被保险人的满期保险金额。

Explanatory Notes on Main Statistical Indicators

Deposit is a form of credit by which enterprises, institutions, organizations or households can put money into banks and other credit institutions for safekeeping and interest earning under the principle of free withdrawal. According to different depositors, deposits are divided into enterprise deposits, fiscal deposits, deposits of government agencies and organizations, savings deposits of rural and household deposits, agricultural savings deposits, entrusted deposits and other deposits. Deposits are major sources of the credit funds of banks.

Loan is a form of credit by which banks and other credit institutions provide funds at certain interest rate to enterprises and individuals in the light of the principle of unconditional repayment. Loans from Chinese banks include short-term loan, medium and long term loans, finance lease and other bill finance.

Amount Insured refers to the maximum that the insurant will get for the claim of the case insured.

Premium is the fee paid by the insurant to the insurer to obtain the obligation of compensation from the insurance within the agreed terms.

Settled Claim is the compensation paid by the insurer to the insurant in accordance with the insurance contract.

Payment includes payment for death, injury or medical treatment and payment at maturity. Payment for death, injury or medical treatment refers to the money paid to the insurant (or the beneficiary) in accordance with the life or health insurance contract when the insurant encounters accidents within the insured period covered in the contract. Payment at maturity refers to the payment to the insurant in accordance with the life insurance contract at the end of the insured period.

20 教育和科技

EDUCATION, SCIENCE AND TECHNOLOGY

资料整理：郝　静　刘志杰
Data management：Hao Jing　Liu Zhijie
数据审核：刘栋婷
Data audit：Liu Dongting

第二十部分　教育和科技

一、简要说明

本章资料包括教育事业、科技事业基本情况，由西安市统计局服务业和社会科技处根据西安市教育局等有关部门提供资料整理。本章资料数据口径见表下备注。科技部分因数据来源较晚，故从2018年起错年使用。

二、主要指标

普通高等学校数（所）	63	与上年	持平
普通高等学校（本专科）在校学生（万人）	74.01	比上年增加	2.73万人
高等学校研究生在校人数（万人）	13.13	比上年增加	1.97万人

20　EDUCATION,SCIENCE AND TECHNOLOGY

Ⅰ.Brief Introduction

Data in this chapter consists of primarily data of educational undertakings, science and technology activities of Xi'an city, compiled by Tertiary Industry and Social & Science and Technology Division of the Xi'an Bureau of Statistics according to data from Xi'an Bureau of Education concerned. Field and range of data are Listed in the explanatory notes below the chart. Due to the late source of science and technology data. the information content provides the data of 2018.

Ⅱ Major Indicators

		Increase over Preceding Year
Number of Regular Institutions of Higher Education(unit)	63	essentially on a par with last year's
Student Enrollment of Regular Institutions of Higher Education (Universities and colleges) (10 000 persons)	74.01	2.73 (10 000 persons)
Postgraduates Enrollment of Regular Institutions of Higher Education (10 000 persons)	13.13	1.97 (10 000 persons)

20-1 主要年份各类普通教育基本情况

Basic Statistics on Regular Eduction in Representative Years

指 标	Item	2010	2012	2013	2014	2015	2016	2017	2018	2019
学校数（所）	**Number of Schools (units)**									
普通高等学校	Regular Institutions of Higher Educatior	50	62	63	63	63	63	63	63	63
普通中等专业学校	Regular Specialized Secondary Schools	28	24	22	22	20	20	16	15	15
普通中学	Regular Secondary School	436	419	418	421	422	422	448	456	469
小学	Primary Schools	1531	1322	1291	1257	1234	1190	1125	1130	1145
幼儿园	Kindergarten	1004	1239	1295	1343	1417	1475	1605	1780	1839
毕业生人数（万人）	**Graduates (10 000 persons)**									
普通高等学校	Regular Institutions of Higher Educatior	18.3	20.9	20.17	21.27	23.23	24.06	23.07	23.21	22.02
普通中等专业学校	Regular Specialized Secondary Schools	2.5	2.1	1.93	1.76	1.32	1.25	1.06	0.84	0.72
普通中学	Regular Secondary School	17.0	15.6	15.24	14.54	13.92	13.96	13.89	13.50	13.89
小学	Primary Schools	9.6	8.9	8.51	8.29	7.85	8.46	9.06	9.32	10.17
幼儿园	Kindergarten	5.4	7.6	8.42	8.90	10.01	9.81	10.79	11.41	11.85
招生数（万人）	**New Enrollment (10 000 persons)**									
普通高等学校	Regular Institutions of Higher Educatior	21.7	25.2	23.88	23.58	23.41	23.08	23.70	23.67	26.88
普通中等专业学校	Regular Specialized Secondary Schools	2.1	1.7	1.35	1.25	0.95	0.88	0.96	0.83	1.12
普通中学	Regular Secondary School	16.2	15.0	14.47	13.97	13.41	13.72	14.08	14.37	15.29
小学	Primary Schools	8.6	8.9	9.56	10.13	10.51	11.65	13.13	15.16	15.80
幼儿园	Kindergarten	8.4	11.6	11.00	9.55	11.96	13.65	13.98	13.03	12.86
在校学生数（万人）	**Total Enrollment (10 000 persons)**									
普通高等学校	Regular Institutions of Higher Educatior	73.3	80.7	83.83	85.42	84.83	83.10	83.02	82.44	87.14
普通中等专业学校	Regular Specialized Secondary Schools	6.8	5.4	4.66	4.07	3.47	3.11	2.74	2.48	2.79
普通中学	Regular Secondary School	48.9	45.3	43.73	42.57	41.37	40.70	41.74	42.46	43.56
小学	Primary Schools	51.6	50.9	51.95	53.79	56.62	59.79	66.68	73.09	78.98
幼儿园	Kindergarten	18.4	27.1	28.56	28.95	30.90	31.80	34.81	35.40	36.05
教职工数（人）	**Staff and Teachers (persons)**									
普通高等学校	Regular Institutions of Higher Educatior	72247	74041	74993	74954	74857	73686	74218	75609	73688
普通中等专业学校	Regular Specialized Secondary Schools	3249	2733	2599	2315	1991	1917	1556	1529	1386
普通中学	Regular Secondary School	39207	41197	41003	40576	40689	41352	44546	45390	47037
小学	Primary Schools	34118	32208	31863	32162	32585	34646	38494	41122	44511
幼儿园	Kindergarten	18710	27735	31989	33062	36004	39753	44895	49604	52442
专任教师（人）	**Number of Full-time Teachers (persons)**									
普通高等学校	Regular Institutions of Higher Educatior	42098	44487	46436	46766	47768	47158	47917	49018	50236
普通中等专业学校	Regular Specialized Secondary Schools	1845	1595	1474	1346	1228	1210	998	958	918
普通中学	Regular Secondary School	31506	31526	31419	32615	33014	33962	36565	37539	39143
小学	Primary Schools	29944	29651	29421	28395	28748	30941	34163	36878	39836
幼儿园	Kindergarten	10638	14293	16238	17337	19096	21395	23789	25823	26496

注：1.本表数据来源于市教育局。

2.本表中普通高等学校毕业生、招生、在校生数含普通高等学校研究生及普通高等学校本、专科学生。

3.本表中小学的学校数是指独立小学个数，其在校生、教职工等指标均为普通初等教育；幼儿园的校数是指独立的幼儿园个数，其在校生、教职工等指标均为学前教育。（下表同）

4.本表中普通中学学生数据为普通中等教育口径，小学学生数为普通初等教育口径，幼儿园学生数为学前教育口径。

5.本表2017年及以后年份数据含西咸新区。

20-2 各级各类学校、教职工情况（2019年）

Situation of All Kinds of Schools and Staff Members at All Levels （2019）

指 标	Item	学校数（所）Number of Schools (units)	教职工数（人）Number of Staff and Teachers (persons)	专任教师数（人）Full-time Teachers (persons)
一、高等教育	**Higher education**	**75**	**75967**	**51393**
（一）研究生培养机构	Postgraduate training institutions	(43)		
1、普通高校	Institutions of Higher Schools	(22)		
2、科研机构	Scientific Research Institution	(21)		
（二）普通高等学校	Regular Institutions of Higher Schools	63	73688	50236
1、本科院校	Universities and Colleges of Undergraduate Course	44	64650	43929
其中：独立学院	Non-university Tertiary	11	5842	3896
2、专科院校	Higher Vocational Colleges	19	9038	6307
其中：高等职业学校	Higher Vocational College	17	7633	5504
（三）成人高等学校	Adult Higher Schools	12	2279	1157
二、中等职业教育	**Secondary Occupation Education**	**157**	**13744**	**10441**
（一）普通中等专业学校	Regular Specialized Secondary Schools	15	1386	918
（二）成人中等专业学校	Adult Secondary Specialized Schools	2	150	68
（三）职业高中学校	Vocational Hight Schools	60	3801	2685
其中：市属	Municipal schools	60	3801	2685
（四）技工学校	Technical Schools	80	8407	6770
其中：市属	Municipal schools	30	2290	1903
三、基础教育	**Elementary Education**	**3464**	**144436**	**105807**
（一）普通中等教育	Regular Institutions Education	469	47037	39143
1、高中	Senior High Schools	167	25344	21104
完全中学	Complete Secondary Schools	103	14649	12343
高级中学	Senior Secondary Schools	49	7512	6222
十二年一贯制学校	Twelve-year Consistency Schools	15	3183	2539
2、初中	Junior Middle Schools	302	21693	18039
初级中学	Junior Middle Schools	241	15729	13127
九年一贯制学校	Nine-year Consistency Schools	61	5964	4912
完全中学	Complete Secondary school	(103)		
十二年一贯制学校	Twelve-year Consistency schools	(15)		
附设普通初中班的学校	Senior Secondary Schools with Regular Junior Secondary Classes	(1)		
（二）普通初等教育	Regular Primary Education	1145	44511	39836
独立小学	Independent Primary Schools	1145	42861	38368
教学点	Teaching Points	(284)	1650	1468
九年一贯制学校	Nine-year Consistency schools	(61)		
十二年一贯制学校	Twelve-year Consistency schools	(15)		
附设小学班的学校	Schools with Primary Classes	(3)		(53)
（三）特殊教育	Special Education Schools	10	404	300
特殊教育学校	Special Education Schools	10	404	300
附设特教班的学校	Schools with Special Edution Classes	(1)		
（四）工读学校	Reformatory Schools	1	42	32
（五）学前教育	Preschool Education	1839	52442	26496
幼儿园	Kindergarten	1839	52442	26496
附设幼儿班的学校	Schools with Nursery Classes	(72)		(59)
另有：职业技术培训机构	Technique Training Institution	2279	28626	20504

注：1.本表数据来源于市教育局。
2.本表为西安市行政区划内各级各类学校全口径数据（不含军事院校、党校）。
3.技工学校数据由西安市人力资源和社会保障局提供。
4.按照事业统计主体校原则，完全中学、十二年一贯制学校的学校数计入普通高中，九年一贯制学校的校数计入普通初中。
5.教职工数和专任教师按照办学类型划分。
6.（）内数据不计入总计，下表同。
7.本表数据包含西咸新区。

20–3 各级各类教育学生情况（2019年）

Basic Facts on Education Student by School Type（2019）

单位：人 (person)

指 标	Item	毕业生数 Number of Graduates	招生数 New Enrollment	在校学生数 Total Enrollment	女生 Female Students
一、高等教育	**Higher education**	**396847**	**475751**	**1375158**	**646145**
（一）研究生	Postgraduates	28619	42653	131982	64290
1、高等学校	Institutions of Higher Schools	28448	42439	131325	64125
2、科研机构	Scientific Research Institution	171	214	657	165
（二）普通高等教育	Regular Institutions of Higher Schools	191757	226339	740106	353195
1、本科	Universities Course Schools	119798	136041	515579	257993
2、专科	Junior Colleges	71959	90298	224527	95202
（三）成人高等教育	Higher Vocational Colleges	46735	82908	166961	79514
其中：成人高等学校	Contains:Adult Higher Education	7089	18345	41059	15526
（四）网络本专科生	Network Undergraduate and clooege students	129736	123851	336109	149146
1、本科	Universities Course Schools	48405	54436	133657	60761
2、专科	Junior Colleges	81331	69415	202452	88385
二、中等职业教育	**Secondary Occupation Education**	**52522**	**77359**	**212133**	**76482**
1、普通中等专业学校	Regular Specialized Secondary Schools	7171	11179	27874	11411
2、成人中等专业学校	Adult Secondary Specialized Schools	79	60	294	122
3、职业高中学校	Vocational high Schools	12559	19797	52553	22898
其中：市属	Municipal schools	12559	19797	52553	22898
4、技工学校	Technical Schools	32713	46323	131412	42051
其中：市属	Municipal schools	12879	14389	33704	11303
三、基础教育	**Elementary Education**	**359489**	**440100**	**1588964**	**754842**
（一）普通中等教育	Regular Institutions Education	138907	152949	435643	206482
1、高中	Senior High Schools	51987	51508	153149	75021
完全中学	Complete Secondary Schools	25160	25903	77218	37995
高级中学	Senior Secondary Schools	24720	23475	69959	34203
十二年一贯制学校	Twelve-year Consistency schools	2107	2130	5972	2823
2、初中	Junior Middle Schools	86920	101441	282494	131461
初级中学	Junior Middle Schools	44664	49653	141024	65327
九年一贯制学校	Nine-year Consistency Schools	6986	8959	23850	11044
十二年一贯制学校	Twelve-year Consistency Schools	3853	5705	16162	7428
完全中学	Complete Secondary school	31417	37124	101458	47662
（二）普通初等教育	Regular Primary Education	101652	157968	789795	374061
独立小学	Pricmary Schools	93118	142514	717686	340407
九年一贯制学校	Nine-year Consistency schools	6340	12498	56690	26593
十二年一贯制学校	Twelve-year Consistency Schools	2194	2956	15419	7061
（三）特殊教育	Special Education Schools	435	541	2967	1130
1、特殊教育学校	Special Education Schools	185	225	1068	407
2、小学附设特教班	Primary Schools with Special Education Classes			3	1
3、小学随班就读	Elementary Inclusive	128	154	1118	449
4、初中随班就读	Junior Mainstreaming	117	131	419	156
5、小学送教上门	Primary School Delivery	3	19	311	100
6、初中送教上门	Junior High School Delivery	2	12	48	17
（四）工读学校	Reformatory Schools	15	7	10	3
（五）学前教育	Preschool Education	118480	128635	360549	173166
1、独立幼儿园	Independent Kindergartens	117436	128222	359817	172806
2、附设幼儿园	Attached Kindergartens	1044	413	732	360
另有：职业技术培训机构	Vocational and Technical Institutions	621048		838107	413263

注：1.本表数据来源于市教育局。
2.本表数据包含西咸新区。

20-4 主要年份普通高等学校和科研机构研究生情况

Basic Statistics of Postgraduates on Regular Institutions of Higher Education and Scientific Research Institution in Representative Years

单位：人 (person)

年 份 Year	毕业生数 Number of Graduates	高等学校 Higher Schools	招生数 New Enrollment	高等学校 Higher Schools	在校学生数 Total Enrollment	高等学校 Higher Schools
1978			232	232	232	232
1980			127	127	651	651
1985	754	754	2819	2819	4799	4799
1990	2051	2051	1662	1662	5275	5275
1995	1769	1769	2712	2712	7974	7974
2000	3236	3236	6924	6924	16620	16620
2001	3881	3770	9274	8966	22564	21855
2002	4103	3952	11282	10882	28446	27471
2003	5971	5765	14322	13882	36936	35790
2004	8384	8127	17310	16871	45402	44169
2005	10416	10127	18583	18106	52699	51310
2006	12914	12552	19581	19105	58433	56951
2007	15506	15124	20570	20167	64137	62801
2008	17234	16788	21892	21443	67296	65834
2009	19025	18574	24879	24400	72366	70908
2010	19526	19129	25971	25477	76993	75483
2011	20965	20605	26686	26256	81696	80332
2012	22963	22578	28065	27618	84712	83306
2013	24778	24385	28786	28333	87002	85570
2014	24092	23881	28636	28436	88518	87826
2015	25322	25104	29487	29293	91448	90790
2016	24779	24562	30263	30079	94720	94102
2017	25808	25616	36296	36084	104092	103458
2018	27276	27088	38582	38399	112250	111626
2019	28619	28448	42653	42439	131982	131325

注：1.本表数据来源于市教育局。
2.本表2017年及以后年份数据包含西咸新区。

20-5 主要年份普通高等学校基本情况（本专科）

Basic Statistics on Regular Institution of Higher Education in Representative Years

单位：所、万人 (units,10 000 persons)

年 份 Year	学校数 Number of Schools	毕业生数 Number of Graduates	招生数 New Enrollment	在校学生数 Total Enrollment	教职工数 Number of Staff and Teachers	专任教师数 Full-time Teachers
1978	21	0.60	1.31	2.88	2.24	0.87
1980	24	0.21	1.08	4.17	2.55	0.97
1985	28	1.17	2.28	6.49	3.40	1.28
1990	31	2.11	2.00	7.50	4.15	1.56
1995	32	2.87	3.13	10.07	4.21	1.59
2000	25	2.71	6.79	17.75	3.81	1.57
2001	32	3.31	8.31	23.24	4.30	1.75
2002	35	3.82	10.75	30.15	4.67	2.06
2003	37	5.89	12.21	36.42	4.92	2.21
2004	41	7.66	13.17	40.29	5.45	2.69
2005	44	10.08	14.68	47.79	5.73	2.95
2006	47	11.75	15.15	51.40	6.14	3.29
2007	48	14.33	16.96	56.03	6.56	3.67
2008	48	15.82	19.31	60.10	6.90	3.89
2009	49	15.04	18.84	63.22	7.08	4.06
2010	50	16.33	19.16	65.74	7.22	4.21
2011	61	17.68	20.52	68.52	7.27	4.27
2012	62	18.64	22.46	72.40	7.40	4.45
2013	63	17.73	21.05	75.27	7.50	4.64
2014	63	18.88	20.74	76.64	7.50	4.68
2015	63	20.72	20.49	75.75	7.49	4.78
2016	63	21.60	20.07	73.68	7.37	4.72
2017	63	20.50	20.10	72.68	7.42	4.79
2018	63	20.50	19.83	71.28	7.56	4.90
2019	63	19.18	22.63	74.01	7.37	5.02

注：1.本表数据来源于市教育局。
2.本表2017年及以后年份数据包含西咸新区。

20-6 主要年份普通中等专业学校基本情况

Basic Statistics on Regular Specialized Secondary Schools in Representative Years

年 份 Year	学校数（所） Number of Schools (units)	毕业生数（万人） Number of Graduates (10 000 persons)	招生数（万人） New Enrollment (10 000 persons)	在校学生数（万人） Total Enrollment (10 000 persons)	教职工数（人） Number of Staff and Teachers(person)	专任教师数（人） Full-time Teachers(person)
1978	19	0.19	0.45	0.82	3937	1110
1980	31	0.18	0.42	1.50	3895	1474
1985	37	0.43	0.76	1.70	6071	2363
1990	44	0.56	0.68	2.09	7136	2891
1995	46	0.97	1.37	3.74	5903	2533
2000	47	1.63	1.90	6.02	6964	3172
2001	47	1.70	1.58	5.63	5252	2467
2002	46	1.60	1.69	5.57	5170	2508
2003	34	1.62	1.80	5.28	4562	2302
2004	35	1.40	2.09	5.71	4676	2388
2005	32	1.44	2.26	6.16	3924	2130
2006	31	1.84	2.61	7.30	3621	2014
2007	30	2.03	2.91	7.97	3548	2011
2008	29	2.58	2.55	8.06	3278	1814
2009	28	2.70	2.15	7.44	2965	1720
2010	28	2.45	2.08	6.75	3249	1845
2011	24	2.34	1.96	6.11	2868	1723
2012	24	2.15	1.67	5.43	2733	1595
2013	22	1.93	1.35	4.66	2599	1474
2014	22	1.76	1.25	4.07	2315	1346
2015	20	1.32	0.95	3.47	1991	1228
2016	20	1.25	0.88	3.11	1917	1210
2017	16	1.06	0.96	2.74	1556	998
2018	15	0.84	0.83	2.48	1529	958
2019	15	0.72	1.12	2.79	1386	918

注：1.本表数据来源于市教育局。
2.本表2017年及以后年份数据包含西咸新区。

20-7 主要年份普通中等教育基本情况

Basic Situation of General Secondary Education in Major Years

年 份 Year	学校数（所） Number of Schools (units)	毕业生数（万人） Number of Graduates (10 000 persons)	招生数（万人） New Enrollment (10 000 persons)	在校学生数（万人） Total Enrollment (10 000 persons)	教职工数（人） Number of Staff and Teachers(person)	专任教师数（人） Full-time Teachers(person)
1978	962	10.85		44.16	27380	20660
1980	1002	12.33	14.03	44.08	29867	22530
1985	563	10.72	13.05	38.24	30063	22050
1990	518	9.11	10.49	30.03	30739	22386
1995	485	8.13	12.40	32.32	30423	21984
2000	466	12.01	17.88	48.31	34385	26230
2001	470	13.85	18.98	52.50	35442	27190
2002	467	15.76	19.68	55.36	36706	28335
2003	467	16.76	18.78	56.44	38252	29887
2004	461	18.01	18.85	56.54	39121	30600
2005	460	18.82	18.83	55.74	39456	31094
2006	457	18.04	18.61	56.11	39341	31203
2007	453	18.37	17.96	54.68	39171	31373
2008	442	17.99	17.16	52.83	39088	31425
2009	439	17.80	16.57	50.63	39002	31415
2010	436	17.01	16.15	48.89	39207	31506
2011	423	16.44	15.42	47.20	41135	31675
2012	419	15.64	14.98	45.33	41197	31526
2013	418	15.24	14.47	43.73	41003	31419
2014	421	14.54	13.97	42.57	40576	32615
2015	422	13.92	13.41	41.37	40689	33014
2016	422	13.96	13.72	40.70	41352	33962
2017	448	13.89	14.08	41.74	44546	36565
2018	456	13.50	14.37	42.46	45390	37539
2019	469	13.89	15.29	43.56	47037	39143

注：1.本表数据来源于市教育局。
2.本表2017年及以后年份数据包含西咸新区。

20-8 各区县普通中等教育基本情况（2019年）

Basic Situation of Ordinary Secondary Education in Various Districts and Counties（2019）

单位：所、人 (unit, person)

区 县	Region	学校数 Number of Schools	毕业生数 Number of Graduates	高中 Senior	招生数 New Enrollment	高中 Senior	在校学生数 Total Enrollment	女生 Female Students	高中 Senior	教职工数 Number of Staff and Teachers	专任教师数 Full-time Teachers
合 计	**Total**	**469**	**138907**	**51987**	**152949**	**51508**	**435643**	**206482**	**153149**	**47037**	**35351**
新城区	Xincheng	25	10968	3901	10904	3818	32236	15463	11475	2765	2198
碑林区	Beilin	36	17034	6691	18385	6864	52239	23805	20463	4189	3378
莲湖区	Lianhu	21	10781	3613	11529	3724	33137	15881	11103	2864	2245
灞桥区	Baqiao	25	7841	2134	9816	2511	26737	12855	7167	2881	2090
未央区	Weiyang	34	10976	4146	15261	4716	39480	18913	12909	4357	2782
雁塔区	Yanta	41	11875	4234	14415	4350	40619	19294	13119	4404	2920
阎良区	Yanliang	12	3294	1278	3337	1105	9644	4942	3332	1057	938
临潼区	Lintong	33	9502	3989	8765	3346	26096	12947	10073	3223	2638
长安区	Chang'an	39	10934	4256	11911	4032	33230	15820	11863	3410	2928
高陵区	Gaoling	15	3546	1251	4222	1395	11725	5895	3882	1025	867
鄠邑区	Huyi	27	7076	3233	6275	2390	20191	9368	8598	2320	1962
蓝田县	Lantian	44	8853	3690	7751	3268	24797	12173	10536	3358	2518
周至县	Zhouzhi	34	9177	4097	8730	3772	25911	11408	10765	2946	2113
西咸新区	Xixian	46	8402	2207	11069	2593	30670	13986	7531	4504	3230
高新区	Gaoxin	37	8648	3267	10579	3624	28931	13732	10333	3734	2544

注：1. 本表数据来源于市教育局。
2. 专任教师按办学层次统计，不含一贯制学校小学部专任教师数。

20–9 主要年份职业高中基本情况

Basic Statistics on Vocational Secondary Schools in Representative Years

单位：所、人 (unit, person)

年 份 Year	学校数 Number of Schools	毕业生数 Number of Graduates	招生数 New Enrollment	在校学生数 Total Enrollment	教职工数 Number of Staff and Teachers	专任教师数 Full-time Teachers
1985	40	1661	8346	17621	1375	868
1990	58	5936	8095	20151	2674	1574
1995	71	8976	12490	32673	2394	1877
2000	95	9949	13903	32188	3311	1997
2001	85	10300	15591	34336	3517	2113
2002	78	8659	17231	39428	3461	2192
2003	87	10755	17310	44033	4036	2458
2004	83	12177	17865	46358	4101	2515
2005	91	15092	20603	51766	4750	2892
2006	96	14887	21158	53828	5193	3126
2007	86	14881	24434	56012	4899	3064
2008	84	15813	30201	62963	4878	3008
2009	84	14691	31042	72388	5129	3179
2010	84	18100	30042	78244	5222	3178
2011	78	22493	27641	75108	4849	3173
2012	77	24048	24995	67969	4775	3148
2013	74	21243	23043	61968	4699	3085
2014	81	19156	19508	60024	4860	3186
2015	80	18565	15060	49092	3239	2214
2016	64	17773	14305	43576	3126	2275
2017	62	14325	17080	45145	3318	2405
2018	60	14064	17295	46380	3499	2584
2019	60	12559	19797	52553	3801	2685

注：1.本表数据来源于市教育局。
　　2.本表2017年及以后年份数据包含西咸新区。

20-10 各区县职业高中基本情况（2019年）

Basic Statistics on Vocational Secondary Schools by Region（2019）

单位：所、人 (unit, person)

区 县	Region	学校数 Number of Schools	毕业生数 Number of Graduates	招生数 New Enrollment	在校学生数 Total Enrollment	女生 Female Students	教职工数 Number of Staff and Teachers	专任教师数 Full-time Teachers
合 计	**Total**	**60**	**12559**	**19797**	**52553**	**22898**	**3801**	**2685**
新城区	Xincheng	8	3182	5283	15564	6409	810	418
碑林区	Beilin	7	1708	2571	7456	2559	427	229
莲湖区	Lianhu	5	1349	1092	3568	2083	275	212
灞桥区	Baqiao	6	609	677	1731	1185	142	117
未央区	Weiyang	3	529	1154	2338	1115	170	120
雁塔区	Yanta	10	981	3093	7064	3108	511	397
阎良区	Yanliang	2	683	839	2537	1319	252	175
临潼区	Lintong	4	876	867	2273	909	178	145
长安区	Chang'an	3	1221	1592	3865	1810	427	359
高陵区	Gaoling	1	277	378	1015	349	101	94
鄠邑区	Huyi	2	196	581	1439	601	209	189
蓝田县	Lantian	2	483	847	1725	639	151	122
周至县	Zhouzhi	3	451	474	1258	535	83	62
西咸新区	Xixian	3		349	683	276	31	21
高新区	Gaoxin	1	14		37	1	34	25

注：本表数据来源于市教育局。

20-11 主要年份普通初等教育基本情况

Basic Situation of General Primary Education in Major Years

年 份 Year	学校数（所） Number of Schools (units)	毕业生数（万人） Number of Graduates (10 000 persons)	招生数（万人） New Enrollment (10 000 persons)	在校学生数（万人） Total Enrollment (10 000 persons)	教职工数（人） Number of Staff and Teachers(person)	专任教师数（人） Full-time Teachers(person)
1978	2667	13.07	14.10	74.03	29744	26428
1980	2337	11.91	12.57	73.36	31770	28360
1985	2337	11.21	9.57	62.16	31075	26430
1990	2343	8.67	10.85	61.87	33788	29090
1995	2360	9.93	14.09	79.36	35568	30270
2000	2323	13.83	11.51	77.81	35336	30215
2001	2277	14.20	11.07	74.51	34257	29281
2002	2137	13.89	10.13	70.78	34143	29428
2003	2084	12.97	9.28	66.78	34080	29531
2004	2016	12.37	9.12	63.75	33794	29367
2005	1980	11.92	8.47	60.47	33907	29674
2006	1929	11.53	9.16	59.33	34460	30018
2007	1872	11.38	8.67	56.83	34901	30533
2008	1781	10.58	8.33	54.66	34653	30382
2009	1666	9.96	7.84	52.52	34389	30334
2010	1531	9.61	8.64	51.56	34118	29944
2011	1424	8.92	8.77	51.39	32457	29900
2012	1322	8.88	8.88	50.85	32208	29651
2013	1291	8.51	9.56	51.95	31863	29421
2014	1257	8.29	10.13	53.79	32162	28395
2015	1234	7.85	10.51	56.62	32585	28748
2016	1190	8.46	11.65	59.79	34646	30941
2017	1125	9.06	13.13	66.68	38494	34163
2018	1130	9.32	15.16	73.09	41122	36878
2019	1145	10.17	15.80	78.98	44511	39836

注：1.本表数据来源于市教育局。
　　2.本表2017年及以后年份数据包含西咸新区。

20-12 各区县普通初等教育基本情况（2019年）

Basic Situation of General Primary Education in Various Districts and Counties（2019）

单位：所、人 (unit, person)

区 县 Region	学校数 Number of Schools	毕业生数 Number of Graduates	招生数 New Enrollment	在校学生数 Total Enrollment	女生 Female Students	教职工数 Number of Staff and Teachers	专任教师数 Full-time Teachers
合 计 Total	**1145**	**101652**	**157968**	**789795**	**374061**	**44511**	**39836**
新城区 Xincheng	36	6164	6910	38122	17922	2220	2011
碑林区 Beilin	42	7785	9291	49533	23128	2767	2366
莲湖区 Lianhu	47	8852	11197	58242	27708	2662	2412
灞桥区 Baqiao	79	7595	13100	64260	30623	3315	3036
未央区 Weiyang	76	11431	24147	111829	52502	5233	4694
雁塔区 Yanta	59	10661	18958	88064	41816	4613	4094
阎良区 Yanliang	23	2422	3343	17514	8502	1061	996
临潼区 Lintong	105	6028	7286	41819	20119	2737	2459
长安区 Chang'an	111	7816	14405	68319	32288	4091	3637
高陵区 Gaoling	72	3117	4898	25246	12242	1758	1510
鄠邑区 Huyi	78	3865	4502	24368	11495	1665	1480
蓝田县 Lantian	83	4588	4622	27805	13281	2554	2334
周至县 Zhouzhi	110	5058	6118	33788	15597	2337	2030
西咸新区 Xixian	137	9276	16308	78609	37367	4374	4003
高新区 Gaoxin	87	6994	12883	62277	29471	3124	2774

注：本表数据来源于市教育局。

20-13 主要年份学前教育基本情况

Basic Conditions of Pre-school Education in Representative Years

年份 Year	幼儿园（个） Number of Kindergartens (unit)	班数（个） Number of Class (unit)	在园幼儿数（万人） Student Enrollment (10000 persons)	教职工数（人） Number of Staff and Teachers(person)	专任教师数（人） Full-time Teachers(person)
1978	191		4.44	3568	1315
1980	186		9.61	5525	2657
1985	310	3135	9.71	6887	2770
1990	256	3816	14.04	6123	2058
1995	257	4464	16.40	6173	2659
2000	367	4142	12.85	6346	2995
2001	366	4306	11.97	6224	3069
2002	378	4186	11.53	6541	3397
2003	610	4470	12.39	8959	4853
2004	660	4507	12.16	9870	5577
2005	737	4712	12.75	10528	5959
2006	863	5037	13.00	12335	7106
2007	830	5081	14.00	13468	7951
2008	905	5506	15.00	14932	8704
2009	896	5710	16.00	15928	9240
2010	1004	6420	18.00	18710	10638
2011	1122	8010	24.00	23680	12577
2012	1239	8729	27.10	27735	14293
2013	1295	9408	28.56	31989	16238
2014	1343	9782	28.95	33062	17337
2015	1417	10457	30.90	36004	19096
2016	1475	11090	31.80	39753	21395
2017	1605	12234	34.81	44895	23789
2018	1780	12970	35.39	49604	25823
2019	1839	13375	36.05	52442	26496

注：1.本表数据来源于市教育局。
2.幼儿园在园人数中包括学前班。
3.本表2017年及以后年份数据包含西咸新区。

20-14 主要年份特殊教育基本情况

Basic Statistics on Special Education in Representative Years

单位：所、人 (unit, person)

年 份 Year	学校数 Number of Schools	毕业生数 Number of Graduates	招生数 New Enrollment	在校学生数 Total Enrollment	教职工数 Number of Staff and Teachers	专任教师数 Full-time Teachers
1980	1	48	64	315	66	43
1985	2	14	36	318	94	59
1990	5	35	111	451	142	96
1995	5	27	147	1363	204	141
2000	5	269	145	1880	230	156
2001	5	237	209	1915	238	162
2002	5	216	148	1661	232	157
2003	5	156	161	1380	237	166
2004	5	137	142	1290	236	167
2005	5	184	182	1445	240	169
2006	6	171	143	1425	254	178
2007	6	169	114	1342	259	190
2008	6	83	96	1286	259	190
2009	7	311	202	1523	335	234
2010	8	214	402	1529	340	235
2011	8	280	222	1393	343	231
2012	8	197	220	1392	352	248
2013	8	194	212	1174	338	243
2014	8	172	222	1225	345	238
2015	8	168	338	1373	352	240
2016	8	214	327	1604	359	246
2017	9	237	774	2498	386	272
2018	9	352	461	2615	379	271
2019	10	435	541	2967	404	300

注：1.本表数据来源于市教育局。
2.包括盲、聋、哑、智力障碍者儿童教育。
3.本表2017年及以后年份数据包含西咸新区。

20–15 基础教育监测评价情况（2019年）

Monitoring and Evaluation of Basic Education（2019）

指 标	Item	2019
入学率（%）	Enrollment Rate(%)	
小学	Primary Schools	99.97
初中	Junior Middle Schools	99.97
巩固率（%）	The Consolidation Rate (%)	
小学（六年）	Primary Schools (six years)	147.74
初中（三年）	Junior Middle Schools (three years)	112.97
毕业率（%）	The Graduate Rate(%)	
小学	Primary school	99.83
初中	Junior middle school	99.02
专任教师学历合格率（%）	Qualified Rate Of Full-time Teacher Education (%)	
小学	Primary Schools	100.00
初中	Junior Middle Schools	99.99
高中	Senior Middle Schools	99.12
幼儿园	Kindergartens	99.14
小学教师专科以上学历达到率（%）	Rate of Primary School Teachers with College degree or Above (%)	99.34
初中教师本科以上学历达到率（%）	Rate of Junior Middle SchoolTeachers with Bachelor degree or Above (%)	94.06
高中教师研究生以上学历达到率（%）	Rate of Senior Middle School Teachers with Postgraduate degree or Above (%)	20.10

注：1.本表数据来源于市教育局。
2.本表数据包含西咸新区。

20-16　主要年份平均每万人口在校学生数及构成

单位：人、%

年　份 Year	平均每万人 高等学校在校学生 Per 10000 people on average Hight Education Students in the school	平均每万人 高中阶段在校学生 Per 10000 people on average Number of Senior high School Students in the school	平均每万人 初中在校学生 Per 10000 people on average Number of Junior Secondary School Students in the school	平均每万人 小学在校学生 Per 10000 people on average Number of Primary School Students in the school
1978	58			1486
1980	84			1434
1985	117			1124
1990	123			1016
1995	168			1224
2000	282			1131
2001	366			1072
2002	470			1007
2003	560			932
2004	618	463	517	879
2005	715	492	489	815
2006	760	534	484	788
2007	817	543	466	744
2008	863	571	444	708
2009	901	619	413	672
2010	939	635	361	660
2011	1090	576	337	604
2012	1132	541	319	595
2013	1146	448	307	605
2014	1157	414	301	626
2015	1125	374	286	650
2016	1080	360	280	641
2017	982	363	270	693
2018	956	335	270	731
2019	1348	358	277	774

注：1.本表数据来源于市教育局。
2.2011年起，表中三个比重指标数据参与计算的学生总数含普通教育、成人教育及网络教育数据。
3.2019年平均每万人高等学校在校学生包含全部高等教育在校生。
4.本表2017年及以后年份数据含西咸新区。

The Average Number of Students in the School every 10000 Individuals in Representative Years

(persons,%)

平均每万人学前教育在校学生 Average Number of Pre-school Students per 10,000 people	普通高等学校在校学生占学生总数比重 Senior high School Students in the school in accounting for the proportion of the total number of students	中等学校在校学生占学生总数比重 Junior Secondary School students in the school in accounting for the proportion of the total number of students	小学在校学生占学生总数比重 Primary School students in the school in accounting for the proportion of the total number of students
	2.3	34.9	58.6
	3.1	33.2	55.3
	5.3	31.3	50.9
	6.7	25.1	51.7
	7.3	28.0	53.6
	11.5	34.8	46.0
	14.6	35.9	42.6
	18.2	36.4	39.0
	20.1	33.8	33.5
	22.2	35.2	31.6
	26.4	36.2	30.1
	27.7	37.1	28.7
	29.3	36.3	26.7
	30.8	36.1	25.2
	31.8	36.5	23.7
217	33.0	35.0	23.2
282	29.8	30.1	19.9
317	31.0	28.2	19.5
333	32.6	25.3	20.2
336	33.2	23.8	20.9
355	32.8	22.2	21.9
360	31.4	21.4	22.6
362	29.1	21.3	23.4
354	27.5	20.2	24.4
353	27.4	20.4	24.9

20–17 民办教育情况（2019年）

单位：所、人

指 标	Item	学校数 Number of Schools	毕业生数 Number of Graduates
一、民办高等教育(民办高校)	**Private higher Education (Institutions)**	**27**	**70072**
二、民办中等教育	**Private Secondary Education**	**105**	**37110**
民办普通高中	Ordinary High School	31	6192
民办普通中等专业学校	Civilian run ordinary secondary vocational school	1	514
民办职业高中	Vocational high school	36	7330
民办普通初中	Ordinary Junior middle school	37	21638
民办的附设中职班	Private primary school class	(10)	1436
三、民办普通小学	**Private Primary School**	**88**	**14662**
四、民办幼儿园	**Private kindergarten**	**1164**	**85411**
另有：民办培训机构	Private Training Institutions	1202	265252

注：1.本表数据来源于市教育局。
2.毕业生数中幼儿园为离园人数。
3.民办高等教育在校生为民办高校普通、成人本专科学生数。
4.聘请校外教师中，小学、中学、幼儿园为代课教师和兼任教师之和。
5.按照教育报表制度，民办的附设中职班教职工计入基础教育主体校教职工总数，专任教师为中职层次，故单独统计。
6.本表数据含西咸新区。

Private Education Situation（2019）

(unit, person)

招生数 New Enrollment	在校学生数 Total Enrollment	教职工数 Number of Teachers and Staff	专任教师 Full-time Teachers	聘请校外教师 Teachers hired from Outside Schools
79647	**254947**	**19804**	**13478**	
50111	**138539**	**12630**	**9739**	**50**
7762	21704	5776	4719	
882	2042	196	135	
12580	34840	1864	1085	50
26792	74883	4794	3800	
2095	5070			
30722	**140998**	**6425**	**5455**	
92316	**261032**	**37222**	**17570**	**8**
	480952	17454	12383	6965

20-18 全市研究与试验发展（R&D）活动情况（2018年）

Scientific and Technological Activities in the Whole City（2018）

指 标	Item	2018
一、单位数（个）	**Number of Units(unit)**	**2479**
#有R&D活动单位数	The Number of R&D active units	680
二、R&D人员（人）	**Personnel Eagaged in R&D（person）**	**107385**
三、R&D人员折合全时当量（人年）	**R&D Stuff Equivalent to Full Time equivalent （person year）**	**76671**
四、R&D经费内部支出（万元）	**R&D Internal Expenditure（10000 yuan）**	**4261408.1**

注：本表数据来源于省统计局反馈。

20-19 规模以上重点行业企业研究与试验发展（R&D）情况（2018年）

R&D Project Status of Key Enterprises above Designated Size（2018）

指 标	Item	2018
一、企业数（个）	**Number of Enterprises(unit)**	**2249**
工业	Industry	1477
非工业	Non-industry	772
#有R&D活动的单位数	The number of R&D active units	504
工业	Industry	416
非工业	Non-industry	88
二、R&D人员（人）	**Personnel Eagaged in R&D (person)**	**50482**
工业	Industry	34510
非工业	Non-industry	15972
三、R&D人员折合全时当量（人年）	**R&D Stuff Equivalent to Full Time equivalent (person year)**	**36038**
工业	Industry	25671
非工业	Non-industry	10367
四、R&D经费内部支出（万元）	**R&D Internal Expenditure (10000 yuan)**	**1696810**
工业	Industry	1220783
非工业	Non-industry	476027

20-20 规模以上工业企业研究与试验发展（R&D）基本情况（2018年）

R&D Project Status of Industrial Enterprises above Designated Size（2018）

指 标	Item	企业数（个）Number of enterprises (unit)	有R&D活动的企业数 The Number of R&D enterprises
总计	**Total**	**1477**	**416**
按企业规模分	**Grouped by Size of Enterprises**		
大型企业	Large-size	66	43
中型企业	Medium-size	176	85
小型企业	Small-size	1182	284
微型企业	Microenterprise	53	4
按登记注册类型分	**Grouped by Registered Status**		
内资企业	Domestic Investment Enterprises	1368	384
国有企业	State-owned Enterprises	21	13
集体企业	Collective-owned Enterprise	5	
股份合作企业	Stock Cooperative Enterprises	4	1
联营企业	Affiliated Enterprise		
有限责任公司	Limited Liability Corporations	612	207
股份有限公司	Share-holding Corporation Ltd	112	62
私营企业	Private Enterprise	613	101
其他	Other Domestic Funded Enterprises	1	
港、澳、台商投资企业	Enterprises with Funds from Hong Kong, Macao And Taiwan	21	3
外商投资企业	Foreign Funded Enterprises	88	29
按国民经济行业分	**Grouped by Sector**		
采矿业	Mining	7	2
煤炭开采和洗选业	Mining and Washing of Coal		
石油和天然气开采业	Extraction of Petroleum and Natural Gas	1	1

20-20 续表1 continued 1

指　标	Item	企业数（个）Number of enterprises (unit)	有R&D活动的企业数 The Number of R&D enterprises
黑色金属矿采选业	Mining of Ferrous Metal Ores		
有色金属矿采选业	Mining of Non-ferrous Metal Ores		
非金属矿采选业	Mining and Processing of Nonmetal Ores		
开采专业及辅助性活动	Mining Professional and Auxiliary Activity	6	1
其他采矿业	Mining of other Ores		
制造业	Manufacturing Industry	1421	410
农副食品加工业	Processing of Food from Agriculture Products	52	1
食品制造业	Manufacture of Food	53	7
酒、饮料和精制茶制造业	Manufacture of Beverages	25	2
烟草制品业	Manufacture of Tobacco	2	1
纺织业	Manufacture of Textile	16	1
纺织服装、服饰业	Manufacture of Textile Wearing, Apparel	4	
皮革、毛皮、羽毛及其制品和制鞋业	Manufacture of Leather, Furs, Feather, Related Products and Footware	2	1
木材加工和木、竹、藤、棕、草制品业	Processing of Timber,Manufacture of Wood, Bamboo, Rattan, Palm and Straw Products	5	
家具制造业	Manufacture of Furniture	15	
造纸及纸制品业	Manufacture of Paper And Paper Products	23	
印刷和记录媒介复制业	Printing and Reproduction of Recording Media	34	4
文教、工美、体育和娱乐用品制造业	Education, Art, Sports And Entertainment Products Manufacturing	12	
石油、煤炭及其他燃料加工业	Processing of Petroleum,Coal and Other Fuels	8	
化学原料和化学制品制造业	Manufacture of Raw Chemical Materials and Chemical Products	84	30
医药制造业	Manufacture of Medicines	62	29

20-20 续表2 continued 2

指 标	Item	企业数（个）Number of enterprises (unit)	有R&D活动的企业数 The Number of R&D enterprises
化学纤维制造业	Manufacture of Chemical Fiber	3	1
橡胶和塑料制品业	Manufacture of Rubber and Manufacture of Plastic	39	7
非金属矿物制品业	Manufacture of Non-metallic Mineral Products	158	10
黑色金属冶炼和压延加工业	Smelting and Pressing of Ferrous Metals	10	1
有色金属冶炼和压延加工业	Smelting and Pressing of Non-ferrous Metals	44	22
金属制品业	Manufacture of Metal Products	95	12
通用设备制造业	Manufacture of General Purpose Machinery	92	24
专用设备制造业	Manufacture of Special Equipment	128	64
汽车制造业	Manufacture of Motor Vehicle	58	19
铁路、船舶、航空航天和其他运输设备制造业	Railways, Ships, Aerospace And Other Transportation Equipment Manufacturing Industry	89	39
电气机械和器材制造业	Manufacture of Electric Equipment and Machinery	145	42
计算机、通信和其他电子设备制造业	Manufacture of Communication Equipment, Computers and Other Electronic Equipment	86	48
仪器仪表制造业	Manufacture of Measuring Instruments and Machinery	60	36
其他制造业	Other Manufacturing	8	5
废弃资源综合利用业	Comprehensive Utilization Of Waste Resources	4	
金属制品、机械和设备修理业	Metal Products, Machinery and Equipment Repair Industry	5	3
电力、热力、燃气及水的生产供应业	Production and Supply of Electric Power,Heat,Gas and Water	49	4
电力、热力生产和供应业	Production and Supply of Electric Power and Heat Power	24	3
燃气生产和供应业	Production and Supply of Gas	15	1
水的生产和供应业	Production and Supply of Water	10	

20-21 规模以上工业企业研究与试验发展（R&D）人员和经费支出情况（2018年）

指标	Item	R&D人员（人）R&D personnel (person)	研究人员 Researchers
总计	**Total**	**34510**	**31575**
按企业规模分	**Grouped by Size of Enterprises**		
大型企业	Large-size	23149	21183
中型企业	Medium-size	5612	5161
小型企业	Small-size	5711	5194
微型企业	microenterprise	38	37
按登记注册类型分	**Grouped by Registion Status**		
内资企业	Domestic Investment Enterprises	32050	29171
国有企业	State-owned Enterprises	4887	4315
集体企业	Collective-owned Enterprises		
股份合作企业	Stock cooperative enterprises	12	12
联营企业	Affiliated companies		
有限责任公司	Limited Liability Corporations	21953	20051
股份有限公司	Share-holding Corperation Ltd.	3100	2872
私营企业	Private Enterprises	2098	1921
其他	Other Domestic Funded Enterprises		
港、澳、台商投资企业	Enterprises with Funds from Hong Kong,Macao and Taiwan	111	104
外商投资企业	Foreign Funded Enterprises	2349	2300
按国民经济行业分	**Grouped by Sector**		
采矿业	Mining	1090	1002
煤炭开采和洗选业	Mining and Washing of Coal		
石油和天然气开采业	Extraction of Petroleum and Natural Gas	659	595
黑色金属矿采选业	Mining of Ferrous Metal Ores		
有色金属矿采选业	Mining of Non-ferrous Metal Ores		
非金属矿采选业	Mining and Processing of Nonmetal Ores		
开采专业及辅助性活动	Mining Professional and Auxiliary Activity	431	407
其他采矿业	Mining of other Ores		
制造业	Mannfacturing Industry	33118	30303
农副食品加工业	Processing of Food from Agricultural Products	14	13
食品制造业	Manufacture of Foods	167	160
酒、饮料和精制茶制造业	Manufacture of Beverages	15	15
烟草制品业	Manufacture of Tobacco	39	36
纺织业	Manufacture of Textile	20	18
纺织服装、服饰业	Manufacture of Textile Wearing Apparel		
皮革、毛皮、羽毛及其制品和制鞋业	Manufacture of Leather, Fur, Feather and Related Products and Footwear	6	4

R&D Personnel and Expenditure Conditions of Industrial Enterprises above Designated Size（2018）

R&D经费内部支出（万元） R&D Intramural Expenditure (10000 yuan)	政府资金 Government funds	企业资金 Enterprise funds	境外资金 Foreign funds
1220783	**313562**	**902213**	**221**
947049	296144	647696	108
144421	10925	133228	107
128016	6464	120022	6
1297	30	1267	
1048488	313553	729975	173
117657	30984	86423	
216		216	
796708	268607	523542	148
94335	11687	82595	26
39573	2275	37199	
1587	9	1578	
170708		170661	47
31066	10088	20978	
20590	5856	14734	
10476	4232	6244	
1188363	303474	879881	221
61		61	
2973	46	2927	
221		221	
774		774	
2412	35	2377	
101		101	

20-21 续表1

指标	Item	R&D人员（人）R&D personnel（person）	研究人员 Researchers
木材加工和木、竹、藤、棕、草制品业	Processing of Timber,Manufacture of Wood, Bamboo,Rattan,aplam and Straw Products		
家具制造业	Manufacture of Furniture		
造纸及纸制品业	Manufacture of Paper and Paper Products		
印刷和记录媒介复制业	Printing,Reproduction of Recording Media	220	199
文教、工美、体育和娱乐用品制造业	Manufacture of Articles For Culture, Education and Sport Activities		
石油、煤炭及其他燃料加工业加工业	Processing of Petroleum, Coal and Other Fuels	186	178
化学原料及化学制品制造业	Manufacture of Raw Chemical Materials and Chemical Products	949	861
医药制造业	Manufacture of Medicines	1113	1004
化学纤维制造业	Manufacture of Chemical Fibers	55	49
橡胶和塑料制品业	Manufacture of Rubber and Manufacture of Plastics	288	228
非金属矿物制品业	Manufacture of Non-metallic Mineral Products	335	301
黑色金属冶炼和压延加工业	Smelting and Pressing of Ferrous Metals	10	10
有色金属冶炼和压延加工业	Smelting and Pressing of Non-ferrous Metals	960	810
金属制品业	Manufacture of Metal Products	1205	1059
通用设备制造业	Manufacture of General Purpose Machinery	665	596
专用设备制造业	Manufacture of Special Equipment	2179	2036
汽车制造业	Manufacture of Motor Vehicle	3587	3419
铁路、船舶、航空航天和其他运输设备制造业	Railways,Shipbuilding,Aerospace and Other Transportation Equipment Manufacturing Industry	9576	8589
电气机械和器材制造业	Manufacture of Electric Equipment and Machinery	3191	2981
计算机、通讯和其他电子设备制造业	Manufacture of Communication Equipment, Computers and other Electronic Equipment	4488	4256
仪器仪表制造业	Manufacture of Measuring Instruments and Machinery	3762	3403
其他制造业	Other Manufacturing	67	57
废弃资源综合利用业	Comprehensive Utilization Of Waste Resources		
金属制品、机械和设备修理业	Metal Products,Machinery and Equipment Repair Industry	21	21
电力、热力、燃气及水生产和供应业	Production and Distribution of Electricity,Heat,Gas and Water	302	270
电力、热力的生产和供应业	Production and Supply of Electric Power and Heat Power	292	264
燃气生产和供应业	Gas mining and supplying industry	10	6
水的生产和供应业	Production and Supply of Water		

continued 1

R&D经费内部支出（万元） R&D Intramural Expenditure (10000 yuan)	政府资金 Government funds	企业资金 Enterprise funds	境外资金 Foreign funds
6460		6460	
5086		5086	
30998	1431	29548	
22047	1333	20687	
162		162	
12870	3684	9186	
7665	997	6668	
248	100	148	
30369	6048	24072	
31572	3322	28247	3
17466	383	17083	
57070	17671	39172	124
225909	20807	202775	
297703	154417	143255	31
85450	3754	79570	63
263743	47369	216374	
83693	42027	41666	
878	49	829	
2431		2431	
1354		1354	
963		963	
392		392	

20-22 规模以上工业企业新产品开发、生产及销售情况（2018年）

指标	Item	新产品开发项目数（项）Number of new product development projects（item）
总计	**Total**	**3504**
按企业规模分	**Grouped by Size of Enterprises**	
大型企业	Large-size	1330
中型企业	Medium-size	828
小型企业	Small-size	1330
微型企业	microenterprise	16
按登记注册类型分	**Grouped by Registion Status**	
内资企业	Domestic Investment Enterprises	3300
国有企业	State-owned Enterprises	310
集体企业	Collective-owned Enterprises	
股份合作企业	Stock cooperative enterprises	2
联营企业	Affiliated companies	
有限责任公司	Limited Liability Corporations	1947
股份有限公司	Share-holding Corperation Ltd.	466
私营企业	Private Enterprises	575
其他	Other Domestic Funded Enterprises	
港澳台商投资	Enterprises with Funds from Hong Kong,Macao and Taiwan	16
外商投资企业	Foreign Funded Enterprises	188
按国民经济行业分	**Grouped by Sector**	
采矿业	Mining	186
煤炭开采和洗选业	Mining and Washing of Coal	
石油和天然气开采业	Extraction of Petroleum and Natural Gas	9
黑色金属矿采选业	Mining of Ferrous Metal Ores	
有色金属矿采选业	Mining of Non-ferrous Metal Ores	
非金属矿采选业	Mining and Processing of Nonmetal Ores	
开采专业及辅助性活动	Mining Professional and Auxiliary Activity	177
其他采矿业	Mining of other Ores	
制造业	Mannfacturing Industry	3292
农副食品加工业	Processing of Food from Agricultural Products	5
食品制造业	Manufacture of Foods	33
酒、饮料和精制茶制造业	Manufacture of Beverages	6
烟草制品业	Manufacture of Tobacco	8
纺织业	Manufacture of Textile	11
纺织服装、服饰业	Manufacture of Textile Wearing Apparel	
皮革、毛皮、羽毛及其制品和制鞋业	Manufacture of Leather, Fur, Feather and Related Products and Footwear	16

New Product Development, Production and Sales of Above-scale Industrial Enterprises（2018）

新产品开发经费支出（万元） New Product Development Expenditure （10 000 yuan）	新产品产值 （万元） New product output value （10 000 yuan）	新产品销售收入 （万元） Sales of new products （10 000 yuan）
1497698	**13796400**	**11422610**
1093647	11205451	9111962
218886	1666024	1472189
183184	905238	820256
1981	19688	18204
1280116	13241561	10973655
129487	494430	378510
124	4303	2701
985080	10140720	8304622
100067	1049525	860037
65358	1552583	1427786
2309	318409	237079
215274	236430	211876
13697	5172	4924
1269	135	
12428	5037	4924
1483206	13790477	11417005
2484	3363	4138
4090	90890	89464
1034	2618	1431
874	92070	98413
5900	24000	23603
2318	20393	38375

20-22 续表1

指标	Item	新产品开发项目数（项） Number of new product development projects（item）
木材加工和木、竹、藤、棕、草制品业	Processing of Timber,Manufacture of Wood, Bamboo,Rattan,aplam and Straw Products	
家具制造业	Manufacture of Furniture	
造纸及纸制品业	Manufacture of Paper and Paper Products	
印刷和记录媒介复制业	Printing,Reproduction of Recording Media	15
文教、工美、体育和娱乐用品制造业	Manufacture of Articles For Culture, Education and Sport Activities	
石油、煤炭及其他燃料加工业	Processing of Petroleum,Coal and Other Fuels	4
化学原料及化学制品制造业	Manufacture of Raw Chemical Materials and Chemical Products	180
医药制造业	Manufacture of Medicines	176
化学纤维制造业	Manufacture of Chemical Fibers	7
橡胶和塑料制品业	Manufacture of Rubber and Manufacture of Plastics	68
非金属矿物制品业	Manufacture of Non-metallic Mineral Products	34
黑色金属冶炼和压延加工业	Smelting and Pressing of Ferrous Metals	1
有色金属冶炼和压延加工业	Smelting and Pressing of Non-ferrous Metals	251
金属制品业	Manufacture of Metal Products	81
通用设备制造业	Manufacture of General Purpose Machinery	151
专用设备制造业	Manufacture of Special Equipment	409
汽车制造业	Manufacture of Motor Vehicle	205
铁路、船舶、航空航天和其他运输设备制造业	Railways,Shipbuilding,Aerospace and Other Transportation Equipment Manufacturing Industry	379
电气机械和器材制造业	Manufacture of Electric Equipment and Machinery	779
计算机、通讯和其他电子设备制造业	Manufacture of Communication Equipment, Computers and other Electronic Equipment	245
仪器仪表制造业	Manufacture of Measuring Instruments and Machinery	207
其他制造业	Other Manufacturing	17
废弃资源综合利用业	Comprehensive Utilization Of Waste Resources	
金属制品、机械和设备修理业	Metal Products,Machinery and Equipment Repair Industry	4
电力、热力、燃气及水生产和供应业	Production and Distribution of Electricity,Heat,Gas and Water	26
电力、热力的生产和供应业	Production and Supply of Electric Power and Heat Power	26
燃气生产和供应业	Gas mining and supplying industry	
水的生产和供应业	Production and Supply of Water	

continued 1

新产品开发经费支出（万元） New Product Development Expenditure （10 000 yuan）	新产品产值 （万元） New product output value （10 000 yuan）	新产品销售收入 （万元） Sales of new products （10 000 yuan）
		2
7631	31509	30168
8374	48134	47976
33648	167477	142865
61864	486088	418097
162		
13330	96498	85010
10376	45235	43009
248	288	244
42790	319949	274737
38724	65020	62625
45821	287488	260123
68714	506928	491493
252886	6596046	4636281
380948	1852398	1836354
155352	2105439	2025312
255870	455515	317676
85761	490947	484603
1433	2185	5004
2575		
796	751	680
796		
	751	680

20-23 规模以上非工业重点行业企业研究与试验发展（R&D）基本情况（2018）

R&D Project Status of Non-Industrial Key Enterprises above Designated Size（2018）

指标	Item	单位数（个）Number of Units (unit)	#有R&D活动单位数（个）# The Number of R&D active units (unit)
总计	**Total**	**772**	**88**
按企业规模分	**Grouped by Size of Enterprises**		
大型企业	Large-size	195	51
中型企业	Medium-size	444	36
小型企业	Small-size	126	1
微型企业	Microenterprise	7	
按登记注册类型分	**Grouped by Registered Status**		
内资企业	Domestic Investment Enterprises	742	85
港、澳、台商投资企业	Enterprises with Funds from Hong Kong, Macao And Taiwan	8	
外商投资企业	Foreign Funded Enterprises	22	3
按国民经济行业分	**Grouped by Sector**		
建筑业	Construction	348	33
交通运输、仓储和邮政业	Traffic, Transport, Storage and Post	39	1
信息传输、软件和信息技术服务业	Information Transmission, Computer Services and Software	118	23
租赁和商务服务业	Leasing and Business Services	32	
科学研究和技术服务业	Scientific Research, Technical Sevice	124	29
水利、环境和公共设施管理业	Management of Water Conservancy, Environment and Public Facilities	37	2
卫生和社会工作	Health, Social Security	29	
文化、体育和娱乐业	Culture, Sports and Entertainment	45	

20-24 规模以上非工业重点行业企业研究与试验发展（R&D）人员和经费支出情况（2018年）

R&D Personnel and Expenditure of Non-Industrial Key Enterprises above Designated Size（2018）

指标	Item	R&D人员（人）R&D personnel（person）	#研究人员 #Researchers
总计	**Total**	**15972**	**14673**
按企业规模分	**Grouped by Size of Enterprises**		
大型企业	Large-size	13516	12367
中型企业	Medium-size	2452	2303
小型企业	Small-size	4	3
微型企业	Microenterprise		
按登记注册类型分	**Grouped by Registered Status**		
内资企业	Domestic Investment Enterprises	15617	14349
港、澳、台商投资企业	Enterprises with Funds from Hong Kong, Macao And Taiwan		
外商投资企业	Foreign Funded Enterprises	355	324
按国民经济行业分	**Grouped by Sector**		
建筑业	Construction	6194	5353
交通运输、仓储和邮政业	Traffic, Transport, Storage and Post	25	24
信息传输、软件和信息技术服务业	Information Transmission, Computer Services and Software	6154	5959
租赁和商务服务业	Leasing and Business Services		
科学研究和技术服务业	Scientific Research, Technical Sevice	3581	3327
水利、环境和公共设施管理业	Management of Water Conservancy, Environment and Public Facilities	18	10
卫生和社会工作	Health, Social Security		
文化、体育和娱乐业	Culture, Sports and Entertainment		

20-24 续表1 continued 1

指标	Item	R&D经费内部支出（万元） R&D Intramural Expenditure (10000 yuan)	#政府资金 # Government funds
总计	**Total**	**476027**	**12637**
按企业规模分	**Grouped by Size of Enterprises**		
大型企业	Large-size	416926	12247
中型企业	Medium-size	59093	390
小型企业	Small-size	8	
微型企业	Microenterprise		
按登记注册类型分	**Grouped by Registered Status**		
内资企业	Domestic Investment Enterprises	442025	12529
港、澳、台商投资企业	Enterprises with Funds from Hong Kong, Macao And Taiwan		
外商投资企业	Foreign Funded Enterprises	34002	108
按国民经济行业分	**Grouped by Sector**		
建筑业	Construction	193657	807
交通运输、仓储和邮政业	Traffic, Transport, Storage and Post	30	10
信息传输、软件和信息技术服务业	Information Transmission, Computer Services and Software	212080	5426
租赁和商务服务业	Leasing and Business Services		
科学研究和技术服务业	Scientific Research, Technical Sevice	70057	6394
水利、环境和公共设施管理业	Management of Water Conservancy, Environment and Public Facilities	204	
卫生和社会工作	Health, Social Security		
文化、体育和娱乐业	Culture, Sports and Entertainment		

20-24 续表2 continued 2

指标	Item	#企业资金 # Enterprise funds	#境外资金 # Foreign funds
总计	**Total**	**457898**	**452**
按企业规模分	**Grouped by Size of Enterprises**		
大型企业	Large-size	400209	165
中型企业	Medium-size	57681	287
小型企业	Small-size	8	
微型企业	Microenterprise		
按登记注册类型分	**Grouped by Registered Status**		
内资企业	Domestic Investment Enterprises	427301	452
港、澳、台商投资企业	Enterprises with Funds from Hong Kong, Macao And Taiwan		
外商投资企业	Foreign Funded Enterprises	30596	
按国民经济行业分	**Grouped by Sector**		
建筑业	Construction	192315	
交通运输、仓储和邮政业	Traffic, Transport, Storage and Post	20	
信息传输、软件和信息技术服务业	Information Transmission, Computer Services and Software	203070	287
租赁和商务服务业	Leasing and Business Services		
科学研究和技术服务业	Scientific Research, Technical Sevice	62290	165
水利、环境和公共设施管理业	Management of Water Conservancy, Environment and Public Facilities	204	
卫生和社会工作	Health, Social Security		
文化、体育和娱乐业	Culture, Sports and Entertainment		

20-25 主要年份知识产权情况

Intellectual Property Rights in Major Years

指　标	Item	2015	2016	2017	2018	2019
一、专利申请合计数（件）	**Patents Application Accepted(piece)**	**60986**	**46103**	**81110**	**56408**	**72377**
发明专利	Inventions	14024	18569	40439	24074	29297
实用新型专利	Utility Models	15735	18369	22461	24313	28087
外观专利	Designs	31227	9165	18210	8021	14993
二、授权专利合计（件）	**Patents Application Granted(piece)**	**25103**	**38279**	**25042**	**31640**	**34123**
发明专利	Inventions	5873	6686	7902	8025	9017
实用新型专利	Utility Models	12030	12344	11595	17070	18937
外观专利	Designs	7200	19249	5545	6545	6169
三、注册商标（件）	**Registered Trade Mark(piece)**	**9600**	**35391**	**28448**	**43205**	**61692**

注：1.本表数据由市场监管局提供。
　　2.本表数据为西安原口径数据。

20-26 主要年份民事知识产权维权情况

Protection of Civil Intellectual Property Rights in Major Years

单位：件　　　　(piece)

指　标	Item	2015	2016	2017	2018	2019
1、专利纠纷	Patent controversies	130	95	112	449	233
2、商标纠纷	Trade mark controversies	277	353	404	892	744
3、著作权纠纷	Copyright controversies	327	404	190	520	1852
4、技术合同纠纷	Technological contract controversies	12	10	36	47	52
5、其他知识产权纠纷	Others IPR controversies	67	25	110	182	366

注：1.本表数据由市中级人民法院提供。
　　2.本表数据为西安原口径数据。

20-27 规模以上工业企业自主知识产权情况（2018年）

The Independent Intellectual Property Rights of Industrial Enterprises above Designated Size（2018）

指 标	Item	专利申请数（件）Number of Patent Applications (piece)	#发明专利 Invention Patent of	期末有效发明专利数（件）Number of Valid Invention Patents At the End of the Term (piece)
总计	**Total**	**6325**	**2891**	**12320**
按企业规模分	**Grouped by Size of Enterprises**			
大型企业	Large-size	2918	1482	4641
中型企业	Medium-size	1446	625	3413
小型企业	Small-size	1908	749	4199
微型企业	Microenterprise	53	35	67
按登记注册类型分	**Grouped by Registered Status**			
内资企业	Domestic Investment Enterprises	6173	2815	11703
国有企业	State-owned Enterprises	571	382	1189
集体企业	Collective-owned Enterprise			
股份合作企业	Stock Cooperative Enterprises			6
联营企业	Affiliated Enterprise			
有限责任公司	Limited Liability Corporations	3547	1630	6639
股份有限公司	Share-holding Corporation Ltd	1091	447	2361
私营企业	Private Enterprise	964	356	1508
其他	Other Domestic Funded Enterprises			
港、澳、台商投资企业	Enterprises with Funds from Hong Kong, Macao And Taiwan	21	6	27
外商投资企业	Foreign Funded Enterprises	131	70	590
按国民经济行业大类分	**Grouped by Sector**			
采矿业	Mining	322	171	889
煤炭开采和洗选业	Mining and Washing of Coal			
石油和天然气开采业	Extraction of Petroleum and Natural Gas	227	127	410
黑色金属矿采选业	Mining of Ferrous Metal Ores			
有色金属矿采选业	Mining of Non-ferrous Metal Ores			
非金属矿采选业	Mining and Processing of Nonmetal Ores			
开采专业及辅助性活动	Mining Professional and Auxiliary Activity	95	44	479
其他采矿业	Mining of other Ores			
制造业	Manufacturing Industry	5818	2609	11265
农副食品加工业	Processing of Food from Agriculture Products	2	2	3
食品制造业	Manufacture of Food	5	5	28
酒、饮料和精制茶制造业	Manufacture of Beverages	16	15	69
烟草制品业	Manufacture of Tobacco	40	7	14
纺织业	Manufacture of Textile	15	10	50
纺织服装、服饰业	Manufacture of Textile Wearing, Apparel			
皮革、毛皮、羽毛及其制品和制鞋业	Manufacture of Leather, Furs, Feather, Related Products and Footware	18	4	5

20-27 续表1 continued 1

指 标	Item	专利申请数（件）Number of Patent Applications (piece)	#发明专利 Invention Patent of	期末有效发明专利数（件）Number of Valid Invention Patents At the End of the Term (piece)
木材加工和木、竹、藤、棕、草制品业	Processing of Timber,Manufacture of Wood, Bamboo, Rattan, Palm and Straw Products			
家具制造业	Manufacture of Furniture			
造纸及纸制品业	Manufacture of Paper And Paper Products			
印刷和记录媒介复制业	Printing and Reproduction of Recording Media	23	6	72
文教、工美、体育和娱乐用品制造业	Education, Art, Sports And Entertainment Products Manufacturing			
石油、煤炭及其他燃料加工业	Processing of Petroleum,Coking and Processing of Nuclear Fuel	61	61	90
化学原料和化学制品制造业	Manufacture of Raw Chemical Materials and Chemical Products	245	187	616
医药制造业	Manufacture of Medicines	138	84	439
化学纤维制造业	Manufacture of Chemical Fiber	7	2	
橡胶和塑料制品业	Manufacture of Rubber and Manufacture of Plastic	99	43	245
非金属矿物制品业	Manufacture of Non-metallic Mineral Products	106	26	170
黑色金属冶炼和压延加工业	Smelting and Pressing of Ferrous Metals	1	1	7
有色金属冶炼和压延加工业	Smelting and Pressing of Non-ferrous Metals	214	143	701
金属制品业	Manufacture of Metal Products	158	102	259
通用设备制造业	Manufacture of General Purpose Machinery	217	75	532
专用设备制造业	Manufacture of Special Equipment	990	347	1748
汽车制造业	Manufacture of Motor Vehicle	699	211	242
铁路、船舶、航空航天和其他运输设备制造业	Railways, Ships, Aerospace And Other Transportation Equipment Manufacturing Industry	965	523	2186
电气机械和器材制造业	Manufacture of Electric Equipment and Machinery	911	276	1155
计算机、通信和其他电子设备制造业	Manufacture of Communication Equipment, Computers and Other Electronic Equipment	550	286	1763
仪器仪表制造业	Manufacture of Measuring Instruments and Machinery	334	189	823
其他制造业	Other Manufacturing	4	4	48
废弃资源综合利用业	Comprehensive Utilization Of Waste Resources			
金属制品、机械和设备修理业	Metal Products, Machinery and Equipment Repair Industry			
电力、燃气及水的生产供应业	Production and Supply of Electric Power,Gas and Water	185	111	166
电力、热力生产和供应业	Production and Supply of Electric Power and Heat Power	171	109	163
燃气生产和供应业	Production and Supply of Gas	14	2	3
水的生产和供应业	Production and Supply of Water			

20-28 规模以上非工业重点行业企业知识产权（2018年）

Intellectual Property Rights of Non-Industrial Key Enterprises above Designated Size（2018）

指 标	Item	专利申请数（件）Number of Patent Applications (piece)	#发明专利 Invention Patent of	有效发明专利数（件）Number of Valid Invention Patents At the End of the Term (piece)
总计	**Total**	**2589**	**1020**	**4249**
按企业规模分	**Grouped by Size of Enterprises**			
大型企业	Large-size	2356	934	3970
中型企业	Medium-size	219	81	266
小型企业	Small-size	14	5	13
微型企业	Microenterprise			
按登记注册类型分	**Grouped by Registered Status**			
内资企业	Domestic Investment Enterprises	2584	1018	4235
港、澳、台商投资企业	Enterprises with Funds from Hong Kong, Macao And Taiwan			
外商投资企业	Foreign Funded Enterprises	5	2	14
按国民经济行业分	**Grouped by Sector**			
建筑业	Construction	754	202	977
交通运输、仓储和邮政业	Traffic, Transport, Storage and Post	2	2	
信息传输、软件和信息技术服务业	Information Transmission, Computer Services and Software	470	209	482
租赁和商务服务业	Leasing and Business Services			
科学研究和技术服务业	Scientific Research, Technical Sevice	1348	606	2784
水利、环境和公共设施管理业	Management of Water Conservancy, Environment and Public Facilities	15	1	6
卫生和社会工作	Health, Social Security			
文化、体育和娱乐业	Culture, Sports and Entertainment			

主要统计指标解释

普通高等学校 指按国家规定的设置标准和审批程序批准举办的，通过全国普通高等学校统一招生考试，招收高中毕业生为主要培养对象，实施高等学历教育的全日制大学、独立设置的学院和高等专科学校、高等职业学校及其他机构（独立学院和分校、大专班）。

大学、独立设置的学院主要实施本科层次以上教育。高等专科学校、高等职业学校实施专科层次教育。其他机构是承担国家普通招生计划任务不计校数的机构，包括独立学院、普通高等学校分校、大专班和批准筹建的普通高等学校等。独立学院指由普通本科高校按新机制、新模式举办的本科层次的二级学院，一些普通本科高校按公办机制和模式建立的二级学院，“分校”或其他类似的二级办学机构不属此范畴。

成人高等学校 指按照国家规定的设置标准和审批程序批准举办的，通过全国成人高等教育统一招生考试，招收具有高中毕业或同等学历的人员为主要培养对象，利用函授、业余、脱产等多种形式对其实施高等学历教育的学校。包括职工高等学校、农民高等学校、管理干部学院、教育学院、独立函授学院、广播电视大学、其他机构等。其他机构是承担国家成人招生计划任务不计校数的机构。

小学学龄儿童净入学率 指调查范围内已入小学学习的学龄儿童占校内外学龄儿童总数（包括弱智儿童，不包括盲聋哑儿童）的比重。计算公式为：

小学学龄儿童净入学率（%）=已入学的小学学龄儿童数/校内外小学学龄儿童总数×100%

研究与试验发展（R&D） 指在科学技术领域，为增加知识总量，以及运用这些知识去创造新的应用进行的系统的创造性的活动，包括基础研究、应用研究、试验发展三类活动。国际上通常采用R&D活动的规模和强度指标反映一国的科技实力和核心竞争力。

基础研究 指为了获得关于现象和可观察事实的基本原理的新知识（揭示客观事物的本质、运动规律，获得新发现、新学说）而进行的实验性或理论性研究，它不以任何专门或特定的应用或使用为目的。其成果以科学论文和科学著作为主要形式。用来反映知识的原始创新能力。

应用研究 指为获得新知识而进行的创造性研究，主要针对某一特定的目的或目标。应用研究是为了确定基础研究成果可能的用途，或是为达到预定的目标探索应采取的新方法（原理性）或新途径。其成果形式以科学论文、专著、原理性模型或发明专利为主。用来反映对基础研究成果应用途径的探索。

试验发展 指利用从基础研究、应用研究和实际经验所获得的现有知识，为产生新的产品、材料和装置，建立新的工艺、系统和服务，以及对已产生和建立的上述各项作实质性的改进而进行的系统性丁作。其成果形式主要是专利、专有技术、具有新产品基本特征的产品原型或具有新装置基本特征的原始样机等。在社会科学领域，试验发展是指把通过基础研究、应用研究获得的知识转变成可以实施的计划（包括为进行检验和评估实施示范项目）的过程。人文科学领域没有对应的试验发展活动。主要反映将科研成果转化为技术和产品的能力，是科技推动经济社会发展的物化成果。

R&D人员 指参与研究与试验发展项目研究、管理和辅助工作的人员，包括项目（课题）组人员，企业科技行政管理人员和直接为项目（课题）活动提供服务的辅助人员。反映投入从事拥有自主知识产权的研究开发活动的人力规模。

R&D人员全时当量 指全时人员数加非全时人员按工作量折算为全时人员数的总和。例如：有两个全时人员和三个非全时人员（工作时间分别为20%、30%和70%），则全时当量为2+0.2+0.3+0.7=3.2人年。为国际上比较科技人力投入而制定的可比指标。

R&D经费内部支出 合计指调查单位用于内部开展R&D活动（基础研究、应用研究和试验发展）的实际支出。包括用于R&D项目（课题）活动的直接支出，以及间接用TR&D活动的管理费、服务费、与R&D有关的基本建设支出以及外协加工费等。不包括生产性活动支出、归还贷款支出以及与外单位合作或委托外单位进行R&D活动而转拨给对方的经费支出。

R&D经费内部支出中政府资金 指R&D经费内部支出中来自各级政府部门的各类资金，包括财政科学技术拨款、科学基金、教育等部门事业费以及政府部门预算外资金的实际支出。

R&D经费内部支出中企业资金 指R&D经费内部支出中来自本企业的自有资金和接受其他企业委托而获得的经费，以及科研院所、高校等事业单位从企业获得的资金的实际支出。

R&D项目（课题）数 指在当年立项并开展研究工作、以前年份立项仍继续进行研究的研发项目（课题）数，包括当年完成和年内研究：工作已告失败的研发项目（课题），但不包括委托外单位进行的研发项目（课题）数。

R&D项目（课题）人员全时当量 指实际参加研发项目（课题）活动人员折合的全时当量。

R&D项目（课题）经费内部支出 指调查单位内部在报告年度进行研发项目（课题）研究和试制等的实际支出。包括劳务费、其他日常支出、固定资产购建费、外协加工费等，不包括委托或与外单位合作进行项目（课题）研究而拨付给对方使用的经费。

新产品产值 指报告期企业生产的新产品的产值。新产品是指采用新技术原理、新设计构思研制、生产的全新产品，或在结构、材质、工艺等某一方面比原有产品有明显改进，从而显著提高了产品性能或扩大了使用功能的产品。新产品产值、新产品销售收入既包括经政府有关部门认定并在有效期内的新产品，也包括企业自行研制开发，未经政府有关部门认定，从投产之日起一年之内的新产品。

新产品销售收入 指报告期企业销售新产品实现的销售收入。

专利 是专利权的简称，是对发明人的发明创造经审查合格后，由专利局依据专利法授予发明人和设计人对该项发明创造享有的专有权。包括发明、实用新型和外观设计。反映拥有自主知识产权的科技和设计成果情况。

发明（专利） 指对产品、方法或者其改进所提出的新的技术方案。是国际通行的反映拥有自主知识产权技术的核心指标。

Explanatory Notes on Main Statistical Indicators

Regular Institutions of Higher Education refer to educational establishments set up according to the government evaluation and approval procedures, recruiting graduates from senior secondary schools as the main target by National Matriculation TEST. They include full-time universities, colleges, institutions of higher professional education, institutions of higher vocational education, institutions of higher vocational education and others (non-university tertiary, branch schools and undergraduate classes) .

Universities and colleges primarily provide undergraduate courses; institutions of higher professional education and institutions of higher vocational education primarily provide professional trainings; and others refer to educational establishments, which are responsible for enrolling higher education students under the State Plan but not enumerated in the total number of schools, including: branch schools of universities and colleges, and universities and colleges that have been approved and under plan for construction. Non-university tertiary refers to the regular undergraduate branch college which is running in new mechanism and mode, excluding the branch schools and other similar branches of educational institutions.

Institutions of Higher Education for Adults refer to educational establishments, set up in line with relevant rules approved by the government, enrolling staff and workers with senior secondary school or equivalent education, and providing higher education courses in many forms of correspondence, spare time, or full time for adults. Professionals thus trained receive a qualification equivalent to graduates studying regular courses at regular universities, colleges and professional colleges. Institutions of higher learning for adults include schools of higher education for staff and workers, schools of higher education for peasants, colleges for management cadres, pedagogical colleges, independent correspondence colleges, Radio and TV universities and other educational establishments. Other educational establishments have undertakings to enrol adult students but not enumerated in the schools under the State Plan.

Net Enrolment Ratio of Primary Schools refers to the proportion of school age children enrolled at schools to the total number of school age children both in and outside schools (including retarded children, but excluding blind, deaf and mute children) . The formula is:

$$\text{Net Enrolment Ratio Of Primary Schools} = \frac{\text{Total Primary School-age Children at Schools}}{\text{Total Primary School-age WnerdlihChether or Not Attending School}} \times 100\%$$

Research and Development (R&D) refers to systematic and creative activities in the field of science and technology aiming at increasing the knowledge and using the knowledge for new application. R&D includes 3 categories of activities: basic research, applied research and experimentation for development. The scale and intensity of R&D are widely used internationally to reflect the strength of S&T and the core competitiveness of a country in the world.

Basic Research refers to empirical or theoretical research aiming at obtaining new knowledge on the fundamental principles regarding phenomena or observable facts to reveal the intrinsic nature and underlying laws and to acquire new discoveries or new theories. Basic research takes no specific or designated application as the aim of the research. Results of basic research are mainly released or disseminated in the form of scientific papers or monographs. This indicator reflects the innovation capacity for original knowledge.

Applied Research refers to creative research aiming at obtaining new knowledge on a specific objective or target. Purpose of the applied research is to identify the possible uses of results from basic research, or to explore new (fundamental) methods or new approaches. Results of applied research are expressed in the form of scientific papers, monographs, fundamental models or invention patents. This indicator reflects the exploration of ways to apply the results of basic research.

Experiments and Development refer to systematic activities aiming at using the knowledge from basic and applied researches or from practical experience to develop new products, materials and equipment, to establish new production process, systems and services, or to make substantial improvement on the existing products, process or services. Results of experiment and development activities are embodied in patents, exclusive technology, and monotype of new products or equipment. In social sciences, experiment and development activities refer to the process of converting the knowledge from basic or applied researches into feasible programmes (including conduct of demonstration projects for assessment and evaluation). There are no experiment and development activities in the science of humanities. This indicator reflects the capability of transferring the results of S&T into technique and products, and measures the realization of S&T in spearheading the economic and social development.

R&D Personnel refer to persons engaged in research, management and supporting activities of R&D, including persons in the project teams, persons engaged in the management of S&T activities of enterprises and supporting staff providing direct service to the research projects. This indicator reflects the size of personnel engaged in R&D activities with independent intellectual property.

Full-time Equivalent of R&D Personnel refers to the sum of the full-time persons and the full-time equivalent of part-time persons converted by workload. For instance, if there are 2 full-time persons and 3 part-time workers (20%, 30% and 70% of working hours respectively on R&D activities), the full-time equivalent are 2+0.2+0.3+0.7=3.2 person-years. This is an internationally comparable indicator of S&T manpower input.

Total Internal Expenditure of Funds on R&D refers to the real expenditure of surveyed units on their own R&D activities (basic research, application study, test and development) including direct expenditure on R&D activities, indirect expenditure of management and services on R&D activities, expenditure on capital construction and material processing by others. Excluding the expenditure on production activities, return of loan, and fees transferred to cooperated and entrusted agencies on R&D activities.

Internal Expenditure of Government Funds refersto the expenditure of funds on R&D activities from government agencies at different levels, including appropriate funds on science and technology from financial departments, scientific funds, operating expenses from education departments and the real expenditure of extra budgetary funds from government agencies.

Internal Expenditure of Funds of Enterprises refers to the expenditure of funds on R&D activities from self-raised funds of enterprises and funds from other enterprises through entrustment, and the expenditure of funds of institutions, such as institution of scientific research and universities, from enterprises.

Number of R&D Projects (subjects) refers to the number of R&D projects (subjects) set up and implemented at the reference year, and the number of R&D projects (subjects) set up in former years and under implementation, including the projects (subjects) finished and failed at the reference year, excluding the projects (subjects) implemented by others through entrustment.

Full-time Equivalent of R&D Personnel refers to the full-time equivalent of persons actually engaged in R&D projects. (subjects)

Internal Expenditure of Funds on R&D Projects (subjects) refers to the real expenditure of internal funds of the surveyed units on research and test of R&D projects (subjects) at the reference year, including service fee, other daily expenditure, cost for capital goods, cost of external process; excluding expenditure of funds transferred to other cooperated and entrusted units of the projects.

Output Value of New Products refers to the output value of new products during the reporting period. The new products refer to brand new products produced with new technology and new design, or product that represent noticeable improvement in terms of structure, material, or production process for improving significantly the character of function of the older versions. The output value and sales income of the new products include those of new products certified by relevant government agencies within the period of certification, as well as new products designed and produced by enterprises within a year without certification by government agencies.

Sales Income of New Products refers to the real sales income of new products of the enterprises at the reporting period.

Patent is an abbreviation for the patent right and refers to the exclusive right of ownership by the inventors or designers for the creation or inventions, given from the patent offices after due process of assessment and approval in accordance with the Patent Law. Patents are granted for inventions, utility models and designs. This indicator reflects the achievements of S&T and design with independent intellectual property.

Patented Inventions refer to new technical proposals to the products or methods or their modifications. This is universal core indicator reflecting the technologies with independent intellectual property.

21 文化、体育、卫生、社会福利和其他

CULTURE,SPORTS,PUBLIC HEALTH,SOCIAL WELFARE INSTITUTIONS AND OTHER SOCIAL ACTIVITIES

资料整理：郝　静
Data management：Hao Jing
数据审核：刘栋婷
Data audit：Liu Dongting

第二十一部分　文化、体育、卫生、社会福利和其他

一、简要说明

本章资料主要包括文化、体育、卫生、社保、公检法等方面的内容，由西安市统计局服务业和社会科技处根据市文旅局、卫健委、民政局、体育局、人社局、公安局、医保局、宣传部、退役军人事务局、团市委、司法局、妇联、应急管理局、消防救援支队、法院、检察院、水务局等部门提供资料整理。本章资料数据口径见表下注释。

二、主要指标

公共图书馆藏量（千册件）	8012	比上年增加	301
医院数（个）	359	比上年增加	16
医院床位数（万张）	6.72	比上年增加	0.38

21　CULTURE,SPORTS,PUBLIC HEALTH,SOCIAL WELFARE INSTITUTIONS AND OTHER SOCIAL ACTIVITIES

Ⅰ.Brief Introduction

Data in this Chapter primarily consists of data of culture, sanitation,civiladministration, physicaleducation,familyplanning, CommunistYouth League, the Women's Federation, public security organs,procuratorial organs and people's court,compiled by Tertiary Industry and Social Science Technology Division of Xi'an Bureau of Statistics according to data from Xi'an Bureau of Cuture,health and Family Planning Commision,Bureau of CivialAdministration, Bureau of PE, the Women's Federation, Municipal Committee of Communist Youth League, Bureau of Public Security, Procuratorate, People's Court and other department concerned. The field and range of data in this chapter are listed in the explanatory notes below the chare.

Ⅱ.Major Indicators

		Increase over Preceding Year
Number of Collections in Libraries (1000 volume-times)	8012	301
Number of Hospitals(units)	359	16
Numbers of Beds(10000 units)	6.72	0.38

21-1 电影基本情况（2019年）

The Basic Situation of Film（2019）

指　标	Item	2019
全年上映本市生产的院线影片数量（个）	Number of Theatrical Films Produced In The Whole Year(unit)	14
电影发行放映管理机构（个）	Film Projection and Publication Administrating Institutions(unit)	2
电影发行放映管理机构从业人员（人）	Film Projection and Publication Administrating Institution Staff(person)	8
电影放映单位（个）	Unit of Film Shows(unit)	285
电影院	Cinema	128
影剧院	Theaters	5
放映队	File Projection Team	152
电影放映单位从业人员（人）	Staff of Unit of Film Shows(person)	2823
电影院	Cinema	2560
影剧院	Theaters	57
放映队	File Projection Team	206
电影放映场数（千场）	Number of Film Shows（1000 shows）	1912
电影观众人数（千人次）	Number of Spectators(1000 person-times)	33565
电影票房收入（万元）	Box-office Receipts(10 000yuan)	105719
平均每一放映场次的观众人次（人次）	Average Audience of Each Projection(person-times)	17
平均每一放映场次的放映收入（元）	Average Income of Each Projcetion(yuan)	564

注：本表数据来源于市委宣传部及文旅局。
本表数据含西咸新区。

21–2 图书馆基本情况（2019年）

The Basic Situation of Library（2019）

指　标	Item	2019
公共图书馆个数（个）	Number of Public Libraries(unit)	13
公共图书馆从业人员（人）	Public Library Practitioners (person)	454
公共图书馆藏量（千册件）	Public Library Reserves(1 000 volume-times)	8012
电子图书（千册）	E-books(1 000 volumes)	6427
阅览室坐席（个）	Number of Seatings in Reading Room(unit)	5298
书刊文献外借人次（千人次）	Number of Books and literature Borrowed by Readers (1 000 person-times)	1226
书刊文献外借册次（千册件）	Volumes of Books and literature Lent to Readers(1 000 volume-times)	3726
图书流通人次（千人次）	Book Circulation Person-time (1 000 person-times)	6008
县以上公共图书馆购书经费（万元）	Book-purchase Fund of Public Library above the County Level(10 000 yuan)	1647
公共图书馆建筑面积（万平方米）	Building Area of Public Library (10 000 sq.m)	9.44

注：本表数据来源于市文广新局。
　　本表数据含西咸新区。

21–3 艺术表演基本情况（2019年）

The Basic Situation of Art Performance（2019）

指　标	Item	2019
艺术表演团体机构数（个）	Number of Organization of Art Performance Troupes(unit)	18
艺术表演团体从业人员（人）	Art Performance Troupes Practitioners (person)	2525
艺术表演团体演出场次（场）	Number of Performances by Art Performance Troupes(show)	5045
#国内演出场次	Domestic Performance	4849
艺术表演观众人次（千人次）	Audience for the Art Performance(1 000 person-times)	5533
艺术表演团体本年创作首映剧目（个）	Art Performance Troupes Creative Premieres of the Year (unit)	14
艺术表演场馆数（个）	Number of Art Performance Places(unit)	16
艺术表演场馆从业人员（人）	Art Performance Place Practitioners (person)	845
艺术表演场馆坐席（个）	Art Performance Place Seatings(unit)	9981
艺术科研机构（个）	Art and Research Institutions(unit)	2
艺术科研机构从业人员（人）	Art and Research Institutions Practitioners(person)	53

注：本表数据来源于市文广新局。
　　本表数据含西咸新区。

21-4 主要年份群众艺术馆、文化馆（站）活动情况

Basic Statistics on Activities of Mass Art Centers and Cultural Centers in Representative Years

指　　标	Item	2010	2013	2014	2015	2016	2017	2018	2019
机构数（个）	Number of Insititutions (unit)	197	198	199	199	190	202	202	202
举办展览个数（个）	Number of Exhibitions (unit)	705	658	627	606	562	649	632	594
举办展览参观人次（千人次）	Number of Exhibition Visitors (1 000 person-times)		301	326	289	287	418	392	442
组织文艺活动次数（次）	Art Performances and Story-telling Sessions (times)	3729	4114	3617	3811	4246	5498	6518	6589
组织文艺活动参加人次（千人次）	Number of Culture Activities attendees (1 000 person-times)		1633	1576	1574	1688	2631	3322	2476
举办训练班班次（个）	Number of Training Courses (unit)	3018	1616	1872	2126	1906	2597	3310	2608
举办训练班结业人次（千人次）	Number of Certificate Trained Persons (1 000 person-times)	133	155	156	207	149	188	209	174
组织各类理论研讨和讲座次数（次）	Number of Theoretical Discussion and Seminars(times)		122	254	216	189	101	113	144
组织各类理论研讨和讲座参加人次（千人次）	Number of Persons in Theoretical and Seminars(1 000 person-times)		19	28	25	18	17	15	20
本年收入（千元）	Income of this year (1 000 yuan)	42937	101365	89520	102567	103706	133378	116324	115525
本年支出（千元）	Expenditure of this year (1 000 yuan)	45160	93485	84827	100749	111942	141012	119354	123727

注：本表数据来源于市文旅局。
　　本表2017年及以后年份数据含西咸新区。

21-5 文物保护业基本情况（2019年）

Basic Statistics on Cultural Relics Protection（2019）

指　　标	Item	机　构（个）Insititution (unit)	人　员（人）Personnel (person)	文物藏品 实际数量（件）Factual Number of Collections (piece)	一级品（件）Grade One (piece)	举办陈列展览次数(次) Times of exhibition (times)	参观人员（千人次）Number of Visitors (1000 person-times)
文物保护管理机构	Cultural Relics administrative Departments	26	544	28933	36	12	1463.72
其他文物机构	Other Agencies	4	69	30844			
博物馆	Museums	100	4390	1870248	3886	552	35599.85
#免费开放馆	Museums Open Free	89	2082	1852092	2091	459	17170.24
文物科研机构	Scientific Research of Historical Relics Preservation	4	237	16814	186		

注：本表数据来源于市文物局。
　　本表数据为西安原口径数据。

21-6 主要年份广播电台及节目制作情况

Basic Statistics of Broadcasting Stations and Program Production in Representative Years

指 标	Item	2010	2013	2014	2015	2016	2017	2018	2019
省、地广播电台（座）	Broadcasting Stations at the Province and District Level(set)	2							
省、地广播电视台（座）	Broadcasting Station at Province and District Level(set)		2	2	2	2	2	2	1
县级广播电视台（座）	Number of Wire Broadcasting Stations and TV Relaying Stations(set)	6	6	6	6	6	6	6	8
中、短波转播发射台（座）	Medium and Short Wave Broadcast Transmitting Station (base)	55	57	57	13	13	13	13	13
节目套数（套）	Number of Programs(set)	18	20	20	20	20	20	20	25
全年播出时间(时)	Broadcasting Hours annually(houe)	124100	138278	143873	137075	139159	132252	132596	131122
广播节目综合人口覆盖率(%)	Broadcasts comprehensive population coverage（%）	99.4	99.47	99.49	99.55	99.62	99.65	100.0	99.99
制作广播节目(时)	Productions of Broadcasting(houe)	110639	106554	104459	116603	119424	100169	117418	112202
#新闻资讯类	News Programs	13786	14355	13208	12208	7590	6362	6761	6719
专题服务类	Special Subject Programs	24451	30181	26884	21864	26957	26907	28463	29278
综艺类	Variety Programs	37720	24516	27148	37885	39735	25793	41535	39475
广播剧类	Literature Programs	2406	3083	3712	6674	3990	4680	5404	4378
广告类	Advertisements	28339	20552	18465	15777	18363	15968	13627	10584
其他类	Service Programs	3937	13867	15042	22195	22787	20459	21628	21768

注：本表数据来源于市文旅局。
中、短波转播发射台2014年之前统计口径为中短波、调频发射台及转播台。数据变化因指标含义变化所致。
本表2017年及以后年份数据含西咸新区。

21-7 主要年份电视台及节目制作情况

Basic Statistics of TV Stations and Production of TV Program in Representative Years

指 标	Item	2010	2013	2014	2015	2016	2017	2018	2019
调频电视转播发射台（座）	FM Television Relay Station (base)	10	11	11	48	48	47	48	43
无线电视节目（套）	Program Productions of Non-cable television Stations (set)	6	6	6	6	2	2	2	2
有线电视节目（套）	Program Productions of cable television Stations (set)	16	16	16	16	20	20	21	20
全年播出时间（时）	Broadcasting Hours annually(houe)	141856	140927	143000	141839	140312	136960	128368	142289
电视节目综合人口覆盖率（%）	TV shows comprehensive population coverage（%）	98.57	98.84	98.96	99.01	99.11	99.13	100	99.99
制作电视节目（时）	Earth Stations of Satellite TV(houe)	29626	46614	35182	43563	54200	49001	45731	58427
#新闻资讯类	News and Information Programs	8930	13360	11797	11839	12891	10517	9387	14172
专题服务类	Special Subject Programs	7762	7751	8289	8073	9346	9769	10808	14581
综艺类	Variety Programs	3942	6508	5014	6242	7883	9080	8789	8728
影视剧类	Film and Television Drama	1729	1820	110	462	490	870	363	3482
广告类	Advertisement	3313	8066	3491	7921	6198	6493	3981	6489
其他类	Service Programs	3950	9109	6479	9026	17390	12272	12403	10975

注：本表数据来源于市文旅局。
调频电视转播发射台2014年之前统计口径为发射台及转播台，数字变化因指标含义变化所致。
影视剧及广告类节目2019年数据变化较大，是因统计口径变化所致。
本表2017年及以后年份数据含西咸新区。

21-8 竞技体育情况（2019年）

The Situation of Competitive Sports（2019）

指　标	Item	2019
奥运会获得奖牌(枚)	Number of Medals Won in the Olympic Games(unit)	
金牌数	Gold	
银牌数	Silver	
铜牌数	Bronze	
全运会获得奖牌(枚)	Number of Medals Won in the National Games(unit)	
金牌数	Gold	
银牌数	Silver	
铜牌数	Bronze	
省运会获得奖牌(枚)	Number of Medals Won in the Provincial Games(unit)	
金牌数	Gold	
银牌数	Silver	
铜牌数	Bronze	
其他国际、国内赛事	Other International and Domestic Events	
金牌数(枚)	Gold(unit)	17
银牌数(枚)	Silver(unit)	12
体育传统项目学校(个)	Sports Traditional Project School(unit)	135
体育传统项目学校在校训练学生数(人)	Number of Students in the Sports Traditional Project School (person)	5960
高水平体育后备人才基地(个)	High Level Sports Reserve Base(unit)	3
省级示范性体校(个)	Provincial Demonstration Sports School(unit)	3
等级教练员人数(人)	Number of Graded Coaches (person)	78
国家级	National Level	1
高　级	Senior Level	14
一　级	One Level	28
二　级	Two Level	24
三　级	Three Level	11
二级运动员人数(人)	Second Grade Athletes (person)	281

注：本表数据来源于市体育局。
　　本表数据不含西咸新区。

21-9 群众体育情况（2019年）

The Situation of Mass Sports（2019）

指　标	Item	2019
全年承办的县级以上群众性体育赛事（个）	Mass Sports Events Held throughout the Year(unit)	600
国家级	National Level	6
省　级	Provincial Level	13
市　级	City Level	281
县　级	County Level	300
全年举办的社会体育指导员培训班（期）	Training Course for Social Sports Instructors Held throughout the Year （time）	23
社会体育指导员人数（名）	Social Sports Instructor（person）	25116
体育先进社区（个）	Advanced Sports Community(unit)	
#国家级	National Level	
省　级	Provincial Level	
群众体育先进单位（个）	Advanced Unit of Mass Sports(unit)	12
#国家级	National Level	
省　级	Provincial Level	12
晨晚健身站点（个）	Morning and Evening Fitness sites(unit)	1902
全民健身活动中心（个）	National Fitness Center(unit)	6
乡镇体育健身工程（个）	Township Sports Fitness Project(unit)	
村级农民体育健身工程（个）	Village Level Farmers' Sports Fitness Project(unit)	186
体育人口（万人）	Sports Population(10 000 person)	485

注：本表数据来源于市体育局。
　　本表数据不含西咸新区。

21-10 体育产业情况（2019年）

The Situation of Sport Industry（2019）

指　标	Item	2019
全市县级标准公共体育场地建设情况	Construction of Standard Public Sports Venues in the County Level	
已建场地个数（个）	Number of Built Sites(units)	8
在建场地个数（个）	Number of Sites in Construction(units)	10
全市全民健身设施建设情况	Construction of National Fitness Facilities in the City	
全民健身园区（个）	National Fitness Park(units)	28
多功能运动场（个）	Multifunction Playground(units)	51
户外营地（个）	Outdoor Camps(units)	
全民健身室内健身房（个）	Fitness Indoor Gymnasium(units)	15
健身步道（千米）	Fitness Footpath(km)	26.5
自行车专用道（千米）	Bicycle Special Road(km)	73
全市体育彩票销售情况	Sales of Sports Lottery in the City	
体育彩票销售网点数量（个）	Number of Sales Outlets of Sports Lottery (units)	1853
体育彩票销售网点数量占全省的比重(%)	Proportion of Sports Lottery Sales Outlets Accounts for the Proportion of the Whole Province（%）	37
本年体育彩票销售金额（万元）	Sales Amount of Sports Lottery in this Year (10 000 yuan)	230417.53
本年体育彩票销售金额占全省的比重(%)	Sales Amount of Sports Lottery in this year Accounts for the Proportion of the Whole Province（%）	43
全市体育产业单位数量（个）	Number of Sports Industrial Units in the City (units)	2025

注：本表数据来源于市体育局。本表数据不含西咸新区。
体育产业单位数包括法人单位及产业活动单位。

21-11 主要年份医疗卫生机构、床位、人员情况

Number of Health Care Institutions, Beds and Personnel in Health Care Institutions in Representative Years

年份 Year	医疗卫生机构数（个）Number of Health Care Institutions（unit）	医院数（个）Number of Health Care Hospital（unit）	医疗卫生机构床位数（张）Number of Health Care Bed（unit）	医院床位数（张）Number of Hospital Bed（unit）	卫生技术人员数（人）Number of Medical Technical Personnel（person）
2009	5284	261	36849	32371	52620
2010	5632	258	39407	34274	57756
2011	5554	268	41010	35976	61281
2012	5576	276	44239	39213	66899
2013	5503	281	47867	42753	71134
2014	5554	281	51065	45561	76005
2015	5802	295	54708	49830	81462
2016	5869	292	56332	51508	86258
2017	6376	329	63942	58219	94221
2018	6638	343	68981	63365	101477
2019	7011	359	72549	67238	112243

注：本表数据来源于市卫健委。
本表2017年及以后年份数据含西咸新区。

21-12 医疗卫生机构、床位及人员情况（2019年）

卫生机构	Health Care Institutions	机构数（个）Number of Institutions (unit)	床位数（张）Number of Beds (unit)
总计	**Total**	**7011**	**72549**
一、医院	**Hospitals**	**359**	**67238**
综合医院	General Hospitals	211	47028
中医医院	Hospitals Specialized in Traditional Chinese Medicine	56	7298
中西医结合医院	Hospitals Integrating Traditional Chinese Medicine with Western Therapeutics in Practice	5	1036
民族医院	Nationalities Hospitals		
专科医院	Specialized Hospitals	85	11717
护理院	Nursing centers	2	159
二、基层医疗卫生机构	**Commuting Health Hare Service Centre**	**6575**	**3638**
社区卫生服务中心(站)	Community Health Care Center(Station)	244	1719
社区卫生服务中心	Community Health Care Center	124	1719
社区卫生服务站	Community Health Care Station	120	
卫生院	Health Center	118	1869
街道卫生院	Urban Health-center	2	119
乡镇卫生院	Rural Health-center	116	1750
村卫生室	Village Clinics	3193	
门诊部	Outpatient Department	362	50
诊所、卫生所、医务室	Clinic, Health Center, Infirmary	2658	
三、专业公共卫生机构	**College of Public Health Institutions**	**51**	**1443**
疾病预防控制中心	Center for Disease Control and Prevention	16	
专科疾病防治院（所、站）	Specialized Disease Prevention and Cure Center (Place, Station)	1	800
健康教育所（站、中心）	Health Education Institute (Station, Center)	2	
妇幼保健院（所、站）	Maternal and Child Health Hospital (Place, Station)	14	643
急救中心（站）	Emergency Center (Station)	2	
采供血机构	Blood Collection Agencies	1	
卫生监督所（中心）	Health Supervision Agencies (Center)	14	
计划生育技术服务机构	Institutions of Technical Service for Family Planning	1	
四、其他卫生机构	**Other Health Institution**	**26**	**230**
疗养院	Nursing Centres	1	230
卫生监督检验(监测、检测)所(站)	Health Supervision and Inspection Agencies (Station)		
医学科学研究机构	Medical Scientific Research Institutions	3	
医学在职培训机构	Medical Training Institutions	4	
临床检验中心（所、站）	Clinical Testing Center (Place, Station)	5	
统计信息中心	Statistical Information Center	2	
其他	Other	11	

注：本表数据来源于市卫健委。
本表人员合计中包括乡村医生2838人和卫生员186人，不含乡镇卫生院在村卫生室工作的执业（助理）医师、注册护士。
本表数据含西咸新区。

Number of Health Care Institutions, Beds and Personnel in Health Care Institutions（2019）

人员合计（人） Total Number of Employed Persons (person)	卫生技术人员 Medical Technical Personnel	执业（助理）医师数 Licensed (Assistant) Doctors	#执业医师 Chartered Doctors
136333	**112243**	**38469**	**34102**
97533	**80979**	**24960**	**23844**
71412	60185	18573	17792
9206	7454	2296	2156
1566	1255	419	410
15284	12027	3658	3474
65	58	14	12
32989	**27188**	**12388**	**9243**
6882	5723	1706	1359
5738	4702	1325	1039
1144	1021	381	320
4037	3405	908	609
277	246	74	46
3760	3159	834	563
4932	1908	1673	440
6426	5825	2499	2099
10712	10327	5602	4736
4724	**3514**	**964**	**876**
1094	835	353	326
658	517	99	95
76	27	1	1
2026	1541	452	399
135	76	49	48
144	87	8	6
558	414		
33	17	2	1
1087	**562**	**157**	**139**
71	40	17	14
145	87	49	48
174	70	3	3
288	88	7	5
43	0		
366	277	81	69

21-12 续表1

卫生机构	Health Care Institutions	人员合计（人）	
		卫生技术人员中	
		注册护士 Registered Nurses	药师（士） Junior Paramedics
总计	**Total**	**51882**	**4709**
一、医院	**Hospitals**	**41028**	**3300**
综合医院	General Hospitals	30707	2292
中医医院	Hospitals Specialized in Traditional Chinese Medicine	3418	469
中西医结合医院	Hospitals Integrating Traditional Chinese Medicine with Western Therapeutics in Practice	594	84
民族医院	Nationalities Hospitals		
专科医院	Specialized Hospitals	6274	451
护理院	Nursing centers	35	4
二、基层医疗卫生机构	**Commuting Health Hare Service Centre**	**9731**	**1280**
社区卫生服务中心(站)	Community Health Care Center(Station)	2193	417
社区卫生服务中心	Community Health Care Center	1756	344
社区卫生服务站	Community Health Care Station	437	73
卫生院	Health Center	1009	223
街道卫生院	Urban Health-center	113	13
乡镇卫生院	Rural Health-center	896	210
村卫生室	Village Clinics	235	
门诊部	Outpatient Department	2350	261
诊所、卫生所、医务室	Clinic, Health Center, Infirmary	3944	379
三、专业公共卫生机构	**College of Public Health Institutions**	**978**	**118**
疾病预防控制中心	Center for Disease Control and Prevention	60	14
专科疾病防治院（所、站）	Specialized Disease Prevention and Cure Center (Place, Station)	265	31
健康教育所（站、中心）	Health Education Institute (Station, Center)		
妇幼保健院（所、站）	Maternal and Child Health Hospital (Place, Station)	608	64
急救中心（站）	Emergency Center (Station)	18	2
采供血机构	Blood Collection Agencies	26	6
卫生监督所（中心）	Health Supervision Agencies (Center)		
计划生育技术服务机构	Institutions of Technical Service for Family Planning	1	1
四、其他卫生机构	**Other Health Institution**	**145**	**11**
疗养院	Nursing Centres	14	5
卫生监督检验(监测、检测)所(站)	Health Supervision and Inspection Agencies (Station)		
医学科学研究机构	Medical Scientific Research Institutions	8	3
医学在职培训机构	Medical Training Institutions	1	
临床检验中心（所、站）	Clinical Testing Center (Place, Station)	2	
统计信息中心	Statistical Information Center		
其他	Other	120	3

continued 1

Total Number of Employed Persons (person)				
Among:Medical Technical Personnel		其他技术人员 Other Technical Personnel	管理人员 Administrative Personnel	工勤技能人员 Logistics Technical Workers
技师（士） Technicians	其他 Others			
6633	**10550**	**936**	**10229**	**9901**
4805	**6886**	**686**	**8049**	**7819**
3493	5120	471	5528	5228
435	836	99	790	863
78	80	4	196	111
795	849	111	1533	1613
4	1	1	2	4
1264	**2525**	**99**	**1337**	**1341**
463	944	67	520	572
398	879	60	442	534
65	65	7	78	38
325	940	26	295	311
15	31		9	22
310	909	26	286	289
400	315	6	335	260
76	326		187	198
422	**1032**	**73**	**622**	**515**
210	198	25	133	101
52	70	3	78	60
	26	28	20	1
145	272	8	220	257
0	7	1	34	24
14	33	1	51	5
	414	4	80	60
1	12	3	6	7
142	**107**	**78**	**221**	**226**
3	1		13	18
18	9	21	20	17
2	64	52	40	12
78	1	5	70	125
			41	2
41	32		37	52

21-13 各区县医疗卫生机构、床位及人员情况（2019年）

Number of Health Care Institutions, Beds and Employed Persons in Health Care Institutions By Region (2019)

区 县	Region	机构（个）Number of Health Care Institutions (unit)	床位（张）Number of Beds (unit)	人员合计（人）Total Number of Employed Persons (person)	#卫生技术人员 Total Number of Medical Technical Personnel
合 计	**Total**	**7011**	**72549**	**136333**	**112243**
新城区	Xincheng	300	7976	15654	12913
碑林区	Beilin	453	9326	17338	14785
莲湖区	Lianhu	428	8788	16205	13244
灞桥区	Baqiao	416	3184	5626	4760
未央区	Weiyang	492	6977	13588	11566
雁塔区	Yanta	552	8951	20176	16928
阎良区	Yanliang	185	1890	3239	2588
临潼区	Lintong	527	2934	4551	3564
长安区	Chang'an	683	6821	10583	8364
高陵区	Gaoling	232	2361	3781	3188
鄠邑区	Huyi	453	3209	5314	4264
蓝田县	Lantian	609	1869	3226	2584
周至县	Zhouzhi	480	2052	4001	2890
西咸新区	Xixian	753	2656	5071	3869
高新区	Gaoxin	392	3467	7633	6466
国际港务区	International Trade&Logistic Park	56	88	347	270

注：本表数据来源于市卫健委。

21-14 各区县农村村级卫生组织情况（2019年）

Village Level Health Organization in the Rural Area by Region (2019)

区 县	Region	村卫生室（个） Village Health Room（unit）	乡村医生和卫生员（人） Rural Doctors and Health Workers（person）	#乡村医生 Rural Doctors	#卫生员 Health Workers
全 市	**Total**	**3193**	**3024**	**2838**	**186**
新城区	Xincheng				
碑林区	Beilin				
莲湖区	Lianhu				
灞桥区	Baqiao	149	150	148	2
未央区	Weiyang	51	27	27	
雁塔区	Yanta	30	38	38	
阎良区	Yanliang	80	100	100	
临潼区	Lintong	342	329	296	33
长安区	Chang'an	405	311	308	3
高陵区	Gaoling	122	155	151	4
鄠邑区	Huyi	358	299	235	64
蓝田县	Lantian	506	353	353	
周至县	Zhouzhi	410	551	478	73
西咸新区	Xixian	503	468	465	3
高新区	Gaoxin	204	208	204	4
国际港务区	International Trade&Logistic Park	33	35	35	

注：本表数据来源于市卫健委。

21-15 各区县社区卫生服务中心（站）情况（2019年）

Situations of Community Health Service Center（Station）by Region（2019）

区 县	Region	社区卫生服务中心（站）（个）Community Health Care Center(Station) (unit)	床位数（张）Number of Beds (unit)	人员数（人）Personnel Number (person)	卫生技术人员（人）Medical Technical Personnel (person)	执业（助理）医师 Licensed (Assistant) Doctors	注册护士 Registered Nurses
全 市	**Total**	**244**	**1719**	**6882**	**5723**	**1706**	**2193**
新城区	Xincheng	19	35	357	297	107	104
碑林区	Beilin	22	60	453	358	145	132
莲湖区	Lianhu	20	195	785	655	200	270
灞桥区	Baqiao	21	76	442	367	116	140
未央区	Weiyang	27	50	730	607	175	273
雁塔区	Yanta	36	80	1147	1007	307	425
阎良区	Yanliang	8	76	172	154	39	70
临潼区	Lintong	28	559	694	582	151	145
长安区	Chang'an	16	317	694	550	160	163
高陵区	Gaoling	8		71	67	13	31
鄠邑区	Huyi						
蓝田县	Lantian						
周至县	Zhouzhi	1		108	80	13	33
西咸新区	Xixian	21	38	355	288	94	125
高新区	Gaoxin	14	145	661	535	152	209
国际港务区	International Trade& Logistic Park	3	88	213	176	34	73

注：本表数据来源于市卫健委。

21-16 主要年份医疗卫生机构各类人员情况

Number of Personnel in Health Care Institutions in Representative Years

单位：人 (person)

指　标	Item	2010	2013	2014	2015	2016	2017	2018	2019
人员合计	**Total**	**71230**	**90129**	**95633**	**102684**	**107906**	**116939**	**125179**	**136333**
卫生技术人员	Medical Technical Personnel	56579	71134	76005	81462	86258	94221	101477	112243
执业（助理）医师	Licensed (Assistant) Doctors	18763	23885	24820	26626	27864	30820	33776	38469
#执业医师	Chartered Doctors	16613	21205	22145	23818	25023	27683	30322	34102
注册护士	Registered Nurses	22640	29967	32136	34819	37518	41603	46450	51882
药师(士)	Junior Paramedics	3030	3551	3709	3957	4075	4280	4423	4709
技师（士）	Technicians	4589	4089	4276	4690	5058	5593	6035	6633
其他	Other	7557	9642	11064	11370	11743	11925	10793	10550
其他技术人员	Other Technical Personnel	1156	590	621	816	835	839	925	936
管理人员	Administrative Personnel	6416	7160	7355	8248	8470	9003	9723	10229
工勤技能人员	Logistics Technical Workers	7079	7437	7944	8326	8913	9179	9707	9901

注：本表数据来源于市卫健委。
本表2011年及以后合计栏数据含乡村医生和卫生员。
本表2017年及以后年份数据含西咸新区。

21-17 医疗卫生机构门诊、住院及病床使用情况（2019年）

指 标	Item	总诊疗人次数 总计 Total
总计	**Total**	**70413747**
一、医院	**Hospitals**	**42582210**
综合医院	General Hospitals	31131439
中医医院	Hospitals Specialized in Traditional Chinese Medicine	3666633
中西医结合医院	Hospitals Integrating Traditional Chinese Medicine with Western Therapeutics in Practice	399077
民族医院	Nationalities Hospitals	
专科医院	Specialized Hospitals	7382993
护理院	Nursing Centers	2068
二、基层医疗卫生机构	**Commuting Health Care Service Centre**	**26483055**
社区卫生服务中心（站）	Community Health Care Center(Station)	5123951
社区卫生服务中心	Community Health Care Center	4207868
社区卫生服务站	Community Health Care Station	916083
卫生院	Health Center	2488163
街道卫生院	Urban Health-center	73276
乡镇卫生院	Rural Health-center	2414887
村卫生室	Village Clinics	10727655
门诊部	Outpatient Department	2401507
诊所、卫生所、医务室	Clinic, Health Center, Infirmary	5741779
三、专业公共卫生机构	**College of Public Health Institutions**	**1304726**
专科疾病防治院（所、站）	Specialized Disease Prevention and Cure Center (Place, Station)	55582
妇幼保健院（所、站）	Maternal and Child Health Hospital (Place, Station)	1059077
急救中心（站）	Emergency Center(Station)	190067
四、其他卫生机构	**Other Health Institution**	**43756**
疗养院	Sanatorium	43756

注：本表数据来源于市卫健委。
本表数据含西咸新区。

Medical and Health Institutions Outpatient, Inpatient and Utilization of Beds (2019)

Total Number of Clinics (person time)				观察室 Observation Room	
门、急诊人次数合计 Total Number of People In Outpatient and Emergency Department	门诊人次数(人次) Number of Outpatients (person time)	急诊人次数小计(人次) The Number of Emergency Subtotal (person time)	死亡人数（人） Number of Deaths (person)	留观病例数(人次) Number of Patients Receiving (person times)	死亡人数（人） Number of Deaths (persons)
69687242	**65344181**	**4343061**	**3551**	**28884**	**21**
42393568	**38413242**	**3980326**	**3551**	**28349**	**21**
31001285	27799070	3202215	3367	23351	21
3646821	3509761	137060	84	459	
397670	360528	37142	35	709	
7345724	6741815	603909	65	3830	
2068	2068				
25945297	**25888377**	**56920**		**115**	
4994817	4955231	39586		44	
4091399	4056898	34501		44	
903418	898333	5085			
2451877	2434543	17334		71	
73276	72556	720			
2378601	2361987	16614		71	
10384313	10384313				
2393688	2393688				
5720602	5720602				
1304621	**999110**	**305511**		**420**	
55477	54909	568			
1059077	944201	114876		420	
190067		190067			
43756	**43452**	**304**			
43756	43452	304			

21-17 续表1

指 标	Item	急诊死亡率（%） Emergency Mortality (%)	入院人数合计（人） Total Number of Admission Patients (person)
总计	**Total**	**0.08**	**2509239**
一、医院	**Hospitals**	**0.09**	**2421161**
综合医院	General Hospitals	0.11	1868442
中医医院	Hospitals Specialized in Traditional Chinese Medicine	0.06	205028
中西医结合医院	Hospitals Integrating Traditional Chinese Medicine with Western Therapeutics in Practice	0.09	30734
民族医院	Nationalities Hospitals		
专科医院	Specialized Hospitals	0.01	315553
护理院	Nursing Centers		1404
二、基层医疗卫生机构	**Commuting Health Care Service Centre**		**43415**
社区卫生服务中心（站）	Community Health Care Center(Station)		23867
社区卫生服务中心	Community Health Care Center		23867
社区卫生服务站	Community Health Care Station		
卫生院	Health Center		19505
街道卫生院	Urban Health-center		375
乡镇卫生院	Rural Health-center		19130
村卫生室	Village Clinics		
门诊部	Outpatient Department		43
诊所、卫生所、医务室	Clinic, Health Center, Infirmary		
三、专业公共卫生机构	**College of Public Health Institutions**		**41224**
专科疾病防治院（所、站）	Specialized Disease Prevention and Cure Center (Place, Station)		7971
妇幼保健院（所、站）	Maternal and Child Health Hospital (Place, Station)		33253
急救中心（站）	Emergency Center (Station)		
四、其他卫生机构	**Other Health Institution**		**3439**
疗养院	Sanatorium		3439

continued 1

出院人数合计 (人) Total Number of Discharge Patients (person)	死亡人数 （人） Number of Hospital Csualty (person)	病床周转次数 （次） Nnumber of Bed Remover (times)	病床使用率 （%） Bed occupancy rate （%）	出院者平均住院日 （天） Average Stay Days in Hospital (day)
2508811	**10909**	**36.1**	**82.68**	**8.4**
2420760	**10870**	**37.6**	**85.84**	**8.3**
1866174	9741	41.5	88.55	7.8
205928	421	29	80.95	10.2
31026	130	26.9	69.61	9.5
316242	578	28.8	80.57	10.1
1390		8.7	20.16	8.5
43160	**7**	**12.3**	**27.53**	**8.1**
23660	7	14.3	30.09	7.6
23660	7	14.3	30.09	7.6
19457		10.5	25.23	8.7
375		3.2	40.22	46.6
19082		11	24.2	7.9
43				
41615	**32**	**29**	**85.21**	**11**
8341	32	10.4	94.28	34.5
33274		52.6	73.74	5.1
3276		**14.2**	**26.62**	**6.7**
3276		14.2	26.62	6.7

21-18 提供住宿的社会服务机构（2019年）

Social Welfare Insititutions Providing Accommodation (2019)

指　标	Item	机构数（个）Number of Institutions（unit）	年末职工人数（人）Number of Staff and Workers at the End of Year（person）	#女性 Female	床位数（张）Number of Beds（unit）	年末在院人数（人）Number of Persons Housed at the Year-end（person）
1、养老服务机构	Pension Service Institutions	140	3512	2385	24629	11910
2、儿童福利院	Baby Welfare Homes	2	77	49	566	551
3、社会福利医院	Social Welfare Hospitals	1	139	61	750	423
4、救助站	Rescue Station	8	103	37	415	64

注：本表数据来源于市民政局。
本表数据含西咸新区。

21-19 主要年份社会福利事业单位机构及人员情况

Number of Social Welfare Institutions and Personnel

单位：个、人　　(unit, person)

指　标	Item	2010	2013	2014	2015	2016	2017	2018	2019
一、机构	**Insititutions**								
烈士纪念建筑物管理单位	Institutions Managing Memorial Buildings of Martyrs	2	2	2	2	2	2	2	2
救助类单位	Units Providing Assistance	8	8	9	9	9	9	9	9
殡仪服务单位	Funeral Service Units	22	25	26	26	25	27	25	26
殡仪馆	Funeral Homes	4	4	3	3	3	3	3	3
公墓	Cemeteries	14	15	16	16	16	19	18	19
殡葬管理单位	Funeral Management Units	4	6	7	7	6	5	4	4
二、人员	**Staff**								
烈士纪念建筑物管理单位	Institutions Managing Memorial Buildings of Martyrs	37	42	44	42	42	44	42	40
救助类单位	Units Providing Assistance	116	137	139	119	121	114	110	113
殡仪服务单位	Funeral Service Units	1371	1430	1392	1510	1510	1518	1337	1282
殡仪馆	Funeral Homes	375	491	470	497	481	484	458	476
公墓	Cemeteries	939	855	838	929	953	959	824	761
殡葬管理单位	Funeral Management Units	57	84	84	84	76	75	55	45

注：本表数据来源于市民政局及退役军人事务局。
本表2017年及以后年份数据含西咸新区。

21-20 社会保障基本情况（2019年）

Basic Situation of Social Security (2019)

单位：万人、万户　　　　（10 000 persons、10 000 households）

指　标	Item	2019
基本养老保险参保人数	Number of Basic Old-age Insurance	720.59
1. 城镇企业职工养老保险参保人数	Number of Town Enterprise Worker Old-age Insurance	442.69
其中：离退休人员	Retired Personnel	69.57
2. 机关事业单位养老保险参保人数	Number of Institution Old-age Insurance	29.77
其中：离退休人员	Retired Personnel	10.19
3. 城乡居民养老保险参保人数	Number of Rural Residents Old-age Insurance	248.13
城镇基本医疗保险参保人数	Number of urban basic medical insurance	598.3
失业保险参保人数	Number of unemployed insurance	219.99
生育保险参保人数	Number of Maternity insurance	252.68
工伤保险参保人数	Number of industrial injury insurance	266.89
城市居民最低生活保障户数	The Number of Minimum Living Guarantee for Urban Resident Households	1.49
城市居民最低生活保障人数	The Number of Minimum Living Guarantee for Urban Residents	2.24
农村居民最低生活保障户数	The Number of Minimum Living Guarantee for Rural Resident Households	2.5
农村居民最低生活保障人数	The Number of Minimum Living Guarantee for Rural Residents	6.86

注：本表数据来源于市人社局、市民政局及市医疗保障局。
本表中"基本养老保险参保人数"不含西咸新区，其他指标均含西咸新区。

21-21 全市及各区县新型农村合作医疗情况（2019年）

Situation of the New Rural Cooperative Medical Care of the Whole City and Area County (2019)

单位：万人　　　　（10 000 persons）

区　县	Region	参加新型农村合作医疗人数 Participate in The New Rural Cooperative Medical Population
合　计	**Total**	**435.31**
新城区	Xincheng	
碑林区	Beilin	
莲湖区	Lianhu	
灞桥区	Baqiao	19.18
未央区	Weiyang	5.30
雁塔区	Yanta	1.77
阎良区	Yanliang	16.59
临潼区	Lintong	55.96
长安区	Chang'an	52.81
高陵区	Gaoling	24.23
鄠邑区	Huyi	34.02
蓝田县	Lantian	55.63
周至县	Zhouzhi	58.64
西咸新区	Xixian	72.63
高新区	Gaoxin	28.29
国际港务区	International Trade&Logistic Park	10.26

注：本表数据来源于市医疗保障局。
本表数据含西咸新区。

21-22 全市及各区县优抚对象人员情况（2019年）

Statistics on Persons Enjoying Favoured Treatment by Region (2019)

单位：人 (person)

区 县	Region	伤残人员 Number of Disabled Veterans	烈军属人员 Number of Family Members of Martyrs and Soldiers	在乡复员军人 Demobilized Soldiers in Hometown	带病回乡退伍军人 Veterans Returning Home in Sick
合 计	**Total**	**5380**	**778**	**2234**	**977**
市本级	City Level	45			
新城区	Xincheng	645	36	6	2
碑林区	Beilin	697	47	6	2
莲湖区	Lianhu	731	45	18	7
灞桥区	Baqiao	262	43	86	89
未央区	Weiyang	242	45	70	13
雁塔区	Yanta	718	58	45	9
阎良区	Yanliang	116	40	153	59
临潼区	Lintong	293	72	378	173
长安区	Chang'an	242	29	138	9
高陵区	Gaoling	143	38	242	117
鄠邑区	Huyi	199	54	206	67
蓝田县	Lantian	226	54	213	159
周至县	Zhouzhi	278	112	274	133
西咸新区	Xixian	351	78	227	69
高新区	GaoXin	163	19	125	32
国际港务区	Interational Trade& Logistic Park	29	8	47	37

注：本表数据来源于市退役军人事务局。

21-23 全市及各区县计划生育和婚姻登记情况（2019年）

Conditions of Birth Control and Marriage Registration by Region (2019)

区 县	Region	计划生育率（%）Family Planning Rate(%)	结婚对数（对）Marriages (couple)	再婚人数（人）Remarriages (person)	离婚对数（对）Divorced Couple (couple)
合 计	**Total**	**99.0**	**87315**	**45436**	**45329**
新城区	Xincheng	100.0	4197	2267	2475
碑林区	Beilin	100.0	6720	2960	3389
莲湖区	Lianhu	99.6	6290	3506	3654
灞桥区	Baqiao	99.8	4451	2306	2446
未央区	Weiyang	99.9	8288	4171	4346
雁塔区	Yanta	99.9	9184	5260	5621
阎良区	Yanliang	99.0	2085	1396	1190
临潼区	Lintong	93.4	4890	2524	2968
长安区	Chang'an	99.8	7884	4987	5202
高陵区	Gaoling	99.0	2752	1808	1568
鄠邑区	Huyi	97.0	3596	1552	1669
蓝田县	Lantian	98.6	4451	1732	1728
周至县	Zhouzhi	98.1	5001	1965	1977
西咸新区	Xixian	99.7	7908	4573	3416
高新区	Gaoxin	99.5	8421	828	591
国际港务区	International Trade &Logistic Park	100.0	1197	3601	3089

注：本表数据来源于市卫健委、市民政局、市法院。
本表中计划生育率、结婚对数、再婚人数含西咸新区，离婚对数西咸包含不完全。

21-24 全市及各区县妇幼卫生保健情况（2019年）

Care Health Conditions of Women and Child by Region (2019)

区县	Region	5岁以下儿童死亡率（‰） Mortality rate of Children under 5-year-old（‰）	新生儿死亡率（‰） Infant Mortality Ratio in 2012（‰）	婴儿死亡率（‰） Neonatal Mortality Ratio （‰）
合　计	**Total**	**2.35**	**1.14**	**1.77**
新城区	Xincheng	3.21	1.15	2.29
碑林区	Beilin	2.84	1.55	2.32
莲湖区	Lianhu	2.78	1.92	2.35
灞桥区	Baqiao	1.34	0.30	0.89
未央区	Weiyang	1.88	1.31	1.50
雁塔区	Yanta	1.70	0.54	1.49
阎良区	Yanliang	2.26	1.61	2.26
临潼区	Lintong	3.09	1.27	1.82
长安区	Chang'an	3.12	1.12	2.00
高陵区	Gaoling	1.73	0.87	1.30
鄠邑区	Huyi	2.47	1.10	1.37
蓝田县	Lantian	5.32	2.31	3.47
周至县	Zhouzhi	2.71	1.28	2.08
西咸新区	Xixian	2.24	1.12	1.73
高新区	Gaoxin	1.51	0.96	1.23
国际港务区	International Trade&Logistic Park	1.97	0.60	1.32

注：本表数据来源于市卫健委。

21-24 续表1 continued 1

区县	Region	孕产妇死亡率（1/10万） Maternal Mortality Ratio (one in hundred thousandth)	产妇住院分娩比例（%） Proportion of maternal Hospital Births（%）
合　计	**Total**	**13.74**	**99.99**
新城区	Xincheng	45.85	100
碑林区	Beilin	51.63	99.97
莲湖区	Lianhu	21.35	100
灞桥区	Baqiao		100
未央区	Weiyang	6.25	100
雁塔区	Yanta	20.35	100
阎良区	Yanliang		100
临潼区	Lintong	18.19	99.85
长安区	Chang'an		100
高陵区	Gaoling	21.67	100
鄠邑区	Huyi		100
蓝田县	Lantian	46.24	100
周至县	Zhouzhi		100
西咸新区	Xixian		100
高新区	Gaoxin	13.71	100
国际港务区	International Trade&Logistic Park		100

21-25 主要年份律师、公证及调解情况

Basic Statistics on Lawyer, Notaries and Mediation in Representative Years

指 标	Item	2010	2013	2014	2015	2016	2017	2018	2019
一、律师工作	**Lawyers**								
律师事务所（个）	Number of Law Offices (unit)	95	116	122	149	176	200	224	254
律师（人）	Lawyers(person)	1202	1639	1846	2198	2462	2836	3796	4220
#专职	Full-time	1139	1560	1738	2092	2337	2716	3476	3751
兼职	Part-time	63	77	88	91	84	120	148	188
刑事诉讼辩护及代理（件）	Criminal Litigation Defense and Agency（case）		3267	3118	3524	3260	5872	5869	7481
民事诉讼代理（件）	Civil Litigation Agency(case)		10754	9985	15308	16743	24593	28810	37116
行政诉讼代理（件）	Administrative Litigation Agency(case)		319	374	532	601	1584	1256	1720
非诉讼法律事务（件）	Nonlitigious Legal Matters（case）		2265	2352	2780	2840	4981	3900	5864
二、公证工作	**Notarization**								
公证处（个）	Number of Notary Offices (unit)	14	14	14	14	14	14	14	14
公证人员（人）	Notarial Personnel (person)	202	222	298	307	293	285	296	328
#公证员	Notaries	112	115	118	121	115	116	116	114
办理公证件数（件）	Number of Notarized Documents Issued (case)	106491	136471	135413	135622	144662	150300	161932	122152
国内	Domestic	72670	98572	90171	86589	95194	96085	110311	75486
涉外	Foreign-related	33410	37444	44773	49033	49468	54215	51621	46666
港澳台	Hong Kong. Macao and Taiwan related	411	455	469	373	512	641	1601	632
三、人民调解工作	**Number of People Mediations**								
已建调委会数（个）	Number of Mediation Committees (unit)	3911	4040	4059	4052	4062	3903	3589	3411
调解人员数（人）	Number of Mediators (person)	15717	15240	15793	14838	14888	14295	14216	13895
调解纠纷数（件）	Number of Civil Disputes Mediated (case)	22247	33651	33641	31696	27455	48690	24868	22377
#调解成功数	Number of Cases Successfully Mediated	22164	32368	32537	30590	26426	47921	24364	21967

注：本表数据来源于市司法局。

2015年开始统计上将港澳台并入国内，表中2015年以后办理公证件数中港澳台所列数据为其中数，2014年及以前年份港澳台数据与国内、涉外数据为并列关系。

本表2017年及以后年份数据含西咸新区。

21–26 主要年份共青团组织情况

Basic Facts on Communist Youth League in Representative Years

单位：个、人 (unit, person)

指 标	Item	2010	2013	2014	2015	2016	2017	2018	2019
一、基层团组织	**Grass-root Youth League Organisations**	**7006**	**10770**	**10152**	**10074**	**10530**	**10237**	**9438**	**10359**
二、共青团员	**Youth League Members**	**308141**	**344096**	**343121**	**331261**	**251706**	**201789**	**162527**	**166284**
#女团员	Female Youth League Members	142379	158287	153212	146213	110092	88182		
三、专职团干部	**Full-time Youth League Cadre**	**311**	**737**	**659**	**496**	**165**	**158**	**96**	**100**

注：本表数据来源于共青团西安市委员会。
本表数据不含西咸新区。

21–27 妇联组织及工作情况（2019年）

The Basic Situation of Women's Federation (2019)

指 标	Item	2019
一、妇联组织	**Women's Organizations**	
市级妇联（个）	Municipal Women's Federation(unit)	1
街道妇联（个）	Street Women's Federation(unit)	139
社区妇联（个）	Community Women's Federation(unit)	1006
县（区）妇联（个）	County (district) Women's Federation(unit)	14
乡（镇）妇联（个）	Township (town) Women's Federation(unit)	49
村妇联	Village Women's Representative Conference	2144
二、妇联工作	**Women's Work**	
巾帼建功标兵（个）	Women Business Model(unit)	235
巾帼建功集体（个）	Group of Women Business Model(unit)	27
巾帼文明岗（个）	Women's Civilized Model Post(unit)	86
三八红旗手标兵（人）	Models of "March 8 Red-Banner Holders" (person)	2
三八红旗手（人）	March 8 Red-Banner Holders (person)	220
三八红旗集体（个）	March 8 Red-Banner Groups(unit)	126
五好家庭（户）	Five-virtue Family (household)	197
本级最美家庭（户）	The Best Family at the Present Level (household)	372
乡镇最美家庭（户）	The Best Family in the Town (household)	342
街道最美家庭（户）	The Best Family in the Street (household)	650
村最美家庭（户）	The Best Family in the Village (household)	1012
社区最美家庭（户）	The Best Family in the Community (household)	868

注：本表数据来源于市妇联。
本表数据为西安原口径数据。

21-28 主要年份交通、火灾及安全生产情况

Transportation, Fire and Safety Production in Representative Years

指 标	Item	2010	2013	2014	2015	2016	2017	2018	2019
道路交通事故	**Road Accidents**								
事故数(起)	Number of Traffic Accident (case)	2323	2252	1970	2392	2943	2858	3153	2973
死亡人数（人）	Number of Deaths (person)	531	460	483	481	476	453	430	381
受伤人数（人）	Number of Injuries (person)	2520	2217	1832	2318	3012	2856	3219	3156
损失（万元）	Economic Loss (10 000 yuan)	736.6	1143.9	1264.0	1470.2	1653.7	1777.3	2190.9	1808.5
火灾事故	**Fire Accidents**								
事故数(起)	Number of Cases (case)	1825	4062	3199	2590	3434	2353	2066	1871
死亡人数（人）	Number of Deaths (person)	13	26	17	20	16	8	26	18
受伤人数（人）	Number of Injuries (person)	7	6	5	7	7	2	37	2
损失（万元）	Economic Loss (10 000 yuan)	2224.2	3011.9	4381.1	2401.5	1901.1	1659.1	1783.1	1886.6
农机事故	**Farm Machinery Accidents**								
事故数(起)	Number of Cases (case)	5	1	24	47	4	2	4	1
死亡人数（人）	Number of Deaths (person)		1	1	1	1		2	1
工矿商贸事故	**Accidents in Industry, Mine,Business and Trade**								
事故数(起)	Number of Cases (case)	20	14	10	10	33	36	33	28
死亡人数（人）	Number of Deaths (person)	24	18	15	11	35	43	41	31

注：本表2019年数据来源于市公安局、市应急管理局及市消防救援支队。2011年及以前年份数据均来自于市安监局；2012-2018年交通、火灾数据来自于市公安局，农机和工矿商贸数据来自市安监局。

2014年农机及工矿商贸事故发生起数统计口径变化，数据与以前年份不可比。

本表中交通火灾数据为西安原口径，农机和工矿商贸事故2017年及以后年份含西咸新区。工矿商贸事故2017年数据以此表为准。

21-29 主要年份刑事案件情况

Data on Criminal Cases in Representative Years

指 标	Item	2010	2013	2014	2015	2016	2017	2018	2019
一、案件数情况	**Data on Number of Cases**								
立案数（起）	Number of Registered Cases(case)	48566	72611	77051	108955	98056	79828	70332	69800
破案数（起）	Number of Cleared up Cases(case)	18906	26587	25830	28629	30730	33128	33616	36566
破案率（%）	Percent of Cleared up Cases(%)	38.9	36.6	33.5	26.3	31.3	41.5	47.8	52.4
抓获作案成员(人)	Number of Criminals Caught(person)	13104	14255	14184	12827	11982	12848	11153	15179
二、查获犯罪集团情况	**Data on Hunted down and Seized Criminal Gangs**								
查获犯罪集团个数（个）	Number of Hunted down and Seized Criminal Gangs (unit)	186	695	359	153	119	97	75	46
查获犯罪集团人数（人）	Number of Members of Hunted down and Seized Criminal Gangs (person)	939	2632	1508	680	492	418	359	254
涉及案件（起）	Number of Cases Involved(case)	1172	2439	1111	291	242	303	180	199
三、涉枪案件情况	**Data on Cases with Guns Involved**								
立案数（起）	Number of Registered Cases(case)	16	17	13	9	21	22	13	14
破案数（起）	Number of Cleared up Cases(case)	11	16	8	6	17	17	7	10
破案率（%）	Percent of Cleared up Cases(%)	68.8	94.1	61.5	66.7	81.0	77.3	53.8	71.4

注：本表数据来源于市公安局。
本表数据为西安原口径数据。

21-30 主要年份治安案件情况

Data on Public Order Cases in Representative Years

指 标	Item	2010	2013	2014	2015	2016	2017	2018	2019
受理数（起）	Number of Accepted Cases(case)	58968	94853	108780	104553	109124	95821	92927	90250
查处数（起）	Number of Investigated and Prosecuted Cases(case)	57151	93546	106811	100954	106999	93634	90563	88898
查处率（%）	Percent of Investigated and Prosecuted Cases(%)	96.9	98.6	98.2	96.6	98.1	97.7	97.5	98.5
查处违法人数（人）	Number of Investigated and Prosecuted Law-breakers and Crime Committer(person)	45856	46253	52922	40838	40126	34625	32185	31219

注：本表数据来源于市公安局。
本表数据为西安原口径数据。

21-31 主要年份西安市人民检察院案件办理情况

Data on Acceptance of Cases of Xi'an People's Procuratorate

指　标	Item	2010	2013	2014	2015	2016	2017	2018	2019
一、审查逮捕案件受理件数（件）	**Examination and Arresting(case)**	**4229**	**5748**	**6443**	**6545**	**7381**	**7184**	**7216**	**8345**
二、逮捕各类案件人数（人）	**Arresting of Criminals of each kind(person)**	**6183**	**7177**	**7534**	**6692**	**7763**	**7511**	**7162**	**9253**
决定逮捕贪污贿赂犯罪嫌疑人（人）	Suspects of Corporation and Bribery to be Arrested (person)	51	49	64	100	26	27	56	29
决定逮捕渎职、侵权犯罪嫌疑人（人）	Suspects of Misprision and Tortious to be Arrested (person)	2		18	4		22	2	5
批准逮捕刑事犯罪嫌疑人（人）	Suspects of Criminal to be Arrested (person)	6130	7128	7452	6588	7737	7462	7104	9219
三、刑事立案监督、侦查活动监督（件）	**Supervision of Acceptance of Criminal Cases and Investigation (case)**	**623**	**368**	**284**	**162**	**118**	**79**	**56**	**62**
四、审查起诉案件受理件数（件）	**Examination and Prosecution (case)**	**4662**	**6371**	**7278**	**6922**	**8090**	**8933**	**9288**	**11107**
五、起诉各类案件人数（人）	**Prosecution of Criminals of each kind(person)**	**5946**	**7615**	**8399**	**8018**	**9445**	**10365**	**10193**	**11894**
起诉贪污贿赂犯罪被告人（人）	Prosecution of Criminals of Corruption and Bribery to be Defendants(person)	163	151	123	153	154	179	101	102
起诉渎职、侵权犯罪被告人（人）	Prosecution of Misprision and Tortious to be Defendants (person)	22	24	44	17	39	38	12	8
起诉刑事犯罪被告人（人）	Prosecution of Criminal to be Defendants (person)	5761	7440	8232	7848	9252	10148	10080	11784

注：本表数据来源于市检察院。
本表数据为西安原口径数据。

21-32 西安市中级人民法院案件基本情况（2019年）

Law Cases Basic Data of Xi'an Intermediate People's Court（2019）

指　标	Item	全市结案（件） the whole City(case)	中级人民法院结案 the Intermediate People's Court	基层人民法院结案 the Basic People's Court
合　计	**Total**	**247607**	**30735**	**216872**
刑事	Criminal	12266	3334	8932
民事	Civil	150456	20178	130278
行政	Administration	1156	38	1118
执行	Execution	78972	5677	73295
其他类型	Other types	4757	1508	3249

注：本表数据来源于市中级人民法院。
本表数据为西安原口径数据。

主要统计指标解释

艺术表演团体 指由文化部门主办或实行行业管理（经文化行政部门审批并领取营业性演出许可证），专门从事表演艺术等活动的各类专业艺术表演团体，含民间职业剧团。（不包括群众业余文艺表演团队）

艺术表演场馆 指由文化部门主办或实行行业管理（向文化行政部门备案或领取合资（合作）演出场所许可证），有观众席、舞台、灯光设备，公开售票、专供文艺团体演出的文化活动场所。附属于文化部门机构内非独立核算的剧场、排演场，公开营业的也应单独统计。

图书馆 指各类图书馆的管理与服务（对文献和信息的搜集、整理、存储、利用和管理，向社会公众开放并提供科学、文化等各种知识普及教育）。包括公共图书馆和各类机构内部举办的或单独举办的图书馆的管理与服务。不包括部队系统以及文化馆（文化中心、群众艺术馆）、文化站内设的图书室。

群众文化活动 指开展群众文化活动的场所的管理和组织活动。包括文化馆（含综合性文化中心、群众艺术馆）、文化站、文化宫、少年宫等群众文化活动。在本制度中，目前暂不统计文化部门以外的文化宫和少年宫。

文化馆 （含综合性文化中心、群众艺术馆）、文化站：指专门从事群众文化活动的群众文化场馆。不包括临时抽调人员组成、没有编制的农村和街道文化工作队、服务站等。

广播节目综合人口覆盖率 根据国家广电总局制定的《广播电视人口覆盖率统计技术标准和方法》进行统计调查的，分别反映中央、省级、地市级、县级广播节目在本行政区域的综合覆盖情况，反应以无线方式传输的广播节目综合覆盖情况，综合反映广播公共服务覆盖的规模、能力、水平。

电视节目综合人口覆盖率 根据国家广电总局制定的《广播电视人口覆盖率统计技术标准和方法》进行统计调查的，分别反映中央、省级、地市级、县级电视节目在本行政区域的综合覆盖情况，反应以无线方式传输的电视节目综合覆盖情况，综合反映广播公共服务覆盖的规模、能力、水平。

博物馆 指为了研究、教育、欣赏的目的，收藏、保护、展示人类活动和自然环境的见证物，向公众开放，非盈利性、永久性社会服务机构，包括以博物馆（院）、纪念馆（舍）科技馆、陈列馆等专有名称开展活动的单位。

等级运动员人数 指经考核正式批准授予等级运动员称号的人数。运动员等级分为国际级运动健将、运动健将、一级运动员、二级运动员、三级运动员、少年级运动员。

等级裁判员人数 指经考核正式批准授予等级裁判员称号的人数。裁判员等级分为国际裁判、国家级裁判、一级裁判、二级裁判、三级裁判。

医疗卫生机构 指从卫生（卫生计生）行政部门取得《医疗机构执业许可证》、《计划生育技术服务许可证》或从民政、工商行政、机构编制管理部门取得法人单位登记证书，为社会提供医疗服务、公共卫生服务或从事医学科研和学在职培训等工作的单位。包括医院、基层医疗卫生机构、专业公共卫生机构、其他医疗卫生机构。

医院 包括综合医院、中医医院、中西医结合医院、民族医院、各类专科医院和护理院，不包括专科疾病防治院、妇幼保健院和疗养院，包括医学院校附属医院。

基层医疗卫生机构 包括社区卫生服务中心（站）、乡镇(街道)卫生院、村卫生室、门诊部、诊所(医务室)。

专业公共卫生机构 包括疾病预防控制中心、专科疾病防治机构、妇幼保健机构（含妇幼保健计划生育服务中心）、健康教育机构、急救中心（站）、采供血机构、卫生监督机构、取得《医疗机构执业许可证》或《计划生育技术服务许可证》的计划生育技术服务机构。

其他医疗卫生机构 包括疗养院、临床检验中心、医学科研机构、医学在职教育机构、卫生监督（监测、检测）机构、医学考试中心、农村改水中心、人才交流中心、统计信息中心等卫生事业单位。

卫生技术人员 包括执业医师、执业助理医师、注册护士、药师(士)、检验及影像技师(士)、卫生监督员和见习医(药、护、技)师(士)等卫生专业人员。不包括从事管理工作的卫生技术人员(如院长、副院长、党委书记等)。

执业(助理)医师 指《医师执业证》"级别"为"执业（助理）医师"且实际从事医疗、预防保健工作的人员，不包括实际从事管理工作的执业（助理）医师。执业（助理）医师类别分为临床、中医、口腔和公共卫生四类。

提供住宿的社会服务机构 包括养老服务机构、精神疾病服务机构、儿童福利机构以及其他提供住宿机构。

烈士纪念建筑物管理机构 指民政部门管理的、独立核算的褒扬烈士的陵园、纪念馆等单位的总称。

殡葬服务机构 指为殡葬服务的单位总称。殡仪馆（含火葬场）、公墓、独立核算的骨灰堂、殡葬管理机构等。

公证人员 指在国家公证机关依法办理公证事务的司法人员，包括公证员、助理公证员和在公证处工作的其他人员。

办理公证文书 指公证处在一定时期内办结的公证文书件数。公证文书按司法部规定或批准的格式制作，包括国内公证和涉外公证两部分。国内公证分为经济合同公证和民事法律关系公证两大类。

调解人员 指在人民调解委员会担负调解民间一般民事纠纷和轻微违法行为引起纠纷的工作人员，包括调解委员会的委员和调解小组的调解员。

Explanatory Notes on Main Statistical Indicators

Arts Performance Troupes refer to the various professional performing arts groups, which sponsored by the cultural sectors or guided by the cultural society (Receive commercial performance license approved by the cultural administration authority),including non-governmental troupes. (The mass amateur arts performance troupes are not included.)

Arts Performance Places refer to the various sites for cultural activities, which sponsored by the cultural sectors or guided by the cultural society (approved by the cultural market administration, or receive joint/cooperative venues permit), with the facility of auditorium, stage and lighting, and selling tickets in public, including the opera halls and rehearse sites, etc. which are affiliated to the culture sectors without independent financial accounts and open to the public.

Library refers to all types of library management and services(collection, collation, storage, use and management of literature and information, open and provide scientific, cultural and other literacy education to the public). Including the management and services of public libraries and the libraries internally or separately organized by various sectors. Excluding the libraries in troops system and cultural palaces (cultural centers, mass art centers),cultural stations.

Mass Culture Center refers to the management and organization of the places where mass culture activities hold. Including cultural palace (cultural center ,mass art center), cultural stations, cultural palaces ,youth palaces and other mass cultural activities. In this system ,cultural palaces and youth palaces beyond cultural sectors are not counted at present.

Cultural Palaces (Cultural Centers, Mass Art Centers),Cultural Stations refers to the mass cultural venues specialized in mass cultural activities. Excluding rural and street cultural teams, service stations which made up by temporary without authorized strength.

Radio Coverage of Population refers to the comprehensive coverage which respectively reflected central, province, city, prefecture and county radio programs by wireless in the administrative region, and comprehensively reflect the size, capacity, level of the public broadcasting services, according to Statistical Standard and Method on Television and Radio Coverage of Population established by the State Administration of Broadcasting ,Film and Television

Television Coverage of Population refers to the comprehensive coverage which respectively reflected central, province, city, prefecture and county television programs by wireless in the administrative region, and comprehensively reflect the size, capacity, level of the public broadcasting services, according to Statistical Standard and Method on Television and Radio Coverage of Population established by the State Administration of Broadcasting , Film and Television

Museum refers to the non-profit, permanent society service sectors which collect ,protect ,show human activities and the witnesses of natural environment, including the units that organize activities with the proper name such as museum, memorial hall , science and technology museum, exhibition hall, etc.

Number of Athletes in Grades refers to the number of athletes who have been given titles through examination. The titles of athletes include international masters of sports, masters of sports, first-grade, second-grade and third-grade sportsmen and young athletes.

Number of Referees in Grades refers to the number of referees who have been given titles after examination. They are classified as international referees, national referees and referees of the first, second and third grades.

Medical and health institutions are the organizations that have got the practice license of medical institution and family planning technical services license from health administrative departments or have obtained legal entity registration certificate from civil, industrial and commercial administration, organization management departments, to provide medical services, public health services or engaged in medical research and medical job training. It includes hospitals, primary medical and health institutions, professional public health institutions, and other medical and health institutions.

Hospitals include general hospital, hospital of traditional Chinese medicine, hospital of integrated traditional Chinese and Western Medicine, National Hospital, various specialist hospitals and nursing homes, excluding specialized disease prevention and treatment centers , Maternity and child care centers and sanatorium, including hospitals affiliated to medical colleges and universities.

Primary medical and health institutions include community health service centers (stations), township (street) health centers, village clinics, outpatient department, clinics.

Professional public health institutions include the center for disease control and prevention, specialized disease prevention and treatment centers, maternity and child care centers (including maternal and child health family planning service center), health education institutions, first aid agencies,collecting and supplying agencies, health supervision institutions, andfamily planning technical service institutions which have got the practice license of medical institution and family planning technical services license.

Other medical and health institutions include sanatorium, clinical inspection center, medical research institutions, medical in-service education institutions, health supervision institutions, medical examination center, Rural change water quality center, personnel exchange center, statistical information center and other health institutions.

Health technical personnel include practicing physician, practicing assistant doctors, registered nurses, pharmacists, inspection and imaging technicians, health supervisors and clerksand other health professionals. It does not include health technical personnel engaged in management work such as Dean, vice president, Secretary of the Party committee, etc.

Practicing physician(assistant) refers to the practitioner who is a practitioner (assistant) doctor and actually engaged in medical care and preventive health care, and does not include the practitioner (assistant) practitioner who is actually engaged in the management work. Practitioners (assistants) are classified into four categories: clinical, Chinese traditional, oral and public health.

Social services providing accommodation include pension services, psychiatric care services, child welfare institutions, and other lodging establishments.

Martyr memorial buildings management organization refers to the floorboard of cemetery, memorial and other units which are independent accounting and managedby civil affairs department to praise the Martyrs

Funeral service agencies refer to the units that serve funeral services. It includes Funeral home (including crematorium), cemetery, independent accounting ashes hall, funeral and interment management organization, etc.

Notary Personnel refers to judicial workers of the state notary offices handling notarization work according to law. They include notaries, assistant notaries, and other people working for notary offices.

Notarized Documents refer to the documents settled by notary offices in a year. The notary documents are drawn up in accordance with the regulations of the Ministry of Justice, including domestic documents and foreign-related documents. Domestic documents are divided into two major categories, documents on economic contracts and documents on civil legal relations.

Mediators refer to workers on peoples mediation committees responsible for mediating in civil disputes and cases of slight infraction of the law. They include members of the mediation committees and mediators of mediation groups.

22 企业调查

ENTERPRISES INVESTIGATION

资料整理：薛　燕
Data management：Xue Yan
数据审核：黄雪冰
Data audit：Huang Xuebing

第二十二部分　企业调查

一、简要说明

1.本章资料主要包括各行业企业景气调查指数和企业家信心指数等，由西安市统计局社会经济调查中心提供。

2.本章资料调查范围：包括规模以上工业、资质内建筑业、限额以上批发和零售业、限额以上住宿和餐饮业、房地产开发业和规模以上服务业。

3.调查方法：采用非全面调查的方法进行统计。

二、主要指标

企业景气指数（第四季度）	128.3
企业家信心指数（第四季度）	129.2

22　ENTERPRISES INVESTIGATION

Ⅰ.Brief Introduction

1.Data in this chapter consists prosperity survey indices of various industries and Entrepreneur Expectation Indicator, provided by Xi'an Municipal Bureau of Statics .

2. The field of investigation and statistics range. The data in this chapter consists of industrial enterprises above designated size, construction enterprises which possess qualification grades, wholesaletrades and retail trades enterprises above designated size, hotels and catering services enterprises above designated size, real estate industry and services above designated size.

3. Methodology on survey. The survey is conducted bynon-overall investigation.

Ⅱ.Major Indicators

Business Climate Index（Fourth Quarter）	128.3
Entrepreneur Expectation Indicator（Fourth Quarter）	129.2

22-1 企业景气指数（2019年）

Business Climate Index（2019）

指 标	Item	一季度 First Quarter	二季度 Second Quarter	三季度 Third Quarter	四季度 Fourth Quarter
企业景气指数	**Business Climate Index**	**130.8**	**127.9**	**127.4**	**128.3**
按行业门类分	**Grouped by Sector**				
工业	Industry	147.0	143.6	144.0	145.0
建筑业	Construction	109.8	111.6	109.3	112.1
批发和零售业	Wholesale and Retail Sales	131.9	119.1	122.3	122.1
住宿和餐饮业	Hotels and Catering Services	115.6	110.9	114.0	112.3
房地产开发业	Real Estate Development	131.5	131.5	128.3	130.3
规模以上服务业	Services above the Designated Size	126.4	124.3	123.0	123.2

22-2 企业家信心指数（2019年）

Entrepreneur Expectation Indicator（2019）

指 标	Item	一季度 First Quarter	二季度 Second Quarter	三季度 Third Quarter	四季度 Fourth Quarter
企业家信心指数	**Entrepreneur Expectation Indicator**	**132.9**	**129.6**	**129.0**	**129.2**
按行业门类分	**Grouped by Sector**				
工业	Industry	146.8	142.0	143.4	145.2
建筑业	Construction	114.5	116.2	113.4	113.3
批发和零售业	Wholesale and Retail Sales	132.8	122.0	123.4	120.2
住宿和餐饮业	Hotels and Catering Services	122.9	119.3	111.2	118.6
房地产开发业	Real Estate Development	132.9	132.6	129.4	131.4
规模以上服务业	Services above the Designated Size	129.5	127.0	126.0	125.2

主要统计指标解释

企业景气指数：是根据企业家对本企业综合生产经营情况所作的判断与预期（通常是对“良好”、“一般”、“不佳”的选择）而编制的指数，用以综合反映企业的生产经营状况。企业景气指数也称“企业综合生产经营景气指数”。

企业家信心指数：是根据企业家对企业外部市场经济环境与宏观政策的认识、看法判断和预期（通常是对“乐观”、“一般”、“不乐观”的选择）而编制的指数，用以综合反映企业家对宏观经济环境的感受与信心。企业家信心指数也称“宏观经济景气指数”。

景气指数的表示方式：景气指数的表示范围在0~200之间，其含义：100为景气指数的临界值，表明景气状况变化不大；100~200为景气区间，表明景气状况趋于上升或改善，越接近于200，状况越景气；0~100为不景气区间，表明经济状况趋于下降或恶化，越接近于0，状况越不景气。

Explanatory Notes on Main Statistical Indicators

Business Climate Index it is an index worked out according to the judgment and anticipation (normally a choice from good, ordinary, not good) of entrepreneurs made based on synthetic productive and operational situation of the enterprise. It is used to reflect synthetically the productive and operational situation of the enterprise. It is also referred to as synthetic and productive operational prosperity index of enterprise.

Confidence index of entrepreneur it is an index worked out according to the judgment and anticipation (normally a choice from optimistic , ordinary , not optimistic) of entrepreneurs made based on their understandings and views of the market and economic environment outside the enterprise and the macro policies. It is used to reflect synthetically the confidence and feelings of the entrepreneurs to the macro economic environment. It is also referred to as macro-economy prosperity index.

The way to express prosperity index the range of prosperity index is from 0 to 200; 100 is the critical value, and means economic situation didn't change largely; from 100 to 200 is the interval of prosperity; and from 0 to 100 is the interval of not prosperity, meaning economic situation is going down or worse, the closer to 0, the worse the economic situation.